POPULATION AND SOCIETY

Population and Society: An Introduction to Demography is an ideal text for undergraduate, as well as graduate, students taking their first course in demography. It is sociologically oriented, although economics, political science, geography, history, and the other social sciences are also used to inform the materials. Although the emphasis is on demography, the book recognizes that at the individual level, population change is related to private decisions, especially in relation to fertility, but also to mortality and migration. The text thus considers in some detail, especially early in the book, the role of individuals in population decision making. At the level of countries, and even the world, changes in population size have an important effect on the environmental and related challenges facing all of the world's inhabitants. Therefore, attention is paid to the broad implications of population growth and change.

Dudley L. Poston, Jr., is Professor of Sociology, Director of the Asian Studies Program, and the George T. and Gladys H. Abell Endowed Professor of Liberal Arts at Texas A&M University. He holds adjunct professorships at Renmin (People's) University, Beijing, China; Fuzhou University, China; and Nanjing Normal University, China. He previously served on the rural sociology and sociology faculties, respectively, of Cornell University and The University of Texas at Austin. Professor Poston has coauthored or edited 17 books and more than 275 journal articles and book chapters on various sociological and demographic topics.

Leon F. Bouvier is Professor of Sociology at Old Dominion University. He is also Adjunct Professor at the Payson Center for International Development at Tulane University. He previously served as Vice President of the Population Reference Bureau in Washington, D.C.; as a demographic consultant to two congressional committees; and as a consultant to the United States Agency for International Development. Professor Bouvier has also taught at the University of Rhode Island, Tulane University School of Public Health, and Georgetown University. He has coauthored or edited 15 books and numerous articles and book reviews.

POPULATION AND SOCIETY

An Introduction to Demography

Dudley L. Poston, Jr.

Texas A&M University, College Station, Texas

Leon F. Bouvier

Old Dominion University, Norfolk, Virginia

CAMBRIDGE
UNIVERSITY PRESS

CAMBRIDGE UNIVERSITY PRESS
Cambridge, New York, Melbourne, Madrid, Cape Town, Singapore,
São Paulo, Delhi, Dubai, Tokyo

Cambridge University Press
32 Avenue of the Americas, New York, NY 10013-2473, USA

www.cambridge.org
Information on this title: www.cambridge.org/9780521872874

First published 2010

Printed in the United States of America

A catalog record for this publication is available from the British Library.

Library of Congress Cataloging in Publication data

Poston, Dudley L., Jr., 1940–
Population and society : an introduction to demography / Dudley L. Poston, Jr.,
Leon F. Bouvier.
    p.   cm.
Includes bibliographical references and index.
ISBN 978-0-521-87287-4 (hardback)
1. Population.   I. Bouvier, Leon F.   II. Title.
HB849.4.P678   2010
304.6–dc22   2009033926

ISBN 978-0-521-87287-4 Hardback

Brief Contents

Contents

Preface

Although the authors did not know it at the time, this book had its genesis when its two authors, Dudley L. Poston and Leon F. Bouvier, met for the first time in April 1974 at the annual meeting of the Population Association of America, held that year in New York City. When two demographers meet for the first time, they usually want to tell each other about the demographic research they are conducting and the interesting and important facts and findings they are producing. Strangely, this was not the case when Poston met Bouvier. They found themselves talking not about their research but, instead, about what was then, and still is today, their first love: the teaching of demography.

In the more than thirty-five years since that first meeting, Poston and Bouvier have become very good friends, as have their families. They see each other once or twice a year and communicate frequently by e-mail. In the last twenty years, they have coauthored a book about the population of Texas and several research articles dealing with immigration, congressional apportionment, and the relationship between the two. But, over the years, whenever they were together, their conversations would always seem to lead to their talking about teaching demography. They would talk about the topics they were covering in their classes, the teaching tools and techniques they were using, the books and readings they were assigning, and the importance and relevance of demography to society and the world. Every now and again, one of them would say, "Some day we need to write our own demography text." But they never did, at least for the first thirty years of their friendship. Finally, in the early 2000s, Poston said to Bouvier, "If we are ever going to write our demography book, we had better do it soon." Thus, in late 2005, they prepared a book prospectus and chapter outline. In early 2006, they shared it with Ed Parsons of Cambridge University Press, who several months later gave Poston and Bouvier a contract to write *Population and Society: An Introduction to Demography*. The book has taken much longer to write than planned, but it is a true labor of love.

Bouvier drafted some of the chapters, and Poston the others. Each then critiqued and edited and rewrote the other's drafts. And this "back and forth" process continued several times for each chapter, and in the case of a few chapters, many times. Poston, with the help of his graduate students, took the responsibility for finalizing each chapter and putting the complete book together.

Poston and Bouvier usually agreed, for the most part, with the final versions of the chapters. However, they had the most difficult time agreeing about the overall tone of Chapter 7, "International Migration," particularly its discussion about the positive and negative aspects of undocumented migration on the sending and receiving societies. This was indeed an issue debated and talked about for a good while. Its tone may still not be entirely satisfactory as far as Bouvier is concerned, but since Poston initially drafted the major parts of the chapter, it was decided in the end to agree to disagree, a little bit, about this very important issue. For the other chapters of the book, the authors had many fewer disagreements and quibbles, working them out fairly satisfactorily in the final drafts.

The writing of a book such as *Population and Society* would not have been possible without the help and patience of many people. First, we want to thank our editor at Cambridge University Press, Ed Parsons, for his many suggestions and encouragement, and especially his patience. We also thank the several reviewers Ed selected to evaluate our prospectus in 2005 and to read and critique the drafts of many of our chapters in 2008 and then the full book in 2009. These reviewers include Stephanie Bohon of the University of Tennessee, Elwood Carlson of Florida State University, Laurie DeRose of the University of Maryland, Hans-Peter Kohler of the University of Pennsylvania, James Raymo of the University of Wisconsin, and Ronald Rindfuss of the University of North Carolina. Their comments and suggestions, and Ed's, certainly resulted in improved clarity and overall quality. We considered seriously and responded to most of the suggestions and critiques raised by the reviewers. It was not possible to respond to every one of their suggestions owing to overall coverage and style issues and the general format of the book. But we are most grateful to them for the time they spent reading and commenting on our chapters.

We thank a number of individuals who read and edited our chapters and provided feedback, suggested improvements, and alerted us to the work of others. Poston asked many of his former and current graduate students to read, edit, and critique chapters; check references, assemble tables and figures, and prepare chapter outlines and PowerPoint slides for classroom use; also, published work with some of his students has been adapted and referenced in various chapters of the book. He thanks his conscientious and very helpful students, listed here alphabetically: Wadha

Alnuaimi, Amanda Baumle, Yuting Chang, Eugenia Conde, Rachel Cortes, Mary Ann Davis, Danielle Deng, Bethany DeSalvo, Nicole Farris, Ginny Garcia, Andrea Green, Christine Guarneri, Lei He, Lindsay Howden, Anna Iwinska-Nowak, Heather Kincannon, Hua Luo, Leslie Meyer, Hilario Molina, Brittany Rico, Chris Russell, Marilyn Venegas, and Li Zhang. Also, Leon Bouvier thanks Mary Boone for her assistance editing his chapters.

Our friends and associates answered questions we raised about chapter topics, geography, and referencing, and listened and sometimes reacted to our discussions about one or more of the chapters and themes; some listened to a lot of our discussions. These friends and colleagues, listed alphabetically, are James Burk, Rafael Cazorla, Nadia Flores, Mark Fossett, Parker Frisbie, Sidney Goldstein, Melanie Hawthorne, Peter Hugill, John Macisco, Kyriakos Markides, Rogelio Saenz, Jane Sell, James Weatherby, and Xiushi Yang.

Lastly, our long and time-consuming efforts in writing this book were assisted by the support, understanding, patience, and love of our families. In this regard, Dudley Poston thanks his wonderful wife Patricia and their children, Nancy and Dudley III, and son-in-law, Rick. Leon Bouvier thanks his children, Thomas, Lynne, Linda, and Kenneth, and his very special best friend, Becky Livas.

Introduction

The media these days are rediscovering population dynamics and the subject of demography. The first real heyday for demography was probably in the 1960s and 1970s with the "discovery" of the global population problem. In recent decades, demographic behavior and demographic characteristics have received increased attention in the popular media. As a result, the term *demographics* has seeped into our vocabulary. For us authors of this text, this is an encouraging sign. Forty years ago when we first began studying and teaching demography, the subject was nowhere near as recognized and discussed as it is today. Now, the importance of population change, whether in size, composition, or distribution, has become increasingly relevant in policymaking at the local, state, national, and international levels. There is an increasing awareness not only of population growth and decline but also of compositional change in age, sex, and racial identity.

Care must be taken, however, to evaluate the works of journalists and others who use demographic data and comment about their dynamics. It is very easy to make errors when reporting on and interpreting population behavior. Hopefully, readers of our book will become attuned to these types of errors that seem to appear every so often in the popular media.

Population and Society: An Introduction to Demography is intended for undergraduate students, as well as graduate students, taking their first course in demography. It is sociologically oriented, although economics, political science, geography, history, and the other social sciences are also used to inform some of the materials we cover and discuss. While the emphasis is on demography, we recognize that at the individual level, population change is related to private decisions, especially in relation to fertility but also to migration and even to mortality. We thus consider in some detail, early in the book, the role of individuals in population decision making. At the level of countries, and even the world, changes in population size have an important effect on environmental and related challenges facing all of the world's inhabitants. We often wonder why the media, when

1

discussing an issue such as global warming, tend sometimes to minimize the role of population and population growth. The final chapter of our book focuses on the broad implications of population growth and change.

A significant and very necessary component of demography is its techniques. The study of demography involves much more than theories, concepts, and data. Demography, more so than any of the other social sciences, has a body of methods and approaches uniquely suited for the analysis of its concepts and events. In our book, we present some of the basic techniques that are needed to better understand demographic behavior. But the methodological discussions in the chapters per se are introductory. Students interested in pursuing the techniques in more detail will need to take a course or two dealing with demographic methods and/or consult any of a number of excellent texts focusing on demographic methods (e.g., Hinde, 1998; Pollard, Yusuf, and Pollard, 1990; Preston, Heuveline, and Guillot, 2001; Rowland, 2003; Siegel and Swanson, 2004; Smith, 1992).

We believe that students of demography should be conversant with the basic sources of demographic data. Thus, on the Cambridge University Press Web page that is maintained for our book, we have placed detailed instructions on how to locate population data through the Internet and other sources. We are hopeful that in addition to learning about the relevance and importance of demography and its concepts, theories, and methods, students will also gain some knowledge about the richness of data available from a wide variety of governmental sources. This knowledge should come in handy in many future endeavors.

In sum, we have tried to provide students and others interested in this exciting and relevant field with as much information as possible in a readable manner mostly absent of professional jargon.

1 "We Are All Population Actors": An Introduction to Demography

This book introduces you to the study of **demography**. What is demography? It is the systematic and scientific study of human populations. The word *demography* comes from the Greek words δημοσ (*demos*) for **population** and γραφια (*graphia*) for "description" or "writing," thus the phrase, "writings about populations." The term *demography* is believed to have first been used in 1855 by the Belgian statistician Achille Guillard in his book *Elements of Human Statistics or Comparative Demography* (Borrie, 1973: 75; Rowland, 2003: 16). There is fair agreement among demographers (Hauser and Duncan, 1959; McFalls, 2003; Micklin and Poston, 2005; Pressat, 1985; Rowland, 2003) about the objectives and definition of demography.

Demography is the social science that studies 1) the size, composition, and distribution of the human population of a given area at a specific point in time; 2) changes in population size and composition; 3) the **components** of these changes (**fertility, mortality**, and migration); 4) the factors that affect these components; and 5) the consequences of changes in population size, composition, and distribution, or in the components themselves. Demography may be defined as the scientific study of the size, composition, and distribution of human populations and their changes resulting from fertility, mortality, and migration. Demography is concerned with how large (or small) populations are; how populations are composed according to age, sex, race, marital status, and other characteristics; and how populations are distributed in physical space (e.g., how urban and rural they are) (Bogue, 1969). Demography is also interested in the changes over time in the size, composition, and distribution of human populations, and how these result from the processes of fertility, mortality, and migration. The chapters of this book discuss these topics in more depth and provide you with a more detailed introduction to demography.

3

In this first chapter, we begin with the following point: Every one of you, whether you are aware of it or not, has already contributed, and will continue to contribute throughout your lives, to the subject matter of demography. We next elaborate on the definition of demography introduced earlier. We then consider the so-called demographic equation. Because two of the most important variables used by demographers are age and sex, we give examples of the relevance of age and sex to demography and to society. We then discuss the issue of population distribution and review briefly some of the major sources of demographic data. Finally, we conclude this first chapter by discussing the phrase "Demography is destiny."

WE ARE ALL POPULATION ACTORS

We are all population actors. This is a major theme of our book. Think about it: Your parents performed a demographic act when you were conceived. You, in turn, perform similar demographic acts when you decide to have, or not to have, children. Sometime during your lifetime you will move – once or perhaps numerous times. These, too, are demographic acts. Finally, you will die.

Now, you may think that your dying is not the same kind of demographic act as the decision making of your parents when you were conceived because you yourself do not really decide how long you will live and when you will die. But we do indeed have a lot to say about how old we will be when we die. That is, we have many options that may, or may not, extend our lives. These include such behaviors as stopping or never beginning smoking, limiting alcohol intake, eating a healthful diet, and exercising. Other behaviors that will extend our lives are more apparent; obtaining a college degree, for instance, will add, on average, one year to our lives, and a graduate degree will add two more. And the list goes on and on. So, there it is: "We are all population actors" even though we hardly ever realize it.

Demography is the study of many of the most important events in our lives, and we are very much involved in these events. Ask yourself: What are the only two times in your life when you will have an almost 100 percent chance of being identified by name and listed in your local newspaper? When you are born and when you die. These are two of the events that demographers study. Other extremely important events in the lives of many of us include getting married and, also for some of us, getting divorced. These are two more behaviors studied by demographers. Another really important event that almost everyone will do at least once, if not many times, is to move from one residence to another. Demographers also study residential changes. So, it is not at all an overstatement to say that demographers study when we are born and when we die, as well as many of the really important events in our lives that occur in between. Or as the eminent demographer Samuel Preston (1987: 620–621) once stated, "The study of population offers something for everyone: the daily dramas of sex and death, politics and war; the interlacings of individuals in all their . . . (groups); and the confrontations of nature and civilization." In the next chapter, we begin elaborating on these and related points.

DEFINITION OF DEMOGRAPHY

We defined demography in the second paragraph of this chapter. Let us return to its consideration. Demography, that is, the scientific study of human populations, is the study of three basic processes: fertility, migration, and mortality. These are referred to as the **demographic processes**. In one sense, that is really all there is to demography. When populations change in size, composition, or distribution, the changes depend solely on one or more of the three demographic processes. Hence, the examination of the three demographic processes comprises a major portion of our text.

THE DEMOGRAPHIC EQUATION

It should be clear that the size of a population can change only through the processes of fertility, mortality, and migration. There are only two ways of entering a population – being born or moving into it. There are also two, and only two, ways of leaving a population – dying or moving out of it. One of the fundamental facts about population change, thus, is that populations only change because of a limited, countable number of events. For example, consider the population size of a country. Suppose that this country at time t contains P_t persons, and that one year later it contains P_{t+1} persons. We may write this as the following equation:

$$P_{t+1} = P_t + B_{t \text{ to } t+1} - D_{t \text{ to } t+1} + I_{t \text{ to } t+1} - E_{t \text{ to } t+1} \qquad (1.1)$$

where $B_{t \text{ to } t+1}$ and $D_{t \text{ to } t+1}$ are, respectively, the number of births and deaths occurring in the population between times t and $t + 1$; and $I_{t \text{ to } t+1}$ and $E_{t \text{ to } t+1}$ are, respectively, the number of immigrants (or in-migrants) to and emigrants (or out-migrants) from the population between times t and $t + 1$.

Equation (1.1) is known as the *basic demographic equation*, or sometimes as the demographic balancing or accounting equation. It states that an area's population size can change because of only three types of events: births, deaths, and migrations. These three events are known as the components of demographic change and also as the three demographic processes.

The quantity $(B_{t \text{ to } t+1} - D_{t \text{ to } t+1})$ refers to the difference between the number of births and the number of deaths occurring during the time period and is known as **natural increase**; if $B_{t\ to\ t+1} < D_{t\ to\ t+1}$, then the number of deaths exceeds the number of births during the interval t *to* $t + 1$, meaning negative natural increase, or natural decrease. The quantity $(I_{t\ to\ t+1} - E_{t\ to\ t+1})$ refers to the difference between the number of immigrants and the number of emigrants occurring during the time period and is known as net international migration (or, in the case of **in-migration** minus **out-migration**, net internal migration). If $I_{t\ to\ t+1} < E_{t\ to\ t+1}$, then more persons leave (emigrate from) the area than enter (immigrate into) the area, and the quantity is known as negative net international migration. Finally, if the quantity $I_{t\ to\ t+1} > E_{t\ to\ t+1}$, then we have positive net international migration.

In the United States, we almost always have positive net international migration because it is the situation in the United States and in most developed countries that $I_{t\ to\ t+1} > E_{t\ to\ t+1}$. The United States is, thus, a receiving country when it comes to international migration. In most developing countries, there is almost always negative net international migration because $I_{t\ to\ t+1} < E_{t\ to\ t+1}$. Countries such as Mexico and China, for instance, have negative net international migration. They are sending countries when it comes to international migration.

Within countries, however, there is significant variation in the demographic equation. Large older cities often have net out-migration. If the extent of natural increase does not surpass the level of out-migration, then the city loses population. Washington, D.C., is an example of such a demographic pattern. Between 2000 and 2005, its population fell by 20,539 inhabitants. Yet it had positive natural increase (42,502 births minus 30,109 deaths). However, although 20,618 persons moved into the District of Columbia, 53,550 left. Thus, the net out-migration of 32,932 more than offset the natural increase of 12,393.

Some places have natural decrease because the population that is elderly is very large proportionally. Flagler County, Florida (located between St. Augustine and Daytona Beach) is one of the fastest-growing counties in the United States. During the five-year period of 2000 to 2005, the county grew by 26,506 persons. But, there were 3,628 deaths and only 2,652 births; thus, the county had 976 more deaths than births. To account for that loss, net migration amounted to 27,482. Why the high number of deaths? The in-migration predominantly comprised of retirees, resulting in an elderly population. There are many of these so-called retirement counties in Arizona, California, Florida, North Carolina, and Texas.

Some counties have negative levels of both natural increase and net migration. Between 2000 and 2005 in Barnes County, North Dakota, for example, there were 578 births and 736 deaths, and there were 528 more people moving out of the county than moving in. The county's high number of deaths reflects an old population. However, in Flagler County, Florida, the population growth was due to the in-migration of elderly. In Barnes County, North Dakota, the population loss was due to the exodus of young people, thereby leaving a large proportion of elderly.

From these examples, we can see that all three of the demographic processes play important roles in determining not only the size but also the composition of any region. Changes in the variables themselves are the result of our behavior as population actors. This is the heart of demography: understanding how the many factors that cause changes in demographic behavior and that are the consequences of this behavior are all interrelated.

AGE AND SEX

Changes in any one of the demographic processes yield equally important information about how populations are composed, that is, their structure. The most important characteristics that tell us about population structure are age and sex. These two characteristics are so important to the study of demography and the demographic processes that they are referred to as the **demographic characteristics.**

Let us consider how closely age and sex are tied in with the three demographic processes. With regard to fertility, that is, the actual production of children, more males are born than females, usually around 105 males for every 100 females. **Fecundity,** that is, the ability to produce children, varies by sex; specifically, the childbearing years of females are, for the most part, between the ages of 15 and 49, and for males they are generally between the ages of 15 and 79 (Poston, 2005).

Regarding mortality, that is, the frequency with which death occurs in a population, females have lower death rates than males at every age of life. Death rates are high in the first year of life and then drop to very low levels. In modern populations, they do not again reach the level of the first year of life for another five to six decades. Also, cause-specific mortality is often age related. For instance, causes of "mortality such as infanticide, parricide and suicide are . . . age (and sex) related" (Goldscheider 1971: 227). Two renowned demographers, Jacob Siegel and Henry Shryock, have written that "in view of the very close relation between age and the risk of death, age may be considered the most important demographic variable in the analysis of mortality" (Shryock, Siegel, and Associates, 1976: 224; McGehee, 2004).

Migration also differs by age and sex. Traditionally, males and females have not migrated to the same places in equal numbers. Long-distance migration has tended to favor males, and short-distance migration, females; this has been especially the case in developing countries. However, with increases in the degree of gender equity in societies, the migration of females tends to approximate that of males. In fact, almost half of the international migrants worldwide are now women, and more than half of the legal immigrants to the United States are women (Population Reference Bureau, 2007b: 9). Migration is also age selective, with the largest numbers of migrants found among young adults (Tobler, 1995).

Age and sex are not the only important compositional variables in demography. Other variables are also related to the three demographic processes. Knowing something about marital status, for example, is important when studying fertility. Race is strongly associated with socioeconomic status. Blacks, whites, Asians, and Hispanics all have somewhat different lifestyles, and these are related to the basic demographic processes. Education is an especially important variable to consider. In general, the higher the education attained, the lower the fertility and the lower the mortality.

These are just hints of the many compositional variables that demographers consider. The number is large, giving demographers a wide field to study. They are interested in anything that is related to demographic behavior.

Finally, compositional variables are both the cause and effect of population changes. In turn, demographic changes can affect the compositional variables. We have much more to say about this later in our book.

AGE COMPOSITION: AN EXAMPLE

Let us now consider an example that illustrates well the central importance in demography of **age composition**. This is an example that is mentioned and discussed later again in the pages of our book. It is the famous **baby boom**, which began in the United States and in some other Western countries around 1947 and lasted until about 1964. Rather suddenly, right after the end of World War II, the young adults of that period decided to have more children than those in previous generations. This resulted in a "bulge" in the age composition – a bulge, as we shall see, that resulted in numerous challenges for every institution in the U.S. society. The bulge is easy to find in Figure 1.1. In 1950, it is evident in the 5-year-and-under age group; in 2000, the bulge appears in the 35–44-year age groups. In future decades, the baby boom bulge will be visible higher and higher up in the country's pyramid. Joseph A. McFalls, Bernard Gallagher, and Brian Jones (1986) have noted, figuratively, that we can think of the people born during the baby boom period as a group or **cohort** that passes through the population from the youngest ages to the oldest ages as a pig that has been swallowed by a python.

Figure 1.1. Age Composition: 1900, 1950, and 2000. *Source*: U.S. Census Bureau, decennial census of population, 1900, 1950, and 2000.

Those people born from the mid-1940s to the mid-1960s are known as baby boom babies because there were so many of them in comparison to the numbers of babies born before and after them. The baby boomers have experienced problems throughout their lives. Their attendance at elementary and secondary school and at college was marked by overcrowded classrooms and a shortage of teachers. When they entered the labor market, many of them discovered there were not enough jobs to go around. Housing for many members of this generation has been scarce. The older members, now reaching retirement age, are finding that their demands on the U.S. Social Security system are producing strains and will continue to produce strains between the financial demands of their large cohort and the smaller number of younger workers who must finance the system. These are examples of some of the problems that are likely to occur when one age group is considerably larger than groups before or after it (Carlson, 2008).

In contrast, the babies born after the baby boomers, say, those born in the 1970s, have had a much easier time during their lives. In the 1970s, there were 33 million babies born in the United States, a figure 10 million fewer than the number born in the ten years between 1955 and 1964, the latter part of the period when most of the baby boom babies were born. The babies born in the 1970s and in later decades, but especially those born in the 1970s, may be referred to as the **baby bust** cohort. They followed the enormously large group of baby boomers and have been in a much more favored position on their march through life. Education facilities have been more than adequate, and many more jobs have been available for them than for the baby boomers who preceded them. But the baby bust babies will have a major responsibility financing the retirement of the baby boomers.

Clearly, being a member of the baby boom or bust generation can have a significant impact on one's chances of success in life. We are not necessarily suggesting demographic determinism. Indeed, individuals can and do succeed on their own. But it goes without saying that being born as a member of a large or a small cohort does in fact alter one's odds for later success in life (Carlson, 2008). We have discussed here the importance of age and age composition in demography and also some of the ways in which the size of one's age cohort can influence many aspects of one's life and livelihood. Let us turn now to a consideration of sex and **sex composition**.

SEX COMPOSITION: AN EXAMPLE

We noted earlier that most societies in the world have **sex ratios** at birth (SRBs) of around 105, that is, 105 boys born for every 100 girls. This so-called biologically normal level of about 105 is probably an evolutionary adaptation to the fact that females have higher survival probabilities than males. Since at every year of life males have higher age-specific death rates than females, around 105 or so males are required at birth per every 100 females for there to be approximately equal numbers of males and females when the groups reach the marriageable ages (although there are often slightly more males than females at the beginning of the marriageable ages).

Later in the book, we discuss in more detail the sex ratio at birth. But we note here that since the mid-1980s and into the 1990s, several countries, for example, China, South Korea, Taiwan, India, and a few others, have been having sex ratios at birth (i.e., the number of male births per 100 female births) that are much higher than the biological average of around 105 (Hudson and Den Boer, 2002, 2004; Jha et al., 2006; Poston and Glover, 2005; Poston and Morrison, 2005; Poston et al., 1997). Indeed, in 2005, China had an SRB of 118; this means that in 2005 in China, there were 118 baby boys born for every 100 baby girls.

We have estimated that there are already in China more than 31 million Chinese boys who, when they reach their mid-twenties and are looking for brides, will not be able to find Chinese girls to marry (Poston and Zhang, 2009). The Chinese government, as a consequence, could well turn to a more authoritarian form of government so as to be better able to control these millions of excess bachelors. Sociological research has shown that when large numbers of men do not marry, they are often more prone to crime than if they were married (Mazur and Michalek, 1998; Sampson and

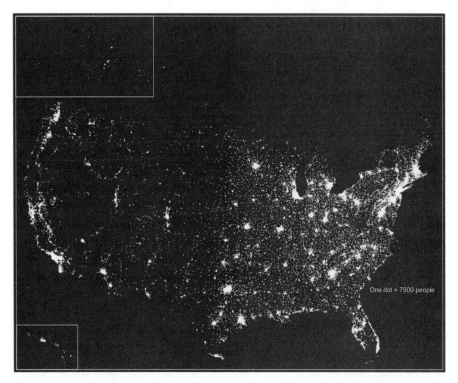

One dot = 7500 people

Figure 1.2. 2000 population distribution in the United States. *Source:* http://www.census.gov/mso/www/pres_lib/index2.html, accessed September 10, 2007.

Laub, 1990). Banditry, violence, and revolutions are likely to occur in areas with large numbers of excess males (Hudson and Den Boer, 2002).

Another implication of this unbalanced sex ratio at birth is the potential for an HIV/AIDS epidemic of a scale previously unimagined. This will occur if many of the excess Chinese bachelors move to the big cities in China, and if China's commercial sex markets in the cities expand to accommodate the many millions of surplus males (Parish et al., 2003; Tucker et al., 2005). These are the kinds of societal impacts that are likely to occur when the sex ratio becomes significantly unbalanced.

POPULATION DISTRIBUTION

In the year 2008, the population of the world numbered more than 6.6 billion people. These billions of inhabitants are not equally distributed across the planet. Some areas are densely populated; others are not. Some areas are deserts; others are mountains. Consider, for instance, the population distribution of the United States. Figure 1.2 is a map of the United States produced by the U.S. Census Bureau showing the distribution of the population using data from the 2000 census. Land area is shown in black and population locations are shown with white dots. Each white dot is meant to represent around 7,500 people. The northeastern region of the country has the highest population density of population per square mile, but the southern region is the most populated.

It is interesting to note that population distribution reflects levels of fertility, mortality, and migration. Earlier in this chapter, we noted how Washington, D.C., was losing population mainly through out-migration. The same is true of many older large cities. Suburbs, on the other hand, tend to grow quite rapidly. We looked at Florida's Flagler County, whose growth is due solely to in-migration. We saw other places where deaths outnumbered births because of a high proportion of elderly residents.

Humans are constantly moving from place to place. We are indeed peripatetic. We always have been and always will be. The interesting point for demographers is that all three demographic processes are involved in this ongoing shift by the residents of the planet.

DEMOGRAPHIC DATA

We need to cover another topic in this introductory chapter, the data that are used to study demography. Where do we find these data? Demographers are more fortunate than many of their social science colleagues who oftentimes must gather and develop their own data. Generally speaking, most of the data that demographers use have already been gathered for us. We cover this topic in more detail in Chapter 2.

The U.S. Census Bureau is an incredible source of demographic data. The data that the Census Bureau makes available and easily accessible to everyone on its Web page apply not only to the United States. The international database maintained by the U.S. Census Bureau is especially thorough and of great relevance.

Another important source of data is the U.S. National Center for Health Statistics (NCHS), particularly data dealing with fertility, **morbidity** (the prevalence of sickness in a population), causes of death, and mortality. The U.S. Citizenship and Immigration Services (USCIS), a branch of the Department of Homeland Security, makes available extensive data on immigration. In addition, most of the U.S. states have their own demographic data centers, and much information can be gleaned there. The United Nations (UN) Population Division also publishes extensive demographic information for every country in the world.

At one time, finding and gathering data from these monumental sources were torturous. One had to go to a library and find the different locations of all the various governmental publications. Then one had to find the actual volumes. And then one had to code the data by hand. But today, most all these sources are available on the Internet. On the Cambridge University Press Web page that is maintained for our book, we have placed specific sources for the various kinds of demographic data discussed in the chapters, with detailed directions about accessing them.

DEMOGRAPHY IS DESTINY

We often hear the expression, "Demography is destiny." Indeed, the founding father of sociology, August Comte, is believed to be the first person to have made such a statement. Today, commentators and news analysts use this as an explanation of how things are, and how they got that way, and how they will be. Many demographers, however, often tend to shy away from the expression. While there is some validity to it, there are far too many other variables that intervene in determining where an individual or a society stands at any given point in time. Nevertheless, there are instances in the study of demography, particularly with respect to population behavior occurring in relatively short periods of time, when it can indeed be argued that demography is destiny. For instance, and again citing the baby boom example introduced earlier, we have known for many years that by the year 2010, there will be a large population increase, indeed, what might be referred to as a **population explosion,** in the numbers of elderly people in the United States and elsewhere. Why? Because we know how many people were born during the baby boom period and can be fairly accurate as to how many will be entering the elderly years of life in the near future. A similar statement can be made with regard to the many, many millions of baby boys already born in China and South Korea and India who, when it is time for them to marry, will not be able to find Chinese or South Korean or Indian brides. These boys have already been born, and we know that they far outnumber the women who will be there for them to marry.

Thus, one could very well argue that demography is destiny. However, the analogy should not be carried too far. Nevertheless, we are convinced that an educated person should have at least a basic knowledge of demography and how it affects every aspect of our lives and our institutions. We hope that the following chapters convince you of this argument.

KEY TERMS

age composition	components of population growth
baby boom	demographic characteristics
baby bust	demographic processes
cohort	demography

fecundity	out-migration
fertility	population
in-migration	population explosion
morbidity	sex composition
mortality	sex ratio
natural increase	

2 The Sources of Demographic Information

INTRODUCTION

We noted toward the end of Chapter 1 that we demographers are more fortunate than many of our social science colleagues who must gather and develop their own databases. Generally speaking, most of the data we use have already been gathered for us, but not always. Indeed, some demographers do gather their own data, especially those who use anthropological perspectives and who engage in ethnographic research (Greenhalgh, 1990b, 1994; Riley, 1998; Riley and McCarthy, 2003). However, most of us use data already gathered and developed by other organizations. This chapter discusses the basic sources of demographic information, of which there are three.

The basic sources of demographic data are national censuses, registers, and surveys. National censuses and registers differ in that the former are conducted on a decennial (or, in some countries, quinquennial) basis, while the latter, theoretically at least, are compiled continuously. Actually, **registration** data of population events are usually compiled and published annually or monthly, but they are gathered continuously. A **census** may be likened to taking a snapshot of a population at one point in time, say, once every ten years, and in this snapshot getting a picture of the size of the population, its characteristics, and its spatial distribution. Conversely, a register may be thought of as a continuous compilation of major population events, often births, deaths, marriages, divorces, and sometimes migrations. As a birth or a death occurs, it is registered with the government; the registrations thus occur continuously.

Censuses and registers are intended to cover the entire population. In a national census, everyone in the population is supposed to be enumerated, and all the demographic events (births, deaths, and so forth) that occur in the population are supposed to be registered. Surveys, on the other hand, are by definition administered to only a fraction of the population. Yet they often gather data on many of the items included in censuses and registers, plus additional items of interest to demographers not included in them. We now cover in some detail each of these three sources of demographic data.

NATIONAL CENSUSES

A national census is "the total process of collecting, compiling, and publishing demographic, economic, and social data pertaining, at a specified time . . . , to all persons in a country or delimited territory" (United Nations, 1958: 3). The principal objective of a census is to obtain data about the size, composition, and distribution of the population. A typical census thus includes information about the size of the population and its social and geographic subpopulations, as well as data on their age and sex composition and their educational composition (levels of literacy and educational attainment and extent of school attendance). Many censuses also contain information on economically active and inactive populations, including data on the industrial and occupational composition of the working population, as well as economic (salary and income) data. Other population data in a typical census include information pertaining to country or area of birth, citizenship, language, recent migration experience, religion, and **ethnic** heritage, which refers to group distinctions based on shared cultural origins (Shryock, Siegel, and Associates, 1976).

In the actual enumeration of the population, there are two ways to count people: by following a **de jure** method or by following a **de facto** method (Shryock, 1964). In the case of a de jure enumeration, the census covers the entire territory of the country and counts persons according to their "usual" or "normal" place of residence in the country. A de facto enumeration also covers the entire territory of the country but counts each person in the population according to his/her geographical location on the day of the census undertaking. For instance, a person who resides with her family in Norfolk, Virginia, but who is traveling on census day and happens to be counted in College Station, Texas, would be counted as a resident of Norfolk if the census was a de jure census but would be assigned to College Station if it was a de facto census. Canada and the United States follow a de jure approach, as do many European countries, for example, Austria, Belgium, Croatia, the Czech Republic, Denmark, Germany, the Netherlands, Norway, Sweden, and Switzerland (United Nations, 1998). The censuses of Colombia have been both de facto (in 1963 and 1973) and de jure (since 1985). Of the more than 230 countries conducting national censuses, however, the de facto type is much more common than the de jure (Wilmoth, 2004: 65).

Shown in Figure 2.1 is an example of a census questionnaire; this one was administered in the United States in the 2000 census. The questions on this instrument were usually answered by one person in every **household** in the United States, and that person typically entered responses to each question for everyone residing in the household; these are known as the 100 percent questions. There were just a few such questions, and they dealt with age, sex, race, Hispanic origin, household relationship, and owner/renter status of the residence. Another much larger questionnaire containing many more questions, for example, dealing with education, occupation, income, mobility, and several other topics, was used in the 2000 census but was only administered to a sample of the population, roughly one in six households. The census questionnaire containing the additional questions has come to be known as the **long-form questionnaire**.

Census taking had its origins in ancient Egypt, China, and Rome, among other places, although only a few of these enumerations have survived. There may have been a census conducted in China as early as 3000 BC, but demographic records for China and other countries for the very early periods no longer exist. Several census counts are mentioned in the Bible; one was undertaken at the time of the Exodus in 1491 BC, and another was conducted during King David's era in 1017 BC. Roman censuses were conducted quinquennially for more than 800 years. The Romans extended the census enumeration to the entire Roman Empire in 5 BC, resulting in the popular biblical census story reported in St. Luke's Gospel (Bryan, 2004: 14).

It is difficult to determine when the first modern census was undertaken. Coverage was highly suspect in early efforts; women and children were seldom included. Censuses were often conducted to determine the fiscal and military obligations of the citizens (Bryan, 2004). Most countries of the world today conduct censuses. Some countries are late to census taking. For instance, Chad and Oman did not take their first censuses until 1993. Of all the countries in the world, only one, Lebanon, has never conducted an official population census. Most likely owing to the way the country was formed by the French, Lebanon has used national population and household surveys for various enumeration estimates and has avoided, likely for political reasons, conducting an actual census (personal communication with Mary J. Chamie, July 10, 2007).

Of the more than 230 countries or areas in the world today, the United Nations reports that all but thirteen (Western Sahara, Guinea-Bissau, Liberia, Togo, Eritrea, Somalia, Democratic Republic of the Congo, Burundi, Angola, Myanmar, Afghanistan, Uzbekistan, and Bosnia and Herzegovina) conducted a national census in the 1993 to 2006 time period (United Nations, 2007). Indeed more than 95 percent of the world's population has been counted in a national census conducted sometime during the decade of the 1990s (P. Johnson, 2000).

Population censuses were conducted relatively early in the United States, starting with Virginia in 1624–1625. Various colonial censuses were

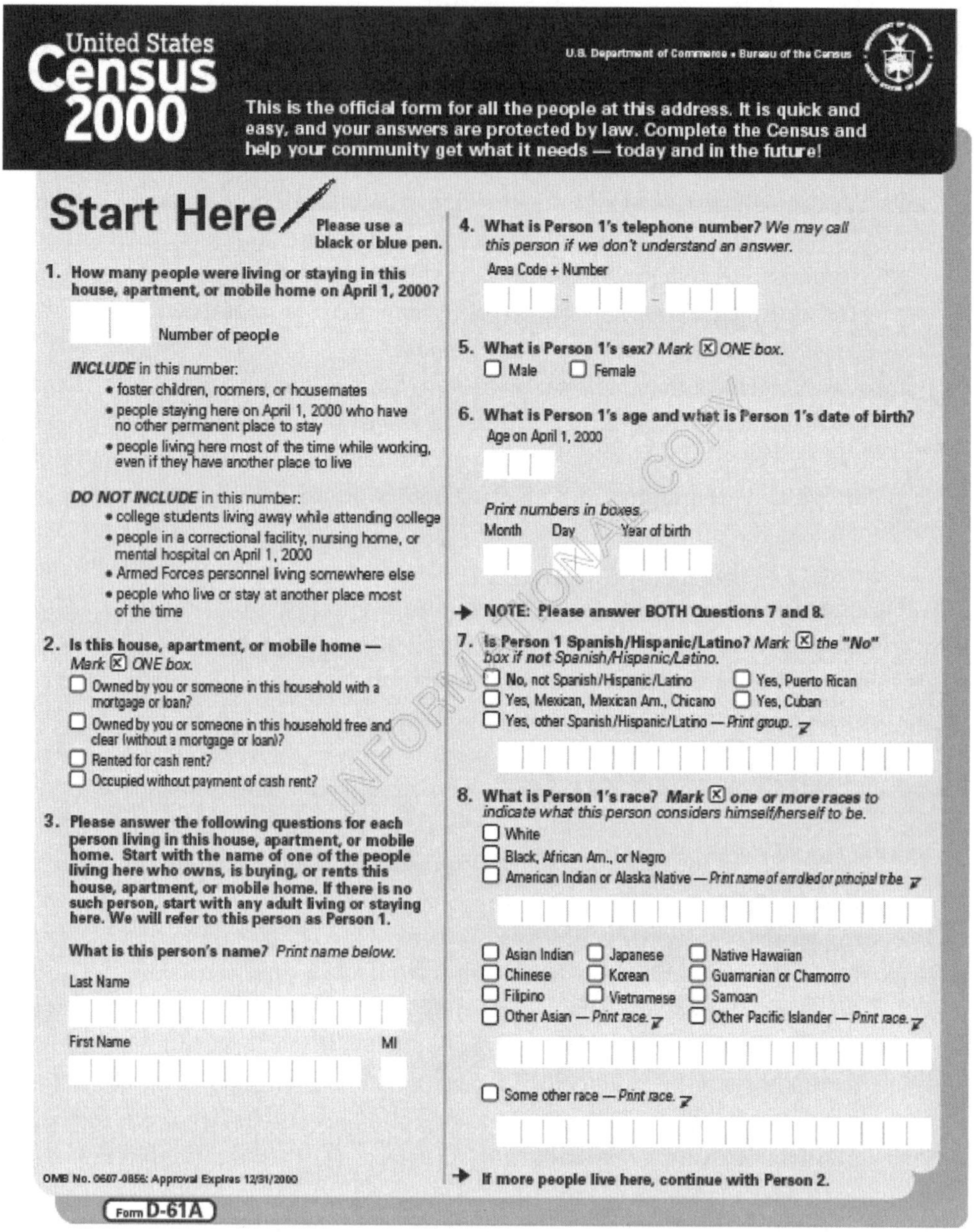

United States
Census 2000

U.S. Department of Commerce • Bureau of the Census

This is the official form for all the people at this address. It is quick and easy, and your answers are protected by law. Complete the Census and help your community get what it needs — today and in the future!

Start Here Please use a black or blue pen.

1. How many people were living or staying in this house, apartment, or mobile home on April 1, 2000?

Number of people

INCLUDE in this number:
- foster children, roomers, or housemates
- people staying here on April 1, 2000 who have no other permanent place to stay
- people living here most of the time while working, even if they have another place to live

DO NOT INCLUDE in this number:
- college students living away while attending college
- people in a correctional facility, nursing home, or mental hospital on April 1, 2000
- Armed Forces personnel living somewhere else
- people who live or stay at another place most of the time

2. Is this house, apartment, or mobile home — *Mark ☒ ONE box.*
- ☐ Owned by you or someone in this household with a mortgage or loan?
- ☐ Owned by you or someone in this household free and clear (without a mortgage or loan)?
- ☐ Rented for cash rent?
- ☐ Occupied without payment of cash rent?

3. Please answer the following questions for each person living in this house, apartment, or mobile home. Start with the name of one of the people living here who owns, is buying, or rents this house, apartment, or mobile home. If there is no such person, start with any adult living or staying here. We will refer to this person as Person 1.

What is this person's name? *Print name below.*

Last Name

First Name MI

4. What is Person 1's telephone number? *We may call this person if we don't understand an answer.*

Area Code + Number

5. What is Person 1's sex? *Mark ☒ ONE box.*
- ☐ Male ☐ Female

6. What is Person 1's age and what is Person 1's date of birth?

Age on April 1, 2000

Print numbers in boxes.

Month Day Year of birth

→ **NOTE: Please answer BOTH Questions 7 and 8.**

7. Is Person 1 Spanish/Hispanic/Latino? *Mark ☒ the "No" box if **not** Spanish/Hispanic/Latino.*
- ☐ No, not Spanish/Hispanic/Latino
- ☐ Yes, Puerto Rican
- ☐ Yes, Mexican, Mexican Am., Chicano
- ☐ Yes, Cuban
- ☐ Yes, other Spanish/Hispanic/Latino — *Print group.*

8. What is Person 1's race? ***Mark ☒ one or more races*** *to indicate what this person considers himself/herself to be.*
- ☐ White
- ☐ Black, African Am., or Negro
- ☐ American Indian or Alaska Native — *Print name of enrolled or principal tribe.*
- ☐ Asian Indian ☐ Japanese ☐ Native Hawaiian
- ☐ Chinese ☐ Korean ☐ Guamanian or Chamorro
- ☐ Filipino ☐ Vietnamese ☐ Samoan
- ☐ Other Asian — *Print race.* ☐ Other Pacific Islander — *Print race.*
- ☐ Some other race — *Print race.*

→ **If more people live here, continue with Person 2.**

OMB No. 0607-0856: Approval Expires 12/31/2000

Form D-61A

INFORMATIONAL COPY

Figure 2.1. The 2000 U.S. Census of Population and Housing, 100% questionnaire.

conducted through 1767. In the United States, the principal reason and justification for conducting a decennial national census is to provide population counts for the states of the country that are used to apportion the House of Representatives. The requirement for a decennial census was written in 1787 into Article 1, Section 2, of the U.S. Constitution as follows: "Representatives and direct taxes shall be apportioned among the several states which may be included within this Union according to their respective

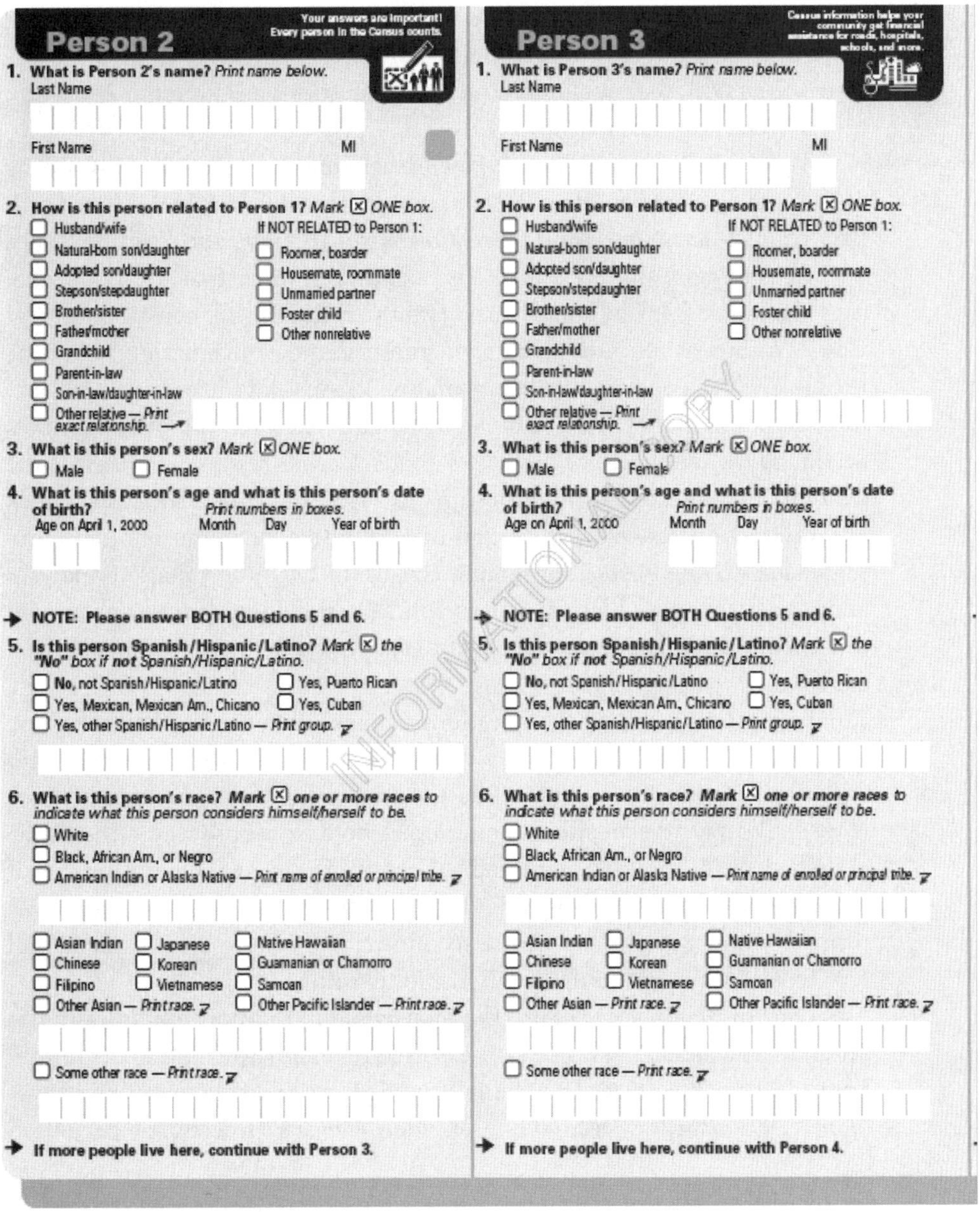
Person 2
Your answers are important! Every person in the Census counts.
1. What is Person 2's name? *Print name below.*
Last Name
First Name MI
2. How is this person related to Person 1? *Mark* ☒ *ONE box.*
☐ Husband/wife
☐ Natural-born son/daughter
☐ Adopted son/daughter
☐ Stepson/stepdaughter
☐ Brother/sister
☐ Father/mother
☐ Grandchild
☐ Parent-in-law
☐ Son-in-law/daughter-in-law
☐ Other relative — *Print exact relationship.*
If NOT RELATED to Person 1:
☐ Roomer, boarder
☐ Housemate, roommate
☐ Unmarried partner
☐ Foster child
☐ Other nonrelative
3. What is this person's sex? *Mark* ☒ *ONE box.*
☐ Male ☐ Female
4. What is this person's age and what is this person's date of birth? *Print numbers in boxes.*
Age on April 1, 2000 Month Day Year of birth
→ NOTE: Please answer BOTH Questions 5 and 6.
5. Is this person Spanish/Hispanic/Latino? *Mark* ☒ *the "No" box if not Spanish/Hispanic/Latino.*
☐ No, not Spanish/Hispanic/Latino ☐ Yes, Puerto Rican
☐ Yes, Mexican, Mexican Am., Chicano ☐ Yes, Cuban
☐ Yes, other Spanish/Hispanic/Latino — *Print group.*
6. What is this person's race? *Mark* ☒ *one or more races to indicate what this person considers himself/herself to be.*
☐ White
☐ Black, African Am., or Negro
☐ American Indian or Alaska Native — *Print name of enrolled or principal tribe.*
☐ Asian Indian ☐ Japanese ☐ Native Hawaiian
☐ Chinese ☐ Korean ☐ Guamanian or Chamorro
☐ Filipino ☐ Vietnamese ☐ Samoan
☐ Other Asian — *Print race.* ☐ Other Pacific Islander — *Print race.*
☐ Some other race — *Print race.*
→ If more people live here, continue with Person 3.

Person 3
Census information helps your community get financial assistance for roads, hospitals, schools, and more.
1. What is Person 3's name? *Print name below.*
Last Name
First Name MI
2. How is this person related to Person 1? *Mark* ☒ *ONE box.*
☐ Husband/wife
☐ Natural-born son/daughter
☐ Adopted son/daughter
☐ Stepson/stepdaughter
☐ Brother/sister
☐ Father/mother
☐ Grandchild
☐ Parent-in-law
☐ Son-in-law/daughter-in-law
☐ Other relative — *Print exact relationship.*
If NOT RELATED to Person 1:
☐ Roomer, boarder
☐ Housemate, roommate
☐ Unmarried partner
☐ Foster child
☐ Other nonrelative
3. What is this person's sex? *Mark* ☒ *ONE box.*
☐ Male ☐ Female
4. What is this person's age and what is this person's date of birth? *Print numbers in boxes.*
Age on April 1, 2000 Month Day Year of birth
→ NOTE: Please answer BOTH Questions 5 and 6.
5. Is this person Spanish/Hispanic/Latino? *Mark* ☒ *the "No" box if not Spanish/Hispanic/Latino.*
☐ No, not Spanish/Hispanic/Latino ☐ Yes, Puerto Rican
☐ Yes, Mexican, Mexican Am., Chicano ☐ Yes, Cuban
☐ Yes, other Spanish/Hispanic/Latino — *Print group.*
6. What is this person's race? *Mark* ☒ *one or more races to indicate what this person considers himself/herself to be.*
☐ White
☐ Black, African Am., or Negro
☐ American Indian or Alaska Native — *Print name of enrolled or principal tribe.*
☐ Asian Indian ☐ Japanese ☐ Native Hawaiian
☐ Chinese ☐ Korean ☐ Guamanian or Chamorro
☐ Filipino ☐ Vietnamese ☐ Samoan
☐ Other Asian — *Print race.* ☐ Other Pacific Islander — *Print race.*
☐ Some other race — *Print race.*
→ If more people live here, continue with Person 4.

Figure 2.1 (*continued*).

numbers. . . . The actual enumeration shall be made within three years after the first meeting of the Congress of the United States, and within every subsequent term of ten years in such manner as they shall by law direct."

The first national census was conducted in 1790, and one has been conducted every ten years since that time. The 1790 U.S. census, however, counted people only according to the following categories: 1) free white males 16 years and over, 2) free white males under 16 years of age, 3) free white females, 4) slaves, and 5) other persons, that is, persons not included in the first four categories. White females were not counted by age, and nonwhite people were counted neither by age nor by sex. Compare these restrictions with the much more inclusive questions asked in the 2000 U.S. census (see Figure 2.1).

Today, censuses and census data are very important for the functioning of government bodies. Box 2.1 shows exactly how the U.S. House was apportioned using data from the 2000 Census (Baumle and Poston, 2004).

Censuses are quite expensive to conduct; the cost of the 2000 U.S. census exceeded 4.5 billion dollars (Gauthier, 2002). But census data provide government officials with useful and necessary information about the people in their country. Governments use census data in virtually all features of public policy, for example, how many children the public schools need to serve and where to place new roads. Census results also provide the denominator data for crime rates, death rates, per capita income figures, and other statistics that are needed to administer local and national governments. Private businesses require census data for their market analyses and advertising activities (M. Anderson, 2003). Many demographers and other social scientists use census data to test their theories and conduct their analyses.

For instance, one of the questions in the 2000 census asked everyone living in a household with two or more persons about their relationship with the person who is known as the "householder." The householder is meant to be "the member of the household in whose name the home is owned, being bought or rented" (Barrett, 1994: 16). Operationally, it refers to the person taking the major responsibility for filling out the census form. Look at question #2 in the second part of Figure 2.1 for the actual wording of the householder relationship question.

One of the responses to the householder relationship question is "unmarried partner." This response is used to identify persons in the household who are not related to the householder but who have a "marriage-like" relationship with the householder. Census procedures permitted

---

BOX 2.1   USING CENSUS DATA TO APPORTION THE U.S. HOUSE OF REPRESENTATIVES

The major objective in apportioning the U.S. House of Representatives is to assign equitably the 435 seats to the fifty states (the District of Columbia is not included in the apportionment and, thus, does not receive representation in the House). There are several constraints: 1) The total number of House seats must equal 435; 2) partial representatives cannot be assigned to states, nor can representatives be given fractional votes; 3) representatives may not be shared by two or more states; and 4) every state must be assigned at least one seat in the House.

The first fifty seats are automatically assigned, one per state; the purpose of the apportionment method is to divide up the remaining 385 seats. The apportionment method of Equal Proportions indicates which states should receive second seats, which states should receive third seats, and so forth. The U.S. Constitution does not provide instructions on how apportionment should be carried out, but the underlying assumption is "one man, one vote." That is, no one person should have more of a voice than another person. As a result, representatives are assigned from states in proportion to their populations. The method of Equal Proportions was first used to apportion the House in 1940 and has been used ever since. It is a divisor method that first develops a target **ratio** of population to representatives that is based on data for the nation. In 2000, the apportionment population (the population counted by the Census Bureau residing in each state plus certain individuals living overseas who claim the state as their "state of residence," namely, military personnel and U.S. government employees and their dependents) of the United States was 281,424,177. Hence, the target ratio in 2000 was 646,952.1 (or 281,424,177 divided by 435). This ratio, also called a divisor, is then divided into the apportionment populations of each of the states to obtain quotients. The method of Equal Proportions endeavors to ensure that "the difference between the representation of any two states is the smallest possible when measured both by the relative difference in the average population per district, and also by the relative difference in the individual share in a representative" (Schmeckebier, 1941: 22). The method gives to a state another representative "when its [apportionment] population, divided by the geometric mean of its present assignment of representatives and of its next higher assignment, is greater than the [apportionment] population of any other state divided by the geometric mean of the assignment to such other state and its next higher assignment" (Schmeckebier, 1941: 22).

The first step in using the method of Equal Proportions is to multiply the apportionment population of each state by the following fraction:

$$\frac{1}{\sqrt{N(N-1)}}$$

where N equals the particular seat being claimed, that is, the second seat or the third seat or the fourth seat, and so on. This provides numbers known as priority values. For instance, the proportion used in determining a state's claim to a second seat is:

$$\frac{1}{\sqrt{2(2-1)}} = \frac{1}{\sqrt{2}} = \frac{1}{1.41421356} = 0.70710678$$

The proportion used in determining a state's claim to a third seat is:

$$\frac{1}{\sqrt{3(3-1)}} = \frac{1}{\sqrt{6}} = \frac{1}{2.44948974} = 0.40824829$$

The rounding rule for this method is to round a state's quotient either up or down, "depending on whether or not the quotient exceeds the 'geometric mean' of these two choices" (Balinski and Young, 1982: 62). The geometric mean of two numbers is the square root of their product. Thus, according to the method of Equal Proportions, if a state had a quotient of 1.39, it would receive one representative because the geometric mean of 1 and 2 is 1.41; however, if a state had a quotient of 1.42, it would receive two representatives.

In the actual apportionment calculations, the rule per se need not be invoked. Instead, one relies entirely on the proportions developed for the various seats. Thus, once the proportions are developed for determining the priorities for the various seats (we have shown the proportions for seats 2 and 3), they are multiplied by the apportionment populations of each of the fifty states. That is, the proportion used for determining the states' priorities for a second seat (0.70710678) is successively multiplied by the apportionment populations of each of the fifty states; this procedure is then repeated using the proportion to determine the states' priorities for a third seat (0.40824829) and so forth. After all of these multiplications have been completed, the resulting priority values are then ranked in order, the largest first and the smallest last. The 385 House seats are assigned to the states with the 385 highest priority values.

In the following table, we report the application of the Method of Equal Proportions in 2000 and identify the states receiving the first six seats and those receiving the last six seats. We also show the states that would have received the three seats beyond the 435th seat if more than 435 seats were assigned. In the 2000 apportionment, California received the 51st seat. Its priority value for a second seat, 23,992,697, was obtained by multiplying its 2000 apportionment population of 33,930,798 by the "second seat" proportion of 0.70710678. Texas received the 52nd seat with its priority value for a second seat of 14,781,356, which was determined by multiplying its 2000 apportionment population of 20,903,994 by 0.70710678. The 51st and 52nd seats were thus assigned to the two largest states, California and Texas. New York was the third largest state in 2000, but New York did not receive the 53rd seat because its priority value for a second seat of 13,438,545 was smaller than California's priority value for a third seat of 13,852,190 (the priority value for California's third seat is obtained by multiplying California's apportionment population of 33,930,798 by the "third seat" proportion of 0.40824829). So California received the 53rd seat and New York the 54th seat. Florida received the 55th seat as its second seat, and California received the 56th seat as its fourth seat.

The table also shows the states receiving the last six seats in the House, the 430th through the 435th seats. Note, for instance, that Georgia's priority value for a 13th seat was slightly larger than Iowa's claim for a 5th seat, so that the 430th seat was assigned to Georgia and the 431st to Iowa. North Carolina received the 435th and last House seat allocated as its 13th seat. The states of Utah, New York, and Texas were next in line to receive the 436th, 437th, and 438th seats had the House allocated three more seats. We have estimated the populations that would have been needed for either Utah or New York or Texas to have been allocated North Carolina's 435th seat. If no other state's population changed, Utah would have needed an apportionment population in 2000 of 2,237,574, which is a mere 860 more persons than its actual 2000 apportionment population. New York would have needed another 47,284 persons in its 2000 apportionment population and Texas another 86,312 persons for either state to have received the 435th seat (Baumle and Poston, 2004).

Application in 2000 of the Method of Equal Proportions: Allocating the first six and last few seats			
Numbered seat in House	State	Numbered seat in the State	Priority value
First six seats			
51	California	2	23,992,697
52	Texas	2	14,781,356
53	California	3	13,852,190
54	New York	2	13,438,545
55	Florida	2	11,334,137
56	California	4	9,794,978
Last six seats			
430	Georgia	13	657,084
431	Iowa	5	655,598
432	Florida	25	654,377
433	Ohio	18	650,239
434	California	53	646,330
435	North Carolina	13	645,931
Three seats beyond the 435th			
436	Utah	4	645,684
437	New York	30	644,329
438	Texas	33	643,276

respondents to check "unmarried partner" whether or not the person's sex is the same as that of the householder. It is thus possible to identify the number of adults in the Unites States who are unmarried partners with persons of the same sex and then calculate the numbers of same-sex adult males and same-sex adult females who are living together. Because this response is meant to reflect a marriage-like relationship between the two persons, demographers make the assumption that these data on same-sex households (male-male or female-female) represent households inhabited by partnered gay men or partnered lesbians (Baumle, Compton, and Poston, 2009; D. Black et al., 2000).

One study used these same-sex data from the 2000 census and cal-culated gay male partnering rates and lesbian partnering rates for the 331 metropolitan areas of the United States (Baumle, Compton, and Poston, 2009). The authors showed that the gay male rate has a mean value of 20.0, meaning that across the 331 metropolitan areas there are, on **average**, 20 gay male cohabiters for every 1,000 never-married males of age 18 and older. (In standard usage, an average is the one value that best represents all cases in a set.) San Francisco has the highest value with a score of almost 61. San Francisco contains the Castro Valley neighborhood, a well-known gay male enclave, making the high prevalence of partnered gay males in San Francisco not a surprise. Dubuque, Iowa, has the lowest score, of about 6 gay male cohabiters per 1,000 never-married males. Dubuque has strong links with the Catholic Church, including the presence of a number of monasteries and motherhouses and two Catholic universities. This strong historical tie with Catholicism may well be linked, at least in part, to the low presence of same-sex male partners in the city, owing to the church's stance against homosexual conduct and gay marriage.

For partnered lesbians living in metropolitan areas, Amanda Baumle and her colleagues (2009) reported an average prevalence rate of almost 27. The Santa Rosa, California, metropolitan statistical area (MSA) has the highest value, a score of more than 72; for every 1,000 never-married women of age 18 and older in the Santa Rosa MSA, there were almost 72 lesbian cohabiters. The Santa Rosa MSA is comprised of a single county bordering the Pacific Ocean, Sonoma County, and is immediately north of Marin County and San Francisco. Its proximity to San Francisco, along with a somewhat more rural locale, perhaps contributes to its high-partnered les-bian prevalence score. The Provo–Orem, Utah, metropolitan area has the lowest score, at 9 per 1,000. Nearly 90 percent of Provo's population is Mormon (Hamby, 2005). Also, Provo is home to Brigham Young Univer-sity, a large private university that is operated by the Church of Jesus Christ of Latter Day Saints. Its adherents oppose marriages of gay males and of lesbians, and they proscribe homosexual behavior in general. Perhaps as a result, gay men and lesbians in Utah have been the subject of a great deal of litigation and restrictive legislation (Hamby, 2005).

Baumle and her colleagues (2009) also found that for the most part, the gay male rates tend to vary in the same way as the lesbian rates. Metropolitan areas with high rates of gay male partnering have high rates of lesbian partnering, and areas with low gay male rates have low lesbian rates. But most of the metropolitan areas, 305 of the 331, have higher lesbian rates than gay male rates. The authors suggest that partnered gay men apparently have a few favorite destinations, including San Francisco, Atlanta, Los Angeles–Long Beach, Miami, Jersey City, Washington, D.C., New York, and Fort Lauderdale, where their prevalence rates surpass those of partnered lesbians. Partnered lesbians, conversely, are concentrated more than are partnered gay men in metropolitan areas in general, tending not to prefer particular areas to the degree that gay men prefer them (Baumle, Compton, and Poston, 2009).

This is but one example of the many and different kinds of demographic research questions that may be answered with data from censuses. We turn next to a discussion of the second source of demographic data, **registration systems**.

REGISTRATION SYSTEMS

Whereas censuses provide a **cross-sectional** (one point in time) portrayal of the size, composition, and distribution of the population, registration systems pertain to the population's demographic events (births and deaths and, in some places, migrations) and measure them as they occur. While censuses are static, registers are dynamic and continuous. Registers apply principally to births and deaths, although many countries also maintain registrations of marriages, divorces, and abortions. Some countries maintain a migration registration system.

Strictly speaking, as Lars Ostby (2003: 763) has noted, a **population register** is a list (i.e., a register) of persons that includes the name, address, date of birth, and a personal identification number. Some registers have been maintained for centuries, such as those in church parishes that record the baptisms and the deaths of the parishioners. In Europe, the Nordic countries and the Netherlands maintain some kind of population register, and many developing countries either have them in place or are planning to implement them. In Eastern Europe under the Communists, "population registers were used for control (of the people) as well as for administrative purposes, and the successor regimes for the most part have not maintained them" (Ostby, 2003: 763). The United States does not maintain any kind of national population register.

The earliest example on record of a population register of families and related household events was in China during the Han Dynasty (205 BC–AD 220). Indeed, as Irene Taeuber (1959: 261) noted, a special demographic tradition of China and the East Asian region as a whole was population registration. Its major function, however, "was the control of the population at the local level" (Bryan, 2004: 25) and not necessarily the collection of continuous data on demographic events.

Population registers are of interest to demographers because they contain birth and death records (certificates). But not all birth and death registrations occur in the context of population registers. In fact, since a large number of countries do not maintain them, the registration of many births and deaths occurs outside population registers.

For most countries in the world, the recording of vital events, that is, births and deaths along with marriages, divorces, fetal deaths (stillbirths), and induced termination of pregnancies (abortions), are recorded in their civil registration systems. But these registration systems need not necessarily be population registers. Indeed, many are not. Although civil registration data are not 100 percent accurate and complete in the more developed nations, their quality is far better than that in the poorer nations. John Cleland (1996: 435) has observed that although civil registration systems in developing countries are "seriously defective, it would not be correct that the data are of little value to demographers." Demographers have developed special techniques for data adjustment and analysis, yielding a rough notion of trends and differentials in these demographic events (Popoff and Judson, 2004).

As articulated by Mary Ann Freedman and James A. Weed (2003: 960), "Vital statistics form the basis of fundamental demographic and epidemiologic measures." **Vital statistics** are the data derived from civil registration systems, as well as from the actual records of vital events. The modern origin of vital statistics and their registration may be traced to the English ordinance in 1532 requiring that parish clerks in London maintain, on a weekly basis, the registration of deaths and christenings (Bryan, 2004: 25). These reports were begun in response to the plagues of the late sixteenth and early seventeenth centuries and were published in a nearly unbroken series for decades. Merchants used those data as a rough gauge of the likelihood of their clientele to flee to the countryside during epidemics (Kraeger, 1988: 129). John Graunt's ([1662] 1939) *Bills of Mortality* is a well-known demographic analysis of these data (see Box 2.2).

With regard to the modern era, Simon Szreter (2007) has written that the registrations of one's birth and death are fundamental human rights. The second clause of Article 24 of the International Covenant on Civil and Political Rights (ICCPR) of the United Nations states that "every child

---

BOX 2.2   JOHN GRAUNT

John Graunt is deemed by many (Bogue, 1969: 9; Poston, 2006a: 254) to be the founder of demography. He was born in London in 1620, raised as a Puritan, and later in life became a Catholic. He died in London in poverty in 1674. Although lacking any higher education and untrained in the sciences or mathematics, he published in 1662 the first-known quantitative analysis of a human population, *Natural and Political Observations Made Upon the Bills of Mortality*.

The "Bills of Mortality" were weekly accountings and reports of the London parish clerks of all the deaths and christenings. These reports were started in response to the plagues of the late sixteenth and early seventeenth centuries and were published in a nearly unbroken series for decades. Merchants used data from the Bills as a rough gauge of the likelihood of their clientele to flee to the countryside during epidemics (Kraeger, 1988: 129). Graunt studied this mass of data searching for regularities. He is credited for being the first to recognize that more males are born than females and that females have greater life expectation than males. He also was one of the first to recognize the phenomenon of rural to urban migration. He also developed a crude mortality table that eventually led to the modern life table; as shown in Chapter 5 of this book, life tables are the basis for calculating life expectancy. Graunt also set a precedent for one of demography's oldest traditions, namely, the evaluation of data "to learn the extent, types, and probable causes of errors" (Bogue, 1969: 9). He "carefully evaluated the bills for their numerical consistency and reliability of compilation, and presented his evidence at length so that his readers might judge it independently" (Kraeger, 1988: 129).

Although Graunt died in obscurity, his lasting monument is his *Natural and Political Observations*, a book that to this day is a joy to read (Poston, 2006a).

---

shall be registered immediately after birth and shall have a name" (Szreter, 2007: 67). The ICCPR also states that "for nation states to take appropriate measures to protect and enhance the life expectancy of their populations, they must have at their disposal accurate and detailed information about patterns and trends of mortality" (Szreter, 2007: 68), thus also requiring death registration. (**Life expectancy** is the average number of years yet to be lived by people attaining a given age, according to a given demographic table.)

How complete is the registration of births and deaths in the world today? For the year 2000, the United Nations (UN) International Children's

Emergency Fund (UNICEF) Research Center has estimated that there were around 50 million babies unregistered, which is more than two fifths of all the babies born in 2000 (UNICEF, 2001). The unregistered children are often found in countries where "there is little awareness of the value of birth registration, where there are no public campaigns, where the registration network is inadequate, or where the costs of registration of children are prohibitive" (UNICEF, 2002: 10). In general, most unregistered babies are born in developing nations, largely because these countries are more likely to face political, administrative, and economic barriers to registration. In some countries, gender discrimination and son preference also lead to female babies being excluded from the birth registration (Hudson and den Boer, 2004). UNICEF has noted that in the year 2000, more than 70 percent and 63 percent of births in sub-Saharan Africa and Asia, respectively, were unregistered. In South Asia alone, there were an estimated 22.5 million unregistered births, the largest number among all the areas of the world.

This does not mean, however, that all developing countries have seriously incomplete birth registration. Many countries in the former Soviet Union have virtually universal coverage of births. This is due likely to their well-established birth registration systems, good medical facilities, and well-trained medical personnel.

Regarding deaths, we do not know as much about the completeness and coverage of death registration around the world. Like the situation with birth registration, incomplete death registration occurs more often in developing nations. For example, only 57 percent of infant deaths were registered in Egypt in the early 1990s (Becker et al., 1996).

The registration of births, marriages, and deaths in the United States began with registration laws in Virginia in 1632 and later in other colonies. We noted earlier that the U.S. Constitution provides the requirement for a decennial census; but there is no such federal requirement for a national vital registration system. Legal authority for the registration of vital events in the United States lies with the individual states. The first U.S. census was conducted in 1790, but the complete coverage of births and deaths occurred much later.

We noted earlier that in seventeenth-century England, the registration and maintenance of baptism, marriage, and burial records were the responsibilities of the clergy. This practice was also followed by the English colonies in North America. In 1639, courts in the Massachusetts Bay Colony declared that birth, death, and marriage reporting would be part of their administrative system. Thomas Bryan has written that the Massachusetts Bay Colony "may have been the first state in the Western world in which maintaining such records was a function of officers of the civil government" (2004: 26; see also Wolfenden, 1954: 22–23). But even here, registration was voluntary and therefore incomplete. By 1865, however, the reporting of deaths was fairly complete, but the same may not be said for births (Bryan, 2004).

Little by little, other U.S. states followed these practices. Since 1919, all of the states have had birth and death records on file for their entire areas, even though registration was not complete. Since 1903, Texas has had birth and death records on file for the entire state. For the state of California, the date is 1905.

The U.S. federal government established a Death Registration Area in 1900 and recommended a standard death certificate form. The U.S. Census Bureau established a Birth Registration Area in 1915. Ten states and the District of Columbia were members, constituting just over 40 percent of the U.S. population. States were added to the registration areas as they qualified. In theory, writes Bryan, "90 percent of deaths, or births, occurring in the state had to be registered for the state to qualify for admission into the Registration Areas; but ways of measuring performance were very crude" (2004: 27). Texas was the last state (of the 48, at the time) to be admitted to the registration areas, and this occurred in 1933.

The U.S. government required that the states in the registration areas transmit copies of their birth and death certificates to Washington every year. Although it is the responsibility of the states to register the births, deaths, and other demographic events, it is the federal government that gathers the materials and publishes them for the country as a whole. Birth and death data are published annually by the National Center for Health Statistics (NCHS) in several series dealing with natality and mortality. These were published in hardcopy volumes into the 1990s but are now published in CD form and on the Internet.

The registration of marriages and divorces in the United States has lagged behind the registration of births and deaths. The National Registration Areas for Marriages and Divorces were not established until 1957 (marriages) and 1958 (divorces). In the 1990s, the government ceased publishing yearly detailed marriage and **divorce** data from the states.

We show in Figure 2.2 an example of a birth certificate and in Figure 2.3 a death certificate. These are the forms used in Texas to register births and deaths.

Birth certificates typically include the names and ages of the parents, their occupations, and, in some states, levels of completed education. The mother normally provides the data, but according to David P. Smith, "If she does not know or does not give the infant's father's attributes, they will not appear on the certificate" (1992: 4). Because birth certificate data about the father are sometimes missing or are incomplete, the study of male

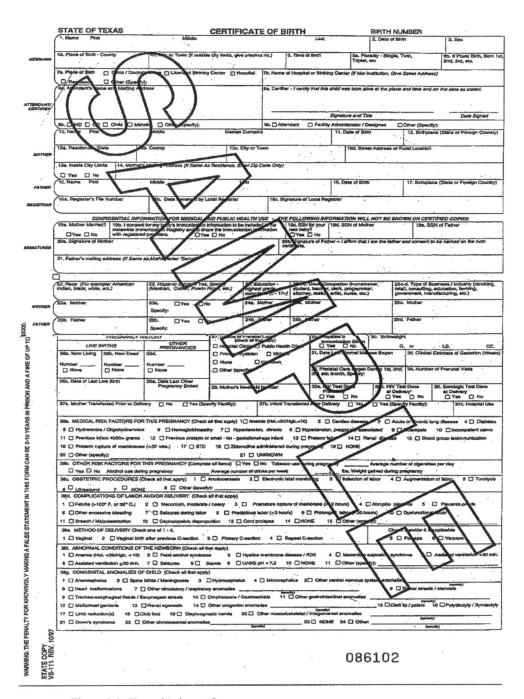

Figure 2.2. Texas birth certificate.

fertility is much more difficult than the study of female fertility. We discuss some of these issues in Chapter 3.

A quick look at the Texas birth certificate reveals that a lot of extra information is gathered about the mother and her baby. For instance, there are sections with respect to pregnancy history, birth weight, obstetric

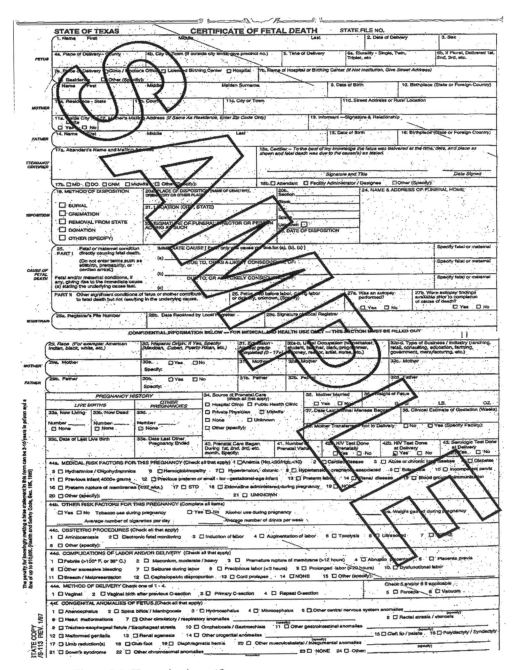

Figure 2.3. Texas death certificate.

procedures, method of delivery, and congenital anomalies of the child. The U.S. states vary somewhat regarding the kinds of supplementary information on their certificates.

The Texas birth certificate also asks if the mother is married. However, this item and several others are reported as confidential information and are not included on the certified copies of the birth certificate. This practice is followed in most states.

A birth is registered in the following way: The physician, the midwife (or person acting as the midwife), the mother of the child, or the father is required to file a certificate of birth with the local registrar of the district where the birth occurred within a certain number of days following the birth of the infant. In most states, the birth must be registered within five days.

Death certificates are usually filled out by funeral homes, with personal information about the decedent provided by one or more of the surviving family members, as well as by the physician in attendance at the death or by the coroner. In addition to the decedent's age, "which may be misreported by surviving family members, particularly for the elderly, the certificates typically include occupation, and place and cause of death information. Space is usually included on the certificate for both immediate and contributing causes of death" (D. Smith, 1992: 4).

The Texas death certificate (Figure 2.3) shows the type of information that is required. Usually, the basic personal information (age, occupation, and so forth) is given by one of the surviving members of the decedent's family (the so-called informant) to a staff member of the funeral home, who fills in the certificate. The certificate also includes data on the facts of the death, and these are filled in by the attending physician or by the medical examiner or justice of the peace. In most states, the person (undertaker or funeral director) in charge of internment or of the removal of the body from the registration district is responsible for filing a certificate of death with the local registrar. Generally, this registration must occur no later than ten days after the date of the death.

We noted previously that at the federal level, the NCHS gathers the birth and death data from each state and tries to make the various birth and death items comparable from state to state. Nosologists, persons who study the classification and categorization of diseases and causes of death, then translate the descriptions of the cause of death into cause-of-death codes of the International Classification of Diseases. At the federal level, the United States also maintains a National Death Index (NDI), "which computerizes names and attributes of decedents as well as cause of death information. Among its . . . uses, the NDI allows tracking of individuals lost to medical studies to confirm any deaths that have occurred" (D. Smith, 1992: 4–5).

One may think that demographic events such as births and deaths are so obvious that they need no definition. Actually, this is not true. Consider the events of births, deaths, and fetal deaths. These are three mutually exclusive categories. A birth must occur before a death. If there is no birth, the **fetus** (the "product of conception") is then classified as a fetal death.

Let us define these terms. First, consider a fetal death, which is defined statistically as follows:

> **Fetal death:** the disappearance of life prior to **live birth**; that is, "the complete expulsion or extraction from its mother of a product of conception, irrespective of the duration of pregnancy. The death is indicated by the fact that after such separation, the fetus does not breathe or show any other evidence of life, such as the beating of the heart, pulsation of the umbilical cord, or definite movement of voluntary muscles" (Shryock, Siegel, and Associates, 1976: 221).

Fetal deaths include miscarriages, abortions, and stillbirths, defined as follows:

> **Miscarriage:** the spontaneous or accidental termination of fetal life that occurs early in pregnancy.

> **Abortion:** the premature expulsion of a fetus, spontaneous or induced, at a time before it is viable of sustaining life. An **induced abortion** is the termination of a pregnancy by human intervention that causes early fetal death, legal or illegal.

> **Stillbirth:** a late fetal death of 20 to 28 weeks or more of **gestation**. (Gestation is the carrying of a fetus in the uterus from conception to delivery.)

A death is different than a fetal death. A death must be preceded by a birth; a fetal death, conversely, is not preceded by a birth. A death is defined statistically as follows:

> **Death:** "the permanent disappearance of all evidence of life at any time after a live birth has taken place (postnatal cessation of vital functions without the capability of resuscitation). A death can occur only after a live birth has occurred" (Shryock, Siegel, and Associates, 1976: 221). Deaths, therefore, do not include fetal deaths.

The third demographic event is a birth. Here is its statistical definition:

> **Birth:** "the complete expulsion or extraction from its mother of a product of conception, irrespective of the duration of pregnancy, which, after such separation, breathes or shows any other evidence of life, such as the beating of the heart, pulsation of the umbilical cord, or definite movement of voluntary muscles, whether or not the umbilical cord has been cut or the placenta is attached" (Shryock, Siegel and Associates, 1976: 273). Strictly speaking, the period of gestation and the state of life or death at the time of registration are not relevant. After being separated from the mother, if the fetus shows any evidence of life (per the definition), it is a live birth.

In the United States, births and deaths are tabulated on a de jure basis. That is, the births and deaths that occur in a state to residents of other states are excluded from the actual tabulations for that state. For example, births and deaths that occur to Virginia residents, regardless of the location of their occurrence, are included in the Virginia birth and death tabulations. A small percentage of births and deaths to residents of a state occurs in other states and places. Knowledge of these events is obtained through an interstate transcript exchange, in cooperation with other states and the NCHS. However, if the death of, say, a Virginian were to occur in California, a California death certificate would be filled out for the decedent; the death information on the California certificate would then be provided to the Virginia registration officials to be included in the Virginia tabulations, and it would not be included in the California tabulations.

SURVEYS

Demographers rely on a third source of demographic data, sample surveys, often because censuses and registration systems do not contain the extensive kinds of information needed to address some of the more critical demographic questions. This is particularly true with respect to the analysis of fertility, although it also applies to mortality and migration. Surveys are required for the collection of more detailed information. By administering surveys to carefully selected random samples of the larger populations, demographers are better able to uncover underlying patterns of demographic behavior than is possible with materials from censuses and registration systems. Here are some of the major surveys that are used by demographers.

World Fertility Surveys

Beginning in the 1970s, coordinated cross-national fertility surveys were introduced in the statistical and demographic communities as an important source of fertility and related demographic information. Between 1974 and 1986, sample surveys to gather data on reproductive behavior and related social and psychological indicators were conducted in 62 countries, representing 40 percent of the world's population, under the auspices of the **World Fertility Survey** (WFS) (Cleland and Hobcroft, 1985; Cleland and Scott, 1987).

Demographic and Health Surveys

The WFS was followed by another coordinated international program of research, the **Demographic and Health Survey** (DHS), with more than 200 sample surveys carried out in 75 developing countries since 1984. DHSs are nationally representative household surveys with large sample sizes (usually between 5,000 and 30,000 households). These surveys provide data for many variables in the areas of fertility, population, health, and nutrition. Typically, the surveys are conducted every five years to permit comparisons over time. Interim surveys are conducted between DHS rounds and have shorter questionnaires and smaller samples than the DHS surveys (2,000 to 3,000 households).

The DHS (as well as the WFS) provides demographic information previously unknown about the countries in which they are implemented. To illustrate, a DHS was recently completed in 2006 in Nepal, a small country of about 26 million people in South Central Asia. The DHS data for Nepal indicated that if current fertility levels were maintained, a Nepalese woman would have, on average, 3.1 children by the time she completed her childbearing. This was a drop from 4.6 births per woman in 1996 and from 4.1 births per woman in 2001, a decrease of 1.5 children in the past ten years. The DHS data also showed that urban women in Nepal have fewer children than rural women, namely, 2.1 children for urban women and 3.3 children for rural women. The DHS data also indicated that fertility varied inversely with the educational and economic status of the mother. Nepalese women with no education were shown to have more than twice as many children as women who completed secondary education or more: 3.9 children versus 1.8 children, respectively. Also, very poor women were shown to have more than twice as many children as wealthy women (Ministry of Population and Health, Nepal, 2007: 3).

Other fertility surveys

Less ambitious demographic surveys, typically focusing on a single country or community, have been part of the demographer's repertoire for decades. Early endeavors included the Indianapolis study (Kiser, 1953; Kiser and Whelpton, 1953), the Princeton study (Westoff et al. 1961; Westoff, Potter, and Sagi, 1963), and surveys of family and reproductive behavior carried out in Puerto Rico (Hill, Stycos, and Back, 1959; Stycos, 1955).

The number of demographic surveys has grown steadily over the years. There are many surveys conducted in the United States, some of which are conducted by the government. Following are two examples of federal surveys.

Current Population Survey

The **Current Population Survey (CPS)** is a monthly nationwide survey conducted by the U.S. Bureau of the Census with the main purpose of collecting

labor force data about the civilian noninstitutional population. Every month there are newspaper stories about levels of unemployment in the United States and its major metropolitan areas, using data gathered in the CPS.

CPS interviewers ask questions concerning the labor force participation of each member 14 years of age and older in every sample household. The survey covers upward of 70,000 households each month and is a nationally representative sample of the U.S. population. A household is in the CPS sample for eight rotations, and the samples are overlapping. Only 25 percent of the households differ between consecutive months. In addition to the basic CPS questions, interviewers also may ask supplementary questions. For instance, the March CPS includes a series of census-type questions (known as the Annual Demographic File) dealing with mobility, marital status, income, poverty, educational status, veteran status, and other census topics.

National Survey of Family Growth

The **National Survey of Family Growth (NSFG)** that was conducted in 2002 is the sixth such cycle of surveys of family growth carried out by the NCHS. Prior surveys were conducted in 1973, 1976, 1982, 1988, and 1995.

The NSFG is a nationally representative multistage survey of male and female respondents between the ages of 15 and 44 that collects information on family life and reproductive health. The 2002 NSFG was the first to include male respondents (National Center for Health Statistics, 2004). Interviews were conducted in person between January 2002 and March 2003. The sample consisted of 12,571 Americans (7,643 women and 4,928 men). The female questionnaire took, on average, 85 minutes to complete and the male questionnaire, 60 minutes. Respondents were offered $40 for participating. Respondent data addressing sensitive topics, such as sexuality, were collected using Audio Computer-Assisted Self-Interviewing (ACASI) "in which the respondent listens to the questions through headphones, reads them on the (laptop computer) screen, or both, and enters the response directly into the computer" (Mosher, Chandra, and Jones, 2005: 7). Such methods have been shown to "yield more complete reporting of sensitive behaviors, and they also avoid the large amounts of missing data often found on paper and pencil self-administered questionnaires" (Mosher, Chandra, and Jones, 2005: 8). The survey had an overall response rate of 79 percent (80 percent for women and 78 percent for men) (Mosher, Chandra, and Jones, 2005). Another important source of demographic information is the National Survey of Adolescent Health, begun in the early 1990s by the Carolina Population Center.

American Community Survey

In the past few years, the U.S. Census Bureau has redesigned its decennial long-form questionnaire (see earlier discussion in this chapter) into an ongoing "continuous measurement" survey, known as the **American Community Survey (ACS)**. Indeed, the ACS will take the place in future census years of the decennial long-form questionnaire. The ACS began on a limited basis in 1996 and is now conducted in all counties in the United States and Puerto Rico. It is intended to provide important economic, social, demographic, and housing data to all the communities in the United States every year, the same types of data that were previously provided to communities only once every ten years. In this sense, the ACS is "the decennial 'long form' spread out over 10 years; that is, the data collection occurs throughout the decade rather than just once in ten years" (Cynthia Taeuber, 2006: 7).

U.S. communities with 65,000 or more population receive ACS data estimates on all the long-form characteristics on an annual basis and have been receiving these data since 2006. Areas with 20,000 to 64,999 population receive data each year based on three-year estimates, which began in 2008. Areas with less than 20,000 population will receive characteristics data each year based on five-year estimates starting in 2010: "Beginning in 2010, and every year thereafter, the nation will have a five-year period estimate available as an alternative to the decennial census long-form sample, a community information resource that shows change over time, even for neighborhoods and rural areas" (U.S. Bureau of the Census, 2006: 2–6). These five-year estimates will be preferred over other ACS estimates because the error will be smaller.

Beginning in 2005, a random sample of households in the United States started to receive the ACS questionnaire each month in the mail. Every year, about one in forty addresses, or 2.5 percent of the community, are included in the ACS. Thus, an address has a chance of about 1 in 480 of being selected in any one year for the ACS. The annual sample size of the ACS is around 3 million addresses. After the mailing, the selected household receives a telephone follow-up; a face-to-face interview then follows for a subsample of the addresses that do not respond. As noted, the ACS questions are very similar to the decennial census long-form questions.

In closing, we need to reemphasize the fact that the ACS is a major change in census operations, indeed, a paradigm shift in census data collection. The ACS was developed so that the U.S. Census Bureau would be able to address various problems encountered in recent censuses. These include, but are not limited to, difficulties in recruiting a sufficient number of qualified enumerators, a decline in the mail return of the census questionnaires, and an uncertainty about the completeness of the census address lists and counts, especially in so-called hard-to-enumerate areas. The ACS plan as summarized here (for more detail, see the ACS Web site, http://www.census.gov/acs/www/) provides an approach for simplifying the enumerators' job by removing the need to learn how to conduct the long-form interview and by identifying hard-to-enumerate areas where special enumeration techniques are needed. The U.S. Census Bureau hopes that the ACS and its timely data will increase the confidence of users in its results, as well as reduce the number and types of problems encountered during the census (for more discussion, see Hillygus et al., 2006).

SUMMARY

In this chapter, we discuss the three basic sources of demographic data: national censuses, registers, and surveys. Each is an important source of data for demographic study. Some demographers rely more on one or two of these than on the other. But demographic analysis in general requires data from all three sources. In the next chapters, we discuss the three demographic processes of fertility (Chapters 3 and 4), mortality (Chapter 5), and migration (Chapters 6 and 7). Our discussions in these and later chapters are based on data from all three sources presented and elaborated on in this chapter.

KEY TERMS

abortion	household
American Community Survey (ACS)	induced abortion
average	labor force
birth	life expectancy
census	live birth
cross-sectional	long-form questionnaire
Current Population Survey (CPS)	miscarriage
death	National Survey of Family
de facto population	Growth (NSFG)
de jure population	population register
Demographic and Health	ratio
Survey (DHS)	registration
divorce	registration systems
ethnic	stillbirth
fetal death	vital statistics
fetus	World Fertility Survey (WFS)
gestation	

3 Fertility

Fertility refers to the actual production of children, which in the strictest sense is a biological process. A **zygote** is produced when the sperm of a male and the egg of a female are united, and around nine months later a baby is born. Most often in this process, though not always, a man and a woman have sexual intercourse, the woman conceives, and the **conception** results in a live birth. Even though the production of a child is a biological process, the various activities and events that lead to the act of sexual intercourse and, later, to giving birth are affected by the social, economic, cultural, and psychological characteristics of the woman and the man, as well as by the environment in which they live. The key to this seeming paradox is that engaging in intercourse, conceiving, and giving birth are themselves behaviors that are influenced by other factors, most of them social and cultural. So while we have no influence at all with regard to the family and parents we receive when we are born, we do have a significant influence on our own fertility, that is, whether or not we produce children, and if so, the number and timing of the children produced. That is, whether we decide to engage in sexual intercourse, whether this intercourse results in a conception, and whether a live birth is the outcome are all driven largely by social and cultural considerations.

Fertility can be studied in different ways, one of which is cross-sectionally, that is, at one point in time; a cross-sectional perspective is also known as a **period perspective**. Were we to study the fertility behavior of women and men in the year 2009, we would develop cross-sectional fertility measures (also called period measures) that would show the number of births to women and men in the calendar year 2009. Most of the fertility measures shown in this chapter are period measures; that is, they refer to a particular time period. A **period rate**, also called a cross-sectional rate, is a rate based on behavior occurring at a particular point or period in time.

Conversely, fertility may be studied over time to give us measures revealing the number and spacing of births to cohorts of women as they pass through the life cycle; this is known as **cohort analysis**. Here we could take the cohort of women who began their childbearing years at age 15 in, say, 1970. We could then follow them each year through 2005 when they were at the end of age 49 and had completed their childbearing years in order to see how many babies they had produced. Fertility may thus be measured on a cohort basis, as well as on a period basis.

The demographic study of the fertility of individual women (and men) is known as *microfertility analysis* because it refers to the fertility of persons. There are several different ways to study fertility at the individual level: 1) examining the number of births a woman (or man) has produced by a given point in time, such as the date of a census or survey; 2) examining the number of births a woman (or man) has had by the end of the childbearing years; and 3) focusing on the timing and spacing of births at various stages of the life cycle (say, between the ages of 25 and 29, or between 45 and 49).

Another way to study fertility is to use a *macro-level approach*, that is, to determine the rate at which births occur in a population or subpopulation during a given period of time. Rather than studying the fertility of persons, macrofertility analysis studies the fertility of populations (Poston and Frisbie, 2005). One reason demographers measure fertility at the macro level is to then compare it with mortality, and to compute rates of reproductive change. They also compare the fertility levels of different types of subpopulations over time.

In this chapter, we first consider the conceptualization and measurement of fertility. Second, we discuss the so-called **proximate determinants** of fertility. These are the mainly biological factors that lead directly to fertility, and are themselves influenced heavily by social factors. Third, we look at some of the main theories generated by demographers to specify the reasons that some women or men or societies have more babies than other women or men or societies. We next consider world fertility patterns and how they have changed over time, then focus on fertility trends and differences in the United States. We follow with a discussion of adolescent fertility, concluding with a section on male fertility.

CONCEPTUALIZATION AND MEASUREMENT OF FERTILITY

There are three main fertility concepts. **Fertility** is the actual production of male and female births and refers to real behavior. **Reproduction** is also actual production, but refers to the production of only female births (there is no demographic term to refer to the production of only male births). **Fecundity** refers to the potential or the biological capacity of producing live births.

The **crude birth rate (CBR)** is the first measure of fertility we consider. It is a cross-sectional (i.e., period) measure and refers to the number of births occurring in a population in a year per 1,000 persons. It is calculated as follows:

$$\text{CBR} = \frac{\text{number of births}}{\text{midyear population}} * 1,000 \qquad (3.1)$$

In 2007, the CBR for the world was 21/1,000. This means that in the world in 2007, there were 21 births for every 1,000 members of the population. Among the continents, the CBR in 2007 ranged from a high of 38 in Africa to a low of 10 in Europe. Almost four times as many children per 1,000 population were born in Africa than in Europe in 2007. North America had a CBR of 14 (the CBR of the United States was also 14); Latin America, 21; Asia, 19; and Oceania, 18 (Population Reference Bureau, 2007a). The major countries of the world had 2007 CBRs ranging from lows of 8 in Macao, South Korea, Germany, and Taiwan to highs of 50 in Liberia and the Democratic Republic of the Congo and 49 in Angola. Generally, CBRs above 30 are considered to be high, and those less than 15 to be low.

The CBR is referred to as "crude" because its denominator, the midyear population of the area, includes many people who are not at the risk of childbearing, such as young women (under age 15) and post-menopausal women (older than age 50). (An **at-risk population** is the population that is at the risk of the event of interest occurring to them.) Another downside is that men are included in the denominator, and, strictly speaking, men do not bear children, so are thus not exposed to the risk of childbearing. However, some demographers do study male fertility, and we consider this topic later in the chapter.

The **general fertility rate (GFR)** is another cross-sectional measure of fertility. It is superior to the CBR because it restricts the denominator to women of childbearing ages. The GFR is calculated as follows:

$$\text{GFR} = \frac{\text{births}}{\text{midyear population}_{f,15-49}} * 1,000 \qquad (3.2)$$

where the numerator is the number of births in the population in the year, and the denominator is the number of females in the midyear population who are in the childbearing ages 15–49.

Table 3.1. Fertility data and rates for the United States in 2005				
Age group	Women in age group (midyear population)	Live births to women in age group	Age-specific fertility rates live births per 1,000 women ASFR	ASFR × 5
Col. 1	Col. 2	Col. 3	Col. 4	Col. 5
15–19	10,240,239	414,406	40.47	202.3
20–24	10,150,079	1,040,399	102.50	512.5
25–29	9,767,524	1,132,293	115.92	579.6
30–34	9,906,365	952,013	96.10	480.5
35–39	10,427,161	483,401	46.36	231.8
40–44	11,475,863	104,644	9.12	45.6
45–49*	11,372,141	6,546	0.58	2.9
TOTALS	73,339,372	4,133,702		2,055.2[a]

* Data are for live births to mothers 45+ per 1,000 women 45–49.
[a] TFR = $\sum$(ASFR * 5) = 2,055.2.
Sources: For population data: U.S. Bureau of the Census, 2008; for birth data: Hamilton, Martin, and Ventura, 2007.

In the United States in 2005, there were 73,339,372 women of ages 15 to 49; and 4,133,702 babies were born in 2005 (see Table 3.1). Dividing the latter figure by the former and multiplying the result by 1,000 yields a GFR value for the United States in 2005 of 56.4. This means that there were more than 56 babies born in the United States in 2005 for every 1,000 women between the ages of 15 and 49.

Sometimes the denominator of the GFR is restricted to women between the ages of 15 and 44. This occurs because, as will be noted, not many babies are born to women in the 45–49 age group. To illustrate, of the 4,133,702 births that occurred in the United States in 2005, only 6,546, or 0.15 percent, occurred to women over the age of 44 (see Table 3.1).

In Figure 3.1, we show GFRs for the United States for individual years between 1970 and 2007. It is important to keep in mind when viewing these GFRs that the denominator is women 15–44, not women 15–49.

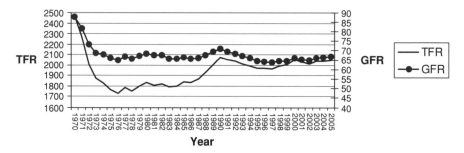

Figure 3.1. TFRs and GFRs: United States, 1970–2005. *Source:* The authors.

The data in the figure show that fertility as measured by the GFR (with a denominator of women 15–44) was high in 1970 but dropped to the 60s by 1980 and has mostly remained in the 60s since then. (Total fertility rates are also shown in Figure 3.1; they are defined later.)

In the definition for the GFR, we referred to its denominator as females in the childbearing ages. We need to consider here what is meant by *childbearing ages*. In practice, as already noted, few women give birth before age 15 and after age 49, and so demographers usually use the age range 15–49 to mark the limits of the childbearing ages. But this range is not universal. In developed countries, not much fertility occurs to women after age 44. Therefore, sometimes (see Figure 3.1) GFRs are calculated only for women of ages 15–44.

Of course, there are exceptions even to these age ranges. To illustrate, in the year 2000, the ages of mothers listed on birth certificates filed in Texas ranged from a low of 11 to a high of 53. The mean age of Texas mothers giving birth in 2000 was 26.1 years. Only 0.3 percent of all births were to mothers under age 15 and 1.6 percent to mothers of age 40 or older. More than half (55.0 percent) of all Texas births were to mothers 20–29 years of age and almost three-fourths (74.4 percent) were to mothers 20–34.

Percentages of U.S. births in 2005 to very young females are even lower than those for Texas. Less than 0.2 percent of all U.S. births in 2005 were to females ages 10–14. More than 2.4 percent of U.S. births in 2005 were to women older than the age of 40. Not many women under age 15 or over age 40, particularly older than age 45, have babies, but some do. Thus, although the denominator of the GFR starts at age 15, the numerator literally comprises of all births, including those to females under age 15.

In July 2008, the British Broadcasting Corporation (BBC) News agency distributed a story about, apparently, the oldest woman ever to give birth. In northern India, Omkari Panwar, 70 years old, gave birth to twins in 2008. She and her husband, Charam Singh, a farmer in his mid-70s, already had two children, both girls. They badly wanted a male, so they took out a bank loan to pay the costs for in vitro fertility therapy, the result being a boy and a girl, both weighing around two pounds (British Broadcasting Corporation News, 2008).

If one has data available only for the CBR but wishes to approximate the value of the GFR, an estimated GFR value (for women 15–44) is given by the following formula:

$$GFR = CBR * 4.5 \tag{3.3}$$

To illustrate, CBR values in the United States in 1950 and in 2005 were 24.1 and 14.0, respectively. If we had no other data available and needed GFR values for these two years, we could multiply each CBR by 4.5 and arrive at estimated GFR values of 108.5 for 1950 and 63.0 for 2005. These estimated GFRs are not far from the actual GFRs of 106.2 for 1950 and 66.7 for 2005. The constant in this formula and those in other formulas to be shown later are based on empirical and analytic relationships between the fertility measures (see Bogue and Palmore [1964] for an example of such an application).

We noted earlier that the GFR addressed the major problem of the CBR by restricting the denominator to women in the childbearing ages. A problem still remains, however, with the GFR. It does not take into account the fact that within the range of the childbearing years for females of 15 to 49, there are differences in the extent to which the women produce children. Fertility is usually low for women 15–19 and is then at its highest for women 20–29; the rates become lower in the 30s and even lower in the 40s. To take into account the fact that fertility varies by age, demographers calculate fertility rates for specific age groups of women.

The **age-specific fertility rate (ASFR)** reflects exactly what its name indicates: It focuses on births to women according to their age. ASFRs are usually calculated for women in each of the seven 5-year age groups of 15–19, 20–24, 25–29, 30–34, 35–39, 40–44, and 45–49. The general formula for the ASFR for women in age group x to x + n is calculated as follows:

$$\text{ASFR}_{x \text{ to } x + n} = \frac{\text{births}_{x \text{ to } x + n}}{\text{females}_{x \text{ to } x + n}} * 1,000 \qquad (3.4)$$

Although most demographic analyses using ASFRs calculate them for these 5-year age groups, sometimes thirty-five single-year age groups are used, for example, age group 15, age group 16, age group 17, all the way up to age group 49.

Table 3.1 shows the numbers of women in the United States in 2005 in each of the seven age groups 15–19 to 45–49 (col. 2) and the numbers of babies born to the women in each of the age groups (col. 3). There were 10,150,079 women in 2005 in the age group 20–24. There were 1,040,399 babies born in 2005 to women in this age group. Dividing the latter figure by the former and multiplying the result by 1,000 produces an ASFR for women 20–24 of 102.5. This means that in the United States in 2005, for every 1,000 women 20–24, 102.5 babies were born to them. All seven ASFRs for U.S. women in 2005 are shown in Table 3.1. The highest ASFR is for women 25–29, the next highest for women 20–24, and the third highest for women 30–34. ASFRs for women in the other four age groups are not as high.

When the seven ASFRs are plotted, they usually form an inverted U. Such a plot is referred to as the *age curve of fertility*. Figure 3.2 shows six age curve of fertility plots for Africa, Asia, Europe, Latin America, North

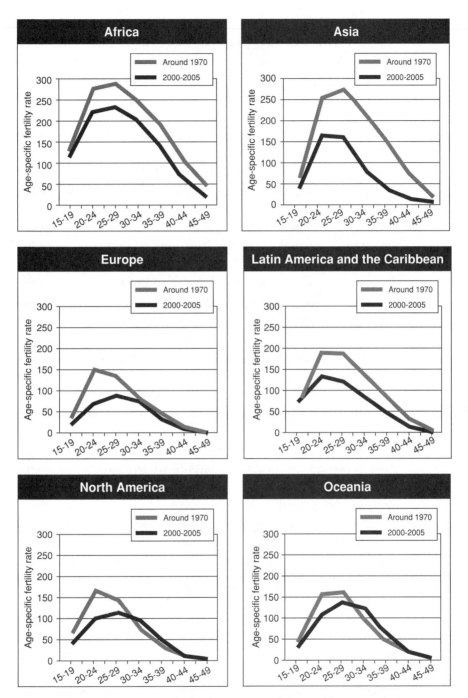

Figure 3.2. Trends in age-specific fertility, regions of the world: 1970 and 2000–2005. *Source:* United Nations, 2008a.

America, and Oceania; the curves for each region are shown for 1970 and for 2000–2005. Fertility as measured by ASFRs in 1970, as well as 2000–2005, is highest in Africa and lowest in Europe and North America. For the most part, fertility was higher in 1970 than 2000–2005. Later in this chapter, we focus on fertility and fertility change in the world.

The **total fertility rate (TFR)** is the most popular of all fertility rates used by demographers. Like the ASFRs, the TFRs take into account the fact that fertility varies by age; unlike the ASFRs, which are expressed quantitatively as a series of **specific rates** (usually seven, one for each age group), the TFR provides a single fertility value. The TFR is most frequently calculated cross-sectionally, that is, for a specific period of time, although as we will show, it may also be calculated for cohorts. A cross-sectional TFR for a particular point in time is an estimate of the number of births that a hypothetical group of 1,000 women would have during their reproductive lifetime, that is, between the ages of 15 and 49 (or, sometimes, 15 and 44), if their childbearing at each of their reproductive years followed the ASFRs for a given period. This number of live births that the hypothetical group of 1,000 women would produce if they were exposed to a particular schedule of ASFRs assumes that none of them die during their reproductive years.

The TFR is calculated by summing the ASFRs after multiplying each by the width of the age interval of the ASFRs. If we use ASFRs based on 5-year intervals, as is usually the case, we would multiply each ASFR by the value of 5:

$$\text{TFR} = \sum (\text{ASFR}_{x \text{ to } x + n} * i) \tag{3.5}$$

where $i =$ the width in years of the age interval; in most cases, this will be 5.

In Table 3.1, we show the calculation of the TFR for the United States for the year 2005. The ASFRs shown in column 4 are multiplied by the constant of 5 and reported in column 5. These values are then summed, to yield a TFR of 2,055. This may be interpreted as follows: If 1,000 women went through their reproductive years of 15 to 49 and were subjected each year to the U.S. ASFRs for the year 2005, by the time they reached age 49, they would have produced 2,055 babies, or an average of 2.1 babies each. The TFR is a standardized rate; that is, it is not influenced by the differences in the numbers of women in each age. Its value is especially useful in interpreting the fertility that is implied by a given set of ASFRs for a particular point in time.

TFRs are shown in Figure 3.1 for the United States for the years 1970 to 2005. In 1970, the TFR was almost 2.5, dropped to lows of 1.73 and 1.75 in 1976 and 1978, and then increased to its 2007 value of just slightly more than 2. There is a fairly close correspondence between the TFR and the GFR for most, but not all, of the years.

If one only has CBR data available for an area or country or, alternately, only GFR data, the TFR may be estimated with the following formulas:

$$TFR = CBR * 4.5 * 30 \tag{3.6}$$

$$TFR = GFR * 30 \tag{3.7}$$

For example, the actual CBR and GFR values for the United States in 2005 were 14.0 and 66.7, respectively. If we only had the CBR data but needed an estimate of the TFR for the United States in 2005, we could use formula 3.6 and obtain an estimated TFR of 1,890. If we only had available the GFR data and desired a TFR estimate, we could use formula 3.7 and get an estimated TFR of 2,001. These two estimated TFR values of 1,890 and 2,001 are fairly close to the true value of 2,055 shown in Table 3.1. Certainly, one would prefer to have the real data, but these two formulas are helpful for providing estimates.

In 2007, the world TFR was 2.7. It was 2.9 for the **less-developed countries (LDCs)** of the world including China, and 3.3 for the LDCs excluding China. The developed countries had an average TFR in 2007 of 1.6. TFRs ranged from a high of 7.1 in Niger and Guinea-Bissau to a low of 1.1 in South Korea and Taiwan (Population Reference Bureau, 2007a). If during their childbearing years, 1,000 women followed the ASFRs for Niger or Guinea-Bissau in 2007, at the completion of their 49th year, they would have produced 7,100 babies, or an average of 7.1 each. In contrast, if during their reproductive lives, 1,000 women were subjected to the ASFRs of either Taiwan or South Korea for the year 2007, by the time they ended their childbearing years, they would have given birth to 1,100 babies, or about 1.1 each. These are tremendous differences in fertility. We discuss TFR trends and differences among the countries of the world in a later section of this chapter.

We noted that the TFR may be calculated cross-sectionally, that is, for a specific period or year, and is referred to as a period or cross-sectional TFR. Alternately, the TFR may be calculated for cohorts. Rather than subjecting a hypothetical group of 1,000 women to a schedule of ASFRs for a given point in time, that is, as with the cross-sectional TFR, the cohort TFR follows a real group of women through their childbearing years and tabulates their actual fertility as they pass through these years. Table 3.2 presents average annual ASFRs for the years 1970–1974, 1975–1979, and so forth, through 2000–2004. Let us use these data to calculate a period TFR and a cohort TFR.

Table 3.2. Age-specific fertility rates, United States, 1970–1974 to 2000–2004

	15–19 years	20–24 years	25–29 years	30–34 years	35–39 years	40–44 years	45–49* years	Total fertility rate
1970–1974	62.3	137.1	124.1	61.9	25.5	6.2	0.4	2,087.5
1975–1979	53.0	111.8	109.1	112.4	19.2	4.2	0.2	2,049.5
1980–1984	51.9	110.7	110.5	63.9	21.2	3.9	0.2	1,811.5
1985–1989	52.4	109.5	112.9	72.7	26.5	11.3	0.2	1,927.5
1990–1994	59.8	113.2	115.5	80.0	32.4	5.9	0.3	2,035.5
1995–1999	52.0	107.8	109.4	83.7	35.9	7.1	0.4	1,981.5
2000–2004	43.7	104.8	114.3	93.0	42.2	8.4	0.5	2,034.5

* Before 1997, data are for 45–49 per 1,000 women; beginning with 1997, rates are for live births to mothers 45–54 per 1,000 women 45–49.
Source: The authors.

The cross-sectional TFR may be calculated for any of these years by summing the ASFRs across the respective row and multiplying the sum by 5. To illustrate, if we wanted the average annual cross-sectional TFR for the period 1970–1974, we would sum the seven ASFRs for that period, namely, 62.3, 137.1, 124.1, 61.9, 25.5, 6.2, and 0.4, and then multiply the total by 5 to produce an annual period TFR for 1970–1974 of 2,087.5 This value reflects the number of children that a hypothetical group of 1,000 women would produce were they to be subjected to the ASFRs of the United States for the 1970–1974 period.

In contrast, if we desired the cohort TFR for those women who started their childbearing years in 1970–1974 (we refer to those women as the 1970–1974 fertility cohort because they initiated their childbearing during those years), we would take the ASFRs on the diagonal line in Table 3.2 and observe the ASFRs for the 1970–1974 fertility cohort of women as they proceeded through their childbearing years. When those women were 15–19 in 1970–1974, they had an ASFR of 62.3; when they were 20–24 in 1975–1979, they had an ASFR of 111.8; when they were 25–29 in 1980–1984, they had an ASFR of 110.5; and so forth until they were 45–49 in 2000–2004 and had an ASFR of 0.5. When we sum these ASFRs and multiply the total by 5, we have a cohort TFR of 1,986.5. This is the actual number of children that were produced on average by 1,000 members of the 1970–1974 fertility cohort.

A period (i.e., cross-sectional) TFR refers to the fertility of a **hypothetical cohort** (an imaginary set) of 1,000 women, whereas a cohort TFR refers to the actual fertility of a real cohort of 1,000 women. A period TFR for a year, say, the year 2007, refers to the fertility produced by women of all ages in the year 2007, a particular period of time. Alternately, a cohort

TFR refers to the fertility of a group of women who have already completed their childbearing years and sometimes may be viewed as out of date. Both period and cohort TFRs are used by demographers, but, as already noted, period TFRs are preferred principally because of their currency.

There are more fertility measures in addition to the four rates just covered, although none is as popular as the TFR. We now discuss two that are based on the concept of *population replacement*. Given a set of fertility rates, what does this mean with regard to replacing the population? Replacement refers to the production of female births, known among demographers as reproduction. Reproduction pertains to the production of female babies, while fertility refers to the production of babies of either sex.

The **gross reproduction rate (GRR)** is a standardized rate similar to the TFR, except that it is based on the sum of age-specific rates that include only female births in the numerators. Sometimes data are not readily available on the number of female live births reported by age of the mothers. Thus, the proportion of all births that are female is usually employed as a constant and is multiplied against the given TFR, as follows:

$$GRR = TFR * \left(\frac{\text{female births}}{\text{births}}\right) \tag{3.8}$$

The value of the constant multiplier, that is, the proportion of births that are female, varies only slightly from population to population. Most societies, but not all, have about 105 male babies born per 100 female babies. This results in about 51.2 percent of all births each year being male births and 48.8 percent being female births. Hence, we may use the following formula to calculate the GRR:

$$GRR = TFR * 0.488 \tag{3.9}$$

We noted previously that the TFR in the United States in 2005 was 2,055.2 (see Table 3.1). We may thus calculate the GRR for the United States in 2005 as follows:

$$GRR = TFR * 0.488 \tag{3.10}$$
$$= 2,055.2 * 0.488 = 1,002.9$$

This value of 1,002.9 may be interpreted as the number of daughters expected to be born alive to a hypothetical cohort of 1,000 women if none of the women died during their childbearing years and if the same schedule of age-specific rates applied throughout their childbearing years.

In Table 3.3, we show the calculation of the GRR for the United States in 2005 in greater detail than in formula 3.10. We start with a listing of the seven age groups (col. 1) and the midpoint of the age interval for each

Table 3.3. Calculation of gross reproduction rate (GRR) and net reproduction (NRR), United States

Age group	Midpoint of interval	Number of women in age group	Number of births to women in age group	Number of female births to women in age group	Female births per woman	Female birth rate during 5-year interval	Proportion of female babies surviving to midpoint of age interval	Surviving daughters per woman during 5-year interval
15–19	17.5	10,240,239	414,406	202,230	0.01974	0.09874	0.9889	0.09765
20–24	22.5	10,150,079	1,040,399	507,715	0.05002	0.25010	0.9848	0.24631
25–29	27.5	9,767,524	1,132,293	552,559	0.05657	0.28286	0.9801	0.27723
30–34	32.5	9,906,365	952,013	464,582	0.04690	0.23449	0.9752	0.22868
35–39	37.5	10,427,161	483,401	235,900	0.02262	0.11312	0.9691	0.10962
40–44	42.5	11,475,863	104,644	51,066	0.00445	0.02225	0.9600	0.02136
45–49*	47.5	11,372,141	6,546	3,194	0.00028	0.00140	0.9462	0.00133
						1.00296 = GRR		0.98218 = NRR

* Before 1997, data are for 45–49 per 1,000 women 45–49; beginning with 1997, rates are for live births to mothers 45–54 per 1,000 women 45–49.

Sources: For population data: U.S. Bureau of the Census, 2008; for birth data, Hamilton, Martin, and Ventura, 2007.

age group (col. 2). For instance, the midpoint for the age group 15–19 is 17.5. Data on the number of women in each age group in the United States in 2005 appear in column 3. Data on the number of babies born to the women in each age group appear in column 4.

As noted earlier, often we do not have data on the sex composition of births by age of mother, so this needs to be approximated. In the United States, as in most other countries, the **sex ratio at birth (SRB)** is around 105 boys per 100 girls. This means that the proportion of U.S. births that are female is 0.488. We multiply the birth data in column 4 by this constant proportion of 0.488, producing in column 5 the data on female births to women in each group. (If the SRB is not around 105, then another constant must be used. For instance, if we were calculating the GRR for China in 2000, we would need to take into account the fact that China's SRB in 2000 was 119. Thus, the proportion of all births in China in 2000 that were female was 0.457. This would be the constant used for calculating the GRR for China in 2000.)

Next, we divide the number of female births at each age (col. 5) by the number of women at each age (col. 3), to produce the age-specific rates of female births (col. 6); these age-specific rates have not yet been multiplied by 1,000.

The age-specific rates of female births in column 6 refer to only a single year, but we want to assume that the hypothetical cohort of women will experience these rates during the entire 5-year interval. So we now multiply the rates in column 6 by 5 to obtain the female birth rates during the 5-year interval; these are shown in column 7.

We then sum the values in column 7 to obtain the GRR. We multiply this sum by 1,000 to get the number of female births born to the hypothetical cohort of 1,000 women. The value of the GRR is 1.00296. We multiply it by 1,000, yielding 1,003.

The GRR makes no allowance for the fact that some of the mothers will die before they complete their childbearing years. Thus, to obtain a more accurate measure of the replacement of daughters by their mothers, we need another rate: the **net reproduction rate (NRR)**.

The NRR is a measure of the number of daughters who will be born to a hypothetical cohort of 1,000 mothers, taking into account the mortality of the mothers from the time of their birth. It may be thought of as the GRR net of mortality. Thus, the NRR subjects the 1,000 mothers not only to a schedule of age-specific reproduction rates but also to the risk of mortality up to the age of 49 (Rowland, 2003: 246). The formula for the NRR is as follows:

$$\text{NRR} = \sum \left(\text{ASFR}_{x \text{ to } x+n} * 0.488 * \frac{L_x}{5 l_0} \right) \qquad (3.11)$$

The first two components of the NRR formula, namely, multiplying each ASFR by the constant of 0.488, are the major features of the GRR, as noted previously. We already know that the GRR refers to the number of female births born to this hypothetical cohort of 1,000 women if none of the women in the hypothetical cohort die from the time they are babies until the end of their reproductive years. The NRR takes into account the probabilities that not all of the women will survive from age 0 to the end of their childbearing years.

So, returning to Table 3.3, column 8 presents *life table values* for females of L_x, multiplied by 500,000, for each of the age intervals. (The life table is discussed in detail in Chapter 5.) The L_x values represent the total number of person years lived in the age interval. Because we want the proportion of women who survive to the midpoint of the age interval, we divide each of the L_x values by $5(l_0)$, or 500,000, giving us the proportion of women who survive from age 0 to the midpoint of each of the seven age intervals. To illustrate, for age interval 15–19, we take from the life table the value of L_{15} and divide it by $5(l_0)$, or 500,000, equaling 0.9889. This means that 98.89 percent of the women in the hypothetical cohort will survive from birth through the midpoint of the age interval 15–19. These proportions of surviving females appear in column 8.

We then multiply the 5-year female birth rates (col. 7) by the proportions of surviving females (col. 8) to obtain in column 9 the number of daughters the women in each age group will bear, if they abide by a certain schedule of age-specific birth rates and a mortality schedule from the life table. We add the values in column 9 to get a total of 0.9822, which is the average net number of female births per woman in the hypothetical cohort after taking into account the mortality of the mothers; the net number of female births is less than one per woman. We multiply this figure by 1,000 for an estimate of the net number of female births for the entire cohort of 1,000 women, or 982.2 female births per 1,000 women.

The NRR is a "measure of how many daughters would replace 1,000 women if age-specific fertility and mortality rates remained constant indefinitely. Consequently, rates above 1,000 mean that eventually the population would increase, and rates below 1,000 mean that eventually the population would decrease, provided that the age-specific (birth and death) rates remained the same and no migration occurred" (Palmore and Gardner, 1994: 101–102).

PROXIMATE DETERMINANTS OF FERTILITY

Social demographers are primarily interested in ascertaining whether, how, and why various social, economic, cultural, and environmental factors influence both the likelihood of a woman having a baby and the number of babies she will have in her lifetime. Variables such as social class, economic status, religious beliefs, psychological disposition, attitudes about children, and many others have all been shown to be important in the decision to have a baby, as well as the number of babies (from zero to some positive number) a woman will have. Demographers have shown, for example, that the more years of education a woman has, the fewer will be her number of children. Why would this be? Why would more years of completed education result, on average, in a woman having fewer children? One reason is that women who are in school longer tend to marry later and also to start a family later, compared to women who have attended school for a shorter period of time. So, the education variable has an influence on fertility through the so-called proximate or intermediate variables that lie between – that is, they are intermediate to – the social, economic, cultural, and environmental variables and fertility.

In 1956, two famous demographers, Kingsley Davis and Judith Blake, wrote an influential paper about the behavioral and biological variables that are "intermediate" and thus directly influence fertility. These particular variables were distinguished from all of the other kinds of variables because the latter, by necessity, influence fertility by operating through the few intermediate variables specified by Davis and Blake. Briefly, the authors stated that the three variables of intercourse, conception, and gestation/**parturition** (the act or process of giving birth) should be considered as intermediate to the many other social, economic, cultural, and environmental factors that influence fertility. These latter variables, they argued, can only be related to fertility if they work through, or pass through, one or more of the intermediate variables.

Davis and Blake expanded on the three intermediate variables in the following ways: 1) the amount of intercourse is affected by the proportion of persons who marry, the length of time these persons are married, and their frequency of sexual intercourse while married; 2) the probability of conception is affected by **contraception** and by voluntary or involuntary **infecundity** (i.e., the inability to conceive); 3) the probability of a birth resulting from a given conception depends on the likelihood of miscarriage and abortion. They further emphasized that each intermediate variable can operate to increase as well as decrease fertility. Not all of them need to operate in the same direction, however. The observed level of fertility in a population depends on the net balance of *all* the intermediate variables.

Let us pause for a moment and mention some of the fertility terms to be used here. We already know the difference between fertility and fecundity. *Fertility* refers to actual reproduction and *fecundity* refers to the ability to reproduce. The opposite terms are *infertility* (also called **childlessness**) and *infecundity* (which is synonymous with **sterility**). Sterility implies the existence of infertility, but the reverse is not necessarily the case. A **fecund** woman may choose to remain infertile by not marrying or by practicing highly effective contraception. Infertility, then, is due to a voluntary decision not to have children or it is caused by (biological) infecundity.

With regard to fecundity, it is sometimes divided into five categories on the basis of the extent of fecundity impairment and the degree of certainty of the evidence (Poston, Zhang, and Terrell, 2008). That is, how able or unable are couples with respect to producing a birth?

First, all couples may be classified as either "fecund" or "subfecund." Fecund couples are capable of giving birth. Second, subfecund couples have impairments of one sort or another and may be subdivided into the following groups: definitely sterile, probably sterile, **semifecund**, and **fecundity indeterminate** (Badenhorst and Higgins, 1962). Definitely sterile couples are those for whom conception is impossible because of certain physical or medical conditions, including an operation, some other impairment, or menopause. Probably sterile couples are those for whom a birth is improbable on the basis of specific medical evidence. Semifecund couples are those who have married or cohabited for a relatively long time without using contraception but have not conceived. Fecundity indeterminate couples are those who meet the criteria for semifecund couples, except that the woman sometimes reports douching "for cleanness only" soon after intercourse. These couples are defined as "fecundity indeterminate" (Badenhorst and Higgins, 1962: 281). Demographic research has shown that the majority of subfecund couples are impaired according to these definitions (Poston, Zhang, and Terrell, 2008).

Returning to our discussion of the proximate determinants, the demographer John Bongaarts, in papers written in 1978 and 1982, respecified the intermediate variables of Davis and Blake in a way that facilitated the quantitative specification of how they influence fertility. He referred to the intermediate variables as the "proximate determinants" of fertility, a term very commonly used these days. The proximate-determinants perspective is one of the most elegant and useful frameworks in demography for understanding the process of fertility and how it is determined.

Bongaarts recognized that the "Davis and Blake framework for analyzing the determinants of fertility has found wide acceptance, [but] it has proven difficult to incorporate into quantitative reproductive models" (1982: 179). He thus set out the following seven proximate determinants: 1) marriage and marital disruption, 2) contraceptive use and effectiveness, 3) prevalence of induced abortion, 4) duration of postpartum infecundability, 5) waiting time to conception, 6) risk of intrauterine mortality, and 7) onset of permanent sterility. Let us consider each of these in turn.

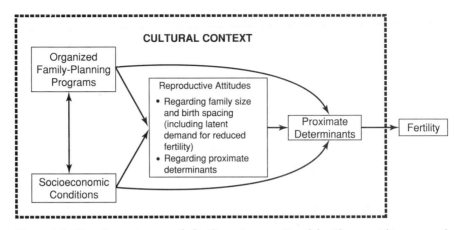

Figure 3.3. The determinants of fertility. *Source:* Knodel, Chamratrithirong, and Debavalya, 1987: 11.

First, with regard to marriage and marital disruption, this variable was intended to reflect the proportion of women in the population who were of reproductive age and engaging in sexual activity on a regular basis. Second, the contraception variable reflects deliberate contraceptive behaviors including abstinence and sterilization that are undertaken to reduce the risk of conception. Third, induced abortion includes all practices and behaviors that deliberately interrupt pregnancies. Fourth, duration of post-partum infecundability, in Bongaarts's terms, may be considered this way: "Following a pregnancy a woman remains infecundable (i.e., unable to conceive) until the normal pattern of ovulation and menstruation is restored. The duration of the period of infecundity is a function of the duration and intensity of lactation" (1978: 107). Fifth, waiting time to conception refers to the fact that a woman who is not contracepting is able to conceive "for only a short period of approximately two days in the middle of the menstrual cycle when ovulation takes place. The duration of this fertile period is a function of the duration of the viability of the sperm and ovum" (Bongaarts, 1978: 107). Sixth, risk of intrauterine mortality reflects the fact that many conceptions do not eventually lead to live births because some of them end as miscarriages, spontaneous abortions, or stillbirths. Seventh, the onset of permanent sterility reflects the fact that "women are sterile before menarche . . . and after menopause, but a couple may become sterile before the woman reaches menopause for reasons other than contraceptive sterilization" (Bongaarts, 1978: 107–108). (**Menarche** is the beginning of the female reproductive period, signaled by the first menstrual flow, and **menopause** is the end of that period, signaled by the termination of menstruation.)

Figure 3.3 summarizes the broad framework incorporating the proximate determinants that demographers use to study fertility. The figure highlights three major kinds of variables that occur in time prior to the proximate determinants: **family planning** variables, socioeconomic variables, and attitudinal variables. All three types of variables must work through the proximate determinants to influence fertility. Moreover, as John Knodel and his colleagues have observed, "since many of the proximate determinants are influenced by volitional actions and choice, attitudes directly concerning fertility as well as attitudes about the proximate determinants themselves are an important feature of any exposition of reproductive change" (Knodel, Chamratrithirong, and Debavalya, 1987: 9).

Bongaarts (1982) has taken the first four of the proximate determinants and quantified them with indices ranging from 0 to 1, with the lowest value of 0 indicating the greatest possible inhibiting effect on fertility of the proximate determinant and the maximum score of 1 representing no inhibiting effect of the determinant. The marriage-pattern index, Cm, has a value of 1 when all women of reproductive ages are in a marital or consensual union and 0 when none of them is in such a union. The contraception index, Cc, equals 1 if no contraception is used in the population and equals 0 if all fecund women are using completely effective modern methods of contraception. The postpartum-infecundability measure, Ci, is an index that ranges from a value of 1 when no women are experiencing postpartum infecundability to a value of 0 when all women are. The index of abortion, Ca, ranges from a maximum value equaling 1 when there is no induced abortion practiced in the population to 0 if every pregnancy that occurs is aborted.

Bongaarts (1982) conducted a quantitative analysis of the fertility of 41 historical and contemporary (developing and developed) countries and populations and showed that 96 percent of the variation in fertility could be explained solely by variation in the four proximate determinants of marriage, contraceptive use, postpartum infecundability, and abortion (see also Bongaarts and Potter [1983]). The other three of the proximate determinants were less important and did not vary significantly among the populations. Bongaarts's demonstration is very important because it shows that virtually all of the variation in fertility is due to variation in only the four major proximate determinants. Thus, the effects of any and all variables to the left of the proximate determinants (see Figure 3.3) can only have an effect on fertility if they operate through the proximate determinants.

THEORIES OF FERTILITY

Demographers have developed several different theories of fertility. Prominent explanations are **demographic transition theory, wealth flows theory, human ecological theory,** political economic theory, feminist theory, proximate determinants theory, bio-social theory, relative income theory, and diffusion theory (Poston and Terrell, 2006). As we have already noted, there is an abundance of theory in demography, indeed, more than in most of the social sciences.

A major explanation of fertility change and dynamics has its origins in demographic transition theory (DTT), as first developed by Warren S. Thompson (1929) and Frank W. Notestein (1945). We discuss DTT in more detail in Chapter 9; it is an important perspective for describing changes in fertility.

Current versions of DTT propose four stages of fertility (and mortality) decline that occur in the process of societal modernization. The first stage is the preindustrialization era, with high birth and death rates and **stable population** growth. (A stable population is a hypothetical population with unchanging birth, death, and growth rates and age composition.) With the onset of industrialization and modernization, the society transitions to lower death rates, especially lower infant and maternal mortality, but maintains higher birth rates with the result of rapid population growth. The next stage is one of decreasing population growth due to lower birth and death rates, which leads then to the final stage of low and stable population growth.

DTT argues that the first stage hinges on population survival. High fertility is necessary because mortality is high. Thus, societies develop a variety of beliefs and practices that support high reproduction, which are centered primarily on the family and kinship systems. The forces of modernization and industrialization alter this state of near-equilibrium, and the first effect is often a reduction in mortality. Indeed, the beginnings of mortality decline in many European countries were stimulated not so much by medical and public health improvements as by a general improvement in levels of living. This intermediate stage resulted in rapid rates of population growth because fertility remained high after mortality had declined. In the next stage, fertility also declines to lower levels. The causal linkages are complex. Underlying the global concepts of industrialization and modernization are specific determinants of fertility such as women's participation in the labor force and the changing role of the family. The normative, institutional, and economic supports for the large family become eroded, and the small family becomes predominant. The increasing importance of urbanization affects the family by altering its role in production. Also, urban families have considerably higher demands for consumption by their children, especially for education and recreation (Browning and Poston, 1980; Coale and Watkins, 1986; Davis, 1963; Hirschman, 1994; Knodel and van de Walle, 1979; McKeown, 1976; Poston, 2000; Poston and Terrell, 2006).

John C. Caldwell (1976) has revised DTT with his fertility theory of wealth flows. It is based on the notion that the "emotional" nucleation of the family is crucial for lower fertility. This occurs when parents become less concerned with ancestors and extended family relatives than they are with their children, their children's future, and even the future of their children's children (1976: 322). Caldwell explained that this depends on the direction of the intergenerational flows of wealth and services. If the flows run from children to their parents, parents will want to have large families. In modern societies where the flow is from parents to children, they want small families or maybe even no children (Poston and Terrell, 2006; Poston, Zhang, and Terrell, 2008).

Two other prominent theories of fertility change are based on human ecology and political economy. Both are extensions of demographic transition theory but in different ways. Human ecological theory is a macro-level explanation and argues that the level of sustenance-organization complexity of a society is negatively related with fertility growth and decline (Poston and Frisbie, 2005). In the first place, high-fertility patterns are dysfunctional for an increasingly complex sustenance organization because so much of the sustenance produced must be consumed directly by the population. High fertility will reduce the absolute amount of uncommitted sustenance resources, thereby limiting the population's flexibility for adapting to environmental, technological, and other kinds of changes and fluctuations. Low fertility is more consonant with the needs and requirements of an expansive sustenance organization. More sustenance would be available for investment back into the system in a low-growth and low-fertility population than in a population with high fertility. Hence, large quantities of sustenance normally consumed by the familial and educational institutions in a high-fertility population would be available as mobile or fluid resources in a low-fertility population. Sustenance organization in this latter instance would thus have the investment resources available for increasing complexity, given requisite changes in the environment and technology. This leads to the hypothesis of a negative relation between organizational complexity and fertility and population change (Kasarda, 1971; London, 1987; London and Hadden, 1989; Poston and Frisbie, 2005).

The political economic approach is another way to analyze fertility. Diverse fields of knowledge are integrated into the political economy approach so that research reflecting this perspective is "multileveled," combining both macro- and micro-level explanations. Its complexity requires a methodology that embraces both quantitative and qualitative approaches (Greenhalgh, 2008; Poston and Terrell, 2006).

The political economy of fertility is not really a theory of fertility per se but an investigative framework, or "analytic perspective," for the study of fertility (Greenhalgh, 1990b: 87). A good example of a political economy approach to fertility is David I. Kertzer and Dennis P. Hogan's 1989 study of Casalecchio, Italy. The authors tracked one small, rural Italian community during a few change-laden decades of the nineteenth and twentieth centuries, using individual-level data and directed by a life-course perspective. They touched on historical events, such as labor and marriage patterns, often ignored by other studies of demographic change. They showed that fertility rates and fertility reduction vary depending on the class or occupation of the family, thus demonstrating that macro-level socioeconomic factors have idiosyncratic effects on different classes of people.

WORLD FERTILITY TRENDS AND PATTERNS

In the world in 2005, the total fertility rate (TFR) was 2.65, but this value hides the tremendous heterogeneity in fertility in the countries around the world (United Nations, 2005). As of 2005, there were 205 countries; a country is an internationally recognized country or a territory with a population of 150,000 or more; or, if smaller than 150,000, is a member of the United Nations (UN). Of these 205 countries, 73 had TFRs at or below the replacement level of 2.1. (Since in most developed countries around 97 to 98 percent of babies survive to become parents, 1,000 females need to give birth to 2,100 babies in order for 2,000 of them to live to become parents.) Of the remaining countries, 35 had TFRs of 5.0 or higher; of these, 30 of the countries are considered by the UN to be the least developed of all countries and are located mainly in Africa (in the countries of Ethiopia, Malawi, Rwanda, Somalia, Uganda, Angola, and Chad, among others) (United Nations, 2005: 6).

The countries with low fertility fall roughly into three groups. The first includes most of the countries in northern and western Europe, as well as Argentina, Australia, Canada, New Zealand, and the United States. These countries had declining fertility rates in the twentieth century until the 1930s, and then their fertility either leveled off or declined, except for some like the United States and many countries in Western Europe where baby booms occurred. The second group of low-fertility countries consists of those in southern and eastern Europe. These nations had fairly consistent fertility declines in the 1930s, 1940s, and 1950s. The third group includes South Korea, China, Japan, Taiwan, and Singapore, which had relatively high fertility rates until the end of World War II and into the 1960s but sharp declines thereafter (United Nations, 2005: 6).

Birth rates in some of the countries of the developing world are high but not as high as biologically possible. CBRs have probably never been higher than 65 to 70 in any countries of the world (Kuczynski, 1936).

A country with a CBR of 70 would have a TFR of roughly 9.5. In pre-revolutionary Russia, the birth rate in several provinces was around this level (United Nations, 1973: 73). Fertility rates approaching this level are possible only when almost everyone is engaged in frequent sexual intercourse, there is little if any contraception, childbearing begins at a young age, and families have many children. There are documented cases of women having twenty or more births. However, the largest *average* family size that seems possible ranges from around nine to thirteen children, and then only in societies where marriage occurs at an early age and birth prevention is not practiced. For instance, rural Irish women who married under age 20 and who had completed childbearing by the date of the 1911 census averaged 8.8 live births (Glass and Grebenik, 1954). T. E. Smith (1960) has reported that Cocos Island women marrying at age 14 or 15 averaged 10.8 children by age 45. Among the Hutterites, a Protestant religious sect living in small agricultural settlements in the Dakotas, Montana, and the adjacent Canadian provinces of Manitoba and Saskatchewan, there was in the 1950s an average of around twelve confinements among women whose last child was born when they were 45 or older (Tietze, 1957). These very high birth rates, however, fall far short of the biological maximum (Bongaarts, 1975).

As of around 2005, the highest TFRs in the world were 7.3 in the Democratic Republic of the Congo and 7.1 in Niger. The lowest TFRs were 0.8 in Macau; 1.0 in Hong Kong; and 1.2 in Ukraine, the Czech Republic, Slovakia, and South Korea. Figure 3.4 shows all the countries of the world ranked by the values of their TFRs in around 2005, high to low, left to right. There is a tremendous range in fertility in the countries, certainly as large a range as ever experienced in the history of the world.

Despite the very high fertility rates in many of the developing countries, some are fairly far along in the transition from high birth rates to low birth rates. However, in fifteen of the countries, "there is either no recent evidence about fertility trends or the available evidence does not indicate the onset of a fertility reduction. Although [their fertility] is projected to decline after 2010 at a pace of about one child per decade, none is expected to reach 2.1 children per woman by 2050" (United Nations, 2005: 7). Most of these countries – namely, Afghanistan, Angola, Burkina Faso, Burundi, Chad, Congo, Democratic Republic of the Congo, Democratic Republic of Timor-Leste, Guinea-Bissau, Liberia, Malawi, Mali, Niger, Sierra Leone, Somalia, Uganda, and Yemen – are classified by the UN as "least developed." Many have been significantly affected by the **human immunodeficiency virus (HIV)/AIDS** epidemic, and some have experienced "civil strife and political instability in recent years, factors that militate against the

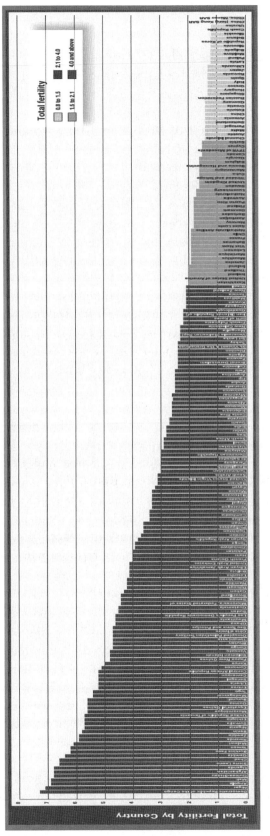

Figure 3.4. Total fertility rates, countries of the world, circa 2005. *Source:* United Nations, 2008a.

provision of basic services for the population" (United Nations, 2005: 8). Certainly, these considerations stand in the way of demographic advances in future years and are serious challenges to the future development of these countries.

As already noted, fertility levels in 73 countries had all declined to replacement levels or below by around 2005. In the 1970s, there were only eighteen countries with fertility below replacement. These included the European countries of Hungary, Denmark, Finland, Sweden, Germany, and Switzerland. In almost all them, fertility continued to decline, attaining "historically unprecedented low levels (below 1.3 children per woman) in fifteen developed countries, all located in Southern and Eastern Europe" (United Nations, 2005: 9; see also Kohler, Billari, and Ortega, 2002; and Morgan, 2003).

Following Francesco C. Billari (2004), we refer to fertility as being "low" when the TFR is below the replacement level of 2.1, as being "very low" when it is below 1.5, and as being "lowest low" when it is below 1.3. In 2005, eleven countries reported lowest-low fertility – that is, a TFR below 1.3; these include South Korea, Taiwan, Poland, the Czech Republic, Slovakia, and Ukraine.

No discussion of world fertility trends would be complete without mentioning depopulation, that is, the decline in the size of the population. This is so because depopulation is projected to occur in most countries of the world in the next fifty to a hundred years. Despite the vast amount of attention paid since the late 1960s to the phenomenon of overpopulation (see esp. Ehrlich [1968]; B. Friedman [2005]; and Meadows, Randers, and Meadows [2004]), declines in population are expected to occur in around fifty or more countries by the year 2050 (Population Reference Bureau, 2006) and in even more countries thereafter (Howden and Poston, 2008).

Even though the population of the world is projected to continue to grow, reaching around 9.1 billion in 2050 according to the United Nation's medium-variant projection, a slowing of the rate of population growth is already underway, and a decline in the size of the world population could begin as early as 2050 (United Nations, 2005). The region most significantly impacted by depopulation is Europe. Between 2000 and 2005, at least sixteen countries in Europe experienced a decline in population size. The largest net loss occurred in Russia, with a loss of almost 3.4 million persons in the five years between 2000 and 2005 (United Nations, 2005).

Indeed, Russia's population is expected to drop from 143 million in 2005 to around 124 million by 2030. Nicholas Eberstadt (2009: 51) has noted the severity of this depopulation in Russia in his statement that

"Russia's human numbers have been progressively dwindling. This slow motion process now taking place in the country carries with it grim and potentially disastrous implications that threaten to recast the contours of life and society in Russia, to diminish the prospects for Russian economic development, and to affect Russia's potential influence on the world stage in the years ahead."

For the majority of countries, including Russia, the reason for depopulation is sustained low fertility. For a population to remain stable, TFRs need to be at or below replacement, that is, no higher than 2.1 children per woman, and the cohorts in the childbearing ages cannot be larger than those in other age groups. If there are large numbers in the population in the parental ages, **replacement-level fertility** alone will not result in depopulation. This is due to what is referred to as negative **population momentum**, that is, the lag between the decline in TFRs and the decline in CBRs that is caused by large numbers of women still in their childbearing years owing to past high fertility. In the 2000–2005 period, the UN noted that sixty-five countries had fertility rates below replacement levels, with fifteen at extremely low levels (i.e., a TFR below 1.3) (United Nations, 2005). In 2006, the Population Reference Bureau reported that as many as seventy-three countries were experiencing TFRs below the replacement level (see also Howden and Poston, 2008).

Many countries with relatively high fertility have started to experience declines in their fertility. The UN has observed that of the thirty-five countries with a TFR of 5 or more, twenty-two have experienced declines in fertility in the past ten to fifteen years (United Nations, 2005). These lower rates of fertility, coupled with low rates of mortality and immigration, are responsible for depopulation in the majority of countries projected to lose population in the next fifty years. For a few countries, population decline is expected to occur even though their fertility is greater than the replacement levels. These countries – namely, Botswana, Lesotho, and Swaziland – are being significantly impacted by the HIV/AIDS epidemic, leading to a net loss in population (Howden and Poston, 2008).

The depopulation of most of the countries in the developed world has significant economic impacts and implications. Major effects will likely be felt through the **aging of a population**. As fertility declines, birth cohorts become progressively smaller. These smaller birth cohorts, coupled with increases in life expectancy, lead to an increasingly larger proportion of the population that is older than age 65 and a smaller proportion of the population in the working ages. The UN has reported that the period between 2005 and 2050 will see a doubling of the **old-age dependency ratio (ADR)** (i.e., the ratio of the population aged 65 and older to the population aged 15–64, times 100) in developed countries from 22.6 to

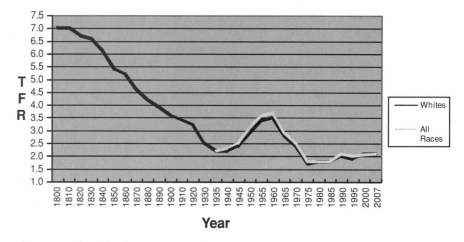

Figure 3.5. Total fertility rates, United States 1800–2007.

44.4 (United Nations, 2005). For many countries, health care and pension programs are ill equipped to handle the large increases in the numbers of elderly, who themselves will live longer than their predecessors (Howden and Poston, 2008).

FERTILITY CHANGE IN THE UNITED STATES

In less than 220 years, the United States has increased tremendously in size from fewer than 4 million people in 1790 to 300 million in 2006 (see Chapter 10 for more discussion). Figure 3.5 shows TFRs for the United States from 1800 to 2007. TFRs for whites are shown for all of the years, and TFRs for all races combined are reported beginning in 1935.

A high fertility rate was an important component of the rapid population increases in the United States in the early years between 1790 and 1860. Indeed, in 1800, the white population had a TFR of 7.0, which was likely the highest fertility rate of any country in the world at the time (Haines and Guest, 2008; Sanderson, 1979). The TFR in 1810 was still around 7.0 but by 1820 had dropped slightly to 6.7. It declined to 5.2 in 1860 and then to just under four births per woman by 1900 (Hamilton, Martin, and Ventura, 2007; Taeuber and Taeuber, 1958; U.S. Bureau of the Census, 1975).

High fertility in the United States resulted from the fact that more than one-half of the population was fecund. The average age of the population was 15.9 in 1790, 17.0 in 1820, and 19.4 in 1860. Another reason for high fertility was the high levels of rural and agricultural activity. When the first census of the United States was conducted in 1790, 95 percent of the population was rural. The rural portion comprised about 90 percent of the population through 1850 and dropped to only 75 percent by 1900 (Kahn, 1974).

Between 1790 and 1860, when agriculture was dominant, income was directly related to the acreage of cultivated fields. Fields in the West were cheap and easy to obtain, and many people tended to have more children in order to have more laborers. Big families were popular and normative.

Every modern, economically developed nation has undergone a demographic transition from high to low levels of fertility and mortality. The United States experienced a sustained fertility decline starting in the nineteenth century (Sternlieb and Hughes, 1978). The TFR (for whites) dropped to 4.6 in 1870 and to 3.6 in 1900 (U.S. Bureau of the Census, 1975). By 1920, just after World War I, the white TFR had dropped to 3.2 (see Figure 3.5).

In the several decades of the early twentieth century, the United States experienced a rapid transition in its economy, industrialization, and urbanization (Taeuber and Taeuber, 1958). In the late 1950s at the height of the baby boom era, the TFR reached its peak at 3.7. The high (baby boom) fertility following World War II was promoted in part by a need to take into account the population losses that occurred during the war.

In the 1960s, the fertility rate started to decline. Many factors influenced this reduction, such as higher living expenses, increases in educational opportunities and expectations, and more women employed in the labor force. The average U.S. family size was reduced. Cheap, easily accessible, and more effective contraceptives, along with abortions (see discussion in Chapter 4), gave couples greater control over births and hence were another factor in the fertility decline. In 1972, the U.S. TFR dropped for the first time below the replacement level of 2.1 (Kahn, 1974); by 1975, it was 1.7. Even during the Great Depression years when fertility was low, it never dropped below 2.2. Total population increase in 1972 was only 0.7 percent, almost one-half of the average annual increase during the 1960s (Kahn, 1974). U.S. birth rates kept declining, although not as rapidly as in earlier years. Since 1990, the TFR has remained at just above two children per woman (see Figure 3.5).

The U.S. population of 281 million people in 2000 has been growing slowly, at a rate of around 1 percent a year. The TFR of 2.05 births in each woman's lifetime is just below the replacement level of 2.1 but, nevertheless, is the highest of any of the developed countries in the world. If these trends continue, the American population is projected to level off at about 408 million by the middle of this century and then begin to decline, even allowing for substantial immigration. People are living longer, and the U.S. population as a whole is aging.

ADOLESCENT FERTILITY

Adolescent fertility refers to the childbearing of young women. The **adolescent fertility rate** is represented by the ASFR for women aged 15–19. Fertility rates for young women in this age group are a particularly important indicator of women's status because women who give birth at this young age "often forego the opportunity to study or find employment away from home" (United Nations, 2005: 1). The adolescent fertility rate for the world for the period 2000–2005 was 55 per 1,000. That is, in 2000–2005, on average each year, for every 1,000 young girls of ages 15–19 in the world, there were 55 babies born to them. Among the developed countries, the adolescent fertility rate was 24, varying from a low of 5 in Belgium and Switzerland to a high of 43 in the United States. Only the United States and two other countries in the developed world have adolescent fertility rates above 30, namely, Bulgaria (40) and Romania (33). In the developing countries, the adolescent fertility rate ranges from lows of 2 in South Korea and 3 in China to highs of 199 in Niger and 192 in Mali. In South Korea and China, for every 1,000 adolescent women, only two or three had babies in an average year in the 2000–2005 period. Almost twenty-two times as many adolescent women in the United States gave birth as in China or South Korea. In both Niger and Mali, almost one in five adolescents gave birth during this period (United Nations, 2007). There is more variation among the countries of the world in adolescent fertility than in fertility per se (as measured by the TFR).

The UN data published in 2007 indicate that the adolescent fertility rate is above 90 in at least fifty-five developing countries; of these, thirty-five are in Africa, fifteen in Latin America, and seven in Asia. The rate is 30 or lower in thirty-two developing countries. It is interesting that the so-called developing countries have the highest and the lowest adolescent fertility rates in the world.

We noted that the United States has by far the highest adolescent fertility rate of all the countries of the developed world: 43 births per 1,000 adolescents, calculated for the year 2002. But adolescent fertility for U.S. females varies considerably by race and ethnic group. The lowest adolescent fertility rate for U.S. women in 2002 was for Anglo females, 28/1,000. The highest was for Hispanic women, 83/1,000. Black adolescents, American Indian or Alaskan Native adolescents, and Asian or Pacific Islander adolescents had fertility rates between these two extremes at 68/1,000, 54/1,000, and 18/1,000, respectively. The very high adolescent fertility rate of U.S.

Hispanics in 2002 was about equal to the rates of Panama, Venezuela, and the African countries of Namibia, Togo, and Mauritania.

The high Hispanic adolescent fertility rate applies only to Hispanics of Mexican origin. (Cubans have lower rates of adolescent fertility.) Current research indicates that young women in the United States of Mexican origin have particularly high rates of adolescent fertility mainly because of the barriers that limit their access to higher education (Conde, forthcoming).

MALE FERTILITY

An important limitation of the our discussion of fertility theories and measures is that they are all derived from calculations and analyses of female fertility. The fertility of men and the determinants of male fertility have rarely been examined and compared with those of females, but they should be. Males are a neglected minority in fertility studies.

Several reasons have been proposed by demographers to justify the exclusion of males from fertility studies. The biological reasons are that the fecundity and the childbearing years of women occur in a more sharply defined and narrower range (15–49) than they do for men (15–79), and that "both the spacing and number of children are less subject to variation among women; a woman can have children only at intervals of 1 or 2 years, whereas a man can have hundreds" (Keyfitz, 1977a: 114). Among the methodological reasons are that data on parental age at the birth of a child are more frequently collected on birth-registration certificates for the mothers than for the fathers, and that when such data are obtained for mothers and fathers, there are more instances of unreported age data for fathers, especially for births occurring outside of marriage. The sociological reasons include the fact that men are regarded principally as breadwinners and "as typically uninvolved in fertility except to impregnate women and to stand in the way of their contraceptive use" (Greene and Biddlecom, 2000: 83; Poston, Zhang, and Terrell, 2008).

In Texas in 2000, among birth certificates that listed information on the father's age (85.4 percent of all birth certificates), the ages of the fathers ranged from a low of 13 to a high of 80, with a mean of age 29.2.

Biological and demographic studies provide us with evidence of the importance of men in fertility and related behaviors. Biologists have found that the male sex in most all species contributes an equivalent amount of genetic information to the next generation as does the female. But the variance contributed by the male sex to the next generation is often greater than that of the female sex, especially in species where **polygyny** (a union where a male is simultaneously married to two or more females) is practiced. That is, most females reproduce, some males do not reproduce, and other males have a large number of offspring. This pattern has been found in most mammalian species (Coleman, 2000). In addition, it has been found that there are more childless males than females in many species.

Demographically, it has been shown that men have different patterns of fertility and fertility-related behavior. Males' age-specific fertility starts later, stops much later, and is typically higher than that of females (Paget and Timaeus, 1994). The TFRs for males and females are not identical either. Research has shown that in most industrialized countries, male TFRs are higher than female TFRs (Coleman, 2000). In the 1990s and later, countries with both male and female TFRs lower than 2.2 tended to have more similar than dissimilar male and female TFRs, and the opposite was found for countries with male and female TFRs higher than 2.2 (Zhang, 2007). This means that for men and women, if they followed the sex- and age-specific fertility rates of an area at one point in time, and if they had fewer than 2.2 children during their childbearing years, these men and women were more likely to have similar than dissimilar fertility and vice versa (also see Myers, 1941; and D. Smith, 1992). (An **age/sex-specific rate** refers to the demographic behavior – for example, regarding fertility – of a subset of the population categorized by age and sex.)

The special importance of male fertility is also seen in the determinants of fertility and fertility-related behaviors, such as cohabitation and marriage. For example, in the United States, men's fertility is more likely to be influenced by their marital and employment status compared to women's. Being married and employed significantly increases men's number of children ever born (CEB), while such factors do not have as strong an impact on women (Zhang, 2007). The relevance of labor-force participation for women's fertility has been emphasized repeatedly. In our own research, we have used several independent variables from various fertility paradigms, namely, human ecology, political economy, and wealth flows, to predict both male and female TFRs for the counties of Taiwan. The variables have consistently performed better when predicting variation in female TFRs than in male TFRs (Poston, Baumle, and Micklin, 2005).

Men also have different cohabitation and marriage patterns compared to women. In the United States, for birth cohorts born during 1958 to 1987, living alone, being foreign-born, and living in fragmented families all tend to increase the likelihood of cohabitation for women but not for men. Foreign-born men are more likely to marry than native-born men. But these factors do not have as significant an impact on women's marriage behavior (Zhang, 2007). Researchers have conducted studies examining male and female transitions to adulthood in twenty-four European countries using survey data for the 1980s and 1990s. They have found that, in general, the negative effect on fertility of educational attainment is stronger for women than for men. Also, unemployment leads to men's postponement of marriage, whereas it affects women in two distinct ways: It either accelerates or slows down the timing of marriage for women. The effect of religion is stronger among women than among men. Furthermore, being Catholic and attending church services affect men's and women's parenthood timing in different ways in Catholic-prevalent countries. Other relevant factors such as parental influence seem to have a different impact for males than for females (Corijn and Klijzing, 2001).

Historically, women have been tied to motherhood, and this is deeply rooted in law and policy in the ways that jobs are structured and that family relations are navigated. Studies of fertility and parenthood have been undertaken by demographers in a similar way (Riley, 2005). These, together with the biological and methodological reasons stated previously, have resulted in the decreased attention given to males in fertility research. It was mentioned earlier that biological and demographic analyses and results have shown that fertility and parenting are not simply female issues; they are issues involving both men and women. The study of fertility should not focus only on females. Greenhalgh (1990b) and Riley (1998; 2005) encouraged more discussion about gender issues among demographers, and critical demography has promoted bringing men into population studies (Coleman, 2000; Horton, 1999). It is necessary to incorporate gender studies and other disciplines into studies of demography in order to gain a more balanced picture of demographic issues. Indeed, male fertility is one of the emerging issues of demographic study. Demographers and sociologists need to give more attention to males in their analyses of fertility variation and change. It is essential to take men's roles and commitments into account when considering factors leading to decisions about the bearing and rearing of children (Poston, Baumle, and Micklin, 2005; Poston, Zhang, and Terrell, 2008).

CONCLUSION

In this chapter, we first considered various measures of fertility and next discussed the so-called proximate determinants of fertility. These are the mainly biological factors that lead directly to fertility and that are influenced heavily by social factors. Indeed, the various social, economic, cultural, environmental, and psychological factors that affect fertility do so only through the "proximate" variables. Both the societal birth rate and the fertility of individual women and men are produced by a combination of those factors. We next looked at some of the main theories generated by demographers to account for the reasons that some women or men or societies have more babies than other women or men or societies. We then considered world fertility patterns and U.S. fertility trends and differences. We concluded with a discussion of adolescent fertility and male fertility.

We close this chapter with a summary of some of the major fertility differentials. Fertility rates are much higher in many developing countries, especially those in sub-Saharan Africa, than they are in developed countries. Likewise, different types of people have different patterns of fertility. Generally, the higher a person's socioeconomic status, the fewer children that person is likely to have. In industrialized societies, women employed in the labor force tend to have fewer children than women who are not so employed. Having a smaller family also increases the woman's availability for employment, and her employment per se encourages a small family. Levels of childbearing also tend to be lower in urban than in rural areas. This is particularly true in more modernized countries, although in the past three or four decades, the difference between rural and urban childbearing rates has diminished. There are few if any differences in childbearing between Catholics and non-Catholics in the United States and other more developed countries. These differences are due mainly to differences in socioeconomic status. The fertility of Moslem women, however, is higher than that of Christian and Jewish women, both in developed and developing countries. These differentials notwithstanding, the most important point to remember about fertility is that fertility rates are heavily conditioned by social, economic, psychological, cultural, and environmental factors, all of which eventually affect fertility through the proximate determinants.

KEY TERMS

adolescent fertility rate	general fertility rate (GFR)
age/sex-specific rate	gross reproduction rate (GRR)
age-specific fertility rate (ASFR)	human immunodeficiency
aging of a population	virus (HIV)
at-risk population	human ecological theory
childlessness	hypothetical cohort
cohort analysis	infecundity
conception	less-developed countries (LDCs)
contraception	menarche
crude birth rate (CBR)	menopause
demographic transition theory	net reproduction rate (NRR)
(DTT)	old-age dependency ratio
family planning	parturition
fecund	period perspective
fecundity	period rate
fecundity indeterminate	polygyny
fertility	population momentum

proximate determinants
reproduction
replacement-level fertility
semifecund
sex ratio at birth (SRB)
specific rate

stable population
sterility
total fertility rate (TFR)
wealth flows theory
zygote

Contraception and Birth Control

A discussion of fertility is incomplete without a consideration and review of **contraception** and **birth control**. Most married couples in the United States and in the other countries of the developed world endeavor to limit their family size and/or to control the timing and spacing of their births. Substantial numbers of unmarried, sexually active women and men also attempt to prevent pregnancy. In the developing countries of the world, slightly fewer married people use birth prevention methods than in developed countries.

There are a variety of methods available to women and men to prevent births. The most popular ones worldwide are contraception, **sterilization**, and **abortion**. Some methods are more effective than others, and each has its advantages and disadvantages. This chapter presents, first, a brief historical review of fertility control. Although fertility-control methods have been widely used and publicly accepted mainly in the last five decades or so, attempts to control fertility have characterized human populations for centuries. This review is followed by a description of the general situation worldwide and in the United States regarding the use of contraception, sterilization, and abortion. The main part of the chapter is a description of the major methods of birth prevention, including a discussion of their **effectiveness**.

BRIEF HISTORY OF FERTILITY CONTROL

The idea or notion of preventing births appeared early in human history. Of the many excellent and comprehensive accounts of contraception available today, three deserve our attention. The classic book is *Medical History of Contraception* by Norman Himes, first published in 1936, with a paperback edition in 1970. This is an exhaustive survey of contraception covering many cultures worldwide over three thousand years. It is a masterful collation of historical and anthropological evidence from preliterate societies to the early twentieth century.

In 1966, John T. Noonan wrote the superb *Contraception: A History of Its Treatment by the Catholic Theologians and Canonists*. As stated in the subtitle, his book traces the very interesting history of contraception from the pre-Christian era to the 1960s, with the heaviest concentration on the interpretation and reception of contraception in the Catholic Church.

The third major treatment is the recent (2008) book by Robert Jutte, *Contraception: A History*, published a few years earlier in German. Jutte's book extends and updates much of the earlier work of Himes and Noonan. All three books remind us that society's "attempts to control the increase in numbers reach so far back into the dim past that it is impossible to discern their real origin. Some forms of limitation on the rate of increase are undoubtedly as old as the life history of man" (Himes, [1936] 1970: 3).

There are written records of contraceptive remedies and abortion techniques in Egyptian papyri (1900–1100 BC), in the Latin works of Pliny the Elder (AD 23–79) and Discorides (AD 40–90), in the Greek writings of Soranus (ca. 100), and in works dealing with Arabic medicine in the tenth century. The oldest surviving documents describing contraceptive methods are the Egyptian papyri. There are five different papyri dating from between 1900 BC and 1100 BC, and each provided different recipes for contraceptive preparations. According to Noonan (1966: 9): "The Kahun Papyrus [mentions] pulverized crocodile dung in fermented mucilage, and honey and sodium carbonate, to be sprinkled in the vulva. . . . In the Ebers Papyrus it is said that pregnancy may be prevented for one, two, or three years by a recipe of acacia tips, coloquintida [a yellow lemon-sized bitter fruit sometimes used as a laxative], and dates, mixed with honey, to be placed in the uterus." Until fairly recently, most contraceptive methods were relatively ineffective, with the exception of induced abortion and **withdrawal**.

Virtually all of the contraceptive methods we review, except for the hormonally based methods, were available and were used by the end of the nineteenth century, some much earlier (Himes, [1936] 1970; Jutte, 2008). Condoms date back to the seventeenth century. Indeed, James Boswell, the famous diarist and author of *The Life of Samuel Johnson*, wrote about "using a condom with a prostitute in London in 1763" (Potts, 2003: 96). Intrauterine devices (IUDs) were first developed in Germany in the 1920s. However, owing to legal and other types of restrictions, it was not possible to undertake IUD research in the United States. The manual vacuum-aspiration method of abortion was first described by the gynecologist of Queen Victoria of England.

In fact, the physiological principles of oral contraception were developed in the 1920s, "but the method made no progress, partly because of the lack of a cheap source of steroid and also because contraceptive research was not academically acceptable" (Potts, 2003: 96). Along these lines, Malcolm Potts and Martha Campbell (2002) have written about the vast historical disconnect between the acquisition of biological knowledge about birth control and its application.

In our presentation later about the specific types of contraceptives, we have occasion to mention the historical precedents for some of them. We turn next to a discussion of fertility control in the world today.

CURRENT PATTERNS OF FERTILITY CONTROL
WORLDWIDE AND IN THE UNITED STATES

The Population Reference Bureau (2008a) has published **family planning** and fertility control data from surveys conducted during the ten-year period from 1997 to 2007 by a host of national governments and international agencies. Fertility control data are presented for women between the ages of 15 and 49 who are married or in informal unions. These are the most comprehensive data available and portray an empirical picture of the reproductive revolution that has occurred in the world since the 1950s.

In the less-developed countries of the world, the percentage of married women using family planning methods has increased from 9 percent in 1960 to more than 60 percent in 2007. According to data from the most recent surveys conducted in the various countries between 1997 and 2007, 63 percent of married women worldwide are using family planning methods: 71 percent of women in the developed countries and 62 percent in the developing countries (Table 4.1). Contraceptive use in the developing countries has now almost reached the level attained in the developed world. This has occurred even though the use of family planning methods in the developing world is quite uneven across the various countries, ranging from lows of 3 percent in Chad and 5 percent in Sierra Leone to highs of 80 percent in Costa Rica, 81 percent in South Korea, and 87 percent in China. China has the highest percentage of family planning use of any country in the world, followed by Australia at 85 percent, the United Kingdom at 84 percent, and Switzerland at 82 percent. The reproductive revolution is one of the most remarkable demographic stories of the past half-century (Population Reference Bureau, 2008a).

These percentage data refer to users of family planning methods. If we subtract the user percentage for a country from 100, we get the percentage of women who are not using contraceptive methods. In China, the percentage of nonusers is 13 percent, whereas in Chad it is 97 percent.

Table 4.1. Percentage of married women using family planning methods, world, most regions, and the United States

	All methods	All modern methods	Pill	IUD	Injection	Male condom	Sterilization Male	Sterilization Female	Other modern methods
WORLD	63	57	8	14	4	6	4	21	1
MORE DEVELOPED	71	61	18	6	–	20	–	13	3
LESS DEVELOPED	62	56	7	15	4	4	3	22	1
Africa	30	25	8	5	7	2	–	2	1
Northern America	74	69	18	2	2	12	12	21	2
Latin America & the Caribbean	72	63	13	7	4	5	2	31	1
Asia	67	61	6	18	3	6	3	25	1
Europe									
Northern Europe	82	77	33	11	–	28	–	–	–
Southern Europe	62	44	10	5	–	18	4	6	1
Oceania	72	64	22	1	3	17	10	9	2
United States	73	69	17	2	2	12	11	22	2

Source: Population Reference Bureau, 2008a.

Who is a nonuser of contraception? There are a number of categories of nonusers, only some of whom are engaging in unprotected intercourse and are thus at the risk of becoming pregnant. The first two categories of nonusers are women 1) who are pregnant, or 2) who have just given birth (for many women there is little risk of pregnancy for several months after giving birth; recall the discussion in the previous chapter of postpartum infecundability). Women in either of these groups would, obviously, not be expected to be contraception users; they are not yet at the risk of becoming pregnant again. Two more categories of nonusers are women 3) who are surgically sterile (via a **hysterectomy**, the surgical removal of the uterus and sometimes the additional removal of the Fallopian tubes and the ovaries, or some other noncontraceptive operation), or 4) who themselves are nonsurgically sterile or their male partners are. These women would also not be expected to be contraception users because they (or their partners) are sterile. A fifth category consists of women who are trying to become pregnant. None of the women in these five categories of nonusers would normally be expected to be using family planning methods. Other women who are not using family planning methods but do not fall into any of the five categories are sometimes split into two groups: a sixth category who are not engaging in sexual intercourse and a seventh category who are participating in sexual intercourse. It is only the women in this last category of nonusers who are truly at the risk of becoming pregnant.

The data in Table 4.1 do not provide information for the various categories of nonusers. We see, for example, that 63 percent, or almost two-thirds, of married women worldwide are using family planning methods; therefore, 37 percent of them are nonusers. But we do not know from the data in the table how many of these nonusers not using methods are at the risk of becoming pregnant involuntarily. That is, we do not know how many of the nonusers would fall into the seventh category of nonusers, as described in the preceding paragraph.

However, these types of nonuser data are available for women in the United States, and we describe them in more detail later. For example, Table 4.1 reports that 73 percent of married women in the United States are using family planning methods; thus, 27 percent of them are not using contraceptive methods. We will see later that of this 27 percent, only 6 percent who are not using contraceptive methods are engaging in sexual activity. Before looking at the contraceptive use of U.S. women, we consider the use of specific methods.

The family planning use data reported in the previous paragraphs pertain to all contraceptive methods, which may be divided into modern and traditional methods. The main modern methods of family planning are the **oral contraceptive (the pill)**, the **intrauterine device (IUD)**, **contraception** injection, the male **condom**, and both male and female sterilization. Other modern methods include the **diaphragm**, vaginal spermicides including various foams and jellies, several kinds of contraceptive implants, the **female condom**, and "natural" family planning methods, also known as **fertility awareness** methods, such as the **Standard Days Method** and the Billings ovulation method. Traditional family planning methods include less effective "natural" methods, such as the calendar **rhythm method** (i.e., periodic abstinence), **coitus interruptus** (i.e., withdrawal), long-term abstinence, and prolonged breast-feeding. We discuss most of these and some other methods in the next section.

Table 4.1 also presents worldwide percentage data for married women using various types of family planning, as well as data for most of the major regions and the United States (only limited survey data are available for Europe); the data are from surveys conducted between 1997 and 2007. Worldwide, the most commonly used family planning method is female sterilization, with more than 20 percent of married women in the reproductive ages having been contraceptively sterilized. The next most popular methods, in order, are the IUD, the oral contraceptive, the male condom, injections, and **male sterilization**. The other modern methods, namely, hormonal implants, the diaphragm, and spermicides, comprise a relatively small percentage of total use.

The traditional family planning methods noted previously are employed by only around 6 percent of married women and men in the world. However, in Africa, where overall family planning use is quite low, one in six married women using a method uses a traditional method, and in sub-Saharan Africa the number is one in four. Indeed, in many sub-Saharan African countries, namely, Niger, Cameroon, Congo, and Gabon, among several others, traditional methods account for more than half of all methods used (Ashford, 2008).

Having examined family planning methods worldwide, we turn next to a discussion of induced abortion. What are the current patterns worldwide of induced abortion?

An induced abortion is a pregnancy that has been terminated by human intervention with an "intent other than to produce a live birth" (Henshaw, 2003: 529). The most complete data on induced abortions are from countries where abortion is legal, but even here the quantity and quality of the data vary considerably. In Table 4.2, we show estimates of the numbers of induced abortions, and the **abortion rates**, for the world and its major regions for 2003 and 1995. In 2003, there were an estimated 42 million induced abortions worldwide, a decline from the approximately 46 million in 1995. For every 1,000 women in the childbearing ages in the world, 29 had an induced abortion in 2003, compared to 35 women in 1995

Table 4.2. Global and regional estimates of induced abortion, 1995 and 2003				
	No. of abortions (millions)		Abortion rate*	
Region and subregion	1995	2003	1995	2003
World	45.6	41.6	35	29
Developed countries	10.0	6.6	39	26
Excluding Eastern Europe	3.8	3.5	20	19
Developing countries†	35.5	35.0	34	29
Excluding China	24.9	26.4	33	30
Estimates by region				
Africa	5.0	5.6	33	29
Asia	26.8	25.9	33	29
Europe	7.7	4.3	48	28
Latin America	4.2	4.1	37	31
Northern America	1.5	1.5	22	21
Oceania	0.1	0.1	21	17

* Abortions per 1,000 women ages 15–44.
† Those within Africa, the Americas (excluding Canada and the United States), Asia (excluding Japan), and Oceania (excluding Australia and New Zealand).
Source: Guttmacher Institute, 2008b.

(Guttmacher Institute, 2008b). Most of the abortions in the world in 2003 occurred in developing countries (35 million) rather than in developed countries (6.6 million). This differential largely reflects the uneven distribution of the population in developing and developed countries. Indeed, the abortion rates are much closer, namely, 29 in developing countries and 26 in developed countries.

Between 1995 and 2003, the abortion rates in the major regions of the world (see Table 4.2) either declined or remained pretty much the same. The greatest decline occurred in Europe, from 48 in 1995 to 28 in 2003. Even though the abortion rates declined throughout Europe, it was, according to Susan A. Cohen (2007: 2–3), "the precipitous drop in Eastern Europe that drove the entire continent's decline and, by extension, literally moved the world's abortion rate downward (from 35 to 29). The former Soviet bloc countries, such as the Russian Federation, Estonia, Bulgaria and Latvia, still possess the dubious distinction of being home to the world's highest abortion rates. In 2003, 44 abortions occurred in this subregion for every 1,000 women of reproductive age. Significantly, however, that rate was less than half of the 1995 rate of 90" for Eastern Europe.

Abortions do not occur more frequently in countries where they are legally performed versus countries where they are not legally performed. To illustrate, the abortion data in Table 4.2 indicate that the rate is 29 in Africa where abortion is, for the most part, illegal, but it is 28 in Europe where it is mostly legal. With regard to safety, abortions are far safer in countries where they are legally performed than where they are illegally performed. It is estimated that 48 percent of the abortions performed worldwide in 2003 were "unsafe." But there is a great disparity between the developed and the developing countries. In the developed regions, "nearly all abortions (92 percent) are safe" but, in developing countries, less than half (45 percent) are safe (Cohen, 2007; Guttmacher Institute, 2008b: 2). It should not be a surprise, therefore, to learn that almost all abortion-related deaths occur to women in developing countries (Guttmacher Institute, 2008b).

We now focus attention on the contraceptive behavior of U.S. women. Data on the bottom row of Table 4.1 indicate that 73 percent of U.S. women who are currently married are using some method of family planning, and 69 percent of U.S. married women are using modern methods. As is the situation worldwide, the most popular method for U.S. married women is female sterilization. But unlike the situation worldwide, for U.S. women the IUD is one of the least favored, not one of the most favored methods. The oral contraceptive is the second most favored method for U.S. women, followed by male sterilization.

To get a better and more comprehensive picture of the family planning method use of U.S. women, we present in Table 4.3 detailed data for the year 2002. Data for all women are shown according to their current marital status: married, cohabiting, never married, and formerly married (see also Figure 4.1). Among all women 15 to 44 years of age (this includes both married and unmarried women), the leading contraceptive method is the oral contraceptive. Almost 19 percent, or 11.6 million, of all women in the reproductive ages were using the pill in 2002. The second most popular method is female sterilization; nearly 17 percent, or 10.3 million, have been contraceptively sterilized. These two methods have been the most popular among U.S. women since 1982 (Mosher et al., 2004: 1).

Table 4.3 also presents data on U.S. women who are nonusers of family planning methods (bottom part). Just over 38 percent of all U.S. women are not currently using any form of contraception (also see Figure 4.1). Around 3 percent of them are sterile and almost 10 percent are pregnant, just gave birth, or are trying to become pregnant. Only 7.4 percent of all women who are nonusers are sexually active (defined as having had intercourse at least once in the three months prior to being interviewed in the survey). Most of the 38 percent who are not using contraceptives, that is, 18.1 percent, are women who are not sexually active (defined as women who have never had sexual intercourse or who have not had sex for at least three months).

How do these patterns differ for the four groups of women according to marital status? As already noted, among currently married women, the most

Table 4.3. Women 15–44 years of age, by current contraceptive status and specific method, according to marital or cohabiting status: United States, 2002

	All marital statuses	Currently married	Currently cohabiting	Never married	Formerly married
	100.0%	100.0%	100.0%	100.0%	100.0%
Using contraception (contraceptors)	61.9	72.9	72.5	44.0	64.4
Female sterilization	16.7	21.7	18.4	4.4	35.3
Male sterilization	5.7	11.2	2.2	0.4	2.2
Pill	18.9	17.2	24.1	21.8	12.3
Implant, Lunelle®, or patch	0.8	1.0	1.1	0.4	0.5
3-month injectable (Depo-Provera®)	3.3	2.2	6.8	4.2	1.7
Intrauterine device (IUD)	1.3	1.9	1.3	0.2	1.9
Diaphragm	0.2	0.2	0.0	0.2	–
Male condom	11.1	12.0	13.1	10.3	8.0
Calendar rhythm method	0.7	1.3	0.7	0.2	0.3
Other natural fertility methods (BBT, Billings)	0.2	0.4	0.0	0.0	–
Withdrawal	2.5	3.0	4.1	1.6	1.3
Other methods	0.6	0.7	0.8	0.2	0.9
Not using contraception	38.1	27.1	27.5	56.0	35.6
Surgically sterile – female (noncontraceptive)	1.5	2.1	1.3	0.4	3.0
Nonsurgically sterile – female or male	1.6	2.0	1.4	1.0	2.5
Pregnant or postpartum	5.3	7.5	8.7	2.3	2.2
Seeking pregnancy	4.2	6.9	5.3	0.8	2.0
Other nonuse					
Never had intercourse or no intercourse in 3 months before interview	18.1	2.3	2.4	42.9	17.7
Had intercourse in 3 months before interview	7.4	6.3	8.3	8.5	8.2
All other nonusers	0.0	0.0	–	0.0	0.1

Source: Mosher et al., 2004.

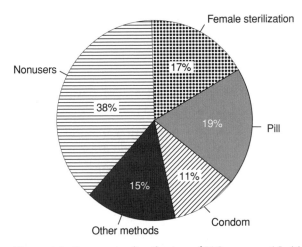

Figure 4.1. Percentage distribution of U.S. women 15–44 years of age, by current contraceptive status, 2002. *Source:* Mosher et al., 2004.

popular method is female sterilization; 22 percent of married women have been contraceptively sterilized. Among cohabiting women and among **single** (never married) women, the most popular method is the pill. Nearly half of single women who are contracepting are using the oral contraceptive.

Among married women, the second most popular method is the oral contraceptive. But for cohabiting women and single women, the second most popular method is the male condom. We noted earlier that the second most popular method worldwide is the IUD. Among U.S. women, the IUD is one of the least favored methods, used by only 2 percent of married women, 1 percent of cohabiting women, and 0.2 percent of single women.

What are the patterns of nonuse of contraception of U.S. women? Among all U.S. women, 7.4 percent are sexually active but not using any family planning method. This is an increase from 5.4 percent in 1995 and represents 1.4 million more women in 2002 than in 1995 who are sexually active but not using any method. This pattern could very well result in an increase in the rate of unintended pregnancy, especially among young women (Mosher et al., 2004: 2).

When we examine U.S. women by marital status, we find that between 27 and 28 percent of married women are nonusers, but of these, 6 percent are nonusers who are sexually active. Among single women and cohabiting women, 8 percent are sexually active but are not using contraceptives. More than three-quarters of single women who are not using any contraceptive method (42.9 percent of the 56 percent) are not sexually active; that is, they have never had sex or have not had sex in the past three months.

Here are some additional observations about the patterns of contraceptive use and nonuse of U.S. women that are not reflected in the data in Table 4.3. Among users, the most popular method for young women is the pill; 53 percent of women 15–24 in age who are contracepting are using the pill. The percentage of pill users drops to 38 percent for contraceptors in their late twenties and to 11 percent for those in their early forties. In contrast, half of all users 40–44 have been contraceptively sterilized; this percentage drops to 28 percent for contracepting women 30–34 and to 4 percent for contracepting women 20–24 (Mosher et al., 2004: 9).

Among contracepting women in the United States, those with less education tend to rely on female sterilization, while those with more education use the pill. Only 11 percent of contracepting women without a high school education use the oral contraceptive, compared with 42 percent of contracepting women holding at least a four-year college degree (Mosher et al., 2004: 2).

About 90 percent of U.S. women in the childbearing ages report having engaged in sexual intercourse prior to marriage. What was their use or nonuse of contraception in their first premarital intercourse? This is an important question because the first premarital intercourse "marks the beginning of exposure to the risk of nonmarital pregnancy and birth and sexually transmitted infections" (Mosher et al., 2004: 5). Also, teenagers who do not use a contraceptive method the first time they have sex are twice as likely to become pregnant and have a baby compared to teenagers who do use a method the first time.

Among U.S. women who had their first nonmarital intercourse prior to 1980, less than half (only 43 percent) used a method. This percentage has risen steadily over the years, reaching 79 percent for women whose first premarital intercourse occurred between 1999 and 2002 (Figure 4.2). Also, the older the woman at first nonmarital intercourse, the greater the likelihood she used a contraceptive method. Of those who used a method at first sexual experience, the condom was by far the most popular method; the pill was one-third as popular as the condom, and withdrawal was the third most favored method. Withdrawal, one of the least effective contraceptive methods, was the method used in one of every ten premarital intercourses occurring in the 1999–2002 period, as well as those occurring prior to 1980 (Mosher et al., 2004: 6, 16).

What is known about abortion in the United States? Between 1973 and 2005, around 45 million legal abortions were performed in the United States. In 2005, an estimated 1.21 million legal abortions were performed in the United States, a decrease from the 1.31 million performed in 2000. Every year, around 2 percent of U.S. women in the childbearing ages have an abortion. Nearly half of all U.S. women in the childbearing ages (47 percent) have had an abortion at some time in their life. Of the women having abortions in 2005, half of them were under age 25; this breaks out with women 20–24 obtaining 33 percent of all abortions and teenagers

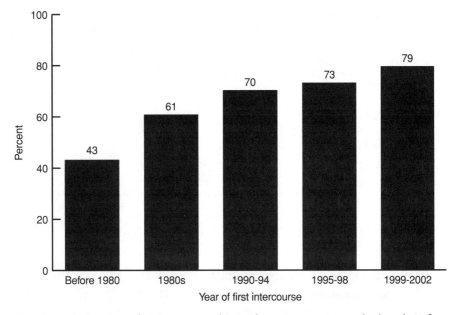

Figure 4.2. Percentage of U.S. women who used a contraceptive method at their first premarital intercourse, by year of first intercourse. *Source:* Mosher et al., 2004.

obtaining 17 percent of the abortions. More than one-third (37 percent) of all abortions were obtained by black women, 34 percent by Anglo women, 22 percent by Hispanic women, and 8 percent by women of other races. Regarding the religions of women having abortions in the United States in 2005, 43 percent of them were Protestants and 27 percent were Catholics. Women who had never been married obtained two-thirds of all abortions, and women with one or more children had about 60 percent of the abortions (Guttmacher Institute, 2008a).

Abortions became legal in the United States in 1973 when the Supreme Court in the *Roe v. Wade* decision declared that "women, in consultation with their physician, have a constitutionally protected right to have an abortion in the early stages of pregnancy, that is, before the fetus is viable, free from government interference" (Guttmacher Institute, 2008a: 2). The abortion rate data (number of abortions per 1,000 women ages 15–44) (see Figure 4.3) was at its low of 16.3/1,000 in 1973, the first year in which abortions were legally permitted. The rate increased to a high of 29.3 in 1981 and has dropped steadily since to a low of 19.4 in 2005. Most women have abortions very early in their pregnancies. The data in Figure 4.4 indicate that in 2004, 61.3 percent of all legal abortions were to women in the first eight weeks of their pregnancies, 17.8 percent to women in the ninth and tenth weeks of their pregnancies, and 9.6 percent to women in the eleventh and twelfth weeks. Almost 89 percent of all abortions

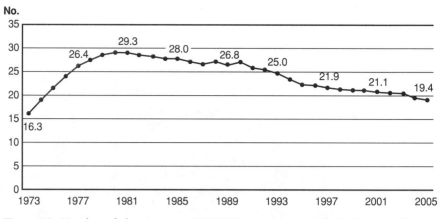

Figure 4.3. Number of abortions per 1,000 U.S. women ages 15–44, by year. *Source:* Guttmacher Institute, 2008a.

performed in the United States in 2004 were to women in the first twelve weeks of their pregnancies.

Having reviewed the patterns of family planning and abortion use and nonuse worldwide and in the United States, we turn in the next section to a discussion of each of the main methods of family planning. There are many kinds of family planning methods; some are controlled by females and others by males. This male–female categorization is "generally determined by which partner's body is most affected by the device's use" (Shepard, 1980: 72).

There are several ways to categorize contraceptives. One way is whether or not the contraceptive serves as a barrier to keep the sperm from entering the woman. Another categorization is whether the contraceptive contains hormones. One could also differentiate contraceptives according to whether they require continuous input (e.g., the pill or the condom) or whether they are long-lasting (e.g., IUDs and implants). Still another way is to categorize or rank them on the basis of their efficacy in preventing

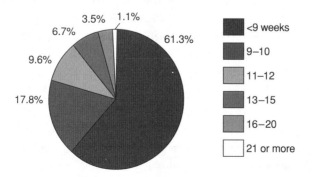

Figure 4.4. Percentage of abortions to U.S. women, by time period of occurrence, 2004. *Source:* Guttmacher Institute, 2008a.

pregnancy. The latter is the approach we follow. In the next section, we first discuss the concept of contraceptive effectiveness and failure and show how failure rates are measured and determined and what they mean. We then review each of the major contraceptive methods.

METHODS OF FAMILY PLANNING

The effectiveness of family planning methods may be measured in two ways, namely, in terms of **theoretical effectiveness** and **use effectiveness**. Theoretical effectiveness refers to the "efficaciousness" of the method when it is used "consistently according to a specified set of rules" and used all the time (Trussell, 2004: 91); one might thus refer to theoretical effectiveness as the degree of effectiveness that would occur with "perfect" use. Alternately, use effectiveness measures the effectiveness of the method taking into account the fact that some users do not follow the directions perfectly or carefully or may not use the method all the time; use effectiveness data reflect how effective the method is in **typical use**.

In Table 4.4, we report contraceptive failure percentage rates based on both use effectiveness and theoretical effectiveness data. Use effectiveness data are empirical data gathered in surveys conducted in the past decade or so that studied the contraceptive and fertility behavior of women, mainly in the United States. Couples were surveyed about their use of specific family planning methods for specific periods of time, usually a year. The percentage of couples "typically" using a specific method and experiencing accidental pregnancies over the course of a year is the **failure rate** for that method according to use effectiveness data. One needs to keep in mind that typical use is broadly defined. In many of the surveys generating contraceptive use data, a woman is stated to be "using" a particular contraceptive method if "she considers herself to be using that method. So, typical use of the condom could include actually using a condom only occasionally" (Trussell, 2004: 91). Or "a woman could report that she is 'using' the pill even though her supplies ran out several months ago" (Trussell, 2007a: 25). Thus, we need to keep in mind that "typical use is a very elastic concept" (Trussell, 2004: 91). It includes imperfect use and is not a measure of the "inherent efficacy of a contraceptive method when used perfectly, correctly and consistently" (Kost et al., 2008: 11).

The contraceptive failure rates based on theoretical effectiveness refer to pregnancies that would be experienced if a particular method was used under ideal, perfect conditions, that is, if the method was always used and used exactly according to the instructions.

We start by asking how many pregnancies will occur if no contraception is used. The failure rate for the nonuse of contraception is based on

Table 4.4. Contraceptive failure rates (percentage of women experiencing an unintended pregnancy during the first year of use), by contraceptive method, according to use effectiveness and theoretical effectiveness, United States, post-1990

Method	Use Effectiveness	Theoretical Effectiveness
No method	85	85
Spermicides	29	18
Withdrawal	27	4
Fertility awareness methods	25	
Calendar rhythm		9
Ovulation method		3
Standard Days		5*
Cap		
Parous women	32	26
Nulliparous women	16	9
Diaphragm	16	6
Female condom	21	5
Male condom	15	2
Combined pill & mini-pill	8	0.3
Patch, Ortho-Evra®	8	0.3
Vaginal ring, NuvaRing®	8	0.3
Injectables		
Depo-Provera®	3	0.3
Lunelle®	3	0.05
Intrauterine device (IUD)		
ParaGard®	0.8	0.6
Mirena®	0.1	0.1
Female sterilization	0.5	0.5
Male sterilization	0.15	0.10
Implants		
Norplant® & Norplant-2	0.05	0.05
IMPLANON®	0.05*	0.05*

Sources: Trussell, 2004. *These data are from Trussell, 2007b.

studies of "populations in which the use of contraception is rare, and on couples who report that they stopped using contraceptives because they want to conceive" (Trussell, 2007b: 748). The failure rate for nonuse is 85 percent. This means that if 100 sexually active couples were to use no contraception (i.e., were to engage in unprotected intercourse) over the course of a year, 85 percent of the women on average would experience an accidental pregnancy. The nonuse of contraception, obviously, has the highest pregnancy (or failure) rate.

Alternately, the contraceptive with the lowest failure rate, determined by both theoretical effectiveness data and use effectiveness data, is the implant; the popular implant brand of IMPLANON® has a failure rate of 0.05 percent (discussed in more detail later). This means that for every ten thousand women using an IMPLANON implant, five would experience an unintended pregnancy in the course of one year.

Failure rates are shown in Table 4.4 for all the major types of contraceptives according to use effectiveness and theoretical effectiveness. They are ranked from the highest failure rate to the lowest failure rate according to use effectiveness data.

Vaginal spermicides are the least effective contraceptive method (based on use effectiveness data), but they are vastly more effective than no contraception. Spermicides are contraceptive creams, jellies, and foams that are inserted into the vagina prior to the onset of genital contact and sexual intercourse. They are "commonly marketed for use with a diaphragm, but they can also be used alone" (Cates and Raymond, 2007: 321). They should be placed in the vagina several minutes before sexual activity commences. To be maximally effective, they should cover the vagina mucus and cervix. Some spermicides require the use of an applicator for correct insertion. The spermicide needs to be reapplied before each coitus. In addition to creating a physical barrier to the movement of sperm, many spermicides contain the sperm-killing chemical nonoxynol-9, which further reduces the chance of **conception** (the beginning of pregnancy) by damaging and killing sperm in the vagina.

The idea of **vaginal contraceptives** is very old. Aristotle described the use of oil of cedar and frankincense in olive oil to block the cervical entrance. During the Middle Ages, rock salt and alum were frequently used as vaginal contraceptives (Himes, 1970: 80). Much later, a sponge moistened with diluted lemon juice and inserted into the vagina was described as an "effective" contraceptive. During the 1920s and 1930s, numerous vaginal suppositories and foam tablets were developed and sold widely.

Vaginal spermicides are available in pharmacies and supermarkets without a prescription under such brand names in the United States as Advantage 24®, Because®, Delfen®, Emko®, Encare®, K-Y Plus®, Ortho Crème®, and VCF®, among many others, and in Canada as Advantage 24®, Delfen®, Emko®, Encare®, Ortho-Gynol®, Pharmatex®, and Ramses Contraceptive Foam®, among several others. Despite their large-scale accessibility and small expense, they are not very effective, from the vantage of either use effectiveness or theoretical effectiveness. Under typical use, the failure rate is 29 percent, and 18 percent under perfect use (Table 4.4). Also, the effectiveness of a spermicide depends on the particular type. Aerosol foams and creams tend to be more effective than jellies and foam tablets. Foam compares favorably with the effectiveness of the calendar rhythm method (see subsequent discussion), but as indicated by the failure rate data just mentioned, produces many more failures than most other methods.

Their relative ineffectiveness is the major disadvantage of vaginal spermicides. Also, as already noted, the vaginal preparations must be administered several minutes before intercourse, which will thus tend to interrupt foreplay and is often inconvenient. They must be inserted high into the vagina to be most effective, and some women may do this only reluctantly or not at all. On the other hand, their use does not require medical supervision. There are no known adverse side effects except for mild burning, which can be experienced by both females and males, and vaginal irritation, which can often be corrected by switching to some other type of preparation. A positive side effect is that spermicides provide some vaginal lubrication.

A very small number of U.S. women use spermicides as their regular contraceptive method, less than half of 1 percent. Their number is so small that they are included in the "Other methods" category in Table 4.3.

The next method we consider is withdrawal, also known as *coitus interruptus* and as the *pull-out* method. With this method, "the couple may have penile-vaginal intercourse until ejaculation is impending, at which time the male partner withdraws his penis from the vagina and away from the external genitalia of the female partner. The male must rely on his own sensations to determine when he is about to ejaculate" (Kowal, 2007: 338). Coitus interruptus may be distinguished from a similar method with the same end result, namely, **coitus reservatus**, also known as **amplexus reservatus**. With the coitus reservatus method, the male enters his partner, does not ejaculate, and endeavors to remain at the plateau phase of sexual intercourse and excitement, thus prolonging and sometimes intensifying pleasure. It differs from coitus interruptus in that ejaculation does not occur or is delayed indefinitely.

Coitus interruptus is one of the oldest known contraceptive practices (Jutte, 2008). It is mentioned in the Old Testament (Genesis 38), and its use has been reported by field researchers in many parts of the world. In fact, demographers believe that withdrawal played a major role in the fertility decline that was part of the demographic transition in France during the nineteenth century (N. Ryder, 1959; Shepard, 1980: 74). As we note in Chapter 9, the changes in the social and economic structure that accompanied industrialization rewarded smaller families and made large families much more costly. Modern contraceptives had not yet been developed, and withdrawal was a culturally acceptable method that was known and available. This illustrates how social, economic, and cultural factors affect the use of birth control methods.

To be used effectively, withdrawal requires a tremendous amount of self-control and trust. The male must have near-complete control of his sexual sensations and know exactly when he is about to reach the time of sexual excitement when ejaculation cannot be stopped or delayed; he must pull his penis out of the woman before this time occurs. But even if he withdraws his penis in time, the preejaculate fluid often picks up enough sperm in the urethra from a previous ejaculation that an unintended pregnancy will sometimes occur. Thus, the man should urinate between ejaculations to rid his urethra of leftover sperm. Even if the male withdraws his penis in time but deposits the ejaculate or preejaculate on or near the woman's vagina, pregnancy will sometimes occur (Segal and Nordberg, 1977).

Some religious groups, namely, Roman Catholics, object to the use of withdrawal on moral grounds, owing to the belief that every act of intercourse must have the possibility of resulting in conception (Jutte, 2008; Noonan, 1966). And some believe that withdrawal is a physically and psychologically damaging technique, although there is no solid evidence to support this view. However, the method does require the complete cooperation of the male partner, as well as practice and considerable motivation. Obviously, coitus interruptus is not a good method for males who tend to ejaculate prematurely. It is also not recommended for males with little or no sexual experience, owing to the fact that a good amount of experience is required before a male can predict with a reasonable amount of certainty that ejaculation is about to occur. On the positive side, there is no financial expense associated with the use of withdrawal, and it requires no special preparation or equipment.

Withdrawal has a high failure rate according to use effectiveness data, 27 percent (Table 4.4). Only a small percentage of all U.S. women report this as their method of contraception (Table 4.3).

Fertility awareness methods refer to several so-called natural family planning methods that employ an awareness of information about the woman's menstrual cycle to predict the time of the month when the probabilities are high that she will become pregnant. In general, these methods are just slightly more effective than spermicides and withdrawal (based on use effectiveness).

These methods require that a woman refrain from having intercourse during the time when the probabilities are high that she will become pregnant. Some of the fertility awareness methods are classified as "modern" and some as "traditional." The more effective ones use various kinds of symptomatic information about the woman and her menstrual cycle.

The traditional and least effective fertility awareness method is the *calendar rhythm method*, known also as periodic abstinence or continence. There are several calendar methods, the first of which was developed independently in 1920 by a Japanese scientist, Kyusaka Ogino, and by an Austrian scientist, Hermann Knaus. It was based on the idea that a women can avoid pregnancy if she refrains from intercourse around the time of ovulation, when the egg is produced. Generally, only one egg is produced per menstrual cycle, and it is potentially fertilizable for around twenty-four hours after ovulation. The sperm is believed to be viable in the female tract for as many as six or seven days (R. Ryder, 1993: 723; Segal, 2003: 171) and is thus capable of fertilizing an egg several days after intercourse occurs. Theoretically, couples who avoid intercourse during the period when the egg and sperm are viable should be able to avoid conception. The trick is finding out the exact time interval during which to avoid intercourse.

The notion that females cannot conceive during most of the menstrual cycle is very old (Himes, [1936] 1970), but some of the early ideas on which part of the cycle was not "safe" were incorrect. For instance, Knaus held that ovulation would always occur fourteen days prior to the start of the next menstrual cycle (Jutte, 2008: 204), a fact that we now know to be untrue. Others held that the woman was most likely to conceive immediately after her menstrual period ended; thus, the rest of the cycle was considered safe because she was thought to be sterile during that time. Frequently, women following these principles became pregnant, and the calendar rhythm method gained a poor reputation. For instance, there is the joke that persons practicing the rhythm method are known as parents. Since the method was defined as "natural" and not "artificial," it was deemed to be acceptable by the Roman Catholic Church, and hence sometimes came to be called "Vatican roulette" or "calendar love."

The calendar rhythm method is typically applied as follows. The woman records the length of her menstrual cycles for a time period of a year or more. The presumed time of ovulation is then determined for the shortest and longest cycles. Nineteen is subtracted from the shortest and ten from the longest. These calculations inform the woman when it is safe and not safe to engage in intercourse. For example, if a woman determines that her menstrual cycles range in length from thirty-one to thirty-five days, it would be safe for her to have intercourse for the first through the twelfth days of the cycle (31 − 19 = 12), not safe on the thirteenth through the twenty-fourth days, and safe again starting on the twenty-fifth day (35 − 10 = 25) (Kipley and Kipley, 1996). There are no failure rate data available based on use effectiveness for this specific method (the failure rate for all fertility awareness methods, combined, is 25 percent). The failure rate based on theoretical effectiveness is 9 percent (Table 4.4). Even if used perfectly – and it is hardly ever used perfectly – the calendar rhythm method will result in nine unintended pregnancies per year for every hundred women using the method.

The estimated time of ovulation may also be calculated by use of a **basal body temperature (BBT)** chart, and the method is known as the **basal body temperature method**. It is based on the principle that ovulation produces a rise in the basic metabolic rate, causing a corresponding increase in body temperature of between 0.3 and 0.9 degrees Centigrade (between 0.5 and 1.6 degrees Fahrenheit). The time of one's ovulation may thus be determined by reading and recording one's temperature daily. This technique greatly reduces the length of abstinence as required in the calendar rhythm method, but there are drawbacks. Changes in body temperature are slight and easily misinterpreted, and the principle of an increase in temperature at the time of ovulation may not necessarily apply to all women (Shepard, 1980). We do not have available (and thus do not show in Table 4.4) validated failure rate data for this method. However, approximate information gives a rate based on use effectiveness data of around 20 percent.

Among the more modern fertility awareness methods are the *Billings Method* and the *Standard Days Method*. The Billings Method, also known as the *ovulation method* or the *Billings ovulation method*, is based on research undertaken by John Billings, Evelyn Billings, and others starting in the 1950s concerning the association between the presence of cervical mucus and ovulation (E. Billings et al., 1972; E. Billings and Westmore, 2000; J. Billings, 1984). Vaginal mucus tends to become more moist and cervical secretions more watery as the body prepares for ovulation. By slipping her finger into her vagina on a daily basis and checking on the moistness of the mucus and the consistency of the secretions, a woman, with appropriate training, can detect when ovulation is about to occur and when it has passed. There are no available failure rate data based on use effectiveness for the Billings method. The failure rate based on theoretical effectiveness is a low 3 percent (Table 4.4).

The Standard Days Method is easy to use for women with menstrual cycles that last between twenty-six and thirty-two days. It is a variant of the calendar rhythm method but is more effective (based on theoretical effectiveness data) and easier to learn and use. Developed by researchers at the Institute for Reproductive Health at Georgetown University, it is based on the principle that "women with regular menstrual cycles lasting 26–32 days can prevent pregnancy by avoiding unprotected intercourse on days eight

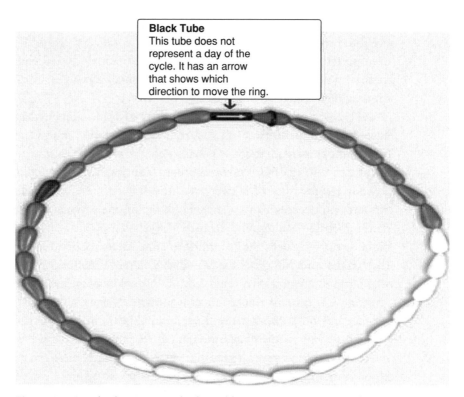

Figure 4.5. Standard Days Method necklace. *Source:* Institute for Reproductive Research, Georgetown University, Washington, D.C., available online at http://www .irh.org/RTP-SDM-MoreCycleBeads.htm (accessed November 10, 2008).

through 19. This 12-day fertile window takes into account the variability in the timing of ovulation and the viability of sperm in the woman's reproductive tract" (Gribble, 2003: 188). Thus, it is safe to engage in intercourse for the first seven days of the cycle, not safe from the eighth through the nineteenth days, and safe again from the twentieth day until the end of the cycle. A necklace of CycleBeads® (Figure 4.5) may be used by the woman to keep track of the days. The beads are colored either red, brown, or white, and the white beads are designed to glow in the dark. There is one red bead on the necklace, and it is used to mark the first day in the woman's menstrual cycle (i.e., the day she starts her menstrual period). Six brown beads follow the one red bead, and they signify the days when it is safe to have intercourse. Twelve white glow-in-the-dark beads follow the brown beads, and they signify days when it is not safe to have intercourse. They are then followed by brown beads signifying safe days until the menstrual period restarts, at which time the woman begins again with the red bead.

The woman is instructed to move a black marker ring each morning from one bead to the next (see Figure 4.5). Prior to engaging in intercourse, she checks the color of the bead; if it is white and glowing in the dark, it is not a safe day.

The Standard Days Method has been introduced in many developing countries to young women who are using contraceptives for the first time, many of whom find the method appealing. According to James M. Gribble (2003: 188): "In trials conducted in El Salvador and India, up to one-half of women who adopted the method had never before practiced family planning, in large part because of concerns about side effects and a perceived threat to future fertility." Like the other fertility awareness methods already discussed, there are also no failure rate data available based on use effectiveness for the Standard Days Method. Its failure rate based on theoretical effectiveness data is 5 percent (Table 4.4).

Be sure and view the one-minute video clip of Flea, from the rock group The Red Hot Chili Peppers, using a necklace of CycleBeads to explain the Standard Days Method in a rural health clinic in Haiti. In this video, available online at http://www.4real.com/tv/details.asp?pageid=12, you will see Flea and a rural health agent of the Haitian Health Foundation. In the right column under "Video," click the box with the header "Birth Control."

Except for the pregnancies that result from method failures, no known serious side effects are associated with any of the fertility awareness methods just reviewed. No special equipment is necessary (except, perhaps, for a calendar or a thermometer, or a set of beads). Their use does not require the interruption of sexual foreplay or the application of mechanical or chemical devices, and all of these methods are acceptable to the Roman Catholic Church. However, their effective use requires a high level of motivation by both partners and the ability to estimate accurately the day of ovulation. There is also a mental disadvantage, that is, the extra worry many users experience knowing in advance the probability of failure. The various fertility awareness methods also have very low use rates among U.S. women (Table 4.3).

The next methods to be considered are the *diaphragm* and the **cervical cap**. The vaginal diaphragm is a device that erects a barrier between the sperm and the ova. It is a soft rubber vaginal cup with a metal spring reinforcing the rim. It should be inserted into the vagina anytime from one to two hours before sexual activity and should be left in place for six to eight hours after the last ejaculation. It functions mainly to block the access of sperm to the cervix (the opening to the uterus) and is held in place by the spring tension rim, the woman's vaginal muscle tone, and the pubic bone. Although the diaphragm acts as a barrier to most of the sperm, it usually does not fit tightly enough to prevent passage of all of the sperm. Thus, it is recommended that diaphragms be used with a spermicidal cream or jelly.

A cervical cap is a small, thimble-shaped cup that also serves as a barrier contraceptive by fitting over the cervix. The first modern cervical caps were developed in 1838 by the German gynecologist Friedrich Wilde when he prepared custom-made rubber molds of the cervix for his patients (Himes, [1936] 1970: 211). Today, caps are made of latex or silicone. They provide a more effective mechanical block against sperm than diaphragms. Thus, spermicidal mixtures are not as necessary with cervical caps as they are with diaphragms but are still recommended. Cervical caps are much more effective when used by nulliparous women (i.e., women who have not yet given birth) than by parous women.

Diaphragms and cervical caps were developed for contraceptive use during the nineteenth century. The diaphragm was popularized in the early twentieth century by Margaret Sanger. However, it lost favor "with the advent of non-event-related methods such as the IUD and oral contraceptive" (Shepard, 1980: 75). In combination with a contraceptive jelly or cream, the diaphragm and cap were the methods most often recommended by physicians in private practice and by birth control clinics throughout the United States and Europe during the 1930s and 1940s (Peel and Potts, 1969: 62–63). About one-third of American couples who tried to plan their families during the 1940s used diaphragms or cervical caps.

Even when properly used with a spermicide, the diaphragm has a relatively high failure rate (16 percent) according to use effectiveness, although lower (6 percent) according to theoretical effectiveness (Table 4.4). The diaphragm is only slightly more effective than spermicides and some other methods. In addition to nonuse because of insufficient motivation, diaphragm failures are due to lack of knowledge regarding proper insertion, an improper fit, displacement during intercourse, and defects in the diaphragm itself. A very small percentage of U.S. women today report using the diaphragm as their main method of contraception (Table 4.3).

Regarding the cervical cap, its failure rate based on use effectiveness data for nulliparous women is the same as for the diaphragm, that is, 16 percent. But its failure rate for parous women is twice as high (Table 4.4).

There are no known serious physiological side effects for either the diaphragm or cervical cap. They do not require the cooperation of the male partner and are used only when needed. Thus, they are both convenient methods for women who engage in sexual intercourse infrequently and do not need continuous protection. Using a spermicidal cream or jelly also produces additional vaginal lubrication during intercourse. However, since the diaphragm or cervical cap should be inserted several hours before intercourse, as already mentioned, its use requires the user to know in advance when she will have intercourse; otherwise, she will have to inter-rupt sexual foreplay to insert the device. Regular use requires considerable motivation. Some women do not like the process of insertion, and other women view it as messy because of the spermicide.

Diaphragms and cervical caps must be fitted by trained personnel, who teach the user the proper insertion techniques. Both seem particularly ill-suited for use in many developing countries, where there is often a lack of privacy for insertion and removal, as well as a convenient source of clean water for washing the devices after use. Moreover, there tends to be a shortage of medical personnel available for fitting the devices, and the need for a constant supply of spermicidal creams or jellies makes this barrier method relatively expensive (Wortman, 1976).

Another barrier method is the condom, for both males and females. The male condom was not popularized until the late nineteenth century. However, it was first mentioned as far back as 1564 in the posthumous writings on syphilis of the Italian anatomist Gabriele Falloppio (who also described the Fallopian tubes). Falloppio recommended that condoms be used to prevent venereal disease (Jutte, 2008: 96). Female condoms, on the other hand, made a much later appearance; they were invented and popular-ized by the Danish medical doctor Lasse Hessel and launched worldwide in 1991. Under the brand name Reality, female condoms were first marketed in the United States in 1992.

The *male condom* is a mechanical barrier that fits snugly over the penis and prevents the ejaculated sperm from entering the vagina. Condoms have many names, namely, rubbers, prophylactics, safes, and jimmies. Himes has written that "the French call the condom 'la capot anglaise' or English cape; the English have returned the compliment; to them it is the 'French letter'" (Himes, [1936] 1970: 194).

As just noted, the condom's first recorded appearance was in the six-teenth century when it was recommended as a prophylactic against venereal disease. Its contraceptive effects at that time were incidental. Condoms were made of linen and were not very effective. Those made from sheep intestines first appeared in the eighteenth century. Christopher Tietze, among others, wrote that this innovation "has been attributed to an Englishman named Cundum, sometimes identified, although erroneously, as a physician at the court of Charles II" (1965: 70; see also Bernstein, 1940; and Himes, [1936] 1970: 191–194). But it was not until the vulcanization of rubber in the mid-nineteenth century that condom use on a large scale became possible. The introduction of liquid latex in the mid-1930s made possible the man-ufacture of condoms with greater tensile strength, allowing them to last longer before decaying.

Female Condom

Figure 4.6. Female condom. *Source:* The Female Health Company, Chicago, Illinois, available online at http://www .femalehealth.com/ (accessed November 10, 2008).

Owing to the important role that condoms now play in HIV intervention, the world market today for condoms is extensive. In 2004, various donors including the United States, Germany, the United Kingdom, and the United Nations Population Fund provided 2.4 billion male condoms to users in more than a hundred developing countries, a slight decrease from the all-time high provision of 2.7 billion condoms in 2001 (Population Action International, 2006).

Condoms are moderately effective. Almost all failures result from nonuse and/or incorrect use rather than from defects in the condoms themselves. The failure rate for male condoms based on use effectiveness is 15 percent (Table 4.4). Male condoms, especially when used with vaginal spermicides, are more effective than most of the other methods we have so far discussed. The male condom requires some interruption of sexual foreplay. An even larger drawback is decreased sensitivity for some males. Its major advantages are its effectiveness and the fact that it has no medical side effects. Condoms are easy to buy and store, and their use requires no special training. Medical examination, supervision, and follow-up are not necessary. Most important, in addition to providing visible postcoital evidence of effectiveness, condoms offer effective protection against venereal disease. More than 11 percent of all U.S. women in the childbearing ages report that the male condom is their main method of contraception.

The *female condom* as a female-initiated barrier method has a failure rate only slightly higher than that of the male condom. It has many of the advantages of the male condom but fewer of its disadvantages. It is a soft and strong transparent polyurethane sheath about the same length as a male condom (around 6.5 inches), with a flexible ring at each end (Figure 4.6). It is inserted into the vagina prior to intercourse. The inner ring at the closed end of the condom is used to insert it into the vagina; the ring then moves into place behind the pubic bone. The outer ring at the open end of the condom is soft and remains outside the vagina. Since its use does not depend on the male having an erection, it usually does not interrupt the spontaneity of the sex act. Moreover, unlike the male condom, it does not need to be removed immediately after ejaculation. Because it lines the vagina loosely, not tightly, some persons, particularly males, find the female condom more satisfying sexually then the male condom.

Failure rate data for the female condom are based on the use of the Reality brand female condom, the first to appear in U.S. markets. Other brands of female condoms now available include Care®, Dominique®, FC Female Condom®, and Myfemy®. The failure rate based on use effectiveness data is 21 percent, slightly higher than the corresponding rate of 15 percent for the male condom (Table 4.4).

The distribution of the female condom has increased worldwide since first becoming available at a reduced cost in the mid-1990s. But the female condom has nowhere near the impact on the world market as the male condom. Only 12 million female condoms were distributed worldwide in 2004, compared to the 2.4 billion male condoms distributed in the same year. More than half of the female condoms distributed in 2004 went to women in sub-Saharan Africa (Population Action International, 2006).

The next most effective and modern type of contraceptives are *hormonal-based methods*, of which the oral contraceptive, that is, the **birth control pill**, or "the pill," is the most popular. Let us first review how hormonal methods work. The first oral contraceptives marketed in the 1960s were known as "combined" pills because they contained the two hormones similar to the estrogen and progesterone produced by the ovary and governed by the pituitary gland. When a woman ingests the hormones contained in the pill, one can say that her pituitary is "fooled" into thinking that she is already pregnant. Thus, there is no need for the pituitary "to send out hormones to stimulate the ovaries [into egg production] if there are already [in the woman] high levels of ovarian-type hormones" (Guillebaud, 2005: 7). The combined birth control pill containing both estrogen and progestin (a type of progesterone) thus prevents conception primarily by preventing ovulation. There are two additional factors that contribute to its contraceptive effect. Because ovulation does not occur, the consistency of the cervical mucus is maintained in a state that the sperm cannot easily penetrate. Also, because the full secretory pattern is not reached, the inner lining of the uterus is usually not suitable for implantation of the fertilized egg.

Today, there are several different hormonal methods, and they differ according to the type of hormone(s) in the contraceptive, the amount of the hormone(s) in the contraceptive, the way the woman receives the hormone(s), and whether the exposure to the hormone(s) is continuous or periodic. As already noted, the hormones are estrogen and progestin, and they may be received by the woman orally or via a patch, injected under her skin, implanted into a tissue, or placed into her vagina.

The first hormonal-based method was the oral contraceptive. In 1950, the Planned Parenthood Federation of America funded a reproductive physiologist and a gynecology professor to develop a simple and effective oral contraceptive: Gregory Pincus (1903–1967), Director of the Worcester Foundation for Experimental Biology in Shrewsbury, Massachusetts, and John Rock (1890–1984), Professor of Gynecology and Obstetrics at the Harvard Medical School. In 1951, Carl Djerassi, a chemist, led a research team in the first synthesis of a steroid oral contraceptive (see Chapter 5 in his autobiography [Djerassi, 1992] for an interesting account of this discovery). Pincus, Rock, and Djerassi are sometimes referred to as the "fathers" of the oral contraceptive, although Djerassi referred to himself as its "mother" (Marks, 2001:11).

In 1953–1954, Pincus and his collaborators tested this steroid and others for ovulation inhibition. Pincus and Rock then began work formulating a birth control pill at the Worcester Foundation. Pincus headed the science side of the research, and Rock directed the clinical trials to show that this new pill was safe and effective. The pill was first tested on some of Rock's patients, but systematic trials could not then be performed because it was a felony in Massachusetts at that time to dispense contraceptives. The tests were moved to Puerto Rico, and later to Haiti, Mexico, and Los Angeles. The work of Pincus and Rock led eventually to G. D. Searle and Company marketing the oral contraceptive in the United States in 1960 as Enovid-10®.

Ironically, Rock was a devoted and devout Roman Catholic who believed that the newly invented birth control pill should be approved by the Roman Catholic Church. He compared the birth control pill to the calendar rhythm method, which had been approved earlier in 1951 by Pope Pius XII. Like the rhythm method, the pill did not kill sperm or obstruct the passage of sperm into the female tract. It suppressed ovulation with a combination of estrogen and progestin, much like a woman's body suppressed ovulation during pregnancy. Rock's landmark book published in 1963, *The Time Has Come: A Catholic Doctor's Proposals to End the Battle over Birth Control*, was a conscientious and honorable effort to justify the pill as a natural method of birth control. Although ghostwritten by professionals of the Planned Parenthood Federation of America, the book clearly represented Rock's views and opinions (Tentler, 2008). It noted that "the pills, when properly taken, are not at all likely to disturb menstruation, nor do they mutilate any organ of the body, nor damage any natural process. They merely offer to the human intellect the means to regulate ovulation harmlessly, means which heretofore have come only from the ovary, and during pregnancy, from the placenta" (Rock, 1963: 169). Rock was deeply disappointed in 1968 when Pope Paul VI published his encyclical *Humanae Vitae* (Latin for "Of Human Life") declaring that oral contraceptives and all other so-called artificial methods of birth control were immoral. Margaret Marsh and Wanda Ronner's (2008) recently

Figure 4.7. Poster from the Bangladesh Family Planning Directorate: "In Bangladesh and around the world, millions of women rely on oral contraceptive." *Source:* Zlidar, 2000.

published biography of John Rock, *The Fertility Doctor*, is "a balanced portrait of a twentieth-century medical giant" (Tentler, 2008: 24) and describes in detail the kinds of conflicts that Dr. Rock had with his Catholic Church.

Once introduced in the United States and other countries in 1960, the oral contraceptive became extremely popular, and remains so today. It is known simply as "the pill." If a woman informs her male friend that she forgot to take her "pill" for the past few days, he does not think to himself, "I wonder if she is referring to an aspirin or a sleeping pill or a vitamin pill or some other kind of pill." He knows exactly and right away that she is referring to the birth control pill.

We reported earlier (see Table 4.1) that 8 percent of married women worldwide and 17 percent of married women in the United States are using the oral contraceptive. Almost 12 million women in the United States use the oral contraceptive, as do an estimated 100 million women worldwide (Zlidar, 2000) (Figure 4.7).

When the oral contraceptive was first introduced in the early 1960s, its major disadvantage was adverse side effects. The negative side effects, particularly in the early versions of the pill, were numerous. Some were nuisances, such as headaches, weight gain, and morning nausea, but many users found these nuisances so discomforting that they discontinued using the pill. Some of the side effects were life threatening. Thromboembolic (blood-clotting) disorders are but one example. Although the more common superficial leg thromboses (or phlebitis) are not very dangerous, cerebrovascular diseases (strokes that are also thrombic) are potentially fatal. The estrogen content of the pill is primarily responsible for the thromboembolic problems. Other negative side effects included increased blood pressure and vaginal dryness (Guillebaud, 2005). There is also a demonstrated interaction between cigarette smoking and pill use and the incidence of heart disease. However, the oral contraceptives produced these days "contain less than one-twentieth of the dose of the original pills, which results in a lower incidence of side effects" (Segal, 2003: 171).

Other side effects of the pill have been shown to be beneficial. Most of the beneficial ones are associated with the physical and emotional aspects of menstruation. These include decreased incidence of menorrhagia (heavy bleeding), dysmenorrhea (cramps), iron deficiency anemia, and premenstrual tension. Thus, for many women, oral contraceptives produce more regular menstrual cycles that are shorter in duration, produce less bleeding and abdominal discomfort, and are accompanied by less premenstrual tension than is normally the case (Potts, Diggory, and Peel, 1977: 38). There are several additional noncontraceptive health benefits, namely, "decreased risk of endometrial and ovarian cancer, decreased risk of colon cancer . . . and maintenance of bone density" (Segal, 2003: 171).

The modern oral contraceptive is either a combined pill containing estrogen and progestin or a pill containing only progestin, known as a **mini-pill**. The combined pill is **monophasic, biphasic,** or **triphasic,** referring to the amounts of estrogen and progestin provided each day. A monophasic pill provides a constant amount of estrogen and progestin every day, while the other two types provide varying amounts. Depending on the manufacturer (there are now around forty different combination pills produced), most combination pills come in either twenty-one- or twenty-eight-day packages. With the former, the woman takes a pill each day for twenty-one days and no pill for seven days when menstruation occurs, and then the process is repeated; with the twenty-eight-day packet, the hormonal medication is present in the pills for the first twenty-one days, and the pills for the last seven days are placebos.

The mini-pill, the other type of oral contraceptive, was first marketed in the United States in 1973. It consists of a small dose of progestin, which is taken daily, even during menstruation. It reduces the side effects of the combined pill, and it also makes available an oral contraceptive for women who breast-feed their children or who should avoid estrogen for health reasons. The mini-pill does not include estrogen; therefore, it does not always result in the suppression of ovulation. Thus, many of the menstrual periods of mini-pill users are natural. The mini-pill functions as a contraceptive mainly "by interfering with the passage of sperm through the mucus at the entrance to the uterus" (Guillebaud, 2005: 176), whether or not an egg has been released. In this sense, the mini-pill acts more like a barrier method of contraceptive, albeit one that is taken orally. The mini-pill also prevents pregnancy; since the **endometrium** (the lining of the uterus) is altered, the result is that a fertilized egg is not being implanted, if indeed ovulation does occur (Raymond, 2007: 182). The mini-pill is not as popular as the combined pill, and currently there are only three brands on the market.

Both the combined oral contraceptive pill and the mini-pill are very effective. Table 4.4 shows that according to use effectiveness data, the combined pill and the mini-pill have a failure rate of 8 percent and a much lower failure rate of 0.3 percent according to theoretical effectiveness. Most of the pregnancies that occur to pill users result from the failure to take it regularly. The major advantages are its high effectiveness and the fact that its use does not interfere with the sexual act in any way. It is not necessary to interrupt foreplay or to conclude sexual activity right after coition. Moreover, the pill allows the female to use contraception independently of any cooperation by the male (or even of his knowledge). Nearly 19 percent of all U.S. women use either the combined pill or the mini-pill.

We noted previously that hormonal contraceptives need not be administered orally. There are several other hormonal contraception delivery systems, one of which is the **contraceptive patch**. The patch is an adhesive device about the size of a 50-cent piece that is placed on the buttocks, arm, or stomach. It works like the combination pill just discussed, except that instead of requiring the user to engage in a daily regimen, it is based on a weekly regimen. A new patch is placed on the skin once every seven days. The two hormones are released from the patch at a constant and continuous level each day. After three weeks, no patch is used for one week, to allow menstruation to occur. The one brand of birth control patch now on the market is Ortho-Evra® and is available in a beige color. The patch has the same effective numbers as the combined pill and mini-pill (see Table 4.4). Less than 1 percent of U.S. women use the patch (Table 4.3).

A woman may also receive the contraceptive hormones by inserting into her vagina a **vaginal ring**, under the brand name **NuvaRing®**. The vaginal ring is a thin, transparent, flexible ring and is similar to the combined pill; it contains both the estrogen and progestin hormones, which are released on a continuous basis into the woman's body. The ring is inserted by the woman into her vagina usually during the first five days of her menstrual period and remains in place for three weeks. The woman then withdraws it, throws it away, and does not use a ring for a week, during which time menstruation occurs. A new ring is then inserted after seven days. Since the vaginal ring is not a barrier method like the diaphragm or cap or female condom, the exact and precise placement of the ring in the vagina is not a major issue. The vaginal ring has the same effectiveness numbers as the pill (Table 4.4).

Another way for women to receive hormonal contraception is through *contraception injection*. There are two forms, namely, Depo-Provera®, which is similar to the mini-pill, and Lunelle®, which is similar to the combined pill. Like the mini-pill, Depo-Provera contains only progestin. It is administered via an injection by a health professional once every twelve weeks in the arm, buttocks, upper thigh, or abdomen. The economic cost is about the same as the birth control pill.

Lunelle contains both hormones so is similar in concept to the combined pill. The user receives an injection monthly. Lunelle is the newer of the two types of injectables. The Depo-Provera and Lunelle injectable contraceptives have the same use effectiveness numbers, very low failure rates of 3 percent (Table 4.4). When failures (pregnancies) occur, they will mainly be due to the fact that the woman did not have her shots at the prescribed intervals. Failure rates based on theoretical effectiveness are 0.3 and 0.05, respectively. With both forms of injectables, a woman typically stops having periods altogether after one year of use. More U.S. women use Depo-Provera than Lunelle (Table 4.3).

Still another way for the woman to receive hormonal contraception is via a **subdermal contraceptive implant**. The first implant was developed in the 1980s under the brand name of Norplant® (Sivin, Nash, and Waldman, 2002). It consisted of six small silicone capsule-type rods, each containing progestin, placed subdermally in the woman's upper arm, to remain in effect for five years. The implants are usually visible and resemble small veins. The Norplant implant has now been phased out in favor of implants with fewer capsule rods. The more popular ones are Norplant-2, two silicone rods with protection for three years; IMPLANON, one rod with protection for three years; and Jadelle®, two rods with protection for five years (Sivin, Nash, and Waldman, 2002).

One obvious advantage of these latter three implants is the reduction in the number of implant rods, making the insertion and removal processes much easier. Another advantage is that a single visit to a clinic once every three years, or once every five years, for an implant is substituted for the daily consumption of birth control pills, or the weekly employment of a patch, or the triweekly insertion of a vaginal ring, or the monthly or trimonthly birth control shot. A third, and likely the major, advantage of the implant is its effectiveness. It is the most effective of all contraceptives, including male or female sterilization. According to both user and theoretical effectiveness data, the failure rate for the Norplant, Norplant-2, and IMPLANON implants (the only three implants for which effectiveness data are available) is a miniscule 0.05 percent (Table 4.4) (Ramchandran and Upadhyay, 2007).

All of the aforementioned family planning methods are reversible; that is, a woman and her partner may use any of them and then decide later to stop using them if a pregnancy is desired.

The next method we discuss, **surgical sterilization** performed for contraceptive purposes, is rarely reversible. Surgical sterilization may be

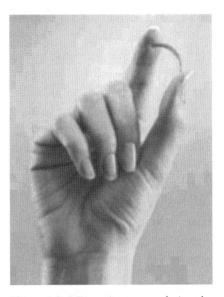

Figure 4.8. Micro insert used in the Essure® procedure of female sterilization. *Source:* Conceptus, Inc., 2008.

performed on both males and females. In the female, the sterilization is known as **tubal ligation** (tying of the tubes). It consists of cutting, tying, and removing a portion of the oviduct, that is, the Fallopian tubes. Female sterilization may be performed in one of several ways.

Laparoscopic sterilization is a sterilizing procedure using a laparoscope (from the Greek words *lapara*, meaning flank; and *skopein*, meaning to examine; the word thus means "look inside the abdomen"). It requires general anesthesia during which a small incision is introduced near the woman's belly button and a second incision may be made right above the pubic hairline. A laparoscope, a telescope-like device, is then inserted through the first incision so that the physician or operator can view the Fallopian tubes. Rings or clips are then inserted through the second incision (or if there is no second incision, through the first) and used to close the Fallopian tubes.

Minilaparotomy is a surgical sterilization procedure performed on a woman a few days after she delivers a baby. A general anesthesia is required. The operator makes a small incision in the woman's abdomen and then cuts and removes a piece of each of the Fallopian tubes.

Hysteroscopic sterilization, also known as the **Essure® procedure**, is performed using only a local anesthesia. A tiny coil insert (Figure 4.8) is introduced into each of the Fallopian tubes through the vagina and uterus. The introduction of the Essure mechanism in each tube causes the development of scar tissues over a three-month period, resulting in both tubes becoming sealed (Conceptus, Inc., 2008) (see the demonstration of this procedure online at http://www.essure.com/PopUps/FlashDemo.aspx?src=/Portals/0/essure_procedure.swf&height=400&width=428&title=The%20Essure%20Procedure).

Female sterilization is very effective (Table 4.4). It has a failure rate of only 0.5 percent based on both user and theoretical effectiveness data. It frees the woman and her partner from ever again having to worry about an accidental pregnancy. But since it is a permanent form of contraception, it is not an appropriate method for persons who wish to delay a pregnancy to a later time or who are not completely certain that they wish to have no more (or no) children. Almost 17 percent of all U.S. women have been sterilized (Table 4.3).

Quinacrine sterilization (QS) is an interesting method of nonsurgical female sterilization currently being researched and evaluated. The renowned family planning researcher and scholar, Malcolm Potts, former President of Family Health International and now Professor of Population and Family Planning at University of California, Berkeley, has noted that "QS is the most important new method of family planning since the Pill" (Donald A. Collins, personal communication with Leon F. Bouvier, May 26, 2008).

QS is a sterilization method that most women worldwide can afford because each application is manufactured for around $1.00 in U.S. dollars. The woman receives two treatments, one month apart, of seven tiny quinacrine pellets. They are placed into the uterus through the vagina using the kind of inserter employed with IUDs. The pellets dissolve and flow into the openings of the Fallopian tubes where they cause a minor swelling that results in scar tissue, which closes the tubes. It is similar in concept to the Essure procedure, except that it is easier to administer, far cheaper, and less taxing on the patient (Collins, 2008 personal communication). But the QS method is not without controversy. Its side effects are not fully known, and research continues regarding this method (Whitney, 2003).

Male sterilization is known as **vasectomy**. It consists of cutting, tying, and removing a portion of the spermatic duct, that is, the vas deferens. There are several ways the surgery may be performed, and we discuss two approaches. The traditional vasectomy is a minor procedure that occurs under local anesthetic. The surgeon makes one incision in the skin on each of the two sides of the scrotum to expose the tubes of the vas deferens from each testicle. The vas deferens tube is lifted from the scrotum, cut, and tied, or sometimes cauterized. The separated tubes are then returned to the scrotum and a few stitches are used to close the two incisions. After having a vasectomy, a man is still capable of ejaculating semen, but the semen no longer contains sperm.

A second approach to male sterilization is the **no-scalpel vasectomy** (also known as **keyhole vasectomy**) and was devised in 1974 by a surgeon in China, Li Shunqiang, and is now employed worldwide. It has been used in the United States since 1988. In this method, as its name indicates, no scalpel is employed, but there is still the need for a small opening to be made in the scrotum. The doctor applies a local anesthetic (which may be introduced without a needle) and then uses his/her hand to find the vas deferens under the scrotal skin. A very small set of pointed forceps then works to separate the scrotal tissue and to create a keyhole-type opening in the skin. Then, as with the traditional vasectomy procedure, the tubes of the vas deferens are lifted from the scrotal sac, cut, and tied, or sometimes cauterized, and then placed back into the scrotum. Because the scrotal skin opening is so small, it may not need to be closed with sutures.

Male sterilization is a very effective contraceptive method; its failure rates of 0.15 percent and 0.10 percent based, respectively, on user effectiveness data and theoretical effectiveness data (Table 4.4) are even lower than those for female sterilization. Moreover, compared to female sterilization, male sterilization is generally faster to perform, requires only a local anesthetic, is less expensive, and presents less risk of complications. Finally, although sterilization reversal is a difficult operation and does not have high rates of success, it is sometimes a little easier to reverse a male sterilization than a female sterilization.

Overall, the effectiveness of sterilization varies according to the techniques used by the physician and the gender of the patient. As noted from the failure rates reported in Table 4.4, there are very few failures. Most result from inadequate surgical procedures or because the tubes grow back together again. Some men who obtain vasectomies have unprotected intercourse too soon after the operation. If this occurs before all the sperm containing semen already stored in the reproductive tract has been expelled, then pregnancy may result. However, this is a short-term problem that is easily avoided.

Because a sterilization is only performed once, this family planning method does not require continuous motivation. It does not interfere with sexual enjoyment in any way. But it is very difficult to reverse sterilization and so is not suitable for persons who might change their mind about not wanting more children. Although the development and use of microsurgical techniques have greatly increased the chance of reversibility among vasectomy patients, most physicians still consider surgical sterilization a permanent form of contraception.

Surgical sterilization does not lower the sexual drive or capabilities of the male or female. Indeed, males with vasectomies often report increased enjoyment of sex, which is usually attributed to freedom from anxiety about their partners becoming pregnant. The male partners of almost 6 percent of U.S. women in the childbearing ages have been sterilized (see Table 4.3).

The *IUD*, a nonhormonal device placed in the uterus, is the most widely used reversible contraceptive method worldwide. The idea of placing devices in the uterus to prevent conception is fairly old. Giacomo Casanova, the eighteenth-century Italian adventurer and libertine, recommended the use of a gold ball for this purpose (Himes, [1936] 1970: 180). The antecedent of the modern intrauterine device was the **stem pessary**, developed in the late 1860s. This was a small button or cap that covered the opening of the cervix and was attached to stems extending into

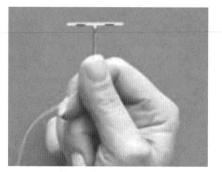

Figure 4.9. ParaGard® intrauterine device (IUD). *Source:* Planned Parenthood Federation of America, 2008, available online at: http://www.planned parenthood.org/health-topics/birth-control/iud-4245.htm#work (accessed November 10, 2008).

the cervical canal. In the 1920s, a German, Ernst Grafenberg, developed a silver ring that was placed in the uterus. In 1934, a Japanese scientist, Tenrei Ota, introduced a gold ring. Neither was accepted widely until the late 1950s (Peel and Potts 1969: 128–129; Tietze, 1965: 79). The Lippes Loop was a popular type of IUD in the 1960s, as were several other types of plastic IUDs.

Research on modern IUDs was initiated at about the time that oral-contraception research was in its final stages. But, as noted by Sheldon J. Segal, "despite intensive research, scientists (still) do not fully understand why the presence of a foreign body in the uterus prevents pregnancy. The evidence clearly indicates that the IUD is a pre-fertilization method: the presence of fertilized eggs in IUD users cannot be demonstrated" (2003: 173).

The main type of IUD available in the United States today, a flexible plastic device shaped like a "T" with copper wire twisted about it, is known as a Copper T; the brand marketed in the United States is the **ParaGard®** **IUD** (Figure 4.9). Adding copper wire to the device increases its contraceptive effectiveness significantly, "although it is not known why the release of copper in the uterus is so effective in preventing pregnancy" (Segal, 2003: 173). The IUD is placed in the uterus by a health-care provider. Small strings extend from its end (see Figure 4.9) into the vagina, where they may be checked periodically by the woman to make sure that the IUD has not been ejected. If the IUD is going to slip out of the uterus, this will most likely occur during the first several months of use and/or during the days of the menstrual period. The ParaGard IUD should be replaced after twelve years of use.

The ParaGard and most earlier types of IUDs are nonhormonal; that is, they do not contain the female hormones used to suppress ovulation. There is available today, however, a **hormonal IUD**, under the brand name of Mirena®. Like the ParaGard, the Mirena IUD is a flexible plastic device shaped like a "T" but, rather than containing copper, it contains progestin, which as we already know usually blocks ovulation and thickens the woman's cervical mucus. We referred earlier to the vaginal ring, for example, the NuvaRing, which is also a foreign body placed in the uterus that contains hormones to be released into the woman's system. The

NuvaRing contains both estrogen and progestin, unlike the Mirena IUD, which contains only progestin. Also, the NuvaRing needs to be replaced monthly, whereas the Mirena IUD remains effective for up to five years.

IUDs are very effective. The ParaGard has failure rates of 0.8 percent and 0.6 percent, based on use effectiveness data and theoretical effectiveness data, respectively (Table 4.4). The Mirena has even lower failure rates, 0.1 percent according to both user and theoretical effectiveness. The undetected expulsion of these devices is the most common cause of pregnancy, a major disadvantage. The major advantages of the IUD are that insertion is necessary only once every twelve years for the ParaGard and once every five years for the Mirena. Also, the IUD does not interfere with intercourse in any way.

IUDs that are expelled involuntarily may usually be reinserted successfully by medical-care professionals. Young women with no or few previous births may have higher rates of expulsion and pregnancy than older women with more previous births.

In addition to the risk of involuntary expulsion, IUDs sometimes need to be removed for medical reasons. Excessive menstrual bleeding and pain are the major medical reasons that IUDs are removed. Another disadvantage is that unlike the case with vaginal rings, trained medical personnel are necessary for the insertion of IUDs. Just over 1 percent of U.S. women now use the IUD (Table 4.3).

We discuss now a special type of contraception, the **emergency contraceptive pill (ECP)**, also known as the **morning-after pill**. ECPs are contraceptive medication taken after unprotected intercourse and are designed to prevent pregnancy by interfering with the implantation of the fertilized ovum in the uterine lining. This is a different strategy from that of oral contraceptives and the other kinds of hormonal contraceptives discussed earlier that prevent pregnancy primarily by preventing ovulation. The designation of "morning after" is actually a misnomer. ECPs are licensed for use for up to 72 hours after an unprotected intercourse.

There are several types of ECPs. One popular brand has the label of Plan B®. The various ECPs are mainly distinguished from combined oral contraceptives and mini-pills (as discussed) in that they contain much higher doses of the hormones. One form is a progestin-only medication taken as either two doses 12 hours apart or (in another brand) as a single dose. Another regimen contains high doses of both estrogen and progestin, typically ingested as two doses in 12-hour intervals. ECPs are not to be confused with abortifacients, that is, abortion pills (to be discussed). ECPs are meant to function after fertilization has occurred but before the fertilized egg has settled into the uterine environment. Because ECPs have their effect prior to implantation, the International Federation of Gynecology and Obstetrics considers them legally and medically to be contraceptives. However, not all researchers and medical practitioners agree with this categorization.

These postcoital methods of birth prevention are particularly convenient for women who have sexual intercourse infrequently, or who did not have an opportunity to use contraceptives before intercourse, or who used a contraceptive that failed in the process, for example, a condom that broke open during use.

ECPs are regarded as a very effective means of preventing an accidental pregnancy. Those pregnancies that do occur result from 1) failure of an already established implantation, 2) an excessive lapse of time between unprotected intercourse and taking the pill, 3) inadequate dosages, 4) regurgitation of the pill, or 5) failure of the drug itself. The major advantages of ECPs are effectiveness and suitability for use among women who had unexpected and unprotected sexual contact, particularly in situations of rape. The most common short-term side effects are nausea, headaches, menstrual irregularities, and breast tenderness (Stewart, Trussell, and Van Lok, 2007).

Finally, we consider **abortifacients**, which are pharmaceutical medications that cause the termination of an early pregnancy by interfering with the viability of an already implanted **zygote** (ferilized egg). A synthetic steroid compound with antiprogestational effects, known as RU-486, was discovered in 1982 by the French reproductive physiologist Etienne-Emile Baulieu and researchers at the Roussel Uclaf Company in France, the eventual designer of the drug (hence, the designation "RU"). Since it contains antiprogestational agents, the medication works in a way opposite to that of progesterone, which functions to prepare and maintain the uterine environment for the fertilized egg. The generic name of the drug is mifepristone and it is marketed in the United States by Danco Laboratories under the trade name Mifeprex®. It is produced in China and has been approved by the U.S. Federal Drug Administration as a drug to terminate an implanted zygote of up to forty-nine days' gestation. A 600 mg dose of mifepristone is administered by a physician, to be followed two days later by a large dose of a prostaglandin, misoprostol, to induce contractions (Spitz et al., 1998).

SUMMARY

A thorough understanding of a population's level of fertility requires knowledge of the extent to which people endeavor to limit family size. Whether or not a person uses a birth prevention method, and how effectively that method is used, depend on the person's motivation and the availability of the various methods. These, in turn, are influenced by social, economic, and religious factors.

The chief means by which people attempt to limit their family size are contraceptive techniques and devices, surgical sterilization, and induced abortion. Some methods are more effective than others. However, there is no perfect method of birth prevention. Each involves risks of failure or adverse effects.

Although the use of birth prevention methods is sometimes associated with medical risks (occasionally including mortality), these are usually much smaller than the mortality risks associated with pregnancy and giving birth. Generally, they are also smaller than the mortality risks associated with many widely accepted activities of daily life.

KEY TERMS

abortifacients	intrauterine device (IUD)
abortion	keyhole vasectomy
abortion rate	male sterilization
amplexus reservatus	mini-pill
basal body temperature (BBT)	minilaparotomy
basal body temperature method	monophasic
biphasic	morning-after pill
birth control	no-scalpel vasectomy
birth control pill	NuvaRing®
cervical cap	oral contraceptive (the pill)
coitus interruptus	ParaGard® IUD
coitus reservatus	quinacrine sterilization (QS)
conception	rhythm method
condom	single
contraception	Standard Days Method
contraception injection	stem pessary
contraceptive patch	sterilization
diaphragm	subdermal contraceptive implant
effectiveness (of family planning)	surgical sterilization
endometrium	theoretical effectiveness (of a
emergency contraceptive pill	contraceptive)
(ECP)	triphasic
Essure® procedure	tubal ligation
failure rate	typical use (of a contraceptive)
family planning	use effectiveness (of a contraceptive)
female condom	vaginal contraceptives
fertility awareness	vaginal ring
hormonal IUD	vasectomy
hysterectomy	withdrawal
hysteroscopic sterilization	zygote

5 Mortality

As population actors, our final behavior on this earth is our death. When this demographic event occurs, it will be at least the second time for most of us to have had our name mentioned in the daily newspaper. When we were born, our name was likely listed in the local paper along with the name of our mother and maybe that of our father. Not much else was reported about us when we were born. But when we die, not only will our name be listed (again) but also other information probably provided in a story, an **obituary**, about our life. Our obituary might include when and where we were born, our surviving family members, and perhaps something about our main occupation while we were alive, our education, and other items of interest.

The Oxford English Dictionary defines "obituary" as an "announcement of a death (in a newspaper) . . . usually comprising a brief biographical sketch of the deceased" (Simpson and Weiner, 2000: X: 640). What other time will a biographical sketch about you be written and published for everyone to read? Perhaps never. Our death is indeed one of the most important events in our life.

Everyone of us has been born and everyone of us will die. This is a certainty. No one escapes death. In fact, all species are born and all species die. But we humans are the only species to actually think about and contemplate the act of dying.

Death will not occur at the same time for everyone. Some of us will die sooner than others. On average, death will come earlier to males than to females, and earlier to members of racial and ethnic minority groups than to members of the majority. If we live in the United States and are white females, we will have the longest average **longevity** (length of life); we will have the shortest longevity if we are African American males. As of the beginning of this new century, white women in the United States could expect to live an average of 80.2 years, compared to 68.6 years for black males.

We ourselves play an important role in deciding when we will die. In a discussion in Chapter 1 of our role as population actors, we noted that our individual decision making is more obvious and apparent, say, with regard to fertility than to mortality. We had absolutely no control over when or where we were born; our birth was the decision or decisions of our parents. But we do have a lot of control and influence over whether, when, and where we ourselves produce children. Our dying is a similar kind of demographic act. We may or may not exercise many options that result in extending or shortening our lives. While death is a certainty, the length of time we will live depends on many factors; over some of them (e.g., our sex and race) we have no control, but over other factors we have a lot of control. Further, we ourselves have some influence not only on the timing and characteristics of our own death but also on the deaths of some others.

The impact of mortality varies significantly according to social and demographic characteristics. People in higher social classes live longer than those in the lower classes. Married people live longer than single, separated, or divorced people. We discuss some of these issues later.

Mortality and its effects are best discussed from the viewpoint of the society. Demographers often consider all individuals together as members of a single society (or state or country) and inquire about the factors that contribute to differences among them in their average length of life. For instance, in the year 2006, a baby born in Japan could expect to live, on average, for about 82 years and a baby born in Sweden about 81 years. A baby born in the United States in 2006 had a **life expectancy** of around 78 years. Compare these enviable life expectancies with those of babies born in 2006 in Botswana or Lesotho (both countries in southern Africa) who may expect to live on average only 34 and 36 years, respectively (Population Reference Bureau, 2006). Why do babies born in Botswana or in Lesotho have such a low average life expectancy compared to babies born in Japan or in Sweden? Levels of development, medical conditions, and a host of other factors are involved, and we discuss some of these later.

We do not wish to leave the impression that the sub-Saharan African countries are the only ones with low life expectancy. Afghanistan's life expectancy at birth of 43 years, and Haiti's and Iraq's of 58 years, are only slightly better than those just mentioned, and they are not sub-Saharan African countries.

There have been major changes over the historical record in the main causes of death. People used to die mainly of infectious and parasitic diseases, but the major causes of death today in developed countries like the

United States are heart disease, cancer, and stroke. These days, the major causes of death are also not the same in countries with high and low levels of life expectancy. This topic, too, will be covered in a later section.

This chapter has several sections. After addressing various issues of measurement, we look at mortality and longevity from an international point of view. Then we discuss the major causes of death in developed and developing countries and how these have changed over time. An important theory that demographers use to help them understand the changing structure of causes of death is **epidemiological transition theory**, which also is covered. Another section is concerned specifically with changes in mortality in the United States, followed by a discussion of a special kind of mortality, that which occurs in infancy. We also provide some speculation about the future course of mortality and improvements in life expectancy. Before addressing these substantive issues, we turn to a discussion of the measurement of mortality.

MEASUREMENT OF MORTALITY

The quantification of mortality is central to demography. The measurement of mortality dates back to John Graunt (1620–1674) and his analyses of the "Bills of Mortality" (see the discussion of Graunt in Chapter 2). Mortality refers to the relative frequency of death in a population.

Demographers use two different concepts when referring to mortality, namely, the **life span**, which is the numerical "age limit of human life" (Kintner, 2004: 307), and life expectancy or expectation, which is the average expected number of years of life to be lived by a particular population at a given time. An exact figure for the human life span or for the life span of any species is not known (Carey, 1997). However, demographers often use the "maximum recorded age at death" as an accepted operational definition of the human life span (Kintner, 2004: 307). As of the writing of this book, the longest known and verified life span was 122 years and 164 days, lived by the Frenchwoman Jeanne Louise Calment (see Box 5.1). The concept of life expectancy, which is used by demographers much more than the concept of the life span, is considered later.

Crude death rate

An easily understood and interpreted method for quantifying mortality, the **crude death rate (CDR)**, is the number of deaths in a population in a given year per one thousand members of the population. It is expressed as

$$\text{CDR} = \frac{\text{deaths in the year}}{\text{population at midyear}} * 1,000 \qquad (5.1)$$

BOX 5.1   THE LONGEST-KNOWN LIFE SPAN (122+ YEARS)

The longest-known and verified life span is 122 years and 164 days, lived by the Frenchwoman Jeanne Louise Calment, who was born in Arles (a city in southern France) on February 21, 1875. She died in a retirement home there on August 4, 1997. On her 120th birthday, Mme Calment reportedly made the following observations:

"I've been forgotten by (a good) God."

"I took pleasure when I could. I acted clearly and morally and without regret. I'm very lucky."

"I've only got one wrinkle, and I'm sitting on it."

"Wine, I'm in love with that."

Sources: Available online at http://images.google.com/images?q=Jeanne±Louise± Calment&hl=en&rls=com.microsoft:*:IE-SearchBox&rlz=1I7DMUS&um=1&sa= X&oi=images&ct=title and http://www.wowzone.com/calment.htm (both accessed July 8, 2007).

As an illustration, using data for the United States for 2004 (National Center for Health Statistics, 2007; U.S. Bureau of the Census, 2007b), equation (5.1) becomes

$$CDR = \frac{2,398,343}{293,028,000} * 1,000 = 8.2 \qquad (5.2)$$

This means that in the United States in 2004, there were just over 8 deaths for every 1,000 persons in the population. Estimates of the CDR for the countries of the world in 2006 ranged from lows of 1 in the United Arab Emirates (UAE) and 2 in Kuwait to highs of 23 in Sierra Leone, Zambia, and Zimbabwe and 22 in Angola and Afghanistan (Population Reference Bureau, 2006). The range of CDRs is narrower than that for CBRs (discussed in Chapter 3).

However, CDRs must be interpreted with caution. When CDR comparisons are made between countries, differences are sometimes due to differences in age composition. The fact that the UAE has a CDR of 1 and the United States has a CDR of 8 means that there are eight times as many deaths per one thousand population in the United States than in the UAE.

Why is the CDR of the United States eight times higher than that of the UAE? Why are there so many more deaths per 1,000 population in the United States than in the UAE? The main reason is that the UAE is much younger in average age than is the United States, and younger people have lower death rates than older people. In other words, countries with large proportions of young people and small proportions of old people will usually have lower CDRs than countries with small proportions of young people and large proportions of old people.

CDRs also should not be used to compare the death experiences of the same population at different points in time, particularly if the population's age structure has changed over time. Thus, it would not be correct to compare the CDR of the United States, say, in 1960, when it was 9.5/1,000, with the CDR of the United States, say, in 1990, when it was 8.5/1,000, and conclude that the mortality experience in the United States hardly changed at all in the thirty-year period. This would not be a correct statement because the United States became older in the thirty-year period; its **median age** (the age that divides a population into equally younger and older groups) increased from 29 to 33. At the same time, the mortality experience in the United States (as measured by the *standardized death rate* – see later discussion) dropped by more than 30 percent, but the CDR hardly changed at all. Much of the reduction in the mortality experience was offset by the fact that the population became older. The CDR is not capable of differentiating between these experiences.

The CDR is referred to as crude because its denominator is comprised of the entire population, the members of which are not all equally at the risk of experiencing death. This is because the risk of death varies by age, sex, race/ethnicity, socioeconomic status, and many other characteristics. Thus, although it is true that all persons in the denominator of the CDR will eventually experience death, they are not all equally exposed to the risk of death.

Death rates vary considerably by age. They are very high in the first year of life, but even then, the likelihood of death is not the same from month to month and day to day. Indeed, in the first year of life, deaths are much higher in the first month of life than in the remaining eleven months, much higher in the first day than in the remaining days of the month, much higher in the first hour than in the remaining twenty-three hours, and much higher in the first minute than in the remaining fifty-nine minutes. This is the main reason why demographers who study mortality give such special attention to the study of infant mortality (Frisbie, 2005), a topic we cover later.

Age-specific death rate

Because death varies so considerably with age, demographers prefer to use **age-specific death rates (ASDR)** as a more precise measurement of mortality. ASDRs are sometimes referred to as "M" rates. The ASDR (or $_nM_x$) is the number of deaths to persons in a specific age group per 1,000 persons in that age group. Its formula is

$$_nM_x = \left(\frac{\text{deaths to persons aged x to x} + \text{n}}{\text{midyear population aged x to x} + \text{n}} \right) * 1,000 \qquad (5.3)$$

where n is the width of the age group and x is the initial year of the age group. For instance, the ASDR for age group 15–19 is referred to as $_5M_{15}$. The ASDR is not crude because deaths to persons in the age group x to x + n are examined in relation to the number of persons in the age group x to x + n.

We have noted that death rates vary by age. They are high in the initial year of life, then drop precipitously, and begin increasing again at around age 40 or so (although in societies highly affected by HIV/AIDS, they tend to increase more so at the young adult ages). ASDRs are very low for young persons after the first year or so of life. When we plot a schedule of $_nM_x$ values, we produce what demographers refer to as the **age curve of mortality**.

In Figure 5.1, we show age curves of mortality for four countries: Afghanistan, China, Japan, and the United States. Japan has one of the lowest levels of mortality in the world. Figure 5.1 displays its ASDRs, that is, its $_nM_x$ values, and you can observe that Japan's rates are very low at all ages. Still, even in Japan with its very low mortality, death during the first year of life is still high. Indeed, the $_nM_x$ value for the first year of life in Japan ($_1M_0$) is not reached again until the Japanese population is in

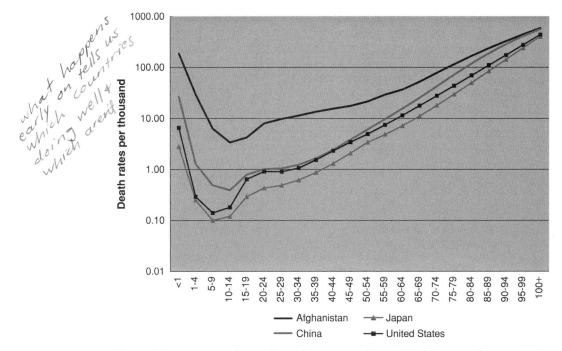

what happens early on tells us which countries which are doing well & which aren't

Figure 5.1. Age curves of mortality: Afghanistan, China, United States, and Japan, 2005.

their late 40s. Afghanistan has one of the highest levels of mortality in the world, yet its display of $_nM_x$ values in Figure 5.1 also shows an age curve of mortality, only at higher age-specific levels than in Japan. In Afghanistan, its $_1M_0$ value is so high that it is not reached again until about age 75. The age curve of mortality characterizes every population whether or not its level of mortality is high as in Afghanistan or low as in Japan.

Standardization

ASDRs and not CDRs should be used to compare the mortality experiences of countries with known differences in age composition. Let us elaborate this point with an example. The United States in 2006 had a CDR of 8, while Venezuela had a CDR of 4. This means that there were twice as many deaths per 1,000 population in the United States in 2006 than there were in Venezuela. But does this necessarily mean that young people and middle-age people and old people in the United States all die at higher rates than they do in Venezuela? To answer this question, we need to look at ASDR data and not CDR data.

In Table 5.1, we present ASDRs for the United States and Venezuela for 2006. Observe the data in columns 1 and 3 of the table. At every age,

Table 5.1. Age-specific death rates (ASDR) and age-specific proportions of the population: United States and Venezuela, 2005

Age group	United States ASDR	United States Proportion of population	Venezuela ASDR	Venezuela Proportion of population
<1	0.00654	0.0139	0.01623	0.0219
1–4	0.00029	0.0548	0.00064	0.0800
5–9	0.00014	0.0675	0.00032	0.1038
10–14	0.00018	0.0719	0.00041	0.1023
15–19	0.00064	0.0724	0.00146	0.1012
20–24	0.00091	0.0702	0.00238	0.0925
25–29	0.00090	0.0671	0.00221	0.0842
30–34	0.00106	0.0679	0.00203	0.0726
35–39	0.00153	0.0706	0.00215	0.0688
40–44	0.00231	0.0766	0.00289	0.0630
45–49	0.00341	0.0757	0.00411	0.0515
50–54	0.00493	0.0675	0.00568	0.0437
55–59	0.00742	0.0575	0.00775	0.0346
60–64	0.01150	0.0437	0.01173	0.0251
65–69	0.01780	0.0339	0.01877	0.0180
70–74	0.02771	0.0284	0.02838	0.0136
75–79	0.04350	0.0248	0.04270	0.0097
80–84	0.06958	0.0187	0.07531	0.0053
85–89	0.11056	0.0107	0.12769	0.0024
90–94	0.17477	0.0045	0.20820	0.0007
95–99	0.27656	0.0013	0.32576	0.0001
100+	0.43892	0.0003	0.48975	0.0001

except one, the United States has lower ASDRs than Venezuela. But we know that the United States has a CDR twice as high as Venezuela's. How can this be? Why is Venezuela's CDR half that of the United States, while all but one of its ASDRs are higher than those of the United States?

The answer is shown in columns 2 and 4 of Table 5.1, namely, the proportions of people by age in the two countries. Venezuela has proportionately many more people in the younger age groups than does the United States. To illustrate, the population of age 10–14 comprises 10.23 percent of Venezuela's total population, versus 7.19 percent of the U.S. population. The opposite holds true with regard to people in the middle and older ages, with higher proportions in the United States than in Venezuela. Starting at age 35–39, the age-specific proportions become larger in the United States than in Venezuela. The population 65–69 is 3.39 percent of the United States versus 1.80 percent of Venezuela. The population in the age group 85–89 comprises 1.07 percent of the United States, compared to 0.24 percent of Venezuela. The United States is an "older" country than Venezuela, that is, it has more older people proportionately than does Venezuela. In contrast, Venezuela is a much "younger" country than the United States. Because younger people die at lower rates than older people, many (but not all) "young" countries have lower CDRs than "old" countries.

Demographers have a method for taking into account such a factor as age composition in their comparisons of the death rates among different countries. It is known as **standardization**. We focus here on age standardization, the most popular form. Young populations tend to have low CDRs, and old populations have high CDRs. One way to consider this issue is to observe that the CDR can be viewed as the sum of the ASDRs weighted by the size of the population in each age group. In other words, the CDR may be viewed as the "weighted mean of the death rates at each age, the weights used being the numbers at each age in the population being studied" (Pollard, Yusuf, and Pollard, 1981: 71–72).

We presented in (5.1) the formula for the CDR. The numerator of formula (5.1), deaths in the year, or D, is nothing more than the sum of each of the ASDRs multiplied by the size of the population in the age group. Consider, therefore, the following formula for the CDR as an alternative to that shown in formula (5.1):

$$\text{CDR} = \sum {}_nM_x \left(\frac{{}_nP_x}{P} \right) * 1{,}000 \tag{5.4}$$

where:

P = total population,

${}_nP_x$ = population in age group x, and

${}_nM_x$ = ASDR for age group x (Palmore and Gardner, 1994: 15)

Here is a very simple way to better understand formula (5.4). Let us imagine a hypothetical population with a CDR of 40. This population may be divided into two broad age groups, 0–34 and 35+. Table 5.2 contains age data for this hypothetical population.

The data in Table 5.2 may be arranged using formula (5.4) as follows:

$$\text{CDR} = \frac{D}{P} * 1{,}000 = \frac{120}{3{,}000} * 1{,}000 = 0.04 * 1{,}000 = 40 \tag{5.5}$$

Age	Midyear population	Deaths	ASDR
Table 5.2. Age data for a hypothetical population			
0–34	2,000	40	20/1,000
35+	1,000	80	80/1,000
Total	3,000	120	40/1,000

Source: Palmore and Gardner, 1994: 15–16.

Next, consider the CDR as a weighted sum of the ASDRs, and arrange the data in Table 5.2 using formula (5.4) as follows:

$$CDR = \left[\frac{2,000}{3,000} * 20 \right] + \left[\frac{1,000}{3,000} * 80 \right] = \left[\frac{2}{3} * 20 \right] + \left[\frac{1}{3} * 80 \right] \quad (5.6)$$

$$CDR = \frac{40}{3} + \frac{80}{3} = \frac{120}{3} = 40 \quad (5.7)$$

This example shows nicely and exactly how the CDR is a sum of the weighted (by population) ASDRs.

Now we may consider comparing the mortality experiences of two or more populations. If a population such as the United States has more persons in the older age groups than in the younger age groups, then the death rates of the older groups (where there is usually more mortality) will be more heavily weighted than the death rates of the younger groups (where there is usually less mortality), and vice versa for a country such as Venezuela that has more persons in the younger age groups than in the older groups. This is seen clearly in the ASDRs in Table 5.1 for the United States and Venezuela. In other words, "if two populations of quite different age distributions are being compared, the weights used are quite different, and this method (i.e., the CDR) could give very misleading results" (Pollard, Yusuf, and Pollard 1981: 72). Hence, demographers need to control for age composition.

Actually, there are other features of population composition, namely, sex, that also need to be considered, that is, controlled, when comparing the death experiences of two populations. If one population has an excess of females and another an excess of males, and if the age compositions of the two are similar, the latter will have a higher CDR than the former because of the heavier representation of males. A similar statement may be made with regard to race and ethnic composition, where the majority race usually has lower mortality rates than the minority group. Also, as noted, it is not correct to compare the CDRs of the same population for different points in time, particularly if the age structure of the population has changed over the time periods under consideration.

Although our discussion here is restricted to standardization for age composition, the basic techniques of standardization are easily extended to sex composition, as well as to any other aspects of composition that the demographer believes could be influencing the death rates.

There are many statistical software programs available that demographers use to execute the statistical calculations for standardizing mortality rates for age composition. We are most familiar with the Stata Statistical Software Program (StataCorp, 2009), although many other statistical software packages have standardization programs based on formula (5.4). We have used Stata's direct standardization program to standardize Venezuela's death rate by assigning to Venezuela the age composition of the United States. Recall that Venezuela has a CDR of 4 and the United States has a CDR of 8. The result of the standardization exercise is that Venezuela has a directly standardized death rate (SDR) of 11.1. This means that if Venezuela had the age composition of the United States, while retaining its own ASDRs, it would have a CDR of 11.1 and not its actual CDR of 4. The fact that Venezuela has such a low CDR of 4 compared to the U.S. CDR of 8 is due to its much younger age composition. Thus, if we assign to Venezuela the same age composition of the United States, Venezuela ends up having a directly SDR of 11.1, which is higher than that of 8 for the United States.

The life table

One of the most important and elegant measures of the mortality experiences of a population is the **life table**. It dates back to John Graunt (1620–1674) and his analyses of the "Bills of Mortality" (see Chapter 2). The life table starts with a population (a radix) of 100,000 at age 0. Setting the radix at 100,000 is arbitrary but conventional. From each age to the next, the population is decremented according to age-specific mortality probabilities until all members have died. The mortality schedule is fixed and does not change over the life of the population. The basic life table consists of eight columns, including the probability of dying between age x and age x + n $(_nq_x)$, the number of survivors at each age x (l_x), the number of deaths in each age interval $(_nd_x)$, the number of years lived in each age interval $(_nL_x)$, and life expectancy at each age (e_x). In Box 5.2, we discuss and develop in more detail a life table for U.S. females for the year 2005.

Life expectancy, a statistic gleaned directly from the last column of the life table in Box 5.2, is a primary indicator of quality of life. In 2006, life

BOX 5.1   THE LIFE TABLE

Demographers use the life table to determine life expectancy, not only at birth but at any age. Like the total fertility rate (see Chapter 3), the life table is a synthetic or hypothetical measure. It tells us many things about a population. One of the most important questions it answers is the following: How many years of life, on average, may a person expect to live if the person during his or her lifetime is subjected to the age-specific probabilities of dying of a particular country or population at a given time? Thus, when we say that females in the United States in 2005 have a life expectancy at birth of 80.1 years, we mean that if a cohort of females throughout their life were subjected to the ASDRs, that is, the $_nM_x$ rates, of females in the United States in 2005, they would live, on average, 80.1 years.

In Table 1, we show an abridged life table for U.S. females for the year 2005. It is referred to as an abridged life table because it is calculated, for the most part, for 5-year age groups, rather than for single-year age groups.

A life table starts with a population of 100,000 persons born alive at age 0 (see the figure of 100,000 at l_0 in column 4). This initial group of 100,000 persons is then subjected to the probabilities of dying at each age, until all 100,000 are dead. We now examine each of the eight columns of the life table for U.S. females in the year 2005.

Column 1 refers to the age intervals of each group. The age groups shown here refer to the range of years between two birthdays. To illustrate, the age group 5–9 refers to the 5-year interval between the fifth and the tenth birthdays.

Column 2 reports the ASDRs (i.e., the $_nM_x$ rates) for each age group. These are the only empirical data that are needed to build a life table. As discussed in the next paragraph, the $_nM_x$ rates are used to generate the age-specific probabilities of dying (the $_nq_x$ rates), and these probabilities are then used to start the mathematical calculations to produce the life table. Since the only purpose of the $_nM_x$ data in column 2 is to develop the $_nq_x$ rates, some life tables do not include the $_nM_x$ rates, and thus only have seven and not eight columns.

Column 3 reports for each age group the probabilities of dying; these probabilities are designated as $_nq_x$. This is the most basic column of the life table. The $_nq_x$ values represent the probabilities that persons who are alive at the beginning of an age interval will die during that age interval, before they reach the start of the next age interval. While it is true that the $_nq_x$ rates resemble the $_nM_x$ rates, there is an important difference between them. The difference has to do with their denominators; the

Table 1. Abridged life table for females, United States, 2005							
(1)	(2)	(3)	(4)	(5)	(6)	(7)	(8)
Age range	nMx	nqx	lx	Ndx	nLx	Tx	Ex
<1	0.00591	0.00588	100000	588	99471	8006245	80.1
1–4	0.00025	0.00100	99412	100	397410	7906774	79.5
5–9	0.00013	0.00064	99313	64	496404	7509363	75.6
10–14	0.00015	0.00076	99249	75	496057	7012960	70.7
15–19	0.00038	0.00192	99174	191	495392	6516903	65.7
20–24	0.00045	0.00227	98983	225	494354	6021511	60.8
25–29	0.00052	0.00258	98758	254	493156	5527157	56.0
30–34	0.00071	0.00353	98504	347	491652	5034001	51.1
35–39	0.00112	0.00560	98157	550	489409	4542349	46.3
40–44	0.00175	0.00870	97607	849	485911	4052940	41.5
45–49	0.00256	0.01273	96758	1231	480710	3567029	36.9
50–54	0.00370	0.01834	95526	1752	473252	3086318	32.3
55–59	0.00578	0.02849	93774	2672	462193	2613066	27.9
60–64	0.00909	0.04446	91103	4050	445387	2150874	23.6
65–69	0.01432	0.06911	87052	6016	420222	1705487	19.6
70–74	0.02252	0.10658	81036	8637	383590	1285265	15.9
75–79	0.03614	0.16574	72400	11999	331999	901675	12.5
80–84	0.06037	0.26226	60400	15840	262400	569676	9.4
85–89	0.10002	0.40008	44560	17827	178231	307276	6.9
90–94	0.16442	0.55054	26732	14717	89510	129045	4.8
95–99	0.26812	0.69160	12015	8310	30992	39535	3.3
100+	0.43376	1.00000	3706	3706	8543	8543	2.3

Source: World Health Organization, 2006a.

denominator of the $_nM_x$ rates is the midyear population (see formula [5.3] earlier in this chapter), whereas the denominator of the $_nq_x$ rates is the population alive at the beginning of the age interval. In most cases, the $_nq_x$ rates may be estimated from the $_nM_x$ rates with this transforming equation:

$$_nq_x = \frac{2(n) * (nMx)}{2 + (n) * (nMx)}$$

where: $_nM_x$ is the ASDR (per person, not per 1,000), and n is the width in years of the age interval. At the oldest age category (100+ in the life table we show here), the value of $_nq_x$ must equal 1.0 because all people alive at the start of that age interval must die. For some of the values in the table, because of rounding error, the transforming equation will produce $_nq_x$ rates with slightly different values at the fifth decimal place. For a few age groups, namely, those less than 1, 1–4, and 100+, different formulas are used (see Kintner, 2004: 312).

Column 4 shows values for the number of people alive at the beginning of the age interval; this column is designated as the l_x column of data and is sometimes known as "the little l column." It may be calculated by subtracting the $_nd_x$ value (column 5) from the l_x value in the age interval immediately preceding the one being calculated. For example, of the 99,249 people alive at the beginning of the age interval 10–14 (i.e., l_{10}), 75 of them die during the age interval between their 10th and 15th birthdays (i.e., $_5d_{10}$). Thus, for the next age group, those ages 15–19, there are 75 fewer people; therefore, the value of l_{15} is 99,174 (i.e., 99,249 minus 75).

Column 5 shows the number of people who die during a particular age interval and is designated as $_nd_x$. It is arrived at by multiplying l_x by $_nq_x$. Thus, for the number of people who die during the age interval of 40–44, the $_5d_{40}$ value is 849; this equals the $_5q_{40}$ value of 0.0087 times the l_{40} value of 97,607.

Column 6 reports for each age interval the total number of years lived by all persons who enter that age interval while in the age interval. It is designated as $_nL_x$ and is often referred to as "the big L column" of data. For instance, the life table shows that 98,504 females are alive at the beginning of age interval 30–34 (i.e., the l_{30} value). If none of those persons died during that age interval, those women would have lived 492,520 years during the period of time between their 30th and 35th birthdays, or 98,504 times 5. But we know that some of them died during the age interval of 30–34, namely, 347 died (see the $_5d_{30}$ value of 347). Demographers assume that these 347 deaths are evenly distributed during the 5-year period. Therefore, the $_nL_x$ values may be roughly given by the following formula:

$$_nL_x = \left(l_x - 1/2 _nd_x\right)(n)$$

With regard to the age interval 30–34, this formula would result in the following: $491,652 = (98,504 - \frac{1}{2} 347) * (5)$.

This equation applies to age intervals after the first few age intervals. With regard to the first year of life, we noted earlier in this chapter that during the first year of life, it is erroneous to assume that deaths are evenly distributed throughout the year. There are several formulas that may be used to produce the $_nL_x$ value for the first few age groups (see Kintner, 2004: 313–315). At the other age extreme, 100+ in the life table, another formula is used (see Kintner, 2004: 314).

Column 7 reports the total number of years lived by the population in that age interval and in all subsequent age intervals; this column of data is designated as T_x. To determine the values of T_x for each age interval, one sums the $_nL_x$ from the oldest age backwards, using this formula:

$$T_x = \sum_{i=x}^{\omega} L_i$$

where: L_i = entry i in the $_nL_x$ column, and $\sum_{i=x}^{\omega} L_i$ = the sum of the $_nL_x$ column starting at entry x through the last $_nL_x$ entry, namely, w.

Let us calculate T_{90} from the life table for U.S. females in 2005, as follows:

$$T_{90} = \sum_{i=90}^{100} L_i$$

$$T_{90} = {}_5L_{90} + {}_5L_{95} + {}_\infty L_{100}$$

$$T_{90} = 89,510 + 30,992 + 8,543 = 129,045$$

Column 8 presents the average number of years of life remaining at the beginning of the age interval. This column of data, known as e_x, provides life expectancy at any age; it is calculated by dividing column 7 by column 4. We noted earlier that females in the United States in 2005 have an average life expectancy at birth of 80.1 years. This is the e_0 value of 80.1 in the life table and is calculated as T_0 (8,006,245) divided by l_0 (100,000) = 80.06. If we wanted to know the average number of years of life remaining for U.S. women in 2005 who had reached their twentififth birthday, we would consult the e_{25} value of 56 in the life table; it is calculated as T_{25} (5,527,157) divided by l_{25} (98,758) = 55.96. This means that women ages 25–29 can expect to live an additional 56 years if they are subjected to the age-specific probabilities of dying of U.S. women in 2005.

Life tables are used for many purposes other than studying human mortality. Examples include estimating the failure rates of contraceptives, tracing the progress of a population of freshmen through college, and measuring marital formation and dissolution. With respect to the second example, one would take the number of freshmen entering college as the radix of the life table and then subject them to age-specific probabilities of dying, of dropping out of college, and of graduating from college. One could then determine, for example, the average number of years of college life for, say, male freshmen who entered four-year public colleges in the state of Texas in the fall semester of 2000, and compare this value of e_x with that for male freshmen who entered four-year private colleges. Is the average number of years of college life larger or smaller for male freshmen in public versus private colleges? An educational life table would provide the answer.

expectancy at birth in the world was 65 for males and 69 for females. In more developed countries, it was 73 and 80, and in less developed countries (excluding China), 62 and 65. The highest life expectancy at birth was in Japan (79 for males, 86 for females), while the lowest were in Botswana (35 for males, 33 for females), Lesotho (35 for males, 36 for females), and Swaziland (33 for males, 35 for females) (Population Reference Bureau, 2006).

We should be aware of the fact, however, that when considering life expectation at birth, e_0, we need to be cognizant of the importance of infant mortality. When e_0 is low, as in Lesotho or Botswana, for example, a major reason is the very high value for infant mortality. When comparing values of life expectation at birth across countries, especially developing countries, we should not think of e_0 as, strictly speaking, a modal age at death.

Whereas John Graunt is referred to by most demographers as the founder of demography, many refer to Alfred Lotka (1880–1949) as the person most responsible for the development of modern demography. Lotka used life tables in the development of his **stable population theory**. The concept of a stable population was actually first set forth by Leonhard Euler ([1760] 1970), but its current development stems from the work of Lotka, who first introduced the concept in a brief note in 1907. Later, F. R. Sharpe and Lotka (1911) proved mathematically that if a population that is closed to migration experiences constant schedules of age-specific fertility and mortality rates, it will develop a constant age distribution and will grow at a constant rate, irrespective of its initial age distribution. We discuss this important demographic concept in more detail in Chapter 8.

Having covered some of the methodological issues involved in the study of mortality, we turn next to substantive issues. In the next section, we discuss the major causes of death in developed and developing countries and how they have changed over time.

MORTALITY IN THE WORLD, CAUSES OF DEATH, AND THE EPIDEMIOLOGICAL TRANSITION

Our knowledge of mortality levels and conditions prior to the Industrial Revolution is very incomplete. We know that mortality then was high, but the availability and completeness of the death data leave many questions unanswered. A life table for ancient Greece prepared from burial records shows a life expectancy at birth of about 30 years (Dublin, Lotka, and Spiegelman, 1949). Age data from census records of Roman Egypt indicate an average life expectancy at birth in the first to third centuries AD of between 22 and 25 years, a finding that has been corroborated by data on tombstones in Roman North Africa (Scheidel, 2003: 45). A life table developed by John Graunt (see Chapter 2) reported that more than 35 percent of babies born in seventeenth-century London were dead by age 6. According to a U.S. life table for 2005, less than 1 percent of U.S. females born are dead at age 6 (see Box 5.2). Graunt's life table showed that by age 56, 94 percent of those born were dead, while the respective figure for U.S. females in 2005 was less than 10 percent.

As late as the eighteenth century, life expectancy ranged from only 30 to 40 years in much of Europe and the United States (Dublin, Lotka, and Spiegelman, 1949). As recently as 1901, U.S. males had a life expectancy at birth of 47.9 years and females of 50.7 years (U.S. Department of Commerce, 1921). Also, mortality levels at this time were not constant from year to year. There were short-term fluctuations caused principally by changes in the major causes of high mortality, namely, famines, epidemics, and wars. These are the "positive checks" noted by Malthus that kept the death rate high (Malthus, [1803] 1989) (see the discussion of Malthus in Chapter 9). Poor living conditions in urban areas also contributed to high levels of mortality (S. Johnson, 2006).

Famines

We first consider famines as a cause of death. Populations in preindustrial times had much less control over their food supply than we do today. Agricultural output was severely limited by the inefficiency of manual labor, by plagues of rodents and insects, and by plant diseases. Abundant harvests usually could not be exploited owing to inadequate food-storage facilities. Transportation technology and roadways were underdeveloped, and so isolated areas with food shortages were unable to import surplus food from other areas. Thus, famine was a major problem.

The demographic consequences of famines were often disastrous. Because famines have almost always taken place in rural and poor populations, the precise nature of their toll is not easy to measure (O'Grada, 1999, 2001, 2003a). There were serious declines in population in much of Europe during the famine years of 1315–1317. In the 1690s, one-sixth of the population in some Swedish provinces died after severe crop failures.

The Irish potato famine of 1846–1851, known in Ireland as the Great Famine, killed around a million people, although some estimates place the number as high as 1.5 million (Foster, 1988: 324; K. Miller, 1985: 284). This is a very large number of deaths when one recalls that the population of Ireland in the early 1840s was but 8.2 million. As an Irish priest at the time observed, "Truly, the Angel of death and desolation reigns triumphant in Ireland" (Miller, 1985: 285). We must also not forget that these deaths do not include "averted births or allow for famine-related deaths in Britain and farther afield" (O'Grada, 2003b: 391; see also 1999).

The last major famine in Europe was the Finnish famine of 1868 (O'Grada, 2001). Also, as many as 19 million persons likely perished in India between 1891 and 1910 as a result of famines (K. Davis, 1951; Wrigley, 1969).

One of the most destructive famines in the demographic record occurred in China between 1958 and 1961. As industrial and grain production dropped to low levels, the standard of living declined, and the birth rate declined to near replacement levels (Peng, 1987). First there were food shortages, followed by famine, and, to make matters worse, food was exported, often from areas in China with food shortages. It is estimated that around 30 million Chinese died as a direct result of the famine, with 12 million of the deaths under the age of ten (Ashton et al., 1984; MacDonald, 2003). The main cause of the famine stemmed from the ill-conceived and overly ambitious Great Leap Forward program, initiated in 1958 by Mao Zedong and designed to "involve a revolutionary struggle against nature to realize the great potential of agriculture by maximizing the advantages of the collective economy" (Aird, 1972: 278). The economic crisis and famine that followed were due to natural disasters, such as floods, plant diseases, and drought, as well as to bureaucratic inefficiency and improper management (Ashton et al., 1984; MacDonald, 2003).

Throughout human history, unless famines occur in very small populations, they seldom result in the deaths of more than a few percent of the people. As disastrous as was China's famine, it killed "at most 2 to 3 percent of the total population" of the country (O'Grada, 2003a: 383). An exception was Ireland's Great Famine, which killed between 12 and 18 percent of the population. We turn next to a consideration of epidemic diseases.

Epidemic diseases

Diseases may be classified as endemic or epidemic. An **epidemic** is a major increase or upswing of an infectious disease in an area that results in a large number of deaths, followed then by a decline. Many infections and contagious diseases have become epidemic, including scarlet fever, chicken pox, measles, influenza, and cholera, among others. If a disease is maintained at a fairly constant level, it is called an *endemic* (Caldwell, 2006). Epidemic diseases "break out, reach a peak, and subside; endemic diseases cause a relatively constant amount of illness and death over time" (Johansson, 2003: 303). Epidemics typically start out on a local level and are then diffused to nearby areas. If an epidemic strikes several countries or continents, it is known as a **pandemic**. Pandemics are much more disruptive demographically, economically, and socially than epidemics.

John Caldwell (2006) has written that epidemics were important to the development of modern demography because it became obvious that the tracking of deaths was necessary and important. For instance, the Spanish flu epidemic (see the following) resulted in the establishment of the Growth Surveillance System by the League of Nations.

One of Europe's worst epidemics, the Black Death, was a virulent outbreak of a disease that probably originated in Central Asia, moved to the Mediterranean via the Silk Road, and then entered Europe from 1347 to 1352, mainly via rats on inbound ships, ultimately spreading into northern Europe. It resulted in the death of around one-third of the continent's population (Caldwell, 2006; Herlihy, 1997; Sean Martin, 2007). Subsequent epidemics were so frequent and intense throughout Europe that the population was reduced by nearly 50 percent, and demographic recovery took more than two centuries (Johansson, 2003).

The Great Plague that hit London in the 1660s had continuing outbreaks for several decades thereafter, but its toll was lower than that of the Black Death. It was once believed to have been a bubonic plague, but many now hold that it was a disease similar to a viral fever (Caldwell, 2006). The "Bills of Mortality" analyzed by John Graunt (see Chapter 2) were produced during this time.

In the nineteenth century, Britain was subjected to four cholera epidemics. It was during this time that the mystery of the transmission of cholera was solved by "an ingenious physician named John Snow [whose discovery also] helped eliminate cholera from Britain and eventually from the Western world" (Epstein, 2007a: 41). Snow showed that certain wells were yielding contaminated water, and that persons drinking water from these sources were mainly the ones who were dying. He mapped the wells and the incidence of cholera for various areas of London, a map that some refer to today as "one of the most famous documents in the history of science" (Epstein, 2007a: 42). This was one of the first times that **geographic information systems (GIS)** were ever used to shape a policy that led to the closing of certain wells (Swanson and Stephan, 2004). Steven Johnson's book *The Ghost Map* (2006) is a delightful, fascinating, and riveting account of Snow's pioneering work.

A more recent epidemic was the Spanish flu epidemic, so named because Spain was the first European country infected. It spread throughout Europe in 1918 and then to the rest of the world. Epidemiologists Niall Johnson and Juergen Mueller (2002) have estimated that the epidemic resulted in the deaths of around 50 million people; others place the toll even higher (Barry, 2004). The Spanish flu may well have infected almost 1 billion people, or nearly half of the population of the world at that time. Some believe that large numbers of influenza deaths went unreported in less developed countries. By the time the epidemic had run its course in North America, nearly 700,000 had died in the United States and around 50,000 in Canada. Some small villages in Quebec and Labrador were almost wiped out entirely. The most common victims of this epidemic were young adults, 20 to 40 years of age (Barry, 2004; Caldwell, 2006; Crosby, 2003; Kolata, 1999). If one examines month-specific death rates in the United States for the years 1911–1917 and for 1918, the impact of the Spanish flu is particularly apparent in the last quarter of 1918, and especially in the month of October.

In 1918 in San Francisco, a law was passed requiring residents to wear masks when venturing outside the home to visit public places, and the following slogan was promulgated by the city's Health Department: "Wear a Mask and Save Your Life! A Mask is 99% Proof Against Influenza" (available online at http://www.pbs.org/wgbh/amex/influenza/sfeature/sanfran.html). Still, more than 3,500 residents of San Francisco and nearby places were victims, including an aunt and three grandparents of Dudley Poston, an author of this book.

A copy of the actual death certificate of Poston's maternal grandmother, Annie Kara, is shown in Figure 5.2. She died on December 20, 1918, at age 42, of "influenza" and was buried the next day in Holy Cross Cemetery in Colma, a small town south of San Francisco. Poston's mother, Kathryn Kara, also contracted the Spanish flu in San Francisco in the fall of 1918, but, thankfully, she survived, married Dudley Poston in 1936, and gave birth to her son Dudley, Jr., in 1940 and her daughter Kathleen in 1943. Kathryn Kara Poston, who died in San Francisco at age 69 in 1979, had a tremendous influence on the lives of her children and grandchildren during her lifetime. So powerful and long-lasting was her influence on Dudley Poston's daughter Nancy that she named her first daughter Kara after her great-grandmother. Had the vagaries of mortality and the 1918 flu epidemic operated in another way, and had Kathryn Kara died in 1918 along with her parents and sister and 3,500 other residents of the San Francisco area in what Barry (2004) has referred to as the deadliest plague in human history, many persons named in this paragraph would not have been born, this demography text would not have been written, and the lives of countless others would be very different today.

Today, a disease of epidemic proportions is ravaging the world. As of the writing of this book, the world is more than twenty-five years into the HIV/AIDS epidemic. **Acquired immune deficiency syndrome (AIDS)** was first noticed in the United States in 1981, initially among gay men

Figure 5.2. Death certificate of Annie Kara, victim of the flu epidemic, San Francisco, 1918.

(Shilts, 1987). Hemophiliac cases of AIDS were first reported in 1982. The human immunodeficiency virus (HIV) causing AIDS was isolated in 1983 at the Pasteur Institute in Paris, and by the late 1980s and into the 1990s, HIV/AIDS had been identified in every region of the world. HIV is spread person to person via contact with body fluids. As Basia Zaba (2003: 37) writes: "This may occur during sexual intercourse, or as a result of mother-to-child transmission during pregnancy, delivery, or breastfeeding. The virus may also be transferred in blood used for transfusions.... [Also] it can be spread by unsterilized hypodermic needles and surgical instruments."

As of 2006, UNAIDS, the United Nations (UN) Joint Program on HIV/AIDS, estimated that 65 million people worldwide have been infected since the virus was first recognized in 1981, and more than 25 million have died. Two-thirds of all people living with HIV in 2006 were in sub-Saharan Africa, where HIV is mainly transmitted via heterosexual sex. One reason for the very high levels of HIV infection in sub-Saharan Africa is partner concurrency, the practice of men and women having more than one partner concurrently, that is, simultaneously. A man might have a wife and one or two steady girlfriends, all at the same time. This pattern adds significantly to the risk of contracting the virus (Epstein, 2007b).

Although sub-Saharan Africa is by far the most affected region in the world, epidemics are also underway in Central Asia and in Eastern Europe where in 2005, an estimated 220,000 people were newly infected (UNAIDS, 2006). There is an enormous potential for a massive HIV/AIDS epidemic in China owing to the more than 30 million excess boys already born in China who will not be able to find Chinese brides (Poston and Zhang, 2009; Tucker et al., 2005).

It is clear that the HIV/AIDS epidemic has had, and continues to have, an impact on the populations of many countries of the world. As noted, an estimated 25 million people have already died of AIDS, and another 40 million persons or so are living with HIV (Lamptey, Johnson, and Khan, 2006). In its 2006 revision of the *World Population Prospects*, the UN (2007) reported that HIV prevalence is estimated to be at least 1 percent among the population of age 15–49 in the fifty-eight most highly affected countries of the world. Four very large countries with HIV prevalence rates below 1 percent, namely, Brazil, China, India, and the United States, should also be considered in this discussion because of their large absolute number of persons currently living with HIV, making a total of sixty-two countries. Of these countries, forty are located in sub-Saharan Africa, eleven are in Latin America, and five are in Asia. As a combined group, they include more than 35 million of the approximately 40 million adults and children in the world who are infected with HIV, or 90 percent of the total. Figure 5.3 charts the annual growth between 1986 and 2004 of the numbers of people in the world living with HIV, by region. The sub-Saharan African region of the world is the area with the largest number of HIV cases by far.

Eight countries, all in Africa, have astoundingly high HIV prevalence rates. In Swaziland, 33.8 percent of its population ages 15–49 is infected with HIV, followed by Botswana at 24.4 percent, Lesotho at 23.1 percent, Zimbabwe at 20.0 percent, Namibia at 19.7 percent, South Africa at 18.9 percent, Mozambique at 16.3 percent, and Zambia at 16.9 percent. Outside of Africa, no other country has an HIV prevalence rate higher than Haiti's of 3.8 percent (United Nations, 2007: 94–95, Table A.20).

The UN has noted that the epidemic continues to expand, and some countries are expected to have increases in their levels of HIV prevalence for many years into the future. AIDS has taken a truly devastating toll with regard to morbidity, mortality, and population loss:

Life expectancy in the most affected countries already shows dramatic declines. In Botswana, where HIV prevalence is estimated at 24 percent in

Millions

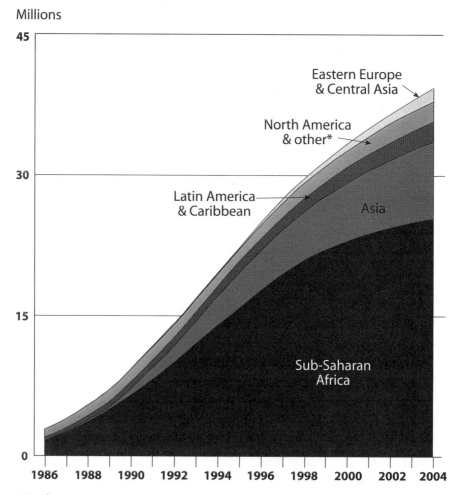

*North America, Europe (except Eastern), North Africa, and the Middle East.

Figure 5.3. People living with HIV by world regions, 1986–2004. *Source:* UNAIDS and World Health Organization, published and unpublished data, 2005. Reproduced from Lamptey, Johnson, and Khan, 2006: 7.

2005 for the adult population, aged 15–49 years, life expectancy has fallen from 64 years in 1985–1990 to 47 years in 2000–2005. By 2005–2010, life expectancy is expected to increase again to 51 years as a result of declining HIV prevalence and increased access to anti-retroviral therapy. In Southern Africa as a whole, where most of the worst affected countries are, life expectancy has fallen from 61 to 49 years over the last 20 years. While the impact in Southern Africa is particularly stark, the majority of highly affected countries in Africa have experienced declines in life expectancy in recent years because of the epidemic. (United Nations, 2007: 18)

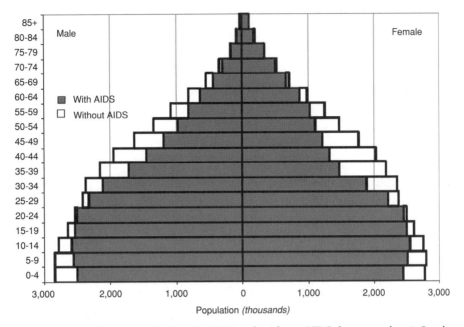

Figure 5.4. Population in 2015, with AIDS and without AIDS, by sex and age, South Africa. *Source:* Population Division of the Department of Economic and Social Affairs of the United Nations Secretariat (2007), *World Population Prospects, The 2006 Revision: Highlights*, New York: United Nations.

The future demographic impact of HIV/AIDS is nicely illustrated by projecting to the year 2015 the age distribution of a country that is now heavily infected by HIV, and comparing its projected age distribution with that under the assumption of no HIV/AIDS–related mortality. Figure 5.4 shows such a comparison for the country of South Africa, with nearly 19 percent of its population now infected with HIV. The figure superimposes the country's age distribution produced under a "No-AIDS" scenario with that produced under a most likely scenario. According to the UN (2007: 18):

> The adult population (ages 15 years and above) projected to 2015 is a smaller fraction of the population than would have been expected in the absence of AIDS (about 16 percent less or about six million smaller). The reduced size of younger cohorts stems from the deaths of large numbers of women during the reproductive ages and to the lower survival prospects of the infected children. The total population in South Africa in 2015 is projected to be 50.3 million or 14 percent lower than in the No-AIDS scenario.

We turn next to a discussion of wars, the last of the Malthusian positive checks.

War

The demographic consequences of war with regard to mortality are not easy to determine. For one thing, there is the issue of definition. What is a war? Some military historians and archeologists define war as all kinds of conflicts involving more than two combatants. But this is an unrealistic approach. Scholars now tend to define war in terms of the number of deaths that have occurred. David Wilkinson (1980) developed a register of wars since 1820 that includes 315 engagements where the number of deaths exceeded 300 (see also Etherington, 2003). In addition to military deaths recorded, there is also the issue of civilian losses that occur as a consequence of war per se, including infection by diseases carried by the soldiers, killings associated with plunder, famine following the destruction of farmland, and hardships occurring as a result of economic and social disorganization.

Mortality data from war are best documented for activities in the twentieth century compared to any previous eras. The greatest number of deaths, unquestionably, occurred during the first part of the last century. The range of estimates is considerable, but "plausible sizes of the military and civilian death toll would be around 8.5 million in World War I and 40 million in World War II" (Etherington, 2003: 964). Often, the number of civilian deaths exceeds the number of military deaths. To illustrate, it is likely that during World War II in Russia, 60 percent of the deaths were civilian (Petersen, 1975: 269).

In the United States, the Civil War resulted in the largest number of deaths to Americans of any war ever experienced by the country, before or after. An estimated 620,000 men, roughly half from the North and half from the South, died during the four years of fighting between 1861 and 1865. This is about the same number of Americans lost in all of the country's other wars, from the Revolutionary War through the Korean War (Faust, 2008). The number of 620,000 Civil War deaths needs to be considered relative to the U.S. population of around 31 million people at the time; approximately 2 percent of the country's total population died. This is the equivalent of around 6 million people in terms of the U.S. population today (Faust, 2008).

MORTALITY TRENDS AND CAUSES OF DEATH IN DEVELOPED VERSUS DEVELOPING COUNTRIES

The eminent demographer Donald Bogue has noted that in many ways "it is superficial to treat death as a single unitary force. . . . In reality death is an event brought about by one or a combination of a great variety of causes, or diseases, and a full understanding of mortality requires an understanding of the trends in each of the major causes of death" (1969: 578).

Even today, data on causes of death are far from complete. Some deaths around the world are not even registered. In many countries, a large proportion of deaths occurs outside the presence of a physician, and the cause is either unknown or incorrectly diagnosed. Sometimes, socially unpopular causes of death, such as suicide, syphilis, or HIV/AIDS, are misrepresented or camouflaged.

Moreover, international comparisons of cause-of-death data are difficult because countries often differ in terminology, method of certification, diagnostic techniques, and the quality of the coding and data-collection system. Nevertheless, some generalizations are possible about the general structure of cause of death.

We report in Chapter 9 that a major explanation of mortality change has its basis in demographic transition theory (DTT). We note that DTT proposes four stages of mortality and fertility decline that occur in the process of societal modernization. The first is the preindustrialization era with high birth and death rates, along with stable population growth. With the onset of industrialization and modernization, the society transitions to lower death rates, especially lower infant and maternal mortality, but maintains high birth rates, with the result of rapid population growth. The next stage is characterized by decreasing population growth due to lower birth and death rates, which lead then to the final stage of low and stable population growth (Poston, Davis, and Lewinski, 2006). There has also occurred during this transition a change in the cause-of-death structure, and this may be summarized with a second theory.

Epidemiological transition theory (ETT) focuses on the society-wide decline of infectious disease and the rise of chronic degenerative causes of death. According to ETT, as postulated by Abdel Omran (1971), there are three stages: The first is the age of pestilence and famine, in which the primary causes of mortality were influenza, pneumonia, smallpox, tuberculosis, and other related diseases, with high infant and childhood mortality and a life expectancy averaging between 20 and 40 years. In developed countries, this stage lasted until around 1875. The second is the age of receding pandemics, in which there was a decline in mortality due to improved sanitation and increases in standards of living and public health, resulting in a steady increase in life expectancy to between ages 30 and 50 years. According to Richard Rogers and Robert Hackenberg (1987), the stage of receding pandemics was approximately 1875 to 1930. The third stage is known as the era of degenerative and manmade diseases (heart disease, cancer, and stroke), in which mortality declines are due to medical advances in the prevention and treatment of infectious diseases. Life expectancy at birth rises rapidly so that fertility becomes the primary factor in population growth as life expectancy exceeds 70 years (Omran, 1971). About three-fourths of deaths in this stage are the result of degenerative diseases in the advanced years (Olshansky and Ault, 1986). Rogers and Hackenberg have noted a fourth "hybristic stage" where mortality is heavily influenced by individual behavior and lifestyle choices. Deaths in this stage are due to social pathologies, such as accidents, alcoholism, suicide, and homicide, as well as to lifestyle issues, such as smoking and diet (Poston, Davis, and Lewinski, 2006; Robine, 2003).

In the world today, most national governments classify causes of deaths according to the **International Classification of Diseases (ICD)** as developed by the World Health Organization (WHO) (World Health Organization, 1992). This classification undergoes periodic revision. Causes of death in the United States have been classified according to the tenth revision since 1999.

In the tenth revision of the ICD (adapted in 1992), the causes of death are classified under twenty-two major headings. These headings, along with a few examples of specific causes for some of them (see World Health Organization, 1992, for more details), are worth listing, as follows:

    I. Certain infectious and parasitic diseases (tuberculosis; viral infections; HIV)

    II. Neoplasms (cancers)

    III. Diseases of the blood

    IV. Endocrine, nutritional, and metabolic diseases (malnutrition; diabetes)

    V. Mental and behavioral disorders (schizophrenia; mental retardation)

    VI. Diseases of the nervous system (meningitis)

    VII. Diseases of the eye (glaucoma)

    VIII. Diseases of the ear

    IX. Diseases of the circulatory system (ischemic heart diseases; cerebrovascular diseases)

    X. Diseases of the respiratory system (influenza; pneumonia)

    XI. Diseases of the digestive system (diseases of liver; hernia)

    XII. Diseases of the skin and subcutaneous tissue

    XIII. Diseases of the musculoskeletal system (disorders of muscles; disorders of bone density)

    XIV. Diseases of the genitourinary system (diseases of male genital organs; disorders of breast)

    XV. Pregnancy, childbirth, and the puerperium

    XVI. Certain conditions originating in the perinatal period (birth trauma)

XVII. Congenital malformations, deformations, and chromosomal abnormalities (spina bifida; cleft palate)

XVIII. Symptoms, signs, and abnormal clinical and laboratory findings, not elsewhere classified (sudden infant death syndrome; unattended death)

XIX. Injury, poisoning, and certain other consequences of external causes (injuries to the head; frostbite)

XX. External causes of morbidity and mortality (traffic accidents; suicide)

XXI. Factors influencing health status and contact with health services

XXII. Codes for special purposes (provisional assignment of new diseases of uncertain etiology)

This listing provides extensive detail about the structure of causes of death. Its presentation makes the general point that death is a complex behavior, and that there are literally many thousand different ways to die. But some causes of death occur more frequently than others.

To illustrate, in 2002, there were approximately 57 million deaths in the world. The top cause of death was cardiovascular disease; coronary heart disease accounted for 7.2 million deaths, and cerebrovascular disease and stroke accounted for another 5.5 million deaths (World Health Organization, 2007). People do not all die of the same major causes, however. There are differences in causes of death, and these are largely due to the socioeconomic levels of the countries.

The WHO (2007) has produced an illustrative example that makes this point very clear. Consider a hypothetical population of 1,000 persons to represent all the women, men, and children of the world who died in 2002. Of these 1,000 decedents, 138 will have come from rich countries, 362 from middle-income countries, and 501 from poor countries. For each group of countries, we examine the distribution of deaths according to the top ten causes. These are neither identical nor are they ranked the same in the three groups of countries.

Concerning the 138 people from the rich countries (chiefly in North America and Europe), slightly more than half (54 percent) experienced death according to one of WHO's top ten causes. Coronary heart disease is the cause of twenty-four of the deaths, stroke the cause of thirteen, and lung cancer the cause of eight. HIV/AIDS is not one of the top ten causes of death in this group of countries (Figure 5.5). Just under 15 percent of the population of the world lives in these countries, but they accounted for only 7 percent of all deaths.

In the middle-income countries, nearly half of the people lived to age 70, and the major causes of death were the chronic diseases, just as in

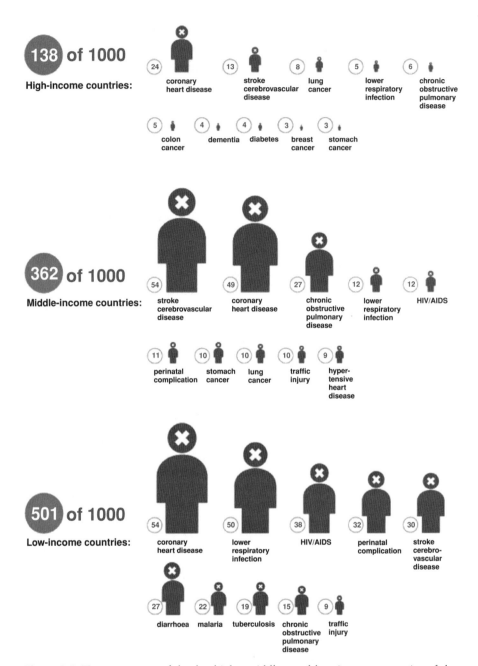

Figure 5.5. Top ten causes of deaths: high-, middle-, and low-income countries of the world, 2002. *Source:* World Health Organization, 2007.

the rich countries. A big difference, however, is the role of HIV/AIDS as a major cause of death in these countries, unlike the situation in the rich countries. Of the 362 people from the middle-income countries, 54 died from stroke or other cerebrovascular diseases and 49 from coronary heart disease. Twelve people died from lower respiratory infection and twelve more from HIV/AIDS (Figure 5.5). More than 56 percent of the decedents from this group of countries died from the group's top ten causes.

In the poor countries (many located in sub-Saharan Africa), less than a quarter of the population attained the age of 70, and nearly a third of all deaths were to children younger than the age of 14. Of the 501 people from these countries dying in 2002, 54 died from coronary heart disease and 50 from a lower respiratory infection. HIV/AIDS was responsible for the deaths of 38 people. Thirty-two infants died from perinatal conditions. Thirty people died of stroke or other cerebrovascular diseases (Figure 5.5). Almost 60 percent of the deaths occurring in the poor countries were due to the top ten causes in this group (World Health Organization, 2007).

There is considerable variation around the world in causes of death. Life expectancy also varies considerably. We noted earlier that in the year 2006, a baby born in Japan, on average, could expect to live for about 82 years, a baby born in Sweden about 81 years, and a baby born in the United States around 78 years. In contrast, a baby born in 2006 in Botswana and a baby born in Lesotho could expect to live on average only 34 and 36 years, respectively (Population Reference Bureau, 2006). We now consider these trends and differences in mortality in greater detail.

In the world in 2006, life expectancy at birth was about 67 years (65 for males, 69 for females). These are averages, and there is considerable variability in them. For the most part, the higher the country's level of economic development, the higher its life expectancy. In the countries of the less developed world in 2006 (accounting for 5.3 billion of the world's 6.6 billion people), life expectancy at birth was 65 years (64 for males, 67 for females). If we exclude China (an economically less developed country but a demographically developed one; i.e., a country with low fertility and low mortality) from these calculations, life expectancy is 63 years (62 for males, 65 for females). Compare these figures with those for the more developed countries of the world, with an overall life expectancy at birth of 77 years (73 for males, 80 for females) (Population Reference Bureau, 2006).

Earlier, we mentioned that in the past, mortality was much higher. In its *World Population Prospects, The 2006 Revision* (2007), the UN noted that the twentieth century was the era characterized by the most rapid decline in mortality in human history. In the early 1950s, life expectancy in the world was but 46 years, and, as just noted, is now 67 years. Figure 5.6 shows the estimated levels of life expectancy for countries of the world in the 2005–2010 period.

The UN has projected that in the next 45 years, life expectancy for the world will reach 75 years. Life expectancy in the developed world is projected to increase from 77 years in 2006 to 82 years by midcentury,

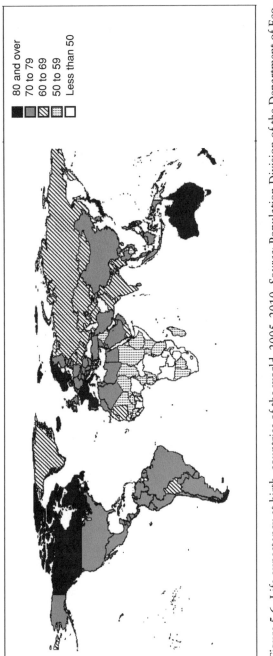

Figure 5.6. Life expectancy at birth, countries of the world, 2005–2010. *Source:* Population Division of the Department of Economic and Social Affairs of the United Nations Secretariat (2007), *World Population Prospects, The 2006 Revision: Highlights,* New York: United Nations. (The boundaries shown on the present map do not imply official endorsement or acceptance by the United Nations.)

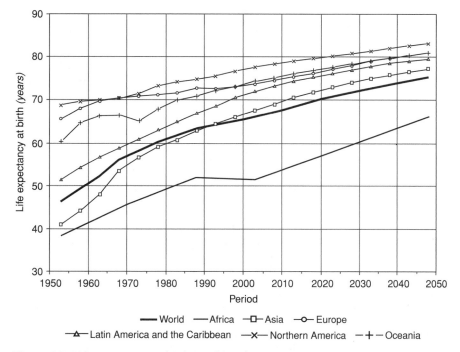

Figure 5.7. Life expectancy at birth, world and major areas, 1950–2050. *Source:* Population Division of the Department of Economic and Social Affairs of the United Nations Secretariat (2007), *World Population Prospects, The 2006 Revision: Highlights,* New York: United Nations.

versus 74 years for the less developed countries. Figure 5.7 shows actual and expected improvements in life expectancy between 1950 and 2050 for the world and its major regions.

The increases in life expectancy just noted for the more developed and the less developed countries tend to hide the variation in these changes among the world's major areas shown in Figure 5.7. The trends in the figure illustrate that on average, the countries of Asia, Latin America and the Caribbean, Northern America, and Oceania have been experiencing increases in life expectancy at a steady pace. Europe, however, shows a slowdown beginning in the late 1960s through the late 1980s. This is due to "severe declines in life expectancy in Eastern Europe, particularly in the Russian Federation and the Ukraine. The remaining regions of Europe have life expectancies equal to or higher than that for Northern America" (United Nations, 2007: 15).

Unlike the situation in the other regions of the world, increases in life expectancy since the late 1980s in Africa have been slowing down:

> This trend is due in large part to the HIV/AIDS epidemic, [but] other factors have also played a role, including armed conflict, economic

stagnation, and resurgent infectious diseases such as tuberculosis and malaria.... [These] recent negative trends in Africa have set back progress in reducing mortality by at least 15 years. Only in 2005–2010 are life expectancy levels in Africa expected to surpass those last seen in 1990–1995. By 2045–2050, life expectancy in Africa is expected to be 66 years, a full 11 years below the life expectancy of the next lowest major area, Asia. (United Nations, 2007: 16)

We turn next to a consideration of trends in mortality and longevity in the United States.

MORTALITY AND LONGEVITY IN THE UNITED STATES

The mortality declines that have taken place in the United States are consistent with demographic transition theory to be described in more detail in Chapter 9. Mortality started dropping gradually in response to changes in the social and economic conditions and the environment that were part of societal modernization. Much of the mortality reduction started to occur before the initiation of any appreciable public health measures.

The decline in mortality

Mortality data for the United States are limited until about the middle of the 1800s. In fact, systematic information on U.S. mortality has only been available since 1933 (see Chapter 2). It is believed that CDRs during the colonial period were moderate, ranging from 20 deaths per 1,000 per population to just under 40 (recall, however, our discussion about problems in using CDRs comparatively). Life expectancy certainly did not exceed age 40, and was much lower in many places. In New Hampshire and Massachusetts, life expectancy was about 35, and had increased to 40 by 1850 (Kitagawa and Hauser, 1973). Indeed, for the states of the United States reporting data as of 1850, we know that life expectancy at birth for whites averaged just over 39 years and for blacks only 23 years. Infant mortality was very high.

Since around 1850, some of the mortality decline has resulted in part from "improvements in public health and sanitation, especially better water supplies and sewage disposal. The improving diet, clothing, and shelter of the American population over the period since about 1870 also played a role. Specific medical interventions beyond more general environmental public health measures were not statistically important until well into the twentieth century" (Haines, 2007). We mentioned earlier that death rates were often high in the urban areas of Europe. The same was true in the

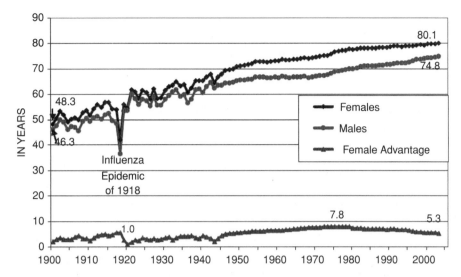

Figure 5.8. Life expectancy at birth in the United States, 1900 to 2003. *Sources:* For 1900–2002, CRS analysis based on data contained in NCHS, United States Life Tables, 2002, *National Vital Statistics Report*, vol. 53, no. 6, Nov. 10, 2004. For 2003, CRS analysis based on NCHS, Deaths: Final Data for 2003, *National Vital Statistics Report*, vol. 54, no. 13, Apr. 19, 2006. Reproduced from Shrestha, 2006.

United States. However, in the 1890s, many of the larger U.S. cities initiated "public works sanitation projects (such as piped water, sewer systems, filtration and chlorination of water) and public health administration" (Haines, 2007). As a result of these efforts, the death rates dropped and rural–urban differences in mortality disappeared. Still, white and black differences remained, as they do to this day.

In Figure 5.8, we show life expectancy at birth data for U.S. males and females for every year between 1900 and 2003. Life expectancy increased dramatically from 46.3 for males and 48.3 for females in 1900 to 74.8 for males and 80.1 for females in 2003. Most of the improvements occurred from 1900 to 1950. These advances were due to the increased recognition of the **germ theory** of disease, resulting in the identification and control of many infectious and parasitic diseases, particularly among infants and children (Preston and Haines, 1991; Shrestha, 2006). The germ theory led to such interventions for the control of infectious disease as "boiling bottles and milk, washing hands, protecting food from flies, isolating sick children, ventilating rooms, and improving water supply and sewage disposal" (Shrestha, 2006: 3). Today, these preventative behaviors are taken for granted and practiced by nearly everyone. Improvements in life expectancy since mid-century have been mostly due to the increased prevention and control of the chronic diseases that affect adults, particularly heart disease and stroke.

Life expectancy has not increased uniformly at all ages. Most of the gains have occurred in the younger age groups. To illustrate, as shown in Figure 5.8, a boy infant born in 1900 could expect to live to the age of 46 and a girl infant to 48. By 2003, a boy infant could anticipate living for 75 years and a girl infant for 80 years. These are gains of 29 years for boy infants and 32 years for girl infants. For people in the older ages, the increases in the past century have not been as striking. A 60-year-old male in 1901 could expect to live for 14.3 more years and a female of the same age for 15.2 more years (Glover, 1921: 57, 61). In contrast, by 2003, a 60-year-old male could anticipate 20.4 more years of life and a 60-year-old female 23.7 more years (Arias, 2006: 10, 12). These are gains during the 100 years of 6.1 years for 60-year-old males and 8.5 years for 60-year-old females. As noted, the greater gains at the younger ages occurred because we can now pretty much control the various infectious diseases that in the past resulted in deaths of infants and young children. But we do not yet have control of the chronic diseases that cause death among older persons.

Race and ethnic differences

Despite the improvements in life expectancy in the twentieth century, a sizable racial difference remains. The gap has narrowed, but there are still differences between the races. Figure 5.9 shows trends in life expectancy at birth by race and by sex in the United States for the years 1900 to 2003. Whites had a much higher life expectancy at birth than blacks at the start of the last century. In 1900, a white female infant could expect to live 51.1 years, compared to 35 years for a black female infant. A white male infant had a life expectancy in 1900 of 48.2 years, compared to 32.5 years for a newborn black male. So the white advantage for female infants in 1900 was 16 years, and for male infants it was 15.7 years.

One hundred years later, whites still had a longevity advantage over blacks, but the white advantage had narrowed slightly. By 2003, the life expectancy advantage for white females over black females had fallen to 4.4 years, and the advantage for white males over black males had dropped to 6.3 years. These gains are impressive, but the racial differences are still present. Blacks still live, on average, around five years fewer than whites. The racial differential in mortality in the United States has been studied and analyzed by medical and social scientists for many decades, but the differences have remained.

A major reason for the racial differential is the socioeconomic consequences of lifelong poverty. Among other possible factors are low birth

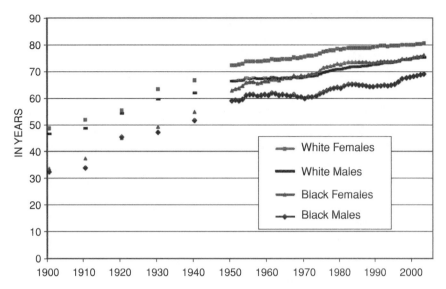

Figure 5.9. Trends in life expectancy at birth in the United States, by race and sex, 1900 to 2003. *Sources:* For 1900 to 2002, CRS compilation from National Center for Health Statistics (NCHS), *National Vital Statistics Reports,* vol. 53, no. 6, Nov. 10, 2004. For 2003, NCHS, *National Vital Statistics Reports,* vol. 54, no. 14, Apr. 19, 2005. Reproduced from Shrestha, 2006.

weight and low levels of childhood nutrition. Factors operating in midlife include the lack of access to health insurance provided by one's employer, "the strain of physically demanding work, and exposure to a broad range of toxins, both behavioral (e.g., smoking) and environmental (e.g., workplace exposures)" (Shrestha, 2006: 17). In addition, one cannot discount the unfortunate experiences of racial discrimination, which not only have serious and adverse psychological and physiological effects but also, in a most important way, limit the potential quantity and quality of health care available (Shrestha, 2006).

Of particular interest in any analysis of majority–minority group differences in mortality is the rather consistent finding that Hispanics in the United States, particularly Mexican Americans, have a life expectancy similar to, and sometimes higher than, Anglos (i.e., non-Hispanic whites) (Bradshaw and Liese, 1991; Rogers et al., 1996; Rogers, Hummer, and Nam, 2000). This is a demographic situation exactly the opposite that of blacks. Thus, despite the fact that Mexican Americans and African Americans "are more likely to be unemployed, poor, and without a high school degree than [Anglos], and...have [also] experienced a long history of discrimination" (Rogers, Hummer, and Nam, 2000: 55; see also Bean and Tienda, 1987), Mexican Americans compared to Anglos are not disadvantaged with regard to life expectancy and other measures of longevity, but African Americans are.

Several hypotheses have been offered to account for this so-called Hispanic **epidemiological paradox** (Markides and Coreil, 1986), also referred to as the Latino mortality paradox (Abraido-Lanza et al., 1999) and the **Hispanic paradox** (Palloni and Morenoff, 2001), that is, the empirical finding that Mexican Americans have death rates of about the same magnitude as and sometimes lower than Anglos. The hypotheses may be subsumed into three groups, namely, data artifacts, migration effects, and cultural effects. Under *data artifacts* are such reasons as the possible under-reporting of Hispanic origin identification on death certificates (Palloni and Arias, 2004; Rosenberg et al., 1999) and the misstatement of age, perhaps overstatement, at the older ages (Rosenwaike and Preston, 1983). There are two principal *migration effects*: First is the **healthy migrant effect**, which states that the longevity advantage is due to the facts that many Mexican Americans in the United States were born elsewhere (Rogers, Hummer, and Nam, 2000: 56) and that migration is known to be selective of persons in better physical and mental health (Palloni and Morenoff, 2001; Rosenwaike, 1991). Second is the *return migrant effect*, also known as the **salmon bias**, which states that Mexican Americans in poor physical health often return to Mexico at old ages and, thus, that their deaths are not counted in U.S. statistics (Abraido-Lanza et al., 1999; Palloni and Arias, 2004). *Cultural effects* may include reasons such as better dietary practices among Mexican American than U.S. residents and the stronger family obligations and relationships among Hispanics than among non-Hispanics (LeClere, Rogers, and Peters, 1997; Markides and Coreil, 1986; Scribner, 1996; Scribner and Dwyer, 1989).

Alberto Palloni and Elizabeth Arias (2004) have studied empirically this paradox and find some support for the salmon bias and the healthy migrant effect, but little if any support for the cultural effects (see Smith and Bradshaw [2006] for an opposite conclusion). Their study does not have all the answers, and the paradox remains a topic of considerable interest among demographers.

Prevailing causes of death

Changes in causes of death in the United States are somewhat predictable. Mortality from infectious and parasitic diseases decreased as major causes of death in the United States many decades ago, and mortality from degenerative diseases has increased. The main causes of death in the United States these days are associated with degenerative and chronic diseases. Table 5.3

shows percentages of deaths in the United States, by sex, for the top ten leading causes for the year 2003.

There were more than 1.2 million deaths of both males and females in 2003. The leading cause of death for both sexes was heart disease, accounting for 28 percent of all deaths for males as well as for females. Cancer was in second place, accounting for 24 percent of all male deaths and 22 percent of all female deaths. Heart disease and cancer accounted for almost half of male and female deaths in 2003 (Heron and Smith, 2007). In 1900, in contrast, these two degenerative causes were much lower in the list of major causes. The top three causes in 1900 were pneumonia and influenza, tuberculosis, and intestinal disorders, for example, diarrhea (Weller and Bouvier, 1981: 187). In 2003, there were two other causes with the same ranking for both sexes, namely, diabetes, sixth place, and kidney disease, ninth place.

There are notable differences by sex, however, with regard to accidents and suicides. Accidents are in third place for males and in seventh place for females; suicide is the eighth ranking cause of death for males versus seventeenth for females. Most accidental deaths in the United States are due to motor vehicles, followed by deaths due to poisoning, falls, suffocating, drowning, and fires. The victims of motor vehicle accidents are more often males than females, usually younger males (Fingerhut, 2003). In most countries, suicide rates are higher for males than for females, and this is also the situation in the United States. Moreover, older men are more often the victims, not younger men. The main reasons for suicides, particularly for older people, are depression and/or the death of a spouse. It has also been found that elderly people are more successful than younger people in attempting suicide (MacKellar, 2003).

Alzheimer's disease (AD) is in the fifth rank for females compared to the tenth rank for males. Males are less likely to die of AD than females at all ages, and the gap increases among the oldest-old. Why? Women live longer than men and thus are more likely to die of chronic and degenerative diseases such as AD (M. Davis, 2006). Most of the other causes of death shown in Table 5.3 have similar ranks for males and females.

Socioeconomic differentials in mortality

Generally, the higher the socioeconomic status (SES), the lower the mortality. This relationship is found whether or not SES is measured in terms of income, occupation, or education (Stockwell, Wicks, and Adamchak, 1978). This inverse association is found in U.S. data from the earliest times to the present, as well as in most other countries (Krieger

Table 5.3. Deaths and percentage of total deaths for the eleven leading causes of death, by sex, United States, 2003

Cause of death	Males			Females		
	Rank[a]	Deaths	Percentage of total deaths	Rank[a]	Deaths	Percentage of total deaths
All cases	...	1,201,964	100.0	...	1,246,324	100.0
Diseases of heart (100–109,111,113,120–151)	1	336,095	28.0	1	348,994	28.0
Malignant neoplasms (C00–C97)	2	287,990	24.0	2	268,912	21.6
Accidents (unintentional injuries) (V01–X59, Y85–Y86)	3	70,532	5.9	7	38,745	3.1
Cerebrovascular diseases (160–169)	4	61,426	5.1	3	96,263	7.7
Chronic lower respiratory diseases (J40–J47)	5	60,714	5.1	4	65,668	5.3
Diabetes mellitus (E10–E14)	6	35,438	2.9	6	38,781	3.1
Influenza and pneumonia (J10–J18)	7	28,778	2.4	8	36,385	2.9
Intentional self-harm (suicide) (*U03,X60–X84,Y87.0)	8	25,203	2.1	17	6,281	0.5
Nephritis, nephrotic syndrome, and nephrosis (N00–N07, N17–N19, N25–N27)	9	20,481	1.7	9	21,972	1.8
Alzheimer's disease (G30)	10	18,335	1.5	5	45,122	3.6
Septicemia (A40–A41)	11	14,987	1.2	10	19,082	1.5

Notes: Cause of death based on the World Health Organization's *International Classification of Diseases, 10th Revision,* 1992.
... Category not applicable.
[a] Rank based on number of deaths.
Source: Heron and Smith, 2007, Table D.

et al., 1993; Rogers, Hummer, and Nam, 2000; Williams and Collins, 1995).

Two extensive and well-known studies of socioeconomic differentials deserve special mention. The first is the analysis of Evelyn Kitagawa and Philip Hauser (1973), *Differential Mortality in the United States*. In this important book, the authors examined a sample of U.S. 1960 death certificates matched with 1960 census data. They showed that income and education have strong negative relationships with mortality, particularly for persons in the 25–64 age group. This was one of the very first analyses reporting the relationship between socioeconomic status and mortality.

A more recent and very noteworthy analysis is by Richard Rogers, Robert Hummer, and Charles Nam (2000), *Living and Dying in the USA*. In this invaluable study of adult mortality, the authors used two matched data sets to analyze the effects of social factors on mortality. One data set, the National Health Interview Survey (NHIS), is a national survey that interviews U.S. residents each year about their health and sociodemographic characteristics. Data from the NHIS for persons ages 18 and older for several years in the late 1980s and early 1990s were then matched with death-certificate data for persons who were included in the NHIS but who subsequently died between 1986 and 1995. Rogers and his colleagues were able to relate socioeconomic characteristics of persons interviewed in the NHIS with whether or not they died in the period through the mid-1990s. They showed statistically and concretely that mortality rates are not the same for all adults. The force of mortality is "stronger for the poor, the less educated, the unemployed and the uninsured rather than for the rich, the highly educated, and the insured.... [Mortality is higher] for those who rarely attend religious services . . . than for those who frequently attend.... [And mortality is higher] for those who smoke, drink heavily, and are inactive [compared to those] who have never smoked, who drink moderately, and exercise regularly" (Rogers, Hummer, and Nam, 2000: 321). The data and results reported in their book provide solid evidence that we are indeed population actors and that personal choices and decisions throughout our lifetime on a number of socioeconomic and behavioral dimensions have dramatic effects on our longevity.

INFANT MORTALITY

An aspect of mortality that receives special consideration from demographers is infant mortality. This is due to at least two considerations. First, as W. Parker Frisbie has written, "few, if any, human experiences are more tragic or emotionally devastating as the death of an infant or child" (2005: 251). Second, as we observed earlier, the death rate in the first year of life is much higher than in the succeeding several decades. Indeed, in high-mortality populations, the mortality rate in the first year of life is not reached again in the society until age 70 or later, and in some high-mortality populations, the highest death rate is in the first year of life. (Recall our earlier discussion about the age curve of mortality in Afghanistan, as in Figure 5.1.)

Infant mortality rate

The **infant mortality rate (IMR)** the most common measure of infant death, is the number of deaths in a year to persons under age 1 per 1,000 babies born in the year. It is expressed as

$$\text{IMR} = \frac{\text{deaths in the year to persons under age 1}}{\text{live births in the year}} * 1,000 \qquad (5.8)$$

Infant mortality rates of 200 or more per 1,000 births were the rule as late as 1800, even in the countries of the presently developed world. This means that around one of every five babies born were dead before reaching their first birthday. IMRs were even higher in countries prior to their completing the demographic transition. During those early periods, "IMRs were probably on the order of 260 to 370 per 1,000 live births" (Frisbie, 2005: 260). As late as the 1870s, the IMR in European countries varied from 100 in Norway to nearly 300 in southern Germany (United Nations, 1973: 124). Infant mortality in China in the early 1900s was likely around 300. Indeed, China probably did not reduce its IMR countrywide to around 200 until the founding of the People's Republic in 1949 (Banister, 1992: 167).

High IMRs led to the cultural practice in China and many other Asian societies of not giving a newborn baby a name until it had lived for several months and showed signs of continued viability. In Korea, for instance, even to this day, a small feast is prepared on the hundredth day after a baby is born. Rice, red bean cakes, and wine are served. This day was originally celebrated as a feast in honor of the child's surviving the first few months of life, the most difficult period of time for survival. In ancient times, the child was not given his/her name until the hundredth-day celebration. It made little sense to invest emotionally in a newborn by assigning it a name if the chances were only around four of ten that it would survive for a year.

During the latter part of the nineteenth century and into the twentieth century, almost all countries in the world experienced decreases in their IMRs. The transition to lower levels of infant mortality in the Western countries, as well as to lower child and adult mortality, was due in large part to reductions in infectious and parasitic diseases. Indeed, prior to the

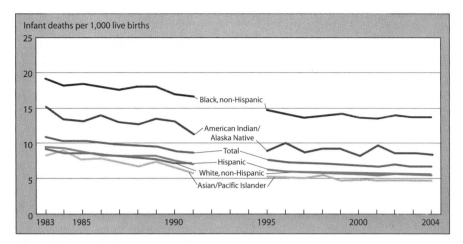

Figure 5.10. Rates of infant deaths per 1,000 live births, by race and Hispanic origin, United States, 1983 to 2004. *Source:* Centers for Disease Control and Prevention, National Center for Health Statistics, *National Linked Files of Live Births and Infant Deaths.* Reproduced from Federal Interagency Forum on Child and Family Statistics, 2007: 61.

third and fourth decades of the twentieth century, "the role played by physicians and drug therapy in the reduction of mortality was relatively slight" (Frisbie, 2005: 260; McKeown, 1976).

In the United States in 2004, the IMR was just under 7 deaths per 1,000 live births. In earlier years and decades, the IMR was much higher. The IMR in the United States was more than 100 in 1915–1916, dropping to 26 by 1960 and to 13 by 1980 (U.S. Bureau of the Census, 2004b). Figure 5.10 shows trends in the IMR in the United States by race and by Hispanic origin of the mother, from 1983 to 2004.

The U.S. IMR dropped from 11 in 1983 to 7 in 2004. Black infant mortality is the highest of the race/ethnic groups; that of American Indians and Alaskan Natives next; followed by those of Hispanics, Anglos, and Asians. These latter three groups have IMRs that are all very similar, at around 6 in 2004. Black infant mortality declined from 19 infant deaths per 1,000 live births in 1983 to 14 in 2004. But black infant mortality in 2004 is higher than that of Anglos in 1983, that is, 14 versus 9, and is considerably higher than Anglo infant mortality in 2004, that is, 14 versus 6.

Infant mortality in the contemporary world varies considerably from country to country. In general, the more modernized the country, the lower its IMR. The IMR of the world in 2006 was about 52 infant deaths per 1,000 live births. This means that in the world in 2006, on average, about one baby died before reaching the age of 1 year for every twenty born. The IMR was 6 in the more developed countries and 57 in the less developed countries.

Table 5.4. Countries with the highest and the lowest infant mortality rates in the world, 2006

Highest infant mortality rates		Lowest infant mortality rates	
Afghanistan	166	Iceland	2
Sierra Leone	163	Singapore	2
Niger	149	Sweden	2
Liberia	142	Finland	3
Angola	139	Norway	3
Somalia	119	Japan	3

Source: Population Reference Bureau, 2006.

We list in Table 5.4 the six countries with the highest IMRs in 2006 and the six with the lowest.

Afghanistan has the highest IMR in the world: 166 infant deaths per 1,000 live births. Sierra Leone is not far behind, with an IMR of 163; the next highest IMRs are in Niger, Liberia, Angola, and Somalia. In 2006, six countries in addition to those shown in the table had IMRs of 100 or higher (i.e., Guinea-Bissau, Chad, Equatorial Guinea, Burundi, Djbouti, and Mozambique) (Population Reference Bureau, 2006). These are astoundingly high levels of infant mortality. Although great success in lowering infant mortality has been achieved in the last century, these benefits have not yet been realized by the countries just mentioned.

The countries with the lowest IMRs in the world in 2006 were Iceland, Singapore, and Sweden, all at 2 infant deaths per 1,000 live births, and Finland, Norway, and Japan, all at 3. IMRs of 2 and 3 are about as low as will ever be attained.

The IMR in the United States in 2006 was 7. Although this is certainly low compared to the IMRs in many other countries, it is higher than the average IMR of 6/1,000 for the developed world. Most developed countries in the world and many developing countries had IMRs in 2006 lower than the IMR of the United States. Indeed, thirty-six countries had IMRs in 2006 lower than that of the United States: Andora, Australia, Austria, Belgium, Channel Islands, Croatia, Cuba, Cyprus, Denmark, Estonia, Finland, France, Germany, Hungary, Iceland, Italy, Japan, Liechtenstein, Luxembourg, Malta, Martinique, Monaco, the Netherlands, New Caledonia, New Zealand, Norway, Poland, Portugal, Singapore, Slovenia, South Korea, Spain, Sweden, Switzerland, Taiwan, and the United Kingdom.

Why was the U.S. IMR higher than those of more than thirty other countries? Part of the reason is surely statistical. The United States counts as a live birth an infant showing any sign of life (see the discussion and definition of a live birth in Chapter 2), whereas many other countries are not as stringent. Dr. Bernadine Healy, former director of the U.S. National Institutes of Health and director and Chief Executive Officer of the American Red Cross, has argued that it is incorrect to

> compare U.S. infant mortality with reports from other countries. The United States counts all births as live if they show any sign of life, regardless of prematurity or size. This includes what many other countries report as **stillbirth**. In Austria and Germany, fetal weight must be at least 500 grams (1 pound) to count as a live birth; in other parts of Europe, such as Switzerland, the fetus must be at least 30 centimeters (12 inches) long. In Belgium and France, births at less than 26 weeks of pregnancy are registered as lifeless. And some countries do not reliably register babies who die within the first 24 hours of birth. Thus, the United States is sure to report higher infant mortality rates. (Healy, 2006)

However, statistical adjustments that attempt to take into account these differences in definitions still do not move the U.S. IMR to the low levels of Japan and Sweden (Haub and Yanagishita, 1991). Also, if one used only the IMR for the U.S. Anglo population, the Anglo IMR would still be twice as high as that of the low IMR countries. One consideration is the powerful influence on infant survival of the mother's socioeconomic status. The leading cause of infant mortality in developed countries such as the United States is congenital malformations, a cause of infant death that can be reduced, if not eliminated, with good nutritional intake and prenatal vitamins. However, poor mothers, especially those in poverty, often lack the needed socioeconomic resources necessary for obtaining these benefits. They also may be forced to forgo full prenatal care, which could result in maternal complications at birth, another prime cause of infant mortality. Many countries in the developed world have socialized medicine that provides universal health care to the entire population, and many of these countries have lower IMRs than the United States.

The further reduction of infant mortality in the United States has been and continues to be a major goal. In fact, one of the objectives of *Healthy People 2010*, a set of health initiatives being pursued by several federal agencies such as the National Institutes of Health, the Food and Drug Administration, and the Centers for Disease Control and Prevention, is to reduce the U.S. IMR in 2010 to 4.5 infant deaths per 1,000 live births.

In the United States and in most countries of the developed world, around two-thirds of infant deaths occur in the first month after birth and are due in large part to "health problems of the infant or the pregnancy, such as preterm delivery or birth defects" (Federal Interagency Forum on Child and Family Statistics, 2007: 61). Deaths to infants during the first

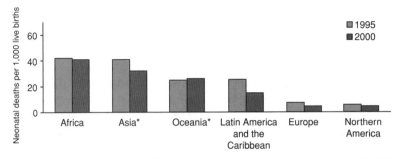

Figure 5.11. Neonatal mortality rates by world region, 1950 and 2000. *Source:* World Health Organization, 2006b.

month of life are frequently analyzed separately from those that occur after the first month but during the first year of life.

Neonatal mortality rate and postneonatal mortality rate

The IMR may be thought of as the sum of two rates, namely, the **neonatal mortality rate (NMR)**, deaths to babies of 28 days of age or less per 1,000 live births, and the **postneonatal mortality rate (PMR)**, deaths to babies of 29 days to 1 year of age per 1,000 live births. These two rates are expressed as follows:

$$\text{NMR} = \frac{\text{deaths to babies 0 to 28 days old}}{\text{live births in the year}} * 1,000 \qquad (5.9)$$

$$\text{PMR} = \frac{\text{deaths to babies 29 days to 365 days old}}{\text{live births in the year}} * 1,000 \qquad (5.10)$$

Neonatal deaths include more than half of the approximately 7.5 million infant deaths that occur each year in the world. We show in Figure 5.11 the NMRs for the regions of the world in 1995 and 2000. The WHO (2006b) has estimated that worldwide in 2000, the NMR was 30 neonatal deaths per 1,000 live births. In countries of the developed world it was 5, and 33 in countries of the developing regions, meaning that "in developing regions, the risk of death in the neonatal period is more than six times that of developed countries; in the least developed countries, it is more than eight times higher" (World Health Organization, 2006b: 19). In the United States, the NMR in 2001 was 4.8 (World Health Organization, 2005: 186–188). An objective of *Healthy People 2010* is to reduce the NMR for the United States to 2.9 by the year 2010.

The main but not only causes of neonatal deaths are **endogenous conditions,** "such as congenital malformations, chromosomal abnormalities, and complications of delivery, as well as . . . low birthweight" (Pebley, 2003: 534). These are usually related to genetic disorders of the birth process itself. It was long thought that neonatal mortality was due primarily to endogenous causes. Research has shown, however, that the endogenous causes dominate infant mortality principally in the early days of life, and not for the entire first month of life (Bouvier and van der Tak, 1976; Poston and Rogers, 1985).

PMRs vary around the world, from highs of 81, 79, and 76 post-neonatal deaths per 1,000 live births in Mozambique, Niger, and Liberia, respectively, to lows of between 1 and 2 in most of the countries of the developed world. The PMR in the United States in 2001 was 2.4 (World Health Organization, 2005: 186–188). The goal of *Healthy People 2010* is to implement policies so that the PMR for the United States will be reduced to 1.2 by the year 2010.

Deaths in the postneonatal period, as well as in the first few years of life, are often due mainly to exogenous causes, such as infectious disease, accidents, and injury. In countries experiencing declining death rates, their PMRs tend to decline much more rapidly than their NMRs. The main reason is that "improved living standards, better health care, and public health programs have greater effects on exogenous causes of death than on endogenous causes" (Pebley, 2003: 534). An **exogenous cause of death** is one caused mainly by environmental or external factors, such as infections or accidents. An **endogenous cause of death** in an infant can occur because of genetic issues or conditions associated with fetal development or the birth process.

Stillbirth rate

Demographers are also interested in the rate at which **stillbirths** (also known as miscarriages or fetal deaths) occur. These are fetuses that are not born alive. They are not registered as deaths because the fetuses were never born. However, they are often identified in hospital reports dealing with obstetric procedures. A fetus may die prior to the onset of labor, that is, in utero, because of pregnancy complications or various maternal diseases. Or a fetus may be alive at the onset of labor but die during the process and, thus, emerge from its mother in a dead state. The WHO has reported that it "is therefore important to know at what point before birth the [fetus] died, so that appropriate interventions can be planned accordingly. . . . Where women receive good care during childbirth, [these] deaths represent less than 10 percent of stillbirths due to unexpected severe complications"

(2006b: 3). The **stillbirth rate (SBR)**, sometimes referred to as the **fetal death rate**, is the following:

$$\text{SBR} = \frac{\text{stillbirths}}{\text{live births plus stillbirths in the year}} * 1{,}000 \qquad (5.11)$$

Not all countries report data on stillbirths, and so the WHO has estimated the SBRs for many countries. The SBR for the world in 2000 was 24 stillbirths per 1,000 live births plus stillbirths; the rate in the developed world was 6; in the less developed regions, it was 26. The SBR was 32 in Africa, 4 in Western Europe, and 3 in North America (World Health Organization, 2006b: 18). The SBRs ranged from highs of 63 in Mauritania, 58 in Liberia, 54 in Afghanistan, and 53 in Cote d'Ivoire, to lows of 2 in South Korea and 3 in several countries (i.e., Australia, Bahamas, Canada, Czech Republic, Italy, Malaysia, Martinique, New Zealand, Singapore, South Korea, Sweden, and Switzerland). The SBR for the United States was 4 (World Health Organization, 2006b: 29–34).

Perinatal mortality rate

Another indicator of mortality at early life and before birth is the **perinatal mortality rate (PeMR)**. Because the "endogenous causes of mortality in the first week after birth are similar to the causes of stillbirths, . . . the two may be combined into the PeMR, which refers to deaths in the period immediately before and after birth" (Rowland, 2003: 202). The PeMR is a measure of what demographers call "pregnancy wastage"; it reflects the number of wasted pregnancies, wasted because they either did not result in a live birth (they were fetal deaths) or resulted in a live birth of an infant who lived for only seven days or less. The PeMR is expressed as

$$\text{PeMR} = \frac{\text{stillbirths} + \text{deaths to babies 0 to 7 days old}}{\text{live births plus stillbirths in the year}} * 1{,}000 \quad (5.12)$$

In 2000, the PeMR for the world was 47 per 1,000 live births plus stillbirths; it was 10 in the developed world and 50 in the less developed regions (World Health Organization, 2006b: 18). Figure 5.12 is a map showing PeMRs for the countries of the world. These rates range from highs of 111 in Mauritania, 104 in Liberia, 96 in both Afghanistan and Cote d'Ivoire, and 90 in Sierra Leone, to lows of 4 in the Czech Republic and Singapore and 5 in Italy, Martinique, and Sweden (World Health Organization, 2006b: 29–34). The PeMR distribution around the world indicates that the highest rates are in sub-Saharan Africa, a story that has been told time and time again in this chapter. The PeMR for the United

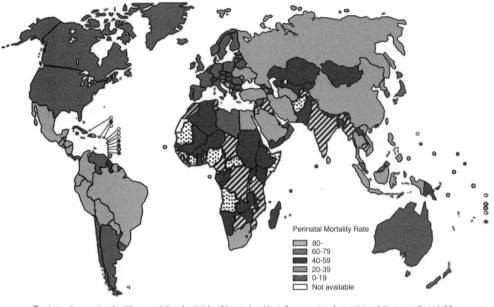

Perinatal Mortality Rate

- 80-
- 60-79
- 40-59
- 20-39
- 0-19
- Not available

The designations employed and the presentation of material on this map do not imply the expression of any opinion whatsoever on the part of the World Health Organization concerning the legal status of any country, territory, city, or area or of its authorities, or concerning the delimitation of its frontiers or boundaries. Dashed lines represent approximate border lines for which there may not yet be full agreement.

Figure 5.12. Perinatal mortality rates, countries of the world, 2000. *Source:* World Health Organization, 2006b: 15.

States was 7.3. The objective of *Healthy People 2010* is to reduce the PeMR for the United States to 4.4 by the year 2010.

Maternal mortality ratio

A final measure, the **maternal mortality ratio** (**MMR**), gauges the extent to which mothers die immediately before, during, or after giving birth because of a problem or problems associated with the pregnancy or childbirth. The WHO (1982) defined a **maternal death** as "the death of a woman while pregnant or within 42 days of termination of pregnancy, irrespective of the duration or site of pregnancy, from any cause related to or aggravated by the pregnancy or its management, but not from accidental or incidental causes" (Maine and Stamas, 2003: 628). The MMR refers to deaths in a year to women dying as a result of complications of pregnancy, childbirth, and the puerperium (that is, the condition of the woman immediately following childbirth, usually ending when ovulation begins again), per 100,000 births occurring in the year. Sometimes the deaths (the numerator) are referred to as deaths due to puerperal causes. The MMR is the following:

$$MMR = \frac{\text{deaths in the year due to puerperal causes}}{\text{live births in the year}} * 100,000 \quad (5.13)$$

Observe that the MMR is multiplied by a constant of 100,000 because since 1940, maternal deaths have become increasingly rare in the developed world (Loudon, 1992). However, as we show in the following, the same may not be said about countries in the developing world.

The WHO (2004) has reported that there were an estimated 529,000 maternal deaths in the entire world in 2000, with about 251,000 in Africa and 253,000 in Asia. The MMR for the world for the year 2000 was estimated to be 400 per 100,000 live births. It was the highest in Africa (830), followed by Asia (330). The highest MMRs ranged from 2,000 in Sierra Leone, 1,900 in Afghanistan, 1,800 in Malawi, 1,700 in Angola, 1,600 in Niger, and 1,500 in the United Republic of Tanzania to 1,400 in Rwanda, 1,200 in Mali, and 1,100 in the Central African Republic, Chad, Guinea-Bissau, Somalia, and Zimbabwe. This means, for instance, that in Sierra Leone in 2000, 20 mothers died in the birthing process for every 1,000 babies born. With the exception of Afghanistan, all the countries with the highest MMRs are in Africa (World Health Organization, 2004: 10).

The lowest MMRs are 1 maternal death per 100,000 live births in Sweden; 3 in Austria, Denmark, Kuwait, and Spain; and 4 in Canada, Ireland, Italy, Portugal, and Switzerland. These are very low levels of maternal mortality. The MMR for the United States is 10 (World Health Organization, 2004: 16–17). The WHO has noted, however, that the number of maternal deaths reported for many of these developed countries are likely understated owing to the misclassification of maternal deaths, and should be inflated by a factor of around 1.5 (World Health Organization, 2004: 11). Regarding the MMR value of 10 in the United States, the *Healthy People 2010* program is endeavoring to reduce it by the year 2010 to a value of 4.3.

Maternal deaths in earlier centuries were very common, even in Europe and the United States. Reliable data on maternal mortality were not collected in the Western world until the mid-nineteenth century. Loudon (2000) has written that the levels were quite high until the 1930s: "The risk of women dying in childbirth in (England) in the 1920s and 1930s was still as high as it had been just after Queen Victoria came to the throne in the 1850s. Today, however, the risk of women in England and Wales dying is between 40 and 50 times lower than it was 60 years ago" (Loudon, 2000: 241S). Annual MMR data for the years of 1890 to 1950 are shown in Figure 5.13 for the United States, England and Wales, and Sweden. It was not until the middle to late 1930s that these countries, and many other developed countries, began to experience the dramatic declines that have resulted in the very low current levels reported here.

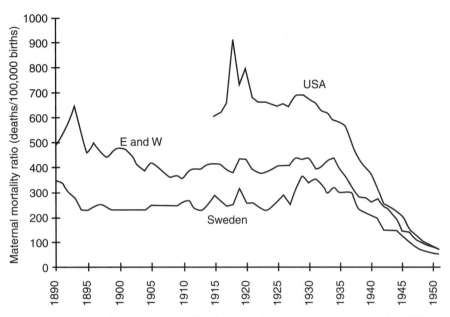

Figure 5.13. Annual maternal mortality ratios in the United States, England and Wales (E and W), and Sweden, 1890–1950. *Source:* Loudon, 2000: 242S.

The two most important factors leading to maternal deaths are age and **parity** (the number of times a woman has given birth; it also refers to **birth order,** for example, a second-born child, who would be a second-parity child). Very young women and older women are more likely to die during pregnancy or childbirth than are women in their twenties and thirties. High-parity women and women with short birth intervals are also at high risk: "Underlying these [factors] are such conditions as chronic disease and malnutrition, poverty, unwanted pregnancies, inadequate prenatal and obstetric care, and lack of access to a hospital" (Lamb and Siegel, 2004: 352).

THE FUTURE COURSE OF MORTALITY

Declining mortality has numerous social and economic implications. The efficiency and productivity of the labor force are increased because healthier adults can work better and longer. More surviving children translate into more potential and hopefully productive workers. Improved childhood survival often weakens and reduces the importance of some of the social, economic, and emotional rationales for high birth rates. At the same time, declining mortality has the direct effect of increasing rates of population growth, unless fertility rates fall as well; the mortality reductions will thus influence the population's age structure. Owing to these social, economic, and demographic implications, there is considerable speculation about the future levels of mortality.

Let us discuss future mortality trends in terms of life expectancy. We noted earlier the high levels of life expectancy reached in this new century by many of the countries of the developed world. In 2006, the developed world as a whole had a life expectancy at birth of 77 years (73 years for males, 80 for females). Japan's life expectancy of 82 years (79 for males, 86 for females) was the highest in the world, followed closely by Australia, Spain, Sweden, and Switzerland, all at 81 years (Population Reference Bureau, 2006).

Is it likely that mortality rates will continue to fall, resulting in even higher levels of life expectancy than those attained by these countries? There are two positions: One argues for a limit and the other argues against one.

A major advocate for an upper limit to human life expectancy is James Fries, who predicted in 1980 that humans have a maximum potential life expectancy averaging about 85 years (Fries, 1980; see also 1983). In a paper published in 2000, he commented on the increases in life expectancy that have occurred since 1980 when he made his stark prediction of 85 years, noting that life expectancy may increase a little beyond his earlier proclaimed average of 85 years, but not by much.

Jay Olshansky and Bruce Carnes (2001) support the contention of Fries and have noted that all living organisms are subjected to a "biological warranty" period. Arguing against an average life expectancy of, say, 100 years, they observed that "if most humans are capable of living to 100, there should be little evidence of significant functional decline and pathology" of older people today who reach ages older than 80. But they noted that there is no such evidence. Indeed, "there is substantial decline in functioning of all human biological systems by age 80" (Sonnega, 2006: 2). They have contended that human life expectancy in the United States is not likely to exceed 90 years at any time in this century (Olshansky et al., 2005).

The major proponent on the other side, proclaiming the real possibility of future and continued mortality declines, is the prominent demographer James Vaupel. He has observed that every time a maximum life expectancy number is published, it is soon surpassed. He and his colleagues have also reported that death rates in human and many nonhuman populations do not continue to increase with increasing age, but that there is a slowing or deceleration of mortality at the oldest ages (Carey, 2003; Carey and Vaupel, 2005; Carey et al., 1992).

Vaupel and his colleague Jim Oeppen have examined what they refer to as "best practice life expectancy" data. They have gathered and graphed data for every year from 1840 to 2000 for the six countries of the world

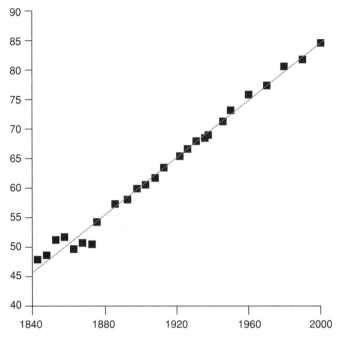

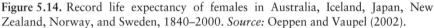

Figure 5.14. Record life expectancy of females in Australia, Iceland, Japan, New Zealand, Norway, and Sweden, 1840–2000. *Source:* Oeppen and Vaupel (2002).

with the highest recorded life expectancy (i.e., Australia, Iceland, Japan, New Zealand, Norway, and Sweden). We show their graph in Figure 5.14. Oeppen and Vaupel have noted that "the gap between the record [highest life expectancy] and the national level is a measure of how much better a country might do at current states of knowledge and demonstrated practice" (Oeppen and Vaupel 2002: 1029). The data in Figure 5.14 illustrate that female life expectancy has increased linearly by about three months per year (or 2.5 years per decade) between 1840 and 2000. Oeppen and Vaupel have extrapolated from this linear trend and predict that if it continues, the average life expectancy at birth for females could well reach 100 years by the year 2060.

We are inclined to take a position closer to that of Vaupel than to that of Fries. Our review of the arguments and the data lead us to conclude against a fixed biological maximum life expectancy. We contend that at the global level, life expectancy will surely increase in the decades of this new century. Whether female life expectancy will reach 100 years by 2060 is not as important as the expectation that it will not stagnate at just above 85. In recent empirical work in sixteen high-income countries, for instance, John Bongaarts has concluded that "the steady upward trend in senescent life expectancy in recent decades confirms the optimists' view that there is no evidence of approaching limits to longevity" (2006: 623). However,

Bongaarts has cautioned that this improvement has not been as great as that predicted by Oeppen and Vaupel (2002).

In the developing world, there will certainly be increases in life expectancy. Many of the developing countries still have high rates of infant mortality and general mortality, including maternal mortality. Infectious diseases remain a dominant cause of death in many of them. Modern medical and public health techniques will surely bring about further reductions in mortality from these causes. The developing countries have a very young age structure, and the young, more so than the old, have benefited and will continue to benefit from reductions in infectious and parasitic diseases. Consequently, further declines in mortality can be expected in many developing countries.

We need to temper this prediction with the realization that progress in reducing the force of mortality in some countries of the world has stalled and has even reversed direction. This phenomenon of **mortality reversals** is a relatively new occurrence in demography. When we authors of this text first began teaching demography to undergraduate students in 1970, evidence of significant mortality reversals was practically unknown. Demographic transition theory proposed, and it was widely believed, that once death rates in a country began to fall, they would never change direction and start to increase (see Chapter 9).

Since the early 1980s, however, we have seen more and more evidence of mortality reversals, first in some of the countries of Eastern Europe and later in sub-Saharan Africa. Russia and many of the countries of the former Soviet Union experienced mortality reversals in the 1980s and 1990s. Life expectancy for males in 2000 in Russia was 59 years, below its value of 60 in the mid-1950s. Meanwhile, other Western countries have increased their life expectancy in the decades of the last century. Life expectancy at birth in the United States increased from around 70 years in 1960 to more than 77 in the year 2000 (Arias, 2006).

What is causing the mortality reversals in Eastern Europe? Possible factors include the "lack of preventative health programs and inadequate quality of medical services; smoking and alcohol abuse; [and] general neglect of individual health." These were caused by "a lack of life choices under the former Communist regimes, [as well as by] unemployment, relative deprivation, and inability to cope with the economic challenges of post-Communist times" (Shkolnikov, 2003: 677).

In many sub-Saharan African countries, there have been drastic increases in mortality and consequent declines in life expectancy since the mid-1980s. Figure 5.15 shows mortality rates in the early years of this decade for children under age 5 per 1,000 live births for the countries of Lesotho, Namibia, South Africa, Swaziland, and Zimbabwe, along with

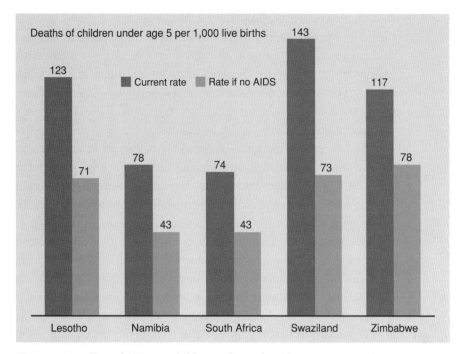

Figure 5.15. Effect of AIDS on child mortality, selected countries, 2002–2005. *Sources:* UN Population Division, *World Population Prospects: The 2004* Revision (2005); and UNAIDS and UNICEF, *A Call to Action: Children, the Missing Face of* AIDS (2005). Reproduced from Ashford (2006).

what the death rates would have been had there been no deaths to children via HIV/AIDS. The differences are striking. The mortality rates for young children are way above what they would be without HIV. In Swaziland, the rate is 143 deaths to children under age 5, per 1,000 live births, but without the presence of HIV/AIDS, the rate would have been 73. In Lesotho, 123 children under age 5 die for every 1,000 births, but without the presence of HIV/AIDS, this rate would be 71. In sub-Saharan Africa, "one-third of children who are born infected with HIV (transmitted through their mothers) die before their first birthday, and about 60 percent die by age 5" (Ashford, 2006: 2).

The AIDS epidemic has halted or reversed gains in life expectancy in many of the sub-Saharan African countries: "For example, in Lesotho, where one-fourth of adults were estimated to be living with HIV/AIDS in 2005, life expectancy was nearly 60 years in 1990–1995, but [will likely plummet] to 34 years by 2005–2010, primarily because of AIDS-related mortality" (Ashford, 2006: 2). Lesotho's life expectancy should have been around 69 years in a decade from now had the HIV/AIDS epidemic not hit the country. Instead, Lesotho's life expectancy will be 50 percent lower. The epidemic has taken a devastating toll on these countries.

Degenerative diseases are the major causes of death in the developed world. It is expected that there will be future improvements in the treatment of these diseases in the next decades. However, only a breakthrough in the area of the physiological process of aging will bring a substantial increase in the length of time people in the developed world will live. Even the total elimination of a specific degenerative disease, say, heart disease or cancer, would not greatly increase life expectancy.

The increases in life expectancy resulting from the elimination of a specific degenerative disease are small mainly because these diseases occur principally in the older age groups. The elimination of one degenerative disease will shift the cause of death from one degenerative disease to another, resulting in a gain in life expectancy of perhaps one or two years. We have already mentioned that the two leading causes of death in the developed world are heart disease and cancer. If heart disease were eliminated as a cause of death in the United States, life expectancy at birth there would increase only by five years. If cancer were eliminated, life expectancy would increase by only three years (Anderson, 1999: 7).

However, this does not necessarily mean that people will not live longer. They will live progressively longer as new medical advances occur and are implemented. But major medical advances, such as a cure for cancer, will not result in huge gains in life expectancy. Instead, it will result only in a modest improvement, as we showed in the previous paragraph, of about three years. This is because of a phenomenon known in demography as the **Taeuber paradox**, named after the demographer Conrad Taeuber, who pointed out many years ago that if a cure is found for one degenerative disease, this will provide the opportunity for death to occur from another. Or, in the words of Nathan Keyfitz, the demographer responsible for attributing the paradox to Taeuber:

> Everyone dies of something sooner or later, so that, when the effects of the eradication of cancer had shaken down, the same number of deaths would occur as before, and the only benefit would be the substitution of heart and other diseases for cancer. A cure for cancer would only have the effect of giving people the opportunity to die of heart disease. [Thus] all that this particular medical advance would do would be to increase the options: one could choose to die of heart disease rather than cancer."
> (Keyfitz, 1977b: 412; see also Rogers, Hummer, and Krueger, 2005).

Few demographers would claim that there will be no future improvements in life expectancy. Although we have experienced setbacks, principally in Eastern Europe and in sub-Saharan Africa, they will hopefully be of short duration.

We close this chapter with a pithy and optimistic observation advanced by Rogers, Hummer, and Krueger (2005: 305): "The question seems to be not whether mortality will improve in the future, but by how much it will improve, and what age, sex, race/ethnic, socioeconomic and geographical groups will reap the greatest benefits. Overall, continued improvements in health behavior, medical technology, and overall quality of life bode for a generally bright future, most likely with steady but deliberate increases in average length of life accompanied by an increasingly healthy population."

KEY TERMS

acquired immune deficiency
  syndrome (AIDS)
age-specific death rate (ASPR)
age curve of mortality
birth order
crude death rate (CDR)
endogenous cause of death
endogenous conditions
epidemic
epidemiological paradox
epidemiological transition
  theory (ETT)
exogenous cause of death
fetal death rate
geographic information systems
  (GIS)
germ theory
healthy migrant effect
Hispanic paradox
International Classification of
  Diseases (ICD)
infant mortality rate (IMR)

life expectancy
life span
life table
longevity
maternal death
maternal mortality ratio (MMR)
median age
mortality reversal
neonatal mortality rate (NMR)
obituary
pandemic
parity
perinatal mortality rate (PeMR)
postneonatal mortality rate
  (PMR)
salmon bias
stable population theory
standardization
stillbirth
stillbirth rate (SBR)
Taeuber paradox

6 | Internal Migration

In previous chapters, we discussed two of the three ways that populations change their size by adding or subtracting members. People are added to a population through births and are taken away through deaths. We now turn to the third and last way that populations change their size, namely, *migration*. Persons may be added to a population by moving into it or subtracted by moving away from it. Unlike birth and death, which occur to each of us once and only once, migration may occur on multiple occasions, or we may never experience migration.

There are two main types of migration, namely, within a country and between countries; the former is **internal migration**, and the latter, **international migration**. The dynamics of the two kinds of migration differ significantly, and many of their concepts and theories are also different. We will see that although their theories are more or less governed by "push" and "pull" factors, they differ in their emphasis and focus. In this chapter, we focus on internal migration; in Chapter 7, we cover international migration.

Internal migration is the change of permanent **residence** within a country, involving a geographical move that crosses a political boundary, usually a county or county-type geographical unit. Not all changes in residence are migrations, however. Indeed, demographers distinguish between "movers" and "migrants." Any person who changes residence, whether the change involves moving across the street or from Maine to Hawaii, is a mover. A migrant is a person whose residential move involves the crossing of a political boundary. The U.S. Bureau of the Census defines migration occurring within the United States as "a move that crosses jurisdictional boundaries. Local moves – for instance, those within a county, are considered residential mobility" (2006: 1). The definition of an internal migrant as one whose change in residence involves moving from one county to another is generally the definition used worldwide; any persons who change residence by moving from one county (or county-type unit) to another is a migrant. Bear in mind that all migrants are movers, but all movers are not necessarily migrants.

Virtually all of us, at least one time in our lives, will be migrants. And usually this happens early in our lives, not later. In modern industrialized countries such as the United States, nearly everyone experiences migration. Since the 1970s, we authors of this text have been teaching demography courses to undergraduate and graduate students in a half-dozen different universities. Of the many thousands of students we have taught, we have found that fewer than a dozen had not yet migrated by the time they took our courses. And, if we broaden the concern from migration to **residential mobility**, the two of us can remember teaching only a couple of students who had never ever moved; that is, they had never moved from the homes in which they lived as infants. Residential mobility and migration affect and will continue to affect virtually all of us.

Migration is a significant event not only for persons but for communities as well. Migration from one area to another has the effect of decreasing the size of the population in the **area of origin** and increasing it in the **area of destination**. Concerning the dynamics of population growth for communities, internal migration is the single most important of the three demographic processes (i.e., fertility, mortality, and migration). Differences in birth rates and death rates between communities of the same country are usually small compared to differences between the communities in migration. Migration is the major method for redistributing the population within a country (Bogue, 1969; Poston and Frisbie, 2005; Poston, Luo, and Zhang, 2006).

Let us start with a few facts about movers and migrants in the United States. Each year since 1947, the U.S. Census Bureau has conducted a survey of the population to determine each member's place of residence one year before the survey date (see Chapter 2 for our discussion of the Current Population Survey). The most remarkable feature of these survey data is their stability over time. There have been no substantial trends, either downward or upward. Each year, about one of every five Americans moves from one house to another, and about one of every fourteen Americans migrates from one county to another (Schachter, Franklin, and Perry, 2003). About half of these migrants move from one state to another. The cumulative effect of this mobility is striking. Some people move many times during their lives; others do not. Americans average about thirteen changes of residence, as well as four migrations, during their lifetimes (Long and Boertlein, 1976). The **geographic mobility** rates in the United States are comparable to those in Canada and Australia, but are much higher than those in many other developed countries like Sweden, Ireland, and Japan. Of course, these latter countries are much smaller geographically than the United States, Canada, and Australia.

The next sections of this chapter cover the basic concepts and definitions used in analyses of internal migration, followed by a discussion of the main theories of internal migration. We conclude the chapter with three detailed discussions of domestic migration in the United States, of temporary internal migration in China, and of the major migration streams in both countries.

CONCEPTS AND DEFINITIONS

Over the years, demographers have developed a standard set of concepts and definitions for studying internal migration. The most basic distinction, already mentioned, is between migration and **local movement**. Local movement is the short-distance change of residence within the same community that does not involve crossing a county jurisdictional boundary. Migration is the geographical movement resulting in the permanent change of residence that involves the crossing of a county boundary. Migration differs from local movement in that a migrant leaves his/her community and moves to a new community. Such a move also usually involves other changes: in one's school, job, church, doctor, dentist, library, pub, shopping center, nightclub, automobile mechanic, and other institutional aspects of daily life. In contrast, with local movement, a permanent change in residence does not involve changing the main institutions in the mover's daily life. "It is customary to define migration as intercounty mobility" because county units, most of the time, "correspond most nearly to the average size of a community" (Bogue, 1969: 756). A person's residential move from one county to another most likely will involve changes in the institutions that govern daily life as well. A migration, but not necessarily a local movement, is a sociological event of major magnitude.

A residential move, be it a local move or a migration, is necessarily defined as a "change in permanent residence, typically of a year or more in duration" (Frey, 2003: 545). Most countries have few or no restrictions on the internal movement of its peoples. In the United States, for example, we are free to move to wherever we wish and whenever we wish. However, in China and in a few other countries, for example, North Korea, internal migration is tightly controlled. In these few countries, therefore, internal migrants may be classified as either permanent migrants or temporary migrants.

A *permanent migrant* in China is the same as a permanent migrant elsewhere; the migration involves a permanent change in residence and the crossing of a county boundary. The difference in China is that the permanent migration must first be approved by the government. A *temporary migrant* in China, and in the few other countries where internal migration is heavily controlled, is one whose residential move does not have governmental approval. In other words, the temporary migrant moves without permission. However, in many if not most cases, the migration is not temporary but becomes permanent, or relatively permanent. Nevertheless, it is a migration that is not officially sanctioned. Later, we discuss in more detail this phenomenon of temporary migration in China, referred to by the Chinese as "floating" migration, which is especially important because its volume is so great. The 2000 Census of China counted more than 140 million temporary internal migrants in the country. The internal migration of "floaters" to China's cities is the largest stream of peacetime mobility in recorded human history (Roberts, 1997).

Other concepts used by demographers in their studies of internal migration are the following: **In-migration** refers to the residential migration of persons to an area of destination; **out-migration** refers to the migration of persons from an area of origin. The area of origin is the area or community where the migration began, and the area of destination is the area or community where the migration ended. **Return migration** is the migration of persons back to their area of origin at some time after their initial out-migration.

Net migration refers to the migration balance of an area, consisting of the number of in-migrants minus the number of out-migrants; the *net balance* may be positive (representing a net population gain to the area) or negative (representing a net loss) or, conceivably, zero (Poston, Luo, and Zhang, 2006). Every time we migrate, we are simultaneously an in-migrant and an out-migrant. But we are never a net migrant. The net migration concept applies only to populations and geographic areas, not to individuals. In contrast, the concepts of in-migration, out-migration, and return migration apply to both persons and geographic areas.

Like the concept of net migration, several other migration concepts apply only to geographic areas. *Gross migration* is the sum of migration for an area and is comprised of the in-migration into the area plus the out-migration from the area. *Migration efficiency* is an area's net migration divided by its gross migration. Migration in an area may be efficient or inefficient. For example, if there has been a lot of in-migration and little out-migration (i.e., most of the migrants have moved in and very few have moved out), then the migration is *positively efficient*. This is a case with little turnover of people, that is, not much milling around. In contrast, the migration could be *negatively efficient* if there has been very little in-migration and a lot of out-migration. Migration is not effective (it is *inefficient*) for an area when there are about the same numbers of persons migrating into the area as there are persons migrating out of the area (Shryock, 1964; Thomas, 1941). High negative migration efficiency characterizes areas of economic hardship, whereas high positive efficiency is often found in areas experiencing economic expansion (Bogue, 1969: 784).

A **migration stream** is a body of migrants departing from a common area of origin and arriving at a common area of destination during a specified time interval. A **migration counterstream** is the migration stream, smaller in size, going in the opposite direction during the same time interval. Later, we discuss the main migration streams in the United States and China.

A *migration interval* refers to the time period during which the migration occurs. Because migration is a process that occurs over time, its analysis requires that time be broken into intervals, so that migration data may be assembled separately for each interval. Time intervals of one year, five years, or ten years are commonly used in studies of internal migration. Irrespective of the length of the intervals chosen by the researcher, they need to be consistent in the analysis: "Two or more sets of migration statistics that have been collected for unequal intervals of time are therefore not fully comparable" (Bogue, 1969: 757).

Differential migration refers to the study of differences in migration according to the demographic, social, and economic characteristics of the population. This is also known as **migration selectivity** and points to the fact that some persons are more likely to migrate than others. The strongest selectivity factor associated with both migration and local movement is age: "The incidence of making each kind of move is highest for persons in their early to middle twenties and then declines precipitously during the thirties and forties, with a sometimes small upturn in the early retirement years" (Frey, 2003: 546). Other selectivity factors vary according to whether the change in residence involves a migration or a local move. Among migrants, there is "strong educational selectivity in movement. College graduates, who are likely to be in a national labor market, show higher (migration) rates . . . than do those with lesser educational attainment. [In contrast], among local movers, there is a large difference between homeowners and renters" (Frey, 2003: 546). Homeowners are much less likely to engage in local moves than are renters. We discuss migration selectivity in more detail later in the context of domestic migration in the United States.

Many of these concepts are used by demographers in the different ways they measure migration. In the next section, we consider a few of these measures and some of the issues involved in measuring migration.

MEASURES OF MIGRATION

There are inherent difficulties in measuring migration that are not generally encountered when analyzing fertility or mortality. Births and deaths are registered at the time of occurrence, but generally the residential movement of a person is not. A few countries, for example, China and those in Scandinavia, require people to register with government officials when they move from one place to another. In most countries, including the United States, there are no such requirements; thus, it is necessary to rely on other types of data for measuring migration.

The U.S. census of population contains two useful items that demographers use to measure migration, namely, the state of birth and the place of residence five years prior to the census. By comparing one's state of birth with one's place of residence at the time of enumeration, it is possible to divide people into the following categories:

1. Those living in a given state and born there;
2. Those living in a given state but born somewhere else; and
3. Those born in a given state but living in some other state.

People in the first category are referred to as *nonmigrants*, or *natives*. People in the second and third categories are classified as *lifetime migrants*. A caveat is needed here. Just because a person lived in, say, Connecticut in 2000 as well as in 2005 does not necessarily mean that the person did not move during the interval and then return to the original state. The same caution applies to place of birth and place of residence at the time of the most recent census.

Data concerning people in these categories can be used to estimate the presence (and size) of migration streams. It is also possible to estimate the proportion of a state's population that was born elsewhere. The "holding power" of a state (or region) can be estimated by calculating the percentage of the people born there who still live there when the census is taken.

Having information about one's residence five years before the census date makes possible the determination of the proportion of a state's population that moved into the state within the past five years. People in this category are known as *recent migrants*.

Measures of migration are usually developed as rates that show empirically the relative frequency of a certain kind of migration. Four of the migration concepts presented here lead directly to rates, and one to a ratio, as follows:

in-migration rate (IMR) $= (I / P) * 1{,}000$

out-migration rate (OMR) $= (O / P) * 1{,}000$

net migration rate (NMR) = [(I − O) / P] ∗ 1,000

gross migration rate (GMR) = [(I + O) / P] ∗ 1,000

migration efficiency ratio (MER) = [(I − O) / (I + O)] ∗ 100

where I refers to the number of in-migrants moving into an area during a certain time interval (usually 1 or 5 or 10 years); O refers to the number of out-migrants moving out of an area during a certain time interval; and P is the denominator and refers to the midyear or average size of the population of the area.

Determining the statistically correct denominator in calculating migration rates can be troublesome. Ideally, every individual in the denominator should have an equal chance to perform the event in the numerator. Obviously, this is not the case with respect to domestic IMRs, where, strictly speaking, the denominator should be the entire U.S. population, excluding the resident population in the area of destination. To make issues of comparison among the migration rates easier, demographers usually use as the denominator for all migration rates the resident population of the area for which the rate is being calculated. As indicated, the four rates are usually multiplied by a constant of 1,000, and the migration efficiency ratio by a constant of 100.

Donald J. Bogue (1969: 758) noted that the OMR is analogous to the crude death rate, and the IMR to the crude birth rate. The parallel to the NMR is the rate of natural increase/decrease. All of these rates may be computed not only for the total population but also for specific subgroups of the population, for example, sex groups, age groups, race groups, and so forth. They may also be calculated for specific education groups and occupational groups.

We now present examples of these migration measures for a few selected states of the United States. In a later section, we provide a more detailed discussion of internal migration flows among the regions and the states of the United States.

Table 6.1 presents domestic migration data for California, Nevada, New York, and Texas for the period 1995 to 2000. The upper panel of the table shows the migration-flow data for each of the four states, and the lower panel, the five migration measures. Between 1995 and 2000, California received more than 1.4 million migrants from other states; for every 1,000 persons in California's population in 2000, 47.1 were in-migrants. By comparison, during the same time period, 2.2 million migrants departed from California for other states, or nearly 72 persons per 1,000 population. The total number of migrants entering and leaving California during this period, that is, gross migration, was almost 3.7 million. Finally, California lost through migration more than 755,000 persons than it gained

Table 6.1. State-to-state domestic migration between 1995 and 2000: California, Nevada, New York, and Texas

| State | Migration flows | | | |
	In-migrants	Out-migrants	Gross migrants	Net migrants
California	1,448,964	2,204,500	3,653,464	−755,536
Nevada	466,123	232,189	698,312	233,934
New York	726,477	1,600,725	2,327,202	−874,246
Texas	1,362,849	1,214,609	2,577,458	148,240

| State | Migration measures | | | | |
	IMR	OMR	GMR	NMR	MER
California	47.1	71.7	118.8	−24.6	−20.7
Nevada	301.8	150.3	452.1	151.5	33.5
New York	40.6	89.4	130.0	−48.8	−37.5
Texas	74.2	66.1	140.3	8.1	5.8

IMR = In-migration rate
OMR = Out-migration rate
GMR = Gross migration rate
NMR = Net migration rate
MER = Migration efficiency ratio
Source: Franklin, 2003.

through migration; that is, between 1995 and 2000, 755,000 more persons departed from California for other states of the United States than entered California from other states. California's net migration rate (NMR) was −24.6, indicating that for every 1,000 persons in the population in 2000, there was a loss of almost 25 persons through net migration. California's MER was −20.7. For every 100 migrants to and from California during the period, there was a loss of almost 21 migrants.

Of all the states in the United States, Nevada, one of the states in Table 6.1, has the highest positive NMR; it gained more than 151 persons through net migration for every 1,000 members of its population. New York had one of the largest negative NMRs, losing nearly 49 persons during the 1995–2000 period for every 1,000 members of its population. The state with the largest negative NMR of all the U.S. states (not shown in the table) was Hawaii, with a NMR of −65.4. The District of Columbia had an even larger negative NMR of −81.7 (Franklin, 2003: 2–4).

Regarding migration efficiency, of the four states shown in Table 6.1, Nevada reported the highest positive efficiency ratio of 33.5, and New York the highest negative efficiency ratio of −37.5. The MER for Texas was the lowest, a ratio of 5.8. In other words, for Texas there was a lot of coming into and leaving the state, which produced a net gain of only 6 persons for every 100 migrants. Migration was rather inefficient in Texas. There was a lot of milling around, that is, coming and going, that ended up in a very small net gain.

Having discussed the major concepts, definitions, and measures used in the analysis of internal migration, we next consider some of the main theories developed by demographers to account for the reasons why people move or do not move, and why some areas grow through migration and others do not.

THEORIES OF INTERNAL MIGRATION

We learned in earlier chapters that fertility and mortality both occur in response to biological/genetic and social factors. For example, the likelihood that a woman will have a child is due in part to her fecundity (biological) and in part to her education (social). Migration, however, has no such biological or genetic component. There is no genetic propensity in people favoring or not favoring residential change. The likelihood that a person will or will not move is due entirely to factors in the physical and social environment at the areas of origin and destination and to personal factors.

Bogue (1969: 753) wrote that the

> human organism tends to remain at rest [that is, in the same residential location] until impelled to action by some unsatisfied need or by the threat of discomfort.... Migration [theories thus begin] with the premise that every departure for a new community, i.e., migratory movement, is either a response to some impelling need that the person believes cannot be satisfied in his/her present residence, or is a flight from a situation that for some reason has become undesirable, unpleasant, or intolerable.

The question of who migrates depends in large part on what are referred to as "push" and "pull" factors. In every consideration of migration, there is usually some combination of factors pushing or not pushing the person from the area of origin and pulling or not pulling the person to the area of destination. **Migration push** factors include loss of a job; discrimination; low availability of social and life partners; community catastrophes such as a flood, epidemic, or hurricane; and so forth. **Migration pull** factors include better chances for employment, education, or income; gentler environment in terms of climate and living conditions, as well as race and sexual orientation; the lure of new or different types of activities; and so forth (Bogue, 1969: 753–754; Lee, 1966).

Demographers have shown that migrants who respond mainly to pull factors at the place of destination tend to be "positively" selected. They generally have more education than those who remain behind (Bouvier, Macisco, and Zarate, 1976). Hence, their departure lowers the overall level of educational attainment in the area of origin and often deprives the area of persons with skills that might be very useful. These migrants tend to be more innovative and are often better planners. Indeed, that is one reason why they chose to move in the first place. They view alternative modes of behavior (e.g., moving from farm to city) and explore them. To the extent that this selectivity is present, the area of origin loses a valuable segment of its population (Macisco, Bouvier, and Weller, 1970).

On the other hand, migrants responding mainly to push factors in the area of origin tend to be "negatively" selected. They are the people who cannot seem to succeed, either because of poor education or lack of needed talents. They are, in a sense, almost forced to leave in order to better their lot in life. They tend to have fewer of the positive characteristics valued in the society. Other things being equal, the area of origin is changed positively by the out-migration of such people (Bouvier, Macisco, and Zarate, 1976).

Everett S. Lee (1966) noted, however, that there is more to migration than a person's calculating the advantages and disadvantages, the positives and the negatives, at both the areas of origin and destination. There are also intervening obstacles that must be considered. Between every two possible areas of origin and destination are various obstacles that may or may not intervene and have an impact on whether the migration will occur. One is distance; other things being equal, the greater the distance between two areas, the less likely the migration. Physical barriers and migration laws may also reduce the likelihood of migration.

Thus, at both the origin and the destination, there are positive and negative factors that the migrant considers when deciding whether or not to migrate. Between the origin and destination are obstacles that may or may not influence the migration decision. The pushes and pulls are thus evaluated in light of the costs of overcoming the intervening obstacles.

Many of the specific theories of internal migration used by demographers to better understand the dynamics of migration begin with this framework; each theory tends to focus more on certain pushes, pulls, or obstacles than on others. The main theoretical models seek to explain internal migration in terms of 1) the effects of distance, 2) income, 3) the physical costs of migration, 4) information, 5) personal characteristics, 6) individual expectations, and 7) community and kinship ties (Poston, Luo, and Zhang, 2006).

As already mentioned, the distance model states that long distance discourages migration (Lee, 1966) because the costs involved in migration are substantial and are closely related to distance. The income model argues that income and job opportunities provide a better explanation of in-migration than they do for out-migration (Perloff et al., 1960); destination characteristics also help determine the location to which the migrant will move (Poston and Frisbie, 2005). The physical costs model suggests that physical costs influence resource allocation and migration by influencing the private costs of migration (Greenwood, 1975). The information model emphasizes that "the availability of information concerning alternative localities plays a prominent role in the potential migrant's decision regarding a destination" (Greenwood, 1975: 405). The personal characteristics model argues that personal demographic characteristics (e.g., age, sex, education, number of dependents, networks, and race) exert important influences on the individual's decision or propensity to migrate (Findley, 1987; Grieco and Boyd, 1998; Nam, Serow, and Sly, 1990). The individual expectations model assumes that the dynamics of migration decision making are based on individual expectations about the advantages and disadvantages of the home community versus possible alternative destination communities (Fischer, Martin, and Straubhaar, 1997). The community and kinship ties model points out that "the presence of relatives and friends is a valued aspect of life [that] . . . encourages migration by increasing the individual's potential for adjustment through the availability of aid in location at an alternative area of residence" (Ritchey, 1976: 389).

These theories focus mainly on individuals and why they move or do not move. Demographers have developed other kinds of theories that focus less on individuals per se than on populations and their geographic areas. Rather than asking why individuals move, the aggregate theories ask why some areas increase in population size through migration, why others decrease through migration, and why still others are not influenced one way or the other via migration. Sociological human ecology provides a perspective for considering the effects of migration on populations and geographic areas.

From the perspective of human ecology, migration is the major mechanism of social change and adaptability for human populations. Knowledge of migration patterns tells us about how "populations . . . maintain themselves in particular areas" (Hawley 1950: 149). The ecological approach asserts that human populations redistribute themselves via net migration in order to attain an equilibrium between their overall size and the life chances available to them (Poston and Frisbie 1998: 30; 2005).

The theoretical foundation of human ecology is based on the interdependence of the four conceptual rubrics of population, organization, environment, and technology. The interrelationships among and between these dimensions inform our understanding of migration patterns. All populations adapt to their environments, and these adaptations vary among populations according to their social and sustenance organization; their technology; and the size, composition, and distribution of their population. The environment is comprised of both social and physical factors, and it sets constraints on the population and the form and characteristics of its organization. The technology at the population's disposal sets the boundaries for the form and type of environmental adaptation that the population assumes. Human ecology posits that of the three demographic processes, migration is the most efficient agent for returning the human ecosystem to a state of equilibrium, or balance, between its size and organization (Poston and Frisbie, 1998, 2005).

An hypothesis typically investigated in ecological studies of migration (e.g., Poston and Frisbie, 1998; Saenz and Colberg, 1988) is that variability among human groups in their patterns of migration is a function of differences in their patterns of sustenance organization, technology, environment, and population. The **ecological theory of migration** thus focuses on characteristics of the population group to predict the level of migration. Individual attitudes and propensities do not play a role in these theories.

Finally, most theories of internal migration, both individual-level theories and aggregate theories, have been influenced in one way or another by the very early work of E. G. Ravenstein who endeavored in two articles written in 1885 and 1889 to identify the so-called *laws of migration*. Ravenstein set forth many laws or theorems of migration based largely on his research in England and a few other countries. Included are the following: 1) Migration is affected by distance; most migrants move only short distances. 2) Migrants often move in stages; as they leave one area, their places are filled by migrants from more distant areas. 3) Every migration stream has a compensating counterstream. 4) Migrants proceeding long distances often stop, temporarily, at major cities or centers of commerce that are located between the area of origin and the intended area of destination. 5) Urban residents are less likely to migrate than rural residents. 6) Females are more likely to migrate than males.

We turn now to three discussions of aspects of migration mentioned earlier. We consider domestic migration flows in the United States, the temporary or **floating migrant** population in China, and migration streams in the United States and China.

DOMESTIC MIGRATION IN THE UNITED STATES

Overall trends

In Chapter 11 on population distribution, we note that the major interregional flows of internal migrants in the United States have been from east to west and from north to south. During the nineteenth and early twentieth centuries, there was a steady movement westward as new areas beyond the Mississippi River were settled. With the exception of California, migration into the western states diminished during the first half of the twentieth century. Since then, it has accelerated considerably. Between 1970 and 1978, the western region of the United States had a net in-migration of 1.4 million people; that is, 1.4 million more people entered the region than left it. This was sufficient to account for almost half of the population increase in that area during that time period.

The southern region of the country had long been an exporter of people, from late in the nineteenth century until well into the 1960s. Long the most underdeveloped and rural area of the nation, the South lagged behind as industrialization surged in the North (Biggar, 1979). The movement from south to north offered an example of rural to urban migration. Blacks often left behind limited economic opportunities in rural areas of the South to find jobs in the big cities of the North (Hamilton, 1964). The adjustment problems facing those migrants were enormous as they tried to adapt to big-city norms of living. The move also contributed to the development of the urban ghetto and its attendant problems.

In recent decades, the trend of movement out of the South has been reversed. The region gained 2.6 million people through migration between 1970 and 1975, compared to only 400,000 in the previous five-year period (Biggar, 1979). The trend has continued. More than 1 million additional people moved into the South than left the region between 1975 and 1978. Net migration into the South amounted to 3.8 million in the 1990s. Since then, more than 1.4 million more people moved into the South than left it between 2000 and 2004. Overall, this indicates that annual net migration into the South since 1990 has averaged around 350,000 people annually (Table 6.2).

The entire southern region is gaining migrants; previously, only the large numbers of migrants into Florida offset net out-migration from the rest of the region. Between 1990 and 2000, and again between 2000 and 2004, states like North and South Carolina, Georgia, and Virginia have exhibited significant amounts of positive net migration. As Table 6.2 indicates, most of the growth in the southern region has taken place in the South Atlantic division. (See the map in Figure 6.1 showing the regions, divisions, and states of the United States.)

Note, too, that while the West region showed positive net migration, it was mainly because of rapid growth in the Mountain division. The Pacific division lost population through net migration between 1990 and 2004 primarily because of large out-migration from California (also shown in Table 6.1). Conversely, the Northeast and Midwest both saw more people leave than enter for the entire period 1990–2004.

Table 6.2. Total and average annual domestic net migration for regions and divisions – 1990–2000 and 2000–2004

Region/division	Total number		Average annual #		Average annual rate	
	1990–2000	2000–2004	1990–2000	2000–2004	1990–2000	2000–2004
Northeast	**−3,144,570**	**−987,262**	**−314,457**	**−246,816**	**−6.1**	**−4.6**
New England	−495,961	−113,536	−49,596	−28,384	−3.7	−2.0
Middle Atlantic	−2,648,609	−873,726	−264,861	−218,432	−7.0	−5.5
Midwest	**−730,087**	**−644,792**	**−73,009**	**−161,198**	**−1.2**	**−2.5**
East North Central	−844,723	−533,163	−84,472	−133,291	−1.9	−2.9
West North Central	144,636	−111,629	11,464	−27,907	0.6	−1.4
South	**3,801,093**	**1,411,172**	**380,109**	**352,793**	**4.1**	**3.4**
South Atlantic	2,538,633	1,250,540	253,863	312,635	5.4	5.8
East South Central	629,824	78,435	62,982	19,609	3.9	1.1
West South Central	632,636	82,197	63,264	20,549	2.2	0.6
West	**73,564**	**220,882**	**7,356**	**55,221**	**0.1**	**0.8**
Mountain	1,804,226	523,353	180,423	130,809	11.6	6.9
Pacific	−1,703,662	−302,353	−173,066	−75,588	−4.1	−1.6

Source: Perry, 2006.

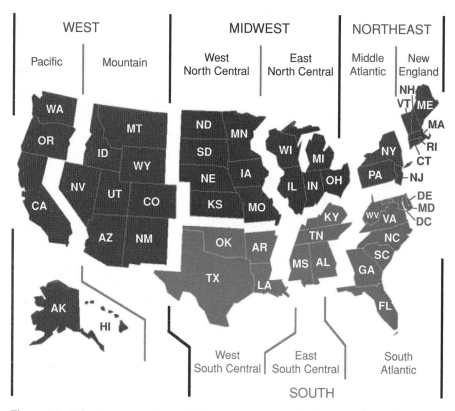

Figure 6.1. U.S. Census regions, divisions, and states. *Source:* Energy Information Administration, available at http://www.eia.doe.gov/emeu/reps/maps/us_census.html (accessed January 14, 2008).

In sum, at this broad geographic level, the pattern is one of net out-migration from the Northeast and the Midwest and net in-migration to the South. Within the Northeast, New England continued to experience net out-migration between 2000 and 2004, but at lower levels than during the 1990s. In the West, net in-migration continued to the Mountain division and net out-migration occurred from the Pacific division. In both cases, these trends moderated the pace of the 1990s. The South continued to have the most net in-migration of any region due to the continued higher levels of net in-migration to the South Atlantic division. Net in-migration to the East South Central and West South Central divisions dropped from their respective average annual levels in the 1990s.

Turning to the state level, Florida had the largest amount of net in-migration of any state, averaging 191,000 per year (Figure 6.2). Arizona and Nevada were the next highest receivers of migrants. New York had the largest annual net out-migration (183,000 per year); California and Illinois were second and third in line. Some migration patterns were different in the

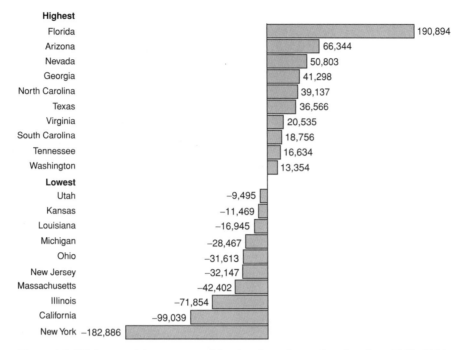

Figure 6.2. Highest and lowest annual levels of net domestic migration: 2000–2004. *Source:* Perry, 2006.

2000–2004 period than in the previous decade. Rhode Island, for example, switched from being a net out-migration state to a net in-migration state. While California continued to experience net out-migration in the later period, its average annual level fell from 221,000 to 99,000. Conversely, Florida increased its in-migration level from 112,000 to 191,000 per year. In general, although with some exceptions, the state patterns reflect those noted for the regions and divisions of the United States.

Migration selectivity

We noted earlier the concept of migration selectivity. This essentially refers to the fact that migrants are not all alike. For example, migration is selective on the basis of age, race, sex, and socioeconomic status. Let us look first at age. Table 6.3 shows the selectivity of mobility and migration by age in 2000. Young adults between the ages of 20 and 29, as well as slightly older adults between the ages of 30 and 39, were more likely to move than anyone else. Those between 20 and 29 leave their family home to seek employment or to attend college. This is also a time when couples get married, which generally involves at least one residential move, if not two.

Table 6.3. Gross and net migration for U.S. population 5 years and over – 2000					
			Different residence 5 years ago		
Age group	Total population (5 and over)	Same residence (nonmovers)	Total movers	Different residence – same area	From abroad
	262,375,152	142,027,478	120,347,674	112,851,828	7,495,846
5 to 9	20,608,282	9,454,270	11,154,012	10,584,770	569,242
10 to 14	20,618,199	11,412,521	9,205,678	8,690,688	514,990
15 to 19	19,911,052	10,905,856	9,005,196	8,221,116	784,080
20 to 24	19,025,980	5,775,043	13,250,937	12,036,005	1,214,932
25 to 29	19,212,244	4,502,548	14,709,696	13,496,068	1,213,628
30 to 34	20,365,113	6,784,152	13,580,961	12,675,662	905,299
35 to 39	23,083,337	10,728,984	12,354,353	11,653,668	700,685
40 to 44	22,822,134	13,007,932	9,814,202	9,314,428	499,774
45 to 49	20,181,127	13,000,521	7,180,606	6,842,874	337,732
50 to 54	17,397,482	11,971,663	5,425,819	5,194,184	231,635
55 to 59	13,383,251	9,649,713	3,733,538	3,578,613	154,925
60 to 64	10,787,979	8,002,390	2,785,589	2,660,793	124,796
65 to 69	9,569,199	7,369,323	2,199,876	2,110,393	89,483
70 to 74	8,931,950	7,093,431	1,838,519	1,775,286	63,233
75 to 79	7,385,783	5,840,932	1,544,851	1,505,089	39,762
80 to 84	4,931,479	3,727,575	1,203,904	1,178,615	25,289
85 and over	4,160,561	2,800,624	1,359,937	1,333,576	26,361

Source: Schachter, Franklin, and Perry, 2003.

The continuing high level of residential movement beyond age 29 differs from previous decades. These days, people are getting married at later ages and divorces are quite common; also, more people are switching jobs. The level of residential movement is also high among the very young. This, of course, reflects the fact that the young are moving with their parents, who themselves are relatively young. Beginning at around age 40, levels of residential mobility and migration drop considerably. The older the people are, the less likely they are to move. There is sometimes a slight surge at around the retirement age of 65, but this trend is not reflected in the data shown in Table 6.3. This lack of an increase in residential mobility at the age of retirement owes in part to the fact that more and more people these days continue working beyond the age of 65 (like the two authors of this text).

For decades after the Civil War, blacks out-migrated from the South, first to the Northeast and later to the Pacific Coast. As recently as 1965–1970, the number of blacks leaving the South was 2.3 times greater than the number coming into the region. Since the 1970s, however, there has been a dramatic turnaround. Between 1995 and 2000, the net migration of blacks into the South amounted to more than 350,000.

Mobility differences between races are minor. Between 2004 and 2005, about 14 percent of the U.S. population moved. However, blacks were somewhat more likely to move locally than were whites. Young blacks are a little more likely to move than others.

Generally speaking, the greater a person's education, the more likely he or she will migrate. Indeed, the farther the move, the stronger the role that education plays in the decision to move. White-collar workers are the most migratory occupational group. Manual workers tend to be as mobile, but their moves are more likely to be local. Farm and service workers are the least-mobile occupational group. People not in the labor force have high mobility. This, of course, is attributed in part to the fact that many are looking for a position in the labor force.

In summary, migration is not randomly distributed. Certain kinds of people are more likely to move than others; some move short distances and others move long distances. Whatever the nature of the moves, there are certain consequences for the areas involved. We now consider some of them.

Consequences of domestic migration

Contrary to fertility and mortality, migration affects two areas: the place of origin and the place of destination. In addition, moving affects the individual lives of movers and nonmovers alike. Often, the consequences for the individual migrant differ from those of the aggregate population. For example, with increased immigration to the United States from Latin America into cities not generally prepared for such newcomers, the experience can be difficult for both the newcomer and the longtime residents of the cities. Let us consider some of these influences at both the origin and destination.

One way that migration affects the area of origin is by reducing its potential for population growth. This can happen in two ways. People who move out of an area represent negative entries in the demographic equation that we discussed in Chapter 2. (The use of the demographic equation to estimate net migration is shown in Box 6.1.) This loss may at least partially compensate for any reproductive increase that occurs. However, as we have seen, those who move out of an area tend to be in the young childbearing age group, which thus tends to reduce the reproductive potential of the population at origin.

BOX 6.1   ESTIMATING NET MIGRATION

In Chapter 1 in formula (1.1), we illustrate the demographic equation:

$$P_2 - P_1 = (B - D) + (I - O)$$

Using the same equation, we can derive the vital statistics method of estimating net migration:

$$(I - O) = P_2 - P_1 - (B - D)$$

- P_1 is the population size at an earlier date
- P_2 is the population size at a later date
- B is the number of births
- D is the number of deaths
- I is the number of in-migrants
- O is the number of out-migrants

B − D = natural increase; I − O = net migration;
Net migration = population growth minus natural increase

Most large cities in the United States owe their population declines to out-migration, not to an excess of deaths over births. The area of origin is affected as well by the type of people who migrate. The question of who migrates depends in part on whether the migration is a response to push or pull factors. We noted earlier that migrants responding to pull factors at the place of destination tend to be positively selected, and migrants responding to push factors in the area of origin tend to be negatively selected.

With regard to the area of destination, migration tends to increase the population in two ways, directly and indirectly. The net number of in-migrants constitutes the direct effect. The number of children born to these in-migrants after their arrival is the indirect effect. The magnitude of the direct effect depends on the relative size of the migrant and the receiving populations. Adding ten people to New York City has far less of an impact on the area of destination than adding ten people to Tonopah, a small mining town in Nevada. The magnitude of the indirect effect depends on the relative levels of reproductive behavior of the migrants and the receiving population. If the in-migrants have considerably more children than those already living in the area of destination, then there will be a larger impact on that area.

Each person added to the population means an additional individual who must be fed, clothed, housed, educated, transported, and given at least occasional medical care. Massive in-migration can put a severe strain on the receiving area to deliver these services. This is particularly true if the original population size of the area is relatively small. The extent to which the strains become real problems depends on the socioeconomic characteristics of the in-migrants and the extent to which the labor force can absorb the newcomers.

In-migration affects the size of the labor force in two ways. First, because of the age composition of the migrants, in-migration may increase the ratio of the economically active persons to the total number of persons. To be sure, there are exceptions, especially in retirement areas where the rapid growth of the elderly population presents special issues. Second, within the same-age categories, the in-migrants may have higher rates of labor-force participation than the receiving population. Both these effects depend on the socioeconomic characteristics and the occupational skills of the in-migrants.

When people with different cultural and linguistic backgrounds migrate to a particular site, a degree of cultural heterogeneity develops. Cultural factors ultimately determine the tolerable levels of in-migration. Only a certain number of newcomers can be absorbed without the receiving population feeling that their social institutions and value systems are being threatened. With the vastly increased levels of immigration into the United States, there are occasions when cities cannot stem the tide of new people moving in. Lewiston, Maine, presents a vivid example of this situation:

> With a population of thirty-six thousand, the town was recently ninety-six percent white and predominantly Catholic – French-Canadian and Irish. . . . Then, practically overnight, the streets seemed to be full of Black African Muslims. Today, there are about three thousand Somalis in Lewiston and dozens more arrive every month. Before the Somalis arrived, the Lewiston school system employed one teacher of English as a second language. It now employs fifteen, for five hundred students, nearly all of them Somalis. (Finnegan, 2006: 46)

The issue is complex and must be addressed in a rational manner. Consideration must be given to the responsibility of the United States to the rest of the world, on the one hand, and to the institutions and values of this nation, on the other. We address some of these issues in Chapter 12. We turn now to the impact of migration on the individual migrant.

Impact on the individual migrant

One important consequence for the migrant is the opportunity to live in an environment with the social, economic, political, or physical characteristics that he or she believes to be preferable to those of the old environment. Whether or not this is the case depends on the accuracy of the migrant's perceptions of the circumstances in both the old and the new environments, as well as the migrant's ability to use the advantageous features of the new environment. The latter, in turn, depends on whether the migrant possesses useful skills and how rapidly he or she is assimilated into the prevailing culture.

In general, the difficulty that migrants experience in being acculturated depends on how different they are from the receiving population. Nonwhite groups have found it much more difficult to be "accepted" into mainstream American life than their white counterparts. Despite having been here for well over three hundred years, the American black is only now beginning to be accepted by the whole society, but this is not yet the case in some isolated heavily white areas. One can only speculate about the problems of adaptation that the newest Americans of Hispanic or Asian nationality will confront.

While immigrants to America perhaps face more daunting problems, the native-born individual moving within the country must also adapt to new situations as he or she joins the residents of a new urban or rural area or leaves the Northeast for the South or Far West. Customs vary somewhat from region to region, and some "assimilating" is usually necessary if a newcomer is to adjust to the unfamiliar surroundings. Despite the "nationalization" emanating from television and the Internet, many Americans still "speak funny" to other Americans.

In the preceding pages, we discuss various aspects of domestic migration in the United States. We turn now to a consideration of domestic migration in China, particularly the so-called temporary internal migration.

TEMPORARY ("FLOATING") MIGRATION IN CHINA

Unlike the process of internal migration in most other countries, "migration" in China is not defined merely as changing a residence from one location to another while crossing a geographical (county-level) boundary. To migrate in China, one needs first to obtain permission to officially transfer his/her household registration (known in Chinese as the *hukou*) from the origin location to the destination location. People in China who move without permission are known as "floaters." These are people "who have crossed over some territorial... boundary, [who] have not altered their permanent registration (*hukou*), and, [who] at least in theory, 'flow in and out'" (Solinger, 1999: 15; see also Fan, 1999). In China, thus, there are two types of internal migration: a move noted by an officially permitted permanent change in the person's place-of-household registration; and a move with no such official sanction (Poston and Mao, 1998; Poston and Zhang, 2008).

In 1948, China enacted the *hukou*, or household registration system. Urban residents were entitled to subsidized housing, social insurance, medical care, and, for the most part, employment. These rights and entitlements were denied to those holding rural *hukous*. In the late 1970s, Deng Xiaoping, the key Chinese leader who succeeded Mao Zedong, established the economic reforms that changed the *hukou* controls. At about the same time, the state relaxed the rules; for instance, these days, one no longer needs coupons to buy grain in stores in China's cities. The economic reforms also resulted in a tremendous requirement for manpower in the cities in low-level construction and manufacturing jobs and, more recently, in many kinds of household service and related jobs. Concurrently, the incentives of Deng's so-called household responsibility system, whereby a household can keep much of what it produces, resulted in the release of millions of workers who in the past, during the communal regime, were inefficiently employed in agriculture (see Nolan, 1991; and Oi, 1999). There has existed in China for the past decade or so a huge agricultural labor surplus that continues to grow because of the implementation of technology that increases even further the efficiency of agriculture (A. Mason, 1997).

So what happens to this agricultural labor surplus? Much of it ends up migrating to the cities to the newly available low-level construction, manufacturing, and household service jobs; they are the so-called floating migrants. The bulk is absorbed in the construction sector; others find jobs in manufacturing, services, and light industry: "The predominance of construction jobs is one reason men migrate more often than women. In areas where light assembly jobs dominate, however, female workers may outnumber males by as much as seven to one" (World Bank, 1997: 55).

The growth of the floating population in Beijing has paralleled the growth of the floating population in the country (Poston and Duan, 2000). In Beijing in the early 1950s, the floating population was very "efficiently controlled" and quite small in size. But by the late 1980s, the number of floaters had reached more than 1.3 million, and by 1994 almost 3.3 million, or almost one-third of its population then of about 11 million. In 1997, the official number of floaters was 2.9 million but, if counted differently, would have been higher, perhaps as high as 5 million (Poston and Duan, 2000).

Who are the floating migrants? They are mainly young and unmarried males and females seeking employment in blue-collar, service, and household jobs. According to the World Bank (1997: 55), the "average [floating] migrant is less educated than the general population but more educated than the rural population. Few [floating] migrants come from the ranks of the absolute poor, who lack even the few years of schooling and basic Mandarin [Chinese language] required for most migrant jobs."

Also, they are young, and males predominate over females (see Yang, 1994, 1996).

Using data from China's 2000 Census, Zai Liang and Zhongdong Ma (2004) noted that there are as many as 140 million floating migrants in China, mainly in the big cities, who migrated from elsewhere in China; more than 100 million come from rural areas. The proportions of floaters in the resident populations of China's large cities typically range from one-third to one-fourth of the total population. The growth trends of the floaters in most of China's cities parallel those noted for Beijing. Since the total number of floaters approximates 140 million persons, this is nearly 40 percent of the country's total urban population (Solinger, 1999: 18). The internal migration of floaters to China's cities constitutes the largest stream of peacetime mobility in recorded human history (Roberts, 1997). This is the main reason why this particular migration is so important.

There is another reason: Many could become international immigrants and leave China, mainly illegally. Let us consider how and why this might happen. The floating migrants in China's big cities earn wages that are several times greater than the wages earned by countrymen in their home villages in the rural areas, and they send as much as half of their salaries back to their home villages. This occurs even though the floaters' wages are quite a bit less than those of the permanent urban workers, as much as 20 to 40 percent less. Usually, 20 to 50 percent of a floater's wage is sent back to the village. In the rural counties of some provinces (e.g., Sichuan and Anhui Provinces), urban remittances from floaters account for almost half of household cash income (World Bank, 1997: 56–57).

If and when the floaters are unable to find jobs or lose their jobs in the cities of China, some may well look elsewhere, likely outside China, where there are jobs and where there are already established Chinese networks. In future years, there will be more rural surplus workers in China, as well as more floaters. Moreover, indications point to increases in unemployment in China's cities in the future. Liang (2001: 693) has written that the "likelihood of competition for jobs between internal migrants [i.e., the floaters] and unemployed workers [among the permanent residents of the cities] is clear. . . . Some members of the floating population and unemployed workers [may be pushed] onto the market for illegal transnational migration."

When floaters lose their jobs in the Chinese cities, some will not likely return home to their rural villages, to which they have been sending remittances. Returning home unemployed would result in tremendous embarrassment and loss of "face." Many floaters could well look elsewhere, most likely outside China, where there are jobs and where there are already established Chinese networks, in countries such as the United States and many in Europe. It is not inconceivable that there could well be between 25 million and 50 million floaters looking for jobs outside China in the next five or so years, and between 35 million and almost 90 million by 2015. The prominent demographer and migration scholar, Douglas Massey, has written that "China's movement towards markets and rapid economic growth may contain the seeds of an enormous migration . . . that would produce a flow of immigrants [to the United States] that would dwarf levels of migration now observed from Mexico" (1995: 649).

We turn now to a consideration of migration streams in the United States and China. This is another way of looking at the topic of internal migration: viewing the streams of migrants from one area to another.

MIGRATION STREAMS IN THE UNITED STATES AND IN CHINA

We noted earlier that a migration stream is a body of migrants departing from a common area of origin and arriving at a common area of destination during a specified time interval. A migration counterstream is the migration stream, smaller in size, going in the opposite direction during the same time interval. We learn a lot about internal migration in a country by considering its major migration streams. Migrants are not randomly sent to all areas of a country. Alternately, they are pushed from and pulled to specific areas. We view these trends and dynamics in the United States and China for the period 1995 to 2000.

In Table 6.4, we present migration flow data for the period 1995–2000 for the ten largest permanent migration streams in the United States (upper panel) and in China (lower panel). We look first at the main U.S. state-to-state migration streams.

Migration streams in the United States

There are fifty U.S. states, plus one statelike unit, the District of Columbia, making fifty-one "states" in total. Each of the fifty-one states may send domestic migrants to fifty other states. Thus, there are 51 times 50 possible domestic migration streams, or 2,550 in all. In the five years between 1995 and 2000, more than 22 million people in the United States changed their state of residence; that is, they were interstate migrants (Franklin, 2003: 1). The data in the top panel of Table 6.4 show the ten largest migration streams of interstate migrants. More than 300,000 of these interstate migrants moved from the New York to Florida, constituting the largest state-to-state migration stream in the country. This New York to Florida stream has been one of the larger migration streams in the United States for several decades, and is comprised, to an important degree, of migrating New York retirees.

Table 6.4. Ten largest permanent state-to-state migration streams in the United States, 1995–2000, and ten largest permanent province-to-province migration streams in China, 1995–2000

Origin	Destination	Number of permanent migrants
United States		
New York	Florida	308,230
New York	New Jersey	206,979
California	Nevada	199,125
California	Arizona	186,151
California	Texas	182,789
Florida	Georgia	157,423
California	Washington	155,577
California	Oregon	131,836
New Jersey	Florida	118,905
Texas	California	115,929
China		
Hunan	Guangdong	252,133
Sichuan	Guangdong	192,993
Guangxi	Guangdong	161,212
Jiangxi	Guangdong	122,664
Hubei	Guangdong	118,670
Henan	Guangdong	82,015
Anhui	Jiangsu	71,801
Anhui	Shanghai	66,866
Jiangxi	Zhejiang	58,907
Anhui	Zhejiang	53,627

Source: Poston and Zhang, 2008.

The next largest U.S. migration stream was from New York to New Jersey, numbering almost 207,000 migrants. The New York to New Jersey stream consisted mainly of younger families moving to suburban areas in the nearby state, not of retirees.

California was the origin state of the next three largest migration streams, people moving to Nevada (almost 200,000 migrants), to Arizona (more than 186,000), and to Texas (almost 183,000). California was also the origin state of the seventh and eighth largest migration streams of migrants, to Washington State (more than 155,000) and to Oregon (almost 132,000). California is a particularly interesting state with regard to inter-state migration streams. It has the largest population of all the U.S. states and also, as we saw earlier, had the second largest number of out-migrants of all the states between 1995 and 2000. California has a great effect on the state-to-state migration streams in the entire country. According to Marc J. Perry (2003: 5):

> By itself, California had an outflow of more than a half-million people (and a net out-migration of 380,000) to the fast-growing states of Nevada, Arizona, Georgia, North Carolina, and Colorado. The most obvious example was Nevada, where migration gains were the result of a large outflow from California. Moreover, 13 other states each had an inflow of more than 50,000 people from California and 27 states had inflows of between 10,000 and 50,000 people. Only the District of Columbia and nine states had inflows from California of fewer than 10,000 people.

Analysis of interstate migration streams also indicates that the largest migration flows into a state and out of a state usually originate and terminate in close-by or adjacent states. To illustrate, Arizona received the largest number of state-to-state migrants from California; the largest migration stream from Arizona was to California (Perry, 2003). These findings affirm the observations made earlier about the negative effects of distance on migration.

The negative effects of distance, however, are frequently overridden by other concerns. The interstate migration data show that large migration flows from many of the cold and wealthy states in the North (e.g., Connecticut, Massachusetts, Michigan, New Jersey, New York, Ohio, and Pennsylvania) ended in Florida. These are good examples of migration streams consisting of retirees and some labor migrants (Perry, 2003).

Finally, some migration streams (e.g., the stream and counterstream between the states of Minnesota and Wisconsin) were near equal, resulting in little net migration gain in either state. Such a situation is in marked contrast to the stream and counterstream between California and Nevada. As shown in Table 6.4, California sent almost 200,000 migrants to Nevada, but Nevada in turn sent just over 60,000 migrants to California, resulting in very unequal streams between the two states (Perry, 2003).

Migration streams in China

China is divided into thirty-one statelike geographical units; there are twenty-two provinces, five autonomous regions set aside largely for minority peoples, and the four central administrative municipalities of Beijing (the capital of China), Tianjin, Shanghai, and Chongqing. These four central municipalities are similar to Washington, DC (see the map in Figure 6.3). There are thus 930 separate migration streams (or 31 times 30) from and to each of the thirty-one provinces or province-like geographical units.

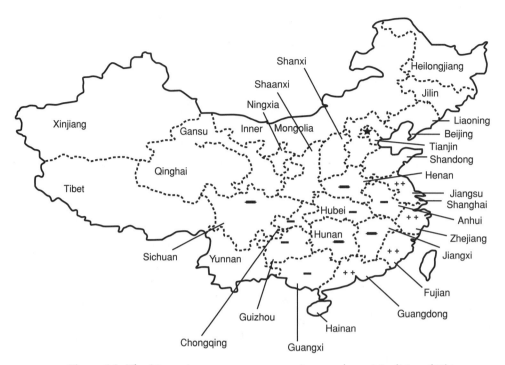

Figure 6.3. The 31 provinces, autonomous regions, and municipalities of China.

The bottom panel of Table 6.4 shows the ten largest province-to-province migration streams in China between 1995 and 2000 (Poston and Zhang, 2008). These are streams of permanent migrants, not floating or temporary migrants – see the earlier discussion – and, hence, these permanent migrant streams are analogous to those just examined in the United States.

Hunan Province, just west of Guangdong Province in southern China, is the major origin province of the permanent migrants. Permanent migrants originating in Hunan comprise 22 percent of all permanent migrants moving to Guangdong between 1995 and 2000. In fact, more than 325,000 left Hunan between 1995 and 2000 and obtained household registrations in other provinces, accounting for 10 percent of the total volume of interprovincial permanent migration. This figure is second only to that of Sichuan Province. During the same period, Sichuan sent out almost 440,000 permanent migrants, or 14 percent of the total volume of interprovincial permanent migration.

Of the ten largest permanent migration streams, only those originating in Sichuan, Hubei, and Henan Provinces are to destination provinces that are not contiguous to them. Seven of the ten largest permanent migration streams have origin and destination provinces that are contiguous. This

Table 6.5. Ten largest temporary (floating) province-to-province migration streams in China, 1995–2000

Origin	Destination	Number of floating migrants
Hunan	Guangdong	3,328,873
Sichuan	Guangdong	2,843,660
Guangxi	Guangdong	2,213,417
Jiangxi	Guangdong	1,611,252
Hubei	Guangdong	1,463,704
Anhui	Jiangsu	1,121,326
Anhui	Shanghai	1,028,508
Henan	Guangdong	1,005,219
Jiangxi	Zhejiang	840,574
Anhui	Zhejiang	781,887

Source: Poston and Zhang, 2008.

reflects the important role that distance plays in determining permanent migration; the closer the destination to the origin, the greater the volume of migration (Poston and Zhang, 2008).

We noted earlier that in China, there are two categories of internal migrants: permanent and temporary (floating). We look now at the province-to-province flows of floating migrants in China between 1995 and 2000. Table 6.5 identifies the ten largest such floating migration streams.

In comparison to the permanent migration streams, there is a very similar overall structure of population movement. The data in Table 6.5 indicate that of the 930 temporary migration streams, the largest is from Hunan to Guangdong, with more than 3.3 million temporary migrants. As a receiving province, Guangdong was the destination of more than 15 million temporary migrants between 1995 and 2000, accounting for almost 36 percent of all interprovincial temporary migration in China. This percentage is very close to Guangdong's percentage share of permanent migration. Table 6.5 also shows that most of the largest temporary migration streams are the same as the largest permanent migration streams.

However, the size of the floating migration streams is much greater than the size of the permanent migration streams. Considering only the ten largest streams, the floating migrant streams are on average fourteen times larger than the permanent migrant streams. Considering all of the interprovincial temporary migrants in China between 1995 and 2000, the number of floating migrants (more than 42 million) is thirteen times larger than the total number of permanent migrants (Poston and Zhang, 2008). This is one reason why the study of floating migration draws so much more attention from migration researchers. It also confirms an earlier statement of Sidney and Alice Goldstein that "temporary movement has become numerically more important than permanent migration" (1991: 44).

SUMMARY

Migration is a permanent shift of residence of such duration and distance that a change in the physical and social environment occurs. It is usually measured as a change of residence across political boundaries, generally between counties. We saw in this chapter that there is a great deal of geographic mobility in the United States, much of it created by people who move repeatedly. On average, every year one person in five changes residence. One person in fourteen migrates by moving from one county to another. Until about 1950, a large part of the interregional migration was from east to west and south to north. Since then, the latter flow has reversed. Both whites and blacks are now moving into the South.

There are marked differences among those who migrate in terms of age, race, and socioeconomic status. Young adults are the most likely to move, as are young children, who move with their parents. Whites are more likely to migrate than blacks, although the latter move locally more often. There is a positive relation between education and the possibility of moving: The better educated tend to migrate more than do the less educated.

In this chapter, we also consider the case of internal migration in China, where movement is tightly controlled. This is referred to as temporary, or floating, migration. Floating migrants are not expected to remain permanently in their areas of destination even though, in fact, most do. There were more than 42 million floating migrants between the provinces of China during the 1995–2000 period; this number is almost twice as large as the number of permanent migrants between the states of the United States in the same time period, and thirteen times larger than the number of permanent migrants between the provinces of China.

Migration is seldom explained in terms of the characteristics of only one place or factor. In any move, a decision has been reached that the area of destination offers advantages that outweigh the disadvantages of moving. Generally, it may be stated that people move "to better their lot" in life. This is happening today and will continue to happen as long as people believe that opportunities and living conditions are better elsewhere. Humankind is indeed peripatetic and will always be so.

KEY TERMS

area of destination	migration counterstream
area of origin	migration efficiency ratio (MER)
differential migration	migration pull
ecological theory of migration	migration push
floating migrant	migration selectivity
geographic mobility	migration stream
gross migration rate (GMR)	net migration rate (NMR)
in-migration rate (IMR)	out-migration rate (OMR)
internal migration	residence
international migration	residential mobility
local movement	return migration

7 International Migration

The first "international" migrations of humans began around 60 thousand years ago, and they continue to this day. Of all the demographic topics presented in this book, none is discussed by both laypeople and social scientists these days as frequently and as forcefully as international migration. **International migration** is migration that occurs between countries. Its dynamics differ significantly from those of internal migration, that is, migration within the geographical boundaries of a single country, the subject of the last chapter. The concepts and theories of international migration are also somewhat different from those of internal migration.

We begin by considering some of the definitions and concepts used in the study of international migration. We next cover world **immigration** patterns over time, followed by a discussion of immigration into the United States. We then look at the major theories of international migration, as well as some of the positive and negative economic issues pertaining to international migration. This is followed by a consideration of legal and unauthorized immigration. We conclude with a discussion of the meaning of the concept of zero **net international migration**.

DEFINITIONS AND CONCEPTS

Somewhat similar to the situation with the study of internal migration, demographers have developed a fairly standard set of concepts and definitions for studying international migration. The first distinction is between immigration and **emigration**. Immigration refers to the migration of people into a new country for the purpose of establishing permanent residence; an **immigrant** is a person who enters a new country of permanent residence and crosses an international boundary in doing so. These concepts are analogous in the study of internal migration to in-migration and in-migrant. Conversely, emigration refers to the permanent departure of people from a country; an **emigrant** is one who migrates away from a country with the intention of establishing a permanent residence elsewhere. The analogous internal migration concepts are out-migration and out-migrant.

In every international migration, a migrant is simultaneously an immigrant and an emigrant. The key element in the definition of an immigrant is the establishment of a permanent residence in the new country. This usually means residence in the destination country for at least one year, and is referred to as *long-term immigration*. The number of long-term immigrants in the world has increased considerably in recent decades, from around 75 million in 1965 to 120 million in 1990 (S. F. Martin 2001) to 190 million in 2006 (United Nations, 2006a). Approximately 3 percent of the world's population in 2006 consisted of long-term immigrants (Cortes and Poston, 2008). Although this is a relatively small percentage, it is a very large absolute number.

Remigration refers to the migration of international migrants back to their original countries of origin. A remigrant is an international migrant who at some later point in time moves back to his or her original country of residence. Oftentimes, international migrants return to their countries of origin in their later years of life (see the last section of this chapter). For example, let's say that a person leaves Ireland and moves to the United States. This person is an emigrant from Ireland and an immigrant to the United States. If at some later point in time the person decides to leave the United States and move back to Ireland, we would refer to him or her as a remigrant. The analogous concept with respect to internal migration is return migrant.

We have already noted that international migration is the permanent movement of people from one country to another. International migrants may be distinguished from tourists and visitors because the latter return home without establishing permanent residence in the destination country. People who move to a foreign country as tourists or to work for a short period, for example, diplomats, are not regarded as international migrants (Münz, 2003).

Twentieth-century immigrants to the major destination countries of the world (i.e., the United States, Spain, Italy, Canada, Germany, the United Kingdom, France, and Australia) may be grouped into four broad (and not necessarily mutually exclusive) categories: refugees/asylum seekers, migrants from former colonies, economic migrants, and "ethnic privileged" migrants (Münz, 2003).

A **refugee** or an *asylum seeker* is one who involuntarily emigrates from his or her native country because of persecution, threat of violence, or extreme deprivation, often going to a neighboring country. Postcolonial migration began in the 1950s as a result of the decolonization of mainly southern nations. Indigenous peoples moved from former colonial countries to the European countries that had colonized them in order to pursue better living conditions or to escape political persecution.

Economic migrants are voluntary migrants motivated by economic aspirations; this flow is more likely to occur from the less to the more developed countries (the latter group is defined as all the countries of Europe and North America plus the countries of Australia, New Zealand, and Japan). Most international migration is economically motivated, and most immigration these days is to the more developed countries. Of the 190 million long-term immigrants in the world in 2006, 115 million resided in more developed countries (United Nations, 2006).

Some countries, for example, Israel, provide priorities for migrants with the same ethnic and religious origins as the majority population (Münz, 2003; Poston, Luo, and Zhang, 2006).

Douglas Massey developed a slightly different set of international migrant categories on the basis of whether the migration is voluntary or involuntary and whether the migrants "are well or poorly endowed with human capital" (2003: 549). People who migrate involuntarily and possess few if any skills are refugees. If their migration is involuntary but they possess significant human capital, they are asylum seekers. If they move voluntarily but possess little if any human capital, they are labor migrants. Massey's final category is skilled immigrants: "their migration decisions reflect the desire to maximize returns to their investments in skills, training and education" (2003: 550).

Most of the population of the world never engages in international migration; "most live and die near their place of birth" (Martin and Zurcher, 2008: 3). Those who are international migrants most often move between countries that are geographically close together. For the United States, this means that most immigrants come from Mexico and Central America. Recently, however, a large number of immigrants have come to the United States from China. Although China is geographically distant from the United States, making migration difficult and expensive, the push and pull factors of China and the United States are strong (Cortes and Poston, 2008; Poston and Luo, 2007).

Regarding the net gain or loss of international migrants, between 2000 and 2005, the United States had a net gain (immigrants minus emigrants) of almost 6.5 million immigrants, far surpassing the more than 2.8 million net gain received by Spain, the country with the second largest number (Figure 7.1). Mexico experienced the largest net loss of immigrants during the 2000–2005 period, with almost 4 million more emigrants than immigrants. China had the second highest net loss, with 1.9 million more emigrants than

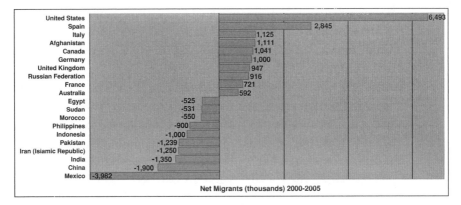

Figure 7.1. Net immigration to countries of the world, 2000–2005. Between 2000 and 2005, the United States received the most (net) international migrants of any country in the world, and Mexico sent the most (net) international migrants of any country. *Source:* United Nations, 2005, Common Database, "Migration, International Net per Year, all Countries, 2000 and 2005," available at http://www.unstats.un.org/unsd/cdb.

immigrants. Most countries of the world, however, discourage immigration and "do not welcome the arrival of foreigners who wish to settle and become naturalized citizens" in their countries (Martin and Zurcher, 2008: 2). (A **naturalized citizen** is a permanent immigrant who has been granted citizenship by the country into which he or she immigrated.)

PATTERNS OF WORLD IMMIGRATION OVER TIME

The residential movement of large numbers of people from one country to another goes far back into human history, way before the beginning of the establishment of nations. The first "fully modern" humans, *Homo sapiens sapiens* (every human being today is a member of this category of Homo sapiens) emerged in sub-Saharan Africa as many as 195,000 years ago and lived there for the first two-thirds of their history. By 35,000 years ago, humans "thrived at opposite ends of Eurasia, from France to southeast Asia and even Australia" (Goebel, 2007: 194). One of the greatest "untold stories in the history of humankind" is how humans "colonized these and other drastically different environments during the intervening 160,000 years" (p. 194). It is believed that humans began to migrate out of Africa between 50,000 and 60,000 years ago, first to southern Asia, China, and Java and later to Europe. Evidence suggests that humans began migrating to the Americas around 14,000 years ago, maybe even earlier ("Before the Exodus," 2008: 101; Goebel, Waters, and O'Rourke, 2008; Meltzer, 2009). These "first Americans used boats, and the [west] coastal corridor would have been the likely route of passage.... Once humans reached the Pacific Northwest, they...continued their spread southward along the coast to Chile, as well as eastward...possibly...to Wisconsin" (Goebel, Waters, and O'Rourke, 2008: 1501).

Years later, movements were often across land areas and over short sea routes. The migration of a population was often preceded by an invasion of its armies. Sometimes the invaders would occupy the new lands permanently, perhaps intermarrying with the subdued population. The Norse peoples from Scandinavia illustrate this principle. They carried out numerous raids in Europe until the ninth century and then settled in England, Ireland, and France (where they were known as Normans). Occasionally, the invaders would occupy the new lands only briefly and later return to their original territory, leaving some of their members in the occupied region.

Prior to the 1400s, many of the international migrations leading to invasion and the conquering of new territory did not involve oceanic crossings. The invasions of the Mongols in the fourteenth century led by Tamerlane, seeking to conquer all of Eurasia, were the last time in human history when massive international migrations and invasions did not cross oceans. Thereafter, international migrations and invasions were global (Darwin, 2008).

Sometimes the international migrations and invasions were accompanied by the enslavement of the defeated peoples and their **forced migration** to the land of the conquerors. For example, a single Roman military campaign might bring in as many as 50 thousand prisoners. During the height of the Roman Empire, the population of the city of Rome probably reached 1 million persons, a large number of whom were slaves who had immigrated involuntarily. Earlier, during the fifth century BC, the population of Athens included between 75,000 and 150,000 slaves, from both Africa and Asia, representing around 25 to 35 percent of the population (K. Davis, 1974: 95).

Exploration also played a role in the dynamics of human migration. In the thirteenth century from China and in the fifteenth and sixteenth centuries from Europe, Zheng He, Columbus, Magellan, and others led large naval expeditions to other parts of the world both to satisfy the curiosity of their governments and to explore parts of the world unknown to them. They brought back treasures and information about the new land. Some settled in the new parts of the world then and later. For example, the Portuguese started colonies in Africa; the Spaniards, English, Dutch, and French in the Americas; the Chinese in Southeast Asia; and the English in Australia and New Zealand (Davis, 1974; Dreyer, 2007; Menzies, 2003).

The greatest period of European migration overseas occurred between 1840 and 1930 when around 52 million people emigrated from European countries, mainly to North America. This number equaled around one-fifth of the population of Europe in 1840 and exceeded the number of Europeans already abroad after more than three hundred years of settlement (Davis, 1974: 98). Michael Haines (2003) has estimated that the transatlantic migration stream from Europe to the Western Hemisphere, from the beginning of colonization around 1500 until 1940, numbered 60 million and was "the greatest and probably the most consequential population movement in modern human history" (p. 942).

Compared to the massive movements out of Europe, intercontinental migration from Asia before World War II was not as large. Asian Indians went to such places as British Guiana, East Africa, Fiji, Mauritius, and Trinidad; Japanese and Filipino migrants went to Hawaii; the Japanese settled in Brazil; and many Chinese migrated to the United States (Poston, Mao, and Yu, 1994).

Intercontinental migration from Africa differed from the preceding movements. The mass outpouring of Africans to other continents was largely involuntary. Around 9.6 million slaves were taken to the New World between 1650 and the nineteenth century, when slavery there was abolished. During these sea voyages, mortality was high; as many as 25 percent who began the voyage would die before reaching the Americas. Thus, the total number of Africans taken from Africa was probably well over 11 million. This was the largest slave migration in recorded human history in terms of distance and the numbers moved (Curtin, 1969).

These massive migrations have had a number of consequences for the world. One reason for the increase in world population after 1750 was that emigration was partly responsible for relieving the pressures of the population on land and resources in the origin areas, postponing an inevitable change in birth and death rates. Although there surely are exceptions, in general, the greater the rate of emigration from a European country, the later the drop in its birth rate. In France, a country characterized by low levels of emigration during this period, the birth rate began to fall as early as the mid-eighteenth century. In Italy, conversely, a significant fertility decline did not occur until early in the twentieth century. In the countries of destination, the immigrants often exhibited high birth rates. Indeed, some of the highest birth rates ever recorded were in French Canada in the latter part of the seventeenth century. Crude birth rates were as high as 65 per 1,000 among some of the immigrant groups to the New World (Bouvier, 1965; Sabagh, 1942).

Another consequence of these international migrations was the geographic redistribution of the global population. Between 1750 and 1930, the population of the main areas of destination of European emigrants increased in size by fourteen times, while the population of all the other areas of the world grew by a factor of only 2.5. In 1750, those areas of destination of European emigrants comprised less than 3 percent of the population of the world; by 1930, they comprised 16 percent. The geographic distribution of races also changed dramatically. By 1930, about one-third of all whites no longer lived in Europe, and more than one-fifth of all blacks no longer lived in Africa (K. Davis, 1974: 99).

There have been several major international migration movements since the 1930s and the period of unrest preceding World War II to the present. Using Massey's categories (mentioned earlier), most of these migrants were refugees and asylum seekers.

First, during Adolf Hitler's rise to power in the 1930s, millions of Jews and political refugees fled Germany. At the end of World War II, there were compulsory large-scale transfers of the European population as a result of repatriation. The uprooting of more than 20 million Eastern and Central Europeans via flight, expulsion, transfer, or population exchange represented a drastic solution to the problems of ethnic minorities in these regions (Bouvier, Shryock, and Henderson, 1977).

Second, after the end of World War II, about 3 million Japanese were returned by decree to Japan from other Asian nations. Third, after the partition of India and Pakistan in 1947, more than 7 million Moslems fled from India to Pakistan, and a comparable number of Hindus fled from Pakistan to India. In the Punjab area of Pakistan alone, those who fled, the refugees, made up more than two-thirds of the population.

Fourth, in 1948, thousands of Palestinians were displaced from the territory that is now Israel, which represents the classic example of an immigrant country drawing a population from dozens of other countries. The United States is another example of a country of immigrants.

Fifth, in the 1970s, millions of Southeast Asians and Africans were uprooted owing to political and economic upheavals, resulting in one of the largest and most tragic refugee migrations in history. In 1971, 10 million refugees migrated from what had been East Pakistan (now Bangladesh) to northern India. Subsequently, millions of Asians escaped from Cambodia, Vietnam, and Laos into Thailand and elsewhere (Patrick, 2003).

Sixth, an often overlooked international migration is that involving refugees fleeing Afghanistan following the Soviet invasion in 1979. There were as many as 6.5 million Afghan refugees between 1988 and 1991, and another 5 million from the early 1990s to 2000. By the early part of this new century, it is estimated that one in four Afghans were refugees (Patrick, 2003: 827).

Finally, the modern refugee era began at the end of the Cold War, when "many, mostly developing countries found themselves embroiled in often violent conflicts after they lost the support of their superpower backer"

(Patrick, 2003: 827). Several million additional refugees were a result of the U.S. invasion of Iraq in 2003. The numbers of refugees and asylum seekers are astoundingly high. As of around the year 2001, there were almost 3.6 million Afghans alone in Pakistan and Iran (Patrick, 2003: 828). In 2005, the following countries were the origins of the largest numbers of refugees: the Palestinian Territories, Afghanistan, Iraq, Myanmar, and Sudan. According to estimates of the United Nations High Commissioner for Refugees, more than 4.2 million Iraqis alone have been displaced since the 2003 U.S. invasion of Iraq; more than 2 million have been displaced within Iraq, and 2.2 million have moved to neighboring countries (UNHCR, 2007).

IMMIGRATION TO THE UNITED STATES

Almost all of the present residents of the United States, more than 98 percent, are immigrants or are the descendents of immigrants. In the United States in 2000, only 4 million people, or just over 1.5 percent of the population, identified themselves as American Indians or as Alaska Natives (Ogunwole, 2006); they were thus neither immigrants to the United States nor descendants of immigrants. These peoples lived in North America for thousands of years before the arrival of the first immigrants. Later, many coexisted with European settlers until the eighteenth century, when most were eliminated through either disease or war. These conflicts continued throughout the late 1800s, when only a fraction of Native Americans remained (Cortes and Poston, 2008; Purcell, 1995).

In terms of the total number of immigrants, the United States is by far the most immigrant-friendly country of all the countries in the world. In 2005, 38.4 million U.S. residents, or almost 13 percent of the total population, were born in foreign countries (Figure 7.2). This is surely the largest number of immigrants residing in any country of the world. The country with the next largest number of **foreign-born** residents is the Russian Federation, with 12.1 million, or 8.5 percent of its total population.

Some countries have larger foreign-born percentages than the United States, but these are much smaller countries, and their foreign-born residents consist mainly of migrant workers and are seldom citizens of the host countries. For example, 78 percent of Qatar's total population of 813 thousand residents are foreign-born, as are 71 percent of the United Arab Emirates' population of 4.5 million and 62 percent of Kuwait's population of 2.7 million residents (United Nations, 2006a). The Gulf countries "tend to extend few rights to migrants; it is very hard for a guest worker to win immigrant status and naturalize in Saudi Arabia or the United Arab Emirates" (P. Martin and Zurcher, 2008: 8).

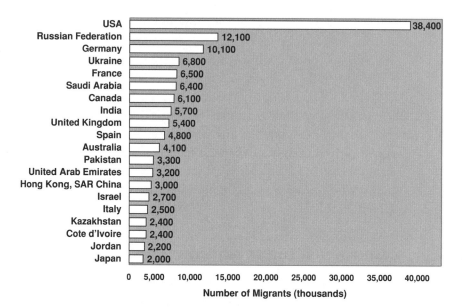

Figure 7.2. International migrant stock, countries of the world, 2005. The United States is the most migrant-friendly country in the world. *Source:* United Nations, 2005, "Trends in Total Migration Stock, The 2005 Revision," http://www.un.org/esa/ population/publications/migration/UN_Migrant_Stock_Documentation_2005.pdf.

One country, the Vatican City State (known officially as the Holy See), has a total population of just over 700 people (United Nations, 2006), and nearly all are foreign-born. Its population consists of the pope, priests and other members of religious orders, and laypeople (and their families) who work at the Vatican. Citizenship is given to people (and their families) who work there and is revoked when they are no longer employed there; thus, not only are almost all the residents foreign-born, but there are also no permanent residents. The Vatican City State is the smallest country in the world with respect to both population size and land mass; it comprises only 0.17 square mile (0.44 square kilometer) and is completely surrounded by the city of Rome. The country is so small that it does not even have street addresses.

Let us now review the history of immigration to the United States, which has clearly played an important part in the American narrative. The size and the numbers of immigrants residing in the United States have varied greatly over time. Figure 7.3 shows the number and percentage of immigrants living in the United States from 1900 to 2007. The 38 million immigrants in 2007 is the largest absolute number of immigrants ever recorded in the United States. The growth of the foreign-born population every decade since 1970 "has been higher than at any other time in history, surpassing the 31 percent increase between 1900 and 1910" (Camarota, 2007: 5).

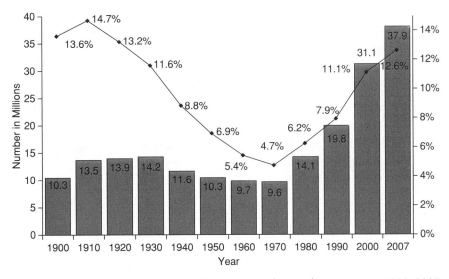

Figure 7.3. Immigrants in the United States, number and percentage, 1900–2007. *Source:* Camarota, 2007.

The streams to the United States from China and Mexico are among the largest and most important historically and currently. Thus, in the paragraphs that follow, we give them special attention.

Spaniards first came to what would become the United States in 1598. They exploited the land and persecuted the indigenous peoples, but they differed from earlier explorers in that many remained permanently in the areas known today as the Southwest and Florida (Purcell, 1995).

The first really large stream of European immigrants to America hailed from England, and they settled mainly in the present state of Virginia (Purcell, 1995). The first permanent settlement was Jamestown, established in 1607. These immigrants largely lived off tobacco crops, which proved to be a profitable but labor-intensive product. This sustenance activity eventually led to the immigration of British indentured servants and African slaves. The arrival of the pilgrims on Plymouth Rock in 1620 marked the beginning of a large migration stream of English people moving to the New World for religious freedom. These early immigrant groups "of the 1600s and 1700s established the basic context of American society. English was the dominant language in America; English legal and government documents were the norm; and culture was for two centuries copied after English literature, drama, and art" (Purcell, 1995: 5). This model of American society set the standard and foundation during the next two centuries for the future discrimination and exclusion of certain immigrants and for the acceptance of others (Cortes and Poston, 2008).

In a previous section, we noted the sizable involuntary migrations of African slaves that also occurred during this period. The first African slaves were purchased in Jamestown in 1619. The slavery of Africans was relatively slow to develop in the colonies because Native Americans and white indentured servants were being used for cheap labor. However, by 1690, there were more African slaves than white indentured servants (Purcell, 1995). After the establishment of the United States as a nation, the slave trade ended in 1807, but slavery persisted until the end of the Civil War. However, to this very day, the system of racism upon which slavery was founded is engrained in the United States and remains a hurdle for African Americans and other racial and ethnic minorities (Bonilla-Silva, 2006; Cortes and Poston, 2008).

The Dutch came to America in the 1600s and claimed much of present-day New York (Purcell, 1995). Swedish immigrants also came to the New World but were less successful than the British and Dutch. Scotch-Irish immigrants came for economic reasons and settled mainly in Pennsylvania. The seventeenth century also saw a considerable migration of German peoples who were motivated primarily by war in Germany. They were the largest non-British and non-English-speaking immigrant group to come to America. The cultural and linguistic differences of the Germans led to their being one of the first European immigrant groups to experience discrimination by earlier settlers in the country (Cortes and Poston, 2008).

Before 1830, the contribution of immigration to population growth in the United States was small. Between 1821 and 1825, for example, the average number of immigrants every year was only about eight thousand; this increased to almost 21 thousand between 1826 and 1830. From 1841 to 1845, immigrants each year numbered more than 86 thousand. In the eight years between 1850 and 1857, the total number of immigrants to the United States was 2.2 million. In sum, between 1790 and 1860, the number of immigrants to the United States was almost 5 million, and most of them were from Europe (Cortes and Poston, 2008; Taeuber and Taeuber, 1958).

Starting on January 1, 1892, many immigrants, mainly from Europe, were processed through the portal of Ellis Island, a small island in New York Harbor. This was not the only port of immigrant entry into the United States but was the major facility until the 1920s. Ports of entry were also located in Boston, Philadelphia, Baltimore, San Francisco, Savannah, Miami, and New Orleans. The Immigration Act of 1924 resulted in many fewer immigrants coming to the United States and also permitted the processing of immigrants at overseas embassies. By the time Ellis Island finally closed in 1954, more than 12 million immigrant steamship passengers had been processed into the United States through this port of entry (Coan, 2004: xiii). Today, more than 100 million Americans, one-third of the U.S. population, trace their ancestry to Ellis Island immigrants (National Park

Service, 2008). Those immigrants had left behind their history, homeland, and people to come to the United States in search of a new and better life.

The first immigrant to enter the United States through Ellis Island was Annie Moore, a young girl from County Cork, Ireland. She and her two brothers traveled alone across the Atlantic Ocean to be reunited with their parents, who had emigrated from Ireland two years earlier (Coan, 2004: xxiv). Annie Moore (1874–1924) has been immortalized in the popular song "Isle of Hope, Isle of Tears," written and composed by Brendan Graham and performed by, among others, the Celtic Women and the Irish Tenors singing groups. Two of the verses and the chorus of the song illustrate well the hopes, fears, dreams, and courage of so many of the immigrants to the United States, feelings and attributes that continue to characterize immigrants to this day:

On the first day of January
Eighteen ninety two.
They opened Ellis Island
And they let the people through.
And the first to cross the threshold
Of the Isle of hope and tears
Was Annie Moore from Ireland
Who was all of fifteen years.

(Chorus)

Isle of hope, Isle of tears
Isle of freedom, Isle of fears
But it's not the Isle
You left behind
That Isle of hunger, Isle of pain
Isle you'll never see again
But the Isle of home
Is always on your mind

In her little bag she carried
All her past and history.
And her dreams for the future
In the land of liberty.
And courage is the passport
When your old world disappears.
'Cos there's no future in the past
When you're fifteen years.

You may view the performance of this song by the Irish Tenors in concert at Ellis Island and/or listen to the audio as performed by the Celtic Women in concert in Trenton, New Jersey, online at http://www.youtube.com/watch?v=BGZaAwD2Mls&feature=related and http://www.youtube.com/watch?v=DbU7u0pr1B4.

As an aside, Brendan Graham, the author of "Isle of Hope, Isle of Tears," has informed us in a personal communication (October 8, 2009) that Annie Moore was actually seventeen years old when she moved from Ireland to the United States, not fifteen as stated in his song. Years after publishing it, Graham obtained a copy of her birth certificate reporting her year of birth as 1874. It was then that he learned she apparently lied about her age and claimed to be fifteen. If she was fifteen, she could remain with her two younger brothers in the "family section" of the ship, but if she was seventeen she would have to travel in the "adult section" of the ship and be separated from her brothers.

The last person to pass through Ellis Island was a Norwegian merchant seaman, Arne Petersson, who was processed on November 12, 1954 (Coan, 2004: xxiv; National Park Service, 2008).

In the 1800s, the combination of pro-immigration campaigns and the reduced cost of transcontinental transportation increased considerably the numbers of immigrants to the United States. Later, there was a second influx of German and Irish immigrants. Germans found work in several established industries, aiding in the overall development of U.S. commerce. The Irish immigrants, mostly Catholics, suffered severe discrimination that reached a peak in the mid-1850s with the emergence of the Know-Nothings, an anti-Catholic organization dedicated to maintaining the dominance of Anglo-Saxon Protestants. Between the early seventeenth century and the 1920s, an estimated 7 million people left Ireland for North America (K. Miller, 1985: 3). In the 2000 U.S. census, 30.5 million Americans (11 percent of the country's population) recorded their ancestry as Irish, second only to the 42.8 million people considering themselves to be of German ancestry (Brittingham and de la Cruz, 2004).

The end of the nineteenth century also saw immigration from some of the Scandinavian countries. These immigrants sought land for farming and developed the mostly unsettled Midwest (Cortes and Poston, 2008).

The Chinese have a long history of immigration to the United States. They first entered shortly after the beginnings of the California Gold Rush in 1849. An estimated 288,000 Chinese came to the United States during this period, although many returned to China before 1882 (I. Black, 1963; Poston and Luo, 2007; Poston, Mao, and Yu, 1994). Like most immigrants, the Chinese came as laborers in search of work and wages. Their port of entry was San Francisco, which is where they hoped to become rich and realize their dreams. To this day, the Chinese name for San Francisco is 舊金山 (*Jiu Jin Shan*), or "Old Gold Mountain." The Chinese were subjected to hostile discrimination because many American workers were threatened by the low wages the newcomers were willing to take. The passing of the Chinese Exclusion Act of 1882 ended the first period of Chinese immigration; it tapered off, eventually stopping by the end of the nineteenth century (Pedraza and Rumbaut, 1996; Poston and Luo, 2007).

The next period of Chinese immigration began in 1882 and extended to 1965. The Chinese Exclusion Act was renewed in 1892, was made permanent in 1902, and was not repealed until 1943. For all practical purposes, Chinese immigration to the United States during this period was banned. The only exceptions were diplomats, merchants, and some students, as well as their dependents, but these were small in number. The Chinese Exclusion Act resulted from a concern about the large numbers of Chinese who had come earlier in response to the need for inexpensive labor, particularly to help with the construction of the transcontinental railroad. Competition with American workers and a growing nativism brought pressure for restrictive action, beginning with the Chinese Exclusion Act. Passed by the 47th Congress on May 6, 1882, this law, as noted, suspended the immigration of Chinese laborers for ten years. It permitted Chinese who were in the United States as of 1880 to stay, travel abroad, and return. It also prohibited the naturalization of Chinese. A few persons were exempt, namely, teachers, students, merchants, and travelers, and they were admitted on the presentation of certificates from the Chinese government.

The next significant exclusionary legislation was the Act to Prohibit the Coming of Chinese Persons into the United States of May 1892, better known as the Geary Act. It allowed Chinese laborers to travel to China and reenter the United States, but its provisions were more restrictive than preceding immigration laws. The Geary Act required Chinese to register and secure a certificate as proof of their right to be in the United States. Those failing to do so could be put into prison or deported. Other restrictive immigration acts affecting citizens of Chinese ancestry followed. The ban continued in force until 1943, at which time an annual quota of 100 immigrants was assigned to Chinese who wished to enter the United States (King and Locke, 1980; Poston and Luo, 2007).

In 1943, President Franklin D. Roosevelt signed the Act to Repeal the Chinese Exclusion Acts, mainly because China and the United States were allies during World War II. The Act of 1943 also lifted restrictions on naturalization. However, until the Immigration Act of 1965, various laws continued to restrict Chinese immigration.

During this second period of Chinese immigration, those Chinese already in the United States were confined to highly segregated Chinatowns in major cities (San Francisco, New York, and elsewhere) and in isolated regions in rural areas across the country. Because the Chinese were deprived of their democratic rights, they sometimes made extensive use of the courts and diplomatic channels to defend themselves.

The U.S. Civil Rights movement of the 1960s, particularly the enactment of the Civil Rights Act of 1964 and the Immigration and Nationality Act of 1965, initiated the third period of Chinese immigration, covering the years from 1965 to the present. The new laws restored many of the basic rights denied earlier to Chinese Americans. Since the 1980s, thousands of Chinese people have come to the United States each year. For instance, during the twenty-three years between 1980 and 2002, the volume of permanent Chinese immigration to the United States numbered more than 911 thousand, almost seven times the number between 1891 and 1979. It is during this latest period that the numbers of Chinese student immigrants increased substantially; in most cases, however, students are not included in the count of permanent immigrants (Poston and Luo, 2007). In Chapter 13, we discuss immigration laws and regulations in more detail.

Overlapping with early Chinese immigration to the United States were population movements from Eastern and Southern Europe. These immigrants were not as welcome as the previous European immigrants had been because the "old" immigrants thought that these "new" immigrants would take their jobs (Purcell, 1995). They were mainly Italians, Greeks, Poles, and Slavs who spoke different languages and had slightly different physical features than the Western Europeans. They were subjected to discrimination but were able to assimilate into white American culture with passing generations (Cortes and Poston, 2008).

Currently, the largest numbers of immigrants to the United States are from certain Asian countries and Mexico. These immigrants come for many of the same reasons that the European immigrants came in earlier decades. Population booms and increased industrialization, combined with the economic opportunities of the United States, created the push and pull factors that increased emigration from Asia. Many Asians move right away into ethnic enclaves where they find jobs and homes among people from their countries of origin. However, they are often criticized for not assimilating into "mainstream" white American culture (Portes and Rumbaut, 1990).

The end of the twentieth century to the beginning of the twenty-first has seen the immigration of many million Mexicans to the United States. There is a long-standing social, economic, and geographical relationship between the two countries. As Massey and his colleagues have written, "the USA has invaded Mexico three times; it annexed one-third of its territory; it is the primary source of capital for Mexican investment; it is Mexico's largest trading partner; and Mexico is the second most important trading partner for the USA" (Massey et al., 2005: 67). Like most other newcomers to the United States, Mexicans are seeking better working conditions and higher wages than are available in their home country. They are subjected to the same discrimination as earlier immigrant groups. Americans of Mexican descent vary in their levels of assimilation, based mostly on how long they or their ancestors have been in the United States (Cortes and Poston, 2008).

The first major migration of Mexicans took place after the Mexican Revolution (1910) and was motivated in large part by labor requirements in the southwestern United States (Donato, 1994). This migration was steadily maintained until the immigrants became subjected to unfair treatment and were deported in large numbers. At about this time, the Immigration Act of 1924 was passed, which, as already noted, gave preference to Northern and Western Europeans. However, there was again a need for agricultural labor, so large-scale Mexican migration was resumed (Donato, 1994; Garcia, 2008).

Mexican migration to the United States may be categorized into three major periods: the *bracero* (i.e., guest worker) period (1942 to 1964), the post-bracero period (1965 through 1986), and the post-IRCA (Immigration Reform and Control Act) period (1987 to the present) (Donato, 1994; Durand, Massey, and Parrado, 1999). The **bracero program** (1942–1964) began as a response to the requirement for temporary agricultural labor. Attitudes toward immigration were tolerable during this twenty-two–year period. Mexicans were brought in on a temporary basis, and they maintained ties with their home country. Only a modicum of unauthorized (i.e., illegal) migration occurred during this period (Reichert and Massey, 1980). The bracero period is important because it established a precedent for Mexican migration to the United States, as an opportunity to obtain earnings in the form of remittances, and for the dynamic of a seasonal migration pattern (Garcia, 2008).

When the bracero program was terminated in 1964, around 200,000 of these guest workers, nearly half of the border population, lost their jobs, "leading to a buildup of social unrest" (Plankey Videla, 2008: 592). Several immigration regulations were then placed into effect. Only a person with family ties to a **green card holder** was allowed to hold a job in the United States (Reichert and Massey, 1980). Thus, persons without such associations would need to use illegal migration as a means to gain U.S. employment, and more and more Mexican immigrants were women and children (Reichert and Massey, 1980). Unauthorized migration also increased because of the caps placed on migration from Europe. In fact, Mexican migrants could enter and leave the United States without much difficulty, and employer sanctions for hiring undocumented workers were minimal.

In the latter part of this period, however, the issue of unauthorized, that is, illegal, migration began to be discussed and debated in the public arena (Bean, Telles, and Lowell, 1987). (An **illegal immigrant** enters a country without authorization or through the use of fraudulent documents.) Jorge Durand and his colleagues have written that "after 1973, wages stagnated, unemployment rates rose, income inequality grew, and the distribution of wealth became progressively more skewed" (Durand, Massey, and Parrado, 1999: 520). Some felt that the United States was losing control of its borders. These concerns and others resulted in the passage of the 1986 IRCA (Garcia, 2008; Warren and Passel, 1987).

IRCA was designed to drastically reduce unauthorized migration from Mexico (Durand, Massey, and Parrado, 1999; White, Bean, and Espenshade, 1990) mainly by imposing strict employer sanctions, providing amnesty to long-term residents of the United States, and instituting stricter border control. It was successful and undocumented migration was reduced. But as Jeffrey S. Passel (2006) has noted, rates began to increase in the early 1990s and have continued to increase to the present (see also Garcia, 2008).

The period following IRCA is known as the *new era of migration* (Durand, Massey, and Parrado, 1999). The immigrant population is no longer temporary, seasonal, geographically concentrated, and predominantly male but is now rather long-term, urbanized, and geographically dispersed. In the past two decades, there has been an increase in nativist sentiment (Espenshade and Hempstead, 1996) due in large part to a stagnating economy, a perceived threat to national security, particularly since the tragedy of 9/11, and the mistaken belief that immigrants, especially Mexicans, are taking away jobs from the permanent residents, even though extensive research indicates that this is not true (Garcia, 2008). The number of unauthorized Mexicans estimated to be residing in the United States in 2006 was about 6.6 million of the roughly 11.6 million total number of unauthorized immigrants, slightly higher than the estimate for the year 2000 (Costanzo et al., 2001; Hanson, 2006; Hoefer, Rytina, and Campbell, 2007; Passel, 2006).

THEORIES OF INTERNATIONAL MIGRATION

There are several theories of international migration, most of which focus on the determinants of voluntary migration. The *neoclassical economic model* may well be the oldest and best-known theory of international labor migration (Harris and Todaro, 1970; Lewis, 1954; Massey et al., 1993; Todaro, 1976). According to **the neoclassical economic theory of international migration**, migration occurs on account of individual cost–benefit decisions to maximize expected incomes through international movement

(Massey et al., 1994). Workers are attracted from low-wage countries with adequate labor to high-wage countries with limited labor.

The *new economics of migration* is a theory developed in recent years to challenge some of the hypotheses and assumptions of neoclassical economics. This theory argues that migration decisions are made not only by isolated individuals but also by larger units, such as families and households (Katz and Stark, 1986; Lauby and Stark, 1988; Massey et al., 1993; Stark 1984, 1991; Stark and Levhari, 1982). Migration occurs not only to increase individual earnings but also to minimize household risks and to protect the family from market failures.

An approach that differs from both of the preceding is the **dual labor market theory**, which argues that migration stems from the demands of the economic structure of industrial societies (Massey et al., 1993, 1994; Piore, 1979). International migration is caused not only by the push factors of the origin countries but also by the pull factors of the destination countries. Inherent tendencies in modern capitalism lead labor markets to separate into two sectors: "the primary sector that produces jobs with secure tenure, high pay, generous benefits, and good working conditions; and the secondary sector typified by instability, low pay, limited benefits, and unpleasant or hazardous working conditions" (Massey et al., 1994: 715). Employers are inclined to turn to migrants to fill the jobs in the secondary sector.

The **world systems theory of migration** argues that international migration is the natural result of the globalization of the market economy (Massey et al., 1994; Portes and Walton, 1981; Sassen, 1988). In the process of global industrialization, a large number of people are released from traditional industries, such as farming, state-owned industries, and handicrafts, and this creates a mobilized population to move both internally and internationally (Massey, 1988; Massey et al., 1994). The development of the global market economy attracts human capital to a relatively small number of global cities, among them, New York, Los Angeles, and Chicago (Castells, 1989; Massey et al., 1994; Sassen, 1991).

Finally, **migration network theory** focuses on networks, that is, the interpersonal ties that connect migrants, former migrants, potential migrants, and nonmigrants in the origin and destination countries. The networks increase the likelihood of international movement by decreasing migrant risks and costs and increasing the net earnings to migration (Massey et al., 1993). Networks make it easier for new migrants to find jobs and gain access to required resources in their destination countries.

These theories and others endeavor to account for the causal process of international migration at different levels of analysis, namely, the individual, the household, the country, and the world. These different perspectives are not necessarily incompatible (Poston, Luo, and Zhang, 2006). Indeed, the key elements of each theory are sometimes all subsumed under the headings of "push" and "pull." There are push and pull conditions facilitating migration in most of the countries of the world. For an individual or group to decide to engage in international migration, there needs to be a push from the origin country and/or a pull to the destination country. In addition to individual push and pull factors leading to international migration, there are also contextual factors that operate. For example, after arriving in destination countries, migrants, particularly Asian migrants, are sometimes pulled into what are called ethnic enclaves. An **ethnic enclave** is a community that helps individuals transition into life as immigrants by providing support and environments much like those in their mother countries. The push and pull factors, individual and contextual, can be one or more of any of the characteristics defining the five theories outlined in this section (Cortes and Poston, 2008).

ECONOMIC EFFECTS OF INTERNATIONAL MIGRATION

We noted at the start of this chapter that no demographic topic is discussed these days by laypeople and social scientists alike as frequently, as emotionally, and as forcefully as international migration. Surveys of U.S. residents conducted in recent years point to increasing levels of negativity about immigrants. A survey conducted in 2008 in Houston, Texas, for instance, found that "residents increasingly carry negative views about immigrants, saying they burden tax-supported services including schools and hospitals, while contributing to crime" (Pinkerton, 2008). Houston residents are not unlike residents of other big cities in the United States regarding their negative views about immigration and immigrants.

These negative sentiments are reflected in numerous popular books in the United States about international migration. In 2002, Patrick Buchanan published *The Death of the West: How Dying Populations and Immigrant Invasions Imperil Our Country*, and in 2007 he published *State of Emergency: The Third World Invasion and Conquest of America*. Other recently published books with similar alarmist views are *In Mortal Danger: The Battle for America's Border and Security* by Tom Tancredo (2006); *Immigration's Unarmed Invasion: Deadly Consequences* by Frosty Wooldridge (2004); *Fighting Immigration Anarchy: American Patriots Battle to Save the Nation* by Daniel Sheehy (2006); and *Alien Nation: Common Sense about America's Immigration Disaster* by Peter Brimelow (1996). We could go on and list another half dozen or more recently published books with gloomy alarmist views about international immigration. Fewer books show the positive contributions of international migration. One is Philippe Legrain's *Immigrants: Your Country Needs Them* (2006).

There is a wealth of published literature by demographers and other social scientists dealing with the positive and negative aspects of international migration, considered from many different vantage points. These include economic effects, cultural effects, environmental effects, health effects, and security effects, to list several of the dimensions that have been surveyed. In this section, we draw on this literature and undertake a review of the positive and negative characteristics of international migration. Our focus is on the economic effects: What is good and what is not good economically about international migration?

Before beginning this review, we note that demographers and social scientists do not always agree about the net economic effects of international migration. That is, is international migration good or bad economically for the sending and receiving countries? For example, the authors of this book hold modestly disparate views on this question. As noted earlier in the book's Preface, we were unable to reach agreement on their appraisal in this chapter of the net economic effects of international migration. The conclusions presented here are more reflective of Poston's views than Bouvier's.

In general terms, there are two basic perspectives on international migration: one permitting it and one denying it. Organizations and bodies such as the Catholic Church and the World Bank argue for more and freer international migration because "people should not be confined to their countries of birth by national borders and that more migration would speed economic growth and development in both sending and receiving countries" (Martin and Zurcher, 2008: 4). An opposite approach is found in organizations in almost every developed country of the world, arguing for reductions in the numbers of international immigrants. In the United States, two such bodies are Negative Population Growth (NPG) and the Federation for American Immigration Reform (FAIR). FAIR argues that "unskilled newcomers hurt low-skilled U.S. workers, have negative environmental effects, and threaten established U.S. cultural values" (Martin and Zurcher, 2008: 4).

The economic arguments about the costs and benefits of international migration, which we concentrate on here, are usually the main ones cited when scholars and laypeople argue for or against immigration. There is an impressive literature on this subject and it is complex and diverse. We draw here on the recent reviews of Bimal Ghosh (2005) and others.

From the vantage point of the receiving (host) countries, there are several related concerns: Are immigrants taking away jobs from the local population, are immigrants driving down wages, and are immigrants a burden on the welfare system of the host country? Most analyses in Western Europe and the United States indicate that the impact of immigration on jobs and wages is weak or nonexistent. Immigrants often wind up in the "dirty, difficult and dangerous jobs . . . shunned by local workers" (Ghosh, 2005: 168). Evidence shows little if any competition in these and in many other types of jobs between immigrants to a country and the local residents. There is a wealth of literature on this topic, and no correlation is found between immigration and employment. Immigrants are often the first ones to be fired, and they are also "found to earn less than local workers in comparable jobs" (pp. 169–170).

There is some literature showing how immigration can have a negative impact on the labor market. This would especially be the case in industries or geographic areas with large concentrations of foreign workers; sometimes this results in "pressure on jobs and working conditions of the local labor force" (Ghosh, 2005: 169; see also Borjas, 2003; Borjas, Freeman, and Katz, 1997).

With regard to wages, some believe that even if immigrants do not take jobs from local workers, they will depress wages. Research from numerous studies in Europe and the United States are mixed, with most indicating little if any depressing impact on local wages. Those showing negative effects of immigration on wages report a very small effect, on the order of −0.3 to −0.8 percent. In a study of U.S. workers, H. Brucker (2002) found that a 10 percent increment in the number of immigrants has essentially a zero effect on nonimmigrant wages (cited in Ghosh, 2005: 169). Other analyses actually show that the presence of immigrants tends to increase local wages, especially those of the highly skilled.

What of the effect of immigration on social welfare costs? Studies in the United Kingdom show that immigrants in the 1999–2000 period contributed the equivalent of U.S. $4 billion more in personal and employment taxes than they received in welfare benefits. Recent analyses conducted in the United States reach similar conclusions. Much depends on the degree to which immigrants depend on welfare. This varies from high levels in many Western European countries, sometimes higher than those of the local people, to levels in other European countries and in Canada, where the welfare dependence of immigrants is lower than that of citizens. Immigrants to the United States, particularly in their early years in the new country, do add to welfare costs, especially for education. But, eventually, the immigrants and their descendants end up paying taxes that result in a net positive contribution (Ghosh, 2005: 171).

There is a real economic gain for many countries in admitting skilled workers. European Union member states, particularly Germany and the

United Kingdom, are experienced users "of highly skilled foreign nationals, [and] are leading the way in selecting qualified workers from abroad" (Papademetriou, 2003: 571).

One study showed that there are approximately 400,000 engineers and scientists from countries of the developing world, representing 30 to 50 percent of the total stock, work in developed countries in research and development industries. Immigrants to the United States from developing countries have roughly twice as much education than their countrymen remaining at home: "An extreme case is that of Jamaica in 2000, when there were nearly four times more Jamaicans with tertiary education in the U.S. than at home. [Also], more Ethiopian doctors are practicing in Chicago than in Ethiopia" (Ghosh, 2005: 173).

Of all the developed countries, the United States has gained the most with respect to attracting skilled immigrants. In 2000, the United States had admitted more than 10.5 million highly skilled immigrants, while losing just over 431 thousand graduates to other countries, for a net gain of 10 million (Legrain, 2006: 95). Skilled immigrants from developing nations play a very important role in the economic activities of developed nations, a point often overlooked by those less accepting of international migrants.

Skilled immigrants have another type of impact on the economies of the host countries. Research has shown, for example, a positive association between the presence of foreign-born workers in California and exports from California to the home country. Specifically, "a one percent increase in the number of first generation immigrants generated a 0.5 percent increase in exports from California to the respective country" (Iredale, 2005: 224).

We turn next to the economic effects that migrants have on the sending countries. Does international migration help or hinder the economic development of the origin countries? On the one hand, emigration may be seen as a safety valve, temporarily, on job losses and labor restructuring in the process of industrial development. But since emigrants involve only a small share of the labor force of the sending countries, no more than 2 to 3 percent, their departure does not have a real and long-term impact on unemployment. In many developing countries, labor emigration does not result in a rise in wages because these countries "generally suffer from a large backlog of unemployed and underemployed; this is one reason why employers normally do not oppose labor emigration" (Ghosh, 2005: 173).

Another economic effect that should be considered is the contribution of remittances to the economies of the origin countries. The many millions of migrants living outside their countries of birth send billions of dollars home. Figure 7.4 uses data from the World Bank and shows the amounts of remittances sent to developing countries between 2000 and 2006. These

US$ (billions)

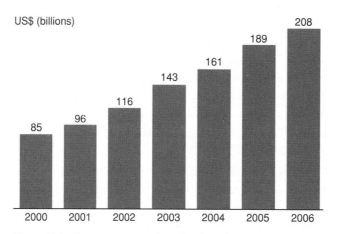

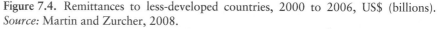

Figure 7.4. Remittances to less-developed countries, 2000 to 2006, US$ (billions). *Source:* Martin and Zurcher, 2008.

are large and growing so rapidly that they are "among the fastest growing international financial flows" (Martin and Zurcher, 2008: 18).

Remittances to developing countries almost doubled, from US $85 billion in 2000 to US $161 billion in 2004, and by 2006 had increased by another US $47 billion. Also, the data in Figure 7.4 are likely underestimates because "some remittances are sent home informally, with friends or relatives or via unregulated transfer agents, rather than through banks or regulated financial institutions" (Martin and Zurcher, 2008: 18).

Remittances are valuable, for one reason, because their recipients have been shown to have a high propensity to save the funds. The remittances also result in credit that may be used as investment capital. Small business ventures grow via remittances. They aid local community development and businesses, and they are an important and sometimes sizable addition to the gross national product (GNP) (i.e., the total dollar value of all goods and services produced for consumption in the society during a particular time period). However, one needs to be careful and not overestimate the effect of remittances on business development: "Businesses established through remittances cannot necessarily rely on their continued flow for sustainability" (Skeldon, 2005: 263).

Studies have also shown a positive association between remittances and poverty reduction: "A 10 percent increase in the share of remittances in country Gross Domestic Product (GDP) [leads] to a 1.2 percent decrease in the percentage of persons living on less than US $1.00 per day, and also reduces the depth or severity of poverty" (Ghosh, 2005: 179). Remittances are indispensable for the economic survival of many developing countries (Skeldon, 2005: 260).

(The difference between GDP and GNP is that GDP refers to goods and services produced in the country, whereas GNP refers to goods and services produced by companies of a country irrespective of their location. For instance, U.S. GNP refers to goods and services produced by American companies everywhere, whereas U.S. GDP refers to goods and services produced in the United States.)

What is the economic cost to the origin countries when they lose skilled personnel via emigration? Is emigration always a "brain drain" that "can act as a serious brake on development and poverty alleviation?" (Laczko, 2005: 287). Actually, in nursing and teaching jobs, the international departure of residents, followed by their return, enables the migrants to obtain new skills, "and in many cases plays a useful role in exposing migrants, as well as the host societies, to new ideas and ways of doing things" (Laczko, 2005: 289). Research on the net effects of return international migration, that is, remigration, shows that the origin countries derive the greatest benefit when the skilled immigrants return home in, say, ten to fifteen years after their departure (p. 289).

The literature on the effects of international immigration is extensive. We have discussed here only a small amount of the relevant research, and have focused only on economic effects. Although there are, indeed, some important economic costs to international migration, on balance there are more benefits, and this generalization may be made with regard to both the host countries and the sending countries.

UNAUTHORIZED INTERNATIONAL MIGRATION

International migrants are often categorized as either legal or illegal. The main adjective we use in this book to refer to an illegal international migrant is *unauthorized*. What does this mean? An **unauthorized immigrant** is a person who immigrates into a host country "through irregular or extralegal channels" (Armbrister, 2003: 512). More specifically, an unauthorized immigrant is an international migrant who resides in the host country of destination, but who is not a citizen of the host country, who has not been admitted by the host country for permanent residence, "and is not in a set of specific authorized temporary statuses permitting longer-term residence and work" (Passel, 2006: 1; see also Passel, Van Hook, and Bean, 2004). An international migrant is classified as unauthorized if 1) during the process of migrating to the host country, the person "avoided inspection by crossing borders clandestinely or . . . traveled with fraudulent documents, e.g., a falsified visa or counterfeit passport"; such persons are referred to as **entries without inspection (EWIs)**; or 2) the migrant "overstayed the time limit of a legally obtained non-immigrant temporary visa"; such persons are referred to as *visa overstayers*; or 3) the migrant "violated explicit visa conditions, e.g., obtaining employment while holding a student visa" (Armbrister, 2003: 512).

The United States is unique among all the countries of the world regarding the most common source of unauthorized immigration. The most frequent type of unauthorized immigrant in almost every country of the world is one who arrives legally in the host country "as a non-immigrant (e.g., tourist, student, or temporary laborer) and [stays] beyond the legally sanctioned period" (Armbrister, 2003: 512), that is, a visa overstayer. The majority of unauthorized immigrants in the United States, however, "entered without inspection over land borders with Mexico and Canada" (Armbrister, 2003: 512); they are EWIs, and most are from Mexico. It is estimated that in 2005, among the unauthorized immigrant population in the United States, 25 to 40 percent were visa overstayers and the balance, the majority, were the so-called EWIs (Passel, 2006: 16).

Whereas most of the unauthorized migrants entering the United States as EWIs are from Mexico, the same may not be said about visa overstayers. Demographers Susan Brown and Frank Bean remind us that "visa-overstays do not come predominantly from any one country" (2005: 369). Nonetheless, in almost all the countries of the world except the United States, most unauthorized immigrants are visa overstayers.

Regarding the volume of unauthorized immigrants worldwide, the International Organization for Migration (2008) estimates the number to be between 30 million and 40 million persons, constituting 15 to 20 percent of the estimated total number of 190 million international migrants. Most unauthorized immigrants go mainly to a few developed countries, and most hail from developing countries. However, visa overstayers in countries of the developed world are now believed to constitute a significant proportion of unauthorized immigrants in developed countries such as Australia and New Zealand (Armbrister, 2003: 513; International Organization for Migration, 2001).

During the 1990s, the volume of unauthorized immigrants increased significantly. Worldwide, most are between the ages of 18 and 35, and more than half are male, although this percentage has decreased in recent years: "With large numbers of women in developed countries working outside the home, opportunities for employment in domestic work and childcare have attracted women from developing countries, swelling both legal and unauthorized migrant numbers" (Armbrister, 2003: 513).

In the major regions of the world, certain countries serve as magnets for unauthorized immigrants. In Africa, South Africa in the post-apartheid era has become the major destination for unauthorized immigrants from other African countries. Right before the start of this new century, it was estimated that South Africa had 3.5 million unauthorized migrant workers, plus another 750,000 who were visa overstayers. These persons comprised around 9.2 percent of the total population of the country; they were "granted no protection under South African law, were targets of widespread violence fueled by high unemployment rates, and remained subject to immediate expulsion on apprehension" (Armbrister, 2003: 513).

In Asia, most of the unauthorized immigrant streams are to Japan, South Korea, and Malaysia. Japan and Malaysia each have around a half million unauthorized immigrants, and in Malaysia they comprise as much as 2 percent of the country's population. In Europe, a half million unauthorized immigrants each year are brought into the European Union by smugglers. The total stock is estimated to be about 3 million. The major destination countries used to be the United Kingdom, Germany, France, Belgium, the Netherlands, and Switzerland, but in the 1990s, these countries introduced strict immigration laws. The unauthorized immigrant streams then moved south to Italy, Spain, and Portugal. Italy now has an estimated 300,000 unauthorized immigrants, constituting 0.5 percent of its population (Armbrister, 2003: 513–514).

In the Western Hemisphere, the United States is the magnet country for unauthorized migrants. The numbers have increased considerably in past decades. In the United States, the estimated number of unauthorized immigrants grew from roughly 4 million in 1990 to around 8.5 million in 2000 and to about 11.6 million in 2006. Between 2000 and 2006, the number increased by 37 percent (Table 7.1). During this period, Mexico maintained its position as the prime source of unauthorized immigrants; the estimated number of unauthorized migrants from Mexico to the United States grew from 4.7 million in 2000 to 6.6 million in 2006, for a 40 percent increase. Countries sending the next largest numbers of unauthorized immigrants to the United States in 2006 were El Salvador (510,000), Guatemala (430,000), the Philippines (280,000), Honduras (280,000), India (270,000), South Korea (250,000), Brazil (210,000), and China (190,000). The top ten origin countries shown in Table 7.1 account for nearly 80 percent of the 2006 unauthorized immigrant population in the United States. Although Mexico is responsible for more than half of the unauthorized migration stream, the largest percentage increases in unauthorized migrants in the 2000–2006 period were from India (125 percent), Brazil (110 percent), and Honduras (75 percent) (Hoefer, Rytina, and Campbell, 2007: 4).

Where in the United States do the unauthorized immigrants reside? Almost 3 million, or 25 percent, of all the unauthorized migrants in the

Table 7.1. Country of birth of the unauthorized immigrant population: United States, January 2006 and 2000

Country of birth	Estimated population in January 2006	Estimated population in January 2000	Percent of total 2006	Percent of total 2000	Percent change 2000 to 2006
All countries	11,550,000	8,460,000	100	100	37
Mexico	6,570,000	4,680,000	57	55	40
El Salvador	510,000	430,000	4	5	19
Guatemala	430,000	290,000	4	3	48
Philippines	280,000	200,000	2	2	40
Honduras	280,000	160,000	2	2	75
India	270,000	120,000	2	1	125
South Korea	250,000	180,000	2	2	39
Brazil	210,000	100,000	2	1	110
China	190,000	190,000	2	2	–
Vietnam	160,000	160,000	1	2	–
Other countries	2,410,000	1,950,000	21	23	24

Source: Hoefer, Rytina, and Campbell, 2007.

United States in 2006 lived in California, whose share in 2006, however, dropped from 30 percent in 2000. Texas is the next leading state, with 1.6 million, and Florida is the third largest with almost 1 million (Table 7.2). The largest percentage increases between 2000 and 2006 in the numbers of unauthorized migrants were in Georgia (a 123 percent increase), in Washington (a 65 percent increase), in Arizona (a 52 percent increase), in Texas (a 50 percent increase), and in North Carolina (a 42 percent increase) (Hoefer, Rytina, and Campbell, 2007: 4).

The geographical distribution of the unauthorized immigrant population in the United States became more diversified between 2000 and 2006. This may be seen in the increased share of unauthorized migrants living in other states: "The percentage of unauthorized immigrants residing in states ranked 6th through 10th in 2006 – Arizona, Georgia, New Jersey, North Carolina, and Washington – increased from 16 percent in 2000 to 18 percent in 2006. In addition, the share of the unauthorized population residing in all other states increased from 21 percent to 26 percent during the period" (Hoefer, Rytina, and Campbell, 2007: 4).

What are some of the characteristics of the unauthorized U.S. migrant population? Around two-thirds have been in the United States for less than ten years and 40 percent for less than five years. Just under half are adult males, a finding that runs counter to the mistaken belief that most unauthorized immigrants are young men. As a matter of fact, the

Table 7.2. State of residence of the unauthorized immigrant population: United States, January 2006 and 2000

State of residence	Estimated population in January 2006	Estimated population in January 2000	Percent of total 2006	Percent of total 2000	Percent change 2000 to 2006
All states	11,550,000	8,460,000	100	100	37
California	2,830,000	2,510,000	25	30	13
Texas	1,640,000	1,090,000	14	13	50
Florida	980,000	800,000	8	9	23
Illinois	550,000	440,000	5	5	25
New York	540,000	540,000	5	6	–
Arizona	500,000	330,000	4	4	52
Georgia	490,000	220,000	4	3	123
New Jersey	430,000	350,000	4	4	23
North Carolina	370,000	260,000	3	3	42
Washington	280,000	170,000	2	2	65
Other states	2,950,000	1,750,000	26	21	69

Source: Hoefer, Rytina, and Campbell, 2007.

age and sex distribution of this population varies considerably. More than 35 percent of unauthorized immigrants are adult females, and 16 percent are children (Passel, 2006: 2–3).

A most interesting fact is that most of the children of unauthorized immigrants are themselves legal residents. Nearly 3.1 million of the children of unauthorized immigrants were born in the United States, and are thus themselves legal residents of the United States. These children comprise almost two-thirds of all the children living in unauthorized migrant families. Two out of three children living in unauthorized immigrant families are legal residents of the United States (Passel, 2006: 7–8).

Of the total population of adult males in the age group 18–64 who are unauthorized immigrants, 94 percent are in the labor force; this may be compared with 86 percent of adult males who are legal immigrants and 83 percent of adult males who are native-born U.S. residents. Adult males who are unauthorized migrants are gainfully employed at a higher rate than adult males who are legal immigrants, who in turn are gainfully employed at a higher rate than U.S.-born adult males. But the opposite trend is found for adult females (Passel, 2006: 9–10).

Unauthorized workers in the United States are found in many occupations but are heavily concentrated in low-wage and low-education occupations. Four percent of the unauthorized immigrants are in agricultural occupations, 19 percent are in construction, and 31 percent are in service occupations. The shares of unauthorized workers in agricultural and construction jobs are three times those of native workers; the share of unauthorized migrants in service jobs is double that of native workers (Passel, 2006: 11).

Another way to view the occupational distribution of unauthorized immigrant workers is by asking what percentage of each occupational category is filled by unauthorized workers. Although only 4 percent of unauthorized migrants are employed in agricultural jobs, they comprise almost a quarter of all agricultural jobs. The unauthorized population comprises 17 percent of all occupations involving building, cleaning, and maintenance; 14 percent of all jobs in construction and extractive occupations; and 12 percent of all jobs in food preparation and serving (Passel, 2006: 10–11).

We conclude this chapter by introducing a concept important in all discussions of international migration and migration policy, *zero net international migration*. This concept is not as easily understood as it should be and often is used incorrectly.

ZERO NET INTERNATIONAL MIGRATION

Net international migration and natural increase (the difference between births and deaths) are the demographic processes that determine the amount of growth or decline in a nation's population. In a country such as the United States and in most of the European countries that are today characterized by low levels of fertility and mortality, the contribution of net international migration to overall population change overshadows the contribution of natural increase. Some hold that international migration to the United States is too large, and thus argue for **zero international migration**. They state that if the number of people who leave the country each year is the same as the number who enter each year, then the effect of net international migration will be zero. For example, proponents of negative population growth (NPG) have stated that we should place a ceiling on annual immigration so that it is balanced by emigration, and thus will not contribute to overall population growth (Mann, 1992). In this last section of the chapter, we draw on our earlier research (Bouvier, Poston, and Zhai, 1997) and show why this reasoning is incorrect.

Zero net international migration should not be confused with no (i.e., zero) international migration. The former is characterized by the same numbers of persons immigrating into a country as emigrating from it. In the latter, there is no international migration. The two are not the same.

Zero net international migration is at least theoretically possible. Indeed, such has always been the intent behind temporary worker programs – whether in Europe or in the Middle East or in the Arabian Gulf.

Workers are typically allowed to enter the country for a specified period of time and then later are expected to return to their homelands. Let us assume that zero net international migration could become a reality even in a country like the United States. If this were to occur, and if each year a number, say, 200,000, were to immigrate to the United States, and 200,000 were to emigrate from the United States, does this mean that immigration will no longer be a main contributor to population growth, as the NPG proponents conclude?

The answer is no. Even with zero net international migration, the impact of the immigration and emigration movements that produce it would result in considerable population increases in receiving countries, such as the United States, and substantial population losses in sending countries, such as Mexico.

In considering the direct impact of zero net international migration, we must first observe that immigrants to a country are usually always younger than remigrants from that country. Immigrants often arrive in their countries of destination when they are in their twenties and early thirties; conversely, remigrants usually depart the host countries either fairly soon after their arrival, or much later when they are in their sixties or older when they reach retirement.

To simplify our hypothetical illustration about patterns of immigration to and remigration from the United States, let us assume that all immigrants enter the country at age 15, and let us further assume that all remigrants leave the country at age 65. Thus, they tend to spend most of their lives in the United States, their country of first destination, for an average of about fifty years.

In this illustration, net international migration each year would be zero because 200,000 people would immigrate in each year and 200,000 would leave each year. We use the life table (discussed in Chapter 5) as a way of keeping track of the immigrants and remigrants. For most people, the life table indicates how many additional years a person can expect to live, on average, after having attained a specific age. If 200,000 people enter the United States at say, age 15, and leave at say, age 65, the total number of person-years spent in the country for any one of these cohorts of 200,000 persons would be 10 million (200,000 immigrants times 50 years) minus the person-years that would have been lived in the United States by those who died there before reaching age 65. If 200,000 persons immigrate to the United States at age 15, stay for fifty years, and then depart at age 65, this one cohort of 200,000 persons will have lived there for more than 9.5 million person-years. Even though 200,000 persons leave the United States each year (at age 65) and 200,000 enter each year (at age 15), there is nevertheless a sizable direct effect of zero net international immigration. In the hypothetical case we have constructed here, the direct effect of the net international migration involving 200,000 emigrants and 200,000 immigrants each year is in excess of 9.5 million person-years lived in the United States for each cohort of 200,000 immigrants who come there at age 15. Therefore, we must not confuse the two concepts of zero net international migration and zero (or no) international migration; they are very different from one another. The direct impact of zero net international migration can be quite substantial.

SUMMARY

This chapter focuses on the demographic dynamics of international migration. No demographic topic is discussed by laypeople and social scientists as frequently, as forcefully, and as emotionally as international migration. Having considered in Chapter 6 the topic of internal migration and now, in this chapter, international migration, it is certainly the case that the dynamics, the concepts, and the theories of the two differ significantly.

We began this chapter by reviewing the definitions and concepts that are used by demographers in their analyses of international migration. World immigration patterns over time were next addressed, followed by a discussion of immigration to the United States. We then summarized some of the major theories of international migration. We next turned to a discussion of the positive and negative economic issues pertaining to international migration, followed by a consideration of legal and unauthorized immigration. We concluded the chapter with a section on the concept of zero net international migration.

This chapter completes our presentation of the three demographic processes of fertility (Chapter 3), mortality (Chapter 5), and migration (Chapters 6 and 7). In the next chapter, we focus on the two most important characteristics studied by demographers, namely, age and sex; these are so relevant for demography that they are referred to as the *demographic characteristics*.

KEY TERMS

bracero program	forced migration
dual labor market theory	foreign-born
entries without inspection (EWIs)	green card holder
emigrant	illegal immigrant
emigration	immigrant
ethnic enclave	immigration

international migration
migration network theory
naturalized citizen
neoclassical economic theory of
    international migration
net international migration

refugee
remigration
unauthorized immigrant
world systems theory of
    migration
zero international migration

8 Age and Sex Composition

INTRODUCTION

Of all the characteristics of human populations, age and sex are the most important and relevant for demographers. They are so important for demographic analysis that they are referred to as "the demographic variables" (Bogue, 1969: 147). The demographic processes of fertility, mortality, and migration produce the population's age and sex structure (Horiuchi and Preston, 1988), and the age and sex structure influences the demographic processes. As we have already shown in Chapter 1, there is a very close relationship between the *demographic variables* and the *demographic processes*.

The importance of age and sex extends considerably beyond demography, however. The division of labor in traditional societies is based almost entirely on age and sex. In fact, age and sex differences of one form or another are found in all known human societies (K. Davis, 1949: Chapter 4; Murdock, 1949: Chapters 1 and 8).

At the individual level, age and sex are of such tremendous importance in our daily life that usually we do not know we are observing them. Whenever we walk across campus or on the streets where we live, what are the first two characteristics we recognize about an approaching person? The person's sex and a rough notion of his or her age, that is, whether the person is a baby, an adolescent, a young adult, a middle-aged person, or a senior. We make these determinations mainly on the basis of outward appearances, and we make them so automatically that they are done subconsciously.

The determination of a person's sex is usually the first item of information we obtain. Often, the person's given name tells us his or her sex. If you inform your mother you just met someone with the name of Nancy, Bethany, or Heather, she will certainly know the person you met is female.

If the person you just met has the given name of David, Daniel, or Mark, your mother will recognize this person to be male. However, if you tell your mother you just met someone with the given name of Pat, Jordan, Leslie, Chris, Jean, or Ryan, the first question your mother will almost certainly ask you is, "Is your friend a male or female?" Try speaking to someone about another person who has an androgynous name, such as the ones just mentioned. Your conversation will not get very far until the other person knows the sex of the person being discussed.

In addition, when a person marries or dies or achieves some important recognition, and these events are written up in stories in local newspapers, the given name usually tells us the person's sex. If the person's name is androgynous, the use of sex-specific pronouns informs the reader of the person's sex. Following the first mention of the person's full name, there appears, almost always, the person's age. We seem to need or want to know not only the person's sex but also the person's age. Indeed, people have a tremendous curiosity about the age of other people when reading about their achievements or recognizing their contributions. Why is this so? Donald T. Rowland has written that this curiosity "reflects a pervasive interest in comparing the timing of events with our expectations or social timetables" (Rowland, 2003: 77; see also Neugarten and Hagestad, 1976: 35).

Changes in the age distribution of a population have consequences for educational, political, and economic life (Keyfitz and Flieger, 1971: Chapter 2). A society's age and sex distribution has important implications for socioeconomic and demographic development (Keyfitz, 1965), as well as for labor-force participation and gender relations (South and Trent, 1988). Indeed, "almost any measurement that can be taken of human beings, or of groups of human beings, will show substantial variation by sex and age" (Bogue, 1969: 147).

In this chapter, we first consider the definition of age and sex. Age is easy to define because it is based on temporal change. Some may think that sex is also easy to define, but it is not. There are many issues to consider in determining one's sex. They are involved and complex, and we spend several pages in this chapter discussing them. Next, some of the theoretical issues in demography dealing with age and sex structure are reviewed; these pertain principally to what demographers refer to as **stable population theory**. We then cover some of the methods and approaches demographers use to represent age and sex structure. We conclude with detailed discussions of two key areas of age and sex structure, namely, the **sex ratio at birth (SRB)** and **population aging**.

CONCEPTS OF AGE AND SEX

Definition of age and sex

To a certain extent, the classification, definition, and enumeration of persons by sex are more straightforward compared to the situation with most other characteristics of human populations. For instance, the characteristics of race, marital status, and occupation "involve numerous categories and are subject to alternative formulation as a result of cultural differences, differences in the uses to which the data will be put, and differences in the interpretations of respondents and enumerators" (Shryock, Siegel, and Associates, 1976: 105). Nevertheless, the classification and definition of age and sex, especially, sex, can be problematic.

Age is defined more straightforwardly than most demographic variables. Age is an ascribed, yet changeable, characteristic. It is usually defined in population censuses in terms of the age of the person at his or her last birthday. The United Nations (UN) (1998a: 69) defined age as "the estimated or calculated interval of time between the date of birth and the date of the census, expressed in complete solar years" (see also Hobbs, 2004). In most censuses, the respondent is asked to give his or her current age, as well as the date when he or she was born. Adjustments are usually introduced by census-editing procedures if the respondent's current age does not correspond to the age denoted by the date of birth. This tends to minimize the phenomenon of **age heaping,** an issue discussed later (Poston, 2005).

Sex is also an ascribed characteristic and, for most people, unchangeable. Although there are some who do indeed change their sex, for most, sex is fixed at birth. When a baby is born, its sex is determined on the basis of his or her genital tubercle. On average, boys are born with penises ranging in length from 2.9 to 4.5 centimeters (Flatau et al., 1975). For girls, clitoral length at birth ranges from 0.2 to 0.85 centimeters (Fausto-Sterling, 2000: 60; Sane and Pescovitz, 1992). When the length of the tubercle is somewhere between the range for penis length and the range for clitoral length, sex determination is open for discussion and decision making by the parents and medical workers. But even in such extreme situations (1–2 cases per 1,000 live births), sex assignment is made soon after birth (Money, 1988). The census definition of sex, therefore, is usually not problematic because everyone knows his or her sex. The question, however, is how one's sex is determined.

There are several biological and social considerations regarding the determination of sex. When demographers identify the sex of a person or its distribution in a population, they almost always rely on the social definition of self-identification. That is, when a person's sex is listed on a census questionnaire or survey or certificate, its designation is based on the person's self-identification of his or her sex, not on biological considerations, such as the person's chromosomes or external genitals. However, sex is also determined biologically, in five ways, discussed next.

Biological definitions of sex

The first biological definition of sex is based on chromosomes, which are structures containing genetic material. Males have an X chromosome and a Y chromosome, and females have two X chromosomes. The X chromosome is larger than the Y chromosome and carries more genetic material (Tavris and Wade, 1984: 135). Chromosome distribution is determined by one's parents. The ovum of the female and the sperm of the male each contain twenty-three chromosomes. When the sperm and the ovum come together in one of the woman's Fallopian tubes, they produce a fertilized egg, known as an embryo. It consists of forty-six chromosomes aligned in twenty-three pairs. One of these constitutes the sex of the embryo. An X chromosome is contributed by the mother and either an X or a Y chromosome is contributed by the father.

The second biological definition of sex is based on gonads, that is, testes in males and ovaries in females. If the embryo is chromosomally male, one theory is that a gene on the Y chromosome produces male gonads (testes) at about the sixth week after conception. If the embryo is chromosomally female, female gonads (ovaries) appear a few weeks later. Scholars are not entirely sure how this occurs.

The gonads produce the sex-specific hormones, which are the basis for the third biological definition of sex. Androgens are a class of hormones, found mainly in males, though also in females, of which testosterone is the most important. Testosterone is responsible for the differentiation of male and female primary sex characteristics at about the seventh week of fetal life; "[o]n average men... have about ten times the testosterone level that women have, but the range among men varies greatly, and some women have levels higher than some men" (Kimmel, 2004: 40). Without the release of testosterone and other androgens, the male fetus will not develop male external genital organs. Males also receive major surges of testosterone at puberty so that the task of sex differentiation can be completed. Estrogen surges also occur at puberty in females.

Every embryo contains "two sets of ducts, one of which will become the internal reproductive structures appropriate to the embryo's sex" (Tavris and Wade, 1984: 137). These internal sexual properties constitute the fourth biological definition of sex. In males, these tissues are referred to as Wolffian ducts, and they result in the vas deferens, the seminal vesicles, and the prostate. In females, they are known as Mullerian ducts, and they become the "Fallopian tubes, the uterus, and the inner two-thirds of the vagina. In each sex, the ducts that do not develop eventually degenerate, except for traces" (p. 137; see also Kimmel, 2004: 39–40).

The sex-specific internal sex structures of the fetus lead finally to the development of sex-specific external genitals, namely, a penis and scrotal sac for males and a clitoris and vagina for females. The external sex structures are the basis for the fifth biological definition of sex. It is this fifth definition that results in the assignment of sex at the birth of the baby.

Intersex

Most embryos are consistent on the five biological definitions of sex. If an embryo is chromosomally a male, it will also be a male gonadally and hormonally, and will possess male internal and male external sex structures; similarly for females. But this is not always the case. In around 23/10,000 births, these five definitions of sex are not consistent, resulting in what is referred to as an intersexed birth. There are numerous types of **intersex**. We discuss some of the major ones.

One intersex category is chromosomal. Occasionally, chromosomal inconsistencies occur, sometimes during sperm production, resulting in what Claire M. Renzetti and Daniel J. Curran (1999: 34) have referred to as an "abnormal complement of sex chromosomes." If the sperm fails to divide properly, that is, if what is called *nondisjunction* occurs, one kind of sperm produced will have neither an X nor a Y chromosome. If this sperm fertilizes a normal egg, the offspring will have only an X chromosome. This type of intersex is known as Turner's Syndrome. The person appears to be a female because although it lacks ovaries, it possesses some external female characteristics. This condition is estimated to occur in about 4/10,000 live births (Fausto-Sterling, 2000: 53).

Another case of nondisjunction is a sperm produced with both an X and a Y chromosome, or two Y chromosomes, resulting in the XXY and XYY chromosome abnormalities. The XXY is referred to as **Klinefelter's syndrome** and occurs in roughly 9/10,000 live births (Fausto-Sterling, 2000: 53). A person born with this chromosomal characteristic has the height of a normal male, with long legs, an absent or weak sex drive, "feminized" hips, some breast development, and a small penis and testes (Money and Ehrhardt, 1972). The XYY is referred to as **Jacob's syndrome** and occurs in about 1/2,000 births. A person born with this chromosomal characteristic is an anatomical male with no physical abnormalities, except for unusual height. The extra Y chromosome does not result in the person's having more androgens than an XY male. Such persons appear to be able to reproduce successfully and rarely come to the attention of investigators, except through large-scale screening of newborns.

The other chromosomal type is the person with three X chromosomes, which is known as the XXX syndrome, or Triple X syndrome, or Trisomy X. This too occurs roughly in 1/2,000 live births. People born with this chromosomal characteristic are anatomically females and show few visible signs of abnormality, although they tend to be taller than XX females and have a slightly higher incidence of learning disorders (Renzetti and Curran, 2003: 36).

These examples of intersex are chromosomal combinations other than the XY male or the XX female. The designation of the sex of these persons at birth is usually based on external sexual organs. There are other forms of intersex in which the persons are chromosomally male (XY) or female (XX), but the sexual distinctions occur at the level of hormones.

One such example is when an XX fetus receives an excessive amount of androgens. This is known as the **adrenogenital syndrome (AGS)**, also referred to as **congenital adrenal hyperplasia (CAH)**. Renzetti and Curran (2003: 37) have estimated the incidence of AGS as between 1/5,000 and 1/15,000 live births. Untreated females with AGS have normally functioning ovaries and normal internal female sexual organs but a masculinized external appearance. This can vary from a slightly enlarged clitoris to a nearly normal-size penis with an empty scrotum. If treated with cortisol from birth on, these females will have a later menarche than normal but will be able to conceive, lactate, and deliver babies normally (Money and Ehrhardt, 1972).

Another type of intersex at the hormonal level is fetuses that are chromosomally male with genitals that are ambiguous or that look more like a clitoris than a penis. This condition is known as **androgen insensitivity syndrome (AIS)**. It cannot be treated by administering androgen after birth because the cells remain incapable of responding to androgen. At puberty, AIS persons develop breasts and a feminine body shape, and identify as females.

These are a few of several examples of intersex occurrences. Such persons are inconsistent on the five biological definitions of sex. But the designation of their sex at birth is most always based on the external organs, that is, the presence or lack thereof of a penis. Sexual consistency on the five biological conditions is not a requirement for sex designation. Indeed, we noted earlier that more than 23/10,000 live births are inconsistent on the five biological definitions.

Several well-known individuals are alleged to be/have been intersexed. These include the historical figure Joan of Arc (Mary Gordon, 2000) and such Hollywood celebrities as Mae West, Greta Garbo, Marlene Dietrich, and Jamie Lee Curtis (Young, 2002). A search on the Internet of "intersex" will bring up these and many more names of historical and contemporary figures. In most of these instances, however, medical verification, for example, in the form of chromosomal data, is lacking.

The case of Joan of Arc is of particular interest. Joan may be "the one person born before 1800, with the exception of Jesus Christ, that the average Westerner can name" (Gordon, 2000: xix). In writings, movies, and plays about her, she is often referred to as a "girl/boy." She reportedly had "beautiful" breasts, yet was not known to have ever menstruated (Gordon, 2000: 144, 145, 169). All of these characteristics are consistent with those of persons with AIS.

Changing sex

We noted earlier that once sex assignment is made, it is usually permanent. However, there are a few instances of persons who change their sex. These persons are usually consistent on the five biological definitions but who voluntarily decide, usually during adulthood, to change their sex; these persons are referred to as *transsexuals*. A transsexual is one whose primary sexual identification is with the opposite sex and who decides to take on such identification by undergoing sex-change surgery and, usually, also hormonal therapy to further the change.

Another term, **transgender**, is a catchall term used to refer to people who live as the opposite sex, whether or not they have had sex-change surgery. This broad category also includes transvestites (sometimes called cross-dressers), that is, persons who dress in a style traditionally associated with persons of the opposite sex, but who do not necessarily undergo sex-change surgery or hormonal therapy.

A male-to-female (MTF) transsexual is a genetic male who thinks of himself as a female. In a similar way, a female-to-male (FTM) transsexual is a genetic female consistent on all five biological definitions who thinks of herself as a male. When a transsexual opts for sexual reassignment through surgery, the external genitals are changed. There are no reliable data on the numbers of people in the population who self-identify as transsexual. However, there appear to be more MTF transsexuals than FTM transsexuals. Many transsexuals report that they felt they were in the wrong body as far back as they can remember, and that even as preschoolers they often preferred clothes, toys, and so forth of children of the opposite sex (Brevard, 2001; Jorgensen, 1967; Khosla, 2006; McCloskey, 2000; Morris, 1974).

Sex determination, self-identification, and the Olympic Games

When demographers measure the sex composition of a population, they almost always rely on self-identification. The census or survey questionnaires contain an item asking about one's sex (or gender). If the person self-identifies as male, that person is counted as a male, and similarly if the person reports her sex as female. Demographers do not base their classification of sex on any one or combination of the five biological definitions just reviewed, only on the social definition of self-identification. Indeed, there is no demographic research of which we are aware that has examined whether males and females who are and who are not consistent on the five biological definitions of sex vary with respect to their fertility, mortality, and migration.

The International Olympic Committee (IOC) has been struggling for many years with the issue of sex determination. In the Olympic Games in the 1960s, female competitors were required to submit themselves for an inspection or examination of their genitalia (Fausto-Sterling, 2000: 3), that is, the fifth biological definition of sex. In later games, chromosomal verification of sex was required (XX equals female, XY equals male), that is, the first biological definition of sex. The IOC decided in 2003 to abandon both kinds of sex testing. For the most part, self-identification of one's sex is now the criterion for determining sex for Olympic competition. With respect to Olympic competitors who are transsexuals, however, such persons must have undergone surgery transforming their genitals to those of the assigned sex and, moreover, there must be verification of the administration of hormonal therapy appropriate for the assigned sex.

Sex versus gender

We have already noted that sex, for the most part though not always, is an ascribed variable whose designation (male or female) is based on biology. In the social sciences, therefore, the concept of *sex* is often used when discussing biological differences between males and females, for example, fertility and mortality differences. The concept of *gender* is most often used when discussing nonbiological differences between males and females, for example, differences in socioeconomic status. However, demographers tend to use the term *sex* when discussing both biological and nonbiological differences owing, perhaps, to demography's major focus on fertility and mortality. We do not mean to suggest that demographers are uninterested in nonbiological differences between the sexes. Differences between males and females in migration, marriage and divorce, and labor-force participation, to name but a few, are nonbiological differences of significant interest to demographers (Poston, 2005; Riley, 2005). But even when demographers study these nonbiological behaviors, they retain the use of the term *sex* (for a broader discussion, see Riley, 2005).

THEORETICAL AND SUBSTANTIVE ISSUES OF AGE AND SEX

The age and sex structure of a population is an important piece of information because in many ways it is a map of the demographic history of the population. Persons of the same age constitute a group or cohort of people who were born during the same period, and therefore have been exposed to similar historical facts and conditions. These experiences may also differ according to sex. For instance, military personnel who participate in wars are usually restricted to a narrow age range and are comprised of more males than females. For decades after the cessation of fighting, one will observe heavier attrition among the male cohorts owing to war casualties. Major events in a population's immediate history, say, those that occurred within the previous eight decades, are easily recognized when only the population's current data on age and sex are examined.

Social scientists in particular are interested in the age and sex composition of populations. The numerical balance between the sexes affects many social and economic relationships, not the least of which is marriage. Later, we describe how the severely imbalanced SRBs in China since the mid-1980s are affecting and will continue to affect the marriage market for the next few decades.

Age is also important theoretically and substantively. Donald Bogue (1985: 42) has written that "almost any aspect of human behavior, from states of subjective feeling and attitudes to objective characteristics such as income, home ownership, occupation, or group membership, may be expected to vary with age." Populations with large proportions of young members differ in many ways from those with large proportions of elders.

Age and sex and the demographic processes

The demographic processes themselves vary significantly by age and sex. With regard to fertility, more males are born than females, usually around 105 males for every 100 females. The fecundity and, hence, the child-bearing years of females and males occurs within certain ages, for females between ages 15 to 49 and for males usually between ages 15 and 79. This is "usually" the situation for males because while "in polygamous populations a man's fertility can remain high well into his fifties and sixties... in controlled fertility societies, it peaks... with a mode in the mid-twenties" (Coleman, 2000: 41). This is due in part to low fertility norms in Western societies, as well as to a small average age difference of about two to three years between men and women in first marriages (Poston, 2005).

Regarding mortality, females have lower death rates than males at every age of life. Death rates are high in the first year of life and then drop to very low levels. In modern populations, they do not again attain the level reached in the first year of life for another five to six decades. Also, as we noted earlier, cause-specific mortality is often age-related.

The sex difference in mortality deserves additional discussion. Females live longer than males. This differential has been observed through the centuries and may be attributed to both behavioral and genetic causes. With regard to behavioral factors, males are more prone than females to engage in risk-taking behavior, and they also engage more so than females in cigarette smoking. Regarding genetic factors, the sex chromosomes and hormones, such as testosterone and estrogen, increase longevity for females, but decrease it for males. Research by the actuary Barbara Blatt Kalben (2003) has shown that "the primarily female hormone, estrogen, is protective for females, while the primarily male hormone, testosterone, is detrimental. Estrogen protects the heart and blood vessels. Testosterone, in contrast, tends to promote higher blood pressure, suppress the effectiveness of the immune system, and increase thrombosis" (2003: 45). Kalben's research provides some evidence for both explanations, but the major determining component, she has argued, are the differing chromosomes and hormones between the sexes.

That the genetic factor is the major reason for the physical superiority of women over men was also a conclusion of Francis C. Madigan (1957) in his interesting study of the mortality patterns of Roman Catholic nuns (sisters) and brothers, all of whom were teachers in Catholic grammar schools and high schools. Madigan's subjects were similar in most all behavioral characteristics, and none were married. The daily regimes of both the "brothers and sisters (were) extremely similar as regards time for sleep, work, study, and recreation, and with respect to diet, housing, and medical care" (Madigan, 1957: 204). Their major difference was their sex.

Madigan found that the "sisters consistently exhibited greater expectations of life, and the brothers shorter expectations" (1957: 210). The title of his research paper was "Are Sex Mortality Differentials Biologically Caused?" He answered in the affirmative: "Biological factors played by far the chief part in differentiating the death rates" of the brothers and the sisters (p. 221).

Migration also differs by age and sex. Traditionally, males and females have not migrated to the same places in equal numbers. Long-distance migration has tended to favor males, short-distance migration, females; and this has been especially the case in developing countries. However, with increases in the degree of gender equity in a society, migration rates of females tend to approximate those of males. Migration is also age-selective, with the largest numbers of migrants found among young adults (Stone, 1978; Tobler, 1995). Calvin Goldscheider noted that "given different political, social, economic, cultural and demographic contexts, age remains as a critical differentiation of migration. . . . [These contexts] determine the specifics of age and mobility" (1971: 311).

Finally, the age and sex structure of human populations sets important limits with respect to sustenance organization. The characteristics of age and sex define a biological entity to which the population's sustenance organization is or must be adapted. Amos H. Hawley observed that the demographic structure (of age and sex) contains the possibilities and sets the limits of organized group life (1950: 78). The age and sex structure of a population at "any given time constitutes a limiting factor on the kinds of collective activities [it] may engage in. . . . In effect, the organization of relationships in a population is an adaptation to its demographic [i.e., age and sex] structure. And to the extent that the [sustenance organization] is differentiated, the adaptation to its demographic features must be precise" (Hawley, 1950: 144). The degree to which a population's age and sex structure limits the kinds and varieties of sustenance activities in which the collectivity may be engaged is an important analytical issue, but one not well explored or understood (Poston and Frisbie, 2005).

Demographic theories of age and sex

Demographers are well known for their formal theories and have developed some of the most mathematically elegant theories in the social sciences. Age and sex, particularly age, comprise the centerpiece of most formal theory in demography. Examples of formal age models include Ansley J. Coale's (1971) development of marriage patterns by age, Andrei Rogers' (1975) elaborate presentation of migration patterns by age, and Louis Henry's (1961) description of fertility patterns by age in the absence of voluntary fertility control. But the most powerful and elegant formal mathematical theory in demography that incorporates a population's age and sex structure, particularly age, is *stable population theory*. Many believe this theory to be the most important aspect of the entirety of the mathematics of population (Pollard, Yusuf, and Pollard, 1990: 104).

We already mentioned stable population theory in Chapter 5. We noted that if a population closed to migration experiences constant schedules of age-specific fertility and mortality rates, it will develop a constant age distribution and will grow at a constant rate, irrespective of its initial age distribution. Its mathematical bases and foundation are laid out and discussed in many places, one of the better expositions being Coale's masterpiece, *The Growth and Structure of Human Populations* (1972) (see also Keyfitz, 1977a; Pollard, Yusuf, and Pollard, 1990: Chapter 7; Preston, Heuveline, and Guillot, 2001: Chapter 7; Schoen, 1988: Chapter 3).

The age distribution of the stable population depends on two items, namely, the underlying age-specific mortality rates, and the rate of growth: "The higher the mortality, the more rapidly the age distribution falls with increasing age; and also the higher the rate of growth, the more rapidly the age distribution falls with age" (Pollard, Yusuf, and Pollard, 1990: 106).

An important point to remember about a stable population is that it eventually converges to a constant age distribution, irrespective of the age distribution with which it began. Thus, demographers sometimes state that stable populations forget their past. In other words, when fixed fertility and mortality rates have prevailed, a stable population eventually ends up with an unchanging age structure that will be completely independent of its form at any earlier time.

Actually, Coale (1957) demonstrated that all human populations, not just stable populations, forget their pasts: "The age distribution of France is no longer much affected by the excess mortality and reduced numbers of births experienced during the Napoleonic wars, and the age distribution of Greece is no longer affected at all by the Peloponnesian Wars" (Coale, 1987: 466). Obviously, when fertility and mortality schedules constantly change, the age structure constantly changes. Thus, following Coale, we may state that all populations, whether or not stable, have forgotten the past. But the stable population, in addition, has a fixed form, and fixed birth and death rates.

This theorem is nicely illustrated by Etienne van de Walle and John Knodel (1970) in their demographic simulation known as "The Case of Women's Island," an exercise that reports quantitatively the "story" of a thousand young women marooned with five men on an island that is forever closed to migration. After a hundred years have elapsed, "one cannot find any evidence that the initial population (of the island was so) . . . distorted in both its [initial] age and sex composition" (van de Walle and Knodel, 1970: 436). This is an interesting demonstration of the statement that a population, stable or not, "forgets" its past and "stabilizes itself in due time with a structure that is entirely dependent on fertility and mortality levels" (p. 436).

Stable population theory has many implications for age and sex distribution. One is that changes and fluctuations in fertility cause far greater change in a population's age distribution than do changes and fluctuations in mortality. Coale and Paul Demeny (1983) have shown that populations closed to migration that have near stable fertility rates but differ only in their mortality schedules will have similar age and sex structures (see also Hinde, 1998: Chapter 13, and Pollard, Yusuf, Pollard, 1990: Chapter 7).

We have limited the discussion of the stable model to the **closed population**, that is, a population in which migration does not occur. However, it has also been shown mathematically that even when migration is taken into consideration, a stable population (indeed, a **stationary population**, that is, one with the same birth and death rates) can eventually be reached. As long as fertility is below replacement levels, a constant number and age distribution of in-migrants (with fixed fertility and mortality rates) will lead to a stationary population. Neither the level of the net reproduction rate nor the size of the in-migration stream will affect this conclusion; a stationary population will eventually emerge (Espenshade, Bouvier, and Arthur, 1982).

We turn now to a consideration of some of the basic methods that demographers use to represent the age and sex structure of populations.

METHODS FOR ANALYZING AGE AND SEX DISTRIBUTIONS

The age and sex structure of a population can be examined and portrayed along several dimensions. The two characteristics of age and sex may be analyzed separately, and a summary evaluation may be conducted of age cross-classified by sex. We first consider the **population pyramid**.

The population pyramid

The age and sex structure of a population at a given moment of time may be portrayed as an aggregation of cohorts born in different years. A graphic representation of the age/sex structure of the population is the *age/sex pyramid*, or population pyramid; it shows for a specific point in time the different surviving cohorts of persons of each sex. A population pyramid is one of the most elegant ways of graphically presenting age and sex data (Poston, 2005).

A population pyramid is nothing more than two ordinary **histograms** (bar graphs), representing the male and female populations in, usually, 1- or 5-year age categories, placed on their sides and back to back. The base of the pyramid, representing the size of each of the age/sex population groups, is presented in either absolute numbers or in percentages. When using percentages as the metric, one must be sure to "calculate the percentages on the basis of the grand total for the population, including both sexes and all ages" (Hobbs, 2004: 162).

Figure 8.1 is a population pyramid for the United States in 2000, presented in absolute numbers. Note first the larger numbers of women,

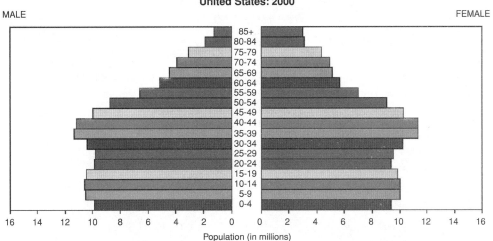

Figure 8.1. Age/sex pyramid, United States, 2000. *Source:* U.S. Bureau of the Census, International Data Base.

compared to men, at the older ages, an illustration of the fact that women survive longer than men at every age. Look also at the larger numbers of males and females between the ages of 30 and 49. Many of these persons, especially the older ones, were born during the "baby boom" years after World War II, when the fertility rate reached its peak level of 3.7 children per woman in the late 1950s. Observe as well the slightly larger cohorts of ages 5 to 19 years. These are the babies of parents born during the baby boom, that is, the babies of the baby boom babies. We see, thus, an echo of the baby boom one generation later, the so-called **echo effect**.

Figure 8.2 is an age/sex population pyramid for France in 2006 and "reflects various irregularities associated with that country's special history" (Hobbs, 2004: 164). This pyramid was constructed with data for individual years of age. There are five special aspects of the pyramid, numbered on the pyramid and identified at the bottom of the figure, that are worth mentioning. The first represents the very small birth cohorts born in France during World War I. One also sees at the older ages of the pyramid the larger numbers of females than males; this latter consideration characterizes all national populations, not only France. The second special feature of the pyramid points to the smaller number of persons born during World War I who reached the reproductive years in 1940. The third feature worthy of note follows closely behind the second and refers to the smaller numbers of babies born in France during World War II. After World War II, France, too, experienced a baby boom, and this is shown in the fourth note on the pyramid. The fifth and last special aspect of the French pyramid refers to the smaller numbers of babies born after the end of the baby

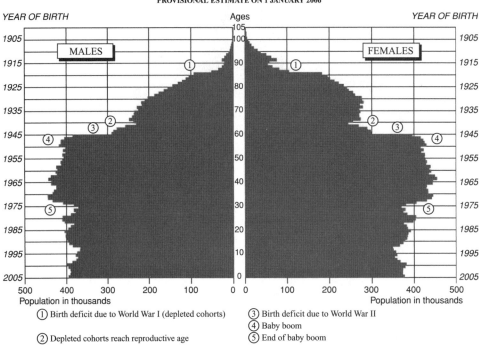

Figure 8.2. Age/sex pyramid, France, 2006. *Source:* Pison, 2006: 3.

boom. We mentioned earlier that knowledge of the age and sex structure of the population tells us a great deal about its history. This is certainly the case for France.

Figure 8.3 is a pyramid for the Republic of Korea in 1995. The bottom bars show the effects of the fertility reduction in Korea since the 1970s. In 1995, less than 12 percent of Korea's population was male of ages 0 to 14 (compared to more than 21 percent in 1970), and also less than 12 percent was female of ages 0 to 14 (more than 20 percent in 1970). The lower bars also indicate the much larger numbers of males, compared to females, born in Korea since the mid-1980s. The lowest two bars of the pyramid indicate that the sex ratio for Koreans in 1995 in the age group 0–4 is 113.4; this suggests a much higher SRB than that regulated by biology, and it is evidence of son preference (also see Poston 2002; Poston, Chu, et al., 2000; Poston et al., 1997; Poston, Walther, et al., 2003; and Zeng et al., 1993). Also seen in the South Korean pyramid is a relatively smaller number of men between the ages of 65 and 74. This is the special population who suffered the most, that is, was heavily depleted through mortality, during the Korean War.

In some subnational populations, usually counties, states, or provinces, their sustenance and livelihood bases may be so restrictive in terms of

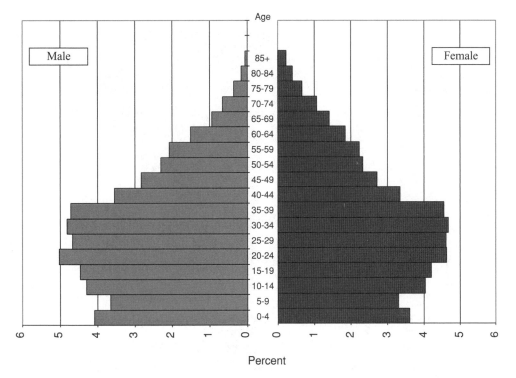

Figure 8.3. Population pyramid, Republic of Korea, 1995. *Source:* The authors.

persons of just one sex, or of just one or a few age groups, that they will often overwhelm the area's demography. Their principal ecological organization and function may be inferred by viewing their population pyramid. Figures 8.4 and 8.5 are pyramids for two counties in Texas in 2000, namely, Llano County and Brazos County.

Llano County (Figure 8.4), located in the Highland Lakes area of central Texas, is demographically an extremely old county, with nearly 40 percent of its population age 60 or older. It is a prime destination of inter- and intrastate elderly migrants and is demographically top-heavy because elderly people have moved into the county and young people have moved out. Llano County's population pyramid is typical of the pyramids of the so-called retirement counties in states such as Texas, Florida, Arizona, and California.

The major sustenance and economic activity of Brazos County, Texas (Figure 8.5) is higher education. Texas A&M University, with a student-body population of more than 45 thousand, is located in Brazos County, and in 2000 was the fifth largest institution of higher learning in the United States. Also located in Brazos County is Blinn College, a community college with a student-body population of more than 8,200 in 2000. Because most of the students attending Texas A&M University and Blinn College live

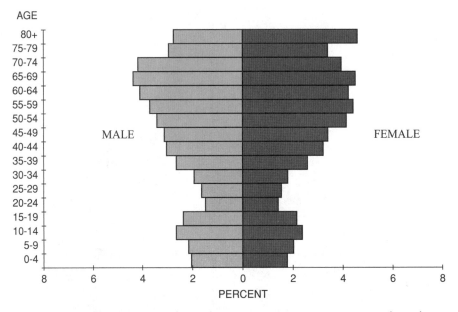

Figure 8.4. Population by age and sex: Llano County, Texas, 2000. *Source:* The authors.

in Brazos County, they overwhelm the county's demography. Almost one-quarter of the county's population is in the age group 20–24, the ages of most of the Texas A&M and Blinn students. Younger undergraduates at Texas A&M and at Blinn comprise a part of the preceding age group 15–19, which is almost 13 percent of the county's population. Many of the approximately seven thousand Texas A&M graduate students are in the 25–29 age group, which comprises more than 8 percent of the county's population.

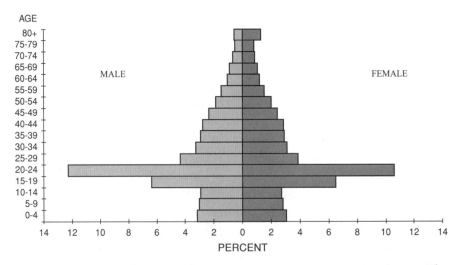

Figure 8.5. Population by age and sex: Brazos County, Texas, 2000. *Source:* The authors.

Despite their descriptive utility, however, population pyramids give only a graphic representation of age and sex structure at a particular point in time. We now discuss several indexes that may be used to examine patterns of age data and patterns of sex data, considered separately.

Age dependency

One may analyze the age distribution of a population in many ways (cf. Arriaga and Associates, 1994: Chapter 2; Hobbs, 2004: Chapter 7). A popular measure of age structure is the **dependency ratio (DR)**. The DR is the ratio of the dependent-age population (both young [persons 0–14 years old] and old [persons 65 years of age and older]) to the working-age population (persons 15–64 years old). The DR is usually multiplied by 100. The higher the ratio, the more people each worker has to support; the lower the DR, the fewer the number of dependents. Demographers usually split the DR into the **youth-dependency ratio (YDR or Youth-DR)** and the **old-age dependency ratio (Old Age-DR)**, or **aged-dependency ratio (ADR or Aged-DR)**; both have the same denominator, namely, the population 15–64. The numerator of the Youth-DR is the population 0–14 and the numerator of the Old Age-DR is the population 65+. The Youth-DR plus the Old-Age DR equals the DR.

An index analogous to the old-age dependency ratio is a measure of elderly support, known as the **parent support ratio (PSR)**. It takes the number of persons 80 years old and older, per 100 persons of ages 50–64 (Wu and Wang, 2004). It represents the relative burden of the oldest-old population, that is, the elderly parents, on the population aged 50–64, that is, the children of the elderly parents. Later, the PSR is illustrated with data for the United States and for China.

Presented in Table 8.1 are values of the Youth-DR, the Old Age-DR, and the **total dependency ratio (Total DR)** for thirteen countries of the world. These countries were chosen because they have low or high values of the Total DR, and low or high values of the component DRs. South Korea and China have Total DRs that are among the lowest in the world. For every 100 persons in the economically producing ages (15–64) in South Korea and China, there are 41 and 43 persons, respectively, in the dependent ages that the producers must support; and more than three-fourths of these dependents are young people (younger than age 15). Compare this situation with that in Italy, Spain, and Japan, countries with only slightly higher Total DRs (47.1 in all three countries), but where just over two-fifths are young dependents. People in the producing ages in Italy, Spain, and Japan have about the same dependency burden as producers in South Korea and China, but they have twice the proportion of elderly dependents. At the

Table 8.1. Values of youth-dependency ratio, old-age dependency ratio, and total dependency ratio, selected countries of the world, 2001

Country	Youth-DR	Old-Age-DR	Total DR
South Korea	31.0	9.9	40.9
China	32.9	10.0	42.9
Italy	20.6	26.5	47.1
Spain	22.1	25.0	47.1
Japan	22.1	25.0	47.1
United States	31.8	19.7	51.5
Yugoslavia	31.8	19.7	51.5
Sweden	29.7	26.6	56.3
Mexico	55.7	8.2	63.9
Nigeria	83.0	5.7	88.7
Yemen	98.0	6.1	104.1
Niger	104.2	4.2	108.4
Uganda	108.5	4.3	112.8

Source: Population Reference Bureau, 2001.

other extreme are Yemen, Niger, and Uganda, with Total DRs that are the highest in the world. For every 100 persons in the economically producing ages in Yemen, Niger, and Uganda, there are 104, 108, and 113 persons, respectively, in the dependent ages that the producers must support; and virtually all of these dependents are young people. The producers in these three countries are supporting more than twice as many dependents as in the five countries mentioned previously.

Age heaping

Demographers use single years of age data to determine whether there are irregularities or inconsistencies in the data. If a population tends to report certain ages (say, those ending in 0 or 5) at the expense of other ages, this is known as **age heaping**.

Age heaping tends to be more pronounced among populations or population subgroups with low levels of education: "The causes and patterns of [age heaping] vary from culture to culture, but preference for ages ending in '0' and in '5' is quite widespread" (Hobbs 2004: 136), particularly in the Western world. In Korea, China, and some other countries in East Asia, there is sometimes a preference for ages ending in the numeral "3" because it sounds like the word or character for "life."

In some cultures, certain numbers and digits are avoided; for example, "13" is frequently avoided in the West because it is considered unlucky.

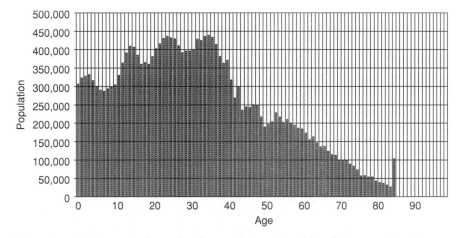

Figure 8.6. Single years of age, female population, Republic of Korea, 1995. *Source:* The authors.

The numeral "4" is avoided in Korea and in China because it has the same sound as the word or character for "death." For example, hotels in the United States and in some Western countries sometimes do not have floors designated as 13. Similarly, many hotels in China, South Korea, and some other East Asian countries do not have floors designated as 4.

Age heaping is easily detected using graphs and indices. Figure 8.6 is a graph of single years of age for females in South Korea in 1995. Aside from some heaping on ages 43, 53, and 63 (note the preference for ages ending in the numeral 3), there is little evidence elsewhere of age heaping. Compare this situation of females in South Korea in 1995 with that of males in Pakistan in 1981 (Figure 8.7). In Pakistan, there is an astounding amount of age heaping on ages ending in 0 and 5.

The extent of age heaping may be ascertained more precisely with indices. One of the more popular is **Whipple's method (WM)**, an index designed to reflect preference for the terminal digits of "0" and "5", usually in the age range of 23 to 62 (cf., Hobbs, 2004). WM varies from 0 (when the digits 0 and 5 are not reported in the census data) to 100 (when there is no preference for 0 or 5 in the census data) to a maximum of 500 (when only the digits 0 and 5 are reported in the census data). The UN (1990) has noted that if the values of Whipple's Index are less than 105, then the age distribution data are "highly accurate." If the WM values are between 105 and 109.9, the age data are "fairly accurate"; if between 110 and 124.9, "approximate"; if between 125 and 174.9, "rough"; and if 175 or more, "very rough" (United Nations, 1990: 18–19). WM is calculated as follows (Hobbs, 2004: 138):

$$\text{WM} = \frac{\sum (P_{25} + P_{30} + \cdots + P_{55} + P_{60})}{1/5 \sum (P_{23} + P_{24} + P_{25} \cdots P_{60} + P_{61} + P_{62})} * 100 \qquad (8.1)$$

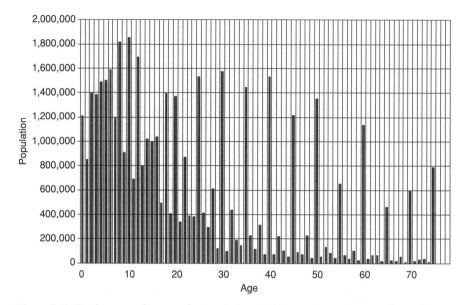

Figure 8.7. Single years of age, male population, Pakistan, 1981. *Source:* The authors.

The UN has reported that "although Whipple's Index measures only the effects of preferences for ages ending in 5 and 0, it can be assumed that such digit preference is usually connected with other sources of inaccuracy in age statements, and the indexes can be accepted as a fair measure of the general reliability of the age distribution" (1990: 20).

The decision in the Whipple's Index to focus on the age range of 23 to 62 is partly an arbitrary one. The ages of early childhood and old age are excluded because, frequently, they are more influenced by other types of errors and issues than digit preference; also, "the assumption of equal decrements from age to age is less applicable" at the older ages (Hobbs, 2004: 138).

The WM value for South Korean females in 1995 (see Figure 8.6) is 100.1; the WM value for Pakistani males in 1981 (see Figure 8.7) is 330.8. Among Korean females, the WM Index indicates virtually no age heaping on digits ending in 0 and 5. This means that in South Korea, the numbers of females counted in 1995 at ages ending in 0 and 5 overstate an unbiased population, that is, one in which there is no age heaping on 0 or 5, by a mere 0.1 percent (cf. Hobbs, 2004: 138). Conversely, in Pakistan in 1981, males counted at ages ending in 0 and 5 overstate an unbiased population by almost 231 percent.

We calculated WM scores for three more developed countries, namely, Japan in 1985, Denmark in 1988, and Hong Kong in 1995; and for two developing countries, namely, Iran and Mexico, both in 1988. Their WM scores are 98.4 for Japan, 101.5 for Denmark, and 101.7 for Hong Kong, versus 122.7 for Iran and 133.4 for Mexico. The WM values for the developed countries, as expected, are lower and closer to 100 than those for the developing countries.

Several other summary indexes of age heaping and digit preference have been developed by Robert J. Myers (1940), R. Bachi (1951), N. H. Carrier (1959), and K. V. Ramachandran (1967). These differ only slightly from one another and from the WM as general indicators of heaping.

Sex structure

Demographers use several methods to index sex composition: 1) the masculinity proportion, 2) the ratio of the excess or deficit of males to the total population, and 3) the sex ratio. The masculinity proportion is often used in nontechnical discussions of sex composition (Hobbs, 2004: 130) and is calculated by dividing the number of males in the population by the number of males and females and multiplying the result by 100.

The ratio of the excess, or deficit, of males to the total population is obtained by subtracting the number of females from the number of males, dividing by the total number in the population and multiplying by 100.

The sex ratio (SR), by far the most popular index of sex composition in demographic and other scholarly analyses, is defined as the number of males per 100 females, as follows:

$$SR = \frac{P_m}{P_f} * 100 \qquad (8.2)$$

An SR above 100 indicates an excess of males and an SR below 100 indicates an excess of females. In some Eastern European countries and in India, Iran, Pakistan, Saudi Arabia, and a few other countries, the SR is calculated as the number of females per 100 (or per 1,000) males. But the SR definition shown in formula (8.2) is used by most demographers and by international bodies such as the UN (Poston, 2005).

In general, "national sex ratios tend to fall in the narrow range from about 95 to 102, barring special circumstances, such as a history of heavy war losses (less males), or heavy immigration (more males); national sex ratios outside the range of 90 to 105 should be viewed as extreme" (Shryock, Siegel, and Associates, 1976: 107).

Most societies have SRBs between 104 and 106, that is, 104–106 boys are born for every 100 girls. This so-called biologically normal SRB is likely an evolutionary adaptation to the fact that females have higher survival probabilities than males (see Clarke, 2000, for another discussion). Since at every year of life males have higher age-specific death rates (ASDRs) than females, slightly more males than females are required at birth for there to

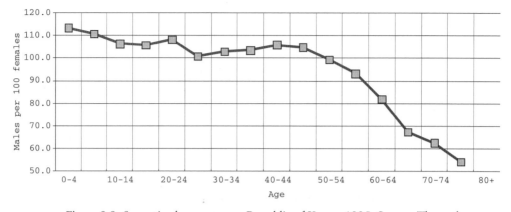

Figure 8.8. Sex ratios by age group, Republic of Korea, 1995. *Source:* The authors.

be around equal numbers of males and females when the groups reach their marriageable ages.

Biology thus dictates that the age-specific SR will be highest at the very young ages, starting around 104–106 at age 0, and should then decline with age, attaining a value of around 100 for persons in their late 20s and continuing to decline to levels around age 50 or 60 in the oldest ages.

Barring extreme forms of human intervention and disturbance, these types of SR patterns by age should occur in most populations. One such intervention would be a major war, such as the Korean War, which would reduce significantly the numbers of males in their 20s and 30s. Another would be high amounts of immigration/emigration. International migration is usually driven economically when, typically, males depart one country and enter another in search of employment. Such disturbances in some countries can be extreme, as we show later for some of the oil-producing countries in the Middle East. Another intervention would be female-specific abortion, resulting in an SRB well above 105.

One way to describe a population's sex structure is to examine sex ratios for each of its 5-year age groups. Figure 8.8 is a graph of the age-specific SRs for South Korea in 1995. The figure shows SRs at the very young ages that are much higher than would be expected biologically. These are the result of human interventions, namely, prenatal sex identification, followed by female-specific abortion (Poston, 2002, 2005). The SRs for age groups 0–4 and 5–9 are 113.4 and 110.6. Other than the higher-than-expected SRs at the very young ages, the declining trend in SRs in 1995 shown in Figure 8.8 for the remaining ages is pretty much as expected.

Some national populations have extreme imbalances by sex in certain age groups. The United Arab Emirates (UAE) is a good example. The UAE is one of several countries in the region of the world known as the Arab Gulf or the Gulf Cooperation Council, the others being Kuwait, Saudi Arabia,

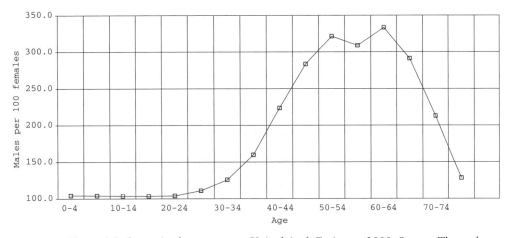

Figure 8.9. Sex ratios by age group, United Arab Emirates, 2000. *Source:* The authors.

Qatar, Bahrain, and Oman. Most of these countries have very large percentages of foreign-born residents. For example, in the UAE, Qatar, and Saudi Arabia, the foreign-born populations comprise more than 70 percent, and as much as 80 to 85 percent, of all the inhabitants. Many of the foreigners are people in the young working ages and are heavily male. They hail from Asia and other countries in the Middle East and are brought to the UAE and the other Gulf countries to work in the oil fields and in construction; "[t]he majority of these labor migrants [are] men unaccompanied by their families" (McFalls, 2003: 26). These high concentrations of foreigners have an especially major impact on the demography of countries that are not large in population size. For instance, Qatar has fewer than 1 million residents and the UAE has just over 4 million. The immigration patterns that favor young working-age males result in extremely unbalanced distributions of SRs by age.

Figure 8.9 is a graph of the age-specific SRs for the UAE in 2000. The SR is balanced at the younger ages, and then at age 25 starts to climb above 100. At age 35, there are around 150 males per 100 females, and more than 200 by age 40. By age 50, there are more than 300 males per 100 females. It is not until the SR is considerably above 300 at age 65 that it begins to decline. These tremendous sex imbalances are concentrated in around thirty years or so of the population's age structure, and they produce the population pyramid shown in Figure 8.10. Not many national populations, other than the few Gulf countries just mentioned, have an age and sex population pyramid like that of the UAE in 2000.

We turn finally to two specific examples of the centrality of age and sex structure. The first pertains to the unbalanced SRBs now being experienced in China, South Korea, Taiwan, and a few other countries such as India. The

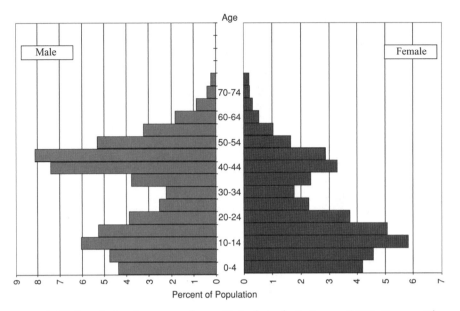

Figure 8.10. Population by age and sex, United Arab Emirates, 2000. *Source:* The authors.

second deals with the process of demographic aging being experienced by the United States and by China and notes its implications for the provision of elderly care that will be required during the next few decades. Both of these are relevant and challenging exemplars of the importance of age and sex composition in human societies.

SEX RATIO AT BIRTH

We have already mentioned that most societies have SRBs of around 105; that is, 105 boys are born for every 100 girls. Figure 8.11 shows time-series data for the SRB for China and the United States for individual years from 1980 to 2005. The United States follows the pattern, but China does not.

The SRB in the United States is invariant, at about 105 for every year. This is expected when there are no human interventions operating to disturb biology. In contrast, whereas in 1980 China had an SRB only slightly above 107, it began to increase in the late 1980s, reaching a value of 115 by 1990, a value of 120 in 2000, and 118 in 2005. Since the 1980s, the SRBs in China have been significantly above normal levels.

If there are no human interferences with the biological processes, the SRB will range from 104 to 107, with an average of around 105. What are the kinds of human interventions that might disturb the biological processes?

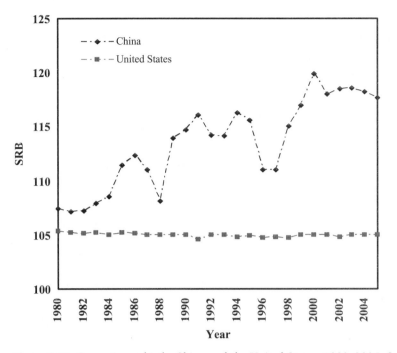

Figure 8.11. Sex ratios at birth, China and the United States, 1980–2005. *Source:* The authors.

China, Taiwan, South Korea, India, and several other Asian countries have been reporting abnormally high SRBs since the 1980s (Arnold and Liu, 1986; Eberstadt, 2000; Goodkind, 1996, 2002; Gu and Roy, 1995; Hudson and den Boer, 2002, 2004; Jha et al., 2006; Kim, 1997; Poston et al., 1997; Sheth, 2006). What are the immediate causes of these abnormally high SRBs? China and the other countries just mentioned are all showing, in varying degrees, the same kinds of intervention leading to abnormally high SRBs, namely, prenatal sex identification followed by gender-specific abortion (Banister, 2004; Chu, 2001; Hull, 1990; Jha et al., 2006; Johansson and Nygren, 1991).

Why would a country such as China resort to an intervention that would produce higher than biologically normal SRBs? The immediate cause is China's dramatic fertility decline. Why would a rapid fertility reduction lead to abnormally high SRBs?

One reason is that China has a Confucian patriarchal tradition where son preference is strong and pervasive (Arnold and Liu, 1986; Gu and Roy, 1995; Kim, 1997; Park and Cho, 1995; Poston et al., 1997). Female subordination is a major characteristic of Confucianism and was exemplified in such behaviors as female foot-binding (from the tenth century forward) and the modification of feminine clothing.

A preference for sons is a part of China's long history and culture. But when fertility was high, the chances that a boy would be born were good (Pison, 2004). When Chinese women were having six children on average, the probability was very low (less than 2 percent) that none of the six children would be male. By comparison, when women have only two children, the probability that neither will be a son is much higher (around 25 percent). When women have only one child, the probability that it will not be a son is just under 50 percent.

Birth-planning policies, as well as social, economic, and industrial transformations in China, have been responsible for the number of babies born per woman falling below replacement levels, and doing so quickly (Poston, 2000). Couples now have fewer children than they had just a couple of decades ago. However, the deeply rooted cultural influences of son preference still make it important for many families to have at least one son. Thus, many families implement strategies and interventions to ensure that they will have a son (Gu and Roy, 1995; Zeng, et al. 1993).

Since the late 1980s, ultrasound technology enabling the prenatal determination of sex has been widely available. Recently, China proposed a ban on the practice and launched a "pro-girl" media campaign to help mediate the strong son preference (*China Daily*, 2004). This campaign, however, is not believed to have had much of an impact.

There is little evidence of female infanticide causing the high SRBs (Banister, 2004; Chu, 2001; Eberstadt, 2000: 228; Zeng et al., 1993). The human interventions that disturb the SRB are mainly due to norms and traditions among Chinese families to have sons, within a more recent policy as well as a normative context to have fewer births.

How many excess boys will there be in China who will be unable to find brides from their countries? Poston and Li Zhang (2009) have taken data for every year from 1978 to 2005 for China's total population size, crude birth rate, and SRB, and have calculated the numbers of males and females born every year. Using data from life tables, they next survived the boys born each year to the ages of 26 and the girls to the ages of 24, which are, or are near, the average ages that boys and girls marry. They estimated that there have already been born in China more than 31 million extra boys who will be looking for wives between 2005 and 2027. There will not be enough Chinese women in the marriage market for them to marry. What will these many millions of young men do when they cannot find brides? Here are some speculations.

While it is true that throughout history, especially in Western Europe, "bachelorhood was an acceptable social role, and the incidence of never-marrying bachelors in the total population was high" (Eberstadt 2000: 230; see also Hajnal 1965), China throughout its thousands of years of history has never been so characterized. Unless in the next few decades China is "swept by a truly radical change in cultural and social attitudes toward marriage [it is] poised to experience an increasingly intense, and perhaps desperate, competition among young men for the nation's limited supply of brides" (Eberstadt 2000: 230).

China could well turn to a more authoritarian form of government to better control the bachelors. In such a scenario, its progress toward democracy could be stalled, if not halted. China could modify the magnitude of the potential unrest of these millions of unmarried young men by dispatching them to public-works projects thousands of miles away from the big cities. For instance, there are several huge construction projects underway, all of which could benefit from a young, male labor force.

When confronted with large numbers of excess males during the Middle Ages, Portugal sent them off to wars in North Africa (Hudson and den Boer, 2002, 2004). With many millions of bachelors in the big cities, all within twenty years of age, bellicose Chinese leaders might be tempted to "kill two birds with one stone"; they could reduce the tensions caused by the bachelors in the cities by sending the excess manpower to pick a fight with or participate in an invasion of another country. What better country with which to engage in such activities than their "renegade province," Taiwan, located less than 100 miles across the Taiwan Straits from the southern province of Fujian.

One solution to the problem would be the immigration into the country of Chinese brides from other countries. This is unlikely for China because it is a poor country, and most of its bachelors will be poor rural workers unable to afford "mail order brides" (Eberstadt, 2000). But even if this kind of marriage immigration were to occur, it would need to be of a substantial magnitude to even begin to offset the gender imbalances of marriage-age males that are expected in the first two decades of this new century. Of course, it would cause shortages of many millions of females in the areas of origin. So if China gains brides, other countries will lose them.

An even less likely solution would be increases in levels of homosexuality. This is an unlikely alternative because most scientific evidence on the origins of homosexuality argues in favor of a strong biological foundation (LeVay, 1991, 1996; also see Murray, 2000, for other views and arguments). It is not likely that when Chinese males are unable to find females to marry they will turn to homosexual relationships as an alternative to (heterosexual) marriage. On the other hand, homosexual behavior could well become more acceptable, so that closeted homosexuals would be freer to openly declare their orientation.

The most likely possibility, of course, is that these Chinese bachelors will never marry and will have no other choice but to develop their own lives and livelihoods. They will likely resettle with one another in "bachelor ghettos" in Beijing, Shanghai, Tianjin, and other big cities, where commercial sex outlets would likely be prevalent. The possible implications of large numbers of bachelors using commercial sex workers need also to be addressed, particularly with regard to the worldwide AIDS epidemic.

There is some historical precedent behind an expected growth of bachelor ghettos. In the nineteenth century, many thousands of young Chinese men immigrated to the United States to work in the gold mines and help build the railroads. When the work projects were completed, many stayed in the United States and resettled in Chinese bachelor ghetto areas in New York, San Francisco, and a few other large U.S. cities (Kwong, 1988; Zhou, 1992). The SRs of the Chinese in these areas were extraordinarily high.

If these Chinese men do not marry, sociological research suggests that they will be more prone to crime than if they married (Laub and Sampson, 2003: 41–46; Sampson and Laub, 1990). This possibility has alerted some to the potential increases in crime in China's future and perhaps political ramifications resulting from these excess males (Hudson and den Boer, 2002, 2004).

No one, of course, knows what this excess number of young Chinese males will do. Several possibilities have been entertained. The only fact known for certain is that there have already been born in China many, many millions more baby boys than there will be girls for them to marry. This issue needs the immediate attention of research scholars and policymakers.

POPULATION AGING

China is the largest country in the world, with a population size of more than 1.3 billion. The United States is the third largest country in the world (after China and India), with a population of more than 300 million. China has a land mass just slightly less than that of the United States (China has 9.6 million square kilometers of surface area compared to the United States with 9.8 million square kilometers) but a population more than 4.4 times larger than that of the United States.

Of even greater interest is the size of the older and oldest-old populations in China and the United States. We follow here the practice of the U.S. Bureau of the Census (Velkoff and Lawson, 1998) and refer to the older population as persons of age 60 and older, and the oldest-old as those 80 and older. In the world in 2000, there were more than 606 million older persons and more than 69 million oldest old. Of the world's older population in 2000, more than 21 percent (or almost 129 million) lived in China, compared to 7.6 percent (or almost 46 million) in the United States.

If the older population of China in 2000 were a single country, it would be the eighth largest country in the world, outnumbered only by the nonelderly population of China and the populations of India, the United States, Indonesia, Brazil, Russia, and Pakistan (United Nations, 2003).

Of the 69 million oldest old in the world, more than 16 percent lived in China in 2000, compared to 13.1 percent residing in the United States. In the early 1970s, China came to grips with the burgeoning size of its population and established a nationwide fertility control program that stressed *later* marriages, *longer* intervals between children, and *fewer* children. However, the large numbers of children born during China's baby boom in the early 1960s caused China's leaders in the middle to late 1970s to become increasingly worried about demographic momentum and the concomitant growth potential of this extraordinarily large cohort. Thus, in 1979, they launched the One-Child Campaign, with a goal of eliminating all births above or equal to three per family, and encouraging most families to have no more than one child, especially those living in urban areas. These two policies, along with increasing levels of socioeconomic development, resulted in a drastic decline in China's fertility rate, from levels greater than six children per woman in the early 1950s to less than two in the late 1990s.

The United States has also experienced a fertility reduction, although not as dramatic as that in China. This fertility reduction has already been discussed in some detail in Chapter 3 and is not repeated here. Suffice it to state that the United States experienced a sustained fertility decline starting in the nineteenth century (Sternlieb and Hughes, 1978). The total fertility rate (TFR) (for whites) dropped to 4.5 in 1870 and to 3.5 in 1900 (U.S. Bureau of the Census, 1975). By 1920, just after World War I, the white TFR had declined to 3.2. In the late 1950s, at the height of the baby boom era, the TFR reached its peak at 3.7. In 1972, the U.S. TFR dropped for the first time below the replacement level of 2.1 (Kahn, 1974). The fertility declines experienced in China and the United States have produced, and will continue to produce, unprecedented increases in the proportions of older populations of the two countries.

It is important to remember that the relatively large numbers of the older and oldest-old populations of China and the United States in 2000 are numbers that were generated during demographic regimes in which fertility and mortality rates declined. A consequence of these transitions, and especially unanticipated in China, are the extremely large older and oldest-old populations projected for the decades of this new century.

Table 8.2. Total population, older population, and oldest-old population: world, China, and the United States, 2000, and 2010 to 2050

World			
Year	Total	Older	Oldest Old
2000	5,995,544,836	591,389,484	68,259,980
2010	6,830,906,857	755,327,646	103,181,481
2020	7,561,076,957	1,018,949,740	136,919,697
2030	8,213,573,346	1,355,545,346	190,254,664
2040	8,809,366,772	1,663,858,895	284,553,277
2050	9,297,023,938	1,981,995,384	399,466,279
China			
Year	Total	Older	Oldest Old
2000	1,268,985,201	128,215,415	11,069,279
2010	1,358,722,700	168,804,989	17,654,658
2020	1,422,937,380	240,217,728	24,018,400
2030	1,432,807,130	341,693,798	35,136,698
2040	1,410,644,753	395,615,825	57,409,084
2050	1,347,624,386	424,395,138	92,505,472
United States			
Year	Total	Older	Oldest Old
2000	272,639,608	44,947,333	8,930,406
2010	298,026,141	55,623,834	11,227,361
2020	323,051,793	73,769,020	12,400,055
2030	347,209,212	87,874,783	18,009,972
2040	370,289,996	93,088,015	26,216,372
2050	394,240,529	99,459,187	30,200,741

Source: The authors.

Table 8.2 shows population projections of the total populations, the older populations, and the oldest-old populations of the world, China, and the United States for the decennial years 2010 through 2050. (A **population projection** is a systematic calculation of the future population size of an area.) These projections are the so-called *middle-range projections* of the UN (2003). They assume for the United States and China that total fertility rates will increase/decrease slowly from their present levels and will stabilize at 1.85 in 2045–2050. Mortality is projected to decline only modestly between 2000 and 2050. International migration for the two countries is "set on the basis of past international migration estimates and an assessment of the policy stance of the countries with regard to future international migration flows" (United Nations, 2003: Vol. I, 23).

In 2020, there are projected to be more than 1 billion older persons in the world; almost a quarter of them (more than 240 million) will be in China and more than 7 percent in the United States. By 2020, there will likely be almost 137 million oldest-old people in the world, with more than 17 percent living in China and more than 9 percent in the United States.

By the midway point of this new century (in 2050), there are projected to be nearly 2 billion older persons in the world out of a total population of 9.3 billion. Of these almost 2 billion older persons, 424 million (more than 21 percent) will be residing in China and nearly 100 million (5 percent) in the United States.

This projected number of 424 million older persons in China in 2050 is a remarkably large number. The number of older persons alive in the world in 2000 (591 million) is only 167 million more than the total number of older persons projected to be living in China in 2050.

In the world in 2050, there are projected to be more than 399 million oldest-old people, with almost 23 percent living in China and more than 7 percent in the United States. The more than 92.5 million oldest old projected to be living in China in 2050 is nearly 1.4 times larger than the total number of 68.2 million oldest old living in the entire world in 2000.

A large number of elderly persons in a population is not problematic if there exists at the same time in the population a large number of producers. It is only when the ratio of elderly to producers becomes high that a host of economic, social, and related problems occur. We now show empirically the degree of the dependency burden in China and in the United States in the year 2000 and how much worse these burdens will become in the years ahead.

Earlier in this chapter, we described the measures of total dependency, youth dependency, and old-age dependency. Figure 8.12 presents the YDRs for China and the United States for every five years from 1950 to 2050. Between 1950 and 2000, the YDRs have dropped for both countries; in 1950, the YDRs were 54 in China and 41 in the United States. By 2000, they had declined to 36 in China and 33 in the United States. Note also the increases in the YDRs for both countries during their baby boom years in the 1950s and 1960s. The YDRs of the two countries in 2000 are modest compared to those of other countries. To illustrate, the Gaza Strip had a YDR in 1995 of 114, the highest in the world, followed by Uganda (99), Ethiopia (97), and Libya (87).

The YDRs in China and the United States are not projected to change significantly between 2000 and 2050. The data shown in Figure 8.12 indicate that in China, the YDR will drop from 36 in 2000 to 26 in 2050. The United States is projected to experience less of a decrease, from a YDR of 33 in 2000 to 29 in 2050. The United States is projected to have a higher

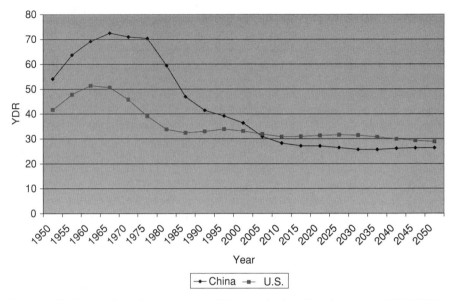

Figure 8.12. Youth-dependency ratios, China and the United States, 1950–2050. *Source:* The authors.

YDR than that of China starting in the year 2005, a situation that would not have been predicted, say, in 1965 when China's YDR was 72 and that of the United States was 50.

Figure 8.13 shows old-age (aged-) dependency ratios for China and the United States for every five years from 1950 to 2050. Unlike the situation with respect to the YDR, in which both the United States and China experienced major net decreases between 1950 and 2000, there have been modest increases in the ADR. In China, the ADR increased from 7 in 1950 to 10 in 2000. The ADR for the United States increased from 13 in 1950 to 18 in 2000.

China's ADR in 2000 is a little higher than average but not appreciably so. The ADR for the United States in 2000 is 8 points higher than in China. But these are not excessively high ADRs. To illustrate using different data that reflect the same phenomenon, in 2000, one-tenth of China's population was older than age 60, compared to 16 percent for the United States. By comparison, in 2000, ten countries, all in Europe, had more than 20 percent of their populations of the 60+ age: Sweden had the highest percentage (22 percent), followed by Norway, Belgium, Italy, the United Kingdom, Germany, Austria, Greece, Denmark, and Switzerland (United Nations, 2003).

The aged-dependency situation changes remarkably when we skip ahead fifty years to 2050. China will have become much older by 2050. China's ADR is projected to increase from 10 aged dependents per 100 producers in 2000 to 37 aged dependents per 100 producers in 2050. The

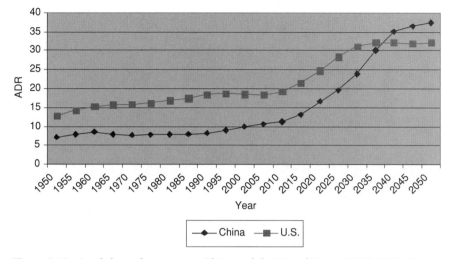

Figure 8.13. Aged-dependency ratios, China and the United States, 1950–2050. *Source:*
The authors.

United States also is projected to have grown older; its ADR will increase
from 13 in 2000 to 32 in 2050.

By 2050, China is expected to have made the transition to a demographically very old country. The United States also will have become quite
old, but not as old as China. In the fifty years since 2000, the two countries will have become demographically top-heavy. In 2050, more than 32
percent of China's population (more than 424 million people) will be 60
years of age or older. The oldest countries in the world today, the European
countries mentioned earlier, are nowhere near as old as China is projected
to be in 2050. In 2050, China will be older than the United States, the latter
in 2050 having "only" one-quarter of its population (more than 99 million
people) of age 60 or older.

As just noted, in 2050, China's ADR will be larger than that of the
United States. For every 100 producers (persons 15–64) in China in 2050,
there will be 37 aged dependents (persons 65+), whereas in the United
States, the figure will be 32.

We also mentioned earlier in this chapter the parent support ratio
(PSR). Figure 8.14 presents PSRs for every five years from 1950 to 2050
for the United States and China. In 1950, both countries had very low
PSRs. In China in 1950, there were fewer than three persons of age 80 and
older per 100 persons 50–64. In the United States, the figure was fewer
than eight. There was not much of an elderly parent burden on the older
children in either country in 1950.

By 2000, the PSRs had increased threefold in both countries, for China
from 2.5 in 1950 to 7.8 in 2000, and for the United States from 7.8 in
1950 to 21.4 in 2000. The burden of elderly parents on their children has

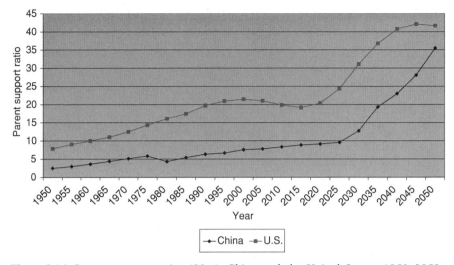

Figure 8.14. Parent support ratios (80+), China and the United States, 1950–2050. *Source:* The authors.

increased in both countries, with the burden almost three times as heavy in the United States as in China. In the United States in 2000, there were more than 21 elderly of ages 80+ for every 100 persons 50–64, whereas in China the PSR was fewer than 8 persons 80+ per 100 of ages 50–64.

Both countries are projected to experience even more dramatic increases by 2050. The PSR is expected to increase almost fivefold in China, from 7.8 in 2000 to 35.5 in 2050. The PSR is projected to double in the United States, from 21.4 in 2000 to 41.7 in 2050. The burden of elderly parents on their children will be extremely high in 2050 in both countries. There are projected to be in the United States almost 42 persons 80+ for every 100 persons 50–64, whereas in China there are projected to be almost 36 persons 80 and older for every 100 persons 50–64. The PSR figure for China is projected to be slightly less than that for the United States. But the change in PSRs between 2000 and 2050 for China will be much greater than for the United States.

By 2050, China will have grown to be one of the oldest populations in the world, and a country with one of the heaviest aged-dependency burdens of any population in the world. The United States will be close behind. What are the implications of this very old population, particularly for China?

Traditionally in China, the support of one's elder parents has been the responsibility of the sons. Often the parents lived with the oldest son and either with or nearby the other sons. The eldest son and his brothers tended to be responsible for providing the parents with economic support. The sons would rely on one of their sisters, or sometimes on one or more of their wives, to provide their parents with emotional support. These norms have been adjusted or modified in past decades, especially since the founding of the People's Republic in 1949, and particularly among urban residents. Nevertheless, the provision of economic and emotional support to one's parents has seldom been a major burden. As one might expect in a population with modestly high levels of fertility, there have usually been many more producers in the Chinese population than aged dependents. Similar traditional norms have not governed the U.S. family to the extent as in China.

However, given the very low levels of fertility in contemporary China, as well as a highly unbalanced SRB since the 1980s, the provision of elder care will be a major concern in this new century. For one thing, as we have already noted, in the decades of this new century in China, there are projected to be many more aged dependents per producers. In 2000, there were 10 aged dependents per 100 producers in China; in 2020, there are projected to be 17 aged dependents per 100 producers, and by 2050 there are projected to be 37 per 100 producers. This is an astonishingly high number of old persons per 100 producing members in the population. The number of aged dependents per 100 producers in China in 2050 is projected to be 3.7 times larger than China's current number. This ADR for 2050 will likely be one of the highest of any country in the world.

When we couple this very high ADR for the year 2050 for China with the abnormally high SRBs in China (Poston et al., 1997), the issue of elder-care provision in this new millennium becomes even more complex. It has been estimated by Poston and Zhang (2009) that based only on the births that have occurred in China between 1980 and 2005, there have already been born more than 31 million boys who will be unable to find Chinese brides when they reach marriageable age (see also Poston and Glover, 2006). If these abnormally high SRBs continue into the decades of the twenty-first century (and there is no indication that they will not), an enormously large number of Chinese males, likely 100 million or more, will find it difficult if not impossible to meet females to marry. These single males will have the responsibility for providing both the economic and emotional support for their parents. Since they are not likely to marry, they will have no sons or daughters to take care of them. Since many of them will be only children, they will have no siblings with whom to grow old.

Unlike the case in past decades in China, where there have usually been several married sons, along with their sisters, available to care for the elderly parents, the situation in the next thirty to forty years will be different: There will be many, many more elderly parents and aunts and uncles requiring care than has been the situation in the recent past. Moreover, many of the providers will be sons, perhaps only-born sons, without wives. The care of the elderly in the decades of this new century will not be without problems.

SUMMARY

In this chapter, we first discussed the definition of age and sex. The definition of sex is not as straightforward as one might imagine; there are many complex issues involved in determining one's sex. We next discussed some of the key theoretical issues in demography dealing with age and sex structure, particularly stable population theory. We then described the major methods and approaches used by demographers to measure age and sex structure. Data reflecting the age and sex structure of the Republic of Korea, China, the United States, and some other countries were used to illustrate these methods. We concluded the chapter with detailed discussions of two key areas of age and sex structure: the SRB, and population aging.

KEY TERMS

adrenogenital syndrome (AGS)

aged-dependency ratio (ADR or Aged-DR)

age heaping

androgen insensitivity syndrome (AIS)

closed population

congenital adrenal hyperplasia (CAH)

dependency ratio (DR)

echo effect

histogram

intersex

Jacob's syndrome

Klinefelter's syndrome

old-age dependency ratio (ADR or Old Aged-DR)

parent support ratio (PSR)

population aging

population projection

population pyramid

sex ratio at birth (SRB)

stable population theory

stationary population

total dependency ratio (Total DR)

transgender

Whipple's method (WM)

youth-dependency ratio (YDR or Youth-DR)

9 World Population Change over Time

INTRODUCTION

Having finished discussion of the three demographic processes in the preceding chapters, we are now in a position to put them all together and analyze overall population change. This chapter deals with the dynamics of world population change over time, and the next chapter (Chapter 10) with U.S. population change.

To help better understand the issues presented in the chapter, we first examine the different ways that writers over the centuries have written about population and population change, and some of the main theories of population change, particularly **demographic transition theory (DTT)**. We then look specifically at the dynamics of world population change, taking both a long and a short view. We conclude the chapter with a discussion of the future of world population.

How large is the population of the world, and how rapidly is it growing? The U.S. Bureau of the Census estimates that the world population numbered more than 6.6 billion people in 2007. The crude birth rate (CBR) was around 21/1,000, and the crude death rate (CDR) about 9/1,000. Thus, the rate of annual growth was about 1.2 percent. So, if these birth and death rates were to continue into the future, the population numbers would double about every 58 years (see our discussion of **doubling time** later in this chapter). Of course, such astronomical numbers are unlikely to occur. Either the birth rate will fall or the death rate will rise.

Figure 9.1 shows that the current growth rate of the world's population of about 1.2 percent has not been constant in past years. We see that the annual rate of growth increased from around 1.5 percent in 1950–1951 to a high rate of more than 2 percent in the early 1960s. It stabilized at 2 percent until the early 1970s, when it began to drop to 1.4 percent just a few years ago, and then to its current level of 1.2 percent.

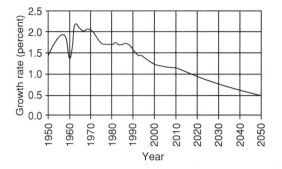

Figure 9.1. World population growth rates: 1950–2050. *Source:* U.S. Census Bureau, International Data Base, July 2007 version.

The increases and decreases in the world's population have not always been steady, however. Indeed, the dramatic decline in the world population's growth rate to almost 1.3 percent in the early 1960s was due almost entirely to events in China, namely, the natural disasters and decreased agricultural production there that resulted in a great famine following the calamitous years of the Great Leap Forward (we discussed this famine earlier in Chapter 5). This points to the fact that the notion of a "world population" may be misguided because there is not really a "world society." Changes and trends in world demographic behavior are often the consequence of the differential demographic behavior of the major world regions. This point is made more apparent later in this and other chapters.

MAJOR WRITINGS AND THEORIES ABOUT POPULATION AND POPULATION CHANGE

Demographers have developed several theories or explanations of why and how populations change their size. Many have written about world population growth and decline. We look first at some of the writings by major thinkers about population and population change.

Writings about population and population change

Demography is the study of human populations. The word *population* is from the Latin *populare*, to populate, and the Latin noun, *populatio*. Geoffrey McNicoll has noted that in ancient times, the verb *populare* "commonly meant to lay waste, plunder, or ravage," and the noun *populatio* "was a plundering or despoliation" (2003: 730). These usages became obsolete by the eighteenth century. According to Adolphe Landry (1945), the modern use of the word *population* first appeared in 1597 in an essay by Francis Bacon (McNicoll, 2003).

Interest and concern about population change have not been limited to demographers. In 1848, the great English philosopher John Stuart Mill wrote:

> If the earth must lose that great portion of its pleasantness which it owes to things that the unlimited growth of wealth and population would extirpate from it, for the mere purpose of enabling it to support a larger, but not a happier or a better population, I sincerely hope, for the sake of posterity, that they will be content to be stationary, long before necessity compels them to it ([1848] 1965, Book 4: 756–757).

Actually, concerns about population per se go back to Genesis 1:28, where humans were encouraged to "be fruitful and multiply and fill the earth." Today, one might ask if the earth has indeed been replenished.

Plato had his own ideas about population size. He believed that a community should not be larger than 5,040 citizens; otherwise, too many people would lead to anonymity. The farsightedness of Plato and some of the other Greek philosophers of that time remains amazing to us today. A major concern of sociologists in the twenty-first century is the lack of face-to-face communication because of the Internet, the cell phone, the iPod, the iPhone, and other new inventions. We can only speculate as to how Plato would react were he alive today!

Plato's ideas resonate well with the writings of the nineteenth-century sociologist, Emile Durkheim, who visualized two types of societies: mechanic and organic. The former was quite small, with a simple division of labor, whereas the latter was considerably larger, with an extensive division of labor as well as increasing anonymity (Durkheim, [1893] 1984).

The fourteenth-century Arab philosopher Ibn Khaldun was also concerned with population growth. He posited that societies pass through stages of population growth as they mature – much like individuals do: "The inhabitants of a more populous city are more prosperous than their counterparts in a less populous one. . . . The fundamental cause of this is the difference in the nature of the occupations carried on in different places" (Issawi, 1987: 93).

The most well-known early scholar who wrote about population growth is Thomas Robert Malthus. He was born in England in 1766 and educated at Jesus College in Cambridge. At the age of 22, he became a curate near his family home in Surrey and later in Lincolnshire. In 1805, he was appointed a professor of history and political economy at East India College, Hailerbury, a position he occupied until his death in 1834 (James, 1979; Petersen, 1964, 1979; Poston, 2006b; Winch, 1987, 2003).

It was during his early years as a rural clergyman that he observed the rapid growth occurring in his native England. In 1798, when he was

32 years of age, he published anonymously the first edition of his famous book, *An Essay on the Principle of Population as It Affects the Future Improvement of Society, with Remarks on the Speculations of Mr. Goodwin, M. Condorcet, and Other Writers*. This publication "immediately established its anonymous author as a controversial figure" (Petersen, 1979: 48). Five years later in 1803, this time under his name, Malthus published the second edition of the essay, with a different subtitle, as *An Essay on the Principle of Population; or a View of Its Past and Present Effects on Human Happiness; With an Inquiry into our Prospects Respecting the Future Removal or Mitigation of the Evils Which It Occasions*. This was indeed a new book. The first edition was a "deductive book" of around 55 thousand words, whereas the second edition expanded the theory and provided a great deal of illustrative data, resulting in approximately 200 thousand words (Petersen, 1979: 52–53). Subsequent editions, ending in the seventh edition published posthumously in 1872, included relatively minor changes. The best edition is the second, with revisions, contained in two volumes and edited by Patricia James (Malthus, [1803] 1989).

The principle of population, according to Malthus, stipulated that if left unchecked, populations tend to double once every generation. Food shortages occur because, while the population every generation tends to grow geometrically (1-2-4-8-16 and so forth), "subsistence" tends to increase at an arithmetic rate (1-2-3-4-5 and so forth). Thus, following this example, at the end of five generations, there would be sixteen units of population but only five units of food and subsistence.

However, Malthus argued, population growth tends to be checked by two types of controls, **preventive checks** and **positive checks**. He referred to the major preventive check as "moral restraint." That is, people tend to restrain themselves, refraining from premarital intercourse and postponing marriage. (Malthus practiced what he preached. He married at age 38 and fathered three children.) As a clergyman, he considered other types of preventive checks (e.g., homosexuality, contraception, and abortion) as unacceptable because they were "vices." For example, he was "opposed to birth control on the grounds that such 'unnatural' experiments ran contrary to God's design in placing humankind under the right degree of pressure to ensure its development" (Winch, 2003: 620). The positive checks included wars, famine, pestilence, and others forms of misery. These checks kept the death rate high, and the preventive checks kept the birth rate low.

We need to keep in mind that the Malthusian concept of moral restraint was targeted primarily at the poverty population: Couples were encouraged to postpone marriage until they could afford to bear children, essentially restricting childbearing to the wealthy and better-off members of the society.

Malthus's essay needs to be placed and considered in historical context. It opposed two very influential schools of thought at the time, namely, mercantilism and utopianism, and cast doubt on the hope of human perfectibility. Donald Winch has written that "Malthus showed that any attempt to create an ideal society in which altruism and common property rights prevailed would be undermined by its inability to cope with the resulting population pressure" (2003: 619).

The writings of Malthus are said to have influenced the work of Charles Darwin, Herbert Spencer, David Ricardo, John Maynard Keynes, and many others. For example, Darwin wrote in his *Autobiography* ([1887] 1958: 42–43) that "[f]ifteenth months after I had begun my systematic enquiry, I happened to read for amusement Malthus on population, and being well prepared to appreciate the struggle for existence which everywhere goes on from long-continued observation of the habits of animals and plants, it at once struck me that under these circumstances favorable variations would tend to be preserved and unfavorable ones be destroyed. The result of this would be a new species. Here, then, I had at last got a theory by which to work."

Karl Marx, the economist and philosopher, disagreed with Malthus about the universal nature of the problem of overpopulation. Marx was writing at a time when the Industrial Revolution was reaching its apex. He argued that there were two classes of people, namely, the bourgeoisie (capitalists) and the proletariat (the workers) (Marx and Engels, [1848] 1935: 32). It was to the advantage of the bourgeoisie to encourage high fertility because this would result in a surplus of workers. Such a surplus would lead to more profits, the goal of the capitalists. According to Malthus, population was an **independent variable** and was the cause of much distress, such as poverty. In contrast, Marx argued that population was the **dependent variable**: "Whenever the reserve army of labor is relatively depleted and the level of wages tends to rise reducing the rate of surplus value, the capitalist class will adopt measures (i.e., technological improvements, foreign investments, and so forth) which, while increasing the productivity of labor and the rate of profit, will render obsolete the number of jobs" (Gimenez, 1971: 4). In other words, Marx believed that capitalism was the culprit that ended up causing poverty, whereas Malthus believed that population growth per se was the main cause.

Marx was aware that population growth could be a problem. Indeed, Friedrich Engels, his longtime friend and collaborator, wrote that "there is, of course, the abstract possibility that the number of people will become so great that limits will have to be set to their increase. But if at some time communist society finds itself obligated to regulate the production of human beings, just as it has already come to regulate the production of things, it will be precisely this society and this society alone which will carry this out without difficulty" (cited in Gimenez, 1971: 4).

Strictly speaking, a population is a group or collection of items. But to a demographer, a population is a group or collection of people. Samuel H. Preston, Patrick Heuveline, and Michel Guillot (2001: 1) have distinguished between a specific population or group of actual people alive at a given period of time (e.g., the population of the United States as of April 1, 2000) and the population that persists over time even though its actual members may change (e.g., the population of China during the past 4,000 years). But as McNicoll has noted, the more common use of the term *population* by demographers and in modern English usage is with regard to a "well-defined set, with clear-cut membership criteria" (2003: 731), such as the population of the People's Republic of China as identified and enumerated in its 2000 census.

In a similar vein, Norman B. Ryder (1964: 448) considered a population to be an aggregate of individuals defined in spatial and temporal terms. It is not necessarily a group, which in sociological terms requires some form of interpersonal interaction and the development of a sense of community. The analysis of human populations is inherently dynamic because attention is focused on changes in the population over time. The **population equation** shown in the next section is an example.

Ryder also stated that the population model is both microdynamic and macrodynamic in nature. This means that processes of change in fertility, mortality, and migration can be identified at both the individual and the aggregate levels. This distinction lies at the very heart of the population model because it introduces Alfred J. Lotka's ([1934] 1998) important distinction between the persistence of the individual and the persistence of the aggregate. All human beings are born, live for some period of time, and then die. But a population aggregate is not temporally limited, provided that enough individuals continue to enter the population, usually through births, to replace those exiting; the population in this sense is immortal.

Population aggregates, both in terms of the changes in numbers and the characteristics of those entering and exiting, can experience changes not reducible to individuals who constitute the population. For instance, when individuals enter a population through birth or through in-migration, they will "age" by becoming older. But the population aggregate cannot only become older; it can also become younger, provided that births exceed deaths and that the in-migrants are younger than the out-migrants. Indeed, all human institutions and organizations may be thought of in these terms. One way that social change may be studied is by the monitoring of compositional change caused by entrances and exits (Ryder, 1964).

Theories of population change and the Demographic Transition Theory

Changes in the size of the world's population over a certain period of time are due entirely to changes during the same time period in fertility and mortality (migration, obviously, does not figure into the equation when the focus is on the world). The world changes its size over a given time interval by adding persons born during the period and subtracting persons dying.

The dynamics of world population change may thus be represented in an abbreviated form of the population equation (shown earlier in Chapter 1, formula [1.1]), also known as the **balancing equation**, namely

$$P_2 = P_1 + B - D$$

where P_2 is the size of the world population at the end of the time interval; P_1 is the size of the world population at the beginning of the time interval; B is the number of births occurring in the world during the time interval; and D is the number of deaths occurring in the world during the interval.

The most prominent explanation of population change is the *demographic transition theory*. Other explanations already discussed in the context of human fertility (see Chapter 3) are **wealth flows theory,** *human ecological theory*, and *political economic theory*. Regarding this general issue of demographic theory, we are often struck by observations from uninformed scholars that demography is void of theory. This is clearly an incorrect statement. Indeed, there is more theory in demography than in most of the other social sciences. We have already provided evidence in Chapter 3 in discussions of fertility theories and in Chapters 5 and 8 in discussions of the more formal (i.e., mathematical) theory of stable populations. Because demographers rely heavily on the analysis of quantitative data, they are sometimes characterized solely as "number crunchers." What needs to be remembered is that their quantitative data analyses are almost always guided by a rich body of demographic theory.

DTT was first developed by Warren S. Thompson (1929) and Frank W. Notestein (1945). The theory proposes four stages of mortality and fertility change that occur in the process of societal modernization. The first stage is the *pretransitional* or *preindustrialization stage*. It lasted for thousands of years when the world was characterized by high birth and death rates and stable population growth. It shows high rates of fluctuating mortality and high fertility. The relative instability of the mortality rates means that during this stage, there were some periods of natural increase and some of natural decrease, but that over the longer period, there was very little change in population size. Because of its high birth rates, it is

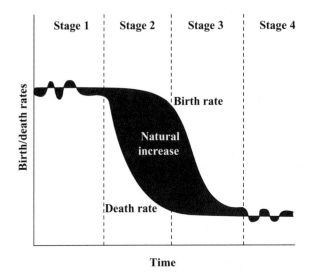

Figure 9.2. The classic stages of demographic transition. Note that natural increase is produced from the excess of births over deaths. *Source:* Population Reference Bureau, available at http://www.prb.org/presentations/g_classic-stages-transit.ppt (accessed May 20, 2009).

also referred to as the *stage of high growth potential* because of the great potential for population growth if mortality were ever to fall. This stage is shown in the left portion of Figure 9.2.

The pretransitional stage was followed by the *first transitional stage* (shown in Figure 9.2 as Stage 2). For numerous reasons (discussed in more detail in Chapter 5 and later in this chapter), mortality began to decline in many countries of the world. With the onset of industrialization and modernization, many societies transitioned to lower death rates, especially lower infant and maternal mortality, but maintained high birth rates; rapid population growth was the result. It would take another generation or so before fertility would begin to fall. Thus, during Stage 2, population growth was intense.

The next stage (Stage 3) was characterized by *decreasing population growth* due to lower birth and death rates; it is during this period that fertility begins to decline. In the final stage (Stage 4), called *incipient decline*, both fertility and mortality are very low. In Stage 4, populations grow only when there are increases in fertility, such as in the baby boom in the United States after World War II. During this stage, however, there are slight fluctuations in fertility; thus, both natural increase and decrease will occur owing to these fluctuations. The term *incipient* is used because it is not really possible to determine how low fertility will go. In recent years, fertility has fallen so low in many European countries and in Japan that the number

Billions

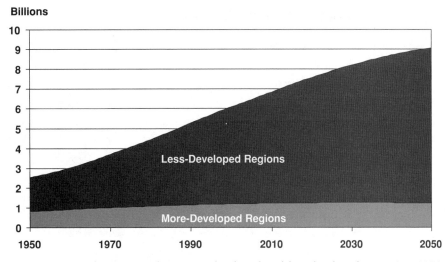

Figure 9.3. Population growth in more-developed and less-developed countries, 1950 to 2050. *Source:* United Nations, *World Population Prospects: The 2004 Revision* (medium scenario), 2005. © 2006 Population Reference Bureau. Available at http:// www.prb.org/presentations/g_growth-MDCs-LDCs.ppt (accessed May 20, 2009).

of deaths exceeds the number of births. This suggests, perhaps, that there could well be yet another stage, Stage 5, one of population decline. Where that might lead us is too early to tell.

The theory of demographic transition is the most popular of the demographic theories of population change. There are numerous applications of the theory in European and other populations; these show that it does not work the same way in every population (Hirschman, 1994; Knodel and van de Walle, 1979; Mason, 1997; Poston, 2000). Its major contribution is its utility less as a predictor than as a general description of population change.

The demographic transition in most less-developed countries is not as yet complete. Most African countries are early in Stage 3 of the transition, with falling death rates and high, though falling, birth rates. This is also the case in much of the Middle East. Some countries in Latin America are moving toward the stage of incipient decline but are not there yet. This is also true of the United States.

These variations in demographic transition between the more-developed and the less-developed countries are resulting in some interesting changes in population distribution. Figure 9.3 shows population growth in the more **developed countries** of the world and in the less-developed countries of the world, from 1950 to 2050. Today, about 82 percent of the world's population (5.4 billion) lives in the less-developed countries and only 18 percent in the more-developed countries (1.2 billion). Just one century ago, the pattern was almost reversed, with a large majority of the earth's population residing in the more-developed countries: "The conclusion is obvious: not only has population growth been enormous in the 20th century, it has also led to a complete reversal of population distribution with the poorer regions gaining and surpassing the richer sections in the process" (Bouvier and Bertrand, 1999: 10). Figure 9.3 projects that the share of population living in the less-developed countries will increase further during the twenty-first century, given the very low fertility rates in the developed nations.

According to the United Nations (UN), the more-developed countries of the world, for the most part, are all the countries of North America and Europe (including Russia), along with Japan, Australia, and New Zealand. The so-called less-developed or **developing countries** are the more than two hundred remaining countries in the world.

John C. Caldwell (1976) called for a restatement of DTT (see also our discussion in Chapter 3). His theory of wealth flows is grounded in the assumption that the "emotional" nucleation of the family is crucial for lower fertility. This occurs when parents become less concerned with ancestors and extended family relatives and more so with their children, their children's future, and even the future of their children's children (Caldwell, 1976: 322). He argued that ideally there are essentially two types of societies; the first is where "the economically rational response is an indefinitely large number of children, and the second where it is childless" (p. 322). But why, from an economic view, would couples want either an unlimited number of children or none at all? Caldwell explains that it depends on the direction of the intergenerational flows of wealth and services. If the flows run from children to their parents, it is entirely rational for parents to want to have large families. In modern societies, where the flow of wealth and services is from parents to children, it is rational to want small families. To say that parents in the less-developed countries today are "irrational" because they continue to have large families is to misunderstand these societies. In Caldwell's view, fertility behavior is rational in virtually all societies, irrespective of their levels of development (Poston and Terrell, 2006).

Doubling time and halving time

How fast or how slow is the world's current population growth rate of 1.2 percent? We noted in the first part of this chapter that in the 1960s, the world was growing at more than 2 percent, and now it is growing at around 1.2 percent. Demographers sometimes use the **Rule of Seventy** to gain an idea about whether a population's growth rate is fast or slow. Where did the Rule of Seventy come from? What does it mean?

One way to determine the significance or relevance of a population's rate of growth is through the concept of doubling time. That is, if a population maintains its present birth and death rates year after year, how long would it take to double its size? The answer may be presented through the use of natural logarithms. The **natural log** of 2 (doubling time) is 0.693 We multiply by 100 and round up to 70.

To illustrate, if we divide 70, or more precisely, 69.3, by the population's positive growth rate expressed as a percentage, the answer tells us how many years it will take for the population to double its size if it maintains its current birth and death rates. The world's CBR in 2007 was 21/1,000 and its death rate, 9/1,000, for a difference between the two of 12/1,000, or 1.2 percent. Dividing 69.3 by 1.2 equals 57.8, which is the number of years it would take the world to double its size from 6.6 billion to 13.2 billion. If its present birth and death rates were maintained, the world would number 13.2 billion in 2065 and 26.4 billion in 2123. A growth rate of 1.2 percent is a relatively rapid rate of growth, leading to a doubling of the population in around 58 years. As we will see, even though this growth rate of the world is not as high as it was in the 1960s when the world was growing at 2 percent (a doubling time of almost 35 years), population growth rates greater than 1 percent have not been common in the world until just a few centuries ago.

Let us compare the population growth rates of two countries of about the same size with very different rates of growth. The West African country of Niger has a population of 14.2 million, with a birth rate of 48 and a death rate of 15, equaling a growth rate of 3.3 percent. The European country of the Netherlands has a population of just over 16 million people, with a birth rate of 11 and a death rate of 8, resulting in a population growth rate of 0.3 percent. How different are these two growth rates of 3.3 percent and 0.3 percent? The difference between the two, one might say, is only 3 percent; this is not very much.

If one answers the question in terms of doubling time, however, there is a vast difference between a doubling time based on 3.3 percent and one based on 0.3 percent. If Niger maintains its current birth and death rates, its population will double in size in only 21 years. If the Netherlands maintains its current birth and death rates, its population will double in size in 231 years. The doubling time concept does not necessarily reflect what will happen in the future because a country's birth and death rates hardly ever remain the same from year to year. But the concept allows us to appraise the relevance or significance of a particular percentage rate of population change.

What happens if the difference between the population's birth and death rates is not positive but negative? May we still use the Rule of Seventy to tell us about the significance or relevance of a negative rate of growth? Yes, we may.

For example, Russia in 2007 had a population numbering 142 million people; its birth rate was 10/1,000 and its death rate 15/1,000, for a percentage rate of population change of −0.5 percent. If we divide this negative percentage rate into 69.3, the answer is 138.6. This means that if Russia were to maintain its current birth and death rates, its population would become half as large in 139 years (i.e., a **halving time**). We noted earlier that Russia is indeed experiencing population decline because of its low birth rate.

We turn next to a discussion of population change in the world. We look first at population growth before 1650 and then since 1650.

WORLD POPULATION GROWTH

Population growth before 1650

Figure 9.4 charts estimated numbers of the size of the population of the world beginning around 65 thousand years before the common era (BCE). The world population then was estimated to number between 400 thousand and 500 thousand people. For thousands of years, the world grew very slowly. About 35 thousand years BCE, at the time of the emergence of *Homo sapiens sapiens* (i.e., the *sapiens* variety of the species Homo sapiens), the population of the world numbered around 4 million. By about 8000 BCE, the world's population was about 6 million. That was about the time when the Agricultural Revolution got underway. With settled agriculture and the domestication of animals, it was possible to support a denser population. There were long periods of stationary growth, that is, no growth, until around the time of Christ, when the world's population numbered approximately 250 million (Biraben, 2003). The population did not double again until about the year 1600. The annual rate of growth was a mere 0.04 percent. To be sure, the growth patterns were uneven. The population would grow fairly rapidly for a few years, and this was followed by epidemics or plagues, and the population would decline in size. Indeed, the size of the world population apparently declined between 1300 and 1400. Overall, death rates were very high, and birth rates had to be at least as high if the population were to grow even very slowly.

These stationary conditions of near zero to very low population growth continued until approximately 1650, when the population of the world numbered around 650 million. During these many thousands of years, the

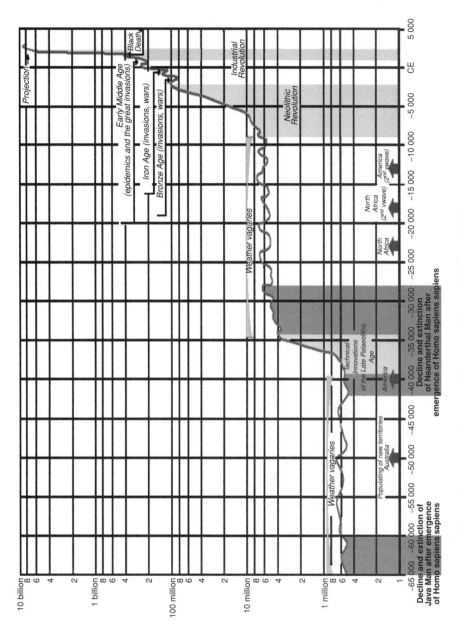

Figure 9.4. World population growth over 65,000 years. *Source:* Biraben, 2003.

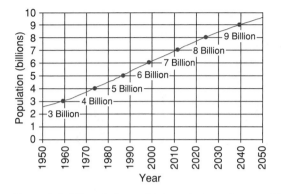

Figure 9.5. Historical world population change: 1950–2050. *Source:* U.S. Census Bureau, International Data Base, December 2008 update. Available at http://www. census.gov/ipc/www/idb/worldpopgraph.html (accessed May 20, 2009).

world's population was kept small in size by the various **Malthusian checks** mentioned earlier. Death rates were high because of the positive checks of plagues, famines, and poor living conditions. Generally, populations had high birth rates so as to compensate for the high death rates.

Population change since 1650

The world's population grew from around 650 million in 1650 to 1 billion by 1850. It then took less than eighty years to double again by 1927 (Pison and Belloc, 2005). As the Agricultural Revolution resulted in more density, so too did the Industrial Revolution. People began to leave their farms and move to cities where factories and mills were humming. An urban revolution occurred along with the Industrial Revolution. This made it possible for density to increase as well. Figure 9.5 charts changes in the size of the world population from 1950 to the present, with projected numbers to 2050.

Much of the growth was attributable to lower death rates while birth rates remained high. The improved standards of living that eventually evolved from industrialization helped explain the declining death rates. However, death rates rose slightly before they fell.

The onset of the Industrial Revolution was not kind to the individuals who joined the urban labor force. Indeed, their situation was a major concern of Karl Marx, who saw this as an attempt by the bourgeoisie to force the proletariat to accept incredibly poor working conditions (Marx and Engels, [1848] 1935). Only later did conditions improve somewhat, and this was accompanied by a lower death rate. With the birth rates remaining high, the result was massive population growth. A latent function of that growth was international migration away from the highly populated

European countries to the underpopulated Americas and elsewhere (discussed in Chapter 7).

The rapid population growth during this period was limited to Western Europe. In other regions, where the Industrial Revolution had not fully taken hold, death rates remained high, as did birth rates. It was only later that death rates fell rapidly in the less-developed regions.

The decline in mortality in the developed nations was later followed by a decline in fertility. By the 1930s, growth rates were approaching zero again. Whereas throughout most of history until the eighteenth century population growth was very slow because of high fertility and high mortality, this time population growth approached zero because of low fertility and low mortality.

The political and economic challenges from these demographic shifts in distribution are considerable. Will the massive numbers of poor people in the less-developed regions rise up against the far fewer rich in the developed nations? Will it be necessary for the rich to increase their contributions to the poor of the world? The lists of questions are endless.

The declines in both fertility and mortality warrant explanations. As we have stated, the Industrial Revolution eventually created a healthier society. With better transportation, food supplies were improved and famines occurred less frequently. New foods were introduced from the colonies in the Americas and elsewhere. Also, better housing was constructed, and better clothing became available as cotton was plentiful. In the nineteenth century, sanitary behavior began to be practiced by the people, and public-health movements were appearing. Medical improvements did not really contribute much to declining mortality until the twentieth century.

Death rates remained very high in the less-developed regions. It was not until after World War II that significant improvements in longevity occurred. Then, death rates in many places fell rapidly. These areas benefited from the knowledge learned in the more advanced nations a decade or two earlier. By then, too, medical knowledge had increased, and the residents were the benefactors of this information.

The decline in fertility is not as easily understood as that for mortality. Note that individual decisions were not that important when it came to lowering mortality. The social system, for the most part, was the major contributing factor. When it came to fertility, however, individual decisions were necessary if the rates were to be lowered. But even those decisions depend on the social situation. As urbanization and industrialization began to occur, the family became less important as an economic unit of production. When most people resided in rural areas, having large families was important. The children, as they grew up, participated in the daily household chores. Having another child was economically feasible since families tended to live mainly off the land. With the move to the city, impersonal systems like the factory took over the allocation of jobs. Those moving from the farm to the city often found themselves living in tenement houses, usually with only one or two bedrooms. It was soon concluded that children who were useful as a cheap supply of labor in farming families were not as useful in industrial working-class families. Furthermore, child labor laws were soon passed and formal education became mandatory. Hence, children did not contribute as much to the family economy as they did prior to the initiation of these legal changes.

Another factor in the process of declining fertility was the fall in infant mortality. Along with overall mortality declines, so too did deaths to infants decrease. Prior to the Industrial Revolution, families would often have nine or ten or more children, perhaps subconsciously realizing that only three or four might survive to adulthood. Now, most survived; the solution, thus, was to limit fertility.

Returning to our earlier point, individual decisions had to be made with reference to limiting family size. (We already discussed birth prevention measures in Chapter 4.) Such decisions were long in the making. For centuries, the culture virtually dictated that women should have as many offspring as possible. Consider how dramatic this shift in sexual behavior was for those couples. It was not at all surprising that it took more than one generation for smaller families to become the norm. This was a major cultural change in familial behavior.

The decline in fertility among people in the less-developed regions has been very slow. With mortality falling swiftly, this slow decline in fertility began in the 1960s to result in large increases in the size of the population. This, in turn, led to a growing concern about overpopulation (Connelly, 2008). The fairly esoteric topic of demographic growth took on a new meaning in the United States and elsewhere with the publication in the 1960s and 1970s of several high-profile books: Frederick Osborn's *This Crowded World* was written in 1960, followed by Paul R. Ehrlich's best-seller, *The Population Bomb*, in 1968 and *Famine 1975* by William and Paul Paddock in 1967. These treatises, sometimes referred to as **neo-Malthusian**, "were designed to be alarmist in tone, and Ehrlich and his wife Ann went on to advocate the need for incentives bordering on coercion to induce couples to have fewer children" (Bouvier and Bertrand, 1999: 64; see also Connelly, 2008).

Since then, however, there have been several success stories among the countries of the developing world. Bangladesh, one of the poorest countries, has seen its total fertility rate fall from well over six births to three births by 2007. Mexico's rate has fallen significantly. There are many other examples of evolving success.

However, the fertility rates for most African countries, especially in Western and Eastern Africa, remain well above five births per woman, and above six births per woman in many middle African countries, for example, Angola, Congo, and Chad. Will fertility begin to fall, or will some of these countries see their mortality rates climb back to premodern levels? The question remains as international agencies continue to try to assist in lowering fertility levels.

THE FUTURE POPULATION OF THE EARTH

Before gazing into the future, let us reexamine the population growth of the last few decades. Recent demographic trends can be described without exaggeration as revolutionary, a virtual discontinuity with all of human history. When we realize that it was not until about 1850 that world population reached the first billion and that it is now well over 6 billion, it becomes altogether clear that for most of the time that *Homo sapiens sapiens* has been on this planet, growth has been infinitesimal. This point is made most clearly in Figure 9.4.

The population projections we present in this chapter suggest that such a demographic balance will necessarily take place again in the not-too-distant future as population approaches the ultimate carrying size of the planet.

Note that we have used the word **projection** rather than "prediction" or "forecast." Predictions of things to come are best left to seers and psychics. Forecasts are best left to meteorologists. A **population projection** refers to the number of people who will comprise the population of an area at some future point in time according to clearly stated demographic assumptions about the demographic variables.

A population projection is intended to answer the question, "What if . . . ?" It need not even be realistic. In fact, population projections are sometimes used to demonstrate the impossibility of maintaining certain rates of growth. For example, Ansley J. Coale (1974) calculated that if the then-current rate of world population growth continued indefinitely, in less than seven hundred years there would be one person for every square yard of the earth's surface. Coale's calculation was definitely not intended as a prediction. Rather, it was meant to illustrate rather vividly that the planet cannot maintain such a rate of population growth indefinitely.

Such examples are extreme, yet they demonstrate what demographer Peter Morrison (1977: 12) meant when he wrote that "the purpose of projecting population is not exclusively, or even primarily, to make accurate predictions. Rather, it is to identify and chart the likely effects of influences and contingencies that will determine future population size."

Most projections, however, try to be realistic. The assumptions generally reflect what appears to be reasonable at a given point in time. Populations rise and fall because of shifts in fertility, mortality, and/or migration. Assumptions are made about the future levels of such demographic behavior. The person making the assumptions must be clear about the intent of the effort. Are the projections realistic or are they intended to show the absurdity of the assumptions? Far too many projections are reified. Looking for quick and easy answers, those not well versed in demographic research too often ignore the assumptions and only emphasize the projections.

In this chapter, we use world population projections prepared by the Population Division of the United Nations. It is our view that these reflect reasonable demographic behavior. Nevertheless, they are just that, namely, projections that indicate what the population of a specific area will be according to stated assumptions. In no way should they be seen as predictions, nor should they be considered the final word. The UN is continuously revising its assumptions based on the latest data available.

Another issue with projections is the length of time for which they are made: The longer the period, the less reliable the projection. Short-term projections are usually grounded in a detailed analysis of current trends. These projections amount to forecasts of a sort, but chiefly forecasts of the near-term future, as long as the underlying trends do not change substantially. Of course, these trends can affect the future, and ultimately falsify themselves, by alerting policymakers to the need for policies to thwart an undesirable future.

Fluctuations have occurred and will continue to occur in the future. The projections set forth here in our book go to the year 2100, but confidence in the first fifty years is far greater than in the latter part of the century.

What do the numbers tell us? The world population was estimated to number 6.6 billion in 2007; it is projected to reach 7 billion in 2013, 8 billion in 2026, and 9 billion in 2046 (United Nations, 2005). The 2050 population is projected to be more than 9 billion people.

You may be asking about the assumptions that the UN demographers used to arrive at these figures, and you are correct in asking such a question. Whether it is the UN or the U.S. Census Bureau making the projections, three alternate projections are usually prepared, namely, a high one, a low one, and one in the middle. In this chapter, we use the middle projection that assumes that all nations will eventually reach a total fertility rate of 1.85 children per woman. Some will reach it sooner than others; those currently with fertility lower than 1.85 will gradually see an increase to the level of 1.85. As for mortality, the projections see gradual improvements in life expectancy, especially among the less-developed nations. Since we are considering the projected population numbers for

Table 9.1. Population projections (in thousands) for the world, 2010 to 2050

Year	Medium variant	High variant	Low variant	Constant-fertility variant
2010	6,842,923	6,903,276	6,781,431	6,881,529
2020	7,577,889	7,873,172	7,280,148	7,819,207
2030	8,199,104	8,784,155	7,618,083	8,855,299
2040	8,701,319	9,709,446	7,753,745	10,092,723
2050	9,075,903	10,646,311	7,679,714	11,657,999

Source: United Nations, 2005.

the entire world, there is obviously no need to make assumptions about migration.

Frankly, we consider these assumptions, especially about fertility, to be somewhat conservative. Yet, by using them, we cannot be accused of being alarmists. It is always better to err on the conservative side in matters like population growth. Table 9.1 indicates the future projected population under the three basic models. Also included is the projected population assuming no change in fertility anywhere in the world. Note that the population in 2050 under this scenario would be fast approaching 12 billion, almost double today's numbers. This may serve as another example of a projection that is not realistic!

The middle scenario we prefer to use indicates that population will continue to grow. This increase will take place despite the fact that the annual growth rate is projected to decline from 1.14 in 2005 to 0.38 in 2050. Again, we repeat that this is a rather conservative projection. For example, in Africa, the total fertility rate (TFR) is posited to fall from 4.68 to 2.52 in the next fifty years. This will be quite a challenge.

How large can a population grow? Or, to borrow the question from Joel Cohen's (1995) book, "How many people can the earth support?" Unfortunately, Cohen never gives us a direct answer, but he does identify the variables that must be considered before arriving at one. For example, at what standard of living will the people of the earth live? That of the United States, France, or Nigeria? He has answered the following:

> The human population of the Earth now travels in the zone when a substantial fraction of scholars have estimated upper limits on human population size. These estimates are no better than present understanding of humankind's cultural, economic, and environmental choices and constraints. Nevertheless, the possibility must be considered seriously that the number of people on the Earth has reached, or will reach within a half century, the maximum number the Earth can support in modes of life that we and our children and their children will choose to want. (Cohen, 1995: 76)

It may seem contradictory to project such momentous increases while the growth rate itself is falling. Three factors account for this apparent anomaly. First, the population itself is expanding. Even though the growth rate is falling, it is based on an ever-growing population. Consider the parallel situation in banking, where one's bank account continues to grow in size despite falling interest rates.

Second, infant and childhood mortality rates have fallen rapidly in many developing countries during the past few decades. The result is a sort of baby boom attributable not to higher fertility, as in the United States, but rather to lower mortality. This baby boom has contributed to a third factor. In any young population, a built-in momentum for growth is present. Looking at the world, and particularly its developing regions, the numbers of young people are enormous, proportionally speaking. Even if these people all decide to lower their fertility, the number of births will increase because there are more and more women of reproductive age who are available to have children. This is called *population momentum* (see Chapter 3) and is discussed again in Chapter 12.

The conclusion is apparent. Despite recent declines in fertility, rapid population growth is in store for the planet for the foreseeable future. However, different regions and countries will exhibit different demographic behaviors, resulting in a growing proportion of the planet's population residing in the developing areas.

Today, major portions of Malthus's line of reasoning are suspect, particularly his doubts concerning people's ability (and willingness) to practice "moral restraint." His rejection of contraception and abortion as immoral (although the latter view is still today held by some) is clearly not in line with the thinking of a majority of the inhabitants of the world. Yet, his concern about a sufficient supply of food for a growing population remains an issue to this very day. We have more to say on this issue of available resources in Chapter 14. For now, it is important to keep **Malthusianism** and its concepts in mind as we learn more about population change.

CONCLUSION

Through most of the human time on earth, the population has grown very slowly. High birth and death rates prevailed. It was not until about 1650 that population growth began to accelerate when death rates fell faster than birth rates. By the early twentieth century, births had fallen; growth in the developed regions began to fall and has recently reached an almost "no-growth" situation. This has not been the case with most developing nations. There, the death rates did not fall until the twentieth century and birth rates are still fairly high, although there are many examples of lower birth rates in some developing countries.

The world continues to grow at about 1.2 percent annually. The possibility of a world population of 9 billion in about fifty years or so is a definite possibility. This growth contributes to several problems: massive malnutrition, pressures on nonrenewable resources, and low standards of living in many countries. Stopping growth would not completely solve these problems, but it would make it easier to deal with them.

Eventually, the world's population must stop growing because we inhabit a finite space. Turning once again to Malthus, we can accomplish that goal by high death rates that balance high birth rates, or it may be accomplished by a combination of low birth rates and low death rates. The latter alternative is definitely preferable.

KEY TERMS

balancing equation	Malthusianism
demographic transition theory (DTT)	natural log
	neo-Malthusianism
dependent variable	population equation
developed countries	population projection
developing countries	positive checks
doubling time	preventive checks
halving time	projection
independent variable	Rule of Seventy
Malthusian checks	wealth flows theory

10 | Population Change in the United States

INTRODUCTION

The United States is the third most populous country in the world after the two demographic billionaires, China and India. In 2007, the population of the United States numbered 302 million inhabitants, compared to 1.3 billion in China and 1.1 billion in India. When the first census was taken in the United States in 1790, the population size of the country (as then defined geographically) was just under 4 million, the size today of the city of Los Angeles. In less than 220 years, the United States has increased tremendously in size, from 3.9 million inhabitants in 1790 to more than 281 million in 2000 (Figure 10.1) to more than 302 million in 2007. In this chapter, we trace the patterns of growth of the United States from colonial times to the present and then examine some projections of the population for the future.

HISTORY OF POPULATION CHANGE IN THE UNITED STATES

The precolonial period

Estimates for the precolonization period of the size of the population in the land now known as the United States are difficult to come by, and they vary considerably: "There is probably no single figure that can be accepted as the 'best' estimate of the late fifteenth century North American population" (Snipp, 1989: 9). According to Howard Zinn (2003: 16):

> The Indian population of [around] 10 million that lived north of Mexico when Columbus came would ultimately be reduced to less than a million. Huge numbers of Indians would die from diseases introduced by the Whites. A Dutch traveler in New England wrote in 1656 that "the Indians ... affirm, that before the arrival of the Christians and before the

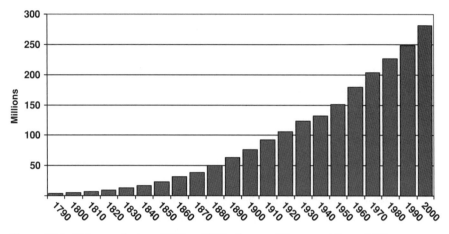

Figure 10.1. U.S. population: 1790 to 2000. *Source:* Gibson and Jung, 2002.

smallpox broke out amongst them, they were ten times as numerous as they now are, and that their population had been melted down by this disease, whereof nine-tenths of them have died."

The number of Native Americans continued to decline over the next centuries and totaled between 125 thousand and 150 thousand by 1900 (Thornton, 1990: 42). This decline resulted in part from attritions during the continual warfare in which they participated in the defense of their tribal lands, as well as from unusual hardships imposed and, as just noted, from diseases introduced by the European settlers. At the beginning of the twentieth century, "there were so few Indians left in America that it was widely believed that they would eventually disappear" (Snipp, 1989: 23).

The colonial period: 1607–1790

On May 14, 2007, the town of Jamestown, Virginia, celebrated the four hundredth anniversary of its first settlement. At its founding in 1607, Jamestown had just over a hundred colonists. By 1610, Virginia counted 350 settlers. The non–Native American population of the colonies was more than two thousand in 1620 and is estimated to have reached 50 thousand by 1650. By 1790, when the first census of the United States was taken, almost four million people were enumerated. The eightyfold increase from 1650 to 1790 is surely one of the most spectacular examples of population growth in history (Weller and Bouvier, 1981: 52–53).

Immigration was the main contributor to growth in the decades immediately following settlement. Later in the colonial period, natural increase became as important as if not more important than immigration. The pattern of population growth in that era follows closely the phases of the demographic equation. At the end of the eighteenth century, the crude birth rate (CBR) was estimated at about 55 per 1,000 and the crude death rate (CDR) at about 25 per 1,000 (Thompson and Whelpton, 1933). This rate of growth alone would increase the population by 3 percent annually. Massive immigration compounded this growth.

As we noted at the start of this chapter, the population of the United States was just under 4 million at the time of the first census in 1790. However, the census count included only the populations of the original thirteen states, along with the districts of Kentucky, Maine, and Vermont, as well as the so-called Southwest Territory, that is, what is now Tennessee (Gauthier, 2002: 5). The actual census questionnaire was quite short. As noted in Chapter 2, the first census only counted people according to whether they were free white males 16 years and older, free white males younger than 16 years of age, free white females, slaves, and "other" persons. Most of the Native American population was not included in the enumeration. About 80 percent of those counted were white. Most were of either English or Scotch-Irish ancestry; others came from Holland, Sweden, Spain, and France. The majority of the remaining 20 percent of the population was black. Most were slaves who had involuntarily immigrated to the United States from Africa. Their forced migration began slowly in the seventeenth century and increased in the eighteenth and early nineteenth centuries. The settlement of blacks was concentrated in the South (I. Taeuber and C. Taeuber, 1971: 5).

The nineteenth century

The United States grew rapidly between 1790 and 1860. The U.S. population numbered 3.9 million in 1790, 5.3 million in 1800, 12.9 million in 1830, and 31.4 million in 1860. The population increased approximately 30 percent per decade from 1790 to 1860, which was amazing considering that the growth rate in Europe at the same time was less than half as large. The numbers of the U.S. population more than quadrupled from 1800 to 1850. The combination of high levels of immigration and a high rate of natural increase explains this phenomenal growth in just a half-century. For example, the total fertility rate (TFR) in 1800 was more than 7.0 and dropped only to 5.4 by 1850 (U.S. Bureau of the Census, 1975).

We just noted that in addition to high fertility, the other component of this population increase was immigration (Hughes and Cain, 2002). Before 1830, the contribution of immigration to population growth in the United States was small. Between 1821 and 1825, for example, the average number of immigrants every year totaled only about eight thousand. This number increased to almost 21 thousand between 1826 and 1830. Between 1841 and 1845, immigrants to the United States each year numbered more than 86 thousand. In the eight years between 1850 and 1857, the number of immigrants was 2.2 million. In sum, between 1790 and 1860, the total number of immigrants to the United States was almost 5 million, and most of these were from Europe (Taeuber and Taeuber, 1958).

Of course, we must also bear in mind that the country grew geographically as well as demographically. The land area of the United States, according to the first census in 1790, comprised only 889,000 square miles (Taeuber and Taeuber, 1958). The Louisiana Purchase in 1803 nearly doubled the land area. The accession of Florida in 1819 added still more land. Between 1840 and 1850, the territory of the United States was increased by two-thirds through the annexation of Texas in 1845, and Oregon in 1846, as well as the cession by Mexico in 1848 (Taeuber and Taeuber, 1958). The addition of these new states brought with them vast increases in the numbers of people.

Most of the population growth between 1800 and 1850 occurred on the Atlantic seaboard. Yet, despite geographic growth to encompass the forty-eight contiguous states, the population density (i.e., the number of persons per unit of land) actually grew from 6.1 persons per square mile in 1800 to 7.9 persons per square mile in 1850. The newly acquired western part of the nation remained relatively underpopulated, except for the Native Americans, who were not counted in the decennial censuses until 1890. After 1850, the rate of population growth slowed down somewhat, although the population still managed to triple in size. The 1900 census counted about 76 million inhabitants. By then, there were 25.6 persons per square mile.

The first major slowdown in the population growth rate in the United States occurred during the years of the Civil War in the 1860s. Compared with a 32 to 36 percent increase in each decade between 1790 and 1860, the increase from 1860 to 1890 was between 26 and 27 percent per decade.

Despite this decline in the rate of population growth, the Industrial Revolution seriously impacted the American population during the second half of the nineteenth century. Urbanization intensified, and both the CBRs and CDRs fell. The CBRs fell from 47.9 in 1850 to 32.2 in 1900. By 1900, the CDR was 17.2 per thousand. Again, we see the demographic transition in action.

By the beginning of the twentieth century, almost 40 percent of the people were living in urban areas, compared to only 15 percent in 1850. The nation was also becoming increasingly heterogeneous. Until the middle of the nineteenth century, most of the population was white, of Anglo-Saxon ancestry. These people, along with the African Americans and the Native

Americans, comprised the bulk of the nation's population. However, during the second half of the century, new waves of immigration brought people from southern Europe and Asia, particularly China and Japan. By 1900, the nation could no longer be classified as predominantly white, Anglo-Saxon, and Protestant (WASP).

The African American population increased from around 1 million in 1800 to 8.8 million in 1900. Yet, the proportion of the total population that was African American fell from almost 19 to 11.6 percent during the period. One reason for the decline was that the mortality rate for African Americans was higher than that for whites. Another reason was that large numbers of whites immigrated to the United States from Europe, while few blacks immigrated from Africa, particularly after the slave trade was abolished in 1808.

The twentieth century

We noted that the first major decline in the population growth rate of the United States occurred during and after the years of the Civil War. The second decline was from 1890 to 1910, when the rate of population growth dropped to about 20 percent per decade. The third major decline was in the decade between 1910 and 1920, when the growth rate dropped to about 15 percent, largely due to World War I. During the period of World War I, immigrant flows were interrupted, fertility rates declined, and death rates rose. The increase in death rates was also due to the influenza epidemic of 1918–1919 (Barry, 2004), a topic already discussed in Chapter 5. Although there was a little rebound in the next decade, the population growth rate in the 1930s dropped to a new record low of 7.2 percent, which was less than half of the lowest decennial increase in earlier decades (Taeuber and Taeuber, 1958). This very low rate of increase resulted mainly from the economic Great Depression of the 1930s, which caused a sharp decline in births (Kahn, 1974). The decline of the 1930s did not continue into the 1940s and 1950s, however. The baby boom after World War II ended in the late 1950s, and the population growth rate began to decline, dropping to almost 10 percent in the 1980s.

Although the size of the U.S. population quadrupled in the twentieth century, increasing from 76 million in 1900 to more than 280 million in 2000 (U.S. Bureau of the Census, 2004b), the rate of population growth slowed slightly. The population merely doubled between 1900 (76 million) and 1950 (151.6 million). Two demographic events then greatly affected the growth of the population. First, the baby boom began around 1947. Fertility rates rose to levels unanticipated in any industrialized nation. In the late 1950s, at the height of the baby boom era, the TFR reached its peak of more than 3.7 children per woman. This high fertility (the *baby boom*) following World War II was promoted by the need to compensate for population losses during the war, as well as to rehabilitate the economy and production. The demographic effects were startling. About 30 million people were added to the population between 1950 and 1960, compared to only 19 million during the 1940s.

The second demographic surprise came in the late 1960s and early 1970s when fertility declined sharply (the *baby bust*). Many factors came together to influence the decline, such as increases in living expenses, the extension of education, increases in voluntary childlessness, and more women employed in the labor force. Cheap and easily accessible contraceptives and abortions, permitting greater control over births, were an added factor. In 1972, the country's TFR dropped for the first time below the replacement level of 2.1 (Kahn, 1974). Total population increase in 1972 was only 0.7 percent, almost half of the average annual increase during the 1960s (Kahn, 1974). U.S. fertility kept declining, although not as rapidly as in earlier years. Since 1990, the TFRs have remained at around 2.1.

People continued to settle in and around cities during the first half of the century. By the time of World War II, about two-thirds of the population lived in urban areas, compared to only 40 percent in 1900. Immigration had dwindled after World War I, slowing the pace of heterogeneity. However, as we already learned in Chapter 7, immigration once again soared after World War II, reaching its largest levels ever. Once again, heterogeneity became a part of American society.

THE UNITED STATES POPULATION: TODAY AND TOMORROW

The 2000 census counted more than 281 million residents. Although the fertility rate has fallen and the rate of population growth has declined, the absolute numerical increase in the U.S. population between 1990 and 2000 of 32.7 million people is the largest census-to-census increase in American history. The previous high was the 28 million people added to the population between 1950 and 1960 (Perry and Mackun, 2001: 1).

In 2009, the estimated U.S. population was more than 306 million. More than 80 percent reside in metropolitan areas. One-third of the U.S. population resides in metropolitan areas with at least 5 million people, and about 14 percent in metropolitan areas with between 2 million and 5 million people. However, the inner cities of the metropolitan areas have tended to lose population, while the suburbs and exurbs have grown rapidly. This is discussed in greater detail in Chapter 11.

Two important phenomena warrant noting. First, heterogeneity has been on the increase. According to the 2000 census, the non-Hispanic white (i.e., Anglo) population represented less than 70 percent of the nation's population – the lowest ever recorded. African Americans comprised 12.7 percent and Hispanics 12.6 percent of the population. Early in 2003, however, the Hispanic percentage of the U.S. population became larger than that of African Americans, so that Hispanics are now the nation's largest minority. As of 2007, the U.S. Census Bureau reported that Hispanics comprised 15.1 percent of the population, followed by African Americans at 13.1 percent ("U.S. Hispanic Population Surpasses 45 Million," 2008).

Second, the United States has become an older population. In 2000, more than 35 million elderly (defined as anyone age 65 and older) were enumerated. This is by far the largest number ever recorded. As with growing heterogeneity, aging in America is just beginning.

The U.S. Census Bureau prepares projections of the nation's population every few years. We center our attention on its so-called *middle scenario* developed in 2005. The projection assumes that fertility will rise just a little, from 2,180 to 2,186 births per 1,000 women by 2050. Life expectancy is assumed to increase from 74.1 to 81.2 years for men and from 81.2 to 86.7 years for women. Net international migration, now assumed to be just below 1 million per year, is expected to rise to almost 1.1 million per year by 2050. (For more information and a detailed explanation of the population projection assumptions, go online to http://www.census.gov and click "Projections.")

The projections also vary by race and ethnicity. For example, Hispanics are assumed to have higher fertility rates than others, but these are assumed to fall off during the next fifty years. Overall, we feel that this projection is definitely conservative. Our prime concern is with the immigration assumption. It does not take into consideration the millions of individuals who cross into the United States illegally. Nevertheless, we use the Census Bureau's projections here, bearing in mind that they probably will end up erring on the low side.

Figure 10.2 illustrates the projected population of the United States in future years. By 2050, there are projected to be well over 419 million people living in the country. That is around 115 million more than at present. How will we adjust to such an increased size and density? We discuss population policy in Chapter 13.

Table 10.1 shows the projected population of the United States by race and ethnicity in the future. The non-Hispanic white proportion of the population (once well over 80 percent of the total) is projected to fall gradually, from 69 percent in 2000 to just over 50 percent in 2050. Conversely, the component of the U.S. population that is Hispanic will almost double, from almost 13 percent in 2000 to more than 24 percent in 2050. The Asian share will also increase, from almost 4 to 8 percent by

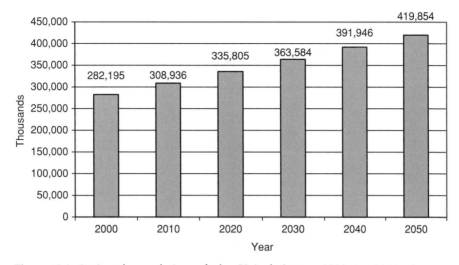

Figure 10.2. Projected population of the United States: 2000 to 2050. *Source:* U.S. Census Bureau, available at http://www.census.gov/population/www/projections/ usinterimproj/ (accessed May 20, 2009).

2050. The African American population, while increasing numerically, will see its share grow very little – from almost 13 percent to almost 15 percent.

In his famous book published more than sixty-five years ago, *An American Dilemma*, social scientist Gunnar Myrdal concluded:

> Mankind is sick of fear and disbelief, of pessimism and cynicism. It needs the youthful, moralistic optimism of America. But empty declarations only deepen cynicism. Deeds are called for. If America in actual practice could show the world a progressive trend by which the Negro became finally integrated into modern democracy, all mankind would be given

Table 10.1. Projected population of the United States by race and ethnicity: 2000–2050, medium scenario

Year	Non-Hispanic White	Black	Asian	Hispanic	Other	Total
2000	69.4	12.7	3.8	12.6	2.5	101.0
2010	65.1	13.1	4.6	15.5	3.0	101.3
2020	61.3	13.9	5.4	17.8	3.5	101.9
2030	57.5	14.3	6.7	20.1	4.1	102.7
2040	53.7	14.6	7.1	23.3	4.7	103.4
2050	50.1	14.6	8.0	24.4	5.3	102.4

Note: Percentages exceed 100% due to some persons claiming more than one race and to rounding.

Source: U.S. Census Bureau, available at http://www.census.gov/population/www/ projections/usinterimproj/ (accessed May 20, 2009).

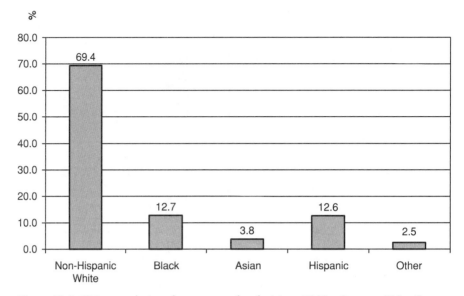

Figure 10.3. U.S. population by race and ethnicity: 2000. *Source:* U.S. Census Bureau, available at http://www.census.gov/population/www/projections/usinterimproj/ (accessed May 20, 2009).

faith again – it would have reason to believe that peace, progress, and order are feasible and America would have a spiritual power many times stronger than all her financial and military resources – the power of trust and support of all good people on earth. America is free to choose whether the Negro will remain her liability or becomes her opportunity. (Myrdal, 1944: 1021–1022)

Today, the issue remains unsolved. Indeed, it has become more complex. Rather than *Negro* (the term used several decades ago to refer to African Americans), one should include all minorities: African Americans, Hispanics, Asians, and Native Americans.

The nation can expect major shifts in its population composition (see Table 10.1 and Figure 10.3). This in itself is not to be seen as negative. Yet one should realize that the challenges will be considerable. Will non-Hispanic whites voluntarily become "just another minority"? How are African Americans adjusting to no longer being the largest minority? A new mode of cultural adaptation will be desirable if current and future Americans are to live in peace with one another. We discuss this issue later in Chapter 12.

The aging of America is a major challenge for today and for the future. In 1990, there were about 30.5 million elderly in the United States, representing 12.1 percent of the population. The 2000 census enumerated about 35 million elderly. As seen in Table 10.2, the future growth of that population will be enormous. By 2020, another 20 million elderly will be added.

Table 10.2. Projected population of the United States: 65 and older, medium scenario

Year	65–84	%	85+	%	Total 65+	%	Total Population
2000	30,794	10.9	4,267	1.5	35,061	12.4	282,195
2010	34,120	11.0	6,123	2.0	40,243	13.0	308,936
2020	47,363	14.1	7,269	2.2	54,632	16.3	335,805
2030	61,850	17.0	9,603	2.6	71,453	19.7	363,584
2040	64,640	16.5	15,409	3.9	80,049	20.4	391,946
2050	65,844	15.7	20,461	4.9	86,305	20.6	419,854

Source: U.S. Census Bureau, available at http://www.census.gov/population/www/ projections/usinterimproj/ (accessed May 20, 2009).

At that time, they will represent some 16 percent of the population. By 2050, the elderly will number almost 87 million – an increase of 52 million since the 2000 census. One in five inhabitants of the United States is projected to be 65 years of age or older.

Finally, let us take a look at the oldest-old population – those persons 85 years of age and older. Their numbers will quadruple between 2000 (4.2 million) and 2050 (20.8 million). This age group is especially vulnerable to chronic diseases and hospital (or nursing-care) confinement.

What is causing this enormous growth? Life expectancy among the older citizens is increasing; that is, more people are living longer. More important is the effect of the baby boom. Those babies born during its peak years, say between 1950 to 1960, will be reaching retirement age in about 2020 to 2030. The huge baby boom cohort of the population that has "haunted" the United States since the late 1940s remains with us and will continue to do so for some time to come, culminating in, as these data show, a gigantic *senior boom*. For now, just consider a few of the obvious problems that will evolve from these age shifts.

The rather dramatic changes that we have noted are the result of variations in demographic behavior (see also our discussions toward the end of Chapter 8). Indeed, any change in the basic demographic processes will affect population size as well as population composition. There have been significant changes in fertility and mortality, and these have contributed to the size and composition of the nation.

FERTILITY

Fertility was high during the colonial period. As noted earlier, women averaged eight to ten births, resulting in a CBR of about 55 per 1,000.

Fertility then began to decline slowly. By 1850, when the CBR was 44.3, women were averaging 5.5 live births. In 1900, the CBR was 29.8; the TFR was 3.6. This drop in fertility continued until after the Great Depression in the 1930s. In 1937, the CBR was 17.4 and the TFR was 2.2. This change in fertility mostly mirrors the demographic transition theory (DTT) model discussed in Chapter 9 and elsewhere in this book.

The birth rate began to increase during the early 1940s. The period after World War II was characterized by rather large increases in fertility; this was expected. Historically, fertility has increased at the conclusion of a war during demobilization as men return home and renew the process of family formation interrupted during wartime. However, the fertility rate was not expected to remain high for so long a period. Instead of dropping after just a few years, fertility climbed steadily for more than a decade. The CBR of 25.3 in 1957 was the highest recorded in the United States since 1924. The TFR in 1957 was 3.7, a figure 60 percent higher than the rate in 1940. What caused this unexpected baby boom?

It can be partially explained by the "catching up" of veterans after World War II; it can be partially explained by the end of the severe economic conditions during the 1930s. But other factors were also at work. Weller and Bouvier (1981: 57) suggested the following:

1. The proportion of women in their childbearing years was greater than normal. This resulted from the high fertility of the 1920s relative to that of the 1930s.
2. The percentage of women who remained single dropped significantly during this period.
3. Voluntary childlessness declined to a new low.
4. The three- or four-child family became the norm, as people moved to the suburbs and had more space, time, and money to raise children.
5. The prosperous postwar economic situation encouraged parents to have an extra child.
6. The average age at marriage decreased, and people began having their children sooner after marriage and closer together.

Together, all these factors contributed to the baby boom. The people born in that period have represented and will continue to represent a bulge in the age and sex composition of the nation's population throughout their lives. This will be happening again as soon as they become the senior boom (Carlson, 2008).

Fertility fell rapidly after the baby boom. By 1961, the CBR was 23.5; by 1968, it was 17.6. By the 1970s, the United States was experiencing a baby bust. It reached a new low of 14.8 in 1975; in 1978, it was 17.8. The

TFR also fell spectacularly from its high level of 3.7 in 1957. By 1968, it had fallen to 2.5 and reached 2.1 in 1972. It fell even more to 2.0 in 1972. Since then, it has hovered around 2.1 and 2.2.

The rapid shift in behavior from the baby-boom period to the baby-bust period was amazing. Admittedly, fertility could not stay high. Sooner or later, it was bound to fall. However, it took only a short time to accomplish this shift. What are some of the causes of such a change in behavior?

Perhaps the unsettled economic conditions that began in the late 1960s were a factor that led people to postpone marriage or childbearing. Perhaps people felt that they could not afford another baby. S. Philip Morgan and Kellie J. Hagewen (2005: 233–234) have offered the following:

> The factors include "structural" changes in the way we live and work that make children costly (in economic terms and in terms of foregone opportunities). Secular forces also include ideologies of self-actualization and individualism that could become even more powerful and pervasive antinatalist ideologies.

In a word, the decline in fertility noted in the United States, Europe, and Japan may be explained by "modernity."

Predicting the future course of fertility is difficult, if not impossible. Norms could change; economic booms could occur; the return of armed-forces personnel from the Middle East could result in an upward blip. Conversely, it is quite likely that we will continue our current pattern of low fertility, and that the two-child (or even smaller) family norm will continue as modernity becomes ever more meaningful in the twenty-first century.

MORTALITY

Death data for the early years of the republic are scant at best. Irene and Conrad Taeuber (1971: 495) have written, nevertheless, that "the mortality of the early American population was low in comparison with that in many areas of the world at that time." It is estimated that the CDR averaged about 25 per 1,000 between 1800 and 1820. From that high level, the rate dropped quite steadily, and by 1900 it was 17.2 per 1,000. Newly born Americans could expect to live on average for about forty-seven years. In 1940, the CDR was 10.8, and it dropped even more to 8.8 in 1980 (Table 10.3). A better measure of mortality is life expectancy. In 1950, a newborn male could expect to live 65.6 years and a newborn female 71.1 years. As Table 10.3 shows, life expectancy has increased since then. The latest data (in 2003) indicate that men can expect to live 74.5 years and women 79.9 years. Yes, it is true: Women live longer than men!

Table 10.3. Mortality in the United States: 1940 to 2003

| Year | CDR | Life Expectancy | |
		Male	Female
2003	8.4	74.5	79.9
2000	8.5	74.3	79.7
1990	8.6	71.8	79.8
1980	8.8	70.0	77.4
1970	9.5	67.1	74.7
1960	9.5	66.6	73.1
1950	9.6	65.6	71.1
1940	10.8	60.8	65.2

Sources: National Center for Health Statistics (NCHS), 2001, 2002: CDC National Center for Health Statistics, National Vital Statistics Reports, Vol. 50, No. 6, "Life Expectancy at Birth, by Race and Sex, Selected Years 1929–98"; CDC National Center for Health Statistics, National Vital Statistics Reports, Vol. 49, No. 12, "Deaths, Preliminary Data for 2000"; U.S. Census "Current Population Reports: Special Studies 65+ in the United States," pp. 23–190.

We have already discussed in Chapter 8 the main reasons for the female advantage.

Some molecular biologists are convinced that we are on the verge of major new discoveries that will increase life expectancy to more than a hundred years in the not-too-distant future (Endres, 1975). No one can say for certain that this will not occur. Some argue it will not. First, there is little evidence that dramatic improvements in disease elimination will come to pass. Heart disease and cancer remain high, and we now have the tragedy of AIDS to consider. Second, the demographic effects of the elimination of a specific disease will be rather small. For example, the noted demographer Nathan Keyfitz (1977b: 411–418), estimated that totally eliminating cancer deaths would increase life expectancy at birth by just 3 percent. This is because deaths from other causes would increase, and the major causes of death are clustered largely in the same age groups. We discussed this in Chapter 5.

INTERNATIONAL MIGRATION

Admittedly, there is a lot of guesswork involved when examining data on international migration. The U.S. Citizenship and Immigration Services (USCIS), formerly the Immigration and Naturalization Service (INS), did not begin gathering immigration data until a few decades into the 1800s. These data reveal nothing about illegal immigration because for all practical purposes, there was no illegal immigration at that time; there were not even any immigration laws in existence then. Moreover, there are few reliable estimates about emigration, that is, the number of people leaving the United States to live elsewhere.

It is estimated that 80 million people are believed to have migrated to the United States since its independence; three-quarters probably remained. We do know that between 1819 and 1850, about 2.5 million people moved to the United States. These newcomers came mostly from England, Ireland, and Germany. Between 1850 and 1900, there were about 17 million more immigrants. By 1890, the emphasis had shifted from Northern and Western Europe to Southern and Eastern Europe, particularly Italy, Poland, and Greece. It was at that time, too, that immigration from Asia, especially from China and Japan, rose significantly. Tensions arose between the older immigrants (mostly WASPs) and these newer immigrants, who were less likely to speak English and were more likely to be Catholic or Jewish rather than Protestant.

The volume of immigration reached what was a historic peak at that time in the first decade of the twentieth century. A total of 6.3 million immigrants came to the United States between 1900 and 1910. Immigration dropped sharply after that, in part because of World War I and the Great Depression of the 1930s. Only 2.5 million came in the 1910–1920 decade. Just about 100 thousand came during the 1930s. In some years, more people left the country than entered it (Taeuber and Taeuber, 1971: 97).

After the Great Depression and World War II, immigration increased dramatically to levels not seen before: 3 million came during the 1950s, 4 million during the 1960s, and almost 5 million in the 1970s. During the 1990s and to this day, more than 1 million immigrants enter the country every year. Again, there has been a shift in the sending countries. Now, a large majority of all immigrants come from either Latin America or Asia. The largest-sending countries are Mexico and India. Once again, tensions have evolved with this shift.

The numbers just cited account solely for legal immigration. Illegal (also referred to as *unauthorized* or *irregular*) immigration movements, especially across the country's southern border with Mexico, are significant, although it is difficult to be precise about the numbers. Perhaps another million cross the border illegally every year, maybe less. This, too, has contributed to major tensions in the nation, and as of the time of the writing of our book, the United States is far from a solution.

Future levels of immigration are difficult to forecast. The levels of immigration into the United States depend on economic conditions in the sending country, as well as those in the United States itself. Even more important, they depend to a considerable extent on legislation passed by Congress determining the number of immigrants who will be allowed to enter in any given year and the countries from which these immigrants may come.

SUMMARY

Since the first census was taken in 1790, the population of the United States has increased from just less than 4 million to more than 300 million (Figure 10.1). The proportion that is urban has grown from 5 percent to well over 75 percent. The U.S. population has aged during the years and will continue to do so in future decades. The population is increasingly heterogeneous and this, too, will continue to increase in future years. The twenty-first century will be an era of major shifts. Americans need to be aware of these changes and prepared to adapt to them.

Birth rates and death rates fell steadily during the nineteenth and twentieth centuries. The death rate is unlikely to fall much more; the birth rate is another story. As we have seen, it has fluctuated wildly during the twentieth century, highlighted by the baby boom and the baby bust. Currently, the TFR is just above 2.1. Although the United States has the highest fertility rate of all the developed countries in the world, the fertility rate of just over 2.1 indicates that the population is just barely replacing itself through "natural increase." That is, birth and death rates are close to being even; hence, most growth is coming from immigration.

The population of the United States will continue to grow during the twenty-first century but at rates below those of the 1950s and 1960s. How large the population will be in 2100 depends on the demographic behavior not only of Americans but also of immigrants coming to the country.

Population Distribution

Whether looking at the planet Earth, or at Africa or the United States, it is clear that the population is far from being equally distributed around the world. The spatial demographer Mark Fossett has written that "structured patterns in spatial distribution are evident from the highest levels of macrospatial scale... to 'fine-grained' patterns in metropolitan areas... and nonmetropolitan hinterlands" (2005: 479).

Most know that China's population numbers more than 1.3 billion, and the population of the United States is just over 300 million. However, many may not be aware that China and the United States are very close in geographic size; China has 9.6 million square kilometers of surface area compared to the United States with 9.8 million square kilometers. But the populations in both countries are not distributed randomly. Most of the people in both countries live in the eastern regions. Figures 11.1 and 11.2 are nighttime satellite maps of the United States and China and illustrate well the uneven distribution of the population in the two countries.

In some countries, people are more likely to be rural than urban dwellers. Generally, however, there is an **urbanization** movement throughout the world: "Without question, the dominant feature of spatial distribution in the United States and other developed countries is the concentration of population in densely settled urban areas" (Fossett, 2005: 479). For that matter, the way in which cities have evolved is a quite interesting phenomenon. In this chapter, we examine how the inhabitants of the world are distributed, and how most of us are becoming **city** dwellers rather than cave dwellers, as was the case thousands of years ago.

DISTRIBUTION OF THE POPULATION OF PLANET EARTH

Only about one-third of the earth's land is permanently inhabited. Areas such as the Arctic and the Antarctic, as well as the vast deserts such as

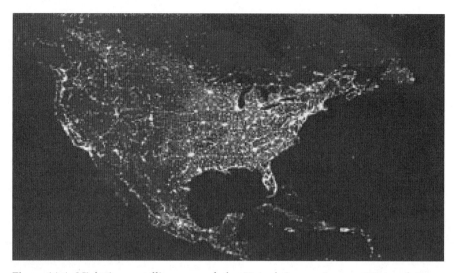

Figure 11.1. Nighttime satellite map of the United States. *Source:* National Aeronautics and Space Administration, available at http://www.gsfc.nasa.gov/topstory/20011027heatisland.html (accessed May 20, 2009).

the Sahara, are scarcely inhabited. The situation is similar where rugged mountains make it almost impossible for humans to survive. The geographic distribution of the global population is shown in Table 11.1. South Central Asia (mainly India) and East Asia (predominantly China) are the most populated of the world regions; Oceania (primarily Australia) is the least.

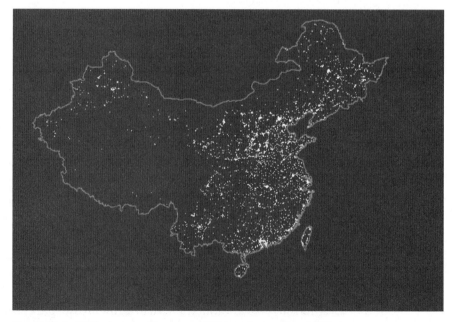

Figure 11.2. Nighttime satellite map of China. *Source:* Lo, 2002.

Table 11.1. Distribution of the world's population by region – 2006 (in millions)		
Major areas and regions	Estimated midyear population	
Africa		924
Northern Africa	198	
Western Africa	271	
Eastern Africa	284	
Middle Africa	116	
Southern Africa	54	
North America		332
Canada	32.6	
United States	299.1	
Latin America/Caribbean	566	
Central America	149	
Caribbean	39	
South America	378	
Asia		2,657
Western Asia	218	
South Central Asia	1,642	
Southeast Asia	565	
East Asia	1,544	
Europe		732
Western Europe	187	
Northern Europe	97	
Eastern Europe	296	
Southern Europe	152	
Oceania		34

Source: Population Reference Bureau, 2006.

Today, four countries have populations that exceed 200 million, and they are led by China and India. Table 11.2 lists the top ten countries by current population size (as of 2006), and also projects the top ten countries for the year 2050.

Back in 1930, Great Britain, France, Germany, and Italy were among the ten largest nations in the world. Changes that have occurred in past decades reflect the rapid growth in developing nations and the slow and even declining growth in many of the developed nations. Peering into the future, Table 11.2 informs us that by 2050, India will have surpassed China as the most populated nation in the world, and this will mainly be the result of the lower fertility of the Chinese. Actually, this crossover is projected by the United Nations (UN) to occur sometime between 2025 and 2030. In

Table 11.2. The world's ten most populous countries: 2006 and 2050 (in millions)

2006		2050	
Country	Population	Country	Population
China	1,311	India	1,628
India	1,122	China	1,437
United States	300	United States	420
Indonesia	225	Nigeria	299
Brazil	187	Pakistan	295
Pakistan	166	Indonesia	285
Bangladesh	147	Brazil	260
Russia	142	Bangladesh	231
Nigeria	135	Congo	183
Japan	128	Ethiopia	145

Source: Population Reference Bureau, 2006.

2030, China is expected to have 1.446 billion people, compared to 1.449 billion in India (United Nations, 2005: 291 and 475).

Note also the two countries projected to be newcomers to the list of the ten most populated countries in 2050: Congo (i.e., the Democratic Republic of the Congo, formerly Zaire) and Ethiopia, replacing Japan and Russia. Again, their entry into the top ten is a reflection of the major population increases projected for the African continent and the very low fertility rates in most of the developed nations.

Earlier, we pointed out that China and the United States are quite similar in areal size, although the former is four times larger in population size than the latter. Thus, regional or national population figures do not fully take into account differences in the size of the areas. A better descriptive measure that demographers use is **population density**, that is, the number of persons per square mile (or square kilometer; a mile equals about 1.6 kilometers).

We show in Figure 11.3 the distribution in population density (persons per square kilometer) for the world in 2000. The world's population density is 45 persons per square kilometer. Several countries with large populations have densities higher than 250 persons per square kilometer, namely, South Korea at 444, Japan at 327, and India at 274. Countries with densities between 500 and 2,000 persons per square kilometer are usually small islands; examples are Bermuda at 1,189, Malta at 1,152, and Barbados at 616. Countries with densities higher than 2,000 persons per square kilometer are usually city-states; examples are Monaco at 31,000, Macao

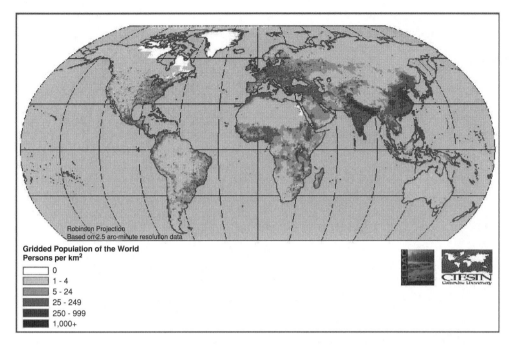

Figure 11.3. Population density in the world, 2000. Copyright 2005. The Trustees of Columbia University in the City of New York. *Source:* Center for International Earth Science Information Network (CIESIN), Columbia University; and Centro International de Agriculture Tropical (CIAT), Gridded Population of the World (GPW). Version 3. Palisades. NY: CIESIN, Columbia University. Available at http://sedac.ciesin. columbia.edu/gpw.

at 21,560, and Singapore at 4,650. The population density of the United States in 2000 was 30 (Plane, 2004: 96).

Western Europe is much more densely settled than Western Asia, although the latter population has more people (see Table 11.1); and East Asia is the most densely settled, and the most populated, of all the regions in the world. Of course, considerable variation in population density exists among countries in the same region, and even greater differences exist within any particular country. In the United States, vast portions of the Mountain states are sparsely inhabited compared to the Northeast and parts of the West Coast (Figure 11.4).

The measure of population density just discussed is a crude measure because it divides the number of persons in the population by the number of square kilometers (or miles) of territory in the country or area. An alternative and perhaps a more accurate measure uses the amount of arable land area as the denominator. One such measure is the *physiological* (or *nutritional*) *measure of population density*. It is calculated by dividing the number of persons in the country by the country's quantity of arable land (in square kilometers or miles).

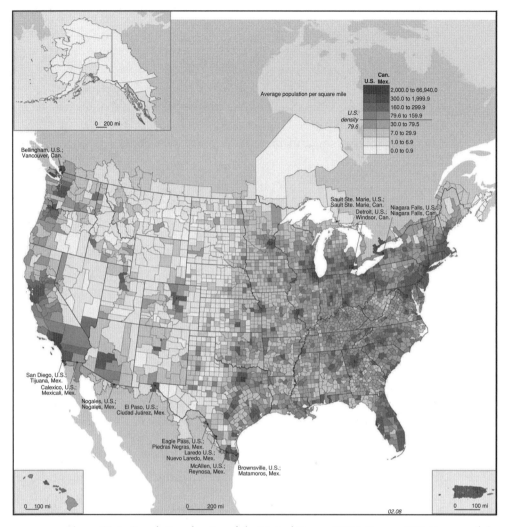

Figure 11.4. Population density of the United States, 2000. *Source:* U.S. Bureau of the Census, 2007a.

Jerome D. Fellmann, Arthur Getis, and Judith Getis have provided an interesting comparison between Bangladesh and Japan using the two measures of population density. Bangladesh has a population density of 921 persons per square kilometer of land, versus Japan's 334. However, since land in Bangladesh is much more devoted to agricultural activity than is the case in highly urbanized Japan, Japan's physiological density is 2,688 persons per square kilometer of arable land, versus 1,292 for Bangladesh (Fellmann, Getis, and Getis, 1999: 125; Plane, 2004: 96). The United States had a physiological density value in 2000 of 145 persons per square kilometer of arable land.

Many factors influence the distribution of the population. These include geographic factors (climate, terrain and soils, and natural resources); economic, social, and political factors (the type of economic activity and the form of social organization); and demographic factors (mainly the rates of population change due to the three demographic processes of fertility, mortality, and migration). These factors continue to contribute to the distribution of the world's population, some more than others. In the sections that follow, some of these factors are considered and their impacts addressed.

RESIDENTIAL DISTRIBUTION AND URBANIZATION

When looking at population distribution, whether for the world or for the United States, it is customary for demographers to examine the percentages of the populations living in rural and in urban areas. More than simply numbers are involved here. The economy of rural areas tends to be overwhelmingly agricultural. The economy of an **urban area** is more likely to be diversified and nonagricultural. Sociologists have long pointed out that lifestyles differ in rural and **urban places**. For example, Emile Durkheim ([1893] 1984) labeled them as mechanical and organic; that is, in rural areas, behavior and relationships more or less follow mechanical rules and approaches. Roles are not complex and are few in number. In contrast, in urban areas the roles are many, and there is a division of labor leading to an "organic" lifestyle, that is, one with increasing complexities and differences.

Typically, there are also sharp demographic differences between rural and urban areas. For example, fertility has usually been higher in rural than in urban areas. Educational attainment has been lower. But in industrialized nations, many of these differences have been reduced, largely through the pervasiveness of the modern media, namely, radio, TV, the Internet, and cell phones. As a result of these means of rapid communication, distinctions between rural and urban areas have become blurred. The differences, however, are still apparent in the less-developed nations of the world.

Throughout most of history, humans have been rural dwellers. Even after the Agricultural Revolution, most people were still "living on the farm." They had simply stopped wandering in search of food and shelter. It was really not until the Industrial Revolution that true urbanization began to occur, especially in the countries of Western Europe and their colonies. True, there were exceptions, like the ancient cities of Chang'an (in China, now known as Xi'an), Rome, Athens, and several others. These housed governments and religious headquarters but were not urban in the modern meaning of the word. Thus, large-scale urbanization – or changes in the proportion of people that dwells in cities – is a modern development. It should not be confused with **urbanism**, which is a reflection of lifestyle and is a sociological, not a demographic, term.

China is the country with the longest urban tradition of any country in the world. Cities made their first appearance in China more than two thousand years ago. By AD 100, the city of Luoyang had reached a population size of 650 thousand, a number equal at the time to that of Rome, another **metropolis** (United Nations, 1980: 6). Ancient Chang'an (the present city of Xi'an, capital of Shaanxi Province) attained a population size of 1 million residents in AD 700, the first million-plus city on record in all of Asia (Chandler and Fox, 1974: 291). Indeed, between 600 and 900, no capital in the Western world could compete with Chang'an "in size and grandeur" (Fairbank and Goldman, 2006: 78). For most of the thousand years between 800 and 1800, China was unsurpassed by any country in the world in both the number and size distribution of its cities.

Three conditions must always be present for urbanization, and cities, to develop. First, there must be a surplus of farm products. That is, farmers must produce more than is needed for their own subsistence. Second, there must be a means of transporting these products to the urban areas, where they may be processed into items of food, clothing, and shelter. Third, there must be a sufficiently developed technology in the urban areas to use the farm products and to provide employment for the urban dweller. Thus, mills and factories emerge in the urban areas where the products coming from the farms are developed into cotton, machinery, and the like.

The United States serves as an example of how the impacts of the Industrial Revolution contributed to the growth of cities. It is especially important here to concentrate on the mode of transportation available at any point in time. Here, we assume that the farm regions of the nation are producing a sufficient amount of goods for export to the cities. We also assume that the mills and factories are being developed to handle such products. How do they get there? Early in the nineteenth century, water was the main source of such major transportation. (Horses and wagons were not really capable of moving large amounts of material.) The first large and important cities thus were all water based, namely, Boston, New York, Baltimore, and Charleston, South Carolina. The latter was among the ten largest cities in the nation in 1800, due primarily to the cotton industry and the acrimonious slave trade. A little later, Chicago and Detroit emerged, mainly because of their locations on the Great Lakes and the St. Lawrence River. New Orleans was another early city, the result of its location near the mouth of the Mississippi River.

Then came the railroad era in the nineteenth century, opening up more areas for **urban growth**. Atlanta, Denver, and Indianapolis, among others, emerged as major urban centers. The automobile and the construction of the interstate highway system also contributed to this urban growth. Another recent contributor is the airline system with its hubs; Charlotte, North Carolina, is an excellent example of such very recent urban growth. On a smaller dimension, consider that wherever two interstate highways intersect, fast-food restaurants and hotel chains open for business and more residents move in; these may not be particularly great in number but, nevertheless, are examples of how growth follows the transportation modes. Indeed, Joel Garreau (1991) has referred to so-called **edge cities**. New "cities" actually are formed at the edges of metropolitan areas to better serve those residing ever more remotely from the true central cities (a **central city** being the largest city in an area).

Returning to a discussion of world urbanization, in 1800, only 3 percent of the population of the world was classified as urban. Later, as technological and economic changes made possible large agricultural surpluses, people began migrating to the cities in search of jobs in the factories. Consequently, massive urbanization was soon underway. By 1950, 29 percent of all residents lived in urban places. In 2007, half of all the world's inhabitants were classified as urban residents (United Nations, 2008b). Recent urbanization has been especially marked in the developing regions. Some concern has been expressed over this growth as faceless migrants multiply in and near metropolitan areas like Mexico City and Mumbai (in India, formerly known as Bombay). There, millions of homeless migrants from rural areas live in slum conditions with little hope of securing employment. This is also true of other large cities such as Lagos in Nigeria and Harare in Zimbabwe.

Is this phenomenon urbanization, or is it simply urban growth? We must be careful to distinguish between the two. As noted earlier, *urbanization* refers to an increase in the percent of a region's or country's population living in an urban area; *urban growth* refers to an increase in the number of people living in urban areas. This is not to minimize the problems exhibited in today's large cities in developing countries; however, it may well be that the rural populations are also growing.

The enormous growth of large urban areas is a recent development. Large cities existed in ancient times; we have already mentioned Chang'an, Rome, and others. But such cities were not common. In 1800, only one city, London, had more than a million residents (LeGates, 2006).

Starting in 1900, however, there began a very rapid urbanization in many parts of the world. The UN (2006b: 1) has reported that the

> global proportion of urban population increased from a mere 13 per cent in 1900 to 29 per cent in 1950 and . . . reached 49 per cent in 2005. Since

Table 11.3. World's 20 largest urban agglomerations in 2005 (in millions)			
Rank	Urban agglomeration	Nation	Population
1	Tokyo	Japan	35.2
2	Mexico City	Mexico	19.4
3	New York–Newark	United States	18.7
4	São Paulo	Brazil	18.3
5	Mumbai (Bombay)	India	18.2
6	Delhi	India	15.0
7	Shanghai	China	14.5
8	Calcutta	India	14.3
9	Jakarta	Indonesia	13.2
10	Buenos Aires	Argentina	12.6
11	Dhaka	Bangladesh	12.4
12	Los Angeles[a]	United States	12.3
13	Karachi	Pakistan	11.6
14	Rio de Janeiro	Brazil	11.5
15	Osaka-Kobe	Japan	11.3
16	Cairo	Egypt	11.1
17	Lagos	Nigeria	10.9
18	Beijing	China	10.7
19	Manila	Philippines	10.7
20	Moscow	Russia	10.7

[a] Refers to the Los Angeles–Long Beach urban agglomeration.
Source: United Nations, 2005.

the world is projected to continue to urbanize, 60 per cent of the global population is expected to live in cities by 2030. The rising numbers of urban dwellers give the best indication of the scale of these unprecedented trends: the urban population increased from 220 million in 1900 to 732 million in 1950, and is estimated to have reached 3.2 billion in 2005, thus more than quadrupling since 1950.

By 2030, there are projected to be 4.9 billion urban residents in the world, out of a total population of 8.2 billion.

Table 11.3 presents population data for the twenty largest urban agglomerations in the world; all have populations of more than 10 million. The UN has defined an **urban agglomeration** as an urban area of at least 1 million inhabitants, including all inhabitants in the surrounding territory living in urban levels of residential density. With more than 35 million residents in 2005, Tokyo is clearly the most populous of the world's urban areas. Tokyo in 2005 had more residents than the country of Kenya, with 34 million residents. Mexico City and the New York–Newark urban agglomeration, each with around 19 million residents, follow Tokyo. Next come São Paulo and Mumbai, each with just over 18 million people (United Nations, 2006b).

In addition to the twenty urban agglomerations in the world in 2005 with more than 10 million residents (Table 11.3), there were thirty urban areas with between 5 million and 10 million residents and 365 urban areas with between 1 million and 5 million residents (United Nations, 2006: Table A.17). As noted, today more than half of the world's population lives in urban areas.

ECONOMIC DISTRIBUTION

Another way to classify the distribution of the world's population is to classify people according to the level of **economic development** of their country of residence. Economic development is not an easily defined concept. Two common measures are 1) per capita income, and 2) per capita energy consumption. Each yields similar results with respect to population distribution: Less than 20 percent of the population of the world resides in the more economically developed regions.

The small proportion of one-fifth of the world's population living in the more economically developed regions is expected to decline in future years. By 2050, it may well be below 15 percent. This is projected to occur because the rates of population growth are much higher in the developing than in the developed nations. For example, in Africa, the annual rate of population growth via fertility and mortality now stands at 2.4 percent (Population Reference Bureau, 2007a). That means that the population of Africa would increase from 944 million in 2007 to almost 2 billion by 2050 if the birth and death rates of 2007 did not change. Conversely, the population of Europe is projected to actually decline between now and 2050, from 733 million to 669 million, because of very low birth rates. These examples suggest why a significant shift in the proportion of people living in developed and developing regions is expected in the coming decades of this new century. Massive migration from developing regions into the developed regions is unlikely because of political barriers erected by the latter to prevent such international movements. However, as we already saw in Chapter 7, despite many and varied limitations, quite a large number of people are estimated to be moving from one country to another without official documents. These migrants are sometimes referred to as "undocumented" or "irregular" or "illegal" or "unauthorized" immigrants; the adjective *illegal* carries considerable emotional baggage, and we have used it sparingly. As already mentioned, most undocumented immigrants are moving from the less-developed countries of the world to the more-developed and richer countries.

Table 11.4. Population (in thousands) of the United States, by region, 1970 and 2000

Region	Population, 2000	% of total, 2000	Population, 1970	% of total, 1970
Northeast	53,594	19.0	49,061	24.1
Midwest	64,393	22.9	56,589	27.8
South	100,237	35.6	62,812	30.9
West	63,198	22.5	34,838	17.1

Sources: U.S. Bureau of the Census, 1994, 2007c.

DISTRIBUTION OF THE UNITED STATES POPULATION

Over history, several trends have occurred to shape the distribution of the population of the United States. Generally, there has been a longtime movement westward. After the end of the Civil War, a migration out of the South also occurred. However, in more recent decades, there has been a resurgence of population movement into the South. Table 11.4 shows population data for each of the four geographic regions of the United States for 1970 and 2000. (Figure 6.1 in Chapter 6 shows these regions, as well as their divisions.) In the thirty years since 1970, the South has grown by almost 60 percent. In 2000, almost 36 percent of the nation's population lived there, compared to but 31 percent in 1970.

As illustrated in Figure 6.1, the United States is divided into four regions and nine divisions. The nation's population is concentrated in the eastern third of the land area. Vast proportions of the land remain sparsely populated (see Figures 11.1 and 11.4). Nevertheless, the long-term trend in geographic distribution has been westward.

Figure 11.5 is a map showing the approximate center of the United States population for each decade from 1790 to 2000. The **center of population** "is determined as the place where an imaginary, flat, weightless, and rigid map of the United States would balance perfectly if all residents were of identical weight" (U.S. Bureau of the Census, 2007a: 11). In 1790, the center of population was located in the upper portion of the Chesapeake Bay. A gradual movement westward followed. By about 1820, the entire middle section of the United States started its growth as agricultural and grazing lands were developed west of the Mississippi. The West began to grow around 1850 as the frontier became more accessible to settlers, rich ore deposits were located, and cheap land became scarcer in the East. As a result of this expansion, the center of population moved farther west with each census. By 1970, the center was located in St. Clair County, Illinois. Since then, the center has continued its movement west and, by 1980, it had

Figure 11.5. United States mean center of population: 1790 to 2000 with territorial expansion. *Source:* U.S. Bureau of the Census, 2007a.

crossed the Mississippi River for the first time. As the map (Figure 11.5) illustrates, by the time of the most recent census in 2000, the center of the population of the United States was in Phelps County, Missouri, between St. Louis and Kansas City. It had moved "12.1 miles south and 32.5 miles west of the 1990 center of population" (U.S. Bureau of the Census, 2007a: Chapter 2, p. 11). By 2000, the center had moved more than 1,000 miles from the center in 1790, near Chestertown, Maryland (2007a: Chapter 2, p. 11).

In the past, most changes in U.S. population distribution resulted from migration movements from one part of the country to another. Historically, there has been a movement out of the South into the East, then the Middle

West, and finally the Far West. In more recent decades, people have been more likely to move into the South from other regions. Especially notable has been the massive migration of retirees into the states of Florida, Arizona, and Texas. As a result, there is a **concentration** of elderly in these states.

In an earlier chapter, we pointed out the situation in Flagler County, Florida, where despite the fact that deaths outnumbered births, the county was the most rapid growing county in the country. Since about 1970, however, the United States has begun to witness a substantial increase in international migration, especially from Latin America and Asia. Many of these newcomers have settled in a few states, namely, Florida, California, New York, and Texas. This, too, has contributed to shifts in population distribution (see our earlier discussions in Chapters 6, 7, and 10).

METROPOLITANIZATION AND MICROPOLITANIZATION

Even more important than the western and, to a certain extent, southern shifts in the nation's population has been the rapid concentration in urban areas, or **metropolitanization**. First, we must ask about the definition of an *urban area* in the United States. How is the urban population defined? In the United States, one type of urban area is known as an **urbanized area** (UA); it consists of a densely settled core of census blocks and block groups that meet minimum population-density requirements, along with adjacent, densely settled surrounding census blocks that together encompass a population of 50 thousand people, at least 35 thousand of whom live in an area that is not part of a military installation. In contrast, an **urban cluster** (UC) consists of a densely settled core of blocks and block groups, along with adjacent densely settled surrounding blocks that together encompass a population of at least 2,500 people, but fewer than 50,000 people, or greater than 50,000 people if fewer that 35,000 of them live in an area that is not part of a military installation. Strictly speaking, any place that is not in an urban area or urban cluster is defined as *rural*.

Within these broadly defined urban areas, we may consider the concept of a **metropolitan area**. There have been numerous changes in past decades in the definition of a metropolitan area by the U.S. Census Bureau. In the 2000 census, a metropolitan area was defined as containing a large population nucleus, together with adjacent communities with considerable economic and social integration with the core. *Counties* are the building blocks for metropolitan areas. Hence, many metropolitan areas have small rural components.

In 1900, there were sixty-one areas that would qualify under this metropolitan area definition. By 1970, the number had grown to 202. The proportion of the U.S. population living in such areas increased from about

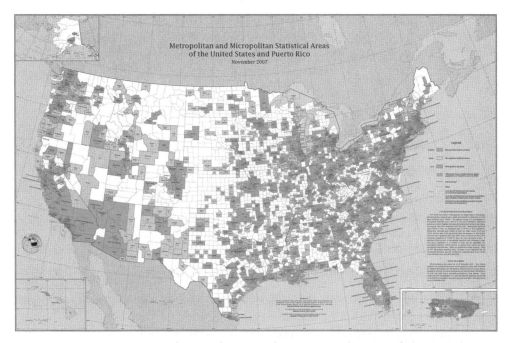

Figure 11.6. Metropolitan and Micropolitan Statistical Areas of the United States and Puerto Rico, November, 2007. *Source:* U.S. Census Bureau, Geography Division: http://ftp2.census.gov/geo/maps/metroarea/us_wall/Nov2007/cbsa_us_1107.pdf (accessed 2-9-2010).

one-third in 1900 to two-thirds by 1970. This increase was caused both by actual population increase and redefinitions of these areas as urban living styles spread beyond what had been the traditional city borders. By the 1990s, there were 331 areas in the United States defined as a **metropolitan statistical area (metro area or MSA)**, and they contained around 83 percent of the nation's population.

Another urban area concept used in the United States is the *micropolitan statistical area (micro area)*; this concept was introduced in 2003. Whereas a metropolitan area contains at least one urbanized area of 50,000 or more people (see previous definition), a **micropolitan area** contains at least one UC of between 10,000 and 49,999 people. Micropolitan areas now contain about 10 percent of the nation's population.

As of November 2007, there were 363 metropolitan areas, comprising 1,092 counties and county equivalents (83 percent of the population); there were 577 micropolitan areas, comprising 694 counties and equivalents (10 percent). This leaves 1,355 rural counties (7 percent). Figure 11.6 is a map of the metropolitan and micropolitan areas of the United States. The gray areas are metro, the light gray are micro, and the white areas are rural. You may access the map at http://ftp2.census.gov/geo/maps/metroarea/

Table 11.5. Population change in the most populous metropolitan statistical areas, 1990–2003

Rank in population size in 2003	Metropolitan statistical area title	Population (thousands)			Numerical (thousands)		Percent	
		1990	2000	2003	1990–2000	2000–2003	1990–2000	2000–2003
1	New York– Northern New Jersey–Long Island. NY-NJ-PA	16,846	18,323	18,641	1,477	317	8.8	1.7
2	Los Angeles–Long Beach–Santa Ana. CA	11,274	12,366	12,829	1,092	464	9.7	3.7
3	Chicago-Naperville-Joliet. IL-IN-WI	8,182	9,099	9,334	916	235	11.2	2.6
4	Philadelphia-Camden-Wilmington. PANJ-DE-MD	5,435	5,687	5,773	252	86	4.6	1.5
5	Dallas–Fort Worth–Arlington. TX	3,989	5,162	5,590	1,172	428	29.4	8.3
6	Miami–Fort Lauderdale–Miami Beach. FL	4,056	5,008	5,289	952	281	23.5	5.6
7	Washington-Arlington-Alexandria. DC-VA-MD-WV	4,123	4,796	5,090	673	294	16.3	6.1
8	Houston-Baytown–Sugar Land. TX	3,767	4,715	5,076	948	360	25.2	7.5
9	Atlanta–Sandy Springs–Marietta. GA	3,069	4,248	4,610	1,179	362	38.4	8.5
10	Detroit-Warren-Livonia. MI	4,249	4,453	4,484	204	31	4.8	0.7
11	Boston-Cambridge-Quincy. MA-NH	4,134	4,392	4,440	258	48	6.3	1.1
12	San Francisco–Oakland–Fremont. CA	3,687	4,124	4,157	437	34	11.9	0.8
13	Riverside–San Bernardino–Ontario. CA	2,589	3,255	3,642	666	388	25.7	11.9
14	Phoenix-Mesa-Scottsdale. AZ	2,238	3,252	3,593	1,013	342	45.3	10.5
15	Seattle-Tacoma–Bellevue. WA	2,559	3,044	3,142	485	98	18.9	3.2
16	Minneapolis–St. Paul–Bloomington. MN-WI	2,539	2,969	3,084	430	115	16.9	3.0
17	San Diego–Carlsbad–San Marcos. CA	2,498	2,814	2,931	316	117	12.6	4.2
18	St. Louis. MO-IL	2,581	2,699	2,736	118	37	4.6	1.4
19	Baltimore-Towson. MD	2,382	2,553	2,616	171	63	7.2	2.5
20	Tampa–St. Petersburg–Clearwater. FL	2,068	2,396	2,532	328	136	15.9	5.7

Source: Mackun, 2005.

us_wall/Nov2007/cbsa_us_1107.pdf. Download the map, enlarge it and look at the metro and micro areas in your state.

Table 11.5 presents data on population change between 1990 and 2003 in the twenty largest MSAs of the United States. The already noted patterns of population movement westward and southward can be seen in the data in this table. Note how the MSAs have kept growing, and also that many of the older metropolitan areas of the Northeast and Midwest (e.g., Cincinnati and Pittsburgh, to mention only two) are not included among the twenty largest. Fifty years ago, these and other big cities in the Northeast and Midwest would have been included.

What about the micropolitan areas of the United States? Which are the most populous micro areas, where are they located, and how fast are they changing the size of their populations? Table 11.6 presents population data for the twenty largest micropolitan areas and their population changes between 1990 and 2003. The Torrington, Connecticut, micro area, with a population of 188,000 and located in the northwestern corner of Connecticut, is the most populous of all the micro areas. All but two of the twenty largest micro areas grew in population between 2000 and 2003. The only micro areas that lost population were Pottsville, Pennsylvania, and Jamestown-Dunkirk-Fredonia, New York. Population growth in the largest micropolitan areas was mainly due to net gains in the numbers of internal migrants. This is a situation unlike that in the largest metro areas, where population growth is often, if not mainly, due to net gains in the numbers of international migrants.

MEGALOPOLIS

A new community form has been emerging in recent decades, namely, the **megalopolis**. The term is taken from the Greek words *mega (megalo)*, meaning "large," and *polis*, meaning "city," for "great (or large) city." This geographic trend was first introduced by the French geographer Jean Gottmann (1961). Generally, the term describes any densely populated social and economic entity encompassing two or more cities and the increasingly urbanized space between them.

One can often drive the entire area of a megalopolis, going from one city to another, with barely any break in nongreen spaces. This vast concentration of people, goods, and services functions as an "economic hinge" for the United States. It links the North American continent with the foreign markets accessible via the Atlantic.

In particular, this urban phenomenon came to describe the urbanized region of the northeastern United States that arose in the second half of the twentieth century. "Boswash" is the most well-known megalopolis,

Table 11.6. Population change in the most populous micropolitan statistical areas, 1990–2003.

Rank in population size in 2003	Micropolitan statistical area title	Population (thousands)			Population change			
					Numerical (thousands)		Percent	
		1990	2000	2003	1990–2000	2000–2003	1990–2000	2000–2003
1	Torrington. CT	147	182	188	8	6	4.7	3.1
2	Lake Havasu City–Kingman. AZ	93	155	171	62	16	65.8	10.5
3	Lebanon. NH-VT	155	167	171	12	4	7.9	2.2
4	Seaford. DE	113	157	168	43	11	38.3	7.9
5	Hilo. HI	120	149	158	28	10	23.6	6.6
6	East Stroudsburg. PA	96	139	154	43	16	44.9	11.46
7	Hilton Head Island–Beaufort. SC.	102	142	154	40	12	39.0	8.7
8	Ottawa-Streator. IL	148	153	153	5	0	3.2	0.2
9	Thomasville-Lexington. NC	127	147	152	21	5	16.2	3.3
10	Daphne-Fairhope. AL	98	140	152	42	11	42.9	8.1
11	Pottisville. PA	153	150	148	−2	−2	−1.5	−1.6
12	Concord. NH	120	136	144	16	7	13.5	5.4
13	Traverse City. MI	106	131	138	25	7	23.3	5.2
14	Jamestown-Dunkirk-Fredonia. NY.	142	140	138	−2	−2	−1.5	−1.5
15	Kahului-Wailuku. HI	100	128	136	28	8	27.6	5.9
16	Salisbury. NC	111	130	134	20	4	17.8	2.8
17	Statesville-Mooresville. NC	93	123	133	30	11	32.0	8.7
18	Chambersburg. PA	121	129	133	8	4	6.8	3.0
19	Tupelo. MS	108	125	128	17	3	16.2	2.4
20	Eureka-Ancata-Fortuna. CA	119	127	128	7	1	6.2	1.1

Source: Mackun, 2005.

with around 55 million people. Stretching between the metropolitan areas of Boston on the northeast side to Washington, D.C., on the southwest side, it includes the metropolitan areas of New York City, Philadelphia, Baltimore, and the District of Columbia. There are other *megalopolitan areas* in the United States, such as the "Chi-Pitts" megalopolis, with around 54 million people. It is located in the Great Lakes area and comprises the metropolitan areas of Chicago, Pittsburgh, Detroit, Cleveland,

Milwaukee, Buffalo, and some others. The largest megalopolis in the world is the Taiheiyo Belt in Japan, with around 82 million residents, consisting mainly of Tokyo, Okayama, Hiroshima, Osaka, and some other large cities. One might expect, perhaps someday, a San Francisco–Los Angeles–San Diego megalopolis, and a Dallas–Waco–Austin–San Antonio megalopolis, or maybe even a Dallas–Waco–College Station–Houston megalopolis. Present geographical barriers and insufficient amounts of intermetropolitan interaction make the emergence of such new urban areas not yet possible.

Let us look at Boswash in more detail. It begins with the northern suburbs of Boston, which extend into southern New Hampshire. To the south, the Boston suburbs extend toward the northern suburbs of Providence, Rhode Island. Then it follows to New London–New Haven, Connecticut, and the large cities that approach New York. It continues on through New Jersey to Philadelphia, Baltimore, and Washington, and then into the southern suburbs of Washington into northern Virginia. Indeed, as suburbs continue to grow, one could make a case that Boswash extends to Richmond, Virginia, and its suburbs.

However, we need to ask whether a megalopolis has the essential characteristics of a community? It does have one such characteristic, namely, a common geographic area that is distinguishable from other areas. To be a community, its people must be linked in a system characterized by a division of labor, increased differentiation of economic activity, and functional interdependence. Without such a pattern of interaction, it is difficult to conceive of a megalopolis as anything other than a grouping of contiguous metropolitan areas sharing a common, heavily populated geographic area.

TRENDS TOWARD DECONCENTRATION

At the same time that the population has become concentrated into metropolitan areas, there has also occurred a **deconcentration** in metropolitan areas. **Suburbanization** has taken place. This represents a shift from the higher-density central cities to the lower-density areas beyond the traditional city limits. Another form of deconcentration is the shift from metropolitan to nonmetropolitan areas.

Since 1900, the proportion of the United States population living in metropolitan areas has increased and, by 2000, 83 percent were residing in these parts of the nation. However, since 1930, the proportion living in the central cities of the metro areas has been falling. Thus, while metropolitan areas have seen population growth, much of that growth has been taking place in the suburban portions. This does not mean that the population of central cities has necessarily declined; rather, it means that it has grown more slowly than in the suburban portions.

Indeed, some of the growth that has occurred in central cities in past decades can be explained by *annexation*, that is, by placing outlying areas under the jurisdiction of the central cities for one reason or another. Jacksonville, Florida, annexed all of Duval County, much of which is actually quite rural. Similarly, Nashville, Tennessee, has annexed all of Davidson County. Houston, Texas, is another example of a city that has grown by leaps and bounds, partly by gradually annexing all of Harris County: "The city of Houston grew by 29 percent during the 1970s – one of the most rapidly growing large cities in the country. But the city also annexed a quarter of a million people. Without the annexation, the city would have grown only modestly" (G. T. Miller, 2004: 31).

A number of older U.S. cities have shown population declines in recent decades. For example, Detroit's population has been reduced by 50 percent since 1970. These older cities are unable to annex contiguous lands because those territories are already incorporated; there are no more unincorporated sections ready to be grabbed by the larger central cities. Although the city of San Francisco has gained population since 1970, increasing from just over 715,000 in 1970 to almost 780,000 in 2000, none of this growth occurred through annexation. San Francisco is bounded on the west, the north, and the east by water, and on the south by the smaller cities of Daly City and Brisbane. There is no available contiguous territory anywhere for San Francisco to annex, a situation not unlike that of many other older U.S. cities.

Social reasons also help explain the declining populations of many central cities. One has been the so-called **white flight**. The large movement of poorer, often nonwhite, residents into the central cities has contributed to the massive out-migration to the suburbs of the mostly white middle and upper classes. The very fact that large, relatively moderate housing developments were being produced in the suburbs after the end of World War II also contributed to this movement away from the cities. Admittedly, some of the white flight is a matter of out-and-out racism and takes place to avoid sending children to the same schools as people of color or living in the same neighborhoods with them. But the attractiveness of living in the suburbs, that is, owning a piece of land, having a yard, and leading a middle-class life, is difficult to overcome. More recently, middle-class minority families have also taken advantage of such benefits. Indeed, the declining population of the central cities cannot be ascribed solely to racial fears inasmuch as black migration to the suburbs has been accelerating for many years. The negative side of this movement is that the central cities have been left to the poor and to the underclass.

International migration must also be considered when population distribution is considered. Whether from Europe or Asia, in the late nineteenth and early twentieth centuries, immigrants were most likely to settle in the poor downtown areas of the big cities. Later, these immigrants (and their children) started moving to the suburbs. A recent upsurge in immigration, some of which is undocumented, represents a new growth for many downtown areas. It is difficult to determine the exact contribution made by such movements, and some undocumented residents are not counted in the census enumerations. It is clear, however, that these newcomers tend to reside near and in close contact with one another, usually in the relatively large cities. However, there are exceptions. For example, certain middle-size cities with a need for low-wage workers often attract undocumented workers. This is especially true in some sections of North Carolina and Alabama, such as Winston-Salem and Huntsville.

There was a time when internal migration was overwhelmingly from nonmetropolitan to metropolitan areas. This has changed. Today, people are more likely to move from the suburb of one area to the suburb of another. In other words, the traditional move "to the city" is now being bypassed. Those who move within a metropolitan area are often more likely to move from the city to the suburbs, and increasingly to the **exurbs**. Furthermore, those who make these moves are apt to be young adults, along with their children. Thus, an area experiencing net in-migration gains population in two ways: 1) through the net number of movers, and 2) through the number of children born to those movers after the migration has occurred.

The 2000 census noted the growth in areas beyond the suburbs of existing metropolitan areas. These are the *exurbs*, that is, those areas beyond the beltways that circle the metropolitan areas. In one sense, they are filling in the "empty spaces" in any megalopolis. For example, the fastest-growing counties in Virginia have been those beyond the Washington metropolitan area but just north of the Richmond metropolitan area. This pattern has been noted throughout the nation.

Summing up our discussion of population deconcentration in the United States, we first saw a movement from rural to urban areas; this was followed by a movement from the urban centers to the inner suburbs. Now we are witnessing a movement even farther away from the historic downtowns into the exurbs. This, in turn, leads to the development of *edge cities*, which then typically contribute to growth ever farther from the "downtown."

The New England Patriots of the National Football League (NFL) are an interesting example of what has been happening in recent decades. Originally, they were called the Boston Patriots. As the size of the population and, hence, the fan base declined in Boston while the suburbs grew rapidly, the team moved from Boston to Foxboro, Massachusetts. But Foxboro is not just a suburb of Boston. It lies in the center of a triangle composed of Boston, Worcester, and Providence. Since other New England states are geographically close to this area, the team wisely chose "New England" as its official name, a truly regional name for a professional football team. Similar statements may be made about the regional appeal, and name, of another NFL team, the Tennessee Titans, as well as at least two Major League Baseball teams, the Texas Rangers and the Colorado Rockies.

CONSEQUENCES OF POPULATION DISTRIBUTION

We have briefly alluded to some of the problems related to the geographical movements of people. One consequence is that particular types of economic activities have also relocated to the ring portions of metropolitan areas. This tends to remove important sources of tax revenues and jobs from the central city. Also, the composition of the population of central cities has changed radically. The out-migrating middle class has been replaced by relatively disadvantaged segments of the population, often poor minority groups, the chronically unemployed, the aged, and the socially disadvantaged.

The significance of this concentration of economically and socially disadvantaged persons in the central cities is twofold. First, the increasing proportion of such persons has added to the demand for related social services, namely, welfare, health, public housing, sanitation, and police protection, to name but a few. At the same time, the economic status of the resident population is lowered because more families move out of the central cities than move in and because the average income of the out-migrants tends to be higher than that of the in-migrants. The lowered economic status of the resident population and the loss of industry and business activity through deconcentration combine to reduce the tax base. This subsequently leads to declines in the financial ability of the central-city governments to support the increased need for services brought about by the spatial concentration of the disadvantaged. Thus, many central cities, especially the older ones, are confronted with a financial crisis: Demands for services are increasing at the same time that taxable resources are diminishing. To meet the demands, the central city often responds by greatly increasing the property tax rate, which has the effect of forcing more homeowners and industries to move out of the central city, further lowering the tax base. It is a vicious circle.

In recent years, however, **gentrification**, that is, the migration of middle-class and affluent peoples into the once poorer areas of cities, has begun to take place in some older central cities. People have begun to move back "downtown" from the outer suburbs as the cities offer new opportunities. New condominiums are being built in many of the areas in the city that were once considered depleted. Other rundown sections have been renovated. New office towers have sprung up as businesses begin to realize that there is much to say about being downtown. These movements back into the cities usually involve older, and sometimes retired, whites, as well as gay men and lesbians, many of them without children (Bradley and Longino, 2009). Whether this will result in sustained population growth in central cities remains to be seen.

SUMMARY

The term *population explosion* and **population implosion** appear contradictory. Yet they are both occurring these days throughout the world. We are already aware of the massive population growth that occurred during the twentieth century (see especially our discussions of world population growth in Chapter 9). But, as an earlier table illustrates, the growth of metropolitan areas has been enormous, while rural areas have lost population. The demographers Avery Guest and Susan Brown have given us an example of this double phenomenon in their very interesting discussion of population distribution in the United States. They have noted that "the Las Vegas metropolitan area tripled between 1980 and 2000, while 46 of the 53 counties in the state of North Dakota lost population" (2005: 59). We can only speculate as to whether this will be the direction of population distribution in the twenty-first century, not only in Nevada and North Dakota but all over the world.

KEY TERMS

center of population	micropolitan area
central city	population density
city	population implosion
concentration	suburbanization
deconcentration	urban area
economic development	urban agglomeration
edge cities	urban cluster (UC)
exurbs	urban growth
gentrification	urbanism
megalopolis	urbanization
metropolis	urbanized area (UA)
metropolitan area	urban places
metropolitanization	white flight
metropolitan statistical area (metro area or MSA)	

12 | Cultural Adaptation and Growth

INTRODUCTION

In this chapter, we discuss the changing race and ethnic distribution of the United States and its implications and consequences. We read in Chapter 10 that between 1980 and 2000, the majority race/ethnic population in the United States (i.e., persons who are white and non-Hispanic, sometimes referred to as *Anglos*) grew much less rapidly than the minority population (i.e., persons who are of a race other than white or are Hispanic); the majority grew by almost 8 percent, and the minority grew by 88 percent. In 1980, almost 80 percent of the U.S. population was of the majority; by 2000, just over 69 percent was of the majority (Hobbs and Stoops, 2002: Table 10).

This faster growth of the minority population occurred in all fifty states. In 1980, as many as twenty-one states had minority populations comprising less than 10 percent of their total populations; by 2000, the number had dropped to six. In 1980, only Hawaii and the District of Columbia had more than 50 percent of its population minority, that is, they were so-called *majority-minority states*. According to the U.S. Census Bureau, "majority-minority is defined as more than half the population being of a group other than single-race, non-Hispanic White" ("Census Bureau Releases State and County Data Depicting Nation's Population Ahead of 2010 Census," 2009). By 2000, California and New Mexico had joined Hawaii as majority-minority states (Hobbs and Stoops, 2002: Table 10).

In 2000, Texas was 48 percent minority but became a majority-minority state in 2004, an occurrence forecasted by the authors of this text in 1993 (Bouvier and Poston, 1993). As of 2008, four states and the District of Columbia were majority-minority: 75 percent of Hawaii was minority, as well as 58 percent of New Mexico, 58 percent of California, 53 percent of Texas, and 67 percent of the District of Columbia ("Census Bureau Releases State and County Data," 2009). The five states of

Arizona, Georgia, Maryland, Mississippi, and New York are next in line to become majority-minority states; they all had minority populations of more than 40 percent (U.S. Bureau of the Census, 2005).

Almost 10 percent of the 3,142 counties in the United States (i.e., 309 counties) were majority-minority counties as of July 1, 2008. Of these, 56 had become majority-minority since 2000. Orange County, Florida, the 35th most populous county in the country and the home to Disneyworld and Orlando, is one of several U.S. counties newly added in 2008 to the majority-minority group. The U.S. county in 2008 with the highest percentage minority was Starr County, Texas (98 percent), followed by Maverick County, Texas (97 percent) and Webb County, Texas (95 percent). The bulk of the minority populations of these three counties is Hispanic. Nationwide in 2008, there were 48 majority-minority Hispanic counties, and the largest 10 were in Texas. There were 77 majority-minority African American counties, and all were in the South. The only majority-minority Asian county in 2008 was Honolulu County, Hawaii, with 58 percent of its population Asian. Ten U.S. counties in 2008 were majority-minority American Indian and Alaskan Natives (AIAN) counties, the largest being Shannon County, South Dakota, with 88 percent AIAN.

By the year 2050, the U.S. population is projected to number well over 400 million people. The Anglo component of the population, that is, non-Hispanic whites, comprising 69 percent of the population in 2000 and 67 percent in 2005, will have dropped to 47 percent of the total (Figure 12.1). The United States in 2050 is projected to have become a majority-minority country. Hispanics are projected by 2050 to comprise 29 percent of the country, blacks 13 percent, and Asians 9 percent. Almost one in five Americans (19 percent) in 2050 are projected to be foreign-born, a significant increase from the 12 percent in 2005 and higher than the "historic peaks for immigrants as a share of the U.S. population, 14.8 percent in 1890 and 14.7 percent in 1910" (Passel and Cohn, 2008: 1–2).

Similar situations are also projected to occur in some of the European countries. The major changes in racial and ethnic composition in the United States and some other countries are the result largely of high levels of immigration, along with low levels of fertility by the residents of the receiving countries. What is likely to occur in the United States and certain European countries in the process of their becoming majority-minority countries? How will the populations interact? What will be the result of these race/ethnic changes? This chapter explores some of the issues of group adaptation.

Some new form of interaction necessarily follows whenever one group migrates into an area already inhabited by another group. Both groups must adapt to a new situation. Humankind has been faced with the challenges

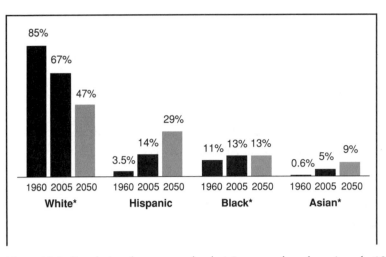

Figure 12.1. Population by race and ethnicity, actual and projected: 1960, 2005, and 2050 (% of total). *Note*: All races modified and not Hispanic (∗); American Indian/Alaskan Native not shown. Projections for 2050 indicated by light gray bars. *Source:* Passel and Cohn, 2008: Figure 6.

of group adaptation ever since migration began many thousands of years ago. In the United States and elsewhere, some form of adaptation begins whenever a new group of immigrants arrives. The immigration of Europeans into what is now the United States during the seventeenth and eighteenth centuries forced a kind of adaptation by them and by their hosts. The earliest immigrants were Native Americans, who first arrived in North America about 14 thousand years ago (see Chapter 7), as their hosts. In America, Native Americans coexisted with European settlers until the eighteenth century, when a large number of them were eliminated through either disease or war. These conflicts continued throughout the late 1800s, after which only a fraction of Native Americans remained (Cortes and Poston, 2008; Purcell, 1995). Admittedly, this adaptation was brutal, but it was nevertheless a form of cultural adaptation. The adaptation is again occurring and will be repeated as long as immigration from one culture to another persists. We turn now to a discussion of cultural adaptation and its variants.

CULTURAL ADAPTATION PROCESSES

Residents of and newcomers to an area must adapt to a new social situation that results from group interaction. At one extreme is **cultural separatism**. Here, the newcomers are socially isolated from the residents either through their own volition or through separatist practices of the host group. The slave–free person relationship exemplifies cultural separatism at its most extreme. Another example is the relationship between the dominant American society and a religious group like the Amish or the Fundamentalist Church of Jesus Christ of Latter-Day Saints (FLDS).

At the other extreme lies **cultural amalgamation**. Here, a new society and culture result from the massive intermingling and intermarriage between two or more groups. The racial blending that occurred in nineteenth-century Latin America between the Spanish newcomers and the indigenous groups resulted in the emergence of the *mestizos*. (A **mestizo** is a person of mixed blood, the result of this racial blending.) A slightly different result occurred in China over the centuries and during many dynasties. Alien groups would conquer and dominate parts of the country, intermingle and intermarry, eventually becoming Chinese. The Chinese have a saying reflecting this form of cultural amalgamation: "Just as all water becomes salty when it flows into the sea, so everyone who comes to China becomes Chinese."

Between these extreme processes of cultural adaptation are **pluralism**, **assimilation**, and the so-called **melting pot**. In pluralism, the society allows its constituted ethnic groups to develop, each emphasizing its own cultural heritage. Assimilation assumes that the new groups will take on the culture and values of the host society and gradually discard their own. The sociologist Milton Gordon (1964) distinguished between cultural assimilation (or acculturation), where a subordinate group takes on many of the characteristics of the dominant group, and structural assimilation, where the subordinate group gains access to the principal institutions of the society.

In the melting-pot process, the host and immigrant groups share one another's cultures and, in the process, a new group emerges. Consequently, the melting-pot concept differs somewhat from that of pure assimilation. While early U.S. advocates of the melting-pot theory encouraged newcomers to "assimilate" into American society, that society was not intended to be totally dominated by Anglo-Saxons but rather was to be a new society formed by the blending of the various groups, albeit with a strong Anglo-Saxon influence.

Throughout American history, immigrants as well as nonimmigrant residents have adjusted to one another. A process of cultural adaptation was necessary if the society was to survive.

ASSIMILATION VERSUS PLURALISM

At the beginning of the twentieth century, the Anglo majority favored the total assimilation of the new European groups into an Anglo-dominated society. It was taken for granted – indeed, it was ordered – that Mexicans,

Asians, and blacks would remain culturally separate. Cultural pluralism and even the melting pot were adamantly opposed. President Theodore Roosevelt felt nothing but disdain for the "hyphenated American," and President Woodrow Wilson actually declared that "any man who thinks himself as belonging to a particular national group in America has not yet become an American" (cited in Adams, 1983: 111).

Assimilation

"Americanization" was in full vogue in the early decades of the twentieth century. It was assumed that all European immigrants would become Americanized. Anglo-conformity was encouraged – indeed, demanded – for all the new immigrants. More than twenty-five years ago, the sociologist Nathan Glazer wrote the following (1983: 335–336):

> The ideal, i.e., Americanization, was the full assimilation of all immigrant groups to a common national type, so that ethnicity would play a declining role in individual consciousness, groups would not be formed around ethnic interests, "hyphenated Americans" would be a thing of the past, and the United States would be as homogeneous in its Americanness as the nations of the old world were once in their Englishness, their Frenchness.

Cultural pluralism

Aligned against total assimilation were the cultural pluralists, who urged a new type of nation in which the various national groups would preserve their identity and their cultures, uniting in a world federation in miniature (Bourne, 1916). With this approach, immigrants would assimilate into the American culture while maintaining and taking pride in the important characteristics of their native culture. This theory has been described as a "salad bowl," with all the "ingredients" being important in their own way.

Horace Kallen argued vehemently against assimilation and the melting pot, convinced that if the course of cultural pluralism was followed, "the outlines of a possibly great and truly democratic commonwealth would become discernible. Its form would be that of the federal republic; its substance a democracy of nationalities, cooperating voluntarily and autonomously through common institutions in the enterprise of self-realization through the perfection of men according to their kind" (1924: 124).

Melting pot

The melting-pot theory was a compromise between cultural pluralism and assimilation. The first recorded mention of this idea is attributed to

Hector St. John de Crevecoeur in 1782 when he noted that "here in America, individuals of all nations are melted into a new race of men" ([1782] 1997: 25). The 1909 play *The Melting Pot* by Israel Zangwill (1864–1926) brought this idea to the attention of many people and made the term more widespread. But the historian Frederick Jackson Turner probably did more than anyone to popularize the concept in 1920 with his remark that "the tide of foreign immigration...has risen so steadily that it has made a composite American people whose amalgamation is destined to produce a new national stock" (1920: 190). In one sense, the melting pot is a form of assimilation in that emphasis is on the formation of an American culture. Nevertheless, its determination not to overemphasize Anglo-conformity makes it a different type of assimilation than that emphasized by the "Americanization" movement. We present in Box 12.1 an interesting excerpt from Laubeová (2000) of "melting pot versus ethnic stew." These are terms we do not come across much these days, but they portend particular significance and relevance in the coming decades in the United States and elsewhere.

RECENT PATTERNS OF CULTURAL ADAPTATION

As we look at the twentieth century, it is clear that the attempt to Americanize everyone to Anglo-conformity through total assimilation did not succeed. Most European groups retained some semblance of ethnicity over the years while at the same time adapting to their new surroundings. Neither has cultural pluralism been particularly successful among European immigrants and their descendants in the United States, despite efforts on the part of some of its advocates to maintain ethnic identities.

By the 1940s, the melting pot was beginning to work fairly well for immigrants from Southern and Eastern Europe. But the melting pot may have been working in different ways than had been anticipated. A new population was in the process of forming the "unhyphenated American." In addition, the power elite, historically almost exclusively white Anglo-Saxon Protestant (WASP), was being replaced by one in which persons of non-WASP heritage were commonplace. Finally, the melting pot, although only among Anglos (non-Hispanic whites), was coming to a boil. Consider several examples of such success, namely, Lee Iacocca, a successful American corporate executive, and A. Bartlett Giamatti, president of Yale University, who later became the commissioner of Major League Baseball. In the 1968 election, both major parties offered second-generation American vice presidential candidates: Spiro Agnew, of Greek parentage, and Edward Muskie, of Polish parentage. Among those mentioned as possible presidential candidates in 1988 were second-generation Italians, Greeks,

---

BOX 12.1. "MELTING POT VS. ETHNIC STEW"

The history of the melting pot theory can be traced back to 1782 when J. Hector de Crevecoeur, a French settler in New York, envisioned the United States not only as a land of opportunity but as a society where individuals of all nations are melted into a new race of men, whose labours and posterity will one day cause changes in the world (Parrilo, 1997). The new nation welcomed virtually all immigrants from Europe in the belief that the United States would become, at least for Whites, the "melting pot" of the world. This idea was adopted by the historian Frederick Jackson Turner (1893) who updated it with the frontier thesis. Turner believed that the challenge of frontier life was the country's most crucial force, allowing Europeans to be "Americanised" by the wilderness (Takaki, 1993)... The metaphor of the "melting pot" symbolized the mystical potency of the great democracy, whereby people from every corner of the earth were fused into a harmonious and admirable blend. A decline in immigration from northwestern Europe and concerns over the problems of assimilating so many people from other areas prompted the passage in the 1920s of legislation restricting immigration, one of the measures reflecting official racism. . . . The concept of ethnic stew is similar to that of melting pot, though the degree of cultural distinctiveness is higher in the former, however not reaching the level of the "salad bowl" thesis (different groups keep their differences, while maintaining relations among each other). . . . The shortages of the melting pot and salad bowl paradigms can be expressed in the following summarising parables: In the case of the melting pot the aim is that all cultures become reflected in one common culture[;] however this is generally the culture of the dominant group – *I thought this was mixed vegetable soup but I can only taste tomato*. In the case of the salad bowl, cultural groups should exist separately and maintain their practices and institutions. However, *where is the dressing to cover it all?* Hopefully the solution may be offered by the concept of the ethnic stew where all the ingredients are mixed in a sort of pan-Hungarian *goulash where the pieces of different kinds of meat still keep their solid structure.*

Excerpted from Laura Laubeová (2000)

---

and Basques. Most important was the fact that the voting public was apparently not that concerned with the diversity of the candidates. Who would argue that Michael Dukakis was less American than George H. W. Bush?

Finally, Barack Hussein Obama, II, formerly the junior senator from the state of Illinois, is now the forty-fourth president of the United States.

Obama was born in Hawaii to a Kenyan father and an American mother. He lived in Hawaii for most of his childhood and adolescent years, and also lived for four years in Jakarta, Indonesia, with his mother and Indonesian stepfather. Is Barack Obama any less American than the Republican Party's candidate for president in 2008, John S. McCain, III, born at the Naval Air Station in Panama to an American father and mother?

While the melting pot has worked fairly well among Americans of European ancestry, islands of dissent have been noted. In the minds of a few, some hesitancy still remains about accepting "ethnics" as truly American, even though the nation has come a long way with its population of European ancestry. However, let us once again bear in mind that this encouraging process has been limited to Anglos. Blacks, Hispanics, and Asians have mostly remained out of the mainstream.

In these early years of the twenty-first century, new adaptation challenges are facing the nation. Today, well over 80 percent of immigrants come from either Latin America or Asia. As we noted at the beginning of this chapter, in 2050 there will be no ethnic majority in the United States. We will all be minorities. What kind of a nation will emerge? While interracial marriages are on the rise, they still remain a relatively rare occurrence. For instance, in 2006, just over 3 percent of black women were married to Anglo men, and less than 1 percent of Anglo women were married to black men (Kincannon, 2009). A "tea colored" society is hardly within our reach. Such might be attained in the more distant future. Indeed, the great African American sociologist W. E. B. Dubois (1921: 21–22) predicted that "some day, on American soil, two world races may give each to each those characteristics both so sadly lack." Dubois called for the maintenance of racial purity only "until this mission of the Negro people is accomplished, and the ideal of human brotherhood has become a practical possibility."

Another factor to consider as we examine the mode of cultural adaptation for today's American society is that the current immigration pattern is not a wave. Earlier immigration movements were actual waves; that is, there was a beginning and an end to the immigration movement. This explains to a large degree the success of the newcomers from Eastern and Southern Europe. Once the wave ended, they were more likely to Americanize than to remain ethnically separated. Today, this does not appear to be the case. There is apparently no end to the movement of people to the United States from Latin America and Asia. Thus, the "breathing time" accorded to the earlier immigrants is not available to the current immigrants.

We must then ask whether the relative success achieved during the twentieth century in the adaptation of Southern and Eastern European immigrants and their descendants into a new kind of America (a true melting pot in the majority population) will be duplicated with the current and future mix of racially and ethnically diverse groups. The question of how the United States is to maintain a unified country composed of people from all over the world cannot be long ignored.

It seems unlikely that a repetition of the successful melting-pot process will occur given the situation in 2000–2010 as compared to 1900–1910. The differences in the economic structure, in the possibilities of interracial marriages, in the increasing emphasis on group rights, and particularly in the levels of immigration are far too great to envision a new interracial melting pot in the near future. What then are the alternatives?

It is to be hoped that cultural separatism is a phenomenon of the past. The nation is well past that period when the various race and ethnic groups were deliberately separated. Neither does the total cultural assimilation of the new minority groups (i.e., the complete surrender of immigrants' cultures and values and their absorption into the core culture) seem to be a realistic goal. In around four decades from now in the United States, there will no longer be a majority in which to assimilate. Indeed, as already noted, right now in four U.S. states and the District of Columbia, the Anglo population is not in the majority; moreover, five more states are rapidly approaching majority-minority status. As a matter of fact, people who are English and of English ancestry are no longer the majority of the population of the United States. In 2005, they comprised less than 10 percent of the population.

The racial- and ethnic-identity consciousness that has emerged during the past few decades, together with the growth of large enclaves of new immigrants in certain parts of the country, preclude any substantive assimilation into the dominant Anglo culture of the nation. Furthermore, there is considerable doubt as to whether the new groups desire total assimilation and, for that matter, whether the majority favors it.

The choices lie between cultural pluralism and what we have called pluralistic assimilation. Whatever direction the nation follows will determine the kind of America that will evolve in this century.

A benign form of cultural pluralism has always been part and parcel of American life. Ethnic enclaves are still present in major cities. Diverse religious and cultural holidays remain on the calendars of many Americans. However, cultural pluralism took on a different meaning in the 1960s. To some people, "cultural pluralism implies the conscious pursuit of a national order in which Americans find their identity primarily as members of ethnic and/or religious groups and only secondarily as individuals engaged in carving out a position in the greater society" (Christopher, 1989: 20). A harder-edged version of cultural pluralism seems to be currently in vogue. The focus is on the contention that the United States is a compact between what some are beginning to lump together as a "Euro-American" population and a limited set of minority groups made up principally of

African Americans, Hispanics, and Asians (Archdeacon, 1990: 18). The non-European immigrants and longtime minorities tend to rely more and more on in-group cohesiveness and cultural reassertion as the only effective means to combat social discrimination.

Too often, Americans confuse the fact that we are a pluralistic nation with an acceptance of cultural pluralism. America is pluralistic in the fact of having many religious groups and ethnicities represented in its population. Nevertheless, it has constantly striven to achieve an overall unity in its basic interests and ideals. A motto of the United States and included on the official seal of the country, *E Pluribus Unum* ("Out of Many, One"), succinctly describes the "ideal" American nation. If cultural pluralism were but a supplement to these common interests and ideals, it would be appropriate. However, cultural pluralism, as currently conceived, nonetheless argues for the primacy of the homeland language and culture. Indeed, as Theodore White once commented, "some...have made a demand never voiced by immigrants before, that the United States, in effect, officially recognize itself as a bicultural, bilingual nation" (1982: 367).

PLURALISTIC ASSIMILATION

The challenge to the nation is to find a way to assure that all of its residents, of whatever background, have equal access to all avenues of success, and in the process are able to adapt to American culture while contributing to its ever-changing content. At the same time, they need also to have the choice of maintaining their own subculture within the broader American society. As the nation becomes more multiracial, it is particularly important that it accept a form of cultural adaptation that takes the best of cultural pluralism and assimilation, while at the same time maintaining the American culture and assuring its acceptance.

The sociologist J. Milton Yinger and the historian John Higham have both addressed this issue and have suggested new forms of adaptation that would take into account pluralism as well as assimilation. Yinger (1981: 261) wrote that some sort of integration that falls short of assimilation may be the right compromise. Higham (1975: 265) stated that "pluralistic integration" does not eliminate ethnic boundaries but upholds the validity of a common culture. However, neither Yinger nor Higham examined the possibility of a truly multiracial society where no one group clearly predominates, a situation that will characterize the United States by 2050. The concept of pluralistic assimilation, while derived from these earlier models, looks at a truly multiracial society.

Pluralistic assimilation would be appropriate if the goal of the society is to be united, insofar as possible, given the population's composition. All groups are assimilated, both culturally and structurally, into the already diverse mainstream American society. This is neither "Anglo-conformity" nor even "white American conformity." This is really *assimilation among* rather than *assimilation into* and reflects the changing demographic picture and the fact that no one ethnic group predominates. It is a "New Americanization."

The inclusion of structural assimilation suggests that all groups will have equal access to power, whether economic or political. Pluralistic, conversely, reflects the fact that the society is no longer dealing with groups of the same race or ethnicity. These multiracial and multiethnic groups may maintain their identity at the same time that they become assimilated into the ever-changing mainstream American society (Bouvier, 1992).

Some form of pluralistic assimilation may have been implied in Benjamin Franklin's first version of the shield for the nation. That shield represented the six European nations that comprised the white population of the new country. In that context, *E Pluribus Unum* was a recognition that the survival of the new government depended on its ability to forge a nation from a population in which ethnic diversity was the norm (Archdeacon, 1990: 11).

The success of Japanese Americans, despite the horror of the concentration camps during World War II, and of Chinese Americans, despite the outright discrimination directed against them as written into early immigration laws (see Chapters 7 and 13), provide us with a working model of pluralistic assimilation. While the Japanese and the Chinese gradually became assimilated, both culturally and structurally, into the mainstream American society, they have remained as identifiable racial groups even though interracial marriages have increased. Perhaps part of their success can be attributed to the fact that immigration from Japan and China to the United States was practically nonexistent until the 1980s, except for the streams that entered the country in the nineteenth century. This eases the adaptation process. It would be naive to pretend that prejudice toward Japanese Americans or Chinese Americans does not exist, although it is declining. Pluralistic assimilation is an ongoing process, and its eventual success requires the cooperation of all groups. Nevertheless, the fact that Japanese Americans and Chinese Americans are often cited as an example of the achievement of a New Americanization is evidence of the powerful integrative forces at work in American society.

Numerous factors must be present if pluralistic assimilation is to succeed.

First, American society must provide the means to make economic and social advancement possible for *all* Americans. This necessarily involves easy and inexpensive access to higher education, as well as to technical training. It necessitates a revamping of the nation's educational institutions to allow for the better preparation of *all* Americans for the occupations of the future. Given the rapid change in the process of information through the Internet and e-mail, this goal is especially vital. A new kind of structural mobility must be developed for the United States economy of the twenty-first century. Should these plans fail and blacks and Latinos find themselves overwhelmingly in lower-paying jobs while Asians and whites are dominant in the higher-paying positions, conflict will be inevitable and pluralistic assimilation will fail.

Second, future immigrants must demonstrate their desire to become "one of us," changing the meaning of "us" in the process. Just as most eighteenth- and early-nineteenth-century immigrants wanted to become American, so too should those of the present era. If the nation is to retain *E Pluribus Unum*, there can be no room for cultural separatism or for irredentist movements on the part of newcomers.

Third, all forms of discrimination must end. This is a strong challenge. The United States is still a racist society (Bonilla-Silva, 2006), and this must change if pluralistic assimilation is to succeed. If pluralistic assimilation is truly desired as the ideal mode of adaptation for the future, Americans must cease thinking of the newest immigrants as "inferior" foreigners. The newcomers need to be accepted wholeheartedly. These motivated individuals are not a "mob at the gates"; Americans should show them that the United States is a benevolent community eager to welcome newcomers into their society (Waltzer, 1981: 10). Every effort must be made to assist the newest residents to participate fully and equally in this dynamic society.

This applies *a fortiori* to longtime American minorities. The Civil Rights legislation of the 1960s, as well as no less than the U.S. Constitution, promised a nation in which all persons would be treated equally. This goal still remains distant on the horizon. Even relations among minorities are fragile. With the newest immigrants' share of the population growing (recall our earlier statement that in 2050 nearly one in five Americans will have been born outside the United States), it is vital for the survival of the American society that a mechanism be found for all groups to know and understand one another.

Pluralistic assimilation, forms of interaction, cultural assimilation, the melting-pot theory, cultural amalgamation, and *group integration* are all examples of terms and concepts that sociologists, demographers, and other social scientists have developed to better understand the relations in a society between people of different groups. Basically, these terms emphasize the fact that whenever one person or group moves into an area inhabited by another person or group, both must adapt to a newly defined situation.

While we have concentrated in this chapter on the United States, the process of cultural adaptation is at work whenever and wherever two different groups find themselves sharing the same land. Indeed, in some ways, the situation in Europe is more challenging than that in the United States. There, as we have already showed in Chapter 3, the fertility of the resident population is so low that without immigration, some European countries could well disappear as economic forces. Yet most of these countries are not familiar with massive movements of individuals from other races and cultures, as is the United States. There, too, some significant modes of cultural adaptation are called for. To date, the prospects for peaceful relations between the residents and the newcomers do not look particularly favorable. All the various modes of cultural adaptation that we have discussed in this chapter may be tried, but as of now, it is too early to determine the eventual result.

IMMIGRATION AND GROWTH

We have been examining cultural adaptation as a means of solving problems caused by immigration and low fertility. But immigration also results in population change. Even if immigration were to come to an end immediately, population change (i.e., growth or decline) would still take place. We are referring to an important demographic concept, that of *population momentum*. Here, immigration is but a minor factor.

As a first example of population momentum, that is, *positive momentum*, let us examine the United States after the baby boom. The total fertility rate (i.e., the number of children a woman could expect to have according to a schedule of age-specific fertility rates at a given time; see Chapter 3) fell considerably between the 1960s and now, from around 3.5 to slightly above 2.0; however, the number of births did not fall. For quite a few years, it remained around 4 million per year. How could this be?

The answer is simply that the number of births does not only reflect the number of children a woman has; it also reflects the number of women available (i.e., in their childbearing years) to have those children. The number of such women in the late 1950s and early 1960s belonged to the cohort of the baby boomers. Proportionally, they were very numerous. Thus, even if these women had only two births on average, there were so many childbearing women producing babies that the number of births did not fall. That is called positive momentum. One cannot simply turn the faucet off. Just because the rate falls, this does not mean that the number immediately falls. Indeed, it usually takes another generation or so for the number to actually fall once the age composition is back to a more normal structure.

Now let us look at the situation in many European countries, where fertility is so low (between 1.2 and 1.5) that without immigration, many could literally disappear if fertility remains low. Picture a government frantically trying to convince the women to have more children so as to avert such a catastrophe: Bonuses are offered; a call for patriotism is issued. As a result, women start having between two and three children. Then, the country's demographers issue the bad news. The number of births is barely rising but not enough to put an end to the population decline. What is going on? It is the reverse of the U.S. situation just described. Because of the very low fertility for the past two decades, there are few women available to have more children. This is called *negative momentum*. Women would have to produce perhaps four children to make up for the lack of potential mothers in the population.

SUMMARY

In this chapter, we consider two important social and demographic phenomena. First, in large part because of immigration movements, policymakers must examine cultural adaptation. If a society is to remain domestically peaceful, some mode of adaptation needs to be followed. This then led us, at the end of the chapter, to a consideration of the concept of population momentum. It is almost impossible to understand population growth, whether through immigration or through natural change, without considering the impact of momentum, positive or negative.

KEY TERMS

assimilation	melting pot
cultural amalgamation	mestizo
cultural separatism	pluralism

Population Policy

A **population policy** is a deliberately constructed arrangement or program "through which governments influence, directly or indirectly, demographic change" (Demeny, 2003: 752). These arrangements typically are "legislative measures, administrative programs, and other governmental actions intended to alter or modify existing population trends in the interest of national survival and welfare" (Eldridge, 1968: 381). The demographer John May has written that "population policies are designed to regulate and, if possible, mitigate the problems [of too rapid growth or decline] by adjusting population size and structure to the needs and aspirations of the people" (2005: 828).

Population policies are usually understood to represent strategies for governments or sometimes, albeit less frequently, nongovernmental organizations (NGOs) to attain specific goals. The procedures or programs are put into place to ensure that the goals of the policy are attained. As already noted, a policy is generally intended to either reduce or increase population levels. Policies are typically developed "in the interest of the greater good . . . in order to address imbalances between demographic changes and other social, economic and political goals" (May, 2005: 828).

We read in earlier chapters of this book that many countries in the world today have high rates of population growth. We also know that many have negative or near-negative rates of growth, and many more have fertility rates below replacement levels. In 2008, for instance, more than seventy countries had total fertility rates below 2.1 (Population Reference Bureau, 2008b). Countries exhibiting demographic conditions of too-high or too-low growth sometimes develop policies whose goals are to try to restore the demographic balance.

Whether the issue is severe or minor, demographic behavior is of interest to all governments. In the United States, the onset of the baby boom resulted in major changes in governmental action in many areas. And, of course, are some governments actually install stated government policies, some of which are reviewed in this chapter.

As we all know by now, there are only three ways to change the size of a population, namely, through births, deaths, and migration. Therefore, any policies aimed at restoring demographic balance must be oriented toward one or more of the three demographic processes. But not all of the options are used as the bases for policies.

To illustrate, a policy with the goal of increasing mortality to lower population growth would be unethical and not considered to be a viable means these days for solving an issue of population growth. This is not to say that governments have not developed policies to explicitly raise the mortality levels of groups or subgroups in their countries. One need only recall the explicit policies in the not-too-distant past of the Nazi government in Germany and the Khmer Rouge government in Cambodia to raise the mortality levels of subgroups in their populations.

Population policies dealing with mortality are usually intended to reduce, not to increase, its levels. Manipulating mortality via reduction, however, is not as popular or prominent a strategy of population policy. Most policies focus on manipulating fertility and/or migration. They receive most of our attention in this chapter.

How do governments affect the demographic processes? Generally, they influence the demographic behavior indirectly. Governments often find ways to persuade people to act voluntarily in a "desired" manner. But oftentimes, mere legislation and propaganda are insufficient to attain the intended goal. Then governments act directly, say, to either raise or lower levels of fertility or to force people to move or not to move.

The task of formulating a population policy is complicated by the fact that often there is no consensus on the appropriate size of the population and/or its fertility or migration rates. There may be some disagreement as to the magnitude of the problem (if, indeed, there is a problem) of population growth or decline. More frequently, there evolves a "laissez-faire" attitude as opposed to a "let's do something about it now" position. For example, today in the United States, there is widespread disagreement as to whether levels of immigration should be reduced or increased. Some groups argue for the former, others the latter.

Furthermore, not everyone agrees on the true meaning of a population policy. Here are some issues of disagreement among demographers as well as nondemographers:

1. Must there be an explicit statement by a government that a policy exists? The United States has no official population policy. Nevertheless, the U.S. government finances and sponsors programs designed to

eliminate unwanted childbearing and to make contraception available to certain target populations.

2. Does there have to be a planned course of action or program? Sometimes doing nothing is a policy. In 2008, U.S. fertility was about at the replacement level of 2.1 children per woman. The U.S. government is not concerned at all about raising its level of fertility, or lowering it, to compensate for increases to the population via immigration.

3. Must the goals of a policy be demographic, or may they be social and economic? In other words, do the goals have to be direct or indirect? For example, it is well known that, on average, increased educational attainment of women results in lower fertility; the higher the education of women, the fewer, on average, the number of children born to them. If a developing country decides to improve the educational levels of its female youth, is this a population policy? Yes, but only indirectly. Similarly, opening job opportunities for women tends to result in lower fertility. This is another example of an indirect population policy.

The point of raising these questions is to illustrate that there are no "correct" answers. Governments may differ in their definitions and the formulation of population policies, and it is sometimes difficult to decide whether a specific country has a population policy. Our concern here is not to make judgments about objectives. Our purpose is to address the question: In what ways may a government influence levels of fertility, mortality, and migration?

THE THREE WORLD POPULATION CONFERENCES

The issue of human population growth as a problem or concern is really a twentieth-century phenomenon. However, as noted in Chapter 9, the concern with overpopulation is not new. Indeed, during the eighteenth century, Malthus declared that overpopulation was bound by nature to occur. He and many others wrote about population growth and its problems. But it was not until the 1960s and the early 1970s that the public became acutely aware of them. Several high-profile books, such as *The Population Bomb* (Ehrlich, 1968), *The Limits to Growth* (Meadows et al., 1974), and *Small is Beautiful* (Schumacher, 1975) brought the issue of overpopulation to the attention of millions of readers. Unlike Malthus, however, many of these authors gave special attention to the degradation of the environment by larger and larger numbers of humans (Poston, DeSalvo, and Meyer, 2009; Russell and Poston, 2008). To this day, there is still some discussion of the issue of overpopulation. Benjamin Friedman (2005) has noted, for instance, that aspects of these themes of overpopulation and environmental degradation are reflected in the contemporary antiglobalization movement.

Starting in the 1970s, there was considerable debate in academic circles with many advocating voluntary family planning. The position among the so-called birth controllers and many population specialists was that inducing Third World women to practice contraception would simultaneously improve these individuals' social and economic situation and alleviate the societal problems of their countries (Connelly, 2008; Hodgson and Watkins, 1997). Affluent countries such as the United States, along with private foundations and other organizations, provided large amounts of financial assistance to the population-control movement and the worldwide endeavor to limit population growth.

In 1965, President Lyndon Johnson established an Office of Population in the Department of State and the U.S. Agency for International Development (USAID). The goal of USAID was to convince governments in developing countries to foster contraceptive usage among its citizens. In many instances, this was a politically charged issue that ran counter to traditional **pronatalist** cultural norms (those advocating increases in fertility). The USAID sent teams of demographers and others to countries all over the world to illustrate visually to their leaders and officials the impacts of continued rapid population growth. One of the authors of this book, Bouvier, made such presentations in several Francophone African countries in the early 1980s.

The attempts by the United States to promote family planning overseas in countries not yet "ready" for this message inevitably met with cries of imperialism. Officials in the host countries asked why the United States was promoting family planning instead of addressing, according to their way of thinking, more pressing needs like assistance in relieving the millions of people suffering from malaria (Connelly, 2008). In part to defuse this issue, the United States worked with the United Nations (UN) to help create in 1969 the **United Nations Fund for Population Activities (UNFPA)**. UNFPA served as a major source of funds for population initiatives in developing countries. Three world population conferences were subsequently held in 1974, 1984, and 1994 and framed the story of international family planning that has unfolded since the 1970s (Bouvier and Bertrand, 1999).

The first World Population Conference was held in Bucharest, Romania, in 1974. Organized by members of the UN, it was an attempt to bring together government officials from around the world and to illustrate for them the facts and consequences of rapid population growth. It was expected by the developed nations in attendance that the rest of the world would recognize the so-called population problem and join the growing movement to curb population growth. To the surprise of many, there was no such endorsement. Rather, most developing nations stressed their preoccupation with the importance of socioeconomic development, both in its own right and as a catalyst for lowering fertility. They called for a "New Economic Order," whose position was encapsulated in the expression "Development is the best contraceptive."

The second such conference was held in Mexico City in 1984. During the ten years since the first conference, many developing countries had changed their opinions about population growth and were now interested in assistance directed toward their fledgling family planning programs. (A **family planning program** is a systematic effort to promote modern fertility control.) African countries, especially, were seeing the benefits of more widespread family planning programs, if not for demographic reasons, then at least for the health of women and children. However, by this time, the political atmosphere in the United States had changed dramatically. The official U.S. delegation under the administration of President Ronald Reagan asserted that "population is a neutral phenomenon" in the development process, and that excessive state control of the economy was more responsible for economic stagnation than population growth (Hodgson and Watkins, 1997). James Buckley, the brother of the late conservative scholar, editor, and journalist William F. Buckley, headed the U.S. delegation.

This unexpected U.S. position stunned the delegates. Instead of rallying the world community behind population issues, the United States introduced to the world its controversial Mexico City policy. The U.S. administration, over strong Congressional objection, decided to police the actions of developing countries with respect to abortion services by refusing to fund the family planning activities of local organizations that also provided abortion, even if abortion was legal in that country and paid for by private funds (Bouvier and Bertrand, 1999).

We note here that one of the first acts of President Bill Clinton's administration when he took office in 1993 was to reverse this policy of President Reagan. But when the administration of George W. Bush came into power in 2001, the Reagan policy was once again restored. With the inauguration of Barack Obama in 2009, the Bush–Reagan policy was changed back to the policy of the Clinton administration with respect to providing funds for family planning. When President Obama reversed the Bush–Reagan policy on January 23, 2009, he remarked that "for the past eight years [the Bush–Reagan restrictions] have undermined efforts to promote safe and effective voluntary family planning in developing countries. For these reasons it is right for us to rescind this policy and restore critical efforts to protect and empower women and promote global economic development" (Filteau, 2009: 1). For the full text of the Obama memorandum, see "Revocation of the Reinstatement of the 'Mexico City Policy' on U.S. Family Planning Assistance" (2009).

The 1994 International Conference on Population and Development (ICPD) was held in Cairo, Egypt. This conference radically altered the international population movement. Its major outcome was a new definition of population policy, giving prominence to reproductive health and downplaying the demographic rationale for population policy (McIntosh and Finkle, 1995). Two radically diverse groups, feminists and neo-Malthusians, joined forces to create a new manifesto that included the following stipulations: 1) population stabilization is a desirable, ultimate goal, although not one warranting the use of compulsion; 2) national programs enhancing access to contraception are justified in terms of individual human rights, not in terms of their development advantages for aggregate populations; and 3) the empowerment of women is a prerequisite for the enduring low fertility that population stabilization requires (Hodgson and Watkins, 1997).

The Cairo conference was considered to be very successful, mainly because it allowed historically opposed and oppressed groups to identify a unified position. Later, however, many officials and scholars working on population matters were surprised that, apparently, discussions of aggregate demographic concerns were being seen as politically incorrect. Indeed, some argued that "programs that are demographically-driven, and are intended to act directly on fertility, are inherently abusive of women's rights to choose the number and timing of their children" (MacIntosh and Finkle, 1995: 260). Others argued that there is nothing inherently abusive or intrusive about demographically driven population policy (Presser, 1997). In sum, Cairo "stressed the importance of individual choices and the necessity to further empower women" (May, 2005: 830).

More recent international conferences have agreed largely with this preoccupation. It was the main theme of follow-up meetings of the ICPD, "which included a meeting in The Netherlands and a meeting of the U.N. General Assembly in 1999" (May, 2005: 830)

One might ask why there was no world population conference in 2004. After three conferences in 1974, 1984, and 1994, a conference was indeed planned for 2004. But when the United States, under the administration of President George W. Bush, withdrew its funding of the UNFPA, it was decided to simply incorporate the goals of earlier conferences for the present and the immediate future.

POLICIES AFFECTING FERTILITY

It is most interesting to note that in all three of the world population conferences, fertility was the only major topic on the agenda. Reductions in mortality were alluded to only briefly in the demand for assistance in combating malaria, issues of international migration were never mentioned. Yet, immigration has become an important phenomenon in recent decades in many parts of the world. In this section, we turn attention to actual policies affecting fertility behavior, whether direct or indirect, that is, whether to raise or lower the level of fertility. Immigration policies are covered in a later section.

A brief history

Prior to the twentieth century, most fertility policies were concerned with increasing population growth; we can thus say that they were pronatalist. These policies usually were of three types: pronatalist propaganda; measures related to the family, such as family allowance programs; and restrictions on the distribution and use of contraceptives and abortion.

Some of the earliest-known population policies were those of the Roman Emperor Augustus, enacted between 18 BC and AD 9. Inheritance laws and rules concerning eligibility for office penalized the childless and favored parents. During the medieval period, high mortality caused by plague, especially the Black Death (see Chapter 5), encouraged the development of pronatalist views and policies. In France, tax exemptions and other privileges were used in the latter part of the thirteenth century to encourage fertility. A Spanish edict in 1623 granted tax exemptions to those who married young and raised large families (Glass, 1940).

It is important to recall that Marxist leaders long believed that population problems in their countries were social and economic rather than demographic. They believed that if matters deteriorated, a social revolution would occur. Thus, in their view, population growth was seen as a spur for the revolution necessary to achieve social, economic, and political change. We discuss this issue later when we address fertility policies in China.

In the twentieth century, the pronatalist movement reached its peak in Germany, Italy, and Japan during the years between World War I and World War II. Intensive pronatalist propaganda, cash payments to families with children, the restriction of access to contraceptives, and the enactment of so-called eugenic laws aimed at encouraging the reproduction of some genetic traits and discouraging others reflected the attempts of some of those governments to have larger and racially "pure" populations. Such measures were adopted because power and prosperity were equated with large numbers of people (Eldridge, 1968: 382).

Countries such as France and Romania also adopted pronatalist policies at various times after World War I. These policies represented a reaction to the low fertility that accompanied modernization. France, Romania, and other nations feared that their national economic and political well-being would decline unless their populations continued to grow.

Sometimes countries have policies that have both pronatalist and antinatalist effects. France is a good example. In 1920, France prohibited the distribution of birth-control propaganda and devices. The Law of 1920 stipulated that it was illegal to distribute contraceptives or information on fertility control, not unlike the Comstock Act in the United States, which was passed in 1873 and overturned by the U.S. Congress in 1971. In 1932 in France, laws prohibiting abortion were tightened. In 1939, the French government adopted a *Code de la Famille*, which incorporated existing family-welfare and pronatalist measures. Allowances were extended to all economically active persons. Marriage loans, premiums on the birth of a first child, and other forms of aid for parents were provided (Glass, 1940). The code was strengthened after 1945 when the crude birth rate (CBR) was less than 15/1,000.

However, in 1967, France legalized the distribution of contraceptives in response to public demand. By 1974, a new statute was passed that provided for the distribution of free contraceptives, and another law lifted the prohibition on abortion. These measures were adopted to achieve the social goal of voluntary parenthood, but they also illustrate how social policies with antinatalist effects can exist in countries with pronatalist population policies (Bouvier and Bertrand, 1999: 139–140).

It does not appear that pronanalist measures in industrialized countries have ever been very effective. In 1979, the French CBR was still under 15/1,000; it is even lower today. Total fertility rates (TFRs) in France, Belgium, Italy, and virtually all of Europe are today well below the level needed to replace the population. However, there has been a slight resurgence in France, where the TFR in 2008 was just under the replacement level of 2.1 (Population Reference Bureau, 2008b). Pronatalist policies have not been sufficient to offset the antinatalist aspects of social and economic policies.

As programs began to develop, program administrators were cautious in the face of legal barriers. Indeed, the Law of 1920 (just discussed) proved to be a serious impediment to the reduction of fertility in Francophone African countries. Most African countries successfully removed the law from their statutes by the late 1980s, and it is not followed in the few countries where it still exists. However, this law unquestionably has had a dampening effect on family planning promotion.

Singapore is another example of a country reversing its policies regarding population growth. Its determination to reduce growth through lowered fertility was very successful. These efforts included indirect measures such as better facilities for health and education: "The initial effort on family planning combined with demographic investments . . . and other productive investments have probably accelerated the transformation of Singapore into a new industrialized country (fertility dropped to sub replacement levels in 1986)" (May, 2005: 843). Its rate of population growth fell from 2.3 to 1.3 percent in the ten-year period between 1968 and 1978. Since then, however, the government has expressed concern over this small country's very low fertility (a TFR of 1.4 in 2008) and is encouraging certain groups (especially Singapore citizens of Chinese ancestry) to elevate their fertility. Indeed, the government organized a commission to devise ways to bring single adults together (Crosette, 1997). A back-to-work program has also been introduced to support the goals and activities of women.

Similarly, South Korea and Taiwan have both adopted incentive programs to increase the number of children per household. To this day, however, there is little evidence of any success in raising fertility, and TFRs remain much below the replacement level. In recent years in both South Korea and Taiwan, the TFR has been an incredibly low 1.1 to 1.2.

Abortion has long been a method used in some countries to reduce fertility. Restricting access to abortion may result in a sharp increase in fertility. Such was the case in Romania in the 1950s. By 1956, the birth rate had fallen to 24.2 births per 1,000 population, primarily due to the widespread use of illegal abortion (David and Wright, 1971). In 1957, the government legalized abortion to allow women to decide whether and when to have children, as well as to reduce the incidence of illegal abortion (Mehlan, 1965). However, the government did not encourage the use of contraception. As a result, induced abortion became the socially accepted means of birth prevention. The CBR fell from 22.9 in 1957 to 14.3 in 1966 (Teitelbaum, 1972: 405).

The Romanian government became concerned about its low birth rate and in November 1966 revised its abortion policy. It restricted legal abortion to cases involving risk to the mother's life, risk of congenital malformation, evidence of rape, pregnancy to women older than 45 years of age, women supporting four or more living children, and a rigorously defined set of physiological conditions, as well as several other limiting social and economic circumstances (Teitelbaum, 1972).

The results of this dramatic change in Romanian population policy were remarkable. The CBR tripled in but nine months from 12.8 per 1,000 in December 1966 to 39.9 in September 1967. Since then it has declined steadily, and fertility is now well below replacement; the TFR in Romania in 2008 was 1.3 (Population Reference Bureau, 2008b). Apparently, the decline has occurred because of a strong preference for small families.

However, it took a little time for Romanian couples to make the sudden transition from a primary reliance on legal abortion to other methods of birth prevention, including the use of withdrawal (coitus interruptus), condoms, illegally imported contraceptives, and illegal abortion (David and Wright, 1971). In that interval, the birth rate increased substantially.

Thus far, we have concentrated on policies aimed at increasing fertility, although in some instances, the policies have tended to be redirected as the situation demanded. Now we examine a few antinatalist policies, both direct and indirect. The two basic approaches are government-sponsored family planning programs and various non–family planning approaches.

Antinatalist policies

Mexico is an example of a country in which the two approaches have been pursued simultaneously (Caldwell, 1997). In the early 1970s, the Mexican government engaged in a historic reversal of its pronatalist policies, embarking on an aggressive family planning initiative. Four branches of the public sector were enlisted to implement this strategy. The program also received additional important support from two private-sector organizations: MEXFAM (the Mexican affiliate of the International Planned Parenthood Federation) and FEMAP (the Mexican Federation of Private Health Assocations and Community Development). Between the early 1970s and 2000, the TFR fell from 6.5 to 2.8. In 2008, the TFR in Mexico was 2.3, just slightly above the replacement level.

There have been other family planning successes leading to dramatic reductions in population growth. Bangladesh, despite its incredible poverty, finances a third of the costs of its very active family planning program (Bouvier and Bertrand, 1999: 109). Other countries with active family planning programs include Colombia, the Dominican Republic, Egypt, El Salvador, India, Indonesia, Jamaica, Peru, Tunisia, and Vietnam.

We have been concentrating to this point on family planning efforts to reduce population growth. But we must go "beyond family planning" to get a more complete picture of population policies intended to reduce growth. Generally speaking, increased education for females and increased labor-force participation contribute to lowering fertility, albeit, as noted earlier, indirectly. But there are other less opaque methods that have been used to achieve this purpose. India provides a good example.

In the 1950s, India was the first country to introduce incentives to influence childbearing behavior. They were targeted at three groups: 1) acceptors, that is, those women and men complying with the government family planning policy; 2) providers, that is, physicians and other health-care personnel; and 3) promoters, that is, individuals in the community who influenced the acceptors to adopt family planning. Payment was usually in the form of cash to the providers, and cash, services, or gifts to the acceptors and promoters (Freedman and Isaacs, 1993). For example, men received gifts such as radios, traditional garments, and money for undergoing sterilization. However, it should be noted that such incentives are sometimes linked to abuses of human rights. For example, in the 1970s, India not only provided incentives to individuals but also penalized local officials for not reaching assigned quotas. Problems arose when public officials allegedly used force on low-status individuals to meet their quotas. This, in turn, created a backlash, contributing to the defeat of Indira Gandhi's government, as well as setbacks for family planning in India (Gillis et al., 1996).

China undoubtedly has one of the most stringent population policies in human history (Poston and Yaukey, 1992: 397–398). Indeed, one reason why China is such an interesting and intriguing country for demographers to study is precisely its fertility policies. Another reason, as noted by Nathan Keyfitz (1984: 45), is that in China the political leaders are "able to control the annual number of births with considerable precision." An important point to make in this regard is that family planning in a socialist country like China differs dramatically from family planning as we know it in the West. In China, "births are planned by the state to bring the production of human beings in line with the production of material goods" (Greenhalgh, 2008: 46). The numbers of babies produced are heavily controlled by the country.

In the period between 1949, when Mao Zedong and the Chinese Communists assumed control of the country and established the People's Republic of China (PRC), and the early 1970s, China's fertility policy was characterized as "on-again-and-off-again." During the early years of the PRC, there was very little attention given to the size of the population. But when the 1953 census data were made public, many leaders expressed anxiety about the size and growth trends of the country. Accordingly, by the summer of 1956, a birth control campaign was underway. However, this fledgling campaign lost its momentum and importance with the introduction in 1958 of communes and the nationalized movement in the country known as the Great Leap Forward, which was intended to move China to the status of an industrialized society. The Leap proved to be a disaster, and there was a tremendous increase in mortality; an estimated 30 million people died as a result of famine (Ashton et al., 1984). China soon recovered and the fertility rate skyrocketed to a TFR in the early 1960s of more than 6.0. In early 1962, China resumed its family planning program, mainly via the publication of propaganda encouraging family size limitation. But this second campaign lasted only until the beginning of the the Great Proletarian Cultural Revolution in 1966, at which time all birth-control efforts in the country were interrupted.

In 1971, China introduced its third family program, the so-called *wan-xi-shao* program, a campaign stressing *later* marriages (*wan*), *longer* intervals between children (*xi*), and *fewer* children (*shao*). However, the large numbers of children born during China's own baby boom in the early 1960s caused government leaders and officials in the middle to late 1970s to be concerned about demographic momentum and the concomitant growth potential of this huge cohort. Population projections for China developed by two scientists, Song Jian and Yu Jingyuan, and their associates showed that under the *wan-xi-shao* program, China would greatly exceed its goal of a population size of 1.2 billion by the year 2000 (Song, Tuan, and Yu, 1985; Song and Yu, 1988). Hence, with arguments and data from Song and his colleagues (Greenhalgh, 2008), the government of Deng Xiaoping approved the "one child is best" norm and intensified its already strong family planning program by launching, in 1979, the so-called One-Child Campaign. Its principal goal was to eliminate births above or equal to three per family, and to encourage families to have no more than one child, especially those in the urban areas. In practice, because of the many exceptions to the policy allowing some couples to have more than one child (Scharping, 2003), China's fertility policy is really best defined as a one-and-a-half child policy (usually one in the cities and sometimes two in the countryside).

China's fertility policy has been characterized by some as especially coercive. For instance, John S. Aird (1990) noted that the policy follows a cycles-of-coercion model of family planning: The Chinese central authorities enforce an unpopular birth-control policy by exerting the local authorities to coerce the people and to force them to accept the program's mandates. The pressure continues until opposition becomes so strong that a relaxation of the policy occurs, which itself leads to more new births than can be allowed, thus leading to another wave of coercion. This causes the kinds of fluctuations one sees in China's vacillating fertility rates, especially in the 1980s and early 1990s.

An alternate view espouses a linear model in which over time, the mandates of an unpopular policy are relaxed and the mechanisms for enforcing the regulations are weakened; more and more couples, especially rural ones, are permitted to have more children. A linear model does not necessarily assume that all of the political directives in China are top-to-bottom in direction, but that *cadres* (the rough equivalent of civil servants) at the local level have considerable influence in not only enforcing but also developing fertility plans and policies (Greenhalgh, 1986; 1990a; 2008).

Pronatalist policies

We now move away from India and China, countries characterized by fertility policies designed to reduce population growth, to countries with policies encouraging population growth. The current situation in virtually all the countries of the developed world is one with fertility rates well below the level needed to replace the population. Such low rates over a long period of time have many consequences, not the least of which is a dramatic aging of the population and, later, a reduction in the size of the population. Thus, there is much concern about below-replacement fertility in the countries of the developed world and in some other countries, for example, South Korea and Taiwan, to mention only two. The concern is not solely about population decline but also about the aging of the population as a result of the very low fertility. This kind of ramification of a below-replacement fertility rate in place for several decades will challenge social security and health-care systems and may even hinder productivity and global competitiveness (Lutz et al., 2003).

Development of pronatalist policies in such countries is difficult to promote. Today, family policies are based on an equal-opportunities rationale and aim to help women combine childrearing with employment (Lutz et al., 2003). Different countries have developed different types of policies to encourage increased fertility. We have already discussed France. In recent years, France has employed numerous policies with two purposes, namely, reconciling family life with work and reversing declining fertility. According to the Rand Corporation:

> To accomplish the first goal, France instituted generous child-care subsidies. To accomplish the second goal, families have been rewarded for having at least three children. Sweden, by contrast, reversed the fertility declines it experienced in the 1970s through a different mix of policies, none of which had the specific objective of raising fertility. Its parental work policies during the 1980s allowed many women to raise children while remaining in the workforce. The mechanisms for doing so were flexible work schedules, quality child care, and extensive parental leave on reasonable economic terms. (Rand Corporation, 1995: 1–4)

Other countries have implemented fertility policies involving financial remittances for each child born, liberal parental-leave benefits, and guaranteed child care and schooling for children. One of the most expansive and generous fertility policies has been enacted in Australia, where remittances per child per year exceed US $3,000 (Balter, 2006). Russia also has initiated an aggressive pronatalist policy involving financial incentives, medals for "baby-making," and an array of other awards (Rodriguez, 2009; see also Eberstadt, 2009). However, the effectiveness of these fertility incentives is hotly debated. Some argue that incentives are beneficial in easing the financial burdens caused by additional children, making families more willing to increase their childbearing. Others emphasize that any increases due to these policies will be small. While financial resources may make it easier for families to pay for the children they already want to have, they are unlikely to raise fertility to the level necessary to stave off population decline (Howden and Poston, 2008).

To be sure, even if successful, these are long-term goals that will take decades to come to fruition. In the meantime, many countries with below-replacement fertility rates are faced with another population-related dilemma: whether they should continue losing population or begin accepting more immigrants. Some have suggested that declining populations and the resulting dramatic imbalances in population age structure can be corrected through increases in migration. Since many developing countries are still experiencing high birth rates and population growth, immigration originating in these countries can supplement small working-age cohorts in other countries (Wattenberg, 2004). While international migration may be beneficial in the redistribution of national populations, immigration policies encouraging migration from developing countries remain the least-favored policies of countries experiencing population declines (Howden and Poston, 2008). We focus on immigration policy in a later section.

In sum, fertility policies vary across the world, and they have for decades. In some regions, birth rates are high; in others, they are low. Both governmental and nongovernmental agencies have been and are involved in attempting to restore some demographic balance in their respective societies.

POLICIES AFFECTING MORTALITY

Some hold that mortality-related policies should not be considered direct population policies. The reduction of mortality should be the goal of all governments, even those wishing to reduce their rates of population growth. Thus, measures taken by governments that deal with mortality may be viewed as indirect population policies as long as they have a demographic effect. For example, most industrialized countries subsidize medical care. Often, medical clinics provide free health care to the public. While these can be said to be examples of health policies, their overall effect is to increase life expectancy. Let us look at some examples of how indirect policies can affect mortality by causing either increases or decreases in the number of deaths.

Mortality policies receiving the most attention are those supporting the development of medical knowledge with the potential to expand life expectancy, as, for example, through the development of new wonder drugs or the facilitation of organ transplants. Beginning in the eighteenth century, there was considerable scientific work in this area of medical knowledge.

The work of scientists like Edward Jenner (1749–1823), Louis Pasteur (1822–1895), and Alexander Fleming (1881–1955) all contributed to the reduction of mortality in Western Europe and elsewhere: "Before the Second World War, colonial powers as well as independent governments in Latin American and Asia had enacted public health measures, launched sanitation and disease vector control programs, and organized targeted campaigns to bring down high mortality levels, notably in cities" (May, 2005: 838).

The demographer Massimo Livi-Bacci (1992) has noted that programs to eradicate malaria in Sri Lanka (then known as Ceylon) were successful as early as the 1940s, and the successes were mainly attributable to the use of DDT. For centuries, mosquitoes had been major killers in Ceylon and elsewhere, where the parasite would afflict "more than half of the population with anemia and chronic fatigue" (Connelly, 2008: 116). In the mid-1940s, public health officials sprayed more than half a million homes in Ceylon with DDT: "Within two years the total number of malaria cases had been cut by three-quarters, and six years later life expectancy had increased from 46 years to 60, largely because of the decline in infant mortality" (Connelly, 2008: 116).

Government policies can directly contribute to lower mortality. Every developed country in the world, with the exception of the United States, offers free or subsidized health care to all of its citizens. This is reflected in comparative levels of life expectancy, as discussed earlier in Chapter 5. Government policies aimed at reducing the incidence of specific diseases are clearly related to mortality. In 1972, then-President Richard Nixon declared a "War on Cancer," and millions of dollars have been spent for this purpose with much success. Thousands of lives are saved each year as a result of government regulations requiring installation of safety features, such as seat belts in new vehicles.

Perhaps the most publicized health policy that affects mortality relates to the use of tobacco. The U.S. National Institutes of Health have for many years cited studies showing a strong positive relationship between smoking and the risk of lung cancer and certain cardiovascular diseases. Even second-hand smoke is detrimental. Today, smoking is banned in many public buildings, including restaurants and bars in some states. Again, these efforts were not directly intended to increase life expectancy; their intent was to improve health.

If we accept the fact that some existing government measures or policies contribute to declining mortality, we must also accept the fact that some government policies can lead to increased mortality. Measures that endanger health, although unintentionally, will eventually raise mortality.

Just as there are policies that decrease mortality, there are also policies that raise it.

International warfare is the most obvious mortality-related governmental policy. Hundreds of millions of people have been killed as a result of humans declaring war on one another. We noted in Chapter 5 that the greatest number of deaths due to wars occurred during the first part of the last century: "Plausible sizes of the military and civilian death toll would be around 8.5 million in World War I and 40 million in World War II" (Etherington, 2003: 964). The number of civilian deaths due to wars usually exceeds the number of military deaths. For example, it has been estimated that during World War II in Russia, 60 percent of the deaths were to civilians (Petersen, 1975: 269). The Civil War resulted in the most number of deaths to Americans of any war ever experienced by the United States, before or after. Around 620,000 men died during the four years of fighting between 1861 and 1865 (Faust, 2008).

Government policies are sometimes deliberately aimed at increasing mortality. We noted earlier the practice of genocide in Nazi Germany as an example. Sadly, the world has witnessed more and more genocides in recent decades, for example, in Rwanda where Hutus tried to eliminate Tutsis, and in Darfur where religious hatred is leading to millions of deaths.

In far less revolting ways, governments frequently, albeit indirectly, affect mortality in a negative manner. Even while state and federal agencies are speaking out against smoking, they continue to subsidize tobacco growers and benefit from cigarette tax revenues. Indeed, cigarette advertising is still allowed in all media except broadcasting. Cigarette smoking, however, is but a minor contributor to air pollution.

For decades, the growth policies of most developed countries have resulted in increased degrees of smog and dangerous chemicals, which infect the environment, both air and water. Epidemiologists have found relationships between polluted air and water and the prevalence of certain respiratory and gastrointestinal diseases. W. J. Nicholson found in the mid-1970s that asbestos and textile workers with twenty years of working in the industry had more than four times the risk of cancer of the respiratory system as the general population (Nicholson, 1976).

Perhaps the strongest example of failure on the part of the U.S. government to do everything possible to improve health and longevity is its policy on medical assistance. For at least a half-century, there has been a growing demand for a national health program. Yet, the United States remains "the only great industrial country without a compulsory nationwide program for health insurance or sickness benefits.... There is ample evidence, however, of a shift of public opinion toward handling medical care as a predictable and insurable risk and responsibility" (Woytinsky and Woytinsky, 1953: 238). Note that this statement was made more than fifty years ago!

Since then, the United States has instituted the Medicare and Medicaid programs to help the poor and the aged. More recently, some assistance has been provided to the elderly for pharmaceutical expenses. And, as of the date of the final editing of this book in February 2010, a comprehensive nationwide program of health insurance has been debated in Congress; whether a final bill will ever become law is unknown; such a program was a centerpiece of the 2008 debates between presidential candidates Barack Obama and John McCain.

For its degree of modernization, the United States has a poor showing on various health indices, such as life expectancy and infant mortality, an issue already discussed in Chapter 5. Perhaps the failure to institute a national health program that would provide better medical care explains in part this poor showing.

Thus far, we have concentrated on policies related to natural population change. We now turn to policies related to immigration.

POLICIES AFFECTING INTERNATIONAL MIGRATION

Throughout most of human history, people have been free to move about in search of a better life. We noted in Chapter 7 that human populations began their migrations out of Africa around 50 thousand to 60 thousand years ago, first going to southern Asia, China, and Java and later to Europe. There were certainly no legal encumbrances then that made such moves difficult or impossible. To a considerable extent, however, such freedom of international movement has been significantly restricted since late in the nineteenth century. Many countries have introduced laws that infringe on the freedom to engage in international migration. In some instances, people have not been permitted to enter a country and, in other instances, people have not been permitted to enter certain parts of a country.

At the same time, some governments have taken measures to encourage movement into some areas and out of others. There have been instances of policies involving both nations and areas within a nation. Policies regarding international migration are much more common and pervasive than those pertaining to internal migration. An example of the latter is China's prohibition of most rural residents to migrate to urban areas, an issue already discussed in Chapter 6. In this section, we restrict our discussions to policies related to international migration.

Some countries encourage immigration in order to increase the size of their population. This was true of the United States during the eighteenth and nineteenth centuries. Immigration from other countries was necessary for the United States to grow in population. Canada, Australia, and New Zealand also fall into this category. Indeed, most of the current residents of these countries are immigrants or the descendants of immigrants. For example, in the United States in 2000, only 1.5 percent of the resident population, or only around 4 million people, were American Indians, Alaskan Natives, or Native Hawaiian or Pacific Islanders. That is, more than 98 percent of the U.S. population were immigrants or the descendants of immigrants. The United States, Canada, Australia, and New Zealand, all of which owe their heritage to immigration, are no longer encouraging large numbers of people to immigrate there.

Today, Israel is one of the few countries that actively seeks immigrants. In fact, immigration is considered the lifeblood of the country. Other nations, faced with rapid population growth, view emigration (movement out of a country) as a safety valve to relieve population pressures; some of the Caribbean countries are examples. In actuality, there are no countries in the world today without some sort of immigration policy, for or against. Some seek immigration, and others, such as Japan, allow little if any immigration. In the few countries that permit modest amounts of immigration, such as the United States, there is often considerable discussion and even disagreement about the numbers and the policies and how those policies should be enforced.

In the developed world today, there are three main types of national immigration regimes. The first is the so-called traditional immigration regime. The United States, Canada, and Australia are the three most important and sizable traditional immigration countries: "Founded by European settlers, they have long experiences with immigration and [to this day] allow the acquisition of citizenship through naturalization or birth within their territory" (Freeman, 2003: 515). The numbers of people legally admitted into these three countries are categorized in terms of family unification, economic needs of the country, and refugees. The United States admits most of their immigrants under the family unification category, whereas Canada and Australia admit most of their immigrants under the skilled worker category. These three countries used to restrict immigrants on the basis of their national origins; persons from certain European countries were usually preferred. But "all three countries ceased to discriminate on the basis of national origin by the early 1970s" (Freeman, 2003: 515).

The second type of national immigration regime includes countries that mainly allow immigrants to enter as guest workers. These are primarily "European countries that recruited temporary labor (guest workers) or received substantial colonial migration during the post–World War II economic expansions" (Freeman, 2003: 516). The immigrants came from

Southern Europe, Eastern Europe, North Africa, Turkey, South Asia, and the West Indies, for the most part. The receiving countries were mainly in Northern and Western Europe, including Germany, Great Britain, France, and the Netherlands. These immigrations stopped in the early 1970s, but not many of the guest workers ever returned to their home countries. Indeed, most of the workers brought members of their families into their new host destinations. As a consequence, by the 1980s, most of the Northern and Western European countries had very large immigrant and foreign-born populations, as well as second-generation immigrants, many of whom were not citizens of these host countries. Today, many Gulf countries, for example, Qatar, the United Arab Emirates (UAE), and Kuwait, among others, fall into this second category.

The third type of immigration regime is the group of Southern and Eastern European countries "more likely to receive than to send immigrants" (Freeman, 2003: 516). The four countries most prominent in this category are Greece, Spain, Portugal, and Italy. These countries serve as entry points for illegal immigrants from other countries who are seeking to enter the European Union. As a consequence, by 2000, there were more than 18.5 million foreigners living in countries of the European Union, or about 7 percent of its population. When one adds in the children of these immigrants, the foreign population becomes larger. As many as 12 million Muslims now reside in the European Union. Gary P. Freeman (2003) has remarked about the difficulties that these countries have experienced in embracing multiculturalism. Their difficulties may be compared with the less difficult and problematic experiences of the United States, Canada, and Australia. To get an idea of the many and varied types of immigration policies, we turn in the next section to a discussion of the history of immigration policies in the United States.

U.S. IMMIGRATION POLICIES

Immigration was not a concern in early America, and there were no formal laws or policies regulating immigration on a national level. But the new U.S. Constitution did deal with the issue of naturalization, that is, the process by which an individual becomes a citizen (Purcell, 1995). The "Articles of Confederation" allowed aliens to naturalize as American citizens after two years residence in the United States, something that was not previously allowed under British rule (Gabaccia, 2002). These policies, however, did not apply to white indentured servants or to blacks. These restrictions were particularly reflected in the Aliens Acts of 1798, which required aliens to register and allowed the president to deport any individuals deemed dangerous. The laws expired in 1801 when Thomas Jefferson became president, and the citizenship waiting period increased to five years (Cortes and Poston, 2008; Purcell, 1995).

One of the most notable laws restricting immigration to the United States was the Chinese Exclusion Act of May 6, 1882, which reflected the public concern about the large numbers of Chinese who had come to provide inexpensive labor for the construction of the transcontinental railroad. This law suspended the immigration of Chinese laborers for ten years; it permitted Chinese who were in the United States as of November 17, 1880, to stay, travel abroad, and return; it prohibited the naturalization of Chinese; and it created the so-called Section 6 exempt status for Chinese teachers, students, merchants, and travelers who were admitted on the presentation of certificates from the Chinese government (Cortes and Poston, 2008).

The next significant exclusionary legislation was the "Act to Prohibit the Coming of Chinese Persons into the United States of May 1892," better known as the Geary Act, and discussed previously in more detail in Chapter 7. It allowed Chinese laborers to travel home to China and reenter the United States, but its provisions were very restrictive. Other restrictive immigration acts affecting citizens of Chinese ancestry followed (King and Locke, 1980). The Chinese Exclusion Act and later exclusionary laws were the first to use the concept of an illegal **alien** (Pedraza and Rumbaut, 1996).

The next major immigration policy was the 1917 Immigration Act that increased the head tax on immigrants to $8.00 and required incoming migrants to pass literacy tests. The Immigration Act also "established several new categories for exclusion, including vagrants, alcoholics, and the psychopathically inferior" (Purcell, 1995: 82). This law required the potential immigrant to be able to read a passage in English or another language. It also extended the exclusion of Chinese and Japanese to all Asians (Cortes and Poston, 2008).

In 1921, further restrictions were passed that set quotas based on nation of origin. In 1924, Congress took this one step further by passing the National Origins Act, which restricted the total number of immigrants to 150 thousand; the division of the quotas reflected the American population enumerated in the 1890 census. This was done in an attempt to allow immigrants only from Great Britain, Scandinavia, and Germany, while reducing immigration from all Asian countries and severely restricting the immigration of Italians, Slavs, Jews, Greeks, and other Southern and Eastern Europeans (Purcell, 1995).

From the 1920s to the 1950s, immigration in the United States changed significantly. The Great Depression and World War II brought in a period of slow and sometimes negative immigration, resulting in net losses in population size due to international migration. The only significant immigration was from Mexico under the *bracero* program, which admitted Mexican male workers while Americans were overseas (see Chapter 7). In 1952, the Immigration and Naturalization Act was passed, maintaining most of the quotas set forth in the National Origins Act of 1924 (Hay, 2001).

The next major U.S. immigration policy was the Immigration and Naturalization Act of 1965, which became law in 1968. This act ended the national origins quota system and allowed the immigration of family members of those already living in the United States, as well as individuals in certain occupations. It also ended the restrictions on Asian immigration, and it limited immigration from the Western Hemisphere as a whole to 120,000 (Hay, 2001). The change in law produced an influx of immigrants from previously unrepresented countries, such as many in Southeast Asia and the Middle East (Cortes and Poston, 2008).

Total permanent immigration to the United States has undergone many changes in recent years, with the numbers increasing from about 600 thousand in 1986 and 1987 to a peak of 1.8 million in 1991, and then falling back to around 660,000 in 1998. The rise in the total number from 1987 to 1991 may be attributed in part to the Immigration Reform and Control Act (IRCA) of 1986 that granted legal status to undocumented immigrants who had been in the United States continuously since 1982. This act has also been cited as a reason for the increased number of pending "adjustment of status" applications and the subsequent reduction in the number of approved applications. Between 1991 and 1999, the total number of admitted permanent immigrants to the United States declined every year except for 1996. The levels of permanent immigration in 1999 were approximately the same as they were eleven years earlier (Poston and Luo, 2007; U.S. Citizenship and Immigration Services, 2004).

Changes in the numbers of permanent immigrants to the United States from all countries in the world are also explained in part by the impact of the Immigration Act of 1990, which revised the annual ceiling on immigration and the preference categories used to regulate immigration. This act, which became effective on October 1, 1991, increased the levels of employment-based immigration and allotted a higher proportion of visas to highly skilled immigrants.

The numbers of permanent immigrants from China have fluctuated from 1989 to 1994. The IRCA, a one-time-only amnesty, does not appear to have had as dramatic an impact on Chinese permanent immigration as it had on total permanent immigration. Indeed, the Chinese immigration rate to the United States has been relatively stable since 1980, except for increases in 1993 and 1994. They were due in part to the influence of the Immigration Act of 1990 but, more important, to the Chinese Student Protection Act of 1992, a bill sponsored by Representative Nancy Pelosi of

California, which granted permanent resident status to Chinese immigrants who were in the United States after June 4, 1989, and before April 11, 1990. Its stated purpose was to prevent the political persecution of Chinese students in the aftermath of the Tiananmen demonstrations and protests of 1989. One of its provisions was that permanent residency status slots granted to Chinese nationals under the act would be subtracted from the immigration spaces available in later years. But, ironically, the primary beneficiaries of this act were reported to be undocumented immigrants from Fujian Province, China, who were not students at all (Poston and Luo, 2007).

In 1996, two laws were passed that impacted the levels of permanent immigration to the United States, namely, the Welfare Reform Act of 1996 and the Immigration Reform and Immigrant Responsibility Act of 1996. The latter, signed into law by President Bill Clinton, eliminated the entitlement of support for poor families, requiring able-bodied persons who received government assistance to work (Espenshade, Baraka, and Huber, 1997). The former circumscribed the eligibility of immigrants for public benefit programs by creating a four-tier system: "The broadest eligibility is reserved for U.S. citizens; next come refugees and asylees; newly limited access is imposed on legal immigrants; and illegal immigrants remain ineligible for almost all social programs" (1997: 771–772). Prior to its enactment, U.S. citizens, legal immigrants, and refugees were all equally eligible for most public benefit programs. (An **asylee** is a person forced to leave home to seek legal refugee status in another country.)

The Immigration Reform and Immigrant Responsibility Act of 1996 was passed to strengthen the effects of the Welfare Reform Act that year by combating illegal immigration and creating higher standards of financial self-sufficiency for the admission of sponsored legal immigrants. This act focused in particular on immigrant access to public benefits: 1) it established measures to control U.S. borders, protect legal workers through worksite enforcement, and remove criminal and other deportable aliens; 2) it placed added restrictions on benefits for aliens; and 3) it introduced miscellaneous limitation provisions, such as a limit on the ability of F-1 students to attend public schools without reimbursing those institutions.

Thomas Espenshade, Jessica Baraka, and Gregory Huber (1997) argued that the combined effects of these two 1996 laws have had important consequences. The welfare reforms of 1996 led to a larger number of eligible legal immigrants becoming nationalized so that the actual cost savings attributable to benefits for immigrants were smaller than expected. In addition, the 1996 immigration and welfare reforms were expected to reduce the future volume of U.S. legal immigration and to produce a legal immigrant stream with higher skill and income levels.

In 1998, the U.S. Congress passed the American Competitiveness and Workforce Improvement Act. It was a response, in part, to the belief in the Congress that the United States was facing a severe shortage of workers qualified to perform skilled jobs in information technology, even though the evidence of a shortage was inconclusive. Under this act, the annual ceiling of certain petitions valid for initial employment was increased from 65,000 to 115,000 in fiscal years 1999 and 2000 and to 107,500 in 2001.

The stated purpose of this act was to protect native-born American workers by preventing employers from hiring low-skilled aliens instead of native-born workers. Employers are required to take good-faith steps to recruit American workers for jobs potentially performed by certain aliens, and to offer the jobs to American workers who are equally or better qualified than the aliens.

The preceding is a summary of many of the immigration and immigration-based laws passed in the United States since the late 1800s. The immigration laws, especially the more recent ones, are numerous and very complex in their meaning and interpretation. Attorneys specializing in immigration law are needed these days to facilitate the entry of immigrants into the United States, and this process, if it is successful, usually takes not months but years. Compare this long-drawn-out and complicated process of entering the country with that of many of our ancestors who entered the United States after undergoing a screening at Ellis Island of, at best, a few days (see Chapter 7).

REPLACEMENT MIGRATION

We noted earlier that in this new era of declining fertility and reductions in population size, countries might consider turning to immigration as a means for redressing the population losses occurring through fertility. In other words, migration could be used as a means for replacing the population lost through fertility. In this last section, we consider the concept of replacement migration (Keeley, 2009) and how it would work and be applied. We do so within the context of South Korea, a country with an extremely low fertility rate: a TFR in 2008 of 1.2.

Population projections prepared for South Korea for the next several decades indicate that the absolute and relative numbers of the older (persons of age 60+) and oldest-old (persons of age 85+) populations will increase tremendously. Figure 13.1 presents South Korea's age and sex population pyramids for the years 2000 and 2050. The two stacked pyramids show graphically that by 2050, South Korea is projected to have made the transition to a top-heavy and demographically very old country. In 2050, almost

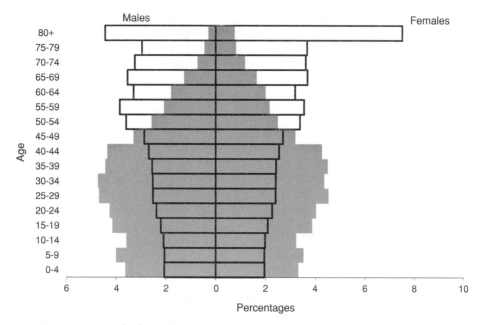

Figure 13.1. Stacked population pyramids: South Korea (ROK), 2000 (Shaded) and 2050. *Source:* The authors.

33 percent of its population will be 60 years of age or older. In 2050, South Korea will be older than the United States, which in 2050 is projected to have only one-quarter of its population of age 60 or older. What are some of the implications of this aging of South Korea's population?

One effect is the tremendous change that will occur in the extent to which the older members of the population will be able to be supported economically and emotionally by the younger members. To appraise quantitatively the extent of this age-structure imbalance, the UN (2001) developed a measure of elderly support, known as the **potential support ratio** (PSR). It represents "the extent that persons of working age [15 to 64] can be seen as supporting the older population [65 years or older], and is the ratio between the two" (United Nations, 2001: 7). The PSR value represents the number of persons in the population who "support" every one old person in the population.

To illustrate, we show in Table 13.1 that in 1950 in South Korea, there were 11,257,000 persons of ages 15–64 and 620,000 persons 65+. Dividing the former by the latter indicates the number of persons in the population who are available to support every one old person. In 1950, the PSR was 18.2. The United States had a PSR in 1950 more than half that of South Korea because the U.S. fertility rate at that time was considerably lower than that of South Korea. The values of the PSR for South

Table 13.1. Total population, population in age groups 0–14, 15–64, and 65+, and potential support ratios (PSR): South Korea and the United States, 1950, 2000, and 2050

	1950	2000	2050
South Korea			
Total population ('000)	20,357	47,471	51,148
Age group 0–14 ('000)	8,479	10,339	7,305
Age group 15–64 ('000)	11,257	33,818	29,937
Age group 65+ ('000)	620	3,314	13,906
Potential support ratio (15–64 / 65+)	18.16	10.20	2.15
USA			
Total population ('000)	152,271	282,339	420,081
Age group 0–14 ('000)	40,998	60,310	82,575
Age group 15–64 ('000)	98,876	186,968	250,800
Age group 65+ ('000)	12,397	35,061	86,706
Potential support ratio (15–64 / 65+)	7.98	5.33	2.89

Source: The authors.

Korea and for the United States for 1950, 2000, and 2050 are shown in Table 13.1.

In the last few decades in South Korea, "life expectancy at birth for both sexes combined increased from 47.5 years in 1950–55 to 70.9 years in 1990–95" (United Nations, 2001: 59). Increasing levels of life expectancy, along with a rapidly declining fertility rate, have resulted in the pace of population aging in South Korea being one of the fastest in the world (United Nations, 2001: 60). The proportion of persons age 65 and older in South Korea's population increased from 3.0 percent in 1950 to 4.0 percent in 1960 to 5.6 percent in 1995 (United Nations, 2001: 59) to 7 percent in 2000, and it is projected to be 27 percent in 2050.

Of even greater interest is the change in the PSRs. The PSR dropped from 18.2 in 1950 to 10.2 in 2000. Whereas in 1950 there were more than eighteen "supporting" persons in the South Korean population for every one old person, this ratio declined by 2000 to ten supporters for every one old person. During this fifty-year period, the PSR also decreased in the United States from 8 to 5. In 2000, the PSR of the United States was half that of South Korea.

By 2050, however, the PSR in South Korea will plummet to 2.15. That is, there are projected to be just over two South Koreans in the population available to support every one elderly South Korean. In South Korea in 2000, ten persons were available to support every one elderly person; in

2050, there will be two supporting persons available for every one South Korean elder.

The United States is also projected to have a low PSR in 2050, a PSR of 2.9, just slightly higher than that of South Korea. But, as noted, the United States had a PSR in 2000 of 5.3, a much lower level of elderly support than in South Korea in 2000. Whereas in the United States in 2000 there were 5.3 supporting persons in the population for every 1 elder, in South Korea in 2000 there were 10.2 supporting persons for every 1 South Korean elder. The process of population aging in the United States has been much less rapid than the process in South Korea.

Given the projected PSR of 2.15 for South Korea for 2050, one may ask what would need to be done to return to a higher PSR. Specifically, what would South Korea have to do demographically to have a PSR of twelve in 2050 instead of the projected PSR for 2050 of two? In other words, what would South Korea have to do to alter its demographic destiny of a highly imbalanced PSR of 2.15 for 2050? How could South Korea obtain more persons in the supporting population so as to offset its very low projected PSR for 2050?

One way would be to increase the fertility rate. The TFR in South Korea is one of the lowest in the world: 1.2 in 2008. Some countries have introduced population policies to raise their fertility rates. Although this is one approach, it would be demographically inefficient because it takes many years before a newborn becomes a supporting member of the population.

A quicker approach would be international migration, a strategy that would permit South Korea to bring supporting members into its population directly and immediately. How many international migrants would South Korea require if the end result would be to maintain, through the first half of this new century, a PSR of around twelve? That is, between the years of 2000 and 2050, how many immigrants would South Korea need to admit into the country if it wished to maintain a PSR of twelve?

The answer is an astonishingly high number of 5.1 billion immigrants! That is, for South Korea to maintain between 2000 and 2050 a PSR of twelve supporters for every one elderly, it would require a total of 5,128,147,000 immigrants, or an average of almost 103 million immigrants each year! The UN reports that this "number is enormous because the initial level of the PSR . . . is relatively high" (2001: 60). This number of immigrants required during the first fifty years of this century is almost equal to the total population of the world. This unrealistic number also indicates that South Korea's current PSR "is transitional and will be considerably lower in the future, irrespective of migration flows" (United Nations, 2001: 60).

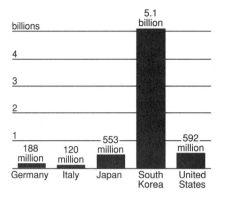

Figure 13.2. Number of immigrants needed by the year 2050 to maintain the potential support ratio (PSR) existing around 2000. *Source:* Tarmann, 2000.

In Figure 13.2, we show the numbers of immigrants that would be required between 2000 and 2050 for the countries of Germany, Italy, Japan, South Korea, and the United States to maintain their PSRs in existence in the late 1990s. South Korea's replacement migration number is much larger than the numbers for the other countries because its PSR in the late 1990s is so much higher than the PSRs of the other four countries.

A less drastic scenario asks how many immigrants South Korea would require if the end result was to not allow the PSR to ever fall below 3.0. We have already seen in Table 13.1 that South Korea's PSR in 2000 was 10.2 and is projected to be 2.15 in 2050. If South Korea's policymakers wished to not allow the PSR to reach the projected level of 2.15 but to stabilize at 3.0, how many immigrants would be needed? To attain this objective, "no immigrants would be needed until 2035, and 11.6 million immigrants would be needed between 2035 and 2050, an average of 0.8 million new immigrants per year" (United Nations, 2001: 60). Under this scenario, South Korea would have a total population in 2050 of 65.7 million, of which "14 million, or 21 percent, would be post-1995 immigrants or their descendants" (United Nations, 2001: 60).

The provision of elder care in South Korea will be a major concern in the years of the twenty-first century. As mentioned, in 2000, there were 10.2 South Koreans supporting every 1 South Korean elder, and this PSR is projected to drop precipitously to a level of 2.15 by 2050. One way for South Korea to offset this dramatic decline in its PSR would be to develop population policies encouraging persons to immigrate to South Korea, that is, turn to international migration for demographic replacement. Although replacement migration is a more efficient strategy than increasing fertility, the number of replacement immigrants is so large that this approach is not quite as easy as one might suspect. Nevertheless, we agree with Charles B. Keeley that "replacement migration will probably continue to be a topic that is redressed from time to time as the demography of the last century and the demographic behaviors of the 21st century play out in a variety of social settings. . . . Its salience, however, is unlikely to become very high" (2009: 403).

SUMMARY

Populations change in size, composition, and distribution via fertility, mortality, and migration. But these changes are not random in their occurrence. Many governments have been known to pass laws and regulations that deal with their levels of fertility, mortality, and migration, particularly migration. Many of the laws represent direct effects to influence national rates of population change, and others involve indirect effects.

Regarding policies intended to influence levels of fertility, there are two main approaches. One is to provide birth-control knowledge and services and related enhancements through massive government-sponsored family and family planning programs. The other is to change the social and economic environments so that people are motivated to have fewer, or to have more, children. Examples of these nonprogram efforts include modernization, payments for having or not having children, increased opportunities for the employment of women, population education, and maternal and paternal employment leaves. The two approaches are often viewed as complementing each other.

Governments influence mortality mainly through their attempts to improve the health levels of the population. But there are several government practices (e.g., war) that serve to increase mortality rather than lower it. The failure of governments to enact remedial laws and programs, say with regard to health insurance coverage, has also been shown to increase mortality.

Governments also have laws and policies influencing the numbers of people coming across their borders, and some have laws related to persons departing. The United States receives the largest number of immigrants of any country of the world and, as a consequence, has a wealth of laws dealing with immigration. At times, countries have expressed a concern in their immigration laws about the "quality" of the population. This was particularly the case with immigration laws invoked in many countries, including the United States, in the last two centuries, regarding the national origins of the immigrants. Quality restrictions are still found in the immigration laws of many countries today regarding the labor-force, educational, and economic qualifications of potential immigrants.

With the increasing number of countries in the world today with below-replacement fertility, we can expect to see more countries writing and implementing policies in an attempt to increase the numbers of babies born. With the growing socioeconomic gap between countries and the desires of persons from the poorer countries to move to the better-off countries, we can expect the receiving countries to continue to prepare policies and laws in an attempt to regulate and balance these streams of migrants from abroad. But the policies, whatever their intention and reason for their genesis, will never be successful unless they take into account the social, cultural, and economic milieu in which demographic behavior occurs, and unless they consider the indirect as well as the direct effects.

KEY TERMS

alien

asylee

family planning program

population policy

potential support ratio (PSR)

pronatalist

United Nations Fund for Population
   Activities (UNFPA)

From the chapters of this book, you have hopefully learned a good deal about population and demography. You likely now know more than you did when you first started to read the book. We have discussed the three demographic processes; we have discussed the basic population characteristics, especially age and sex; we have discussed population growth as well as population decline. In this final chapter, we look at the population itself, the number of inhabitants on this planet now and in the future, and how these may be related to other major factors of life on earth. We look at the future of the earth's population from the standpoint of ecology, sociology, and philosophy. Hence, this last chapter has less to do with demography per se and more to do with other topics.

In Chapter 9, we noted that the world population is estimated to number about 7 billion in 2013, 8 billion in 2026, and 9 billion in 2046 (United Nations, 2005). The 2050 population of the world is projected to be more than 9 billion. What do these numbers mean, and what are their implications?

ECOLOGICAL CONSIDERATIONS

We look first at resources, at pollution, and at technology. What might be the impact of 9 billion inhabitants of the earth were we to take an *ecological* view of the population? In this first part of the chapter, we use what demographers and human ecologists refer to as the *ecological complex*, that is, the interaction of population, organization, environment, and technology (POET) (O. Duncan, 1959; Hawley, 1950; Poston and Frisbie, 2005).

First, a brief review of population. As we have already noted, today the world population is well over 6 billion and is expected to reach more than 9 billion by 2050. An ever-growing proportion of that population resides in the developing regions of the world. More than 95 percent of the projected growth in the world population between 2010 and 2050 is expected to occur in developing countries. By 2050, 85 percent of the world's projected population will hail from developing countries. This population growth will come disproportionately from people on the margins, those with limited resources and life opportunities.

The U.S. population now stands at more than 300 million and is likely to reach 420 million by midcentury. Like the situation with the world's population, the subpopulations in the United States that are increasing disproportionately are mainly those with limited resources and life opportunities, namely, minorities. In the United States, the Latino population has accounted for half of the population growth in recent decades and is projected to comprise nearly two-thirds of the nation's population growth between 2010 and 2050. In contrast, the non-Hispanic white (i.e., Anglo) population will account for only 2 percent of the population increase during this period. Between 2010 and 2050, projections indicate that the Latino share of the U.S. population will increase from 16 percent (1 in 6) in 2010 to 30 percent (3 in 10) in 2050.

Let us use these numbers and consider how they are related to resources, pollution, and technology. We first look at resources, specifically oil and water. To maintain any kind of ecological balance in a social system, there must be sufficient resources for the system to maintain itself. While it is not our intention here to delve deeply into resource issues, it is appropriate to point out that today the world is very much concerned about the availability of petroleum. The term *peak oil* is commonly used when trying to determine the availability of petroleum. This is the date when the peak production of crude oil is expected to be reached. M. King Hubbert, who coined the phrase, predicted in 1974 that peak oil would occur between 1995 and 2000, if current trends continued (Deffeyes, 2005; see also Juvkam-Wold and Dessler, 2009), and it would be due mainly to continued population growth. If these estimates are close to being accurate, then continued high prices for gasoline and heating supplies can be expected. A worldwide energy crisis is not beyond reason, and we already are aware of the growing tensions in the Middle East and elsewhere, in large part because of the desperate need for oil.

There may be some room for optimism. Recent analyses suggest that the year for peak oil was 2005 ("Peak Oil," 2006). But there is a problem distinguishing between resources and reserves. We have a fairly good idea of the extent of resources. Reserves are more plentiful, but the cost of mining these areas is so high as to question the economics of such undertakings.

Another cause for optimism is the determination on the part of many countries both to foster limitations on petroleum use and to find alternative sources of energy. The Kyoto Treaty, a protocol calling on nations to stabilize greenhouse gases in the atmosphere, is an example. Of the 180 countries that both signed and ratified the treaty, the United States, unfortunately, has not been one of them. Although the United States signed the protocol, it has neither ratified nor withdrawn from it. Thus, its signature is merely symbolic. With the Kyoto Treaty scheduled to expire in 2012, 170 countries met at the Copenhagen Conference on Climate Change in December 2009 to develop another agreement. The new document recognizes that climate change is one of today's greatest challenges. However, the final document is not legally binding and does not contain any legally binding commitments for reducing carbon dioxide emissions.

It is interesting that none of these suggestions to relieve the pains of petroleum depletion mention possible reductions in population growth. Indeed, scholars concerned with oil production seem to take population growth as a given: "Because of world population growth, oil production per capita" reached a high in the 1970s (R. Duncan, 2001: 3). In addition, "it is expected that worldwide oil production in the year 2030 will be the same as it was in 1980. The world's population in 2030 is expected to double from 1980 and be much more industrialized and oil-dependent than it was in 1980. Consequently, worldwide demand for oil will significantly outpace worldwide production of oil" ("Life After Oil," 2008).

Why must it be assumed that the population of the world will double between 1980 and 2030? The noted physicist Albert Bartlett has given a possible answer, noting that "some physicists maintain that the non-sustainability of oil production per capita was not addressed due to political correctness implications of suggesting population control" (2004: 8–27). Most certainly, a billion fewer inhabitants of the planet in 2050 would at least postpone the oil crisis that we likely will eventually face. It would give us more time to develop alternate sources of energy. Yet it seems highly probable that by the middle of this century, we will be faced with serious petroleum problems.

Another resource is water. To most readers of this book, water is probably taken for granted. Yes, we know of polluted water but, overall, "What's the problem?" First of all, it should be pointed out that water is a far more unreliable resource than oil. It is fundamental to life, human and otherwise; indeed, it is a prerequisite for all living things. Second, there are no substitutes for most of its uses, unlike oil, which can be replaced by other forms of energy. Finally, while water is a renewable resource, it is also finite. In the twenty-first century, the scarcity of water may be the single greatest threat to global food production.

Sandra Postel, a leading authority on water resources, has noted the following in her book about water and sustainability:

> We are entering an unprecedented period of water stress globally. In 2015, nearly 3 billion people – 40 percent of the projected world population – will live in countries that find it difficult or impossible to mobilize enough water to satisfy the food, industrial, and domestic needs of their citizens. How nations respond to this dilemma individually and collectively will have serious implications for food security, for the health of the aquatic environment, and for social and political stability. A new mindset for water policy and management is required if we are to meet the needs of 9 billion people while protecting the health of the aquatic environment that our economies and all life depend upon (Postel, 1992: 12).

As population grows, there is an increased pressure to deplete our aquifers that are essential to so much of life. Aquifers are crucial to our water supplies. Consider aquifers as huge water-storage reservoirs. Whereas groundwater is a renewable source, the reserves replenish slowly. We put water in and we take water out: "Falling water tables have already curtailed irrigation from some aquifers, and the competition for water between irrigated agriculture and urban population growth has already led to a systematic diversion of water from agriculture to cities in Arizona and California" (Bouvier and Grant, 1994: 15). Increasing numbers of cities are beginning to note water shortages: "Cities like San Antonio, El Paso and Phoenix could run out of water in 10 to 20 years. San Diego's water company has resorted to a once-unthinkable option, namely, recycling toilet water for drinking" (Rubenstein, 2008/2009: 5). Today in the United States, groundwater is utilized about four times faster than it is naturally replaced. The great Ogallala Aquifer that covers parts of eight states is gradually being depleted but remains a primary source of water for much of the Great Plains. It is so important that attempts have been made by billionaire industrialists to purchase much of the land that covers the aquifer. The end result is more expensive water for ordinary users.

Again, as with petroleum, population growth is taken as unchangeable; it is a constant. In his usual pithy manner, Benjamin Franklin said it best: "When the well runs dry, we know the worth of water" (cited in Bartlett, 1968). We repeat here our earlier statement that a billion fewer inhabitants of the planet in 2050 would at least postpone the water crisis that will likely be felt eventually. We should not take out more water than enters the system, although we do. We should not see our aquifers dry up and disappear, although we do indeed face that prospect. The water wars of the nineteenth century made famous, or infamous, by western movies could return to haunt us in the twenty-first century, if population growth continues unabated. This could, in turn, lead to food shortages and significant increases in the cost of food.

We turn now to considerations of the environment. What do we mean by *environment*? The term is extremely broad and vague. Amos H. Hawley has defined it as "whatever is external to and potentially or actually influential on a phenomenon under investigation" (1968: 330). Leo F. Schnore has written that it is "a set of limiting conditions, which may be narrow or broad, depending on the technological devices and modes of organization that prevail in a given population" (1958: 628). These definitions are useful in limiting the term. For our purposes in this chapter, however, the concept "social environment" is not really an environmental issue. Hence, we limit our discussion here to issues of the *physical environment*, namely, global warming and pollution, and the related problem of waste. These are environmental issues and significantly related to the human population.

Global warming is the evidence of a rise in the earth's temperature. It is sometimes referred to as *climate change*. There is a general, although not unanimous, agreement among scientists that global warming is taking place perhaps at a rate even more rapid than had been anticipated. Furthermore, "most of the observed increase in globally averaged temperatures since the mid-20th century is very likely due to the observed increase in anthropogenic greenhouse gas concentrations" (Intergovernmental Panel on Climate Change, 2007: 8).

To be sure, other factors are involved, but greenhouse gases seem to be the prime cause of this momentous change in the earth's temperature. Evidence is already being noted near the Arctic Circle where Greenland is losing some of its ice foundation, causing massive increases in oceanic water to be sent in a southward direction.

Our primary concern is with the contribution of population to the problem, not with an in-depth discussion of climate change. Carbon dioxide is a major contributor to greenhouse gas. Motor vehicles are a major contributor to carbon dioxide. As a general rule of thumb, we can add 700 motor vehicles to every 1,000 persons added to a population. This is true in developed nations, and also in China and India, although less so in the other regions of the world. Now let us add a billion inhabitants to the planet. You do the math and see what the result will be. So, once again, we point out that although reductions in population growth will not solve all these problems, they would be drastically alleviated if such reductions were at least discussed. In an otherwise excellent article in the *American Prospect*, Ross Gelbspan (2007) has failed to even mention population limitation as a possible aid to solving the planet's problems. He has cited a report from the insurance giant Swiss Re in which it was noted that "there is a danger that human intervention will accelerate and intensify climate change to such a point that it will become impossible to adapt our socio-economic systems in time" (Gelbspan, 2007: 47). One wonders what he meant by the phrase "human intervention."

Pollution is closely related to global warming. There are, of course, numerous types of pollution, such as air, water, and noise. Here, we concentrate on air pollution that involves the release of chemicals into the atmosphere. Examples are carbon monoxide and nitrogen oxide, both of which are produced by industry and motor-vehicles. Motor vehicle emissions are among the leading causes of air pollution. For decades, we have lamented the dense smog over such cities as London, Los Angeles, and Houston and, more recently, some of the major cities in China. The cause has overwhelmingly been the result of too many vehicles. As noted, adding 1,000 people to an area, especially in the industrialized world, results in around 700 more vehicles. Indeed, the ratio may be even more damaging given the increased number of automobiles per household in economically advanced nations. So, once again, we repeat our observation that limiting population growth could well reduce many of our problems; this time, it is pollution.

Of all the problems associated with continued rapid population growth, garbage and waste disposal may be among the most visible. Today, cities in the United States produce more than twice as much solid waste as they did in 1960 (Bouvier and Grant, 1994: 15). The problems associated with waste disposal are critical: "Because they were polluting, or simply full, the number of landfills declined from 20,000 in 1978 to 6,000 in 1990 and down to 3,581 by 1995. Cities have unsuccessfully tried to unload the waste on third world countries. . . . Eastern cities [in the United States] have been negotiating with rural counties as far away as New Mexico and Texas to accept the stuff. The nation is on a treadmill" (1994: 16). The challenge of waste disposal continues, and some states today, for example, Virginia, are beginning to question the wisdom of accepting waste from northern cities.

Let us sum up the overall environmental problems faced by the planet. These include "encroaching deserts, rising sea levels, deforestation, acid precipitation, resultant forest dieback, toxic contamination of food supplies, soil oxidation and pollution of water tables, ozone depletion, greenhouse gas buildup and climatic change" (Rees, 2004: 12). Population growth is a contributor, direct or indirect, to all of these challenges for our planet.

SOCIOLOGICAL CONSIDERATIONS

Thus far, we have presented a rather dismal picture of population growth and its impact on the world. Some might even refer to us as **doomsters**. However, there are **boomsters** among social scientists, sometimes referred to as **cornucopians**. Two economists associated with this line of thought are Ester Boserup and Julian Simon. Boserup, a Danish economist, argued that population growth was a stimulus to social change (1965). For example, it was population growth that contributed to the move from an agricultural to an industrial society. She also wrote that a growing population is more likely to experience economic development than a society where growth is limited or even nonexistent (Boserup, 1981).

Simon, the late American economist, would also be considered a boomster. Politically conservative, he was a major proponent for the argument that "population growth is neutral." This was the basis for the U.S. position at the Second World Population conference in Mexico City, discussed previously in Chapter 13. Simon argued in his highly influential and very interesting book, *The Ultimate Resource* (1981), that population growth and the ability to innovate go together. Indeed, the "ultimate resource" referred to more people. People innovate, and the more people there are, the more likely innovation will occur. In his later years, Simon paid less attention to population growth and more to the commercial market: "Misplaced attention to population growth has resulted in disastrously unsound advice being given to developing nations" (1992: xiii).

While the views of cornucopians such as Boserup and Simon may have had merit in the past, it is more difficult for such arguments to hold sway in a world with more than 6 billion inhabitants that could very well double in less than fifty years. Perhaps one area where doomsters and boomsters can agree is technology. The technological changes in the world, developed and developing, especially during the last half of the twentieth century, have been remarkable. We immediately think of the computer and the Internet. The computer chip has made communications incredibly rapid. A person in New York can be in contact with a person in Beijing in seconds. Recall, too, our earlier discussion of the interstate highway system. Consider how this has increased our ability to get almost anywhere in the United States faster than previously possible. Now we have more speed in our communications and in our travel capabilities. What will the future bring? What technological changes will take place in this century that might impact our lifestyles even more than have been observed in recent decades?

If one thinks that the recent advancements in technology were amazing, we have only seen the beginnings. We, as a species, are constantly evolving. This is nothing new. Auguste Comte, generally considered to be the father of sociology, believed that humanity progressed through three stages of thought and development: theological, metaphysical, and positivist (1853). Emile Durkheim saw a gradual evolving of society from what he called "mechanical" to "organic" ([1893] 1984). Herbert Spencer believed there to be "an inexorable tendency toward differentiation both in the case of organisms into species and in the case of societies into more differentiated structures" (Wallace and Wolf, 2005: 160).

Recently, Anthony Giddens (2002: 7) has remarked that

> we live in a world of transformations, affecting almost every aspect of what we do. For better or worse, we are being propelled into a global order that no one understands, but which is making its effects felt upon all of us. Globalization may not be a particularly attractive or elegant word, but absolutely no one who wants to understand our prospects . . . can ignore it. . . . The global spread of the term is evidence of the very developments to which it refers. . . . [E]ven in the late 1980s the term was hardly used. . . . It has come from nowhere to be almost everywhere.

Thomas Friedman's recent books, *The World Is Flat* (2005) and *Hot, Flat and Crowded* (2008), are yet additional examples of the rapid changes that are occurring as globalization intensifies and as Friedman finds himself communicating instantly from Boston to Bangalore and elsewhere.

PHILOSOPHICAL CONSIDERATIONS

Humankind is evolving. We see it in our behavior, in our changing activities, in the globalization of knowledge, and in our relationships. When do we stop evolving? The Jesuit priest and psychic Pierre Teilhard de Chardin (1959, 1969b) argued that reaching the noosphere (or the Omega point) will mark the end of human evolution. Indeed, the noosphere could be easily interpreted as heaven for believers, although Teilhard made no such assertion. For others, perhaps Karl Marx's dictum, namely, "From each according to his abilities to each according to his needs," will mark the end of social evolution.

In the process of human evolution, our numbers have increased at an ever-increasing rate. This has been noted several times in earlier chapters. Now let us bring back a term we used earlier, **exponential growth**. Important to bear in mind is the fact that the number of "items" doubles in size in every doubling time. Two exponential concepts concern us as we look at the future of the world, namely, population, that is, human exponentialism, and noetic exponentialism.

We have already discussed **population exponentialism**; we referred to this in Chapter 9 as *doubling time*. For example, at a rate of increase of 2 percent per year, a population doubles its size every thirty-five years. We cannot continue to double the size of the world population for very much longer, given the earlier discussion about resources: "Human society is presently breaching the biophysical limits to growth, but this time on a global scale. As a result, the very qualities that once assured humanity's remarkable evolutionary success are threatening to do us in" (Rees, 2004: 11).

Exponentialism is present in many areas of human life. "Thought" is such an area. Our knowledge, be it technical, medical, or scientific, grows exponentially. This is a result of human thinking. Consider all that has evolved over recent generations, not only with regard to computers and the Internet but also with respect to medicine, the genome project, and stem-cell research. Indeed, more has happened in this recent generation (the last thirty to thirty-five years) than in earlier generations. This, too, is exponentialism.

We might, however, consider here the remarks made in 1981 by the biologist Lewis Thomas, namely, that "the greatest single achievement of science in this most scientifically productive of centuries is the discovery that we are profoundly ignorant; we know very little about nature and we understand even less. . . . There is no limit to the ingenuity of the nature of this planet" (quoted in Gellerman, 2003: 1). This suggests that care is necessary in integrating human technologies with those of the natural world. It warns us about the challenges of noetic (i.e., thought and intellectual) exponentialism.

Humans rely on the knowledge acquired in previous generations and build on it. What, then, will transpire in the next generation? Our consciousness may improve, but one wonders about the growing complexity that will also occur. Will humankind be able to adapt to an exponentially growing availability of knowledge? With increasing complexity, will we be able to adjust to these rapidly growing challenges? Already we note a generational gap in computer knowledge, with children of elementary school age often knowing more about computer basics than their parents and grandparents.

As both numbers and thoughts grow exponentially, what will happen to social interactions? We are already witnessing a significant decrease in our number of actual face-to-face interactions, especially as a result of the computer and, more recently, e-mail, the cell phone, and handheld electronic devices. On the pessimistic side, does this mean an end to social interactions? Will we lose the capability to simply "talk" to one another face-to-face? Will college professors, for example, be replaced by computerized lessons? On the more optimistic side, improved technology should allow us to communicate with more people, although much of that communication will be "artificial." Perhaps we are entering a new phase in the evolutionary process of humanity where, increasingly, social interactions will take place through ever-improving technologies. If so, we must all adapt to a new paradigm of communication.

Population exponentialism is also related to human evolution. For example, how are increasing numbers related to human interaction? Perhaps surprising to some demographers, Teilhard de Chardin had a serious concern about population growth. He wrote that

> after rising slowly until the seventeenth century, when it reached about 400 million, the earth's population began to shoot up again in an alarming fashion. It was 800 million by the end of the eighteenth century, 1,600 million by 1900 and over 2,000 million by 1940. At the present rate of increase, regardless of war and famine, we must expect a further 500 million in the next 25 years. This demographic explosion is closely connected with the development of a relatively unified and industrial earth. Clearly it gives rise to entirely new necessities and problems, both quantitative and qualitative. (Teilhard, 1969a: 242–243)

He then asked, "[H]ow are we to prevent this compression of mankind on the closed surface of the planet from passing the critical point beyond which any increase in numbers will mean famine and suffocation?" (p. 243).

Teilhard was clear in his concern about population growth interfering with the ultimate evolution of humankind. He anticipated the writings of the neo-Malthusians, some of whom we mentioned in Chapter 9 and elsewhere in this book. Indeed, it appears that he may well have been the first scholar to use the term *population explosion*.

So here we are now in 2010, faced with the challenge of adapting to both evolution and exponentialism. Will we be able to support 3 billion or more additional inhabitants on this small planet? These are questions that face us today, questions of which we must be aware if we are to handle the increasing complexity that comes with these types of exponentialism.

Furthermore, increasing complexity can be directly related to social interaction. What kind of social interaction can be expected in the kind of world foreseen for the twenty-first century? Virtually all social scientists note that without human social interaction, any group or any nation, for that matter, is bound to fail. Yet, as we continue into the twenty-first century, it is clear that actual face-to-face human interaction is declining. Electronic technology has contributed to this dangerous decline. This is not to say that these new technologies are not beneficial. The sociologist Robert Merton (1968) pointed out many years ago that there are manifest functions and there are latent functions. We know the manifest functions of these technologies, most of which are positive. But a latent function has been a serious decline in the real face-to-face interactions that must occur if the society is to prevail.

All of us must develop a "self" if we are to maintain some sort of identity. More than a hundred years ago, the social psychologist Charles Horton Cooley (1902) coined the term "looking glass self." To a certain extent, we develop a personal self by looking at how others react to us through social interaction. How does one develop a self if there is no longer a "looking glass?"

What can be done about this growing malaise, which could eventually get worse? Obviously, we cannot turn back the clock and bar all new technology. But perhaps we can all try just a little harder to talk more to friends and even strangers and, yes, even enemies. How much more difficult might this be with 9 billion people inhabiting the earth, rather than 6 billion?

In Chapter 1, we mentioned the phrase "demography is destiny." While journalists occasionally use it, some demographers tend to shy away from it. Upon reflection, however, there may be some truth to "demography is destiny," at least in the short term. For example, the world population will most likely grow to around 9 billion. That actual number may prove to be a little off the mark, but the population of the world will grow. Here in the United States, we can forecast the problems associated with the baby boom now reaching its retirement ages. In that sense, demography *is* destiny. In a recently published book, *The Post-American World*, the noted journalist Fareed Zakaria has concluded that "as the industrial world ages, India will continue to have lots of young people – in other words, workers. China faces a youth gap because of its successful 'one-child' policies; India faces a youth bulge because, ironically, its own family planning policies of the past failed. If demography is destiny, India's future is secure" (2008: 132).

In conclusion, in this final chapter, we have looked very broadly at the remaining years of the twenty-first century and the implications of a world population of around 9 billion. Some, if not all, of these musings may appear dismal to many readers. Certainly, we are facing monumental population and environmental challenges; we are witnessing enormous advances in technology. Both population and noetic exponentialism are becoming even more problematic. The era of the Industrial Revolution is long over; now we are experiencing the Information Revolution. Indeed, we are at the onset of dramatic transformations never before imagined. Population size and change are in the middle of this incredible phenomenon. In this looming era of globalization, we once again ask the question, "Will we all get along?" The answer depends on how we adapt to one another in this twenty-first century.

KEY TERMS

boomsters	exponential growth
cornucopians	population exponentialism
doomsters	

Glossary

abortifacients (Chap. 4): pharmaceutical medications that cause the termination of an early pregnancy by interfering with the viability of an already implanted **zygote**; intended to terminate an implanted zygote of up to forty-nine days gestation.

abortion (Chaps. 2, 4): termination of a pregnancy after the implantation of the fertilized egg in the uterine wall, but before the **fetus** is viable; includes both spontaneous and induced abortions.

abortion rate (Chap. 4): the number of abortions in a given year per 1,000 women age 15–44 (or sometimes 15–49).

acquired immune deficiency syndrome (AIDS) (Chap. 5): a disease of the human immune system caused by the human immunodeficiency virus (HIV); a person is said to have AIDS when the virus has weakened the immune system to the point that it is difficult to fight any type of infection.

adolescent fertility rate (Chap. 3): the age-specific fertility rate for women ages 15–19.

adrenogenital syndrome (AGS) (Chap. 8): characteristic of an XX fetus that receives an excessive amount of androgens; also know as **congenital adrenal hyperplasia (CAH).**

age composition (Chap. 1): the composition of a **population** with respect to age (i.e., the distribution of a population among age categories).

age curve of mortality (Chap. 5): a plot that shows the changing values of mortality over the life course, best reflected with data from the full schedule of age-specific death rates (ASDRs).

aged-dependency ratio (ADR or aged-DR) (Chap. 8): the ratio of persons 65 years of age and older to the working-age population (i.e., persons 15–64 years old), multiplied by 100; also known as **old-age dependency ratio.**

age heaping (Chap. 8): irregularities or inconsistencies in the age data for a **population** due to an overreporting of certain ages (e.g., those ending in 0 or 5) at the expense of other ages.

age/sex-specific rate (Chap. 3): a rate referring to the demographic behavior (e.g., regarding fertility), of a subset of the **population** categorized by age and sex.

age-specific death rate (ASDR) (Chap. 5): the number of deaths to persons in a specific age group per 1,000 persons in that age group; also known as "M" rate.

age-specific fertility rate (ASFR) (Chap. 3): births to women according to their age; ASFRs are usually calculated for women in each of the seven 5-year age groups of 15–19, 20–24, and so forth to 45–49.

aging of a population (Chap. 3): an increase in the average age of a population.

alien (Chap. 13): a person living in a country who is not a citizen of that country.

American Community Survey (ACS) (Chap. 2): a survey conducted continuously by the U.S. Census Bureau that gathers economic, social, demographic, and housing data.

amplexus reservatus (Chap. 4): see **coitus reservatus**.

androgen insensitivity syndrome (AIS) (Chap. 8): a condition of fetuses that are chromosomally male with genitals that are ambiguous or look more like a clitoris than a penis.

area of destination (Chap. 6): in the context of migration, the area where the migration ended.

area of origin (Chap. 6): in the context of migration, the area where the migration began.

assimilation (Chap. 12): the sociological concept that new groups to a society will take on the culture and values of the host society and gradually discard their own.

asylee (Chap. 13): a person forced to leave his or her country of birth or nationality and move to another country seeking legal refugee status.

at-risk population (Chap. 3): the set of people who could have produced a specified type of population event (e.g., a birth, a death, a migration); the at-risk population is usually the denominator of a rate.

average (Chap. 2): in statistical usage, the one value that best represents all cases in a set; one such measure is the *median*, the score above which and below which half of the cases fall; another is the arithmetic *mean*, which is the total of all scores divided by the number of cases.

baby boom (Chap. 1): the increase in fertility that occurred after World War II during the late 1940s and 1950s in most developed nations; more generally, a baby boom is any dramatic and extended increase in the birth rate.

baby bust (Chap. 1): the decrease in fertility that occurred during the 1970s in most developed nations; more generally, a baby bust is any dramatic and extended decline in the birth rate.

balancing equation (Chap. 9): the equation that shows that the size of the population of an area at the end of the time interval equals the size of the population at the beginning of the time interval plus the number of births and in-migrants, minus the number of deaths and out-migrants, occurring in the time interval; also sometimes known as the **population equation**.

basal body temperature (BBT) (Chap. 4): the lowest body temperature measured in the morning before walking and eating.

basal body temperature method (Chap. 4): the contraceptive method based on the principle that ovulation produces a rise in the basic metabolic rate, causing a corresponding increase in body temperature of between 0.3 and 0.9 degrees Centigrade (between 0.5 and 1.6 degrees Fahrenheit); the reading and recording of one's basal body temperature on a daily basis may thus assist in determining the time of ovulation.

biphasic pills (Chap. 4): type of birth control pills containing different amounts of progestin and/or estrogen to be ingested during the menstrual cycle.

birth (Chap. 2): "the complete expulsion or extraction from its mother of a product of conception, irrespective of the duration of pregnancy, which, after such separation, breathes or shows any other evidence of life, such as the beating of the heart, pulsation of the umbilical cord, or definite movement of voluntary muscles, whether or not the umbilical cord has been cut or the placenta is attached" (Shryock, Siegel, and Associates, 1976: 221).

birth control (Chap. 4): deliberate measures taken to delay or avoid a birth, including contraception, sterilization, and induced abortion.

birth control pill (Chap. 4): a contraceptive substance that is taken orally; also called an **oral contraceptive** and sometimes more generally "the pill."

birth order (Chap. 5): the numerical order in which a person is born (e.g., first born, third born); also known as **parity**.

boomsters (Chap. 14): persons who argue that **population** growth is a stimulus to social change; also known as a **cornucopians**.

bracero program (Chap. 7): an immigrant guest worker program established from 1942 to 1964, allowing laborers from Mexico to work temporarily in the United States.

census (Chap. 2): a complete count of every inhabitant in a given geographic entity at a specific point in time; censuses are typically conducted once every ten years or once every five years.

center of population (Chap. 11): the geographical point or location in a country at which an imaginary flat, weightless, and rigid map of the country would balance perfectly if all persons distributed in the population were of identical physical weight.

central city (Chap. 11): the largest city in a **metropolitan area** or **micropolitan area**.

cervical cap (Chap. 4): a small, thimble-shaped cup used to prevent conception by blocking the cervix.

childlessness (Chap. 3): the behavior of having no children, either voluntarily or involuntarily.

city (Chap. 11): a place that is incorporated and has been granted certain powers, as defined in its charter, by the state or country in which it is located.

closed population (Chap. 8): a population in which migration does not occur.

cohort (Chap. 1): a group of people who experience a major demographic event in the same time period (e.g., one- or five-year period); for example, a birth cohort (persons born in the same year or five-year period) or a marriage cohort (persons married in the same year or five-year period).

cohort analysis (Chap. 3): examination of a cohort's demographic behavior over time (e.g., children ever born to a specific birth cohort or marriage cohort of women); this is in contrast to an examination of a demographic event at one point in time (i.e., a period or **cross-sectional** analysis).

coitus interruptus (Chap. 4): also known as the "pull-out" contraceptive method; with this method, "the couple may have penile-vaginal intercourse until ejaculation is impending, at which time the male partner withdraws his penis from the vagina and away from the external genitalia of the female partner; the male must rely on his own sensations to determine when he is about to ejaculate" (Kowal, 2007: 338).

coitus reservatus (Chap. 4): the behavior in which the male enters his partner, does not ejaculate, and endeavors to remain at the plateau phase of sexual intercourse and excitement; also known as **amplexus reservatus**.

components of population growth (Chap. 1): the only events by which a population's size can be determined directly; these are births, deaths, and migrations.

concentration (Chap. 11): the clustering of **population** in areas of high population density surrounded by areas of low population density.

conception (Chaps. 3, 4): the fertilization of an ovum by a sperm, marking the beginning of pregnancy, or **gestation**.

condom (Chap. 4): a type of barrier to conception or disease, usually a male condom, a sheath designed to cover the penis during sexual intercourse; see also **female condom**.

congenital adrenal hyperplasia (CAH) (Chap. 8): see **adrenogenital syndrome (AGS)**.

contraception (Chaps. 3, 4): measures taken to prevent coitus from resulting in conception.

contraception injection (Chap. 4): an injection containing hormones to prevent pregnancy; typically administered by a health professional once every three months or so in the arm, buttocks, upper thigh, or abdomen.

contraceptive patch (Chap. 4): an adhesive device about the size of a 50-cent piece placed on the buttocks, arm, or stomach; it releases estrogen and progestin at a constant and continuous level each day to avoid pregnancy.

cornucopians (Chap. 14): see **boomsters**.

cross-sectional (Chap. 2): a one-point-in-time portrayal, for instance of the size, composition, and distribution of the **population**, as in a census.

crude birth rate (CBR) (Chap. 3): the number of live births in a given year per 1,000 total **population** at the midpoint of the given year.

crude death rate (CDR) (Chap. 5): the number of deaths in a given year per 1,000 total **population** at the midpoint of the given year.

cultural amalgamation (Chap. 12): the theory that a new society and culture result from the massive intermingling and intermarriage of two or more groups.

cultural separatism (Chap. 12): the theory that newcomers are socially isolated from the residents either through their own volition or through separatist practices of the host group.

Current Population Survey (CPS) (Chap. 2): a monthly nationwide survey conducted by the U.S. Bureau of the Census for the Bureau of Labor Statistics to gather labor-force data and other data about the civilian noninstitutional population.

death (Chap. 2): "the permanent disappearance of all evidence of life at any time after a live birth has taken place[;] a death can occur only after a live birth has occurred" (Shryock, Siegel, and Associates, 1976: 221).

deconcentration (Chap. 11): a shift in **population** distribution from the higher-density central cities to the lower-density areas located beyond the traditional city limits; or a shift from metropolitan to nonmetropolitan areas.

de facto population (Chap. 2): the population physically present in an area at a given moment in time, such as a **census** moment.

de jure population (Chap. 2): the population that usually, habitually, or legally lives in an area.

Demographic and Health Survey (DHS) (Chap. 2): a survey carried out mainly in developing countries that gathers data dealing with fertility, **population**, health, and nutrition.

demographic characteristics (Chap. 1): usually, the variables of age and sex.

demographic processes (Chap. 1): the three processes of **fertility**, **mortality**, and migration that account for any change in the size of a **population**.

demographic transition theory (DTT) (Chaps. 3, 9): generally, the theory that describes the transition from a situation in which **fertility** and **mortality** are high and the economy technologically less developed, to a situation in which fertility and mortality are low and controlled and the economy and technology are more developed.

demography (Chap. 1): the scientific study of the size, composition, and distribution of human **populations,** and their changes resulting from **fertility, mortality,** and migration.

dependency ratio (DR) (Chap. 8): the number of persons under 15 years of age and age 65 and older, divided by the number of persons age 15 to 64, multiplied by 100.

dependent variable (Chap 9): a variable whose value depends on one or more other variables; also known as the outcome variable or the Y variable.

developed countries (Chap. 9): those countries that have higher levels of per capita income and modernization than other countries; according to the United Nations, the developed countries of the world, sometimes referred to as "more developed" countries, usually include all the countries of North America and Europe (including Russia), along with Japan, Australia, and New Zealand.

developing countries (Chap. 9): those countries that have lower levels of per capita income and modernization than the **developed countries;** they include the 200 or so countries not classified as "developed" (see previous definition).

diaphragm (Chap. 4): a contraceptive device consisting of a flexible disk that covers the uterine cervix.

differential migration (Chap. 6): differences in migration behavior according to the demographic, social, and economic characteristics of the **population;** also known as **migration selectivity.**

divorce (Chap. 2): the marital status of currently nonmarried persons whose previous marriage has been legally dissolved.

doomsters (Chap. 14): persons with a dismal picture of the effects of **population** growth.

doubling time (Chap. 9): the number of years required for a **population** to double its size were it to maintain its present rate of growth; this will occur if the growth rate is positive; at a +1.0 percent rate of growth, the doubling time is 69.3 years.

dual labor market theory (Chap. 7): the theory that argues that migration stems from the demands of the economic structure of industrial societies.

echo effect (Chap. 8): the tendency toward repetition, one generation hence, of any span of abnormally high (or low) fertility, which is caused by the effect of the initial fertility level on the age structure.

ecological theory of migration (Chap. 6): the theory that focuses on characteristics of the **population** to predict the level of migration; individual attitudes and propensities do not play a role in this theory.

economic development (Chap. 11): the level of economic activity in a **population**; two common measures are 1) per capita income, and 2) per capita energy consumption.

edge cities (Chap. 11): new cities formed at the edges of metropolitan areas.

effectiveness (of family planning) (Chap. 4): 1) theoretical effectiveness, and 2) use effectiveness; theoretical effectiveness refers to the "efficaciousness" of the method when it is used exactly as prescribed; use effectiveness refers to the effectiveness of the method taking into account the fact that some users do not follow the directions perfectly, thus representing how effective the method is in "typical" use.

emergency contraceptive pill (ECP) (Chap. 4): a contraceptive medication taken after unprotected intercourse designed to prevent pregnancy by interfering with the implantation of the fertilized ovum in the uterine lining; also known as the **morning-after pill**.

emigrant (Chap. 7): one who migrates away from a country with the intention of establishing a permanent **residence** in another country.

emigration (Chap. 7): the permanent departure of people from one country to establish permanent **residence** in another country.

endogenous cause of death (Chap. 5): a cause of death that originates from within the body or genetic makeup; endogenous causes of infant death typically include "congenital malformations, chromosomal abnormalities, complications of delivery, as well as . . . low birth weight" (Pebley, 2003: 534).

endogenous conditions (Chap. 5): conditions (usually of infant death) caused by factors within the organism or system "such as congenital malformations, chromosomal abnormalities, and complications of delivery, as well as . . . low birthweight" (Pebley, 2003: 534).

endometrium (Chap. 4): lining of the uterus.

entries without inspection (EWIs) (Chap. 7): international migrants who during the process of migrating to the host country "avoid inspection by crossing borders clandestinely or . . . traveling with fraudulent documents, e.g., a falsified visa or counterfeit passport" (Armbrister, 2003: 512).

epidemic (Chap. 5): a disease that spreads and then disappears within a fairly short time, if it can be controlled. Where it appears in a large number of countries, it is sometimes called a **pandemic**.

epidemiological paradox (Chap. 5): the empirical finding that Mexican Americans have death rates of about the same magnitude as, and sometimes lower than, Anglos; also known as the Latino mortality paradox or **Hispanic paradox.**

epidemiological transition theory (ETT) (Chap. 5): the theory that focuses on the societal-wide decline of infectious disease and the rise of chronic degenerative causes of death.

Essure® procedure (Chap. 4): a female sterilization method performed using a local anesthesia; a tiny coil insert is introduced into each of the Fallopian tubes through the vagina and uterus; this causes the development of scar tissues over a three-month period, resulting in both tubes becoming sealed, in turn preventing pregnancy.

ethnic (Chap. 2): refers to group distinctions based on shared cultural origins.

ethnic enclave (Chap. 7): a community with distinctive cultural characteristics that can help migrants transition into life as immigrants by providing support and environments much like those in their mother countries.

exogenous cause of death (Chap. 5): a cause of death that is external to the body or genetic makeup; exogenous causes of infant death include infectious disease, accidents, and injuries.

exponential growth (Chap. 14): a constant rate of growth applied to a continuously growing **population.**

exurbs (Chap. 11): geographic areas beyond the beltways that circle the metropolitan areas.

failure rate (Chap. 4): the number of pregnancies per hundred person years of use of a birth control method.

family planning (Chaps. 3, 4): attempts by couples to regulate the number and spacing of their births.

family planning program (Chap. 13): a systematic effort, often government sponsored, to provide the information, supplies, and services for modern **fertility** control.

fecund (Chap. 3): capable of giving birth.

fecundity (Chaps. 1, 3): the biological capacity or capability of a man, a woman, or a couple to produce a live birth.

fecundity indeterminate (Chap. 3): referring to couples who meet the criteria for being **semifecund,** except that the wife sometimes reports douching "for cleanness only" soon after intercourse.

female condom (Chap. 4): a female-initiated barrier to conception and disease. The female condom is a sheath about the same length as a male **condom** (around 6.5 inches) with a flexible ring at each end; the inner ring at the closed end of the condom is inserted into the vagina and remains in place behind the pubic bone; the outer ring at the open end is soft and remains outside the vagina during sexual intercourse.

fertility (Chaps. 1, 3): the frequency with which a birth of either sex occurs in a **population**.

fertility awareness (Chap. 4): several "natural" family planning methods, such as the **Standard Days Method**, the Billings ovulation method, and others.

fetal death (Chap. 2): the disappearance of life prior to live birth.

fetal death rate (Chap. 5): the number of fetal deaths (i.e., stillbirths), divided by the sum of live births and still births in the year, times 1,000; also known as the **stillbirth rate**.

fetus (Chap. 2): the product of conception when it matures from being an embryo, after about twelve weeks (or three months) of intrauterine life.

floating migrant (Chap. 6): in China, an internal migrant who moves from one place to another without government authorization.

forced migration (Chap. 7): in the modern context, a kind of migration in which individuals are compelled by public authorities to move; includes flight or displacement and the creation of refugees (see **refugee**); historically, it would also include migration for slavery and involuntary indentured servitude.

foreign-born (Chap. 7): referring to a person residing in one country but born in another; the foreign-born **population** of a country is that portion of the population born outside that country.

general fertility rate (GFR) (Chap. 3): the number of live births per 1,000 women ages 15–44 (or 15–49) in a given year.

gentrification (Chap. 11): the migration of middle-class and other affluent peoples into the once poorer areas of cities.

geographic information systems (Chap. 5): mapping of areas used to analyze data.

geographic mobility (Chap. 6): any change of **residence** within a country, including both local movements and migration beyond specific boundaries.

germ theory (Chap. 5): the identification of the microorganism as the cause of many infectious diseases, particularly among infants and children.

gestation (Chap. 2): the carrying of a **fetus** in the uterus from conception to delivery.

green card holder (Chap. 7): an immigrant to the United States who has an identification card documenting that he or she is a legal permanent resident. Known officially as a United States Permanent Resident Card, the green card is no longer green but is called so owing to its color in earlier versions.

gross migration rate (GMR) (Chap. 6): the sum of migrants into and out of a given area in a given period of time, per 1,000 members of the **population**.

gross reproduction rate (GRR) (Chap. 3): the average number of daughters that would be born to a hypothetical group of 1,000 women if they completed their childbearing following the age-specific fertility rates of a given year; similar to the **total fertility rate** but does not include male births.

halving time (Chap. 9): the number of years required for the size of a **population** to become half as large were it to maintain its present rate of growth; this will occur if the growth rate is negative. At a −1.0 percent rate of growth, the halving time is 69.3 years.

healthy migrant effect (Chap. 5): the theory that states that the longevity advantage of Latino immigrants compared to other minority groups (i.e., African Americans) occurs because many Latinos in the United States were born elsewhere, and that migration is known to be selective of persons in better physical and mental health.

Hispanic paradox (Chap. 5): see **epidemiological paradox**.

histogram (Chap 8.): a graphical representation of tabulated data frequencies shown as bars.

hormonal IUD (Chap. 4): an intrauterine (contraceptive) device of flexible plastic, often shaped like a "T," that contains progestin, which usually blocks ovulation and thickens the woman's cervical mucus.

household (Chap. 2): a group of individuals who reside together, whether related or not.

human ecological theory (Chap. 3): a macro-level explanation of **population** growth and decline.

human immunodeficiency virus (HIV) (Chap. 3): the virus that causes AIDS; it destroys the T cells or CD4 cells that the body needs to fight infections.

hypothetical cohort (Chap. 3): an imaginary set of people traced through a series of specified risks in order to detail the cumulative impact of those risks.

hysterectomy (Chap. 4): the surgical removal of the uterus; it may also involve the additional removal of the Fallopian tubes and the ovaries.

hysteroscopic sterilization (Chap. 4): see **Essure® procedure**.

illegal immigrant (Chap. 7): a person who is residing in a country illegally through entry without inspection, as a visa abuser, or through the use of fraudulent documents; more appropriately called an unauthorized or undocumented resident.

immigrant (Chap. 7): a person who enters a country with the intention of residing there permanently.

immigration (Chap. 7): the migration of people into a new country from any other country for the purpose of establishing **residence** there.

independent variable (Chap. 9): a variable that is believed to have an effect on the **dependent variable**; also known as an X variable and as a co-variate.

induced abortion (Chap. 2): a pregnancy that has been terminated by human intervention with an intent other than to produce a live birth; an induced early fetal death, legal or illegal; specifically, the premature expulsion of the **fetus** at a time before it is viable of sustaining life.

infant mortality rate (IMR) (Chap. 5): the number of deaths among infants under one year of age per 1,000 live births in the same year.

infecundity (Chap. 3): the physiological inability to produce a live birth.

in-migration (Chap. 1): the residential migration of persons into a specific political subdivision (e.g., a county or state) from another subdivision of the same country.

in-migration rate (IMR) (Chap. 6): the number of persons migrating into an area usually during a one- or five-year time interval, divided by the **population** of the area at the start of the interval, times 1,000.

internal migration (Chap. 6): the geographical movement within a country for a permanent change of **residence** that involves the crossing of a county boundary.

International Classification of Diseases (ICD) (Chap. 5): the classification of diseases developed by the World Health Organization; the present classification (the Tenth Revision) was adapted in 1992 and categorizes causes of death under twenty-two major headings.

international migration (Chaps. 6, 7): migration between countries.

intersex (Chap. 8): referring to people with atypical combinations of physical attributes (e.g., chromosomes, gonads, genitalia), usually used to distinguish males from females.

intrauterine device (IUD) (Chap. 4): a small device that is inserted directly into the uterus to prevent conception.

Jacob's syndrome (Chap. 8): characteristic of a person born with an extra (i.e., third) sex chromosome, in the configuration of XYY.

keyhole vasectomy (Chap. 4): alternate term for **no-scalpel vasectomy**, a male sterilization procedure.

Klinefelter's syndrome (Chap. 8): characteristic of a person born with an extra (i.e., third) sex chromosome, in the configuration of XXY.

labor force (Chap. 2): the portion of the **population** that is employed or is actively seeking work.

less-developed countries (LDCs) (Chap. 3): countries with the lowest indicators of socioeconomic and human development, as classified by the United Nations.

life expectancy (Chaps. 2, 5): the average number of years yet to be lived by people attaining a given age, according to a given **life table**; it is the value given by the value of "e," usually the last, column of data in the life table.

life span (Chap. 5): the maximum number of years a person can expect to live; the numerical age limit of human life.

life table (Chap. 5): a statistical table used for tracing the cumulative effect of a schedule of age/sex specific death rates over a life cycle for a **hypothetical cohort**.

live birth (Chap. 2): "the complete expulsion or extraction from its mother of a product of conception, irrespective of the duration of pregnancy, which, after such separation, breathes or shows any other evidence of life, such as the beating of the heart, pulsation of the umbilical cord, or definite movement of voluntary muscles, whether or not the umbilical cord has been cut or the placenta is attached" (Shryock, Siegel, and Associates, 1976: 221).

local movement (Chap. 6): the short-distance change of **residence** within the same community that does not involve crossing a county jurisdictional boundary.

longevity (Chap. 5): the length of an individual life; collectively, average length of life of a **cohort**.

long-form questionnaire (Chap. 2): census questionnaire containing detailed questions regarding education, occupation, income, mobility, and several other topics; used in the 2000 census and administered roughly to one in six households.

male sterilization (Chap. 4): a surgical procedure in which a portion of the spermatic duct is cut, tied, and removed; also known as **vasectomy**.

Malthusian checks (Chap. 9): The two kinds of controls, preventive checks and positive checks, argued by Thomas Malthus as tending to check **population** growth. The major preventive check is "moral restraint"; the main positive checks are war, famine, and pestilence.

Malthusianism (Chap. 9): the theory or belief, based on the writing of Thomas Malthus, that if left unchecked, the **population** tends to outstrip the means for its subsistence.

maternal death (Chap. 5): "the death of a woman while pregnant or within 42 days of termination of pregnancy, irrespective of the duration or site of pregnancy, from any cause related to or aggravated by the pregnancy or its management, but not from accidental or incidental causes" (Maine and Stamas, 2003: 628).

maternal mortality ratio (MMR) (Chap. 5): deaths in a year to women dying as a result of complications of pregnancy, childbirth, and the puerperium (the condition immediately following childbirth), per 100,000 live births occurring in the year.

median age (Chap. 5): the age that divides a **population** into two equal groups, half younger and half older.

megalopolis (Chap. 11): a popular term referring to any densely populated social and economic area encompassing two or more contiguous metropolitan areas and the increasingly urbanized space between them.

melting pot (Chap. 12): the theory stating that the host and immigrant groups share each other's cultures and, in the process, a new group emerges.

menarche (Chap. 3): the beginning of the female reproductive, or childbearing, period signaled by the first menstrual flow.

menopause (Chap. 3): the end of the female reproductive, or childbearing, period signaled by the termination of menstruation.

mestizo (Chap. 12): a person of mixed blood, the result of racial blending that occurred in nineteenth-century Latin America between the Spanish newcomers and indigenous groups.

metropolis (Chap. 11): a very large and/or important city.

metropolitan area (Chap. 11): a large concentration of **population** usually consisting of a **central city** (or cities) of at least 50,000 people and the surrounding settlements.

metropolitanization (Chap. 11): the relative growth of the **metropolitan area** population, compared with other populations.

metropolitan statistical area (metro area or MSA) (Chap. 11): a geographic area containing a large **population** nucleus, together with adjacent communities with considerable economic and social integration with the core.

micropolitan area (Chap. 11): a geographic area that contains at least one urban cluster of between 10,000 and 49,999 people.

migration counterstream (Chap. 6): a body of migrants, smaller in size than its corresponding **migration stream**, going in the opposite direction during the same time interval.

migration efficiency ratio (MER) (Chap. 6): the number of gross migrants divided by the number of net migrants, multiplied by 100.

migration network theory (Chap. 7): the theory that focuses on networks, such as interpersonal ties that connect migrants, former migrants, potential migrants, and nonmigrants in the origin and destination countries.

migration pull (Chap. 6): attraction to a place of destination, for a migrant.

migration push (Chap. 6): repulsion from a place of origin, for a migrant.

migration selectivity (Chap. 6): selection on the basis of age, race, sex, socioeconomic status, and other migration characteristics.

migration stream (Chap. 6): a body of migrants departing from a common area of origin and arriving at a common area of destination during a specified time interval; compare with **migration counterstream.**

minilaparotomy (Chap. 4): surgical sterilization procedure performed on a woman a few days after she has delivered her baby.

mini-pill (Chap. 4): oral contraceptive containing only progestin.

miscarriage (Chap. 2): the spontaneous or accidental termination of fetal life that occurs early in pregnancy.

monophasic (Chap. 4): type of birth control pill that provides a constant amount of estrogen and progestin every day.

morbidity (Chap. 1): the prevalence of sickness in a **population.**

morning-after pill (Chap. 4): a contraceptive medication taken after unprotected intercourse that is designed to prevent pregnancy by interfering with the implantation of the fertilized ovum in the uterine lining; also know as the **emergency contraceptive pill.**

mortality (Chap. 1): the frequency with which death occurs in a **population.**

mortality reversal (Chap. 5): the increase in mortality after a **population** has experienced a decrease in mortality.

mortality transition (Chap. 5): that part of the demographic transition in which mortality declines from a high, variable, and relatively uncontrolled level to a low, constant, and controlled level; see **demographic transition theory.**

National Survey of Family Growth (NSFG) (Chap. 2): nationally representative U.S. multistage survey of male and female respondents ages 15–44 that collects information on family life and reproductive health.

natural increase (Chap. 1): the change between two points in time in the number of births minus the number of deaths in a **population,** also known as reproductive change and as vital change.

naturalized citizen (Chap. 7): a permanent **immigrant** who has been granted citizenship by the country into which he or she immigrated.

natural log (Chap. 9): the natural logarithm of a number is the power to which e (an irrational constant approximately equal to 2.7182) would have to be raised to equal the desired number; thus, the natural log of 2 is 0.693; i.e., $e^{0.693} = 2$, or $2.7182^{0.693} = 2$.

neoclassical economic theory of international migration (Chap. 7): the theory that migration is based on individual cost–benefit decisions to maximize expected incomes through geographic movement.

neo-Malthusianism (Chap. 9): belief (according to Thomas Malthus) in the tendency for populations, if left unchecked, to outstrip the means for their subsistence; also advocacy (but not by Malthus) of the promotion of birth control as a solution to this dilemma.

neonatal mortality rate (NMR) (Chap. 5): deaths to babies of 28 days of age or less, per 1,000 live births.

net international migration (Chap. 7): immigration minus **emigration**.

net migration rate (NMR) (Chap. 6): the number of persons moving into an area minus the number of persons moving out of that area, divided by the **population** size of the area, times 1,000.

net reproduction rate (NRR) (Chap. 3): the average number of daughters that would be born to a female birth cohort if the mothers completed their childbearing years subject to the schedules of age-specific fertility and mortality rates of a given place and time.

no-scalpel vasectomy (Chap. 4): a male sterilization procedure in which a small opening is made in the scrotum with local anesthetic, and then, as with the traditional **vasectomy** procedure, the tubes of the vas deferens are lifted from the scrotal sac, cut, tied, or sometimes cauterized, and then placed back into the scrotum. Because the scrotal skin opening is so small, it may not need to be closed with sutures; also known as **keyhole vasectomy**.

Nuva Ring® (Chap. 4): a foreign body placed in the uterus to prevent pregnancy that contains estrogen and progestin. It is a brand of **vaginal ring**.

obituary (Chap. 5): an announcement or story in a newspaper of a person's death that usually includes a brief biographical sketch.

old-age dependency ratio (ADR or Aged-DR) (Chaps. 3, 8): the ratio of persons 65 years of age and older to the working-age **population** (i.e., persons 15–64 years old), multiplied by 100; also known as **aged-dependency ratio**.

oral contraceptive (the pill) (Chap. 4): a pill containing both estrogen and progestin that is used to prevent conception primarily by preventing ovulation.

out-migration (Chap. 1): the residential migration of persons out of a specific political subdivision (e.g., a county or state) into another subdivision of the same country.

out-migration rate (OMR) (Chap. 6): the number of persons migrating from an area usually during a one- or five-year time interval, divided by the **population** size of the area at the start of the time interval, times 1,000.

pandemic (Chap. 5): an **epidemic** spreading throughout a large area, such as a continent, or even the world, and affecting a very large portion of the **population**.

ParaGard® IUD (Chap. 4): a flexible plastic (contraceptive) device shaped like a "T" with copper wire twisted about it, placed into the uterus to prevent conception.

parent support ratio (PSR) (Chap. 8): the ratio of the number of persons 80 years of age and older per 100 persons ages 50–64: meant to represent the relative burden of the oldest-old **population,** i.e., the elderly parents, on the population 50–64, i.e., the children of the elderly parents.

parity (Chap. 5): the number of times a woman has given birth; also refers to **birth order.**

parturition (Chap. 3): the act or process of giving birth.

perinatal mortality rate (PeMR) (Chap. 5): the sum of the number of still-births and the number of deaths to babies age 0 to 7 days, divided by the sum of the number of live births and stillbirths in the year, multiplied by 1,000; also known as pregnancy wastage.

period perspective (Chap. 3): the viewing or studying of a **population** process cross-sectionally as the combined experience of population groups in a specified short period of time, normally one year.

period rate (Chap. 3): a rate based on behavior occurring at a particular point or period in time, such as one year; also known as a **cross-sectional** rate.

pluralism (Chap. 12): the concept that the host society allows its constituted ethnic groups to develop, each emphasizing its own cultural heritage.

polygyny (Chap. 3): the marital union of a male to two or more females simultaneously.

population (Chap. 1): a set of people residing in a given area at a specific time.

population aging (Chap. 8): the increase in the proportion of the population that is old, usually defined as persons of ages 60 and older, or as persons 65 and older.

population density (Chap. 11): the relationship between the size of a population and the size of the area in which it lives, usually expressed as the number of persons per square mile (or kilometer) of land.

population equation (Chap. 9): see **balancing equation.**

population explosion (Chap. 1): a dramatic increase in population size.

population exponentialism (Chap. 14): see **doubling time.**

population implosion (Chap. 11): a dramatic decrease in population size.

population momentum (Chap. 3): the growth of a population attributable to the high proportion of people in the childbearing years; the growth continues to occur even after replacement-level **fertility** has been attained. A negative version appears when the proportion of people in their childbearing years is proportionally small.

population policy (Chap. 13): a deliberately constructed arrangement or program "through which governments influence, directly or indirectly, demographic change" (Demeny, 2003: 752); measures instituted by governments that influence demographic behavior.

population projection: (Chaps. 8, 9): a systematic calculation of the future population size of an area based on an assumed level of population growth and/or the assumed levels of **fertility, mortality,** and migration.

population pyramid (Chap. 8): a conventional form of bar graph representing the age/sex structure of a population at a particular point in time.

population register (Chap. 2): the continuous recording of population events for individual members of a population in such a way that a current reading of all members' demographic characteristics is available.

positive checks (Chap. 9): in Malthusian theory, the checks on **population** growth operating through increases in the death rate; these include war, famine, and pestilence.

postneonatal mortality rate (PMR) (Chap. 5): deaths to babies between the ages of 29 days and 1 year, per 1,000 live births.

potential support ratio (PSR) (Chap. 13): a measure that represents the extent that people of working age can support the older population.

preventive checks (Chap. 9): in Malthusian theory, those checks on **population** growth operating through the decrease in the birth rate; these include delayed marriage and abstinence.

projection (Chap. 9): see **population projection.**

pronatalist: (Chap. 13): referring to advocating an increase in fertility.

proximate determinants (Chap. 3): the most immediate causes of a **population** process such as **fertility;** those biological and behavioral variables that are "intermediate" or "between" the broad social factors that influence fertility, and fertility per se.

quinacrine sterilization (QS) (Chap. 4): nonsurgical female sterilization in which a woman receives treatments of tiny quinacrine pellets placed into the uterus; the pellets dissolve and flow into the openings of the Fallopian tubes and cause a minor swelling resulting in scar tissues that close the tubes.

ratio (Chap. 2): comparison of the sizes of two categories in a series by dividing one by the other.

refugee (Chap. 7): a person who has immigrated into a new country in response to strong pressure because his or her continued stay in the country of origin may have exposed that person to danger of persecution.

registration (Chap. 2): the recording in a register of **population** events on a continuous basis for all members of a population.

registration systems (Chap. 2): continuous recordings of a **population's** demographic events (births and deaths and, in some places, migrations) as they occur.

remigration (Chap. 7): the **international migration** of persons back to their original country of origin at some time after their **emigration** from that country.

replacement-level fertility (Chap. 3): the level of fertility at which a **cohort** of women, on average, has only enough children to replace themselves in the **population**, at current **mortality** levels; in low-mortality populations, replacement fertility equals around 2.1 children per woman.

reproduction (Chap. 3): the production of female births (there is no demographic term to refer to the production of only male births); analogous to **fertility**, but only refers to female births.

residence (Chap. 6): the location with which an individual is affiliated, where he or she usually or habitually lives.

residential mobility (Chap. 6): the movement within and across geographic units that includes not only migration but also residential moves not involving migration (e.g., a residential move within a county); all migrations are residential movements, but not all residential movements are migrations.

return migration (Chap. 6): the migration within a country of persons back to their area of origin at some time after their initial **out-migration**.

rhythm method (Chap. 4): the method of contraception based on abstinence from coitus around the period when a woman is believed to be ovulating.

Rule of Seventy (Chap. 9): a formula based on the natural logarithm of 2 (**doubling time**) to determine the length of time before the **population** would double its size, if its birth and death rates did not change and the difference between the two was positive.

salmon bias (Chap. 5): the theory stating that some Mexican Americans return to Mexico at old ages and, thus, their deaths are not counted in U.S. statistics; also known as the return migrant effect.

semifecund (Chap. 3): descriptive of couples who have married or cohabited for a relatively long time without using contraception but have not conceived.

senior boom (Chap. 10): babies born between 1950 and 1960 who will be reaching retirement age in about 2020 to 2030.

sex composition (Chap. 1): the composition of a **population** with regard to sex.

sex ratio (Chap. 1): the number of males in a **population** per 100 females.

sex ratio at birth (SRB) (Chaps. 3, 8): the number of males of age 0 divided by the number of females of age 0, times 100.

single (Chap. 4): the never-married category of marital status.

specific rate (Chap. 3): any rate for some subset of the **population** (e.g., an age group) rather than for the total population.

stable population (Chap. 3): a hypothetical population with an unchanging birth and death rate, rate of growth, and age composition.

stable population theory (Chaps. 5, 8): the theory stating that a population closed to migration that experiences constant schedules of age-specific fertility and mortality rates will develop a constant age distribution and will grow at a constant rate, irrespective of its initial age distribution.

Standard Days Method (Chap. 4): the contraceptive method based on the principle that "women with regular menstrual cycles lasting 26–32 days can prevent pregnancy by avoiding unprotected intercourse on days eight through 19" (Gribble, 2003: 188).

standardization (Chap. 5): a statistical technique that controls for the effects of factors (e.g., age and/or sex) that may contaminate the comparison of populations with respect to demographic processes such as **mortality** and **fertility**.

stationary population (Chap. 8): a stable population in which the birth rate equals the death rate, resulting in no change in the size of the population, in the absence of migration.

stem pessary (Chap. 4): antecedent form of the modern intrauterine device, developed in the late 1860s.

sterility (Chap. 3): infecundity.

sterilization (Chap. 4): an operation or procedure performed on either a male or a female to prevent conception.

stillbirth (Chaps. 2, 5): a late fetal death at 20 to 28 weeks or more of gestation.

stillbirth rate (SBR) (Chap. 5): number of miscarriages or fetal deaths (stillbirths) divided by the total number of live births plus stillbirths, times 1,000.

subdermal contraceptive implant (Chap. 4): a device consisting of several small silicone capsule-type rods, each containing progestin, placed subdermally, usually in a woman's upper arm, to prevent conception.

suburbanization (Chap. 11): the process of **population** movement from the core city to the fringe area around and nearby the core city.

surgical sterilization (Chap. 4): a procedure performed on either males or females to prevent conception; for females, known as **tubal ligation** (tying of the tubes); for males, known as **vasectomy**.

Taeuber paradox (Chap. 5): the paradox, attributed to demographer Conrad Taeuber, that a cure found for one degenerative disease will provide the opportunity for death to occur from another.

theoretical effectiveness (of a contraceptive) (Chap. 4): degree of effectiveness that would occur with "perfect" use of the contraceptive.

total dependency ratio (Total DR) (Chap. 8): aged-dependency ratio plus **youth-dependency ratio**.

total fertility rate (TFR) (Chap. 3): a usually **cross-sectional** estimate of the number of births that a hypothetical group of 1,000 women would have during their reproductive lifetime, if their childbearing followed the age-specific fertility rates for a given period; alternately, a **cohort** TFR is the actual fertility of a real (marriage or birth) cohort of 1,000 women, i.e., the actual number of children they have in their childbearing years.

transgender (Chap. 8): referring to people who live as the opposite sex, whether or not they have had sex-change surgery.

triphasic (Chap. 4): type of birth control pills containing three different doses of hormones to be administered throughout the menstrual cycle.

tubal ligation (Chap. 4): female sterilization consisting of cutting, tying, and removing a portion of the oviduct (i.e., the Fallopian tubes).

typical use (of a contraceptive) (Chap. 4): broadly defined as the actual use in practice of a contraceptive; thus, it does not refer to the "inherent efficacy of a contraceptive method when used perfectly, correctly and consistently" (Kost et al., 2008: 11).

unauthorized immigrant (Chap. 7): an international migrant residing in the host country of destination who is not a citizen of the host country and has not been admitted for permanent **residence,** nor is "in a set of specific authorized temporary statuses permitting longer-term residence and work" (Passel, 2006: 1).

United Nations Fund for Population Activities (UNFPA) (Chap. 13): a major source of funding for population initiatives in developing countries, created in 1969.

urban agglomeration (Chap. 11): according to the United Nations, an urban area of at least 1 million inhabitants, including all inhabitants in the surrounding territory living in urban levels of residential density.

urban area (Chap. 11): a **central city,** or cities, and the surrounding closely settled territory.

urban cluster (UC) (Chap. 11): a densely settled core of blocks and block groups, along with adjacent densely settled surrounding blocks that together encompass a **population** of at least 2,500 people but fewer than 50,000 people.

urban growth (Chap. 11): an increase in the number of people living in urban areas.

urbanism (Chap. 11): a lifestyle characteristic of urban places.

urbanization (Chap. 11): the process of change in the proportion of the total **population** living in urban places.

urbanized area (UA) (Chap. 11): a densely settled core of census blocks and block groups that meet minimum **population** density requirements, along with adjacent densely settled surrounding census blocks that together encompass a population of 50,000 people.

urban places (Chap. 11): densely populated places; in the United States, incorporated and unincorporated places of 2,500 or more inhabitants.

use effectiveness (of a contraceptive) (Chap. 4): measure of the effectiveness of a method, taking into account the fact that some users do not follow directions perfectly or carefully, or may not use the method all the time. Use effectiveness data reflect how effective the method is in "typical" use.

vaginal contraceptives (Chap. 4): foams, jellies, or pastes that are inserted into the vagina to prevent conception by chemically immobilizing or destroying the sperm.

vaginal ring (Chap. 4): a thin, transparent, flexible device similar in content to the combined **oral contraceptive** pill, which contains both estrogen and progestin that are released on a continuous basis into the woman's body to prevent conception.

vasectomy (Chap. 4): male sterilization involving the surgical excision of a part of the vas deferens.

vital statistics (Chap. 2): the processed results of registrations of vital events; strictly speaking, vital events are deaths and births only, but the term often is broadened to include other **population** events such as marriages and divorces.

wealth flows theory (Chaps. 3, 9): the theory stating that if the wealth flows run from children to their parents, parents will want to have larger families; if the flow is from parents to children, they will want smaller families, or maybe even no children.

Whipple's method (WM) (Chap. 8): an index of age data of a **population** designed to reflect preference for the terminal digits of "0" and "5."

white flight (Chap. 11): the massive **out-migration** to the suburbs from the core cities of the mostly white middle and upper classes.

withdrawal (Chap. 4): a birth control method that consists of removing the penis from the vagina before ejaculation; also known as **coitus interruptus**.

World Fertility Survey (WFS) (Chap. 2): one of a number of sample surveys conducted between 1974 and 1986 in 62 mainly **developing countries**, representing 40 percent of the world's **population**, to gather data on reproductive behavior and related social and psychological indicators.

world systems theory of migration (Chap. 7): the theory arguing that international migration is the natural result of the globalization of the market economy.

youth-dependency ratio (YDR or Youth-DR) (Chap. 8): the number of persons under 15 years of age, divided by the number of persons age 15 to 64, multiplied by 100.

zero international migration (Chap. 7): the equal number of persons immigrating into a country in comparison to the number emigrating from the country.

zygote (Chaps. 3, 4): a fertilized egg, produced when the sperm of a male and the egg of a female are united.

References

Abraido-Lanza, A. F., B. P. Dohrenwend, D. S. Ng-Mak, and J. B. Turner. 1999. "The Latino Mortality Paradox: A Test of the 'Salmon Bias' and Health Migrant Hypotheses." *American Journal of Public Health* 89: 1543–1548.

Adams, Willi Paul. 1983. "A Dubious Host." *Wilson Quarterly* (New Year's): 110.

Aird, John S. 1972. "Population Policy and Demographic Prospects in the People's Republic of China." In *People's Republic of China: An Economic Assessment*, a Compendium of Papers Submitted to the Joint Economic Committee, Congress of the United States, 18 May (92nd Congress, 2nd Session). Washington, DC: U.S. Government Printing Office.

Aird, John S. 1990. *Slaughter of the Innocents: Coercive Birth Control in China.* Washington, DC: AEI Press.

Anderson, Margo. 2003. "Census." In Paul Demeny and Geoffrey McNicoll (eds.), *Encyclopedia of Population*, I: 122–126. New York: Macmillan Reference USA.

Anderson, Robert N. 1999. *U.S. Decennial Life Tables for 1989–91.* Vol. 1, no. 4: *United States Life Tables Eliminating Certain Causes of Death.* Hyattsville, MD: National Center for Health Statistics.

Archdeacon, Thomas J. 1990. "Melting Pot or Cultural Pluralism: Changing Views of American Ethnicity." *Revue Europeene des Migrations Internationelles* 6: 1–18.

Arias, Elizabeth. 2006. "United States Life Tables, 2003." *National Vital Statistics Reports* 54 (14).

Armbrister, Adria N. 2003. "Immigration, Unauthorized." In Paul Demeny and Geoffrey McNicoll (eds.), *Encyclopedia of Population*, II: 512–515. New York: Macmillan Reference USA.

Arnold, F., and Z. Liu. 1986. "Sex Preference, Fertility, and Family Planning in China." *Population and Development Review* 12: 221–246.

Arriaga, Eduardo E., and Associates. 1994. *Population Analysis with Microcomputers.* Vol. 1: *Presentation of Techniques.* Washington, DC: U.S. Bureau of the Census.

Ashford, Lori S. 2006. "How HIV and AIDS Affect Populations." *Population Reference Bureau BRIDGE Policy Briefs* (July).

Ashford, Lori S. 2008. *Ensuring a Wide Range of Family Planning Choices.* Washington, DC: Population Reference Bureau.

Ashton, Basil, Kenneth Hill, Alan Piazza, and Robin Zeitz. 1984. "Famine in China, 1958–61." *Population and Development Review* 10: 613–645.

Bachi, R. 1951. "The Tendency to Round Off Age Returns: Measurement and Correction." *Bulletin of the International Statistical Institute* (*Proceedings of the 27th Session, Calcutta*) 33: 195–221.

Badenhorst, L. T., and Edward Higgins. 1962. "Fecundity of White Women in Johannesburg." *Population Studies* 15: 279–290.

Balinski, Michael L., and H. Peyton Young. 1982. *Fair Representation: Meeting the Ideal of One Man, One Vote.* New Haven, CT: Yale University Press.

Balter, Michael. 2006. "The Baby Deficit." *Science* 312 (5782): 1894–1897.

Banister, Judith. 1992. "China's Changing Mortality." In Dudley L. Poston, Jr., and David Yaukey (eds.), *The Population of Modern China*, 163–223. New York: Plenum.

Banister, Judith. 2004. "Shortage of Girls in China Today." *Journal of Population Research* 21: 19–34.

Barrett, R. E. 1994. *Using the 1990 U.S. Census for Research.* Thousand Oaks, CA: Sage.

Barry, John M. 2004. *The Great Influenza: The Epic Story of the Deadliest Plague in History.* New York: Viking.

Bartlett, Albert A. 2004. "Thoughts on Long-Term Energy Supplies: Scientists and the Silent Lie." *Physics Today* (August 27). http://pppl.gov/energy_population±pt_0704.pdf (accessed November 23, 2008).

Bartlett, John. 1968. *Bartlett's Familiar Quotations.* 14th ed. Boston: Little, Brown.

Baumle, Amanda K., D'Lane R. Compton, and Dudley L. Poston, Jr. 2009. *Same Sex Partners: The Demography of Sexual Orientation.* Albany: SUNY Press.

Baumle, Amanda K., and Dudley L. Poston, Jr. 2004. "Apportioning the House of Representatives in 2000: The Effects of Alternative Policy Scenarios." *Social Science Quarterly* 85: 578–603.

Bean, Frank D., Edward E. Telles, and B. Lindsay Lowell. 1987. "Undocumented Migration to the United States: Perceptions and Evidence." *Population and Development Review* 13: 671–690.

Bean, Frank D., and Marta Tienda. 1987. *The Hispanic Population of the United States.* New York: Russell Sage Foundation.

Becker, Stan, Youssef Waheeb, Bothaina El-Deeb, Nagwa Khallaf, and Robert Black. 1996. "Estimating the Completeness of Under-5 Death Registration in Egypt." *Demography* 33: 329–339.

"Before the Exodus." 2008. *The Economist* 387 (April 26): 101.

Bernstein, E. L. 1940. "Who Was Condom?" *Human Fertility* 5: 172–175, 186.

Biggar, Jeanne C. 1979. "The Sunning of America: Migration to the Sunbelt." *Population Bulletin* 34 (March).

Billari, Francesco C. 2004. "Choices, Opportunities, and Constraints of Partnership, Childbearing, and Parenting: The Patterns in the 1990s." Paper presented at the European Population Forum 2004: Population Challenges and Policy Responses, Geneva.

Billings, Evelyn, John J. Billings, J. B. Brown, and H. G. Burger. 1972. "Symptoms and Hormonal Changes Accompanying Ovulation." *Lancet* 1: 282–284.

Billings, Evelyn, and Ann Westmore. 2000. *The Billings Method: Controlling Fertility without Drugs or Devices*. Toronto: Life Cycle Books.

Billings, John J. 1984. *The Ovulation Method: Natural Family Planning*. 5th ed. Collegeville, MN: Liturgical Press.

Biraben, Jean-Noel. 2003. "The Rising Numbers of Humankind." *Population & Societies* 394: 1–4.

Black, Dan A., Gary Gates, Seth G. Sanders, and Lowell J. Taylor. 2000. "Demographics of the Gay and Lesbian Population in the United States: Evidence from Available Systematic Data Sources." *Demography* 37: 139–154.

Black, I. 1963. "American Labour and Chinese Immigration." *Past and Present* 25: 59–76.

Bogue, Donald J. 1969. *Principles of Demography*. New York: Wiley.

Bogue, Donald J. 1985. *The Population of the United States*. New York: The Free Press.

Bogue, Donald J., and James A. Palmore. 1964. "Some Empirical and Analytic Relations among Demographic Fertility Measures, with Regression Models for Fertility Estimation." *Demography* 1: 316–338.

Bongaarts, John. 1975. "Why High Birth Rates Are So Low?" *Population and Development Review* 1: 289–296.

Bongaarts, John. 1978. "A Framework for the Proximate Determinants of Fertility." *Population and Development Review* 4: 105–132.

Bongaarts, John. 1982. "The Fertility-Inhibiting Effects of the Intermediate Fertility Variables." *Studies in Family Planning* 13: 179–189.

Bongaarts, John. 2006. "How Long Will We Live?" *Population and Development Review* 32: 605–628.

Bongaarts, John, and Robert G. Potter. 1983. *Biology and Fertility Behavior: An Analysis of the Proximate Determinants*. New York: Academic Press.

Bonilla-Silva, Eduardo. 2006. *Racism without Racists: Color-Blind Racism and the Persistence of Racial Inequality in the United States*. Lanhan, MD: Rowman & Littlefield.

Borjas, George J. 2003. "Benefits and Cost of Immigration." In Paul Demeny and Geoffrey McNicoll (eds.), *Encyclopedia of Population*, II: 509–512. New York: Macmillan Reference USA.

Borjas, George J., Richard B. Freeman, and Lawrence F. Katz. 1997. "How Much Do Immigration and Trade Affect Labor Market Outcomes?" *Brookings Papers on Economic Activity*: 1–67.

Borrie, W. D. 1973. "The Place of Demography in the Development of the Social Sciences." In International Population Conference, Liege, 73–93. Liege: International Union for the Scientific Study of Population.

Boserup, Ester. 1965. *The Conditions of Agricultural Growth*. Chicago: Aldine.

Boserup, Ester. 1981. *Population and Technological Change: A Story of Long-Term Trends*. Chicago: University of Chicago Press.

Bourne, Randolph S. 1916. "Trans-national America." *Atlantic Monthly* 118 (July).

Bouvier, Leon F. 1965. "A Genealogical Approach to the Study of French-Canadian Fertility." *Sociological Analysis* 26: 148–156.

Bouvier, Leon F. 1992. *Peaceful Invasions*. Lanham, MD: University Press of America.

Bouvier, Leon F., and Jane T. Bertrand. 1999. *World Population: Challenges for the 21st Century*. Santa Ana, CA: Seven Locks.

Bouvier, Leon F., and Lindsey Grant. 1994. *How Many Americans? Population, Immigration and the Environment*. San Francisco: Sierra Club Books.

Bouvier, Leon F., John J. Macisco, and Alvan Zarate. 1976. "Toward a Framework for the Analysis of Differential Migration: The Case of Education." In Anthony H. Richmond and Daniel Kubat (eds.), *Internal Migration: The New World and the Third World*, 24–36. Beverly Hills, CA: Sage.

Bouvier, Leon F., and Dudley L. Poston, Jr. 1993. *Thirty Million Texans?* Washington, DC: Center for Immigration Studies.

Bouvier, Leon F., Dudley L. Poston, Jr., and Nan Bin Zhai. 1997. "The Population Growth Impacts of Zero Net International Migration." *International Migration Review* 31: 294–311.

Bouvier, Leon F., Henry S. Shryock, and Harry W. Henderson. 1977. "International Migration, Yesterday, Today, and Tomorrow." *Population Bulletin* 30 (September).

Bouvier, Leon F., and Jean van der Tak. 1976. "Infant Mortality: Progress and Problems." *Population Bulletin* 31 (April).

Bradley, Don E., and Charles F. Longino. 2009. "Geographic Mobility and Aging in Place." In Peter Uhlenberg (ed.), *International Handbook of Population Aging*, 319–339. Newark, NJ: Springer.

Bradshaw, Benjamin S., and Karen A. Liese. 1991. "Mortality of Mexico Origin Persons in the Southwestern United States." In Ira Rosenwaike (ed.), *Mortality of Hispanic Populations*, 81–94. New York: Greenwood.

Brevard, Aleshia. 2001. *The Woman I Was Not Born to Be: A Transsexual Journey*. Philadelphia: Temple University Press.

Brimelow, Peter. 1996. *Alien Nation: Common Sense about America's Immigration Disaster*. New York: Harper Perennial.

British Broadcasting Corporation News. 2008. "Woman in India 'Has Twins at 70.'" http://news.bbc.co.uk/1/hi/world/south_asia/7491782.stm (accessed July 8, 2008).

Brittingham, Angela, and G. Patricia de la Cruz. 2004. "Ancestry, 2000." *Census 2000 Brief*, C2KBR-35. Washington, DC: U.S. Census Bureau.

Brown, Susan K., and Frank D. Bean. 2005. "International Migration." In Dudley L. Poston, Jr., and Michael Micklin (eds.), *Handbook of Population*, 347–382. New York: Springer.

Browning, Harley L., and Dudley L. Poston, Jr. 1980. "The Demographic Transition." In Rochelle N. Shain and Carl J. Pauerstein (eds.), *Fertility Control*, 197–203. New York: Harper and Row.

Brucker, H. 2002. "Can International Migration Solve the Problems of European Labour Markets?" Paper presented at the UNECE Economic Analysis Division's Spring Seminar: Labour Market Challenges in the ECE Region, Geneva.

Bryan, Thomas. 2004. "Basic Sources of Statistics." In Jacob S. Siegel and David A. Swanson (eds.), *The Methods and Materials of Demography* (2d ed.), 9–41. San Diego, CA: Elsevier Academic.

Buchanan, Patrick J. 2002. *The Death of the West: How Dying Populations and Immigrant Invasions Imperil Our Country*. New York: St. Martin's Griffin.

Buchanan, Patrick J. 2007. *State of Emergency: The Third World Invasion and Conquest of America*. New York: St. Martin's Griffin.

Caldwell, John C. 1976. "Toward a Restatement of Demographic Transition Theory." *Population and Development Review* 2: 321–366.

Caldwell, John C. 1997. "Reaching a Stationary Global Population: What We Have Learned, What We Must Do." *Health Transition Review* 7, Supplement 4: 37–42.

Caldwell, John C. 2006. "Epidemics." In David Lucas and Others, *Beginning Australian Population Studies*, Chapter 3a. Canberra: Australian National University. http://demography.anu.edu.au/Publications/Books/BAPS.php (accessed July 18, 2007).

Camarota, Steven A. 2007. "Immigrants in the United States, 2007: A Profile of America's Foreign-Born Population." *Backgrounder* 10–07. Washington, DC: Center for Immigration Studies.

Carey, James R. 1997. "What Demographers Can Learn from Fruit Fly Actuarial Models and Biology." *Demography* 34: 17–50.

Carey, James R. 2003. *Longevity: The Biology and Demography of Life Span*. Princeton, NJ: Princeton University Press.

Carey James R., P. Liedo, D. Orozco, and James W. Vaupel. 1992. "Slowing of Mortality Rates at Older Ages in Large Medfly Cohorts." *Science* 258: 457–461.

Carey, James R., and James W. Vaupel. 2005. "Biodemography." In Dudley L. Poston, Jr., and Michael Micklin (eds.), *Handbook of Population*, 625–658. New York: Kluwer Academic/Plenum.

Carlson, Elwood. 2008. *The Lucky Few: Between the Greatest Generation and the Baby Boom*. New York: Springer.

Carrier, N. H. 1959. "A Note on the Measurement of Digital Preference in Age Recordings." *Journal of the Institute of Actuaries* 85: 71–85.

Castells, Manuel. 1989. *The Information City: Information Technology, Economic Restructuring, and the Urban-Regional Process*. Oxford: Basil Blackwell.

Cates, Willard, Jr., and Elizabeth G. Raymond. 2007. "Vaginal Barriers and Spermicides." In Robert A. Hatcher, James Trussell, Anita L. Nelson, Willard Cates, Jr., Felicia Stewart, and Deborah Kowal (eds.), *Contraceptive Technology* (19th rev. ed.), 317–335. New York: Ardent Media.

"Census Bureau Releases State and County Data Depicting Nation's Population Ahead of 2010 Census." 2009. *U.S. Census Bureau News*, CB09–76, May 14.

Chandler, Tertius, and Gerald Fox. 1974. *3000 Years of Urban Growth*. New York: Academic Press.

China Daily. 2004. "China Bans Selective Abortion to Fix Imbalance." http://www.chinadaily.com.cn/english/doc/2004–07/16/content_349051.htm (accessed January 11, 2005).

Christopher, Robert C. 1989. *Crashing the Gates: The De-Wasping of America's Power Elite*. New York: Simon and Shuster.

Chu, J. 2001. "Prenatal Sex Determination and Sex-Selective Abortion in Rural Central China." *Population and Development Review* 27: 259–281.

Clarke, J. I. 2000. *The Human Dichotomy: The Changing Numbers of Males and Females*. Amsterdam: Pergamon.

Cleland, John. 1996. "Demographic Data Collection in the Less Developed Countries." *Population Studies* 50: 433–450.

Cleland, John, and J. Hobcroft. 1985. *Reproductive Change in Developing Countries: Insights from the World Fertility Survey*. New York: Oxford University Press.

Cleland, John, and C. Scott. 1987. *The World Fertility Survey: An Assessment*. New York: Oxford University Press.

Coale, Ansley J. 1957. "How the Distribution of Human Population Is Determined." *Cold Spring Harbor Symposium on Quantitative Biology* 22: 83–89.

Coale, Ansley J. 1971. "Age Patterns of Marriage." *Population Studies* 25: 193–214.

Coale, Ansley J. 1972. *The Growth and Structure of Human Populations*. Princeton, NJ: Princeton University Press.

Coale, Ansley J. 1974. "The History of the Human Population." *Scientific American* 231: 51.

Coale, Ansley J. 1987. "Stable Populations." In J. Eatwell, M. Milgate, and P. K. Newman (eds.), *The New Palgrave: A Dictionary of Economics*, IV: 466–469. London: Macmillan.

Coale, Ansley J., and Paul Demeny. 1983. *Regional Model Life Tables and Stable Populations*. 2d ed. New York: Academic Press.

Coale, Ansley J., and Susan Cotts Watkins (eds.). 1986. *The Decline of Fertility in Europe*. Princeton, NJ: Princeton University Press.

Coan, Peter Morton. 2004. *Ellis Island Interviews: Immigrants Tell Their Stories in Their Own Words*. New York: Fall River.

Cohen, Joel. 1995. *How Many People Can the Earth Support?* New York: W. W. Norton.

Cohen, Susan A. 2007. "New Data on Abortion Incidence, Safety Illuminate Key Aspects of Worldwide Abortion Debate." *Guttmacher Policy Review* 10: 2–5.

Coleman, David A. 2000. "Male Fertility Trends in Industrial Countries: Theories in Search of Some Evidence." In Caroline Bledsoe, Susana Lerner, and Jane I. Guyer (eds.), *Fertility and the Male Life-Cycle in the Era of Fertility Decline*. 29–60. Oxford and New York: Oxford University Press.

Comte, Auguste. 1853. *The Positive Philosophy of Auguste Comte*. New York: Calvin Blanchard.

Conceptus, Inc. 2008. *When Your Family Is Complete, Choose Essure*. Mountain View, CA: Conceptus, Inc.

Conde, Eugenia. "Racial and Ethnic Difference in Adolescent Pregnancy and Fertility in the United States." Ph.D. diss., Texas A&M University, College Station, forthcoming.

Connelly, Matthew. 2008. *Fatal Misconception: The Struggle to Control World Population*. Cambridge, MA: Harvard University Press.

Cooley, Charles Horton. 1902. *Human Nature and the Social Order*. New York: C. Scribner's Sons.

Corijn, Martine, and Erik Klijzing. 2001. *Transitions to Adulthood in Europe*. New York: Kluwer Academic.

Cortes, Rachel Traut, and Dudley L. Poston, Jr. 2008. "Immigrants to North America." In William A. Darity (ed. in chief), *International Encyclopedia of the Social Sciences* (2d ed.), III: 576–580. Detroit: Macmillan Reference USA.

Costanzo, Joe, Cynthia Davis, Caribert Irazi, Daniel Goodkind, and Roberto Ramirez. 2001. "Evaluating Components of International Migration: The Residual Foreign Born." Working Paper #61. Washington, DC: U.S. Census Bureau.

Crosby, Alfred W. 2003. *America's Forgotten Epidemic: The Influenza of 1918.* 2d ed. New York: Cambridge University Press.

Crosette, Barbara. 1997. "How to Fix a Crowded World." *New York Times,* November 2.

Curtin, Philip. 1969. *The Atlantic Slave Trade.* Madison: University of Wisconsin Press.

Darwin, Charles. [1887] 1958. *Autobiography and Selected Letters.* Ed. Francis Darwin. New York: Dover.

Darwin, John. 2008. *After Tamerlane: The Global History of Empire Since 1405.* New York: Bloomsbury USA.

David, Henry P., and Nicholas H. Wright. 1971. "Abortion Legislation: The Romanian Experience." *Studies in Family Planning* 2: 205–210.

Davis, Kingsley. 1949. *Human Society.* New York: The Macmillan Company.

Davis, Kingsley. 1951. *The Population of India and Pakistan.* Princeton, NJ: Princeton University Press.

Davis, Kingsley. 1963. "The Theory of Change and Response in Modern Demographic History." *Population Index* 29: 345–366.

Davis, Kingsley. 1974. "The Migrations of Human Populations." *Scientific American* 231: 92–105.

Davis, Kingsley, and Judith Blake. 1956. "Social Structure and Fertility: An Analytical Framework." *Economic Development and Cultural Change* 5: 211–235.

Davis, Mary Ann. 2006. "Will Our Final Years Be Golden? Mortality by Alzheimer's Disease in the United States." Unpublished Ph.D. diss., Texas A&M University, College Station.

de Crevecoeur, J. Hector St. John. [1782] 1997. "Letter III." In *Letters From an American Farmer,* ed. Susan Manning. Oxford and New York: Oxford University Press.

Deffeyes, Kenneth. 2005. *Beyond Oil: The View from Hubbert's Peak.* New York: Hill and Wang.

Demeny, Paul. 2003. "Population Policy." In Paul Demeny and Geoffrey McNicoll (eds.), *Encyclopedia of Population,* II: 752–763. New York: Macmillan Reference USA.

Djerassi, Carl. 1992. *The Pill, Pygmy Chimps, and Degas' Horse: The Autobiography of Carl Djerassi.* New York: Basic Books.

Donato, Katharine M. 1994. "U.S. Policy and Mexican Migration to the United States, 1942–92." *Social Science Quarterly* 75: 705–729.

Dreyer, Edward L. 2007. *Zheng He: China and the Oceans in the Early Ming Dynasty, 1405–1433.* New York: Pearson Longman.

Dublin, Louis, Alfred J. Lotka, and Mortimer Spiegelman. 1949. *Length of Life.* Rev. ed. New York: Ronald Press.

Dubois, W. E. B. 1921. *The Souls of Black Folks*. Greenwich, CT: The Greenwood Press.

Duncan, Otis Dudley. 1959. "Human Ecology and Population Studies." In Philip M. Hauser and Otis Dudley Duncan (eds.), *The Study of Population*, 678–716. Chicago: University of Chicago Press.

Duncan, Richard C. 2001. "The Peak of World Oil Production and the Road to the Olduvai Gorge." http://dieoff.org/page224.htm (accessed November 23, 2008).

Durand, Jorge, Douglas S. Massey, and Emilio A. Parrado. 1999. "The New Era of Migration to the United States." *Journal of American History* 86: 518–536.

Durkheim, Emile. [1893] 1984. *The Division of Labour in Society*. Trans. W. D. Halls. London: Macmillan.

Eberstadt, Nicholas. 2000. *Prosperous Paupers & Other Population Problems*. New Brunswick, NJ: Transaction Publishers.

Eberstadt, Nicholas. 2009. "Drunken Nation: Russia's Depopulation Bomb." *World Affairs* 171 (Spring): 51–62.

Ehrlich, Paul R. 1968. *The Population Bomb*. New York: Ballantine Books.

Eldridge, Hope T. 1968. "Population Policies." In David L. Sills (ed.), *International Encyclopedia of the Social Sciences*, XII: 380–388. New York: Macmillan Company.

Endres, Michael E. 1975. *On Diffusing the Population Bomb*. New York: John Wiley and Sons.

Epstein, Helen. 2007a. "Death by the Numbers." *New York Review* (June 28): 41–43.

Epstein, Helen. 2007b. *The Invisible Cure: Africa, the West, and the Fight Against AIDS*. New York: Farrar, Straus, and Giroux.

Espenshade, Thomas J., J. L. Baraka, and G. A. Huber. 1997. "Implications of the 1996 Welfare and Immigration Reform Acts for US Immigration." *Population and Development Review* 23: 769–801.

Espenshade, Thomas J., Leon F. Bouvier, and W. Brian Arthur. 1982. "Immigration and the Stable Population Model." *Demography* 19: 125–133.

Espenshade, Thomas J., and Katherine Hempstead. 1996. "Contemporary American Attitudes Toward U.S. Migration." *International Migration Review* 30: 535–570.

Etherington, Norman. 2003. "War." In Paul Demeny and Geoffrey McNicoll (eds.), *Encyclopedia of Population*, II: 963–966. New York: Macmillan Reference USA.

Euler, Leonhard. [1760] 1970. "General Research on Mortality and Multiplication." Trans. Nathan Keyfitz and B. Keyfitz. *Theoretical Population Biology* 1: 307–314.

Fairbank, John K., and Merle Goldman. 2006. *China: A New History*. 2d enlarged ed. Cambridge, MA: Belknap Press.

Fan, C. Cindy. 1999. "Migration in a Socialist Transitional Economy: Heterogeneity, Socioeconomic and Spatial Characteristics of Migrants in China and Guangdong Province." *International Migration Review* 33: 954–987.

Faust, Drew Gilpin. 2008. *This Republic of Suffering: Death and the American Civil War*. New York: Alfred A. Knopf.

Fausto-Sterling, Anne. 2000. *Sexing the Body: Gender Politics and the Construction of Sexuality*. New York: Basic Books.

Federal Interagency Forum on Child and Family Statistics. 2007. *America's Children: Key National Indicators of Well Being, 2007*. Washington, DC: U.S. Government Printing Office.

Fellmann, Jerome D., Arthus Getis, and Judith Getis. 1999. *Human Geography: Landscapes of Human Activities*. 6th ed. New York: WCB McGraw-Hill.

Filteau, Jerry. 2009. "Obama Rescinds Family-Planning Aid Restrictions." *National Catholic Reporter* 45 (February 6): 1, 12–13.

Findley, Sally E. 1987. "An Interactive Contextual Model of Migration in Ilocos Norte, the Philippines." *Demography* 24: 1963–1990.

Fingerhut, Lois A. 2003. "Accidents." In Paul Demeny and Geoffrey McNicoll (eds.), *Encyclopedia of Population*, I: 2–6. New York: Macmillan Reference USA.

Finnegan, William. 2006. "New in Town." *The New Yorker* (December 11): 46.

Fischer, Peter A., Reiner Martin, and Thomas Straubhaar. 1997. "Should I Stay or Should I Go?" In Thomas Hammar, Grete Brochmann, and Kristof Tamas (eds.), *International Migration, Immobility and Development*, 49–90. Oxford: Berg.

Flatau, E., Z. Josefsberg, S. H. Reisner, O. Bialik, and Z. Laron. 1975. "Penis Size in the Newborn Infant." *Journal of Pediatrics* 87: 663–664.

Fossett, Mark. 2005. "Urban and Spatial Demography." In Dudley L. Poston, Jr., and Michael Micklin (eds.), *Handbook of Population*, 479–524. New York: Kluwer Academic/Plenum.

Foster, R. F. 1988. *Modern Ireland: 1600–1972*. New York: Penguin Books.

Franklin, Rachel S. 2003. "Domestic Migration Across Regions, Divisions and States, 1995–2000." *Census 2000 Special Reports*, CENSR-7. Washington, DC: U.S. Census Bureau.

Freedman, Lynn P., and Stephen L. Isaacs. 1993. "Human Rights and Reproductive Choice." *Studies in Family Planning* 24: 18–30.

Freedman, Mary Anne, and James A. Weed. 2003. "Vital Statistics." In Paul Demeny and Geoffrey McNicoll (eds.), *Encyclopedia of Population*, II: 960–962. New York: Macmillan Reference USA.

Freeman, Gary P. 2003. "Immigration Policies." In Paul Demeny and Geoffrey McNicoll (eds.), *Encyclopedia of Population*, II: 515–519. New York: Macmillan Reference USA.

Frey, William H. 2003. "Internal Migration." In Paul Demeny and Geoffrey McNicoll (eds.), *Encyclopedia of Population*, II: 545–548. New York: Macmillan Reference USA.

Friedman, Benjamin M. 2005. *The Moral Consequences of Economic Growth*. New York: Knopf.

Friedman, Thomas L. 2005. *The World Is Flat: A Brief History of the Twenty-First Century*. New York: Farrar, Straus and Giroux.

Friedman, Thomas L. 2008. *Hot, Flat and Crowded: Why We Need A Green Revolution, and How It Can Renew America*. New York: Farrar, Straus and Giroux.

Fries, James F. 1980. "Aging, Natural Death, and the Compression of Morbidity." *New England Journal of Medicine* 303: 130–136.

Fries, James F. 1983. "The Compression of Morbidity." *Milbank Memorial Fund Quarterly* 61: 397–419.

Fries, James F. 2000. "Compression of Morbidity in the Elderly." *Vaccine* 18: 1584–1589.

Frisbie, W. Parker. 2005. "Infant Mortality." In Dudley L. Poston, Jr., and Michael Micklin (eds.), *Handbook of Population*, 251–282. New York: Kluwer Academic/Plenum.

Gabaccia, Donna R. 2002. *Immigration and American Diversity: A Social and Cultural History.* Malden, MA: Blackwell.

Garcia, Ginny E. 2008. "An American Irony: The Story of Mexican Immigrant Poverty in the Land of Immigrants." Unpublished Ph.D. diss., Texas A&M University, College Station.

Garreau, Joel. 1991. *Edge City: Life on the New Frontier.* New York: Doubleday.

Gates, Gary J., and J. Ost. 2004. *The Gay and Lesbian Atlas.* Washington, DC: The Urban Institute Press.

Gauthier, Jason G. 2002. *Measuring America: The Decennial Censuses from 1790 to 2000.* Washington, DC: U.S. Census Bureau.

Gelbspan, Ross. 2007. "Two Paths for the Planet." *The American Prospect* (August): 45–47.

Gellerman, Jo. 2003. "Medical Ignorance Conference to Explore Timely Challenges and Questions." http://uanews.org/node/8144 (accessed February 8, 2009).

Ghosh, Bimal. 2005. "Economic Effects of International Migration: A Synoptic Overview." In Irena Omelaniuk (ed.), *World Migration, 2005: Costs and Benefits on International Migration*, 163–184. Geneva: International Organization for Migration.

Gibson, Campbell, and Kay Jung. 2002. *Historical Census Statistics on Population Totals by Race, 1790 to 1990, and by Hispanic Origin, 1970 to 1990, for The United States, Regions, Divisions, and States.* http://www.census.gov/population/www/documentation/twps0056/twps0056.html (accessed May 20, 2009).

Giddens, Anthony. 2002. *Runaway World: How Globalization Is Reshaping Our Lives.* London: Macmillan.

Gillis, Malcolm, D. H. Perkins, M. Roemer, and D. R. Snodgrass. 1996. *Economics of Development*, 4th ed. New York: W. W. Norton.

Gimenez, Martha E. 1971. "The Population Issue: Marx vs. Malthus." Revised version of a paper presented at the annual meeting of the Pacific Sociological Association, Honolulu.

Glass, David V. 1940. *Population Policies and Movements in Europe.* New York: Augustus M. Kelley.

Glass, David V., and Eugene Grebenik. 1954. *The Trend and Pattern of Fertility in Great Britain.* London: Her Majesty's Stationery Office.

Glazer, Nathan. 1983. *Ethnic Dilemma.* New York: Hawthorne.

Glover, James W. 1921. *United States Life Tables, 1890, 1901, 1910, and 1901–1910.* Washington, DC: U.S. Government Printing Office.

Goebel, Ted. 2007. "The Missing Years for Modern Humans." *Science* 315: 194–196.

Goebel, Ted, Michael R. Waters, and Dennis H. O'Rourke. 2008. "The Late Pleistocene Dispersal of Modern Humans in the Americas." *Science* 319: 1497–1502.

Goldscheider, Calvin. 1971. *Population, Modernization and Social Structure.* Boston: Little, Brown.

Goldstein, Sidney, and Alice Goldstein. 1991. *Permanent and Temporary Migration Differentials in China.* Honolulu: The East-West Population Institute, East-West Center, Hawaii.

Goodkind, Daniel. 1996. "On Substituting Sex Preference Strategies in East Asia: Does Prenatal Sex Selection Reduce Postnatal Discrimination?" *Population Research and Policy Review* 22: 111–125.

Goodkind, Daniel. 2002. "Recent Trends in the Sex Ratio at Birth in East Asia." Paper presented at the Conference on Chinese Populations and Socioeconomic Studies: Utilizing the 2000/2001 Round Census Data, Hong Kong University of Science and Technology.

Gordon, Mary. 2000. *Joan of Arc.* New York: Penguin Putnam.

Gordon, Milton. 1964. *Assimilation in American Life.* New York: Oxford University Press.

Gottmann, Jean. 1961. *Megalopolis: The Urbanized Northeastern Seaboard of the United States.* Cambridge, MA: MIT Press.

Graunt, John. [1662] 1939. *Natural and Political Observations Made Upon the Bills of Mortality.* American ed. with Introduction by Walter F. Willcox. Ed. Jacob B. Hollander. Baltimore: Johns Hopkins University Press.

Greene, Margaret E., and Ann E. Biddlecom. 2000. "Absent and Problematic Men: Demographic Accounts of Male Reproductive Roles." *Population and Development Review* 26: 81–115.

Greenhalgh, Susan. 1986. "Shifts in China's Population Policy." *Population and Development Review* 12: 491–515.

Greenhalgh, Susan. 1990a. "The Evolution of the One-Child Policy in Shaanxi, 1979–1988." *China Quarterly* 122: 191–229.

Greenhalgh, Susan. 1990b. "Toward a Political Economy of Fertility: Anthropological Contributions." *Population and Development Review* 16: 85–106.

Greenhalgh, Susan. 1994. "Controlling Births and Bodies in Village China." *American Ethnologist* 21: 3–30.

Greenhalgh, Susan. 2008. *Just One Child: Science and Policy in Deng's China.* Berkeley: University of California Press.

Greenwood, Michael J. 1975. "Research on Internal Migration in the United States: A Survey." *Journal of Economic Literature* 13: 397–433.

Gribble, James M. 2003. "The Standard Days Method of Family Planning: A Response to Cairo." *International Family Planning Perspectives* 29: 188–191.

Grieco, Elizabeth M., and Monica Boyd. 1998. "Women and Migration: Incorporating Gender into International Migration Theory." Working Paper WPS98-139. Tallahassee: Florida State University, Center for the Study of Population.

Gu, Baochang, and Krishna Roy. 1995. "Sex Ratio at Birth in China, with Reference to Other Areas in East Asia: What We Know." *Asia-Pacific Population Journal.* 10: 17–42.

Guest, Avery M., and Susan K. Brown. 2005. "Population Distribution and Suburbanization." In Dudley L. Poston, Jr., and Michael Micklin (eds.), *Handbook of Population*, 59–86. New York: Kluwer Academic/Plenum.

Guillebaud, John. 2005. *The Pill and Other Hormonal Contraceptives*. 6th ed. New York: Oxford University Press.

Guttmacher Institute. 2008a. "Facts on Induced Abortion in the United States." New York: Guttmacher Institute.

Guttmacher Institute. 2008b. "Facts on Induced Abortion Worldwide." New York: Guttmacher Institute.

Haines, Michael R. 2003. "Trans-Atlantic Migration." In Paul Demeny and Geoffrey McNicoll (eds.), *Encyclopedia of Population*, II: 942–946. New York: Macmillan Reference USA.

Haines, Michael R. 2007. "Fertility and Mortality in the United States." http://eh.net/encyclopedia/article/haines.demography (accessed July 26, 2007).

Haines, Michael R., and Avery M. Guest. 2008. "Fertility in New York State in the Pre-Civil War Era." *Demography* 45: 345–361.

Hajnal, J. 1965. "European Marriage Patterns in Perspective." In D. V. Glass and D. E. C. Eversley (eds.), *Population in History*, 101–143. London: Edward Arnold.

Hamby, Chris. 2005. "Utah's Mormon Influence Creates First Amendment Challenges." First Amendment Center, July 21, 2005. http://www.firstamendmentcenter.org/news.aspx?id=15569 (accessed May 9, 2006).

Hamilton, B. E., J. A. Martin, and Stephanie J. Ventura. 2007. "Births: Preliminary Data for 2005." *National Vital Statistics Reports* 55 (11). Hyattsville, MD: National Center for Health Statistics.

Hamilton, C. Horace. 1964. "The Negro Leaves the South." *Demography* 1: 273–295.

Hanson, Gordon H. 2006. "Illegal Migration from Mexico to the United States." NBER Working Paper Series No. 12141. Cambridge, MA: National Bureau of Economic Research.

Harris, J. R., and Michael P. Todaro. 1970. "Migration, Unemployment, and Development: A Two-Sector Analysis." *American Economic Review* 60: 126–142.

Haub, Carl, and Machiko Yanagishita. 1991. "Infant Mortality: Who's Number One?" *Population Today* 19: 6–8.

Hauser, Philip M., and Otis Dudley Duncan (eds.). 1959. *The Study of Population: An Inventory and Appraisal*. Chicago: University of Chicago Press.

Hawley, Amos H. 1950. *Human Ecology: A Theory of Community Structure*. New York: Ronald Press.

Hawley, Amos H. 1968. "Human Ecology." In David L. Sills (ed.), *International Encyclopedia of the Social Sciences*, 328–337. New York: Crowell, Collier, and Macmillan.

Hay, Jeff (ed.). 2001. *Immigration*. San Diego, CA: Greenhaven.

Healy, Bernadine. 2006. "Beyond the Baby Count." *U.S. News and World Report* (September 24). http://health.usnews.com/usnews/health/articles/060924/2healy.htm (accessed July 31, 2007).

Henry, Louis. 1961. "Some Data on Natural Fertility." *Eugenics Quarterly* 8: 81–91.

Henshaw, Stanley K. 2003. "Induced Abortion, Prevalence." In Paul Demeny and Geoffrey McNicoll (eds.), *Encyclopedia of Population*, II: 529–531. New York: Macmillan Reference USA.

Herlihy, David. 1997. *The Black Death and the Transformation of the West.* Cambridge, MA: Harvard University Press.

Heron, Melonie P., and Betty L. Smith. 2007. "Deaths, Leading Causes for 2003." *National Vital Statistics Reports* 55 (March 15).

Higham, John. 1975. *Send These to Me.* New York: Athenaeum.

Hill, R., J. Mayone Stycos, and Kurt Back. 1959. *The Family and Population Control: A Puerto Rican Experiment in Social Change.* Chapel Hill: University of North Carolina Press.

Hillygus, D. Sunshine, Norman H. Nie, Kenneth Prewitt, and Heili Pals. 2006. *The Hard Count: The Political and Social Challenges of Census Mobilization.* New York: Russell Sage Foundation.

Himes, Norman E. [1936] 1970. *Medical History of Contraception.* New York: Schocken Books.

Hinde, Andrew. 1998. *Demographic Methods.* London: Arnold.

Hirschman, Charles. 1994. "Why Fertility Changes." *Annual Review of Sociology* 20: 203–233.

Hobbs, Frank. 2004. "Age and Sex Composition." In J. S. Siegel and D. A. Swanson (eds.), *The Methods and Materials of Demography* (2d ed.), Chapter 7, 125–173. San Diego, CA: Elsevier Academic.

Hobbs, Frank, and Nicole Stoops. 2002. *Demographic Trends in the 20th Century.* Census 2000 Special Reports, Censr-4. Washington, DC: U.S. Government Printing Office.

Hodgson, Dennis, and Susan Watkins. 1997. "Feminists and Neo-Malthusians: Past and Present Alliances." *Population and Development Review* 23: 469–523.

Hoefer, Michael, Nancy Rytina, and Christopher Campbell. 2007. "Estimates of the Unauthorized Immigrant Population Residing in the United States: January 2006." In *Population Estimates* (August). Washington, DC: U.S. Department of Homeland Security, Office of Immigration Statistics.

Horiuchi, S., and Samuel H. Preston. 1988. "Age-Specific Growth Rates: The Legacy of Past Population Dynamics." *Demography* 25: 429–441.

Horton, Hayward Derrick. 1999. "Critical Demography: The Paradigm of the Future?" *Sociological Forum* 14: 363–367.

Howden, Lindsay, and Dudley L. Poston, Jr. 2008. "Depopulation." In William A. Darity (ed. in chief), *International Encyclopedia of the Social Sciences* (2d ed.), II: 301–302. Detroit: Macmillan Reference USA.

Hudson, Valerie M., and Andrea M. den Boer. 2002. "A Surplus of Men, a Deficit of Peace." *International Security* 26: 5–38.

Hudson, Valerie M., and Andrea M. den Boer. 2004. *Bare Branches: Security Implications of Asia's Surplus Male Population.* Cambridge, MA: MIT Press.

Hughes, Jonathan, and Louis P. Cain. 2002. *American Economic History.* 6th ed. Boston: Addison-Wesley.

Hull, T. H. 1990. "Recent Trends in Sex Ratios at Birth in China." *Population and Development Review* 16: 63–83.

Intergovernmental Panel on Climate Change. 2007. *Climate Change, 2007: The Physical Science Basis.* Geneva: IPCC.

International Organization for Migration. 2001. *World Migration Report 2000.* New York: International Organization for Migration and United Nations.

International Organization for Migration. 2008. "Global Estimates and Trends." http://www.iom.int/jahia/Jahia/pid/254 (accessed May 1, 2008).

Iredale, Robyn. 2005. "Balancing the Benefits and Costs of Skilled Migration in the Asia-Pacific Region." In Irena Omelaniuk (ed.), *World Migration, 2005: Costs and Benefits on International Migration,* Chapter 11, 221–237. Geneva: International Organization for Migration.

Issawi, C. 1987. *An Arab Philosophy of History: Selections from the Prolegomena of Ibn Khaldun of Tunis (1332–1406).* Princeton, NJ: Princeton University Press.

James, Patricia. 1979. *Population Malthus: His Life and Times.* London: Routledge and Kegan Paul.

Jha, P., R. Kumar, P. Vasa, N. Dhingra, D. Thiruchelvam, and R. Moineddin. 2006. "Low Male-to-Female Sex Ratio of Children Born in India: National Survey of 1.1 Million Households." *Lancet* 367 (9506): 211–218.

Johansson, S. Ryan. 2003. "Epidemics." In Paul Demeny and Geoffrey McNicoll (eds.), *Encyclopedia of Population,* I: 302–307. New York: Macmillan Reference USA.

Johansson, S., and O. Nygren. 1991. "The Missing Girls of China: A New Demographic Account." *Population and Development Review* 17: 35–51.

Johnson, Niall, and Juergen Mueller. 2002. "Updating the Accounts: Global Mortality of the 1918–1920 'Spanish Influenza Pandemic.'" *Bulletin of the History of Medicine* 76: 105–115.

Johnson, Peter D. 2000. "Population Censuses: Observations on the Past 50 Years and a Peek at the New Century." Paper presented at the Workshop on Gridding Population Data, Columbia University, New York.

Johnson, Steven. 2006. *The Ghost Map: The Story of London's Most Terrifying Epidemic, and How It Changed Science, Cities, and the Modern World.* New York: Riverhead Books.

Jorgensen, Christine. 1967. *Christine Jorgensen: A Personal Autobiography.* New York: Paul S. Eriksson.

Jutte, Robert. 2008. *Contraception: A History* (in German). Trans. Vicky Russell. Malden, MA: Polity.

Juvkam-Wold, H. C., and A. J. Dessler. 2009. "Using the Hubbert Equation to Estimate Oil Reserves." *World Oil* (April): 107–115.

Kahn, E. J. 1974. *The American People: The Findings of the 1970 Census.* New York: Weybright and Talley.

Kalben, Barbara Blatt. 2003. *Why Men Die Younger: Causes of Mortality Differences by Sex.* Society of Actuaries (SOA) Monograph M-Ll101. http://www.soa.org/news-and-publications/publications/other-publications/monographs/pub-life-monographs.aspx (accessed January 19, 2009).

Kallen, Horace M. 1924. *Culture and Democracy in the United States.* New York: Boni and Liveright.

Kasarda, John D. 1971. "Economic Structure and Fertility: A Comparative Analysis." *Demography* 8: 307–317.

Katz, E., and Oded Stark. 1986. "Labor Migration and Risk Aversion in Less Developed Countries." *Journal of Labor Economics* 4: 131–149.

Keeley, Charles B. 2009. "Replacement Migration." In Peter Uhlenberg (ed.), *International Handbook of Population Aging*, 395–403. Newark, NJ: Springer.

Kertzer, David I., and Dennis P. Hogan. 1989. *Family, Political Economy, and Demographic Change: The Transformation of Life in Casalecchio, Italy, 1861–1921*. Madison: University of Wisconsin Press.

Keyfitz, Nathan. 1965. "Age Distribution as a Challenge to Development." *American Journal of Sociology* 70: 659–668.

Keyfitz, Nathan. 1977a. *Applied Mathematical Demography*. New York: John Wiley.

Keyfitz, Nathan. 1977b. "What Difference Would It Make If Cancer Were Eliminated? An Examination of the Taeuber Paradox." *Demography* 14: 411–418.

Keyfitz, Nathan. 1984. "The Population of China." *Scientific American* 250 (February): 38–47.

Keyfitz, Nathan, and W. Flieger. 1971. *Population: Facts and Methods of Demography*. San Francisco: W. H. Freeman.

Khosla, Dhillon. 2006. *Both Sides Now: One Man's Journey Through Womanhood*. New York: The Penguin Group.

Kim, D. 1997. "The Pattern of Changing Trends and the Regional Difference in the Sex Ratio at Birth: Evidence from Korea and Jilin Province, China." *Korea Journal of Population and Development* 26: 19–24.

Kimmel, Michael S. 2004. *The Gendered Society*. 2d ed. New York: Oxford University Press.

Kincannon, Heather Terrell. 2009. "Interracial Marriage in the U.S. in 2006." Unpublished Ph.D. diss., Texas A&M University, College Station.

King, H., and F. B. Locke. 1980. "Chinese in the United States: A Century of Occupational Transition." *International Migration Review* 14: 15–42.

Kintner, Hallie J. 2004. "The Life Table." In Jacob S. Siegel and David A. Swanson (eds.), *The Methods and Materials of Demography* (2d ed.), 301–340. San Diego, CA: Elsevier Academic.

Kipley, Sheila K., and John F. Kipley. 1996. *The Art of Natural Family Planning*. 4th ed. Cincinnati, OH: Couple to Couple League International.

Kiser, Clyde V. 1953. "The Indianapolis Fertility Study: An Example of Planned Observational Research." *Public Opinion Quarterly* 17: 496–510.

Kiser, Clyde V., and Pascal K. Whelpton. 1953. "Resume of the Indianapolis Study of Social and Psychological Factors Affecting Fertility." *Population Studies* 7: 95–110.

Kitagawa, Evelyn, and Philip M. Hauser. 1973. *Differential Mortality in the United States*. Cambridge, MA: Harvard University Press.

Knodel, John, Aphichat Chamratrithirong, and Nibhon Debavalya. 1987. *Thailand's Reproductive Revolution: Rapid Fertility Decline in a Third-World Setting*. Madison: University of Wisconsin Press.

Knodel, John, and Etienne van de Walle. 1979. "Lessons from the Past: Policy Implications of Historical Fertility Studies." *Population and Development Review* 5: 217–245.

Kohler, Hans-Peter, Francesco C. Billari, and Jose Antonio Ortega. 2002. "The Emergence of Lowest-Low Fertility in Europe during the 1990s." *Population and Development Review* 28: 641–680.

Kolata, Gina. 1999. *Flu: The Story of the Great Influenza Pandemic of 1918 and the Search for the Virus That Caused It.* New York: Farrar, Straus, and Giroux.

Kost, Kathryn, Susheela Singh, Barbara Vaughan, James Trussell, and Akinrinola Bankole. 2008. "Estimates of Contraceptive Failure from the 2002 National Survey of Family Growth." *Contraception* 77: 10–21.

Kowal, Deborah. 2007. "Coitus Interruptus (Withdrawal)." In Robert A. Hatcher, James Trussell, Anita L. Nelson, Willard Cates, Jr., Felicia Stewart, and Deborah Kowal (eds.), *Contraceptive Technology*, 337–342. 19th rev. ed. New York: Ardent Media.

Kraeger, Philip. 1988. "New Light on Graunt." *Population Studies* 42: 129–140.

Krieger, N., D. Rowley, A. Herman, B. Avery, and M. Phillips. 1993. "Racism, Sexism and Social Class: Implications for Studies of Health, Disease and Well-Being." *American Journal of Preventive Medicine* 9 (Supplement): 82–122.

Kuczynski, Robert R. 1936. *The Measurement of Population Growth.* New York: Oxford University Press.

Kwong, Peter. 1988. *The New Chinatown.* New York: Hill and Wang.

Laczko, Frank. 2005. "Enhancing the Benefits of Return Migration for Development." In Irena Omelaniuk (ed.), *World Migration, 2005: Costs and Benefits on International Migration*, Chapter 16, 287–295. Geneva: International Organization for Migration.

Lamb, Vicki L., and Jacob S. Siegel. 2004. "Health Demography." In Jacob S. Siegel and David A. Swanson (eds.), *The Methods and Materials of Demography* (2d ed.), 341–370. San Diego, CA: Elsevier Academic.

Lamptey, Peter R., Jami L. Johnson, and Marya Khan. 2006. "The Global Challenge of HIV and AIDS." *Population Bulletin* 61 (1): 1–28.

Landry, Adolphe. 1945. *Traité de Démographie.* Paris: Payot.

Laub, John H., and Robert J. Sampson. 2003. *Shared Beginnings, Divergent Lives: Delinquent Boys to Age 70.* Cambridge, MA: Harvard University Press.

Laubeová, Laura. 2000. "Melting Pot vs. Ethnic Stew," *Encyclopedia of the World's Minorities.* Chicago: Fitzroy Dearborn. http://www.tolerance.cz/english/melting.htm (accessed June 31, 2006).

Lauby, Jennifer, and Oded Stark. 1988. "Individual Migration as a Family Strategy: Young Women in the Philippines." *Population Studies* 22: 139–191.

LeClere, Felicia, Richard G. Rogers, and Kimberley Peters. 1997. "Ethnicity and Mortality in the United States: Individual and Community Correlates." *Social Forces* 76: 169–198.

Lee, Everett S. 1966. "A Theory of Migration." *Demography* 3: 47–57.

LeGates, Richard. 2006. "Visualizing World Urbanization with GIS and Data Graphics." Paper presented at the annual meeting of the Association of American Geographers, Chicago.

Legrain, Philippe. 2006. *Immigrants: Your Country Needs Them.* Princeton, NJ: Princeton University Press.

LeVay, Simon. 1991. "A Difference in Hypothalamic Structure Between Heterosexual and Homosexual Men." *Science* 252: 1034–1037.

LeVay, Simon. 1996. *Queer Science: The Use and Abuse of Research Into Homosexuality.* Cambridge, MA: MIT Press.

Lewis, W. Arthur. 1954. "Economic Development with Unlimited Supplies of Labor." *Manchester School of Economic and Social Studies* 22: 139–191.

Liang, Zai. 2001. "Demography of Illicit Emigration from China: A Sending Country's Perspective." *Sociological Forum* 16: 677–701.

Liang, Zai, and Zhongdong Ma. 2004. "China's Floating Population: New Evidence from the 2000 Census." *Population and Development Review* 30: 467–488.

"Life After Oil." 2008. http://www.lifeafteroilcrash.net/ (accessed November 23, 2008).

Livi-Bacci, Massimo. 1992. *A Concise History of World Population.* Cambridge, MA: Blackwell.

Lo, C. P. 2002. "Urban Indicators of China from Radiance-Calibrated Digital DMSP-OLS Nighttime Images." *Annals of the Association of American Geographers* 92: 225–240.

London, Bruce. 1987. "Ending Ecology's Ethnocentrism: Thai Replications and Extensions of Ecological research." *Rural Sociology* 52: 483–500.

London, Bruce, and Kenneth P. Hadden. 1989. "The Spread of Education and Fertility Decline: A Thai Province Level Test of Caldwell's 'Wealth Flows' Theory." *Rural Sociology* 54: 17–36.

Long, Larry H., and Celia G. Boertlein. 1976. "The Geographic Mobility of Americans." *Current Population Reports*, Series P-23, no. 64. Washington, DC: U.S. Government Printing Office.

Lotka, Alfred J. 1907. "Relation Between Birth Rates and Death Rates." *Science*, New Series, 26 (653): 21–22.

Lotka, Alfred J. [1934] 1998. *Analytical Theory of Biological Populations.* Trans. David P. Smith and Helene Rossert. New York: Plenum.

Loudon, Irvine. 1992. *Death in Childbirth: An International Study of Maternal Care and Maternal Mortality, 1800–1950.* Oxford: Clarendon.

Loudon, Irvine. 2000. "Maternal Mortality in the Past and Its Relevance to Developing Countries Today." *American Journal of Clinical Nutrition* 72 (Supplement): 241S–246S.

Lutz, Wolfgang, Brian C. O'Neil, and Sergei Scherbov. 2003. "Europe's Population at a Turning Point." *Science* 299 (March 29): 1991–1992.

MacDonald, Alphonse L. 2003. "Famine in China." In Paul Demeny and Geoffrey McNicoll (eds.), *Encyclopedia of Population*, I: 388–390. New York: Macmillan Reference USA.

Macisco, John J., Jr., Leon F. Bouvier, and Robert H. Weller. 1970. "The Effect of Labor Force Participation on the Relation between Migration Status and Fertility." *Milbank Memorial Fund Quarterly* 48: 51–69.

MacKellar, F. Landis. 2003. "Homicide and Suicide." In Paul Demeny and Geoffrey McNicoll (eds.), *Encyclopedia of Population*, I: 496–499. New York: Macmillan Reference USA.

Mackun, Paul J. 2005. "Population Change in Metropolitan and Micropolitan Statistical Areas, 1990 to 2003." *Current Population Reports, Population Estimates and Projections*, P25, 1134, September.

Madigan, Francis C. 1957. "Are Sex Mortality Differentials Biologically Caused?" *Milbank Memorial Fund Quarterly* 35: 202–223.

Maine, Deborah, and Katrina Stamas. 2003. "Maternal Mortality." In Paul Demeny and Geoffrey McNicoll (eds.), *Encyclopedia of Population*, II: 628–631. New York: Macmillan Reference USA.

Malthus, Thomas R. [1803] 1989. *An Essay on the Principle of Population (with the Variora of 1806, 1807, 1817, 1826)*. 2 vols. Ed. Patricia James. Cambridge: Cambridge University Press.

Mann, Donald. 1992. "Why We Need a Smaller U.S. Population and How We Can Achieve It." A Negative Population Growth Position Paper, July 3.

Markides, Kyriakos S., and Jeannine Coreil. 1986. "The Health of Hispanics in the Southwestern United States: An Epidemiologic Paradox." *Public Health Reports* 101: 253–265.

Marks, Lara V. 2001. *Sexual Chemistry: A History of the Contraceptive Pill*. New Haven, CT: Yale University Press.

Marsh, Margaret, and Wanda Ronner. 2008. *The Fertility Doctor: John Rock and the Reproductive Revolution*. Baltimore: Johns Hopkins University Press.

Martin, Philip, and Gottfried Zurcher. 2008. "Managing Migration: The Global Challenge." *Population Bulletin* 63 (March): 1–20.

Martin, Sean. 2007. *The Black Death*. Edison, NJ: Chartwell Books.

Martin, Susan F. 2001. "Global Migration Trends and Asylum." UNHCR, The UN Refugee Agency, Evaluation and Policy Analysis Unit Working Paper 41 (April 30). http://www.unhcr.org/cgi-bin/texis/vtx/search?page=search&docid=3af66ccc4&query=susan martin (accessed January 17, 2010).

Marx, Karl, and Friedrich Engels. [1848] 1935. "The Communist Manifesto." In Marx and Engels, *Selected Works*, Vol. 1. London: Lawrence and Wishart.

Mason, Andrew D. 1997. "Dimensions of the Labor Market in China: Rural Labor Markets, and Rural, Urban, and Regional Linkages." Background paper. Washington, DC: The World Bank.

Mason, Karen Oppenheim. 1997. "Explaining Fertility Transitions." *Demography* 34: 443–454.

Massey, Douglas S. 1988. "International Migration and Economic Development in Comprehensive Perspective." *Population and Development Review* 14: 383–414.

Massey, Douglas S. 1995. "The New Immigration and Ethnicity in the United States." *Population and Development Review* 21: 631–652.

Massey, Douglas S. 2003. "International Migration." In Paul Demeny and Geoffrey McNicoll (eds.), *Encyclopedia of Population*, II: 548–553. New York: Macmillan Reference USA.

Massey, Douglas S., Joaquin Arango, Graeme Hugo, Ali Kouaouci, Adela Pellegrino, and J. Edward Taylor. 1993. "Theories of International Migration: A Review and Appraisal." *Population and Development Review* 19: 431–466.

Massey, Douglas S., Joaquin Arango, Graeme Hugo, Ali Kouaouci, Adela Pellegrino, and J. Edward Taylor. 1994. "An Evaluation of International Migration

Theory: The North American Case." *Population and Development Review* 20: 699–751.

Massey, Douglas S., Joaquin Arango, Graeme Hugo, Ali Kouaouci, Adela Pellegrino, and J. Edward Taylor. 2005. *Worlds in Motion: Understanding International Migration at the Dawn of the Millennium.* New York: Oxford University Press.

May, John F. 2005. "Population Policy." In Dudley L. Poston, Jr., and Michael Micklin (eds.), *Handbook of Population*, 827–851. New York: Kluwer Academic/Plenum.

Mazur, A., and J. Michalek. 1998. "Marriage, Divorce, and Male Testosterone." *Social Forces* 77: 315–330.

McCloskey, Deidre N. 2000. *Crossing: A Memoir.* Chicago: University of Chicago Press.

McFalls, Joseph A., Jr. 2003. "Population: A Lively Introduction." *Population Bulletin* 58 (4): 1–40.

McFalls, Joseph A., Jr., Bernard Gallagher, and Brian Jones. 1986. "The Social Tunnel Versus the Python: A New Way to Understand the Impact of Baby Booms and Baby Busts on a Society." *Teaching Sociology* 14: 129–132.

McGehee, Mary A. 2004. "Mortality." In Jacob S. Siegel and David A. Swanson (eds.), *The Methods and Materials of Demography* (2d ed.), 265–300. San Diego, CA: Elsevier Academic.

McIntosh, C. Alison, and Jason L. Finkle. 1995. "The Cairo Conference on Population and Development: A New Paradigm." *Population and Development Review* 21: 223–260.

McKeown, Thomas. 1976. *The Modern Rise of Population.* New York: Academic Press.

McNicoll, Geoffrey. 2003. "Population." In Paul Demeny and Geoffrey McNicoll (eds.), *Encyclopedia of Population*, II: 730–732. New York: Macmillan Reference USA.

Meadows, Donella H., Dennis L. Meadows, Jorgen Randers, and William W. Behrens, III. 1974. *The Limits to Growth: A Report for the Club of Rome's Project on the Predicament of Mankind.* 2d ed. New York: Universe.

Meadows, Donella, Jorgen Randers, and Dennis L. Meadows. 2004. *Limits to Growth: The Thirty-Year Update.* White River Junction, VT: Chelsea Green.

Mehlan, K. H. 1965. "Legal Abortions in Romania." *Journal of Sex Research* 1: 31–38.

Meltzer, David J. 2009. *First Peoples in a New World: Colonizing Ice Age America.* Berkeley: University of California Press.

Menzies, Gavin. 2003. *1421: The Year China Discovered the World.* New York: William Morrow.

Merton, Robert K. 1968. *Social Theory and Social Structure.* New York: Simon and Schuster.

Micklin, Michael, and Dudley L. Poston, Jr. 2005. "Prologue: The Demographer's Ken: 50 Years of Growth and Change." In Dudley L. Poston, Jr., and Michael Micklin (eds.), *Handbook of Population*, 1–15. New York: Springer.

Mill, John Stuart. [1848] 1965. *Principles of Political Economy with Some Applications to Social Philosophy.* 2 vols. Eds. V. W. Bladen and J. M. Robson. Toronto: University of Toronto Press.

Miller, G. Tyler. 2004. *Living in the Environment: Principles, Connections, and Solutions.* 13th ed. Belmont, CA: Brooks/Cole Thomson Leaning.

Miller, Kerby A. 1985. *Emigrants and Exiles: Ireland and the Irish Exodus to North America.* New York: Oxford University Press.

Ministry of Population and Health, Nepal. 2007. *Nepal Demographic and Health Survey 2006: Key Findings.* Kathmandu, Nepal, and Calverton, MD: Ministry of Health and Population, New ERA and Macro International Inc.

Money, John. 1988. *Gay, Straight, and In-Between: The Sexology of Erotic Orientation.* New York: Oxford University Press.

Money, John, and Anke Ehrhardt. 1972. *Man and Woman, Boy and Girl.* Baltimore: Johns Hopkins University Press.

Morgan, S. Philip. 2003. "Is Low Fertility a Twenty-First-Century Demographic Crisis?" *Demography* 40: 589–603.

Morgan, S. Philip, and Kellie J. Hagewen. 2005. "Fertility." In Dudley L. Poston, Jr., and Michael Micklin (eds.), *Handbook of Population,* 229–249. New York: Kluwer Academic/Plenum.

Morris, Jan. 1974. *Conundrum: From James to Jan, an Extraordinary Personal Narrative of Transsexualism.* New York: Harcourt Brace Jovanovich.

Morrison, Peter. 1977. *Forecasting Population of Small Areas: An Overview.* Santa Monica, CA: Rand Corporation.

Mosher, William D., Anjani Chandra, and Jo Jones. 2005. "Sexual Behavior and Selected Health Measures: Men and Women 15–44 Years of Age, United States, 2002." *Advance Data from Vital and Health Statistics* 362: 1–56.

Mosher, William D., Gladys M. Martinez, Anjani Chandra, Joyce C. Abma, and Stephanie J. Willson. 2004. "Use of Contraception and Use of Family Planning Services in the United States: 1982–2002." *Advance Data from Vital and Health Statistics* 350: 1–46.

Münz, Rainer. 2003. "Immigration Trends in Major Destination Countries." In Paul Demeny and Geoffrey McNicoll (eds.), *Encyclopedia of Population,* II: 519–523. New York: Macmillan Reference USA.

Murdock, George P. 1949. *Social Structure.* New York: The Macmillan Company.

Murray, S. O. 2000. *Homosexualities.* Chicago: University of Chicago Press.

Myers, Robert J. 1940. "Errors and Bias in the Reporting of Ages in Census Data." *Transactions of the Actuarial Society of America* 41 (Part 2): 411–415.

Myers, Robert J. 1941. "The Validity and Significance of Male Net Reproduction Rates." *Journal of the American Statistical Association* 36: 275–282.

Myrdal, Gunnar. 1944. *An American Dilemma: The Negro Problem and Modern Democracy.* New York: Harper and Row.

Nam, Charles B., William J. Serow, and David F. Sly (eds.). 1990. *International Handbook on Internal Migration.* New York: Greenwood.

National Center for Health Statistics. 2001. "Deaths, Preliminary Data for 2000." *National Vital Statistics Reports* 49 (12).

National Center for Health Statistics. 2002. "Life Expectancy at Birth, by Race and Sex, Selected Years 1929–98." *National Vital Statistics Reports* 50 (6).

National Center for Health Statistics. 2004. *National Survey of Family Growth, Cycle 6, 2002.* CD-ROM Series 23, Number 4A. Hyattsville, MD: National Center for Health Statistics.

National Center for Health Statistics. 2007. "Fast Stats, A to Z, Deaths/Mortality." http://www.cdc.gov/nchs/fastats/deaths.htm (accessed July 7, 2007).

National Park Service. 2008. "Ellis Island History." http://www.nps.gov/archive/stli/serv02.htm (accessed April 27, 2008).

Neugarten, Bernice L., and Gunhild O. Hagestad. 1976. "Age and the Life Course." In Robert H. Binstock and Ethel Shanas (eds.), *Handbook of Aging and the Social Sciences*, 35–55. New York: Van Nostrand Reinhold.

Nicholson, W. J. 1976. "Case Study I, Asbestos – The TLV Approach." *Annals of the New York Academy of Science, Occupational Carcinogenesis* 271 (May 28): 152–159.

Nolan, Peter. 1991. "Petty Commodity Production in a Socialist Economy: Chinese Rural Development Post-Mao." In Jan Breman and Sudipto Mundle (eds.), *Rural Transformation in Asia*, 218–255. Delhi, India: Oxford University Press.

Noonan, John T., Jr. 1966. *Contraception: A History of Its Treatment by the Catholic Theologians and Canonists.* Cambridge, MA: Harvard University Press.

Notestein, Frank W. 1945. "Population – The Long View." In Theodore W. Schultz (ed.), *Food for the World*, 36–57. Chicago: University of Chicago Press.

Oeppen, Jim, and James W. Vaupel. 2002. "Broken Limits to Life Expectancy." *Science* 296: 1029–1031.

O'Grada, Cormac. 1999. *Black '47 and Beyond: The Great Irish Famine in History, Economy and Memory.* Princeton, NJ: Princeton University Press.

O'Grada, Cormac. 2001. "Markets and Famines: Evidence from Nineteenth Century Finland." *Economic Development and Cultural Change* 49: 575–590.

O'Grada, Cormac. 2003a. "Famine, Concepts and Causes of." In Paul Demeny and Geoffrey McNicoll (eds.), *Encyclopedia of Population*, I: 382–385. New York: Macmillan Reference USA.

O'Grada, Cormac. 2003b. "Famine in Ireland." In Paul Demeny and Geoffrey McNicoll (eds.), *Encyclopedia of Population*, I: 390–392. New York: Macmillan Reference USA.

Ogunwole, Stella U. 2006. *We the People: American Indians and Alaska Natives in the United States.* Census 2000, Special Reports, CENSR 28. Washington, DC: U.S. Census Bureau.

Oi, Jean C. 1999. *Rural China Takes Off: Institutional Foundations of Economic Reform.* Berkeley: University of California Press.

Olshansky, S. Jay, and Brian Ault. 1986. "The Fourth Stage of Epidemiologic Transition: The Age of Delayed Degenerative Diseases." *Milbank Quarterly* 64: 355–391.

Olshansky, S. Jay, and Bruce A. Carnes. 2001. *The Quest for Immortality.* New York: W. W. Norton.

Olshansky, S. Jay, Douglas J. Passaro, Ronald C. Hershow, Jennifer Layden, Bruce A. Carnes, Jacob Brady, Leonard Hayflick, Robert N. Butler, David B. Allison, and David S. Ludwig. 2005. "A Potential Decline in Life Expectancy in the United States in the 21st Century." *New England Journal of Medicine* 352: 1138–1145.

Omran, Abdel R. 1971. "The Epidemiologic Transition: A Theory of the Epidemiology of Population Change." *Milbank Quarterly* 49: 509–553.

Osborn, Frederick. 1960. *This Crowded World*. New York: Public Affairs Committee.

Ostby, Lars. 2003. "Population Registers." In Paul Demeny and Geoffrey McNicoll (eds.), *Encyclopedia of Population*, II: 763–765. New York: Macmillan Reference USA.

Paddock, William, and Paul Paddock. 1967. *Famine, 1975*. Boston: Little, Brown.

Paget, W. John, and Ian M. Timaeus. 1994. "A Relational Gompertz Model of Male Fertility: Development and Assessment." *Population Studies* 48: 333–340.

Palloni, Alberto, and Elizabeth Arias. 2004. "Paradox Lost: Explaining the Hispanic Adult Mortality Advantage." *Demography* 41: 385–415.

Palloni, Alberto, and Jeffrey D. Morenoff. 2001. "Interpreting the Paradoxical in the 'Hispanic Paradox': Demographic and Epidemiological Approaches." In M. Weinstein, A. Hermalin, and M. Stoto (eds.), *Population Health and Aging*, 140–174. New York: New York Academy of Sciences.

Palmore, James A., and Robert W. Gardner. 1994. *Measuring Mortality, Fertility and Natural Increase*. 5th ed. Honolulu: East-West Center.

Papademetriou, Demetrios G. 2003. "International Labor Migration." In Paul Demeny and Geoffrey McNicoll (eds.), *Encyclopedia of Population*, II: 570–574. New York: Macmillan Reference USA.

Parish, W. L., E. O. Laumann, M. S. Cohen, S. M. Pan, H. Y. Zheng, I. Hoffman, T. F. Wang, and K. H. Ng. 2003. "Population-Based Study of Chlamydial Infection in China: A Hidden Epidemic." *Journal of the American Medical Association* 289: 1265–1273.

Park, C. B., and N. Cho. 1995. "Consequences of Son Preference in a Low-Fertility Society: Imbalance of the Sex Ratio at Birth in Korea." *Population and Development Review* 21: 59–84.

Parrilo, Vincent. 1997. *Strangers to These Shores: Race and Ethnic Relations in the United States*. Boston: Allyn and Bacon.

Passel, Jeffrey S. 2006. "The Size and Characteristics of the Unauthorized Migrant Population in the U.S.: Estimates Based on the March 2005 Current Population Survey." Research Report (March 7). Washington, DC: Pew Hispanic Center.

Passel, Jeffrey S., and D'Vera Cohn. 2008. *U.S. Population Projections: 2005–2050*. Washington, DC: Pew Hispanic Center.

Passel, Jeffrey S., Jennifer Van Hook, and Frank D. Bean. 2004. "Estimates of Legal and Unauthorized Foreign Born Population for the United States and Selected States, Based on Census 2000." Washington, DC: Urban Institute.

Patrick, Erin. 2003. "Demography of Refugees." In Paul Demeny and Geoffrey McNicoll (eds.), *Encyclopedia of Population*, II: 825–830. New York: Macmillan Reference USA.

"Peak Oil." 2006. http://www.energybulletin.net/21696.html, October 28 (accessed November 23, 2008).

Pebley, Anne R. "Infant and Child Mortality." 2003. In Paul Demeny and Geoffrey McNicoll (eds.), *Encyclopedia of Population*, II: 533–536. New York: Macmillan Reference USA.

Pedraza, Sylvia, and Ruben G. Rumbaut. 1996. *Origins and Destinies: Immigration, Race and Ethnicity in America*. Belmont, CA: Wadsworth.

Peel, John, and Malcolm Potts. 1969. *Textbook of Contraceptive Practice*. New York: Cambridge University Press.

Peng, Xizhe. 1987. "Demographic Consequences of the Great Leap Forward in China's Provinces." *Population and Development Review* 13: 639–670.

Perloff, Harvey S., E. S. Dunn, E. E. Lampard, and R. F. Muth. 1960. *Regions, Resources, and Economic Growth*. Baltimore: Johns Hopkins University Press.

Perry, Marc J. 2003. "State to State Migration Flows: 1995 to 2000." *Census 2000 Special Reports*, CENSR-8. Washington, DC: U.S. Census Bureau.

Perry, Marc J. 2006. "Domestic Net Migration in the United States: 2000 to 2004." *Current Population Reports*, P25–1135 (April).

Perry, Mark J., and Paul J. Mackun. 2001. "Population Change and Distribution." *Census 2000 Brief*, C2KBR/01–2. Washington, DC: U.S. Census Bureau.

Petersen, William. 1964. *Population*. 2d ed. New York: Macmillan.

Petersen, William. 1975. *Population*. 3d ed. New York: Macmillan.

Petersen, William. 1979. *Malthus*. Cambridge, MA: Harvard University Press.

Pinkerton, James. 2008. "Anti-immigrant Mood Here Rising, Survey Says." *Houston Chronicle*, April 23.

Piore, Michael J. 1979. *Birds of Passage: Migrant Labor in Industrial Societies*. Cambridge: Cambridge University Press.

Pison, Gilles. 2004. "Fewer Births, but a Boy at All Costs: Selective Female Abortion in Asia." *Population and Societies* 404 (September).

Pison, Gilles. 2006. "The Population of France in 2005." *Population and Societies* 421 (March).

Pison, Gilles, and Sabine Belloc. 2005. "The World Population, and What About Me? An Exhibition at the Cité des Sciences et de l'Industrie in Paris." *Population and Societies* 412: 1–4.

Plane, David A. 2004. "Population Distribution: Geographic Areas." In Jacob S. Siegel and David A. Swanson (eds.), *The Methods and Materials of Demography* (2d ed.), Chapter 5. San Diego, CA: Elsevier Academic.

Plankey Videla, Nancy. 2008. "Maquiladoras." In William A. Darity (ed. in chief), *International Encyclopedia of the Social Sciences* (2d ed.), IV: 591–594. Detroit, MI: Macmillan Reference USA.

Pollard, A. H., Farhat Yusuf, and G. N. Pollard. 1981. *Demographic Techniques*. Sydney: Pergamon.

Pollard, A. H., Farhat Yusuf, and G. N. Pollard. 1990. *Demographic Techniques*. 3d ed. Sydney: Pergamon.

Popoff, Carole, and Dean H. Judson. 2004. "Some Methods of Estimation for Statistically Underdeveloped Areas." In Jacob S. Siegel and David A. Swanson (eds.), *The Methods and Materials of Demography* (2d ed.), 603–641. San Diego, CA: Elsevier Academic.

Population Action International. 2006. *Condoms Count: Meeting the Need in the Era of HIV/AIDS, 2006 Data Update*. Washington, DC: Population Action International.

Population Reference Bureau. 2001. *2001 World Population Data Sheet*. Washington, DC: Population Reference Bureau.

Population Reference Bureau. 2006. *2006 World Population Data Sheet*. Washington, DC: Population Reference Bureau.

Population Reference Bureau. 2007a. *2007 World Population Data Sheet*. Washington, DC: Population Reference Bureau.

Population Reference Bureau. 2007b. "World Population Highlights." *Population Bulletin* 62 (3).

Population Reference Bureau 2008a. *Family Planning Worldwide, 2008 Data Sheet*. Washington, DC: Population Reference Bureau.

Population Reference Bureau. 2008b. *2008 World Population Data Sheet*. Washington, DC: Population Reference Bureau.

Portes, Alejandro, and Ruben G. Rumbaut. 1990. *Immigrant America: A Portrait*. Berkley: University of California Press.

Portes, Alejandro, and John Walton. 1981. *Labor, Class, and the International System*. New York: Academic Press.

Postel, Sandra. 1992. *Water and Sustainability: Dimensions of the Global Challenge*. Amherst, MA: World Watch Institute.

Poston, Dudley L., Jr. 2000. "Social and Economic Development and the Fertility Transition in Mainland China and Taiwan." *Population and Development Review* 26 (Supplement): 40–60.

Poston, Dudley L., Jr. 2002. "South Korea's Demographic Destiny: Marriage Market and Elderly Support Implications for the 21st Century." In *International Conference on the Longevity and Social, Medical Environment of the Elderly*, 69–83. Taegu, South Korea: Institute of Gerontology, Yeungnam University.

Poston, Dudley L., Jr. 2005. "Age and Sex." In Dudley L. Poston, Jr., and Michael Micklin (eds.), *Handbook of Population*, 19–58. New York: Kluwer Academic/Plenum.

Poston, Dudley L., Jr. 2006a. "John Graunt." In Bryan Turner (ed.), *The Cambridge Dictionary of Sociology*, 254. Cambridge: Cambridge University Press.

Poston, Dudley L., Jr. 2006b. "Malthus." In Bryan Turner (ed.), *The Cambridge Dictionary of Sociology*, 347–348. Cambridge: Cambridge University Press.

Poston, Dudley L., Jr., Amanda K. Baumle, and Michael Micklin. 2005. "Epilogue: Needed Research in Demography." In Dudley L. Poston, Jr., and Michael Micklin (eds.), *Handbook of Population*, 853–881. New York: Kluwer Academic/Plenum.

Poston, Dudley L., Jr., Iris H. J. Chu, Jaime M. Ginn, Godfrey Jin-Kai Li, Catherine Hong Vo, Carol S. Walther, Ping Wang, Juan J. Wu, and Ming M. Yuan. 2000. "The Quality of the Age and Sex Data of the Republic of Korea and Its Provinces, 1970 and 1995." *Journal of Gerontology* 4: 85–126.

Poston, Dudley L., Jr., Mary Ann Davis, and Chris Lewinski. 2006. "Fertility." In Bryan Turner (ed.), *The Cambridge Dictionary of Sociology*, 403–405. Cambridge: Cambridge University Press.

Poston, Dudley L., Jr., Bethany S. DeSalvo, and Leslie D. Meyer. 2009. "Malthusian Theory of Population Growth." In Dennis L. Peck and Clifton D. Bryant (eds.), *Encyclopedia of Death and the Human Experience*, 684–687. Thousand Oaks, CA: Sage.

Poston, Dudley L., Jr., and Charles Chengrong Duan. 2000. "Nonagricultural Unemployment in Beijing: A Multilevel Analysis." *Research in Community Sociology* 10: 287–301.

Poston, Dudley L., Jr., and W. Parker Frisbie. 1998. "Human Ecology, Sociology, and Demography." In Michael Micklin and Dudley L. Poston, Jr. (eds.), *Continuities in Sociological Human Ecology*, 27–50. New York: Plenum.

Poston, Dudley L., Jr., and W. Parker Frisbie. 2005. "Ecological Demography." In Dudley L. Poston, Jr., and Michael Micklin (eds.), *Handbook of Population*, 601–623. New York: Springer.

Poston, Dudley L., Jr., and Karen S. Glover. 2005. "Too Many Males: Marriage Market Implications of Gender Imbalances in China." *Genus* 61: 119–140.

Poston, Dudley L., Jr., and Karen S. Glover. 2006. "China's Demographic Destiny: Marriage Market Implications for the 21st Century." In Dudley L. Poston, Jr., Che-Fu Lee, Chiung-Fang Chang, Sherry L. McKibben, and Carol S. Walther (eds.), *Fertility, Family Planning and Population Policy in China*, 172–186. London: Routledge.

Poston, Dudley L., Jr., Baochang Gu, Peihang Liu, and Terra McDaniel. 1997. "Son Preference and the Sex Ratio at Birth in China." *Social Biology* 44: 55–76.

Poston, Dudley L., Jr., and Hua Luo. 2007. "Chinese Student and Labor Migration to the United States: Trends and Policies Since the 1980s." *Asian and Pacific Migration Journal* 16 (3): 323–355.

Poston, Dudley L., Jr., Hua Luo, and Li Zhang. 2006. "Migration." In Bryan Turner (ed.), *The Cambridge Dictionary of Sociology*, 384–386. Cambridge: Cambridge University Press.

Poston, Dudley L., Jr., and Michael Xinxiang Mao. 1998. "Interprovincial Migration in China, 1985–1990." *Research in Rural Sociology and Development* 7: 227–250.

Poston, Dudley L., Jr., Michael X. Mao, and Mei-Yu Yu. 1994. "The Global Distribution of the Overseas Chinese Around 1990." *Population and Development Review* 20: 631–645.

Poston, Dudley L., Jr., and Peter A. Morrison. 2005. "China: Bachelor Bomb." *International Herald Tribune*, September 14.

Poston, Dudley L., Jr., and Richard G. Rogers. 1985. "Toward a Reformulation of the Neonatal Mortality Rate." *Social Biology* 32: 1–12.

Poston, Dudley L., Jr., and Heather K. M. Terrell. 2006. "Fertility." In Bryan Turner (ed.), *The Cambridge Dictionary of Sociology*, 201–203. Cambridge: Cambridge University Press.

Poston, Dudley L., Jr., Carol S. Walther, Iris H. J. Chu, Jaime M. Ginn, Godfrey J. Li, Catherine H. Vo, Ping Wang, Juan J. Wu, and Ming M. Yuan. 2003. "The Age and Sex Composition of the Republic of Korea and Its Provinces, 1970 and 1995." *Genus* 59: 113–139.

Poston, Dudley L., Jr., and David Yaukey (eds.). 1992. *The Population of Modern China*. New York: Plenum.

Poston, Dudley L., Jr., and Li Zhang. 2008. "Ecological Analyses of Permanent and Temporary Migration Streams in China in the 1990s." *Population Research and Policy Review* 27: 689–712.

Poston, Dudley L., Jr., and Li Zhang. 2009. "China's Unbalanced Sex Ratio at Birth: How Many Surplus Boys Have Been Born since the 1980s?" In Joseph Tucker, Dudley L. Poston, Jr., Qiang Ren, Baochang Gu, Xiaoying Zheng, Stephanie Wang, and Chris Russell (eds.), *Gender Policy and HIV in China: Catalyzing Policy Change*, 57–69. New York: Springer.

Poston, Dudley L., Jr., Li Zhang, and Heather K. M. Terrell. 2008. "Fertility." In William A. Darity (ed. in chief), *International Encyclopedia of the Social Sciences* (2d ed.), 126–130. Detroit, MI: Macmillan Reference USA.

Potts, David Malcolm. 2003. "Birth Control, History of." In Paul Demeny and Geoffrey McNicoll (eds.), *Encyclopedia of Population*, I: 93–98. New York: Macmillan Reference USA.

Potts, David Malcolm, and Martha Campbell. 2002. "History of Contraception." *Gynecology and Obstetrics* 6: Chapter 8.

Potts, David Malcolm, Peter Diggory, and John Peel. 1977. *Abortion*. New York: Cambridge University Press.

Pressat, Roland. 1985. *The Dictionary of Demography*. Oxford: Blackwell.

Presser, Harriet B. 1997. "Demography, Feminism, and the Science-Policy Nexus." *Population and Development Review* 23: 295–331.

Preston, Samuel. 1987. "The Social Sciences and the Population Problem." *Sociological Forum* 2: 619–644.

Preston, Samuel H., and Michael R. Haines. 1991. *Fatal Years: Child Mortality in Late Nineteenth-Century America*. Princeton, NJ: Princeton University Press.

Preston, Samuel H., Patrick Heuveline, and Michel Guillot. 2001. *Demography: Measuring and Modeling Population Processes*. Malden, MA: Blackwell.

Purcell, L. Edward. 1995. *Immigration: Social Issues in American History*. Phoenix, AZ: The Oryx Press.

Ramachandran, K. V. 1967. "An Index to Measure Digit Preference Error in Age Data." *World Population Conference, 1965, Belgrade*, III: 202–203.

Ramchandran, Deepa, and Ushma D. Upadhyay. 2007. "Implants: The Next Generation." *Population Reports*, Series K, No. 7. Baltimore: INFO Project, Johns Hopkins Bloomberg School of Public Health.

Rand Corporation. 1995. *Low Fertility and Population Ageing: Causes, Consequences, and Policy Options*. Santa Monica, CA: Rand.

Ravenstein, E. G. 1885. "The Laws of Migration." *Journal of the Royal Statistical Society* 48: 167–277.

Ravenstein, E. G. 1889. "The Laws of Migration, Part II." *Journal of the Royal Statistical Society* 52: 241–301.

Raymond, Elizabeth G. 2007. "Progestin-Only Pills." In Robert A. Hatcher, James Trussell, Anita L. Nelson, Willard Cates, Jr., Felicia Stewart, and Deborah Kowal (eds.), *Contraceptive Technology* (19th rev. ed.), 181–191. New York: Ardent Media.

Rees, William. 2004. "Sustainable Development and the Ecosphere." In Arthur Fabel and Donald St. John (eds.), *Teilhard in the 21st Century*, 1–12. Maryknoll, NY: Maryknoll Publications.

Reichert, Josh, and Douglas S. Massey. 1980. "History and Trends in U.S. Bound Migration from a Mexican Town." *International Migration Review* 14: 475–491.

Renzetti, Claire M., and Daniel J. Curran. 1999. *Women, Men, and Society*. 4th ed. Boston: Allyn and Bacon.

Renzetti, Claire M., and Daniel J. Curran. 2003. *Women, Men, and Society*. 5th ed. Boston: Allyn and Bacon.

"Revocation of the Reinstatement of the 'Mexico City Policy' on US Family Planning Assistance." 2009. *Population and Development Review* 35: 215–216.

Riley, Nancy E. 1998. "Research on Gender in Demography: Limitations and Constraints." *Population Research and Policy Review* 17: 521–538.

Riley, Nancy E. 2005. "Demography of Gender." In Dudley L. Poston, Jr., and Michael Micklin (eds.), *Handbook of Population*, 109–142. New York: Springer.

Riley, Nancy E., and James McCarthy. 2003. *Demography in the Age of the Postmodern*. Cambridge: Cambridge University Press.

Ritchey, P. Neal. 1976. "Explanations of Migration." *Annual Review of Sociology* 2: 363–404.

Roberts, Kenneth D. 1997. "China's 'Tidal Wave' of Migrant Labor: What Can We Learn from Mexican Undocumented Migration to the United States?" *International Migration Review* 31: 249–293.

Robine, Jean-Marie. 2003. "Epidemiological Transition." In Paul Demeny and Geoffrey McNicoll (eds.), *Encyclopedia of Population*, I: 307–310. New York: Macmillan Reference USA.

Rock, John. 1963. *The Time Has Come: A Catholic Doctor's Proposals to End the Battle over Birth Control*. New York: Alfred A. Knopf.

Rodriguez, Alex. 2009. "'Parental Glory' Counts in Russia." *Houston Chronicle*, January 29.

Rogers, Andrei. 1975. *Introduction to Multiregional Mathematical Demography*. London: Wiley.

Rogers, Richard G., and Robert Hackenberg. 1987. "Extending Epidemiologic Transition Theory: A New Stage." *Social Biology* 34: 234–243.

Rogers, Richard G., Robert A. Hummer, and Patrick M. Krueger. 2005. "Adult Mortality." In Dudley L. Poston, Jr., and Michael Micklin (eds.), *Handbook of Population*, 283–309. New York: Kluwer Academic/Plenum.

Rogers, Richard G., Robert A. Hummer, and Charles B. Nam. 2000. *Living and Dying in the USA*. San Diego, CA: Academic Press.

Rogers, Richard G., Robert A. Hummer, Charles B. Nam, and Kimberley Peters. 1996. "Demographic, Socioeconomic, and Behavioral Factors Affecting Ethnic Mortality by Cause." *Social Forces* 74: 1419–1438.

Rosenberg, H. M., J. D. Maurer, P. D. Sorrie, N. J. Johnson, M. F. MacDonald, D. L. Hoyert, J. F. Spitler, and C. Scott. 1999. "Quality of Death Rates by Race and Hispanic Origin: A Summary of Current Research, 1999." *Vital Health Statistics* 2 (128): 1–13.

Rosenwaike, Ira. 1991. *Mortality of Hispanic Populations*. Westport, CT: Greenwood.

Rosenwaike, Ira, and Samuel H. Preston. 1983. "Age Overstatement and Puerto Rican Longevity." *Human Biology* 56: 503–525.

Rowland, Donald T. 2003. *Demographic Methods and Concepts*. New York: Oxford University Press.

Rubenstein, Edwin S. 2008/2009. "The Twin Crises." *The Social Contract* 19: 3–83.

Russell, Chris, and Dudley L. Poston, Jr. 2008. "Overpopulation." In William A. Darity (ed. in chief), *International Encyclopedia of the Social Sciences* (2d ed.), VI: 95–96. Detroit, MI: Macmillan Reference USA.

Ryder, Norman B. 1959. "Fertility." In Philip M. Hauser and Otis Dudley Duncan (eds.), *The Study of Population*, 400–436. Chicago: University of Chicago Press.

Ryder, Norman B. 1964. "Notes on the Concept of a Population." *American Journal of Sociology* 69: 447–463.

Ryder, Robert E. J. 1993. "Natural Family Planning: Effective Birth Control Supported by the Catholic Church." *British Medical Journal* 307 (September 18): 723–726.

Sabagh, Georges. 1942. "The Fertility of French Canadian Women during the 17th Century." *American Journal of Sociology* 47: 680–689.

Saenz, Rogelio, and E. Colberg. 1988. "Sustenance Organization and Net Migration in Small Texas Nonmetropolitan Communities, 1960–1980." *Rural Sociology* 53: 334–345.

Sampson, Robert J., and John H. Laub. 1990. "Crime and Deviance over the Life Course: The Salience of Adult Social Bonds." *American Sociological Review* 55: 609–627.

Sanderson, W. C. 1979. "Quantitative Aspects of Marriage, Fertility and Family Limitation in Nineteenth Century America: Another Application of the Coale Specification." *Demography* 16: 339–358.

Sane, K., and O. H. Pescovitz. 1992. "The Clitoral Index: A Determination of Clitoral Size in Normal Girls and in Girls with Abnormal Sexual Development." *Journal of Pediatrics* 120: 264–266.

Sassen, Saskia. 1988. *The Mobility of Labor and Capital: A Study in International Investment and Labor Flow*. Cambridge: Cambridge University Press.

Sassen, Saskia. 1991. *The Global City: New York, London, Tokyo*. Princeton, NJ: Princeton University Press.

Schachter, Jason P., Rachel S. Franklin, and Marc J. Perry. 2003. "Migration and Geographic Mobility in Metropolitan and Non-Metropolitan America: 1995–2000." *Census 2000 Special Reports*, CENSR-9 (April).

Scharping, Thomas. 2003. *Birth Control in China 1949–2000: Population Policy and Demographic Development*. London: Routledge Curzon.

Scheidel, Walter. 2003. "Ancient World, Demography of." In Paul Demeny and Geoffrey McNicoll (eds.), *Encyclopedia of Population*, I: 44–48. New York: Macmillan Reference USA.

Schmeckebier, Laurence F. 1941. *Congressional Apportionment*. Washington, DC: The Brookings Institution.

Schnore, Leo F. 1958. "Social Morphology and Human Ecology." *American Journal of Sociology* 63: 620–634.

Schoen, Robert. 1988. *Modeling Multigroup Populations*. New York: Plenum.

Schumacher, E. F. 1975. *Small Is Beautiful: A Study of Economics As If People Mattered*. New York: Harper Colophon.

Scribner, Richard S. 1996. "Paradox as Paradigm: The Health Outcomes of Mexican Americans." *American Journal of Public Health* 86: 303–304.

Scribner, Richard S., and James H. Dwyer. 1989. "Acculturation and Low Birthweight Among Latinos in the Hispanic HANES." *American Journal of Public Health* 79: 1263–1267.

Segal, Sheldon J. 2003. "Modern Methods of Contraception." In Paul Demeny and Geoffrey McNicoll (eds.), *Encyclopedia of Population*, I: 170–174. New York: Macmillan Reference USA.

Segal, Sheldon, and Olivia S. Nordberg. 1977. "Fertility Regulation Technology: Status and Prospects." *Population Bulletin* 31 (March): 1–25.

Sharpe, F. R., and Alfred J. Lotka. 1911. "A Problem in Age Distribution." *Philosophical Magazine* 21: 435–438.

Sheehy, Daniel. 2006. *Fighting Immigration Anarchy: American Patriots Battle to Save the Nation*. Bloomington, IN: Rooftop Publishing.

Shepard, Marguerite K. 1980. "Nonsurgical Methods of Contraception." In Rochelle N. Shain and Carl J. Pauerstein (eds.), *Fertility Control: Biological and Behavioral Aspects*, Chapter 6, 71–84. New York: Harper and Row.

Sheth, S. S. 2006. "Missing Female Births in India." *Lancet* 367 (9506): 185–186.

Shilts, Randy. 1987. *And the Band Played On: Politics, People and the AIDS Epidemic*. New York: St. Martin's.

Shkolnikov, Vladimir M. 2003. "Mortality Reversals." In Paul Demeny and Geoffrey McNicoll (eds.), *Encyclopedia of Population*, II: 676–679. New York: Macmillan Reference USA.

Shrestha, Laura B. 2006. "Life Expectancy in the United States." *CRS Report for Congress*, RL 32792. Washington, DC: Congressional Research Service.

Shryock, Henry S. 1964. *Population Mobility within the United States*. Chicago: Community and Family Study Center.

Shryock, Henry S., Jacob S. Siegel, and Associates. 1976. *The Methods and Materials of Demography*. Condensed edition by Edward G. Stockwell. New York: Academic Press.

Siegel, Jacob S., and David A. Swanson (eds.). 2004. *The Methods and Materials of Demography*. 2d ed. San Diego, CA: Elsevier Academic.

Simmons, Tavia, and Martin O'Connell. 2003. "Married Couple and Unmarried-Partner Households: 2000." *Census 2000 Special Reports*, CENSR-5. Washington, DC: U.S. Bureau of the Census.

Simon, Julian L. 1981. *The Ultimate Resource*. Princeton, NJ: Princeton University Press.

Simon, Julian L. 1992. *Population and Development in Poor Countries: Selected Essays*. Princeton, NJ: Princeton University Press.

Simpson, J. A., and E. S. C. Weiner (eds.). 2000. *The Oxford English Dictionary*. 2d ed. Oxford: Oxford University Press.

Sivin, Irving, Harold Nash, and Sandra Waldman. 2002. *Jadelle Levonorgestrel Rod Implants: A Summary of Scientific Data and Lessons Learned from Orogrammatic Experience*. New York: Population Council.

Skeldon, Ronald. 2005. "Migration and Poverty: Some Issues in the Context of Asia." In Irena Omelaniuk (ed.), *World Migration, 2005: Costs and Benefits on International Migration*, Chapter 13, 253–268. Geneva: International Organization for Migration.

Smith, David P. 1992. *Formal Demography*. New York: Plenum.

Smith, David P., and Benjamin S. Bradshaw. 2006. "Rethinking the Hispanic Paradox: Death Rates and Life Expectancy for U.S. Non-Hispanic White and Hispanic Populations." *American Journal of Public Health* 96: 1686–1692.

Smith, T. E. 1960. "The Cocos-Keeling Islands: A Demographic Laboratory." *Population Studies* 14: 94–129.

Snipp, C. Matthew. 1989. *American Indians: The First of This Land*. New York: Russell Sage Foundation.

Solinger, Dorothy J. 1999. *Contesting Citizenship in Urban China: Peasant Migrants, the State, and the Logic of the Market*. Berkeley: University of California Press.

Song, Jian, Chi-Hsien Tuan, and Jingyuan Yu. 1985. *Population Control in China: Theory and Applications*. New York: Praeger.

Song, Jian, and Jingyuan Yu. 1988. *Population System Control*. Berlin: Springer-Verlag.

Sonnega, Amanda. 2006. "The Future of Human Life Expectancy: Have We Reached the Ceiling or Is the Sky the Limit?" *Research Highlights in the Demography and Economics of Aging* 8 (March): 1–4.

South, Scott J., and Katherine Trent. 1988. "Sex Ratios and Women's Roles: A Cross-National Analysis." *American Journal of Sociology* 93: 1096–1115.

Spitz, I. M., C. W. Bardin, L. Benton, and A. Robbins. 1998. "Early Pregnancy Termination with Mifepristone and Misoprostol in the United States." *New England Journal of Medicine* 338 (18): 1241–1247.

Stark, Oded. 1984. "Migration Decision Making: A Review Article." *Journal of Development Economics* 14: 251–259.

Stark, Oded. 1991. *The Migration of Labor*. Cambridge, UK: Basil Blackwell.

Stark, Oded, and D. Levhari. 1982. "On Migration and Risk in LDCs." *Economic Development and Cultural Change* 31: 191–196.

StataCorp. 2009. *Stata: Release 11, Statistical Software*. College Station, TX: Stata Corporation.

Sternlieb, George, and James W. Hughes. 1978. *Current Population Trends in the United States*. New Brunswick, NJ: Center for Urban Policy Research.

Stewart, Felicia, James Trussell, and Paul F. A. Van Lok. 2007. "Emergency Contraception." In Robert A. Hatcher, James Trussell, Anita L. Nelson, Willard Cates, Jr., Felicia Stewart, and Deborah Kowal (eds.), *Contraceptive Technology* (19th rev. ed.), 87–116. New York: Ardent Media.

Stockwell, Edward G., Jerry W. Wicks, and Donald J. Adamchak. 1978. "Research Needed on Socioeconomic Differentials in U.S. Mortality." *Public Health Reports* 93: 666–672.

Stone, L. O. 1978. *The Frequency of Geographic Mobility in the Population of Canada*. Ottawa: Statistics Canada.

Stycos, J. Mayone. 1955. *Family and Fertility in Puerto Rico: A Study of the Lower Income Group*. New York: Columbia University Press.

Swanson, David A., and G. Edward Stephan. 2004. "A Demography Time Line." In Jacob S. Siegel and David A. Swanson (eds.), *The Methods and Materials of Demography* (2d ed.), 779–786. San Diego, CA: Elsevier Academic.

Szreter, Simon. 2007. "The Right of Registration: Development, Identity Registration, and Social Security: A Historical Perspective." *World Development* 35: 67–86.

Taeuber, Conrad, and Irene B. Taeuber. 1958. *The Changing Population of the United States.* New York: John Wiley.

Taeuber, Cynthia M. 2006. *American Community Survey Data for Community Planning.* Victoria, BC, Canada: Trafford.

Taeuber, Irene B. 1959. "Demographic Research in the Pacific Area." In Philip M. Hauser and O. Dudley Duncan (eds.), *The Study of Population*, 259–285. Chicago: University of Chicago Press.

Taeuber, Irene B., and Conrad Taeuber. 1971. *People of the United States in the 20th Century.* Washington, DC: U.S. Government Printing Office.

Takaki, Ronald. 1993. *A Different Mirror: A History of Multicultural America.* Boston: Little, Brown.

Tancredo, Tom. 2006. *In Mortal Danger: The Battle for America's Border and Security.* Medford, OR: WND Books.

Tarmann, Allison. 2000. "The Flap over Replacement Migration." Population Reference Bureau. http://www.prb.org/Articles/2000/TheFlapOverReplacement Migration.aspx (accessed September 26, 2008).

Tavris, Carol, and Carole Wade. 1984. *The Longest War: Sex Differences in Perspective* (2d ed.). New York: Harcourt Brace Jovanovich.

Teilhard de Chardin, Pierre. 1959. *The Phenomenon of Man.* New York: Harper and Row.

Teilhard de Chardin, Pierre. 1969a. *The Future of Man.* New York: Harper and Row.

Teilhard de Chardin, Pierre. 1969b. *The God of Evolution.* Orlando, FL: Harcourt.

Teitelbaum, Michael S., 1972. "Fertility Effects of the Abolition of Legal Abortion in Romania." *Population Studies* 26: 405–417.

Tentler, Leslie Woodcock. 2008. "Bitter Pill." *Commonweal* 135 (20): 22–24.

Thomas, Dorothy Swaine. 1941. *Social and Economic Aspects of Swedish Population Movement, 1750–1933.* New York: Macmillan.

Thompson, Warren S. 1929. "Population." *American Journal of Sociology* 34: 959–975.

Thompson, Warren S., and P. K. Whelpton. 1933. *Population Trends in the United States.* New York: McGraw Hill.

Thornton, Russell. 1990. *American Holocaust and Survival.* Norman: University of Oklahoma Press.

Tietze, Christopher. 1957. "Reproductive Span and Rate of Reproduction among Hutterite Women." *Fertility and Sterility* 8: 89–97.

Tietze, Christopher. 1965. "History of Contraceptive Methods." *Journal of Sex Research* 1: 69–85.

Tobler, Waldo. 1995. "Migration: Ravenstein, Thornthwaite, and Beyond." *Urban Geography* 16: 327–343.

Todaro, Michael P. 1976. *Internal Migration in Developing Countries.* Geneva: International Labor Office.

Trussell, James. 2004. "Contraceptive Failure in the United States." *Contraception* 70: 89–96.

Trussell, James. 2007a. "Choosing a Contraceptive: Efficacy, Safety, and Personal Considerations." In Robert A. Hatcher, James Trussell, Anita L. Nelson, Willard Cates, Jr., Felicia Stewart, and Deborah Kowal (eds.), *Contraceptive Technology* (19th rev. ed.), 19–47. New York: Ardent Media.

Trussell, James. 2007b. "Contraceptive Efficacy." In Robert A. Hatcher, James Trussell, Anita L. Nelson, Willard Cates, Jr., Felicia Stewart, and Deborah Kowal (eds.), *Contraceptive Technology* (19th rev. ed.), 748–826. New York: Ardent Media.

Tucker, Joseph D., Gail E. Henderson, T. F. Wang, Y. Y. Huang, William Parish, S. M. Pan, X. S. Chen, and M. S. Cohen. 2005. "Surplus Men, Sex Work, and the Spread of HIV in China." *AIDS* 19: 539–547.

Turner, Frederick Jackson. [1893] 1920. *The Frontier in American History*. New York: Henry Holt.

(UNAIDS) United Nations Joint Program on HIV/AIDS. 2006. "Global Facts and Figures, 2006." http://data.unaids.org/pub/GlobalReport/2006/200605-FS_globalfactsfigures_en.pdf (accessed July 18, 2007).

(UNHCR) United Nations High Commissioner for Refugees. 2007. *Statistical Yearbook 2006: Trends in Displacement, Protection and Solutions*. Geneva: UNHCR.

(UNICEF) United Nations International Children's Emergency Fund. 2001. *Progress since the World Summit for Children*. New York: UNICEF.

(UNICEF) United Nations International Children's Emergency Fund. 2002. "Birth Registration Right from the Start." Florence: UNICEF.

United Nations. 1958. *Principles and Recommendations for National Population Censuses*. New York: United Nations.

United Nations. 1973. *The Determinants and Consequences of Population Change*. Vol. 1. New York: United Nations.

United Nations. 1980. *Patterns of Urban and Rural Population Growth*. New York: United Nations.

United Nations. 1990. *1988 Demographic Yearbook*. New York: United Nations.

United Nations. 1998a. "Principles and Recommendations for Population and Housing Censuses, Revision 1." *Statistical Papers*, Series M, No. 67/Rev. 1. New York: United Nations.

United Nations. 1998b. *World Population Prospects: The 1998 Revision*. New York: United Nations.

United Nations. 2001. *Replacement Migration: Is It a Solution to Declining and Ageing Populations?* New York: United Nations.

United Nations. 2003. *World Population Prospects: The 2002 Revision*. 2 vols. New York: United Nations.

United Nations. 2005. *World Population Prospects: The 2004 Revision and World Urbanization Prospects: The 2003 Revision*. New York: United Nations. http://esa.un.org/unpp (accessed June 6, 2006).

United Nations. 2006a. *International Migration 2006 Wall Chart*. New York: United Nations.

United Nations. 2006b. *World Urbanization Prospects: The 2005 Revision*. New York: United Nations.

United Nations. 2007. *World Population Prospects, The 2006 Revision: Highlights*. New York: United Nations.

United Nations. 2008a. *World Fertility Patterns 2007, Wall Chart*. New York: United Nations.

United Nations. 2008b. *World Urbanization Prospects: The 2007 Revision*. New York: United Nations.

U.S. Bureau of the Census. 1975. *Historical Statistics of the United States*. Washington, DC: U.S. Government Printing Office.

U.S. Bureau of the Census. 1994. *Statistical Abstract of the United States: 1994*. 114th ed. Washington, DC: U.S. Government Printing Office.

U.S. Bureau of the Census. 2004a. *Census Bureau International Data Base*. Updated April 30, 2004. http://www.census.gov/ipc/www/idbnew.html.

U.S. Bureau of the Census. 2004b. *Statistical Abstract of the U.S.: 2003*. Washington, DC: U.S. Government Printing Office.

U.S. Bureau of the Census. 2005. "Texas Becomes Nation's Newest 'Majority-Minority' State, Census Bureau Announces." U.S. Census Bureau News, CB 05–118, August 11.

U.S. Bureau of the Census. 2006. *American Community Survey, Design and Methodology*. Technical Paper 67. Washington, DC: U.S. Government Printing Office.

U.S. Bureau of the Census. 2007a. *Census Atlas of the United States*. Series CENSR-29. Washington, DC: U.S. Bureau of the Census.

U.S. Bureau of the Census. 2007b. "International Data Base Summary Demographic Data for the United States." http://www.census.gov/cgi-bin/ipc/idbsum.pl?cty=US (accessed July 7, 2007).

U.S. Bureau of the Census. 2007c. *Statistical Abstract of the United States: 2008*. 127th ed. Washington, DC: U.S. Government Printing Office.

U.S. Bureau of the Census. 2008. *Annual Estimates of the Population by Sex and Five-Year Age Groups for the US: April 1, 2007 to July 1, 2007 (NC-EST2007-01)*. Washington, DC: U.S. Bureau of the Census.

U.S. Citizenship and Immigration Services. 2004. Yearbook of Immigration Statistics. http://uscis.gov/graphics/shared/statistics/archives/index.htm (accessed March 11, 2006).

U.S. Department of Commerce. 1921. *United States Life Tables, 1890, 1901, 1910, and 1901–1910*. Washington, DC: U.S. Government Printing Office.

"U.S. Hispanic Population Surpasses 45 Million." 2008. *U.S. Census Bureau News*, CB08–67 (May 1). http://www.census.gov/PressRelease/www/releases/archives/population/011910.html.

van de Walle, Etienne, and John Knodel. 1970. "Teaching Population Dynamics with a Simulation Exercise." *Demography* 7: 433–448.

Velkoff, Victoria A., and Valerie A. Lawson. 1998. "Gender and Aging Caregiving." *International Brief*, IB/98–3 (December). Washington, DC: U.S. Bureau of the Census.

Wallace, Ruth, and Alison Wolf. 2005. *Contemporary Sociological Theory*. Upper Saddle River, NJ: Prentice-Hall.

Walther, Carol S., and Dudley L. Poston, Jr. 2004. "Patterns of Gay and Lesbian Partnering in the Larger Metropolitan Areas of the United States." *Journal of Sex Research* 41: 201–214.

Waltzer, Michael. 1981. "The Distribution of Membership." In Peter G. Brown and Henry Shue (eds.), *Boundaries: National Autonomy and its Limits*, 221–235. Totowa, NJ: Rowman & Littlefield.

Warren, Robert, and Jeffrey S. Passel. 1987. "A Count of the Uncountable: Estimates of the Undocumented Aliens in the United States 1980 Census." *Demography* 24: 375–393.

Wattenberg, Ben J. 2004. *Fewer: How the New Demography of Depopulation Will Shape Our Future*. Chicago: Ivan R. Dee.

Weller, Robert H., and Leon F. Bouvier. 1981. *Population: Demography and Policy*. New York: St. Martin's.

Westoff, Charles F., Robert G. Potter, and Phillip C. Sagi. 1963. *The Third Child: A Study in the Prediction of Fertility*. Princeton, NJ: Princeton University Press.

Westoff, Charles F., Robert G. Potter, Philip C. Sagi, and Elliot G. Mishler. 1961. *Family Growth in Metropolitan America*. Princeton, NJ: Princeton University Press.

White, Michael J., Frank D. Bean, and Thomas J. Espenshade. 1990. "The U.S. 1986 Immigration Reform and Control Act of 1986 and Undocumented Migration to the United States." *Population Research and Policy Review* 9: 93–116.

White, Theodore. 1982. *America in Search of Itself: The Making of the President: 1956–1980*. New York: Harper and Row.

Whitney, R. B. 2003. "Quinacrine Sterilization (QS) in a Private Practice in Daytona Beach, Florida: A Preliminary Report." *International Journal of Gynecology and Obstetrics* 83 (Supplement 2): S117–S120.

Wilkinson, David O. 1980. *Deadly Quarrels: Lewis F. Richardson and the Statistical Study of War*. Berkeley: University of California Press.

Williams, David R., and Chiquita Collins. 1995. "U.S. Socioeconomic and Racial Differences in Health: Patterns and Explanations." *Annual Review of Sociology* 21: 349–386.

Wilmoth, Janet. 2004. "Population Size." In Jacob S. Siegel and David A. Swanson (eds.), *The Methods and Materials of Demography* (2d ed.), 65–80. San Diego, CA: Elsevier Academic.

Winch, Donald. 1987. *Malthus*. Oxford: Oxford University Press.

Winch, Donald. 2003. "Malthus, Thomas Robert." In Paul Demeny and Geoffrey McNicoll (eds.), *Encyclopedia of Population*, II: 619–621. New York: Macmillan Reference USA.

Wolfenden, Hugh H. 1954. *Population Statistics and Their Compilation*. Chicago: University of Chicago Press.

Wooldridge, Frosty. 2004. *Immigration's Unarmed Invasion: Deadly Consequences*. Bloomington, IN: Authorhouse.

World Bank. 1997. *China 2020: Sharing Rising Incomes: Disparities in China*. Washington, DC: The World Bank.

World Health Organization. 1992. *International Classification of Diseases*. 10th revision. Geneva: World Health Organization.

World Health Organization. 2004. *Maternal Mortality in 2000*. Geneva: World Health Organization.

World Health Organization. 2005. *World Health Report 2005: Make Every Mother and Child Count*. Geneva: World Health Organization.

World Health Organization. 2006a. *Life Tables for WHO Member States*. Geneva: World Health Organization.

World Health Organization. 2006b. *Neonatal and Perinatal Mortality: Country, Regional and Global Estimates*. Geneva: World Health Organization.

World Health Organization. 2007. "The Top 10 Causes of Death." Fact Sheet No. 310. Geneva: World Health Organization. http://www.who.int/mediacentre/factsheets/fs310/en/index2.html (accessed July 24, 2007).

Wortman, Judith. 1976. "The Diaphragm and Other Intravaginal Barriers: A Review." *Population Reports*, Series H, No. 7. Baltimore: INFO Project, Johns Hopkins School of Public Health.

Woytinsky, Wladimir S., and Emma S. Woytinsky. 1953. *World Population and Production*. New York: Twentieth Century Fund.

Wrigley, E. A. 1969. *Population and History*. New York: McGraw-Hill.

Wu, Cangping, and Lin Wang. 2004. "Contribution of Population Control in Creating Opportunities for China Arising from Fertility Decline Should Not Be Neglected." Paper presented at the International Symposium on the 2000 Population Census of China, Beijing.

Yang, Xiushi. 1994. "Urban Temporary Out-migration under Economic Reforms: Who Moves and for What Reasons?" *Population Research and Policy Review* 13: 83–100.

Yang, Xiushi. 1996. "Labor Force Characteristics and Labor Force Migration in China." In *Changes in China's Labor Market: Implications for the Future*, 13–44. Washington, DC: U.S. Department of Labor.

Yinger, J. Milton. 1981. "Towards a Theory of Assimilation and Disassimilation." *Ethnic and Racial Studies* 4: 261.

Young, Paul. 2002. *L. A. Exposed: Strange Myths and Curious Legends in the City of Angels*. New York: St. Martin's Griffin.

Zaba, Basia. 2003. "AIDS." In Paul Demeny and Geoffrey McNicoll (eds.), *Encyclopedia of Population*, I: 37–43. New York: Macmillan Reference USA.

Zakaria, Fareed. 2008. *The Post-American World*. New York: W. W. Norton.

Zangwill, Israel. 1909. *The Melting Pot*. New York: The Macmillan Company.

Zeng, Yi, Ping Tu, Baochang Gu, Y. Xu, B. Li, and Y. Li. 1993. "Causes and Implications of the Recent Increase in the Reported Sex Ratio at Birth in China." *Population and Development Review* 19: 283–302.

Zhang, Li. 2007. "Bringing Men In: Analyses of Male and Female Fertility." Unpublished Ph.D. diss., Texas A&M University, College Station.

Zhou, Min. 1992. *Chinatown: The Socioeconomic Potential of an Urban Enclave*. Philadelphia: Temple University Press.

Zinn, Howard. 2003. *A People's History of the United States*. New York: HarperCollins.

Zlidar, Vera M. 2000. "Helping Women Use the Pill." *Population Reports*, Series A, No. 10. Baltimore: Johns Hopkins University School of Public Health.

Author Index

Subject Index